For Jon Saxton

with my very best
wishes. — Welcome
to Emory — you will
like it!

J Willis Hurt MD
3/11/98

The Quest for Excellence

Emory University
Archives and Libraries
Sources and Guides to Research

Cor prudentis possidebit scientiam

EMORY

Number 3

The Quest for Excellence
*The History of the Department of Medicine at
Emory University School of Medicine*
by
J. Willis Hurst

The Quest for Excellence

*The History of the
Department of Medicine at
Emory University School of Medicine*

by
J. Willis Hurst

SCHOLARS PRESS
Atlanta, Georgia

EMORY UNIVERSITY
Archives and Libraries
Sources and Guides to Research

The Quest for Excellence
by
J. Willis Hurst

© 1997
Emory University

Library of Congress Cataloging in Publication Data
Hurst, J. Willis (John Willis), 1920–
    The quest for excellence : the history of the Department of
Medicine at Emory University School of Medicine, 1834–1986 /
J. Willis Hurst.
        p.   cm. — (Archives and libraries ; 3)
    Includes index.
    ISBN 0-7885-0394-4 (cloth : alk. paper)
    1. Emory University. Dept. of Medicine—History. 2. Medical
colleges—Georgia—Atlanta—History. I.. Title. II. Series.
    [DNLM: 1. Emory University. Dept. of Medicine. 2. Schools,
Medical—history—Georgia. 3. Faculty, Medical—biography. W 19
H9661 1997]
R747.E46H87   1997
610'.9758'231—dc21
DNLM/DLC
for Library of Congress   97-29007
                                                 CIP

Published by Scholars Press
for
Emory University

Table of Contents

Dedicated to
the patients who came,
the benefactors who helped,
and the students, house officers, fellows,
and colleagues who participated in
the *quest for excellence.*

PROLOGUE

If . . . history . . . teaches us anything it is that man, in his quest for knowledge
and progress, is determined and cannot be deterred.

John F. Kennedy Address at Rice University Houston (1962)

This book, *The Quest for Excellence: The History of the Department of
Medicine at Emory University School of Medicine,* is filled with biographies.
Why was this approach used to chronicle events that occurred in the
Department of Medicine of Emory University School of Medicine?
Because, as Thomas Carlyle wrote in his 1838 essay, *On History*: "history is
the essence of innumerable biographies."

I have worked at Emory University for forty-seven years. The growth
and development of the University and its schools have been mind-
boggling. I learned over the years that things happened because men and
women made them happen. Accordingly, as this book was written, I
became increasingly interested in the people who were responsible for
the enormous forward thrust of Emory University, its School of Medicine,
and its Department of Medicine. It seemed appropriate to include the
biographies of some of them. I wish I had studied the lives of the
Candlers, the Woodruffs, and the others discussed here when I first
became chairman of the Department of Medicine. I believe I would have
been a better chairman if I had done so, and I now encourage any and all
faculty members to become familiar with the lives of the wise benefactors
of this jewel we call Emory.

Another reason for including biographies in this book has to do with
an honest effort to entertain those who read it. The mere listing of events
and dates can numb the mind. On the other hand, when the events and
dates are a part of the stories of the people involved, they become far
more interesting. Because of this, many of the events and dates appear
more than once; they are both discussed as part of the lives of people and
recorded as historical events that simply occurred.

The epigraph from John F. Kennedy emphasizes that there is
something in some men and women that stimulates them to seek
knowledge and progress. Such people do not tolerate mediocrity. They
congregate around a noble idea and enable its further development. The
noble idea at Emory was, and is, to create a great university of higher

vii

learning. Of course there is no end to such an endeavor because the more we learn, the more we realize we don't know. The more progress we make, the more we understand that the job is never done. This is why the word "quest" appears in this book's title. I would not dare say that excellence was achieved in the Department of Medicine during the years discussed in this book. I can say that the *quest* for excellence was intense, determined, and persistent. As the future years pass, Emory University, the Emory University School of Medicine, and its Department of Medicine will continue to improve. If not, I will haunt those who fail to seize the opportunities that will surely come their way.

I cannot leave this portion of the prologue without pointing out that Emory succeeded because its leaders loved the institution. This fact made the obstacles that always stand in the way of progress seem small.

Writing this book was not easy. The actual composition was simple enough, but gathering the facts and dates that were associated with the events was more complicated. When photographs of certain people were selected, equity sometimes demanded that photographs of other individuals also be shown. A problem arose when there were no photographs of the other individuals. Many photographs were not labeled with dates, and the dates of certain events were differently listed in different documents. The deep-down inner feelings—the emotional status—of people could not be documented. Therefore, when feelings and emotions are discussed, they usually represent the belief of several people who were on the scene and surmised what was happening.

Chapter 5 of the book was the most difficult to write. How could I, as chairman of the Department of Medicine for thirty years, write about those years without excessive use of the pronoun "I"? Dr. Mark Silverman wrote my biography, but what was to be done about the remainder of the chapter? Impersonal formulations—"the narrator of this book," or "the author of this book"—were initially tried, but even they seemed distasteful and awkward. After fretting endlessly about the matter, I elected to barge on and beg the reader's indulgence. I wish to emphasize, however, that the forward thrust of the Department of Medicine from 1957 to 1986 was due to many, many devoted faculty members, to hundreds of brilliant students, house officers, and fellows, and to several generous benefactors.

Perceptive readers will detect in these pages the medical and social mores of a time that has passed. For example, it was the custom of the day to refer to the Emory Division of Grady Memorial Hospital as "colored

Grady." This habit persisted from 1921 to 1958, when the new Grady Memorial Hospital was occupied. I have always found this language offensive and never used it myself. But I have retained such terms in this book because, in being true to history, they reflect the custom of the day.

J. Willis Hurst, M.D.
Candler Professor of Medicine,
Chairman of the Department of Medicine 1957–1986
Consultant to the Division of Cardiology from 1986 to Present

ACKNOWLEDGMENTS

The information used to write this book came from many places and many people. In some instances the text was created by paraphrasing and combining information that was obtained from multiple sources. These sources are listed in the "General References" section at the end of each chapter. When, however, a portion of the text is indented and in a smaller typeface, it indicates that the passage is a direct quotation. In such cases the source is cited in the text itself or in the footnotes. Most of the information is from Emory-owned sources and has been used with permission of Emory University. When non-Emory sources have been used, permission has been obtained from the author and publisher.

The information came from the following sources:

• The Special Collections section of the Robert W. Woodruff Library of Emory University was a rich source of interesting material. This remarkable collection of documents includes: my own annual reports written during 1957–1986 to the dean of Emory University School of Medicine, as well as the annual reports of Drs. Eugene A. Stead Jr., Paul B. Beeson, and Eugene B. Ferris; the dean's annual reports to the president of the university; the president's reports to the board of trustees or its executive committee; and the private papers of Mr. Robert Mizell, Dr. Glenville Giddings, Mr. Robert Woodruff, Dr. J. Elliott Scarborough Jr., and others.

I wish to acknowledge the enormous help provided me by Kathy Shoemaker, Beverly Allen, Virginia Carr, and Keith Nash, who assisted me in finding important material needed to document certain aspects of the text. The very important 1946 Emory Medical School Planning Report was initially missing. This report, which led to the "defining moment" for Emory University School of Medicine, was eventually found by the very competent "detectives" on the staff who searched the files for several months until it was found.

• The archives housed in the Robert W. Woodruff Health Sciences Center Library were very useful. I thank Mrs. Elaine Keefer and Mrs. Carol Burns for assisting me in locating material, including photographs, old newspaper clippings, old Emory Medical School Bulletins, and letters germane to the development of the Department of Medicine.

- Some of the material used in this book was originally published in the official publications of Emory University. The exact source of such material is cited in the text or in the references.

- Important information was located in the office of the dean of the School of Medicine.

- Dr. Mark Silverman was of considerable help by providing me with a letter he had received from Dr. Eugene A. Stead Jr., and in providing me with the audiotape of a speech Dean Arthur Richardson made on July 13, 1982, at a meeting of the Atlanta Medical History Society. In the talk, Dr. Richardson discussed the history of Emory University School of Medicine including the "ruckus" of 1955–1957. Dr. Silverman owns that audiotape. Dr. Silverman also wrote my biography and critiqued every page of the book.

- When Dean Arthur Richardson retired in 1979 he and Dr. Evangeline Papageorge began writing the history of Emory University School of Medicine. Unfortunately, Dr. Richardson died in 1993 before the project was completed. Dr. Richardson had given Dr. Papageorge a copy of the manuscript he had written about the early days of the medical school. Dr. Papageorge made his document as well as hers available to me. They will be placed in Special Collections of the Robert W. Woodruff Library.

- Most of the photographs were provided by Biomedical Media of Emory University School of Medicine. I especially thank Eddie Jackson and Jack Pierce for their expert help.

- The photographs and text related to Grady Memorial Hospital are in the public domain. Accordingly, no permission was needed for their use.

- Much of the information came from the interviews I had with the members of the Department of Medicine who served with me during the years 1957 to 1986. I am grateful for the help they gave the department during that period, and I thank them for the help they gave me in writing this book.

- My own personal file, which contains letters from Drs. Eugene A. Stead Jr., Paul Beeson, and others, as well as hundreds of photographs, was a major source of information.

- Dr. Charles Hatcher, former Vice President for Health Affairs of Emory University and Director Emeritus of the Robert W. Woodruff Health Sciences Center, supported the project that took more than two years to complete. Half of the financial support came from the dean's office, and the other half came from the Department of Medicine. I especially thank Dr. Juha Kokko, chairman of the Department of

Medicine, for his support of this project. The book could not have been produced without this help.

• The completed manuscript was given to: Dr. William M. Chace, President of Emory University; Dr. Gary S. Hauk, Secretary of Emory University; Dr. Michael M. E. Johns, Executive Vice President for Health Affairs and Director of the Robert W. Woodruff Health Sciences Center; Dr. Charles R. Hatcher Jr., former Vice President for Health Affairs of Emory University and Director Emeritus of the Robert W. Woodruff Health Sciences Center; Dr. Thomas J. Lawley, Dean of Emory University School of Medicine; Dr. Juha P. Kokko, Chairman of the Department of Medicine; Dr. Judson C. Ward Jr., former Executive Vice President and Dean of Faculties, Emory University; Dr. Rein Saral, Director of The Emory Clinic; Dr. Sylvia Wrobel and Ms. Karon Schindler, in the Health Sciences News and Information Office of Emory University School of Medicine; Dr. Eugene A. Stead Jr. and Dr. Paul B. Beeson, former Chairmen of the Department of Medicine at Emory; Dr. R. Bruce Logue, Dr. Mark E. Silverman, Dr. Thomas F. Sellers Jr., and Dr. Joseph E. Hardison, faculty members who lived the times with me; and Dr. William Hollingsworth, who wrote a fine book about Soma Weiss, Stead, and Beeson.

• I especially thank Dr. Gary Hauk, secretary of Emory University, for reading the manuscript and for his useful suggestions. He also speaks for Emory University on issues that deal with copyright law. He gave me permission to use the Emory sources of information which found their way into this book.

• Many people reviewed and corrected each part of the book. Their names are listed at the end of each chapter. I thank them for their excellent suggestions and corrections.

• The books that served as general information for each chapter are listed at the end of that chapter. The specific sources used for the text are cited in the footnotes.

• Typing and keeping order was in the capable hands of Mary Cotton and Carol Miller. Mary worked at home and Carol worked at the office. Somehow they managed to take my barely legible scribbling and convert it into typewritten pages. I thank them both.

• I express my gratitude to Dr. Harry Gilmer, Director of Scholars Press, for his suggestions. His scholarly approach to the publishing of this book is very much appreciated. I also thank the very competent Ted Brelsford of Scholars Press for shepherding the book through the publishing process. Eugene H. Lovering Jr. has an eagle's eye; he saw errors in the manuscript that no one else had seen. He is a superb copy-editor.

• Finally, I acknowledge the help of my wife, Nelie. She is accustomed to the clutter I create in our home when I am on a writing binge. All tables, several beds, and part of the floor are used to support books, magazines, and files that are needed to write a book. This time it was different in one major aspect. The book did not deal with a scientific subject. It dealt with our lives. So, I babbled incessantly to her. She listened. Almost all of the writing brought back pleasant memories. There were a few sad memories as we both thought of the colleagues that had left us. Also, I came face to face with the fact that, during the thirty years, most of my actions were acceptable, but a few were not. When I remarked that I wish I had acted differently, Nelie said, in typical fashion, "let it go." She is emotionally strong and has made my private life serene and happy. Therefore, she deserves much of the credit for the success of the Department of Medicine. No Nelie—no department. No Nelie—no book.

CHAPTER 1
Roots of the Department of Medicine
1834–1942

The Department of Medicine of Emory University School of Medicine was catapulted into the front ranks of American medicine when, in 1942, Dr. Eugene A. Stead Jr. was appointed as Emory's first full-time professor and chairman of the Department of Medicine. Stead promptly attracted a group of brilliant young men who, over the years that followed, had a major impact on academic medicine at Emory and at other institutions where they became department chairmen. Dr. Paul Beeson was one of them. Beeson followed Stead as chairman of the Emory's Department of Medicine in 1946. Stead and Beeson deserve the credit for creating the high standards of medical education, patient care, and research that have challenged all who have followed them. They taught us all a lesson, because they accomplished what they did with little money and very poor facilities.

Chapter 1 of this book is designed to give the reader a glimpse of the events that preceded the giant steps made by Stead, Beeson, and their associates. The story, which began in 1834, is long, complex, and fascinating. The writing is done with a soft pencil—the literary equivalent of painting with a broad brush—because, if every detail were included, the events that are germane to the evolution of the development of the Department of Medicine at Emory would be lost. Accordingly, the names of most of the movers and shakers of the era are absent. The few people who are mentioned stood tall among many individuals who contributed to the evolution of what is now the Department of Medicine of Emory University School of Medicine.

In order to understand the genesis of the Department of Medicine it is necessary to understand the creation of Emory University, to know about the early medical schools in Atlanta and how they coalesced to become Emory University School of Medicine, to understand the relationship of certain hospitals to Emory University, and to meet some of the people who had the vision, energy, and resources to develop a mixture of ingredients that we now call the Department of Medicine.

The reader will find that the stories related in the biographies of some of the people overlap with narratives about the events of the period. Such

1

overlap, if unavoidable, at least has the benefit of reinforcing a chronology of the interesting events that occurred in the birth and metamorphosis of Emory University School of Medicine and its Department of Medicine.

Finally, the account you are reading is not merely a record of events. I initially planned simply to document the times and places of certain actions; however, as numerous source materials were reviewed and many individuals were interviewed, it became increasingly obvious that it was the people who made the story interesting. So the book is filled with biographies, statements, and anecdotes that not only give the historical record but add a dash of wholesome spice to the story.

The Genesis of Emory University

The Birth of Emory College

The Rebellion of "Uncle Allen" Turner

I would like to have known "Uncle Allen" Turner. His action, which could be classified as courageous, outrageous, or ornery, created the spark that ignited the fire that eventually led to the creation of Emory University. I choose to call his action courageous. Here is the story.

When the Georgia Methodist Conference met in Washington, Georgia, in 1834, the president of Randolph-Macon, the famous college located in Virginia, attended the meeting in order to make his annual plea to those with money to assist his college. Obviously, the Methodist church was interested in any educational institution that fostered the growth of Methodism. The members of the conference would have voted in the affirmative, but "Uncle Allen" Turner rebelled. He rose to state that the Methodists from Georgia should develop their own school rather than send their money and sons to another state. "Uncle Allen" Turner, having made an earthshaking contribution to the potential education of Georgians, never again entered the annals of history.

Because of the rebellion of "Uncle Allen" Turner, a manual labor school was created in Covington, Georgia, in 1835. Covington was located about thirty miles east of Atlanta. The school had thirty students but was not a roaring success and did not survive.

Creation of the Town of Oxford and Emory College

The Methodist leaders of the time continued to dream of the creation of a college in Georgia. The members of a subsequent Methodist Conference agreed with the plan for a college and obtained a charter from the Georgia state legislature. In 1836, this led to the simultaneous creation of the village of Oxford, Georgia, and of Emory College. The village and college were to be located adjacent to Covington, Georgia, on 1,453 acres of wooded land bought for $14,950.

The town was named Oxford because John Wesley, the founder of Methodism, was a graduate of Oxford University in England. The college was named Emory in memory of the educated-minded bishop John Emory of Maryland, who died in a carriage accident in 1835. He had been the presiding officer of the Methodist conference held in Washington, Georgia, in 1834 when "Uncle Allen" Turner spoke his mind.

Emory College thrived. The little village of Oxford was soon filled with teachers and preachers. If you close your eyes, you can still see them in your mind's eye. See them there—the scholars of the age walking slowly across the tree-shaded campus while reading Shakespeare, Homer, and the writings of John Wesley. Should you visit Oxford today, you can sense the scholarship that was characteristic of the era.

The Civil War and the Closing of Emory College

The college was closed during the Civil War because most able-bodied men were inducted into the Confederate Army. The major building at Emory College was converted into a hospital. Sherman, in his march to the sea, was supposed to destroy Covington, Georgia. He did not do so because several of Sherman's former West Point classmates lived there. The village of Oxford, however, did not escape the ravages of war. The village was invaded by Sherman's men in 1864. The homes were destroyed, as was the railroad. Medical supplies were no longer available, and the hospital was closed.

The Reopening of Emory College

The terrible war ended and Emory College reopened its doors in 1866. The former beautiful buildings were in shambles and there was little money. The Georgia legislature provided the money for the poor or disabled veterans to go to college. This act has been referred to as the first "GI bill" for education. So, in 1866–1867, 120 students enrolled in Emory College. Ninety-three of them were Civil War veterans.

Emory College continued to improve. Its high academic standards and excellent curriculum caught the attention of a New York banker named George I. Seney, who gave $130,000 to Emory College. Seney was impressed by a pamphlet in which Atticus G. Haygood, the college president, indicated that slavery had been wrong. His gift was used to pay off debts, construct a building, and add to the endowment of the school. Seney Hall on the Oxford campus is named for him.

The name of Candler appears early in this story because members of the Candler family became deeply involved in the development of all that is Emory. Warren Akin Candler, an Emory College alumnus, was appointed president of Emory College in 1888. He remained president until 1898, when he was elected bishop of the Methodist Episcopal Church, South. Because of his leadership and subsequent relationship to Emory, he is sometimes considered to be the founder of Emory University. The story of Warren Candler's brother, Asa Griggs Candler, and that of Coca-Cola will be told in a subsequent discussion. For the moment, we can merely emphasize that without the Candlers there would be no Emory University.

As will be discussed subsequently, the goals of the Oxford school changed several times before it became a part of Emory University in 1915. The beautiful Oxford campus was retained by the university and is now called Oxford College, following action by the Emory Board of Trustees in 1954. Two years of liberal arts education are offered there.

The Birth of Emory University

The Vanderbilt Controversy

The birth of Emory University was not the simple expansion of Emory College. Just as Emory College was created by the controversy that developed after "Uncle Allen" Turner rebelled at sending money and young Georgia men to Randolph-Macon College in Virginia, Emory University was established as a by-product of a controversy that involved Vanderbilt University in Nashville, Tennessee, and the Methodist Episcopal Church, South (MECS).

The controversy that raged between the Church and Vanderbilt University came about as follows. Representative members of the Methodist Episcopal Church, South, met in Memphis in 1872 and proposed the development of "Central University." Cornelius Vanderbilt gave $500,000 for its development. The new school was to be located in Nashville, Tennessee. The first students entered Vanderbilt in 1875. A controversy developed over the degree of control that the Church claimed over the university. This debate dominated the agenda of both the Church and Vanderbilt University for many years. In 1914, following a lawsuit brought by the MECS against Vanderbilt to determine the Church's control, the bond between the two was severed. In May of that same year, at the General Conference of the MECS, an Educational Commission was appointed by the conference officials. The commission was charged with the task of creating two institutions that were to be closely related to the Church. The officials suggested that one university should be located east of the Mississippi River and the other west. Bishop

Warren Candler of Georgia was named chairman of the commission. The officials of the conference also suggested that members of the commission should look at Southern Methodist University in Texas as the university that might possibly be designated as the university to be located west of the Mississippi. The Educational Commission was then charged with the responsibility of finding an appropriate location in the southeast where the new university that was to be located east of the Mississippi, could be located. The members of the conference dreamed of the creation of a major university where a school of theology could be developed. ·

The trustees of Emory College at Oxford, undoubtedly influenced by the Candlers, indicated to the members of the Educational Commission that they were prepared to work with them to achieve their goal. It is likely that some of the leaders of Emory College hoped that the university would be located in Oxford, while others preferred that it be in Atlanta.

How and Why Atlanta Was Chosen for the University

The Educational Commission met in Atlanta in July 1914. It had met previously in several other southern cities. Two important events occurred in the Atlanta meeting. The two events, in many ways, offered a preview of what was to happen over the next 80 years, and together they symbolized the vision, spirit, and generosity of the leaders of the city who forged the development of the new South. The forward-thinking Atlanta Chamber of Commerce, undoubtedly influenced by Asa Griggs Candler, proposed a gift of $500,000 if the new university were located in Atlanta. Furthermore, Asa Griggs Candler donated the land where the university could be built. He offered the commission a beautifully wooded area in his Druid Hills, a suburb on the northeastern edge of Atlanta. The Chamber of Commerce agreed to provide temporary classrooms, offices, and dormitory facilities so that the school of theology could open immediately. This part of the offer was possible because Warren and Asa Griggs Candler were the major spokesmen for the Wesley Memorial Church where some of the seminary's facilities would be located. The Chamber also promised the use of other facilities, including those in the Grady Memorial Hospital area, that could be used for the creation of a school of medicine. Apparently this was the first time a medical school had been mentioned.

The other earthshaking event came from one man, Asa Griggs Candler, who had already promised the land for the new university. His "million dollar letter" was sent to his brother, Bishop Warren A. Candler, chairman of the Educational Commission. Asa Griggs Candler gave $1,000,000 to create the university and wrote: "I do not seek a sectarian end." He hoped the new university would "benefit the people of my section and country without regard to denominational lines."[1]

A charter was procured in 1915, but the development of the university was actually begun in 1914 with the opening of the theology school. What would be the name of the new university? Several names were suggested, including Candler University, Emory-Candler University, Central University, Asbury University, and Candler-Asbury University. The Candlers would not permit the school to be named Candler. They chose to remain the builders but did not aspire to being recognized. Because Emory College was to be deeply involved in the creation of the university, the planners elected to continue to use the name Emory. So Emory University was born.

The Metamorphosis of Emory College at Oxford

The plan was to move Emory College at Oxford to the new Emory University campus in Atlanta. As part of a gradual transfer, in 1915 the Emory University Academy was created to replace Emory College at Oxford. The academy was an excellent high school that offered the usual college preparatory courses. The academy did not thrive, but powerful alumni of the old Emory College at Oxford were adamant that they did not want the Oxford campus closed. So, in 1929, after obtaining the funds to refurbish many of the buildings, a junior college was added to the academy. An associate dean for Emory-at-Oxford was appointed to oversee the academy and the junior college. The academy was eventually phased out, and a building program was initiated that not only restored the old buildings but also created new ones. This permitted the development of a two-year college that was commonly referred to as Emory at Oxford. The name of the college was officially changed in 1954 to Oxford College by the Emory Board of Trustees.

Oxford College is, sometimes considered to be the mother of Emory University; actually it is more like an older sister. It is a gem of an educational facility. It continues to serve the university well, because the students profit enormously from the small student body and a desirable teacher-student ratio. In addition, the alumni are emotionally and financially supportive of the two-year college. A visit to Oxford College today reminds one that there was once a group of scholars who walked between the buildings and trees reading bits of classic literature as they ambled along.

---

[1] T. H. English, *Emory University 1915–1965: A Semicentennial History* (Atlanta: Emory University, 1966), 13.

Emory also developed a two-year college in Valdosta, Georgia, in 1928. The school was discontinued in 1953 when Georgia State Women's College, located nearby, became coeducational. This eliminated the regional need for another two-year college.

Early Medical Schools that Preceded Emory University School of Medicine

Early Medical Schools

The first medical school in Atlanta was established in 1854 and was named the Atlanta Medical College. The medical school building was erected in 1859 in an area of Atlanta where Grady Memorial Hospital would eventually be erected (see Figure 1-1). The curriculum was entirely didactic, and clinical experience was gained through preceptorships. The medical school activities were discontinued during the Civil War, and the medical school building became a confederate hospital.

Another medical school was given a charter in 1878 and was named the Southern Medical College (see Figure 1-2). The two schools coexisted until 1898, when they merged to become the Atlanta College of Physicians and Surgeons (see Figure 1-3).

Dr. W. S. Kendrick, who had been Dean of Atlanta Medical College, became the Dean of the Atlanta College of Physicians and Surgeons. In 1905, however, Dr. Kendrick left and started another school called the Atlanta School of Medicine. The faculty used a hospital located on Luckie and Barton Streets for clinical teaching (no photographs are available of the facilities used by this school and hospital).

The two schools, the Atlanta College of Physicians and Surgeons and the Atlanta School of Medicine, coexisted until 1913. Although the keen competition between the two schools had improved both of them, it was to the advantage of both to pool their resources and seek university affiliation. Three years earlier the Carnegie Foundation had financed a survey that was designed to assess the quality of American medical schools. The survey, conducted by Abraham Flexner, was critical of both medical schools. Responding to the Flexner report, both schools made recommendations for improvements, and this led to the union of the two in 1913. The new school was named the Atlanta Medical College, adopting the name of the first medical school that was established in Atlanta in 1854.

The creation of medical schools and their subsequent disappearance always led to turmoil within the medical profession. Many physicians who taught in these early schools profited from the tuition paid by the students. They also developed a referral practice when their former students referred patients to them. Accordingly, the closing of a school adversely affected the careers and incomes of many physicians.

The Birth of Emory University School of Medicine

Following the Flexner report, there was increasing pressure for medical schools throughout the nation to be associated with universities. The pressure to do so was applied rather rigidly by the American Medical Association. To meet desired standards, the officials of the new Atlanta Medical College approached their counterparts who were planning the newly chartered Emory University and suggested a merger. The officials of the Atlanta Medical College proposed that the new university take over the assets and debts of the Atlanta Medical College. Emory University agreed to do so. Accordingly, on June 28, 1915, Emory University School of Medicine was born.

From 1915 to 1917 the entire Emory University School of Medicine was located in the building formerly used by the Atlanta College of Medicine, which was located across the street from the relatively new Grady Memorial Hospital (see Figure 1-3).

When the new anatomy, physiology, and chemistry buildings were completed on the Emory campus in Druid Hills in 1917, some of the basic science departments were moved to the new facilities. Medical students lived in Dobbs Hall on the Emory campus.

There was no hospital on the Emory campus until 1922, when the new Wesley Memorial Hospital was completed (its name was changed in 1932 to Emory University Hospital). This important development is discussed on page 14. The new Wesley Memorial Hospital almost closed because economic conditions in the South were dismal and sick patients could not afford doctors or hospitals. At one point there were only twenty-five hospitalized patients in the excellent facility. Nonetheless, two devoted physicians, Dr. Cyrus W. Strickler Sr. and Dr. Stewart Roberts, continued to admit their patients to the hospital. They are credited with saving the hospital from financial ruin.

The financial problems just mentioned prevented the use of the new hospital on the Emory campus for clinical instruction. Consequently the school continued to use the facilities in the old Atlanta Medical College for its clinical teaching of junior and senior medical students. The old building, owned by Emory, was leased to the city of Atlanta for one dollar a year. The building was converted into a hospital for African American patients by the city of Atlanta, with the understanding that Emory medical school's faculty and students could attend the patients there.

The Gray Clinic building, adjacent to the old Atlanta Medical College, was completed in 1917. It was owned by Emory and used as an outpatient clinic and educational facility.

The so-called "colored hospital," across Butler Street from Grady Memorial Hospital, was then designated as the Emory Division of Grady Memorial Hospital (see Figure 1-3). Prior to the development of the "colored hospital," all patients were admitted to the original Grady Memorial Hospital, where they were segregated according to race, as was the law then. After the old Atlanta Medical College building was converted into a hospital, the African-American patients were admitted there, and the original Grady Memorial Hospital, became the "white hospital." This development produced even more segregation. The two hospitals were staffed by different professional staffs and, in the beginning, the "white hospital" was not used by Emory for clinical teaching. The "white hospital" was not opened for clinical training of Emory students until 1931.

Thus there were two Grady Memorial Hospitals: one hospital served white patients and the other hospital served African-American patients. This is why the facilities were affectionately called "the Gradys." The separation of the races continued until 1965.

Hospitals Related to Emory University School of Medicine

Prior to 1942 there were three hospitals involved in the educational and patient care activities of Emory University School of Medicine. The first of these, as discussed above, was the hospital for black patients in the former Atlanta Medical College building across the street from Grady Memorial Hospital. The second was Grady Memorial Hospital itself, and the third was Wesley Memorial Hospital.

Grady Memorial Hospital and Its Adjoining Facilities

Towards the end of the nineteenth century the caring citizens of Atlanta saw the need for a hospital that would serve the poor patients of the city. The money needed to build the hospital was raised by public subscription. One hundred beds were allocated for indigent patients, and ten beds were allocated for paying patients. The hospital, located on Butler Street in Atlanta, was completed in January 1892, and formally dedicated on May 25 (see Figure 1-4). It was named for Henry W. Grady, the young, dynamic, editor of *The Atlanta Constitution* (see Figure 1-5). A photograph of the horse-drawn Grady Hospital ambulance is shown in Figure 1-6.

Henry W. Grady died of pneumonia in 1889 at the age of thirty-eight, before the hospital was completed. Why did the citizens of Atlanta name the hospital for him? Henry W. Grady was a forward-thinking, concerned Southerner, who became the leading emotional voice of the region. He was a great orator and writer. Like a Winston Churchill with a southern accent, he could move and improve those who listened to him or read his words. The following account of him can be found in the 1935 Grady Memorial Hospital Annual Report.

> Henry Woodfin Grady was born in Athens, Georgia, in 1851. In the short compass of thirty-eight years, he wove a web of good will over a war-torn country, "Literally loving a nation into peace."
>
> He was a far-sighted and constructive citizen whose activities gave a distracted and despairing section a new vision of its possibilities of again taking its proper place in the life of the reunited nation.
>
> From his golden pen came words of comfort that glowed upon his editorial pages, awakening hope in the hearts of the discouraged, giving energy to the dispirited and, flooding love into many saddened souls.
>
> From his silver tongue came words of wisdom and inspiration that brought the City of Atlanta out of the ashes, giving impetus to his industrial and commercial growth, and a spirit that lives as an evidence of his genius.
>
> He founded the Young Men's Library Association, which later became our Carnegie Library. He established the Y.M.C.A. in Atlanta. He motivated the Atlanta Exposition, which did so much to attract the attention of the nation to the possibilities of Atlanta as one of the important cities of the South.
>
> Out of the constructive spirit that he awakened, came this hospital, that as an enduring memorial to his greatness now bears his honored name. Here it stands as a living expression of his benevolent attitude toward his fellowman, and the generous and unselfish spirit that prompted his many acts of innate kindliness and great good will.
>
> Henry W. Grady died in 1889 but prior to his death he had waged an unremitting and successful campaign in behalf of the building of a general hospital to serve the indigent sick of Atlanta and vicinity.
>
> The cornerstone of the first building was laid December 23, 1890, by John S. Davidson, Grand Master of Georgia Free and Accepted Masons. It bears the following inscription:
>
> "Erected in memory of Henry Woodfin Grady whose heart, so easily moved by others' woes, would get no fitter monument."

The patients were segregated in the original Grady Memorial Hospital because that was the law of the day. The hospital staff included a pharmacist, a head nurse, four graduate nurses, and sixteen undergraduate nurses. There were four or five general house officers who were appointed for a period of two years (see Figure 1-7). They were selected by the score they made on an examination. The practicing physicians of Atlanta gave their services to the indigent patients of

Atlanta. The first Atlanta Medical College and the Southern Medical College existed before Grady Memorial Hospital was opened in 1892. After Grady Memorial Hospital was built, the medical schools did not use the hospital for the training of medical students, although faculty members were on the staff. The lecture system was used for teaching medical students because Osler's contention that students should work with patients on the wards of a hospital had not been heeded by all of the "educators" of the day. The four general house officers who worked at Grady were not appointed by the officials of the medical schools of that period. Students were, however, permitted to see patients in the clinics. Following graduation it was customary for a young physician to serve a preceptorship with a practicing physician. Apparently, the first "ward walk" in Grady Memorial Hospital for medical students occurred in 1908. Such a "walk" consisted of the students moving from bed to bed under the strict supervision of an instructor. The assignment of students to patients who were hospitalized there did not occur until many years later.

A children's ward was added to Grady Memorial Hospital in 1896, and a maternity ward was added in 1903. The Butler Street building was constructed as an annex to Grady Memorial Hospital and was occupied in June 1912 (see Figure 1-8). This addition provided 110 additional beds. This facility also provided space so that all the patients in the hospital could be exposed to the open air, as was the custom of the day.

A contagious-disease hospital was built near Grady Memorial Hospital in 1907–1908 and taken over by Grady Memorial Hospital in 1933. Florida Hall was built in 1922. Patients with venereal disease were treated there by personnel from the city health department. Later, in 1945, Florida Hall was converted into an isolation hospital.

Hirsch Hall was built in 1922 and was used to house ninety white nurses. Feebeck Hall was completed in 1944 and housed 122 nurses. The Butler Street home for African-American nurses was formerly located just north of the "colored hospital" (see Figure 1-8). It was later demolished and became a parking lot. In 1952, the Hughes Spalding private hospital for African-American patients was erected on that site.

The Atlanta Medical College occupied the building on the corner of Butler Street and Armstrong Street until 1915, when it became Emory University School of Medicine. The building, owned by Emory University, was located across the street from the original Grady Memorial Hospital. The city of Atlanta leased the building and converted the facility into a hospital for African-American patients who went to Grady, although Emory faculty continued to occupy part of the building (see Figure 1-3). Emory permitted the development with the understanding that Emory would supervise the patient care and utilize the patients in the educational programs of the new medical school. The African-American patients were moved from the original Grady Memorial Hospital to the "new" hospital across the street. This created the "Gradys" because there was a "white hospital" and a "colored hospital." The lower floor, or basement, of the "colored hospital" contained a large classroom, autopsy room, laboratories, and the medical school library, and offices. The African-American patients were housed in the upper three floors.

In 1917 the Emory University-owned J. J. Gray building was erected on Armstrong Street adjacent to the "colored hospital" (see Figure 1-9). It served as an outpatient facility and emergency room for African-American patients. It also housed some of Emory Medical School faculty. The members of the house staff assigned to the "colored hospital" lived on the fourth floor. The fifth floor was used for animal quarters and animal operating facilities. (As will be discussed later, the building, with the help of Robert W. Woodruff, was converted into an Emory research facility in 1965.)

The Albert Steiner Clinic was created in 1924 as a separate hospital for the research and care of patients with cancer (see Figure 1-10). Initially administered by Grady Memorial Hospital, it was later governed by a separate board of trustees, whose members were closely related to the Steiner family and estate. Steiner had made his money in the Atlanta breweries. Still later its operation was returned to Grady Memorial Hospital.

The Albert Steiner Clinic was a complete hospital, and excellent work was accomplished there. The clinic was one of the first to be devoted solely to neoplastic diseases. New methods of treatment were tested, and patients were given medical care that was not available elsewhere. The hospital was not accepted by everyone, and a controversy developed that was settled when Steiner officials agreed to accept only indigent Grady patients at the facility. This, in turn, led to a financial crisis that was solved when Grady Memorial Hospital absorbed the facility and discontinued its use as a separate hospital. The building was later used for many different activities, including the cardiac catheterization laboratory and offices for Emory faculty members. Later, in 1975, the building was leased by Emory and used for faculty offices. A new auditorium was added to the building to accommodate the increase in educational activities.

Physicians who remember the Steiner Clinic believe that the lessons learned there are important. They see a bit of the Steiner concept in famous cancer centers such as Sloan-Kettering and M. D. Anderson neoplastic hospitals. Its presence and use by Grady patients also stimulated the development of the Robert Winship Memorial Clinic in

Emory University Hospital for nonindigent patients who suffered from cancer.

The Grady Clay Eye Clinic was added to the Grady complex in 1949. Supervised by Emory faculty, it was later used as the Grady Memorial Hospital branch of the Communicable Disease Center (now called the Centers for Disease Control and Prevention). Still later, it was demolished.

The units of the sprawling Grady Memorial Hospital complex were connected by an underground tunnel in 1936.

Grady Memorial Hospital was initially owned by the City of Atlanta and governed by a private, self-perpetuating board of trustees. In 1921 a committee associated with the Atlanta City Council assumed the trustee duties and responsibilities. A scandal occurred when members of the committee were convicted of graft. Because of this an effort was made to free the governance of Grady Memorial Hospital from the politics of that period. In 1941 the Georgia legislature passed a law allowing the creation of the Fulton-DeKalb Hospital Authority so that the hospital would no longer be the responsibility of the city of Atlanta but would fall under Fulton and DeKalb Counties' jurisdiction. Because of World War II the activation of the Hospital Authority was delayed until January 1, 1946. This important governing authority consisted of concerned citizens who were appointed by Fulton and DeKalb Counties. The citizens who served on the Hospital Authority were wise, caring people. These leading citizens deserve much credit for the success Grady Memorial Hospital has attained. The Fulton-DeKalb Hospital Authority effectively removed Grady Memorial Hospital from the hands of the politicians and established an important contractual relationship with Emory University School of Medicine.

Despite some irritating day-to-day problems, the partnership of Grady Memorial Hospital and Emory University School of Medicine survived, and the facility became recognized as an excellent place for medical students and house officers to train. Prior to Dr. Eugene A. Stead Jr.'s arrival in 1942 (and for a time afterwards), Emory University School of Medicine did not fully utilize "white Grady" for teaching students and house staff. Emory's activity was predominantly limited to the "colored hospital."

Grady Memorial Hospital developed a School of Nursing and graduated superb nurses. For many years the hospital supported two nursing schools—one for African-American nurses and one for white nurses.

Prior to 1942 and for several years afterwards, all of the clinical departments of Emory University School of Medicine and the dean's office were located in the "colored hospital," where instruction in the clinical years took place. Some of the basic sciences were taught on the Emory campus. Hugh Wood was the first Emory dean to develop an office on the Emory campus. He first established a small secondary office in the Physiology Building, later moving his major office into the new Woodruff Memorial Research Building on the Emory campus in 1954.

Prior to 1942 there was only one full-time clinical department chairman at Emory, Dr. J. R. McCord, who was chairman of the Department of Obstetrics. Dr. McCord was referred to as a "dollar-a-year" man. He was able to devote his time to teaching at Grady Memorial Hospital because he had a private income and enjoyed teaching and patient care. The remaining faculty members for the "colored hospital" were volunteers. The medical school was held together by Dean Russell Oppenheimer, who was for a time also chairman of the Department of Medicine. The Department of Medicine was blessed by having devoted volunteer teachers such as Strickler, Roberts, Paullin, and others. The physicians who attended patients in "white Grady" were also volunteers but were in a separate category from the staff assigned to "colored Grady." The physicians assigned to "white Grady" were appointed by the Grady Hospital Board.

Even before 1942, the administrators of Grady Memorial Hospital played key roles; they were not only involved in the administration of the hospital but were also major movers in the relationship of Emory University School of Medicine to Grady Memorial Hospital.

The working arrangement of Emory University School of Medicine and Grady Memorial Hospital was not always perfect, but it worked to the advantage of both institutions. It should be remembered that Emory University School of Medicine had few facilities on the Emory campus for clinical instruction, and Emory University Hospital was utilized very little for clinical teaching prior to, and for some time after, 1942. Because of this situation, Emory needed Grady for its clinical teaching, and Grady needed Emory physicians for the professional supervision of patients who were admitted there.

Wesley Memorial Hospital

Wesley Memorial Hospital was opened in 1904 (see Figure 1-11). The forty-bed hospital was named for John Wesley, the founder of Methodism. The hospital was located on the corner of Courtland Street and Auburn Avenue in the Old Calico House. This historic house had been the headquarters of General Sherman during his occupation of the city of Atlanta. The hospital was managed by the North Georgia Methodist Conference.

By 1920, the need for a new facility became apparent, and Asa Griggs Candler donated the land and more than $1,000,000 to build a new Wesley Memorial Hospital on the Emory campus. It was completed in 1922 (see Figure 1-12). The planners of the new hospital had originally planned to build the new hospital in the Grady Memorial Hospital area, but Asa Griggs Candler, always a visionary, insisted that the new Wesley Memorial Hospital be built on the Emory University campus where education was to be emphasized.

A small house staff, consisting of four rotating interns, was trained in the new Wesley Memorial Hospital, although the hospital was not associated with the medical school until 1925. In the beginning, the degree of clinical teaching conducted there was limited because the hospital barely survived from the lack of patients. The name of the hospital was changed to Emory University Hospital in 1932. For many years the hospital stationery was embossed with both names, and finally the name Wesley Memorial Hospital was omitted. The new 150-bed hospital served as an open-staffed community hospital. There were two wings plus a separate, three-story building called the Lucy Elizabeth Pavilion (LEP), which was named for Asa Griggs Candler's wife. The Lucy Elizabeth Pavilion was financed by the children of Asa Griggs Candler as a memorial to their mother. It housed the obstetrical service and a large auditorium. The building was later connected to the hospital.

As the medical library grew, it was moved from the third floor of the Anatomy Building to one location after another in Emory University Hospital. As will be discussed later, in 1954 the medical library was moved to the new Ernest Woodruff Memorial Research Building, which was connected to the hospital. On February 6, 1985, when the undergraduate Emory dental school was closed, two floors of the redesigned building were designated for the use of the Robert W. Woodruff Health Sciences Center Library.

Before the forties only a few full-time basic science faculty members gained national recognition: Dr. Roy Kracke in pathology and hematology, Dr. Jean George Bachmann in physiology, and Dr. Homer P. "Butch" Blincoe in anatomy. There were no full-time faculty in the clinical departments except for Dr. J. R. McCord, who was in charge of obstetrics and Dean Oppenheimer who also served as Chairman of the Department of Medicine.

With the development of the anatomy, physiology, and chemistry buildings, and Emory University Hospital, on the Emory campus there were two powerful magnets operating in the medical school: the magnetic pull of the Emory campus, where basic sciences were taught and where clinical training was potentially possible, and the magnetic

pull of Grady Memorial Hospital, where most of the clinical training was
being implemented.

Major Leaders

It is always risky to name a few individuals who stand tall in a field
populated by many capable and loyal workers. Obviously, hundreds of
people gave their time, talent, and money to the development of Emory
University School of Medicine and its Department of Medicine. They
expected and received no reward except for the satisfaction they felt for
being involved in a noble cause. Ten of these people will be discussed.

"Uncle Allen" Turner and Others

We must not forget *"Uncle Allen" Turner*, whose single rebelling voice
eventually led to the creation of the college at Oxford; the controversy
involving Vanderbilt University and the Methodist church, out of which
came the call for a new university east of the Mississippi; and the leaders
of Emory College at Oxford who indicated that they stood ready to help
establish the new university. These three factors, it seems, created the
circumstances underlying the formation of Emory University.

Asa Griggs Candler and the Candler Family

Emory University would not exist, had it not been for Asa Griggs
Candler, his family, and Coca-Cola. Photographs of the portraits of Asa
Griggs Candler, and his wife Lucy Elizabeth, are shown in Figures 1-13A
and 1-13B. Few stories can be told that are more fascinating and
heartwarming than this one.[2]

Asa Griggs Candler was born on December 30, 1851, on a farm in
Carroll County near Villa Rica, Georgia. His father, Samuel Charles
Candler, owned two farms and managed a mercantile business in Villa
Rica. Charles Howard Candler, Asa's son, records the effect of the Civil
War on his grandfather's home:

> . . . [The Civil War] reduced the standard of living of his home from near
> affluence to one of bare subsistence. It resulted in financial ruin and loss of
> everything except the land, almost denuded of everything animate and
> inanimate that might have been of service to marauding bands of both armies.
> It meant the death-knell of father's hopes and those of my grandfather for a
> medical career for him. More than that, it meant that [father] had, by present
> day standards, almost no formal education beyond the elementary grades.[3]

---

[2] The following biography of Asa Griggs Candler was excerpted from the book *Asa Griggs Candler*, written by his son, Charles Howard Candler Sr. (Atlanta: Emory University, 1950).

[3] C. H. Candler, *Asa Griggs Candler* (Atlanta: Emory University, 1950), 19.

Samuel Charles Candler and Martha Beall Candler named their son Asa Griggs in honor of the former tutor of their two older sons. The tutor, Asa W. Griggs, was a medical student (he later became a prominent professor at the Atlanta Medical College, before it became Emory University School of Medicine). He had been a student of Dr. Milton Anthony of Augusta, who was related to Samuel Charles Candler. Dr. Anthony eventually became prominent in the development of the University of Georgia School of Medicine—now the Medical College of Georgia—in Augusta. It was Dr. Anthony who recommended Asa W. Griggs to be the tutor for the two older sons of Samuel Charles Candler.

Martha Beall Candler, the mother of Asa, married Samuel Charles Candler when she was fourteen years old. She had eleven children. It is interesting to note that Martha's father gave her a slave girl named Mary and an Indian pony for wedding presents. Martha Beall Candler instilled a deep-seated religious faith in her eleven children.

Samuel and Martha Candler had high hopes for their children and dreamed that Asa Griggs Candler would go to medical school. The Civil War changed their plans. The family barely survived the ravages of war, and Asa had no opportunities and little education.

He earned his first dollar selling mink skins. As a boy he chased and caught a mink that ran from under the family's house. He reasoned he could sell the skin in town for twenty-five cents. He sold it for one dollar. Seeing an opportunity to make more money, he proceeded to organize the neighbors to catch mink and sell them to him. He then sold them for a profit. He also earned $100 by selling straight pins he bought in town to his country neighbors. He learned how to make a profit.

Asa Griggs Candler had only seven years of schooling. He had been in school for five years when the schools were closed because of the Civil War. Later he spent a year with his sister in Huntsville, Alabama, where he attended school. When he returned to his home in Villa Rica, he attended school for one more year. He continued to study, however, because he did not give up the idea of becoming a physician until he was in his twenties. He recognized that his father had no resources to send him to college and medical school. This being true, he turned his mind toward working in a drug store. He became an apprentice to two physicians, Drs. Best and Kilpatrick, who operated a drug store in Cartersville, Georgia. He lived in the store and, when he was not working, studied Latin, Greek, chemistry, and medicine.

After learning to be a prescriptionist, he decided to leave Cartersville for a larger town, because Cartersville was not large enough to support a prescriptionist. He wrote Dr. Asa Griggs, who was, by then, a member of the faculty at the Atlanta Medical College. Apparently, Dr. Griggs advised him to move to Atlanta. Following this encouragement, Asa Griggs Candler moved from Cartersville to Atlanta in 1873.

He arrived in Atlanta wearing homemade clothes and with $1.75 in his pocket. He walked the streets looking for work as a pharmacist. He visited almost every drug store in town. He was turned down by Pemberton-Pullman Drug Company located in the Kimball House. Pemberton would reenter Asa Candler's life at a later time. Asa was hired at last by George Jefferson Howard to work in his drug store near the Kimball House on Peachtree Street. Paid nothing until he proved himself, Asa lived in a small room on the first floor of the three-story building.

He worked hard and eventually became the chief clerk at George Howard's drug store. He was twenty-one years of age when his father died. Because of his father's death he moved back to the farm in Carroll County to take care of his mother and the younger members of his family. During that period he engaged in manual labor and undoubtedly learned more about the business of farming. He remained there for more than two years until his mother and family moved to Cartersville, where one of his sisters lived.

Asa moved back to Atlanta in January 1875 to resume his position as chief clerk at the drug store owned by George Howard. He remained there for two years and learned more about business and the business world. He then moved to a higher plane of business activity. Leaving Howard's drug store, he formed a partnership with Marcellus B. Hallman and created the name Hallman and Candler, Wholesale and Retail Druggist. The exact location of the store is unclear—it was either forty-seventh or forty-ninth Peachtree Street. Asa Candler would, from then on, own his own business, never again working for another man. Parenthetically, it should be noted that Dr. J. S. Pemberton, a pharmacist and nonpracticing physician, replaced Asa Candler at George Howard's drug store.

In the years that followed, Asa Candler began to spread his interests. He began to invest in Atlanta real estate. He married Lucy Elizabeth Howard, the daughter of his former boss. George J. Howard had been against the relationship and sent his daughter, known as Lizzie, away to college in Winston-Salem, North Carolina, when she was thirteen years of age. Four years later he sent her to LaGrange College, in LaGrange, Georgia. Lizzie Howard and Asa Griggs Candler decided to marry at Christmas in 1877, and she refused to return to LaGrange College. George Howard refused to go to the wedding. But later, when his daughter became pregnant, Howard wrote a brief note to her stating that he would "bury the hatchet."

Asa Candler bought his first home and bought out his partner, Mr. Hallman, who was retiring. The drug store continued as Candler and Company. In April 1882 he sold a half-interest in the store to his father-in-law and former employer. As Atlanta continued to grow, so did the business at the drug store.

The firm of Howard and Candler bought out Pemberton, Iverson and Denison. Pemberton, who had replaced Asa Candler at Howard's first store, had later joined Iverson and Denison. Pemberton and his son now started the Pemberton Chemical Company.

In 1886, Asa Candler bought out George Howard, who was retiring. Candler was becoming an excellent businessman. He would, from time to time, invest in side ventures that seemed likely to succeed. He bought the formulas for: Botanic Blood Balm; Delectalane, a dentifrice; and Everlasting Cologne, a perfume. On April 14, 1888, Asa Griggs Candler bought one-third of a formula for an elixir called Coca-Cola. On August 30, 1888, he became the sole owner of Coca-Cola. (The details of his ownership of Coca-Cola will be told subsequently.)

His investments increased, but he was not a wealthy man. He concluded, with much courage, that he would sell his successful business and devote full time to the production and marketing of Coca-Cola. Accordingly, at the age of thirty-eight he sold his business for $50,000 and devoted himself to the production and marketing of Coca-Cola.

The story of Coca-Cola begins with Dr. J. S. Pemberton. Pemberton was a native of Columbus, Georgia. After Asa Candler bought out Pemberton, Iverson and Denison, Pemberton created the Pemberton Chemical Company in his home on Marietta Street in Atlanta, across from the Glenn Memorial Building. It was in the kitchen and backyard of this home that the compulsive Pemberton created his magic formula. It is interesting to note that he concocted about 2,600 different drinks. Only one drink survived, and an associate, F. M. Robinson, named it Coca-Cola. Pemberton sold the "extract" to local drug stores. But when he became too ill to manage the business, he offered to sell two-thirds of his interest in the formula to George S. Lowndes. Lowndes asked Willis E. Venable to join him in buying the two-thirds interest in the formula. Venable, who was the manager of Jacobs' Drug Store, had no money but agreed to handle the production of Coca-Cola if Lowndes would pay the $1,200 required to buy the two-thirds interest. The $1,200 was to be repaid to Lowndes from the profits of the company.

Lowndes and Venable, as the new controlling partners, bought all of the materials and fixtures used by Pemberton to make the "extract." The bill was $283.29. Venable was to produce Coca-Cola in the basement of Jacobs' Drug Store. Although sales increased, Lowndes was not happy with the progress Venable was making and bought his share of the partnership. Lowndes then owned two-thirds of the interest in the formula. Lowndes could not assume the responsibility of producing and marketing the product and sold his share to Woolfolk Walker and Mrs. M. C. Dozier, who was Walker's sister, for $1,200. Walker wanted to buy Pemberton's one-third interest in Coca-Cola as well, but did not have the money to do so. He asked Asa Griggs Candler and Dr. Joseph Jacobs to join him and to supply the money for the purpose of buying Pemberton's share. They paid Pemberton $550 for his share, making Asa Griggs Candler a holder of one-ninth of a share.

It soon became apparent, however, that Asa Candler had paid all of the $550 himself, making him the owner of Pemberton's third. This action, however, was not duly recorded. He quickly bought one half of the two-thirds owned by Walker and Dozier for $750 and later bought the final third from Walker and Dozier for $1,000. In order to avoid confusion about the $550 used to buy Pemberton's interest, Asa Candler subsequently prepared an official record to document the action on April 22, 1891, in which Walker, Candler and Company, and Jacobs assigned all interest in Coca-Cola to Asa Candler. Asa Candler had become the sole owner of the formula, trademark, and all other rights. The charter permitting the creation of The Coca-Cola Company was issued on January 29, 1892. Asa Candler paid a total of about $2,300 for the formula.

This is not the place to discuss the success of The Coca-Cola Company. Suffice it to state that if one had invested $40 in the Coca-Cola Company in 1919, he or she would be worth about $3,500,000 today.

Asa Candler became wealthy, and so did the members of his family and his friends. Most of his wealth came from the success of The Coca-Cola Company, but he made other successful investments. He bought the land and developed Druid Hills in Atlanta. He owned large buildings in Atlanta, Baltimore, and New York. He built a huge warehouse in Atlanta for the storage of bales of cotton, a move that helped stabilize the cotton business. He also developed a successful bank in Atlanta and was a director in the Southern States Life Insurance Company, the Georgia Railway and Power Company, the Georgia and Florida Railway, and the Southeastern Fair Association.

Asa Candler was not interested in wealth for himself. Above all, he wanted to be useful. He found rest only when he worked. He was profoundly religious and brought his Christian views to the world of business. He believed that all wealth belonged to the Creator. He loved people, the Methodist Church, Atlanta, and Emory University. He gave almost all of his time and talent to the Methodist Church and Emory University.

It is not possible to list all of the gifts Asa Griggs Candler made to the State of Georgia, Atlanta, the Methodist Church, Emory University, and other educational institutions. The following, incomplete list of his benefactions will give the reader an idea of the contributions he made to the betterment of the community in which he lived.

• He provided the money to build several churches.
• He gave land for a park.
• His warehouse, and his influence with important banks, saved many cotton farmers.
• As mayor of Atlanta for two years (1917 to 1919), he eliminated a debt and loaned $360,000 to the city to improve its water works and water supply system. He personally contributed another $250,000. The city of Atlanta built the nurses' dormitory, Hirsh Hall, on the Grady Hospital campus while he was mayor.
• His earliest contribution to an educational institution was to build and finance the Moreland Park Military Academy.
• He contributed $20,000 to a Methodist mission school in Cuba.
• Asa Candler's first gift to Emory College was in the late 1890's. He was interested in the little college at Oxford, Georgia, because his brother, Bishop Warren Candler, had served as its president and two of his sons had graduated from there. He gave $500 to establish the Quillian Lectureship. He also accepted a position on the board of trustees. He became chairman of the finance committee in 1900. He gave several thousand dollars toward the cost of a gymnasium. He contributed $50,000 to a $300,000 endowment drive, later increasing the amount when the goal was not reached. He gave $67,000 for the construction of the Haygood dormitory. Later, when financial difficulty arose at the college, he made up the deficit with a gift of $30,000. When the General Conference of the Methodist Episcopal Church, South, voted to terminate the relationship with Vanderbilt University in 1914, the Educational Commission of the Methodist Episcopal Church, South, was formed. It was to:

> "provide at the earliest possible time for the establishment and maintenance of a Biblical School or Department of Theology," and was directed, if necessary, "to arrange for the temporary establishment of such a school or department . . . either separate from or in conjunction with some institution now under the control and management" of the church.[4]

---

[4] T. H. English, *Emory University 1915–1965: A Semicentennial History* (Atlanta: Emory University, 1966), 12.

As discussed earlier, Bishop Warren A. Candler was chosen as the chairman of the commission, and Asa Candler was elected to be the treasurer.[5] Several cities, including Birmingham, Alabama; Washington, D.C.; Hendersonville, North Carolina; and Atlanta were competing for the new institution.

The leaders of Emory College at Oxford indicated that they were prepared to support the view of the commission. At the time, Asa Candler was president of the Emory College board and the treasurer of the commission. Wesley Memorial Church and the old Wesley Memorial Hospital were offered as temporary facilities for a school of theology and a school of medicine. This was possible because Asa Candler and Warren Candler were on the board of trustees of the Wesley Memorial Enterprise, which controlled the Wesley Memorial Church and the old Wesley Memorial Hospital. In fact, Asa Candler had personally contributed heavily to the erection of the church and the maintenance of hospital. The Atlanta Chamber of Commerce, of which Asa Candler was an influential past president, offered to give $500,000 to the new university. Asa Candler, who had founded and financed Druid Hills, offered a seventy-five acre tract of land to the new institution. Later the size of the campus was enlarged many times by gifts of Asa Candler. Asa Candler wrote his "million dollar letter" on July 16, 1914, to Bishop Candler, making clear his views as to the goals of the University and pledging $1,000,000 for its development. This was heralded at the time as the largest gift ever made to a southern educational institution.

• Asa Candler was on the Emory Committee that met with the trustees of Atlanta Medical College to determine the terms under which the medical college would be accepted by Emory University. The terms of the merger were accomplished on May 24, 1915, and on June 28 the entire holdings of the Atlanta Medical College were deeded to Emory University, thus transforming the medical college into a medical department of the university. Asa Candler established a trust fund of $250,000 for the development of Emory University School of Medicine.

• In 1916 four buildings were completed on the Emory campus for the school of theology, which was later named the Candler School of Theology for Warren Candler. The Lamar School of Law occupied its own building the same year. The anatomy, physiology, and chemistry buildings were added to the complex the next year on land that was given to Emory by Asa Candler. The buildings were first used in 1917

---

[5] This text is somewhat similar to that presented earlier. It is repeated here, in more detail, in order to preserve the continuity of discussion regarding the contributions made by Asa Candler to the creation of Emory University.

for the teaching of freshmen and sophomore students of Emory University School of Medicine.

• In 1918 more buildings were erected on the Emory campus using funds advanced by Asa Candler. During the year, Asa Candler made a large gift to the university. It included the notes used to secure the erection of the buildings. The gifts to Emory University and Emory College that year totaled $1,054,834.29, of which a large part was given by Asa Candler.

• In 1918 there were no residential houses near the Emory campus, and there was no place for the members of the faculty to live. Asa Candler used more of his land to build about fifteen homes, later selling them to Emory for a fraction of the cost.

• Asa Candler contributed a large amount of money to the development of Wesley Memorial Hospital. By 1914, Wesley Memorial Hospital and the buildings for its school of nurses had become outdated. A new hospital was needed. Warren and Asa Candler went to work and, as was customary for them, succeeded in creating the atmosphere in which a new hospital was assured. Asa Candler indicated he would give $3.00 for every $1.00 raised by the women of Wesley Memorial Church. The new hospital was to be built on Washington Street-Trinity property and was to be offered to the newly formed Emory University School of Medicine. The Candlers were on both of the boards at that time, so of course the gift was accepted by Emory. Strangely, and apparently without Asa Candler's approval, another site was selected for the location of the new hospital. Many people wanted to build the new hospital on the Grady Memorial Hospital campus near the old Atlanta Medical College, which was by then the Emory University School of Medicine. The Washington Street-Trinity Avenue site was given up but Asa Candler retained the land at a cost of $95,000. Plans were then created for a new Wesley Memorial Hospital and outpatient department to be erected on Butler Street. The plans were actually published in the *Atlanta Constitution* on November 6, 1916. This surprised and concerned Asa Candler, who usually avoided controversy and was not satisfied with the idea. His son, Charles Howard, wrote the following about his father's view.

> He realized for the future years and generations, the campus of Emory University was the logical and best place for a great hospital.[6]

Asa Candler reasoned that the hospital would offer opportunities for the medical students who were already spending the first two years of

---

[6] C. H. Candler, *Asa Griggs Candler* (Atlanta: Emory University, 1950), 367.

their schooling on the Emory campus. Not everyone accepted this view, but Asa Candler persisted, and the Emory campus was eventually selected for the location of the new hospital. The building would cost $1,000,000, and Emory University did not have the resources to build the structure. Asa Candler said it would be built "because he knew the donor." The hospital actually cost him $1,750,000 and became his pride and joy.

Twenty-five patients were moved from the old "Calico House" to the new Wesley Memorial Hospital on the Emory campus on December 11, 1922. The name of the hospital was changed to Emory University Hospital in 1932.

• In 1923–24 Asa Candler gave Emory University $1,000,000 to cover the deficits most of the schools at Emory University were incurring. He also gave sixty-five more acres of land to expand the campus.

• He gave $500,000 for the creation of the Asa Griggs Candler library in 1926, although he did not approve the use of his name.

• Many of his gifts, including the establishment of a chair in medicine, directly and indirectly assisted the Department of Medicine of Emory University School of Medicine.

• In 1924 he gave Emory University a $2,000,000 annuity with the understanding that he would receive the income of the annuity during his lifetime. At his death the entire amount could be added to the university's endowment.

• Other members of the Candler family contributed enormously of their time and resources to Emory University. His brother, Bishop Warren Candler, worked closely with Asa to develop Emory University. The school of theology is named for Warren.

Obviously, Asa Candler, who gave so much of his time and money to Emory University, contributed to Emory's rise to be one of the great universities in our nation. Asa Candler viewed his contributions to Emory University as the "crowning achievement" of his career. He also viewed Emory University Hospital as the "jewel in the crown."

Charles Howard Candler Sr., Asa's son, contributed time and money to the university. In 1996 there are twenty-four Howard Candler professorships spread among several schools within the university. I was a Charles Howard Candler Professor of Medicine.

The children of Asa Candler provided the funds to add the Lucy Elizabeth Pavilion (LEP) for obstetrics to Emory University Hospital. This facility also contained an auditorium. The building, named for Asa Candler's wife, Lizzie, was later attached to the hospital. I joined Dr. Bruce Logue in Dr. Paul Beeson's Department of Medicine in 1950; our offices were located in the ground floor of the Lucy Elizabeth Pavilion.

Asa Candler became profoundly depressed after the death of his wife on February 22, 1919. He deteriorated until he had to be confined in Emory University Hospital for the last three years of his life. During most of the time he did not recognize his family or friends. He died in the hospital he loved on March 12, 1929. The information available suggests that he had Alzheimer's disease and suffered the consequences and complications of that devastating condition.

No one can determine the exact amount of money he poured into the state of Georgia, Atlanta, the Methodist Church, Emory College at Oxford, Emory University and Emory University Hospital. In addition, he gave the University large amounts of priceless land. More than that, he gave his life to the university. He spent most of his life on committees that welded Emory College in Oxford, Emory University, Emory University Hospital, and Emory University School of Medicine into a single magnificent whole.

It has been estimated that Asa Candler gave over $8,000,000 and a great deal of land to Emory University. I cannot accurately translate this figure into current equivalent dollars; however, if we assume he gave the money and land to the university from 1915 to 1930, the equivalent current dollars would be about $240,000,000 or more, and the land value would have increased in value to at least as much. Accordingly, his gifts to Emory would be worth more than $480,000,000. Just as important, he gave himself to the development of the university. He taught the citizens of Atlanta to give their time and money for just causes. One wonders how he developed his Coca-Cola empire when he spent so much time working for the development of the university. The whole affair seems like a miracle of some gigantic proportion. How did this unschooled, unselfish, highly religious man accomplish all that he did? With it all, he never felt he was successful, because he really wanted to be a physician.

When he died, the city of Atlanta and the nation mourned the loss of this great man. He, along with the great orator, Henry W. Grady, had moved Atlanta and the South into a new magnificent era.

No one who loves Emory University can read Howard Candler's book about his father, Asa Candler, without being emotionally moved by the sheer goodness of the man and his family.

Dean Simpson Elkin[7]

Dr. Simpson Elkin deserves much credit for his role in the evolution of several antecedent schools that led eventually to Emory University

---

[7] A portion of the profile on Dean Simpson Elkin was written by Dr. Evangeline Papageorge.

School of Medicine, of which he was the first dean (1915–1925; see Figure 1-14).

W. S. Elkin was born in 1858 in Lancaster, Kentucky. The son of a prosperous farmer, he had the advantage of a liberal college education before entering one of the leading medical schools in the country, and this at a time when most physicians rarely had more than two years of high school before entering medical school. In 1879 he received the A.B. from Center College in his home state, and in 1882 he was graduated from the University of Pennsylvania School of Medicine. In that same year he came to Atlanta, where he lived until his death on April 24, 1944.

With his background, the young Dr. Elkin became prominent soon after this arrival in Atlanta. In 1884 we find him serving as president of the newly established Atlanta Academy of Medicine and a member of the faculty of Southern Medical College. It was he who in 1898 proposed to Dr. W. S. Kendrick, dean of the Atlanta Medical College, that the two schools merge. And thus the Atlanta College of Physicians and Surgeons was formed with Dr. Kendrick as dean. When the latter left the newly formed college in 1905 to form and head the Atlanta School of Medicine, Simpson Elkin was made dean of Atlanta College of Physicians and Surgeons. Both schools struggled to raise their standards under difficult financial circumstances. The American Medical Association and the Association of American Medical Colleges were putting pressure on many of the medical schools throughout the country to meet standards that neither of the two could meet. When in 1913 the Atlanta School of Medicine agreed to the proposal of the Atlanta College of Physicians and Surgeons to reunite, Dr. Elkin became dean of the merged institution, which took the historic name of Atlanta Medical College.

The famous report of Abraham Flexner of 1910 had criticized both of the rival schools and had strongly recommended university affiliation. Thus, soon after Emory University received its charter in January 1915, Dean Elkin approached his friend Asa Candler about accepting the Atlanta Medical College as part of the new university. Negotiations were begun in March, and on June 28, 1915, the Atlanta Medical College became legally the property of Emory University. Dr. Simpson Elkin continued as dean as well as professor of obstetrics and gynecology until 1925, when ill health forced him to resign the deanship. He continued to teach until his retirement from Emory University in 1933. On that occasion, President Harvey Cox of Emory stated that Dr. Elkin had "done more than any other man for medical education in the South."

Dean Arthur Richardson addressed the Atlanta Medical Historical Society on July 13, 1982, and emphasized Dean Elkin's enormous abilities. Richardson observed how Dean Elkin could rally the Emory volunteer faculty behind his quest for excellence. Elkin pointed out in 1922 that Vanderbilt had received $1,000,000 to build a hospital and medical school and that Emory must move quickly if Atlanta was to become the medical center of the South. He recalled with appropriate emotion that little Center College, where he graduated, had once beaten mighty Harvard in football. He said, "Center College had comparatively few resources and students but had vision, courage, ability, and organization. Center won against Harvard with its resources and numbers. The lesson to us is clear."

Richardson pointed out how Elkin had to accept many disappointments. For example, he had been led to believe that Emory would receive a large Rockefeller grant from the General Education Board. The grant was not awarded, and this was a terrible blow, but Elkin did not give up. He intended to create an excellent school of medicine at Emory University. He obviously loved Emory.

Dr. Russell Oppenheimer

The credit for survival of the Emory University School of Medicine as a whole belongs to Dr. Russell Oppenheimer (see Figure 1-15). He was a "one man" medical school in that he alone held numerous administrative positions. The following profile of Dr. Oppenheimer was found in the Emory archives. The author is unknown.

> Dr. Oppenheimer was born January 26, 1888, in Fremont, Ohio. He graduated from high school in Fremont and in 1911 received an A.B. degree from Ohio State University. His M.D. degree was awarded by the University of Michigan in 1917, after which he interned at the City Hospital, New York City. Following this, he spent sixteen months in the Army Medical Corps with terms of duty at the Base Hospital, Camp Jackson, at General Hospital No. 2 in Baltimore, and at Camp Hospitals in France.
>
> After nineteen months in general practice, Dr. Oppenheimer in 1921 came to Emory University and has been associated with the school continuously for thirty-three years until his retirement in August, 1954. He has served the University and the School of Medicine particularly in many more capacities than could be told, but through the years he has held the following titles:
>
> Resident Physician, Emory Division at Grady Memorial Hospital, 1921–23[8]
> Resident Physician and Pathologist, Grady Memorial Hospital, 1923–24
> Superintendent, Emory University Hospital, 1924–37
> [Superintendent, Grady Memorial Hospital, 1936][9]
> Medical Director, Emory University Hospital, 1927–44

---

[8] Sources in special collections suggest that the designation "resident physician" implies that he was the first full-time chief of medicine at Grady Hospital. As such he started the Emory University house staff training program.

[9] Added to original manuscript (see letter of Dr. Papageorge on page 29).

Dean, Emory University School of Medicine, 1925–45
Director, Postgraduate Education, 1947–54
Professor of Medicine, Emory University School of Medicine, 1930–54
Chairman, Department of Medicine, 1931–41

His leadership in medical education was recognized by the Association of American Medical Colleges when he was elected to the vice presidency of that organization in 1935–36 and to the presidency in 1940–41. He also served as a member of that body's Executive Council.

Under the sponsorship of the Kellogg Foundation of Battle Creek, Michigan, Dr. Oppenheimer was named director of a program of graduate medical education which was formulated to bring to doctors and outlying hospitals of the region the newest advances in medicine as well as improvement and development of the internship and residency programs of these hospitals. While little progress has been made in expanding the program beyond affiliation with two hospitals in Georgia and the presentation of ten or more postgraduate courses each year for doctors in the specialties, results have been encouraging enough to warrant the Kellogg Foundation's continued support of the project.

No eulogy of Dr. Oppenheimer's life would be complete without mentioning his care and devotion to the indigent and sick of this area. For many years he has served without compensation as chief physician at Battle Hill Haven, and in the outpatient department of Grady Hospital, far beyond the requirements of his positions, he has fulfilled to the highest degree the role of a physician.

Dr. Evangeline Papageorge, the long-time anchor and Associate Dean of Emory University School of Medicine, wrote the following letter to Dr. Max Michael in Jacksonville, Florida, on February 9, 1966, at the time of Dr. Oppenheimer's death.

When news of Dr. Oppenheimer's death reached us at Emory University, those of us who had known him felt the loss of a colleague who in our hearts was still a part of the medical school, even though he had "retired" over eleven years ago to take up another career in Jacksonville. Dr. Oppenheimer's association with Emory began in 1921, when he came to Atlanta as resident physician of the Emory Division at Grady Memorial Hospital. It ended officially 33 years later, in 1954. He was at that time given the title Professor Emeritus of Medicine, and he left Atlanta to undertake new tasks in Jacksonville. However, his career as a physician and a medical educator did not end until his death.

Four years after he came to Atlanta, Dr. Oppenheimer was appointed Dean of the School of Medicine, to succeed Dr. W. S. Elkin, who first served as Dean when the medical school became part of Emory University. During the 20 years of his deanship, 1925–1945, Dr. Oppenheimer carried the responsibilities of several other offices on his tireless shoulders and gained prominence as a medical educator on a national level. He was Superintendent of Emory University Hospital from 1924 until 1937, when a lay superintendent took over most of the administrative duties, and then "Dr. Opp" became "Medical Director," a capacity in which he served until 1944. In 1930, he was given the title of Professor of Medicine and the job of Chairman of the Department. He administered this department until 1942 when he brought Dr. Eugene A. Stead back to Emory as the first full-time Chairman of the Department of Medicine. In 1936 Grady was without a superintendent, and Dr. Oppenheimer filled this job, too, until a full-time man could be found. In 1945, "Dr. Opp," as his faculty affectionately called him, resigned from the deanship because of ill health and was succeeded by Dr. Stead. After a few brief months of rest, however, he came back to continue his duties as Professor of Clinical Medicine and as Director of the Regional Hospital Plan which was supported by a grant to Emory from Kellogg Foundation. His professional title was changed to Professor of Medicine but his duties remained essentially the same until his retirement in 1954. He taught medical students and house staff, he directed Grady Hospital's outpatient department, he organized Emory's postgraduate medical education program, and he worked towards improvement of internship and residency programs in smaller hospitals in the region. In addition he undertook the medical supervision, on a purely voluntary basis, of the chronically ill and elderly patients at Battle Hill Haven and Happy Haven Home.

Emory University conferred the honorary degree of *Doctor of Science* on Dr. Oppenheimer in June of 1957, making an exception to the general policy excluding former faculty and administrative officers from nomination for honorary degrees. I well remember that Commencement Day and the memories that flitted through my mind as I watched the present dean, Dr. Arthur P. Richardson, hood the man who headed the medical school for the first seventeen years of my affiliation with Emory. My duties were entirely those of a member of the faculty in that period, and thus my contacts with "Dr. Opp" were in his function as Dean of the School of Medicine.

Those were years of unbelievably tight budgets, when understaffed basic science departments carried heavy teaching loads and when practically all clinical instruction was offered by dedicated volunteers who earned their income through private practice. The years of the depression and the ensuing years of World War II presented problems hard to envision by those who did not experience the financial and educational struggles of those days. Today's faculty would never dream of accepting the teaching loads we carried then, and thus we needed desperately the encouragement which our Dean never failed to give us when we ventured to think also of research. The dean himself lent his skill as a diagnostician and his talent as a teacher to the instruction of our juniors and seniors. As one can surmise, he was always hurried, but he never lost his sense of humor and I can still see him rushing by yet never failing to greet us with his warm smile. During these same years, Dr. Oppenheimer was active in the Association of American Medical Colleges. He was elected vice-president of the Association for 1935–36, and served on the Executive Council from 1935 until 1944. The esteem in which his fellow Deans held him is evidenced by his election to the presidency of the Association in 1940–41. One can well understand why Dr. R. Hugh Wood, Emory medical school Dean in 1954, answered Dr. Oppenheimer's request for retirement with words such as these:

It was with deep regret and a feeling of loss that I read your letter of resignation . . . It has been my role to attempt to follow in your footsteps during the past thirty years. I have often found your long stride difficult to measure. . . .

One can only ponder on how many of us—physicians, teachers and administrators—have tried to follow in his footsteps and measure his giant stride. He has left with us for always the example of his selfless devotion to medicine and to medical education and the warmth of his friendship and smile.

Note that Dr. Oppenheimer was the appointed Chairman of the Department of Medicine. He could hardly be called full time because he simultaneously held numerous other administrative posts. He was an administrative genius who saved the medical school almost single-handed and gained the love of all who knew him.

Three Practicing Physicians

Three practicing physicians deserve special recognition because they contributed an enormous amount of time and talent to the clinical teaching in the Department of Medicine. They were: Dr. Cyrus W. Strickler Sr., Dr. Stewart Roberts, and Dr. J. Edgar Paullin.

Cyrus W. Strickler Sr., M.D.

Cyrus W. Strickler Sr., was born the first of November 1873, near Staunton, Virginia (see Figure 1-16). In 1882, his father, who had been a Confederate soldier and had fought in the battle of Gettysburg, moved his family to Atlanta, Georgia, where he became pastor of the Central Presbyterian Church.

Cyrus W. Strickler Sr. graduated from preparatory school in Atlanta and then graduated from Washington and Lee University, where he was elected a member of Phi Beta Kappa. He graduated from the Atlanta Medical College in 1897 with honors. He completed two years of internship at Grady Memorial Hospital and two years of residency at the W. S. Elkin-Cooper Sanatorium.

During his internship at Grady Memorial Hospital he developed the first clinical laboratory in Atlanta. He entered private practice, which initially entailed the care of all types of patients—delivering babies, performing surgery, and caring for the full range of routine patient ills. He later restricted his work to internal medicine.

His academic appointments were clarified in a 1937 letter to Miss Mary Strickler from Anna Thurman, who worked in Dean Oppenheimer's office. The letter is shown here in its entirety (see Figure 1-17), not only because it evidences Dr. Strickler's academic appointments but also because it shows the stationery used by the School of Medicine in 1937. Note that in 1918 Dr. Strickler was said to be "head" of the Department of Medicine. Note too, that the Dean's office was located at 50 Armstrong Street. During his academic career, Dr. Strickler introduced bedside teaching to Emory students and organized the first clinical pathology conferences to be given at Grady Memorial Hospital.

Dr. Strickler served as co-chief, with Dr. Stewart Roberts, of the "white hospital" at Grady and admitted his private patients to the new Wesley Memorial Hospital (later the University Hospital) on the Emory Campus. Dr. Cyrus Strickler Jr. wrote the following paragraph that sheds light on the early days of Emory University Hospital.

> Prior to becoming Emory University Hospital, the hospital was known as Wesley Memorial Hospital. In those early days hard times nearly closed Wesley Memorial Hospital and the credit for saving the hospital in this crisis was given to Dr. Cyrus Strickler, Sr. and Dr. Stewart Roberts who did not move out in the emergency. They were able to admit enough patients to allow the hospital to survive.

Dr. Cyrus Strickler Sr. authored several scientific papers on typhoid fever, hypertension, pneumonia, encephalitis, and the preservation of health. He was among the first to use oxygen by funnel and worked with Lederle Laboratories to test a pneumonia vaccine. He served as Chief of Medicine in the Emory unit in World War I, specializing in treating the victims of war-gas. He was honored by France when he was made an *Officier d'Académie*. More could be written about the numerous positions Dr. Strickler held within the medical school, Emory University Hospital, and Grady Memorial Hospital. During the same period, he was a busy practitioner. He practiced day and night, including Saturday, and visited patients in their homes on Sunday afternoon. He gave group therapy to young girls in his office on Sunday morning. He was a member of the committee that organized the Medical Service Bureau in 1942 to offer medical services to low income families.

Dr. Cyrus Strickler Jr. states that by age forty-eight his father was "burned out." So he changed his lifestyle. He took up golf and played the game on the afternoons of Wednesday, Saturday, and Sunday. He had played end on the football team at Washington and Lee and loved that game, too. In fact, he was the head coach of the football team at Georgia Tech in 1901 while he served his residency in medicine at the Elkins-Cooper Sanatorium. He won four games and tied one for the Yellow Jackets.

Dr. Strickler Jr. points out his father's great love of people. He appeared stern but was kind and considerate. He read one or more chapters in the Bible each evening and kneeled in prayer every night.

I remember this tall, thin, distinguished man because when I arrived at Emory in 1950, he was still admitting patients to Emory University Hospital. What had he done to cause the nurses on the medical floor to place a fresh red carnation in his lapel each morning when he arrived to see his patients? At times, when he went to another floor he received a new carnation from the group of nurses assigned to that floor. When he went to still another floor he received another carnation. He received the carnations because, for many years, he had shown the nurses how very much he appreciated their work. He respected them, and they respected him.

He was kind enough to ask me, a thirty-year-old consultant in cardiology, to see patients with him. Following the manners of his time, he was always there when a consultant examined his patients to discuss the suggestions for treatment. Accordingly, poor communication did not occur between him, the patient, and the consultant.

Cyrus W. Strickler Sr. died on July 23, 1953, at the age of seventy-nine years. He devoted much of his career to Emory without financial recompense. His friends and colleagues honored him by establishing the Cyrus Strickler Student Fund for needy students. They raised $30,115. In 1996 the Fund had grown to $288,000. He also specified in his will that $5,300 should be bequeathed to support a chair in the Department of Medicine. This gift had grown to $62,000 in 1996.

Stewart R. Roberts, M.D.

Stewart Roberts was born in Oxford, Georgia, in 1878 (see Figure 1-18). He attended Emory College at Oxford for two years, distinguishing himself as a brilliant student. He worked in the railroad office in Atlanta for one year, then entered the Atlanta College of Physicians and Surgeons, where he graduated in 1900. He returned to Emory College in Oxford and remained there for four years, teaching biology for $1500 a year. He later taught physiology and the principles and practice of medicine in the various medical schools in Atlanta, and in 1915 he became professor of clinical medicine at the new Emory University School of Medicine. One year later he was appointed a member of the Emory board of trustees. He was co-chief of medicine at Grady's "white hospital."

Early in his career he admitted his patients to the original Wesley Memorial Hospital, and when the new hospital was built on the Emory campus he admitted his patients there. This was an important act, because without his and Dr. Cyrus Strickler Sr.'s paying patients, the new Wesley Memorial Hospital might well have closed from lack of revenue.

He was a superb teacher, and his orations and writing prompted many to label him as the "Osler of the South." He influenced many physicians as he demonstrated how to deal successfully with the problems exhibited by his patients.

In 1912, when he was thirty-four years old, he wrote a book on pellagra, long before it was recognized as a deficiency disease. At that time the disease was killing hundreds of Southerners every year. His first scientific paper on angina pectoris was published in 1913. He published over ninety articles and urged his colleagues to do likewise. The subjects of his articles show his wide interests, but later in his life he considered himself a heart specialist. He became president of the American Heart Association in 1933.

A powerful leader, he always influenced the other leaders of Emory University School of Medicine. In 1941 he represented the Medical Faculty Council and recommended to Dean Oppenheimer that two full-time, young professors be recruited for the Department of Medicine. The time had come, he and many other faculty members thought, for the Department of Medicine to add full-time professors if it aspired to become first rate. He recommended that one of the new professors be in charge of "white Grady" and the other be in charge of "colored Grady." In time, he pointed out, one of them could be appointed chairman of the Department of Medicine. He suggested that Emory recruit two former Emory medical school graduates. One was Dr. Eugene Stead, who had made a national reputation at the Peter Bent Brigham Hospital in Boston, and the other was Dr. Purcell Roberts (no relation to Stewart Roberts) who also had a fine reputation and was being recruited by both Boston University and Tufts University. The decision makers of the day chose to appoint one of them as chairman; they chose Eugene Stead.

Stewart Roberts was president of the Southern Medical Association and was active in Emory Medical alumni affairs. In 1923 he created and edited the Emory Medical Review. (The journal was discontinued in 1925 because of lack of funds.) In 1923 he was a founding member of the Emory University Medical Historical Club, of which he was president in 1924. The club disbanded in 1927.

Roberts served with distinction in World War I. He collected books about medicine and the Civil War and perfected his teaching technique, lecturing, and medical skills.

He had a myocardial infarction in 1938 and died at his Stone Mountain home in 1941. He was buried in Oxford, Georgia. A large plaque hangs on the wall of the fourth floor of Emory University Hospital commemorating this great physician.

His two sons graduated from Emory University School of Medicine. Stewart Ralph Roberts Jr., M.D., is currently a professor in the Department of Radiology at Emory University, and William Clifford Roberts, M.D., is considered to be one of the leading cardiac pathologists in the world. After many productive years at the National Institutes of Health, Bill currently directs a Cardiac Institute at Baylor University in Dallas, Texas.

The book, *Life and Writings of Stewart R. Roberts, M.D.*, written by his grandson Charles Stewart Roberts, M.D., who also graduated from Emory University School of Medicine, is an inspiring document.

James Edgar Paullin, M.D.

James Edgar Paullin was born November 3, 1881, in Fort Gaines, Georgia (see Figure 1-19). He graduated from Mercer University in 1900 and remained for one additional year as a graduate student. He entered the Johns Hopkins Medical School and graduated in 1905. At Hopkins he was influenced profoundly by Dr. William Osler, who had become the leading physician in the world. This experience undoubtedly encouraged Paullin to study pathology and internal medicine, to work hard, teach, and write, to create medical organizations, and to develop a philosophy of medicine and life in general.

After graduating from Johns Hopkins, Paullin trained in pathology at the Rhode Island Hospital and Piedmont Hospital in Atlanta. He entered the private practice of internal medicine in Atlanta in 1906 and admitted his patients to Piedmont Hospital. Because Osler influenced him during medical school at Johns Hopkins, he was driven to teach and to influence others. Accordingly, from 1907 to 1911, he served as pathologist to the Atlanta College of Physicians and Surgeons, which later joined the Atlanta School of Medicine to become the Atlanta Medical College and in turn, Emory University School of Medicine. During this period, he was also pathologist to the Georgia State Board of Health. Despite the demands of private practice, which he met with great professionalism, he became Chief of Medicine of the Emory University Division of Grady Memorial Hospital. He was considered to be chairman of the Department of Medicine from 1930 to 1942, although Dr. Oppenheimer did much of the administrative work. Eugene Stead, who had a personal and professional relationship with Paullin, wrote the following to Dr. Mark Silverman on November 26, 1990:

> Around 1914 my sister, age 4, and I age 6, had bilateral broncho-pneumonia and bilateral otitis media. My mother was not satisfied with our

medical care and required that Dr. Paullin be placed in charge. My memory of the events is vague. I remember the cold baths used to control high febrile spikes and the pain from the ears. From that time on Dr. Paullin cared for my family usually in the office, but on rare occasions in our home. He remains in my memory as the ideal physician. When my mother had extensive surgery he was in the operating room.

Dr. Paullin came to Grady on Tuesday and Wednesday. His patients knew that these times at Grady as a member of the Emory faculty assured them that their doctor was up to date. He arranged for coverage and because he was the best doctor, charged accordingly. The arrangement was profitable for Paullin and his patients.

In my third and fourth year I attended Paullin's Tuesday morning sessions with the Grady interns and residents, cutting my assigned third and fourth year lectures. Dr. Paullin greeted me warmly and never asked why I was the only student who came to his Tuesday morning rounds.

Paullin gave the clinical presentation at the weekly clinical pathology conference. These were open to all students and staff. I particularly remember his discussion of renal clearance and in particular urea clearance. This was the first time I heard of Donald Van Slyke and his gas machines.

Dr. Paullin advised me to apply for internship at the Peter Bent Brigham Hospital. Henry Christian was the physician-in-chief and a friend of Paullin. I found that Hugh Wood and Carter Smith were Brigham alumni and I wanted to join the club.

Paullin's reputation as a clinician increased until he was recognized at the national and international level. He brought many "firsts" to his native Georgia. He was the first physician in Georgia to use insulin for diabetes mellitus, the first in Georgia to identify typhus fever, the first in Georgia to use the Wasserman test for the diagnosis of syphilis, and the first in Georgia to feed patients with typhoid fever. His opinion was sought in virtually all aspects of medicine. Read what Eugene Stead wrote in his 1990 letter to Mark Silverman about smoking:

> Paullin was a chain cigarette smoker. One day I missed the cigarettes and asked Paullin why. He said that a few weeks earlier he was playing with his grandchild. She stopped and asked, "why do you wheeze?" "That was my last cigarette!"

I recall reading his entry of -Tobacism- as a diagnosis on the record of a patient he saw at Emory University Hospital in 1950.

Paullin is the only physician who became president of the American Medical Association, the American College of Physicians, and the American Clinical and Climatological Society. He sponsored two medical organizations: the Southeastern Clinical Club, which consisted of physicians from New Orleans, Nashville, Birmingham, and Atlanta, and a study club that became the Atlanta Clinical Society. At the beginning of the latter organization, the members met at his home, where his influence was felt by many young physicians.

He served as special consultant to the Surgeon General of the U.S. Navy. He received the Presidential Medal of Merit for his study of the medical care and education of the natives of the Pacific islands.

His honors and awards increased as the years passed. He became known by the public at large as one of President Franklin Roosevelt's physicians. His final act for the President was to rush to Warm Springs, Georgia, when the President died.

Paullin died on August 13, 1951. He himself diagnosed the dissection of the aorta that caused his death. Former students, former house officers, colleagues, and patients mourned the great loss.

Paullin's contribution to Emory was made without financial gain. His accomplishments for Grady and Emory were made possible because he was good at what he did and enjoyed it. His acceptance of the 1946 planning report was testimony to his greatness (see page 93). He was responsible for the enduring Emory-Piedmont connection. The Paullin Scholarship Fund had, at the time of this writing in 1997, reached more than $1,000,000. This endowment is used for the yearly financial assistance of five Emory medical students.

Important Developments from 1930 to 1942

Whereas many fascinating events happened during the period 1930–1942, I have chosen to discuss the following events because they have had a lasting impact on the Department of Medicine of Emory University School of Medicine.

The secretary of the Association of American Colleges in 1930 notified the School of Medicine that there should be less lecturing and more teaching at the bedside of patients. Emory responded by limiting the didactic "teaching" to the junior year and using patient-oriented teaching in the senior year. This required more patients than could be supplied by the Emory Division of Grady Hospital, which was known as "colored Grady." So in 1931, "white Grady" was used to some degree for teaching Emory senior medical students. Wesley Memorial Hospital, later renamed Emory University Hospital, was under financial stress in the thirties and was used very little for teaching.

Two important events happened in 1937. First, Emory purchased a rather large tract of land adjacent to Grady Memorial Hospital. The plan was to erect additional buildings that would satisfy the needs of Emory University School of Medicine. The land was later sold to Grady, and the new Grady Memorial Hospital was erected on that location. The money paid to Emory was used to refurbish the Emory Division of Grady Memorial Hospital and the J. J. Gray Clinic buildings, which were owned by Emory.

The second major event was the organization, by Dr. J. Elliott Scarborough Jr., of the Robert Winship Memorial Clinic in Emory University Hospital. Robert W. Woodruff financed the project with a gift of $50,000. The clinic was named for Mr. Woodruff's maternal grandfather. This development was important for three reasons. First, the gift in 1937 by Mr. Woodruff was the first of his numerous large gifts to Emory University. Initially, the Robert Winship Memorial Clinic was virtually separate from the medical school. But Scarborough, noting what had happened to governance and support of the Steiner Clinic, developed a closer arrangement with Emory Medical School in order to ensure the long-term survival of the new clinic. Second, the clinic was devoted to the recognition, treatment, and research of neoplastic diseases. The goals were similar to those of the Steiner Clinic. Accordingly, the participating doctors included surgeons, hematologists, radiologists, and researchers. Third, this development, as discussed later, was a major stimulus to the development of other "organizations" at Emory University Hospital that eventually coalesced to form the Emory University Clinic.

Woodruff and Scarborough became close friends, and this friendship profoundly influenced the future development of Emory University School of Medicine and the Department of Medicine.

The creation of the Winship Memorial Clinic in Emory University Hospital located on the campus of Emory University and the new purchase of land in the Grady area by Emory—highlight a problem that plagued Emory for many years. The question was: would Emory University School of Medicine be centered in the Grady Hospital area or on the Emory campus?

J. Elliott Scarborough Jr.

Dr. Elliott Scarborough deserves a special place in the history of Emory University, its School of Medicine, Emory University Hospital, and the Emory University Clinic (see Figure 1-20). For it was he who established the unshakable bond between Emory and Robert Woodruff.

Dr. Scarborough was born in Mount Willing, Alabama, on July 26, 1906. He was a Harvard Medical School graduate and specialized in oncology at Memorial Hospital in New York. Mr. Woodruff was familiar with the medical care given to the patients with cancer admitted to the Memorial Hospital, because his mother had been a patient there. Woodruff was distressed that he could not obtain the medical care he wanted for his mother in Atlanta. The Steiner Clinic was functioning but by then admitted only Grady patients. Therefore, in 1937, Robert Woodruff gave $50,000 to develop the Robert Winship Memorial Clinic in Emory University Hospital. He chose Dr. Scarborough to be the first medical director of the multidisciplinary facility.

The $50,000 for the development of the Winship Memorial Clinic was Robert Woodruff's first gift to Emory University. Scarborough became Woodruff's physician, close friend, and confidant, and without a doubt stimulated Woodruff's interest in the health field and in Emory University. Woodruff's gift not only established the Robert Winship Memorial Clinic but also signaled that further medical development would take place on the Emory campus. It was similar to the signal Asa Candler sent in 1922 when he insisted that the new Wesley Memorial Hospital be built on the Emory campus rather than in the Grady Memorial Hospital area.

When Elliott Scarborough died of cancer of the pancreas on January 31, 1966, Robert Woodruff said, "He was the greatest man I have ever known." Posthumously, Scarborough was given the Shining Light Award, the greatest award the city of Atlanta can bestow on a citizen. The central building of the Emory University Clinic bears his name.

Robert W. Woodruff and Brother George

Robert Woodruff was born in Columbus, Georgia, on December 6, 1889 (see Figure 1-21), the eldest son of Ernest and Emily Woodruff. His grandfather, George Waldo Woodruff, developed a flour milling business and made a fortune, only to lose it during the Civil War. After the war, Robert's grandfather borrowed the money to start over and created Empire Mills.

Robert's father, Ernest, married Emily Winship, who lived next door to his sister, Annie Bright Hurt, in Atlanta. The newly married couple settled in Columbus, where Ernest became vice president of his father's flour mill. Ernest sold flour to merchants in south Georgia, Alabama, and Florida. This caused him to be away from home for weeks at a time. Even though the family regained its fortune, Ernest decided that a long career in the flour business was not for him.

During the Civil War, the Winships had developed a munitions factory and sold arms and ammunition to the Confederate army. The family left Atlanta as Sherman moved in to destroy it; they returned to find their factory and home in ruins. They rebuilt the company, made farm equipment, and their fortune was eventually restored.

Robert Winship Woodruff was a determined child. This attribute reminded people of his father. He was also a brooding child, a trait that others associated with the Winships.

While Ernest Woodruff was living in Columbus, Joel Hurt, the husband of Ernest's sister, was making a fortune in Atlanta. He was involved in banking, real estate, streetcars, and electric power. He needed help and asked Ernest to join him in Atlanta. Ernest, of course, was waiting for an opportunity to leave the flour mill business, and he accepted Hurt's offer. Ernest Woodruff became increasingly successful in Atlanta and, with it all, became increasingly aggressive, bossy, domineering, and stingy.

The second son of Ernest and Emily Woodruff died of meningitis. Their next two sons were named George and Henry. As will be discussed later in the story, Henry died a tragic death and George became a successful businessman and philanthropist.

As Ernest Woodruff became increasingly prominent, the family had the best of everything. But Ernest did not want his wealth to ruin his children. He failed with Robert, however, because Robert had his own view of the world and his role in it. Robert somehow attracted friends and admirers but was a terrible student. Even as a youngster he gave parties and made more and more friends, but despite extra tutoring, he continued to do poorly in school. In hindsight it is likely that he had dyslexia. He never liked to read, and years later it was obvious to those who watched him that he paused and stumbled over every word he read.

The tension between Ernest and Robert Woodruff increased. Their relationship was not psychologically conducive to the proper development of an adolescent boy. Robert flunked out of Atlanta's famous Boys High School. Ernest then sent him to Georgia Military Academy, an excellent boarding school in College Park, located adjacent to Atlanta. (In later years the school became Woodward Academy). Robert liked the military aspect of the school.

Severe dental problems, which required Robert to wear braces, prevented him from participating in sports, so he took over the leadership positions of almost all of the nonathletic activities of the school. He was clearly a leader who had the ability to get things done. At that early age he discovered that he had a knack for raising money for noble causes. He became an effective fund-raiser for the school. He avoided classes when he could, however. He simply was not teachable in a classroom. Although he graduated from GMA, Colonel Woodward advised Ernest not to send Robert to school any more. He believed that formal schooling would ruin young Woodruff. The wise Colonel must have seen a streak of genius in young Robert that was beyond the influence of organized schooling. Woodward also knew that Robert would not be able to handle the broad curriculum of a college.

Ernest Woodruff did not heed Woodward's advice and sent Robert to Emory College, which was then still in Oxford. Robert did not do well. For a while he convinced his parents that he had turned over a new leaf, but he continued to avoid classes and spend beyond his allowance. On his visits home to Atlanta, he was a ladies' man, a young playboy. He continued to rebel against his father in many ways, frequently charging items to his father's account and even, as an act of arrogance, confiscating some of his father's clothes as well as other items. The relationship of father and son deteriorated even further.

The president of Emory at Oxford, James Dickey, gave up on Robert Woodruff and, after a few months, dismissed him from the school. With that, Ernest also gave up on Robert's schooling and insisted he go to work.

Robert Woodruff, then twenty years old, began to work as a laborer at the General Pipe and Foundry Company, making sixty cents a day. He then became an apprentice to a machinist at the company, where he impressed everyone; he liked the work. His father tried to interest him in the "finer things," but Robert seemed content to be a laborer. He performed well at the General Pipe and Foundry Company. People liked him, and the owners of the company recognized his talent as a leader and salesman. So they promoted him to stock clerk and then salesman for the General Fire Extinguisher Company, the parent company of the General Pipe and Foundry Company. As predicted, Robert became a very successful salesman of fire extinguishers.

Robert was settling down, and his father was beginning to forgive him for his rebellion against him and schooling. Ernest hired his son as a purchasing agent for one of his companies, The Atlanta Ice and Coal Company. Prior to Robert's marriage to Nell Hodgson of Athens, Georgia, his father agreed to pay him $150 a month. After the marriage, he agreed to pay Robert $250 a month. This plan was actually devised to encourage Robert to marry Nell.

Two events destroyed the newfound relationship between father and son. The first occurred when Robert visited an auto show in New York and met Walter White. White displayed his new trucks to Robert and pointed out that it was old-fashioned to deliver ice and coal in a wagon. White said Robert should buy White Trucks to transport such merchandise. Young Robert bought fifteen trucks but, promoter that he was, told White to keep the trucks on display and to point out to potential customers that The Atlanta Ice and Coal Company had already bought them. Robert had not discussed the purchase with his father, who, when he was told about them, was very much against the idea. In fact, he was furious with Robert. Ernest Woodruff believed that horse-drawn wagons could be used to deliver ice and coal. Robert then discovered that his promised raise to $250 a month was not awarded to him after his marriage. This was the final blow. Young Robert Woodruff declared he would never work for his father again, although he said he would always love him.

Robert Woodruff had made quite an impression on Walter White, who hired him as a salesman. White also hired him because Robert Woodruff knew the right people in Atlanta and White wanted to gain a foothold in the truck business in Atlanta.

Young Woodruff became a star salesman of White Trucks. He sold them to county commissioners and to national parks. He learned the names of the individuals in an organization that could make decisions and talked only to them. He learned not to waste time on those who could not make final decisions.

It was becoming clear to everyone that there really was a streak of genius in Robert Woodruff. It obviously did not come from schooling— he was born with it. He was promoted up the ladder in Walter White's Atlanta office and soon had a fleet of salesmen working under him. He was making $300 a month plus expenses and a commission on sales. He formed friendships with Bobby Jones, Ty Cobb, and many others. Everyone enjoyed being in the circle of friends that surrounded Robert Woodruff.

World War I was raging, and Robert Woodruff was drafted and assigned to the army's ordnance department. He helped design army vehicles that would be used to transport troops. Of course they were built, in part, with material produced by the White Motor Company.

After the war, Woodruff began to cultivate a number of friends who were the financial leaders of the day. He borrowed money in order to invest it. He would place the stocks he bought in a drawer and hold them as if he had forgotten them. During this period, Woodruff was invited to join a hunting club near Thomasville, Georgia. This action, as will be discussed later, played an important part in Woodruff's later life.

During this period, Robert moved up in the world without the aid or hindrance of his father. Forever, it seems, the father wanted to control his son's life and the son rebelled against it. Later in life, Ernest Woodruff confided that he was jealous of Robert.

Robert Woodruff was made Vice President of White Motor Company in 1921. An old friend, Harrison Jones of The Coca-Cola Company, ordered thirty trucks as a congratulatory message. Woodruff got the commission on the trucks. Obviously, Jones was planning to use the trucks to transport Coca-Cola.

Robert and Nell Woodruff moved from Atlanta to apartments in Cleveland and New York. Woodruff was enormously successful as the number-two man at White's Motor Company.

The Coca-Cola Connection

In 1919, Charles Howard Candler Sr., and the other stockholders of Coca-Cola sold the Coca-Cola Company for $25,000,000. The Trust Company of Georgia, the Guaranty Trust of New York, and the Chase National Bank of New York formed a syndicate to buy the Coca-Cola Company from the Candler family. The Trust Company of Georgia was the manager of the syndicate. At that time, Ernest Woodruff controlled the Trust Company of Georgia.

Ernest Woodruff was plotting how to take over the Coca-Cola Company and have Robert return to Atlanta. Although he did not get along with Robert, he wanted to be near him. Ernest Woodruff bought additional Coca-Cola stock in order to be in a strong position to dominate his northern partners in the control of the Coca-Cola Company. When the showdown came with his northern partners, Ernest Woodruff won the battle, and he and the other southern shareholders took over the Coca-Cola Company. To accomplish this goal Ernest Woodruff bought stock in the name of his sons—Robert, George, and Henry—without telling them. Robert later discovered that he owned an increasing amount of stock in the Coca-Cola Company but knew little about it and cared even less. Later, Robert bought some Coca-Cola stock at $5 a share because shareholders and directors of the Trust Company of Georgia could buy shares at a cheap rate. By then he was on the Board of Directors of the Trust Company of Georgia. He also bought shares in his father's newly created company, Coca-Cola International, when it was created. Despite this, he still had little interest in the company. At that point the Coca-Cola Company meant no more to him than the other companies in which he invested his money.

During this time Charles Howard Candler Sr. was president of the Coca-Cola Company. Howard Candler did not enjoy being president of the company and did not do well at the job. By 1923 it was obvious that the company needed a new president. Ernest Woodruff, who now owned controlling interest in the company, wanted his son Robert to become president of the company. There were several Candlers working at Coca-Cola who probably aspired to the job. At that time, however, Asa Candler was caught up in a serious scandal with a New Orleans woman, and this made it easier for the directors of the Coca-Cola Company to move away from appointing a Candler as president. Harrison Jones wanted to be the new president, but Ernest Woodruff thought his flamboyant friend was not the right person for this position. Robert Woodruff was offered the position but was reluctant to take it. An oil tycoon promised to hire Robert "in any job at any price" if he did not like his move to Coca-Cola. Finally, in 1923, at the age of thirty-three, Robert Woodruff accepted the presidency of the Coca-Cola Company, though he confessed that he knew nothing about soft drinks. He remained active as president and chairman of the board, serving as a strong and listened-to-advisor of the Coca-Cola Company for the next sixty years. When his time ran out he was recognized as one of the geniuses of the century and one of the greatest philanthropists of all time. His marketing strategy was to have his product "within arm's reach of desire."

Robert Woodruff's Compassion and Philanthropy

Most of what is good in Atlanta, Georgia, can be traced to the benevolence of the Candlers, Robert and George Woodruff, and the Coca-Cola family. The contribution of the Candlers was discussed on pages 22–24. The Woodruffs and the foundations they controlled gave money for parks, the arts center, Emory University, Mercer University, Georgia Tech, the African-American colleges in Atlanta and in Tuskegee, Alabama, and the University of Georgia. They supported efforts to protect the environment and contributed in many ways to the excellent race relations that has characterized Atlanta.

Mayor William Hartsfield and Mayor Ivan Allen Jr. called Robert Woodruff the "mayor of Atlanta" because of his philanthropy and wise advice. His benevolence was endless, ranging from sending his grammar school teacher a monthly check until she died and buying supplies for an Emory student laboratory at Grady, to financing many huge buildings on the Emory campus.

As time passed, the medical facilities on the Emory campus were named the Woodruff Medical Center. After additional growth and development the medical center was renamed the Robert W. Woodruff Health Sciences Center in order to honor him for all that he did for research and clinical care in the health sciences at Emory.

Robert Woodruff, like Asa Candler, was relatively unschooled but for very different reasons. Asa Candler had no opportunity to attend school—he only completed the seventh grade. Woodruff was not a self-made scholar as was Asa Candler. Woodruff had every opportunity but was not teachable. Woodruff, however, was a genius at what he did. In that regard, there was no school that could improve his innate ability. He was a salesman par excellence, a leader, a forward-thinking developer, a visionary of the highest order.

Candler and Woodruff died unhappy men. Following the loss of their wives, they became depressed, and finally the ravages of age ended their lives.

This is not the place to recount the growth and development of the Coca-Cola Company under the rule of Robert Woodruff. Suffice it to say that at Woodruff's death, Emory University and the Trust Company of Georgia each held $1 billion in Coca-Cola stock, and his personal foundation was worth $1.5 billion.

This is the place to discuss what Robert Woodruff, and his brother George, who served on the Board of Directors of the Coca-Cola Company, did with their money. The state of Georgia, the city of Atlanta, and several educational institutions, especially Emory University and its School of Medicine, benefited enormously from the benevolence of the Woodruff Foundations.

Robert Woodruff's method of giving was different from that of Asa Candler. Candler gave money that he obtained by selling Coca-Cola stock or from other sources. Woodruff decided he wanted to use his gifts to improve the minds and health of people who lived in the area, and he wanted others to give as well. He decided not to sell Coca-Cola stock to obtain the money he donated. He elected to keep the family stock in Coca-Cola intact and to give away the income derived from it. He commonly gave half or more of the cost of a project in order to stimulate others to provide the remaining amount. He believed that the citizens would be more likely to appreciate the development if they also contributed to the project. His gifts to Emory University were exceptions to that rule, because they were direct gifts with no strings attached. He expanded his sources of money by creating a number of Woodruff foundations whose directors reported to him.

For many years Woodruff's gifts were given "by an anonymous donor." Everyone knew who it was, but he did not like for his name to be used in the newspaper. His creed was "There is no limit to what a man can do or where he can go if he doesn't mind who gets the credit." Once, however, he was given credit for someone else's "anonymous gift." From then on, he allowed his name to be used freely. He even discovered that he liked it and wondered why he had formerly objected to the use of his name.

Woodruff was also adept at urging others in the wealthy Coca-Cola family to give their money away. He and his lawyer, Hughes Spalding, actually maneuvered the Whiteheads and Evanses into creating foundations that Woodruff controlled or exerted considerable influence over.

Woodruff saw Emory University as his personal responsibility. He was a member of the ad hoc committee of the Ford Foundation that had the opportunity to distribute $90,000,000 to medical schools. He requested that the committee give none of the money to Emory. He said, "Don't worry about Emory. I will take care of Emory myself." He also convinced the members of the committee to give the money to fledgling medical schools rather than to the rich schools.

Robert Woodruff's concern for the needs of sick people came about when, in the thirties, he observed the impact of disease in Baker County, Georgia. He had built his plantation there. It was called Ichauway, a Creek Indian word that means "where the deer sleep." At that time malaria was prevalent, and residents were dying from the ravages of the disease. Profoundly influenced when he observed a black man suffering a terrible chill due to malaria, he spent a fortune to eliminate malaria from the area. He stimulated the development of the Malaria Field Station, a cooperative effort involving Emory University, the state, and the national government. This field station was the fore-runner of the Communicable Disease Center, which was build adjacent to the Emory University campus on land given to the U.S. government by Robert Woodruff. The huge facility is now called the Centers for Disease Control and Prevention.

As discussed earlier, Woodruff was distressed when he could not obtain the medical care he wanted in Atlanta for his mother, who had cancer. This led to his first gift to Emory University. The gift of $50,000, made in 1937, was designated to create the Robert Winship Memorial Clinic in Emory University Hospital. Woodruff selected J. Elliott Scarborough Jr. as its director.

Woodruff and his brother George (see Figure 1-22), who was also a great benefactor, jointly engineered the gift of $105,000,000 to Emory University in 1979. As trustees of the Emily and Ernest Woodruff Fund, they decided to give the remaining corpus of the fund to Emory. At that time it was the largest gift that had ever been given to a university.

Robert Woodruff had no children. His brother Henry, who never married, was profoundly depressed and committed suicide on Thanksgiving Day 1947. Woodruff blamed himself for not being able to help him. Later, when the Glenn Memorial Building at Grady Memorial Hospital was converted into a research facility, it was renamed in honor of Henry.

Woodruff lost his wife, Nell Hodgson Woodruff, from a cerebral hemorrhage on January 23, 1968. Like Asa Candler before him, he never regained his spirit and energy after his wife died. For many years, he had difficulty hearing and gradually lost considerable vision. He died at the age of ninety-five on March 7, 1985, in Emory University Hospital.

The Crawford W. Long Connection

In 1939 Crawford W. Long Hospital was given to Emory University by Drs. Luther Fischer and E. C. Davis. However, it was stipulated that the hospital was not to be operated by Emory until Dr. Fischer died. He died in 1953. Much more will be written later in this book about Crawford W. Long Hospital, which in the years ahead became increasingly important in the development of Emory University School of Medicine and its Department of Medicine.

Scenes of the Atlanta Medical College Just Before It Became Emory University School of Medicine

The scenes shown in Figure 1-23A, B, C, D, and E depict the buildings that made up the medical complex known as the Atlanta Medical College in 1915, when it became Emory University School of Medicine. Note the scene showing Grady Memorial Hospital.

The School As Depicted in the Early Bulletins of Emory University School of Medicine

The *Bulletin of Emory University School of Medicine*, prepared annually as a source of information for those who wish to apply to the School of Medicine, also serves as a repository of historical facts. Because of space limitations, parts of three bulletins have been chosen because they reveal landmark information of considerable value and interest in the period 1915–1942.

A part of the July 1915 *Bulletin* is reproduced because it reveals the beginning of Emory University School of Medicine (see Appendix 1). This was the transition year. The name of the Atlanta Medical College is prominently displayed on the bulletin's cover, although it is the Emory Bulletin. Tuition was $150 annually, and board and lodging could be obtained for $18 to $25 a month.

A part of the June 1917 *Bulletin* is reproduced because it documents the shift of the first two years of medical school teaching from the Grady Memorial Hospital campus to the Emory University campus (see Appendix 2).

A part of the May 1942 *Bulletin* is reproduced because it reveals information about Emory University School of Medicine immediately before Dr. Eugene A. Stead Jr. arrived to become Emory's first full-time professor and chairman of the Department of Medicine (see Appendix 3). The tuition was $112.50 a quarter, and the hospitalization fee was $2 a quarter. A single dormitory room in Dobbs Hall was $30 a quarter, and meals in the Emory campus cafeteria were $17 to $25 a month. It is an historical curiosity to note the emphatic statement, "Only men are admitted."

The View of an Emory Medical Student

Dr. Bruce Logue wrote the following account of his perception of the Department of Medicine during the years prior to 1942. Dr. Logue was a medical student at Emory in the late thirties. He later joined the Emory faculty and was a major contributor to the development of Emory University Hospital and the Emory Clinic. Much more will be written about Dr. Logue in later pages of this book.

> When I was a medical student at Emory, we did not have a full time professor and chairman of the Department of Medicine. Dr. Russell Oppenheimer was dean of the medical school, superintendent of Emory University Hospital, and chairman of the Department of Medicine, in addition to holding many other positions. Teaching was done by volunteer practitioners. The outstanding teacher was Dr. James Paullin, who trained at Johns Hopkins and was the leading internist in Atlanta. He made rounds once a week at "colored Grady" and had a Clinical Pathological Conference (CPC) on one other day. The CPC was outstanding, and he had a great background in pathology as well as medicine. Dr. Cyrus Strickler taught at "white Grady," but the service there was totally separate from "colored Grady," where the best teaching in all specialties was carried out. Dr. Stewart Roberts was another great teacher, very fluent, and later became president of the American Heart Association. Dr. Carter Smith ran the Grady cardiac clinics and taught electrocardiography. Dr. Minor Blackford was an expert in syphilitic heart disease and taught in the Grady clinic. Dr. Merrill Monfort, an internist, also taught medicine.
>
> Dr. J. R. McCord was the full-time professor and chairman of the Department of Obstetrics, but there were no other full-time faculty members in the clinical years."

Analysis of Events Prior to 1942

Emory University, Emory University School of Medicine, and its Department of Medicine evolved from a coalition of several institutions. There had been controversy along the way. Recall "Uncle Allen" Turner's rebellion against sending the money and sons of Georgia to Randolph-Macon in Virginia. Then there was the controversy that occurred when the Methodist Church and Vanderbilt University decided to go their separate ways. Remember also that the faculty members of Emory College urged the development of Emory University; and it is highly likely that some controversy ensued when some of them wanted the new university to be located in Oxford.

In the beginning (1915) the entire Emory University School of Medicine was in the Grady Memorial Hospital area in the Emory-owned old Atlanta Medical College building, which eventually became the "colored Grady" hospital. In 1917 the Anatomy, Physiology, and Chemistry buildings opened so that the basic sciences could be taught on the Emory University campus in Druid Hills. Because there was no hospital on the Druid Hills campus, the clinical departments and the dean's office were located in the medical school building in the Grady Memorial Hospital area. This split campus led to varying degrees of controversy that persisted over the years. This was the second split campus of Emory University, the first being the Oxford College campus and the Emory University campus in Atlanta. A controversy developed when the new Wesley Memorial Hospital was built on the Emory campus in 1922. Some individuals had wanted it located in the Grady Memorial Hospital area to be used by Emory Medical School located there. Others, especially Asa Candler, wanted it to be built on the Emory campus. Asa Candler won—he paid for it, and it later became the Emory University Hospital. Despite the addition of the hospital on the Emory campus, the clinical departments and clinical teaching were still predominantly centered in the "colored hospital" on the Grady Memorial Hospital campus.

Emory University located in Druid Hills was a strong magnet. Academic standards were high. Scholarship filled the air. Flexner's brilliant idea of linking medical schools to universities was fulfilled at Emory.

Grady Memorial Hospital was also a strong magnet because, in the beginning, Emory University had no hospital. In addition, in those days, patients in private hospitals did not participate, or participated very little, in teaching programs. Historically, most of the former medical schools in Atlanta had been located in the Grady area, and those that started elsewhere eventually moved to the Grady area.

Emory faculty became skilled at dealing with split campuses. Perhaps this prepared the future Emory leaders and decision makers for the enormous changes that were coming. In the years ahead, Emory University School of Medicine was destined to include four additional hospitals, a large clinic, and numerous satellite clinics under its umbrella. Accordingly, these additions created many new split campuses.

Who Chaired the Department of Medicine Prior to 1942?

The *Bulletins* of Emory University School of Medicine from 1915 to 1927 do not list the names of the chairmen of the Department of

Medicine. The bulletins from 1915 through 1926 list the following individuals as senior clinical professors:

1915 William S. Kendrick, M.D., C. W. Strickler, M.D., Stewart R. Roberts, M.D.

1916 William S. Kendrick, M.D., C. W. Strickler, M.D., Stewart R. Roberts, M.D., Rufus T. Dorsey, M.D., J. Edgar Paullin, M.D.

1917 William S. Kendrick, M.D., C. W. Strickler, M.D., Stewart R. Roberts, M.D., J. Edgar Paullin, M.D.

1918 C. W. Strickler, M.D., Stewart R. Roberts, M.D., J. Edgar Paullin, M.D.

1919 C. W. Strickler, M.D., Stewart R. Roberts, M.D., J. Edgar Paullin, M.D.

1920 C. W. Strickler, M.D., Stewart R. Roberts, M.D., J. Edgar Paullin, M.D.

1921 C. W. Strickler, M.D., Stewart R. Roberts, M.D., J. Edgar Paullin, M.D.

1922 C. W. Strickler, M.D., Stewart R. Roberts, M.D., J. Edgar Paullin, M.D.

1923 C. W. Strickler, M.D., Stewart R. Roberts, M.D., J. Edgar Paullin, M.D.

1924 C. W. Strickler, M.D., Stewart R. Roberts, M.D., J. Edgar Paullin, M.D.

1925 C. W. Strickler, M.D., Stewart R. Roberts, M.D.

1926 through 1931 J. Edgar Paullin, M.D.

Apparently Dr. W. S. Kendrick was designated as the first Chairman of the Department of Medicine. He served from 1915 to 1918. Dr. Cyrus Strickler Sr. was considered to be the Chairman of the Department of Medicine from 1918 to 1926 and Dr. J. Edgar Paullin was designated as the Chairman of the Department of Medicine from 1926 to 1931. Dr. Russell Oppenheimer was listed as Chairman of the Department of Medicine from 1931 through 1941. During that period he also served as Dean. But Dr. J. Edgar Paullin was the most active teacher in the department and was perceived by many students and house officers as the "one in charge." Dr. Eugene A. Stead Jr. became the first full-time chairman of the Department of Medicine in 1942.

Dr. Henry C. (Jake) Sauls, another Piedmont Hospital physician, became chief of the medical service at the "colored hospital" at Grady Memorial Hospital, and Dr. Carl C. Aven became chief of the medical service at the "white hospital" at Grady Memorial Hospital, but neither of them was considered to be chairman of the Department of Medicine. They were, however, in place when Eugene A. Stead Jr. arrived in 1942 (see discussion on page 74).

It is apparent that Emory had no long-range plans for development, because the institution bought land for further medical school development at Grady and almost simultaneously created the Woodruff-supported Robert Winship Memorial Clinic at Emory University Hospital.

The 1834–1942 era ended when the Emory decision-makers and leaders moved toward the appointment of full-time faculty members in the Department of Medicine. Even though facilities were poor, and money scarce, the leaders of the Medical School believed that generous benefactors were in the wings and that Atlanta showed indisputable signs of becoming the premier city of the South.

Acknowledgments

General References

Allen, Frederick. *Secret Formula: How Brilliant Marketing and Relentless Salesmanship Made Coca-Cola the Best-Known Product in the World.* New York: HarperBusiness, 1994.

Allen's book is filled with interesting information about the people who developed the Coca-Cola Company. His account of the life of Robert W. Woodruff served as a major source of information for the creation of the profile of Woodruff for this book. The source was used with the permission of Mr. Allen, who holds the copyright, and the publisher.

Blumberg, Richard W. *A Department Comes of Age: The History of Pediatrics at Emory University 1854–1981.* Atlanta: Emory University (Fulton, Mo.: Ovid Bell Press), 1993.

Dr. Blumberg was professor and chairman of the Department of Pediatrics for thirty years. Certain parts of his book contain information that is germane to the story of the history of the Department of Medicine. The copyright is owned by Emory University.

Candler, Charles Howard. *Asa Griggs Candler.* Atlanta: Emory University, 1950.

This book by Howard Candler, the son of Asa Griggs Candler, is a beautifully written account of the first great benefactor of Emory University. Anyone who joins the Emory faculty should read this book because it chronicles the creation of the University and discusses the life of its major early donor. This source was used in developing the profile of Asa Griggs Candler. The copyright is owned by Emory University.

Elliott, Charles. *A Biography of the "Boss": Robert Winship Woodruff.* N.p.: R. W. Woodruff, 1979.

This remarkable book by Charles Elliott is entertaining and beautifully written. It was published privately in 1979 and the copyright was originally held by Mr. Robert Woodruff. It is now held by Emory University.

English, Thomas H. *Emory University 1915–1965 A Semicentennial History.* Atlanta: Emory University, 1966.

This excellent account of the creation of Emory University and its various schools gives a broad view of the development that spanned more than 100 years. This source was used to supply much of the information regarding the genesis of Emory University. The copyright is held by Emory University.

Martin, John D., Jr., in collaboration with Garland D. Perdue. *The History of Surgery at Emory University School of Medicine.* Atlanta: Emory University (Fulton, Mo.: Ovid Bell Press), 1979.

Dr. J. D. Martin was professor and chairman of the Department of Surgery at Emory University from 1957 to 1971. Dr. Martin was involved with the growth and development of Emory University for more than fifty years. His insight is priceless. The book, written with Dr. Garland Perdue, relates many details of the development of Emory University School of Medicine and its hospitals and clinic. Much of the information and some of the photographs used in the present book came from Dr. Martin's book. The copyright is held by Emory University.

Paris, Betty B. *Coca-Cola Trivia.* N.p.: n.p. [Betty B. Paris], 1995.

This little book gives interesting one-liners about the people who developed the Coca-Cola empire. If you can answer the true-false questions, you make an A in the class on Coca-Cola.

Richardson, Arthur P. Audiotape.

Speech made at the July 13, 1982 meeting of the Atlanta Medical History Society on the History of Emory University School of Medicine.

Roberts Charles S. *Life and Writings of Stewart R. Roberts, M.D. Georgia's First Heart Specialist.* Spartanburg, S.C.: The Reprint Company Publishers, 1993.

This book, written by Stewart Roberts's grandson, Dr. Charles Roberts, not only tells the story of his grandfather, Stewart Roberts, but sheds light on the development of Emory University School of Medicine and its Department of Medicine. This source of information is used with the permission of the author, who holds the copyright.

The Help of Others

I acknowledge the generous help of Dr. Paul B. Beeson, Dr. Joseph E. Hardison, Dr. Charles R. Hatcher Jr., Dr. Gary S. Hauk, Dr. William Hollingsworth, Dr. R. Bruce Logue, Mr. J. W. Pinkston Jr., Dr. Charles S. Roberts, Dr. Thomas F. Sellers Jr., Dr. Mark E. Silverman, Dr. Eugene A. Stead Jr., Dr. Cyrus W. Strickler Jr. and Dr. Judson C. Ward Jr. who critiqued the manuscript and offered many suggestions—which I accepted.

I especially thank Mr. Frederick L. Allen and Mr. Joseph W. Jones, who are experts on the life of Mr. Robert Woodruff, for discovering and correcting certain aspects of my rendition of this remarkable man.

I am deeply indebted to Dr. Evangeline Papageorge for her help in the preparation of this chapter of the book. She "knows Emory" and is a skillful editor as well.

Figure 1-1
The first Atlanta Medical College was located on the corner of Butler and Armstrong Streets. It was built in 1859.

Figure 1-2
The Southern Medical College (center building). It was built on Butler Street during the last part of the 19th century. The building to the left housed the Atlanta Medical College. The photograph was made looking south on Butler Street.

Figure 1-3

The Atlanta College of Physicians and Surgeons was located on the corner of Butler and Armstrong Streets from 1906 to 1913. It later became the second Atlanta Medical College (1913–1915). The entire Emory University School of Medicine was located in this building from 1915 to 1917. The Emory-owned building was converted to a hospital in 1917. It was referred to as the "colored" division of Grady Memorial Hospital. The building was used for the administrative offices of the clinical departments of Emory University School of Medicine from 1917 to 1954. The hospital was officially called the Emory Division of Grady Memorial Hospital from 1921 to 1958, when the new Grady Memorial Hospital was built.

Figure 1-4
    The original Grady Memorial Hospital, circa 1892. The building was located on Butler Street, across the street from the Atlanta College of Physicians and Surgeons.

Figure 1-5
    Henry W. Grady (1850–1889) for whom Grady Memorial Hospital was named.

Figure 1-6
Grady Memorial Hospital ambulance, 1896.

Figure 1-7
Grady Memorial Hospital house staff, 1902. Dr. Clyde Jeffries, Dr. W. E. Persons, Dr. O. T. White, Dr. W. A. Selman, and Dr. James Randall. The house staff was selected by the officials of Grady Memorial Hospital; there was no relationship to any of the medical schools that existed at the time.

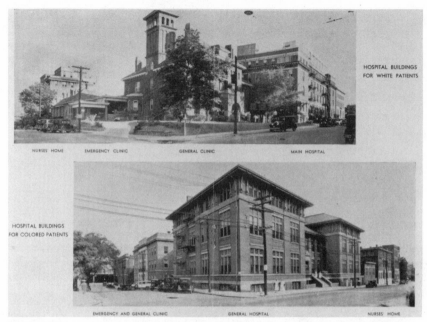

Figure 1-8
  Top: The Butler Street Building (shown to the right) was built as an annex to Grady Memorial Hospital in 1912. After 1917, when the Atlanta Medical College building, located across the street, was converted to a "colored" hospital, the Butler Street Building was referred to as the "white" hospital.

  Immediately above: The "colored" hospital. The building to the right housed the African-American nurses.

Figure 1-9
  The Emory-owned J. J. Gray Building was erected on the Grady Memorial Hospital campus in 1917. It was originally used for the "colored" outpatients and Emergency Clinic. It was later used for Emory faculty and house-staff quarters. Years later, in 1965, it was converted  into the Henry Woodruff Memorial Research Building for Emory University faculty. Henry Woodruff was Robert Woodruff's brother.

Figure 1-10

Side view of the Steiner Building, designed by the noted Atlanta architect, Neel Reid. The Steiner Hospital was, for a while, a free-standing hospital for cancer patients. It was later utilized by Grady Memorial Hospital. In 1950 it housed Emory faculty and the famous Cardiac Catheterization Laboratory. Still later it was leased by Emory and used exclusively for Emory faculty. The structure to the right shows the entrance to a large auditorium that was created for the use of Emory University School of Medicine.

Figure 1-11

The original Wesley Memorial Hospital was located on Courtland Street and Auburn Avenue. In earlier days, it was known as the Calico House. It was headquarters for General William Tecumseh Sherman after the Battle of Atlanta.

Figure 1-12

Wesley Memorial Hospital was built on the Emory campus in 1922.
The hospital was renamed Emory University Hospital in 1932. The building and the land were given to Emory University by Asa Griggs Candler.

Figure 1-13A
    Asa Griggs Candler (1851–
1929) gave his money, time,
and energy to the development of Emory University. He
and his brother, Bishop Warren Candler, were the major
figures in the development of
Emory University. This portrait hangs in the lobby of
Emory University Hospital.

Figure 1-13B
   Lucy Elizabeth Candler (1859–1919) played an important role in creating a religious environment for her family and supported Asa Griggs Candler's work with the Methodist Church and Emory University. The Lucy Elizabeth Pavilion of Emory University Hospital was built by her children to honor her. This portrait hangs in the lobby of Emory University Hospital.

Figure 1-14
   William Simpson Elkin (1858–1944). This extremely capable man was the last dean of the Atlanta Medical College and the first dean of Emory University School of Medicine. His tenure as dean extended from 1900 to 1925.

Figure 1-15

Russell H. Oppenheimer, M.D. (1888–1966). Oppenheimer was a "one-man medical school." He simultaneously held numerous administrative posts that kept the fledgling Emory University School of Medicine together. He was dean of Emory University School of Medicine from 1925 to 1945. He was also chairman of the Department of Medicine from 1931 through 1941. This photograph was made of a photograph that hangs in the Oppenheimer Room in the Glenn Memorial Building, across the street from Grady Hospital.

Figure 1-16

Cyrus W. Strickler Sr., M.D. (1873–1953), a respected teacher in the early days of Emory University School of Medicine. He was considered to be the second volunteer chairman of the Department of Medicine, serving from 1918 to 1926.

Figure 1-17

This letter documents that Dr. Cyrus W. Strickler Sr. was designated as "head" of the Department of Medicine of Emory University in 1918. The letterhead reveals the location of Dean Elkin's office.

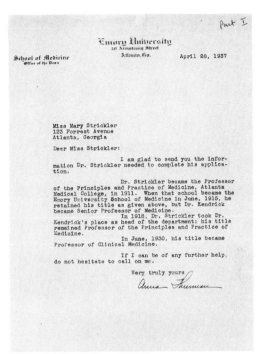

Figure 1-18

Stewart R. Roberts, M.D. (1878–1941). He was known as the "Osler of the South" for his superb teaching and oration.

Figure 1-19
    J. Edgar Paullin, M.D. (1881–1951) was considered to be professor and chairman of the Department of Medicine on a voluntary basis from 1926 to 1931. It was he who influenced Eugene A. Stead Jr.

Figure 1-20
    J. Elliott Scarborough Jr., M.D. (1906–1966). Dr. Scarborough was the first director of the Robert Winship Memorial Clinic and long-time friend of Robert W. Woodruff. He had profound influence on the development of Emory University School of Medicine, the Emory University Clinic, and the Robert W. Woodruff Health Sciences Center. The portrait shown in this photograph hangs in the atrium of the entrance of the original Emory University Clinic building, which is now known as the Scarborough Memorial Building.

Figure 1-21
Robert W. Woodruff (1889–1985), benefactor of Emory University. The Robert W. Woodruff Health Sciences Center is named for him. The portrait shown in this photograph hangs in the atrium of the entrance to the original Emory University Clinic building, which is now known as the Scarborough Memorial Building.

Figure 1-22
George W. Woodruff (1895–1987) contributed enormously to Emory University, Emory University School of Medicine, and the Department of Medicine. The portrait shown in this photograph hangs in the office of Mr. John Henry at Emory University Hospital.

Figure 1-23A
   Photographs from a 1915 brochure showing scenes of the Atlanta
Medical College when it became Emory University School of Medicine.
The legend has been modified for clearer communication.
   Buildings of the Atlanta Medical College. The Microscopic Anatomy
Building is shown on the left (down Armstrong Street). The Main Build-
ing is on the corner of Armstrong and Butler Streets. The Practical
Anatomy Building and the Carnegie Pathological Institute are shown to
the right of the main building (north on Butler Street). One of these
buildings was later used as a home for nurses (see figure 1-8).

Figure 1-23B
   Grady Me-
morial Hospital
buildings on
the left and the
Atlanta Medi-
cal College
buildings on
the right. The
photograph
was taken look-
ing south on
Butler Street.

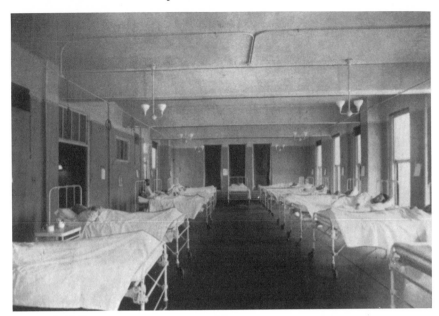

Figure 1-23C

Photograph from a 1915 brochure showing scenes of the Atlanta Medical College when it became Emory University School of Medicine. The original photograph is accompanied by the following legend:

"One of the wards in Grady Hospital. This cut shows one of the many wards in the Grady Hospital, and is typical of the cleanly condition maintained in all the wards. The members of the faculty of the Atlanta Medical College, owing to their official connection with the hospital, are able to give ample clinical and ward instruction to the students."

Figure 1-23D

Photograph from a 1915 brochure showing scenes of the Atlanta Medi-cal College when it became Emory University School of Medicine. The legend reads:

"Surgical amphitheatre. This amphitheatre is located in the Main Building, occupying parts of the third and fourth floors, and seats 350 students. It has been the endeavor of the faculty to make it as nearly per-fect as possible. It has a marble wainscoting, and the floor is laid in white marble tile."

Figure 1-23E
Photograph from a 1915 brochure showing scenes of the Atlanta Medical College when it became Emory University School of Medicine. The legend reads:
"Partial view of College campus, showing rear of Main Building and Microscopic Anatomy Building."

CHAPTER 2
A Giant Step Forward and the
"Defining Moment" 1942–1946

The four and one-half years from July 1942 to January 1947 will never be forgotten at Emory University School of Medicine. During those years, Eugene Stead, Emory's first full-time chairman of the Department of Medicine, stamped his own brand of excellence on the department (see Figure 2-1). He, and the colleagues he gathered around him, were by every measure the best and brightest in American medicine. Emory's Department of Medicine was the beneficiary of their enormous skill, talent, and wisdom. They created a future for the department.

Books have been written about the life and achievements of Eugene Stead (see acknowledgments at end of this chapter). The short story that follows emphasizes only his monumental contribution to the Department of Medicine at Emory University School of Medicine, before he continued his work at Duke University. When the history of medicine is recorded by those who look back at the twentieth century, they will see two medical giants. One will be Sir William Osler, and the other will be Eugene Stead.

The Biography of Eugene A. Stead Jr., M.D.

Stead's Early Years

Eugene Stead was born in Decatur, Georgia, on October 6, 1908. His sister Emily was born before him, and his sisters Cleo and Joyce and brother William were born after him. Gene's mother was Emily Bertha White; his father, Eugene Auson Stead, was a pharmacist and a deeply religious Methodist. Gene's father was advised, for health reasons, to give up his position at the drug store where he worked and become a pharmaceutical salesman. He could be viewed as an early version of the modern pharmaceutical representative or "detail man or woman." As a youngster, Gene traveled with his father and was obviously influenced with him with one exception—Gene did not become deeply involved with religion.

Gene was taught to read by his sister Emily before he entered school. When they were very young, Stead and Emily had pneumonia, and Dr.

J. Edgar Paullin was called to see them. Paullin advised Gene's parents not to force him to attend school when he did not feel well. Paullin also advised young Stead to read and then read some more. So Stead became an avid reader. As years passed, he excelled in school and graduated from Decatur High School with top honors and a one-year scholarship to attend Emory University. As will be seen later, Paullin became a guiding figure in his early career.

He did well at Emory and earned extra money by tutoring other students in biology. As Stead tells it, he tutored students who were doing well but wanted to do even better. One of the students was Arthur Merrill, who later played an important role in Stead's life. Stead graduated from Emory in 1928 with Phi Beta Kappa honors.

Stead's Medical School Days at Emory

Stead says he entered medical school because "it offered an intellectual challenge." He has also stated that "the other graduate schools had no vacancies." He found the early years of medical school too easy, and he, along with a few other classmates, was given a more difficult curriculum in anatomy. Later, in the clinical years, he was dissatisfied with the textbooks that were recommended because he recognized they were out of date. He obtained copies of Paul Dudley White's *Heart Disease* and Henry Christian's *Oxford System of Medicine*. He then lived with these books.

Stead socialized very little with his peers. Today, he might be called a "loner." He read and, as we all learned later, did a lot of thinking. Even then, he was undoubtedly developing his own unique way of cutting through the husk that seems to be wrapped around the kernels of truth. He was, without a doubt, learning who he was and what he could do with his brain. He graduated from Emory University School of Medicine in 1932.

As a medical student Stead recognized the brilliance of Dr. J. Edgar Paullin, one of his Emory teachers and his family's doctor. The Stead-Paullin relationship was always close, but as years passed it was to become increasingly important to the Department of Medicine of Emory University School of Medicine.

Stead's House-Staff and Research Training

Stead was also impressed with Dr. Hugh Wood and Dr. Carter Smith who were among his Emory teachers. He learned that they had interned at Harvard's Peter Bent Brigham Hospital in Boston. He decided to do the same.

Dr. Paullin knew Henry Christian, who was chief of medicine at the Brigham. Paullin, along with Drs. Wood and Smith, arranged for Stead to be interviewed for one of the intern positions at the Brigham. The interns at the Brigham were selected after the competitive interviews of top-flight students had been completed. Gene's interview was with the cardiologist Dr. Sam Levine, who asked Stead some questions about coarctation of the aorta. Stead, having read Paul White's book, was ready for the questions. He and Dr. Levine undoubtedly had an interesting discussion, which Stead very likely stamped with his own unique brand of thinking and talking.

Stead was selected for the sixteen-month-long internship at the Brigham. His chief, Dr. Christian, then offered him an eight-month research fellowship to work in his laboratory, paying him $75 a month. He was given a room to sleep in and his meals. During the eight months, Stead gained insight into the mechanisms responsible for edema. Throughout this period of study and thinking, he began to wonder if the edema from heart failure was caused by the kidney's retaining salt and water. This insight, of course, eventually led to the search for diuretics to prevent the kidney from retaining abnormal amounts of salt and water.

Stead then became an intern in surgery at the Brigham. It seems to me that he decided to do this for all the wrong reasons. But Stead's thinking apparatus was different from that of the rest of us. He learned to respect surgeons, but decided not to be one because they spent their days working on people who were asleep, and he liked to work with people who were awake.

Stead then worked in Dr. Jack Gibson's laboratory, where he learned to use Evans Blue Dye to determine blood volume.

Stead continued his house-staff training at Cincinnati General Hospital under the wing of Dr. Marion Blankenhorn, chairman of the Department of Medicine at the University of Cincinnati. He spent six months as a senior resident and then became chief resident in medicine. Stead's leadership talent began to emerge during this period. He taught, he organized, and he led the house staff to achieve more than they were accustomed to achieving.

Stead's Relationship to Dr. Soma Weiss

Dr. Soma Weiss came to Cincinnati General Hospital to visit Dr. Eugene Ferris, a member of the faculty there. Dr. Ferris had trained with Dr. Weiss in Boston (see Chapter 4 of this book). Stead made teaching rounds with Dr. Weiss, and at the end of the visit Weiss offered Stead a research fellowship in the Thorndike Laboratory at Boston City Hospital. Offered $900 a year by Weiss, Stead said he needed $1,800 because he was helping his brother, Bill, through medical school. When Weiss said he did not have $1,800, Stead replied that he had planned to go into practice in Atlanta, but if Weiss found the $1,800 he should let Stead know; Stead did not want to work for anyone else.

Weiss found the money by combining two jobs. Stead became Weiss's research fellow at the Thorndike Laboratory and Dr. Minot's chief resident at the Boston City Hospital. Dr. Stead performed both jobs without difficulty. After five years in research at the Thorndike Laboratory under the tutelage of Soma Weiss, Stead's reputation was made. He was accepted as the premier student of the circulation and was perceived as an original thinker who worked hard and led others to perform better than they thought they could. Soma Weiss then became chief of medicine at the Brigham, and Stead moved with him to that institution.

Weiss selected Evelyn Selby as his secretary. Stead was attracted to her and, with typical Stead strategy, won her hand in marriage. Soma Weiss gave the bride away, because Evelyn's father had died.

Soma Weiss, who had achieved international recognition for his teaching, research, and leadership ability, died on January 21, 1942, of a ruptured berry aneurysm. Stead, who had already accepted the chairmanship of medicine at Emory but had not left Boston, became Acting Chief of Medicine at the Brigham. He could have remained there as the chief of medicine but kept his word to Emory.

Why Stead Accepted the Emory Offer

There are three reasons why Stead accepted the offer to become Emory's first full-time chairman of the Department of Medicine. His mother had said, "If you have anything to give, give it to the South." Soma Weiss, his chief, advised him to accept the offer, although everyone else in academic medicine advised him not to do so. Finally, and equally important, Stead loved Emory. On July 10, 1989, Stead sent me the following letter with the request that I place it in the medical archives at Emory. Note that the information deals with his decision to accept the offer made by Emory. Stead's letter was published in the *Emory University Journal of Medicine* under the title "Some Weiss's Contribution to the Department of Medicine at Emory."

> During the spring and summer of 1941 I was approached by Dean Oppenheimer of Emory about arrangements to bring me back to my alma mater as Professor of Medicine and Chairman of the Department. I was then 32 years of age and had spent seven of the 10 years after graduation in a white suit. The deal was finally arranged because of the persistence of Dr. Arthur Merrill. I first met Art when I was a student instructor in biology at Emory. I

tutored selected students for $5 an hour and usually selected students who were in the B+ range and wanted to move up to A. Art was one of my students. He really wanted me to return to Emory and in spite of the reluctance of others he had his way.

By the summer of 1941 I had joined the Harvard Unit as a captain and knew that this unit would be the first to go when war was declared. Emory obtained my release from the unit with the understanding that I would not volunteer for active service and that I would take no steps to avoid being called into the service by the Fulton-DeKalb County Procurement and Assignment Committee.

My friends and professional colleagues at Harvard advised strongly against accepting the Emory offer. They said that the outlook for weak private schools was dim and that even with money I could never attract a distinguished faculty. The one exception was my chief—Soma Weiss. *He said one should go where one was needed and that it was time to determine whether I could move from a man of promise to a man of achievement.* If I were better suited for practice than academia—the sooner I found this out the better.[1]

Stead showed his love for Emory when he wrote the following:

I have always been grateful for Emory, my alma mater. This small, struggling college had the audacity to attach to itself a failing proprietary medical school. At the time I entered, it was on and off the probation list. It was 1928 and the Great Depression had already begun in the South. The only question anyone asked when I applied for admission was, "Son, can you borrow the money for tuition?" I said that the Atlanta Rotary Club would lend me the money. Each year I cheerfully send Emory a check. No Emory medical school, no Dr. Eugene Stead.[2]

Emory's Offer to Stead
and His Early Days as Chairman

The Emory officials offered Stead an annual income of $6000. Stead, unsure how he could care for his wife and future children on $6000 a year, requested $8000. After much haggling, the Emory officials agreed to pay him $8000 annually. The discussion, however, left some of the Emory officials believing Stead "liked money." This, of course, was totally untrue.

His task at Emory as chairman of the Department of Medicine was not an easy one. He had to have loved the institution, or he would not have tolerated the problems he found on arrival. He quickly realized that he was to work at the Grady "colored hospital," which was officially named

---

[1] J. W. Hurst, "Soma Weiss' Contribution to Emory's Department of Medicine," *Emory University Journal of Medicine* 4, no. 1 (1990): 63–64. Reproduced by permission.

[2] E. A. Stead Jr., *What This Patient Needs Is a Doctor*, ed. G. S. Wagner, B. Cebe, and M. P. Rozear (Durham, N.C.: Carolina Academic Press, 1978). Reproduced by permission.

"The Emory Division of Grady Hospital." He had no problem with that. He discovered, however, that Dr. Jake Sauls was Chief of the Medical Service there, and that Dr. Carl C. Aven was Chief of the Medical Service at the "white hospital." This placed him in an awkward position—he was not in charge of the medical service in the institution where he was to work. How could he function? How could he recruit anyone to join him?

It was Stead's love for Emory and his self-assurance, maturity, and leadership that saved the school. As will be discussed subsequently, several brilliant people wanted to follow him to Emory, even though they knew he could offer them very little except himself. He thought, in Stead-like fashion, that he would remain at Grady Hospital every night and day, and that the chiefs of the "colored and white" hospitals would be there only a few hours several days a week. He reasoned that if he could not at least be *perceived* as the chief, then he was not suited for academic medicine and would go into practice. So he and his new brilliant recruits taught medicine night and day. They began their research. An aura of excitement prevailed. Within a year he was appointed Chief of the Medical Service of both hospitals. Stead wrote his view of the difficulties in the book *E. A. Stead Jr.*:

> When I went to Grady Hospital, the heads of the colored and white hospitals said there wasn't a place for me. So I got up a little earlier and went to bed a little later and before long I ran Grady. The world belongs to those who work a little harder.
>
> The year 1942 opened with me facing up to the fact that I was going to Emory with a total budget of $23,500 and very little chance of succeeding in academic medicine. I was very hesitant about asking people to come to Emory. The turning point in my career came one night when Jim Warren, Eddie Miller, John Hickam and Abner Golden announced that they would be in Atlanta in July. I said that I doubted the wisdom of that decision. I was informed that I was not being asked for my opinion: I was merely being informed about what would happen.
>
> The Grady days were glorious days. We were very short of money. We had to have a defense contract to study shock in order to survive. Al Blalock visited us and recommended that we be given a small contract to study shock in animals and that we try to develop a program to study shock in man. Jim Warren suggested that he visit Cournand and see if the cardiac catheter was the tool we needed to develop a program to study shock at the Gradys.
>
> After Jim's visit of several weeks with Cournand, we were able to propose a program to the War Resources Development Board for the study of shock in patients. Our first budget grossly underestimated our costs. We were saved by a transcription error. A decimal point was shifted one point to the right and we had just enough money for the project. This project allowed the air conditioning of the basement laboratories and we at least were protected from

heat and from the dust of the cars parked in the dirt lot between our basement laboratories and Coca Cola Place.

I can still feel the excitement of the ventures of the team of Warren, Merrill, Brannon, Weens and Stead. The decision to study patients with heart failure was always with us. Looking back over those times I can think of only one major opportunity that we dropped. We did not link the increased renin output of patients with chronic heart failure with the control of aldosterone.

At Emory our first assignment was to arrange the department's teaching program within the block of time allotted to the department of medicine. We decided first to free the faculty of any compulsion to cover a very large block of knowledge. We would teach from the patients and attach knowledge already acquired to the particular patient the student was caring for. The student would re-investigate those phases of the basic sciences which applied to the particular patient and learn that part of clinical medicine which applied to the same patient. The patient would be the stimulus for learning, because this stimulus would last as long as the student practiced medicine. The role of the faculty would be to see that the student enjoyed his learning experiences and developed a desire to continue them. This system of "slow" learning required that the faculty be willing to tolerate ignorance of many specific areas of medicine. If we laid down no hard and fast body of knowledge that had to be learned, we could not criticize the student for ignorance of a particular fact. We had to base our judgments on his ability to use those facts he did have. If he could manipulate these facts, tear them down and rebuild new structures with them—in short, think—we would be satisfied.

My Emory students are now well established in practice, teaching and research. I have heard from them often about their experiences as interns in other hospitals. They realized that they had memorized fewer facts than students from any other schools; but they were not dismayed when new situations arose and they were satisfied with their ability to learn from each new experience. I am satisfied that their performance since graduation vindicates the method by which they were taught.

Thus my Emory years were spent in freeing the members of the department from the need for compulsive coverage of the field of internal medicine and in freeing the medical student from the idea that he worked because he was in school. Instead, the student learned to work for the fun of learning and to give his patients good care.

The use of research as an important component of education can be defended only anecdotally. I went to Grady to a house staff who had had access to the library. They were very widely read. Their reading was totally uncritical. Never having had a hand in creation of knowledge, they were not aware of the pits into which all authors at one time or another fall. They believed everything they read and were puzzled by the fact that one paper said one thing and a second just the opposite. I decided at that time not to engage in major educational ventures without a faculty engaged in creating new knowledge and publishing it in well-edited journals.[3]

---

[3] Ibid, 154–57. Reproduced by permission.

The Recruitment of Paul Beeson

When, in 1942, Drs. Warren, Hickam, Miller, and Golden called Stead and said they were going to join him, he pointed out to them that they were not very wise. They responded that they were not asking for his opinion but simply telling him they would join him at Grady. Warren was to be Stead's research fellow and the others were to become assistant residents on the medical house staff.

The recruitment of Paul Beeson, who was in England with the Harvard Red Cross unit, was different from the recruitment of the others. Before Soma Weiss died, he made Beeson an offer to return to the Brigham as an assistant professor at Harvard with an annual income of $3000. Stead had, by then, accepted the offer to return to Emory and had decided to ask Beeson to join him at Emory. Weiss knew of Stead's interest in Beeson and, before he died, wrote Beeson the following letter in December 1941. Anyone who reads this letter can see the greatness of Soma Weiss and his faith in the future of Emory University School of Medicine. Stead sent me a copy of Weiss's letter to Beeson on July 10, 1989. Apparently, Weiss had sent Stead a copy of his letter to Beeson. The letter was published in *The Emory University Journal of Medicine* under the title "Soma Weiss' Contribution to the Department of Medicine at Emory."

> You have received or will soon receive a letter from Gene Stead about simultaneously with this letter of mine. You well know how much I am interested in your future progress, and therefore I thought that I would like to write you about how I feel about Gene's undertaking. Emory University School of Medicine has always been an important center in the South, but I am certain that with the recent development there in surgery and now in medicine and with the future plans, it will become one of the most important centers in the South. You know Gene's ability, so I don't have to add anything on that point. He is taking several younger men from the Brigham in the capacity of assistant residents. The clinical material and opportunities there will be very great. I am also confident that the various foundations will see the significance of Atlanta as a medical center, not only in undergraduate but also in graduate education, and it is my sincere belief that they will support worthwhile undertakings. The understanding and treatment of infectious diseases have been particularly neglected in the South, and therefore if you decide to go to Emory, you will be certain of a good opportunity to develop yourself clinically. I also believe that if you do good work, you will have no difficulty in getting other even more important positions if that is your ambition. I don't want to influence you, because the decision is up to you, but I thought these lines might be helpful. . . .[4]

---

[4] J. W. Hurst, "Soma Weiss' Contribution to Emory's Department of Medicine," *Emory University Journal of Medicine* 4, no. 1 (1990): 63–64. Reproduced by permission.

Weiss's death led to a moderate amount of administrative confusion at the Brigham. Stead, who had not at that point in time left the Brigham for Emory, assumed the role of Chief of Medicine at the Brigham until George Thorn was appointed. Stead then moved on to Emory and began his recruitment of Beeson. Here are some further lines from Stead's July 20, 1989, letter to me:

> I offered Paul the rank of associate professor and a salary of $4000. Meanwhile David Barr at Cornell had decided to establish an infectious disease unit at New York Hospital and opened negotiations with Beeson. I gave Paul a deadline for my offer and to my great joy he accepted. Shortly thereafter Barr made a definitive offer and upped the salary to $5000. Beeson regretted his acceptance of my Emory offer but being a gentleman as well as a scholar he came to Emory. After four and a half years he succeeded me as chairman.
>
> Barr, with space on his hands approached Walsh McDermott who was deferred from service because of tuberculosis. He said that Walsh could take the position offered Beeson. If he was successful he could stay on at Cornell and if unsuccessful he would have delayed going into practice by only 12 months. McDermott stayed on and became one of the most distinguished members of the Cornell faculty. In time Beeson and McDermott edited five editions of the Cecil Text Book of Medicine. When they learned many years later that they had been candidates for the same job, they laughed about it because instead of being warm friends they might have become hated rivals.[5]

Paullin's Helping Hand

Not everyone helped Stead when he arrived at Emory, but J. Edgar Paullin did. Stead wrote in his November 26, 1990, letter to Mark Silverman that Paullin, who had the most to lose, helped him enormously. Here is a portion of that letter:

> From 1932 until 1946 I visited Paullin in his office each summer. He was always gracious and interested in my work and the Stead family. When I returned to Grady in 1942 he gave me support at every turn. He knew that I would replace him in the minds and hearts of the Emory students and Grady residents. He continued his Tuesday conferences with the residents. As Paullin and I predicted these gradually became less popular. He was now competing with Beeson, Hickam, Warren, Engel and Stead. These young people lived at Grady. As chief of service I made attendance compulsory when patients were being cared for. I made all conferences not directly related to the care of the intern's or resident's patient optional. There was only one exception. Attendance at Paullin's Tuesday sessions was compulsory and I took attendance.[6]

---

[5] Ibid.

[6] Private correspondence shared with me by Mark Silverman. Reproduced by permission.

Stead also wrote in his July 10, 1989, letter to me how he was permitted to remain at Emory during the years of the second World War. Note how Paullin saved the Department of Medicine:

> Meanwhile in Atlanta, I was attending each quarter a meeting of the Procurement and Assignment Committee (draft board). In 1932 when I was a senior student there were no paid members of the department of medicine and these men on the committee were my teachers. They asked me how I had gotten along and whether I was a competent doctor. I answered in the affirmative. Who taught you? You did. Why can't we teach the current students? Why do we need you? That is a question that you will have to decide. They decided the question quickly and processed my papers for immediate active duty. The next day James Edgar Paullin, who for many years had served as Chairman of Medicine without pay, would take the train to Washington and appeal the decision. My orders would be revoked.
>
> I remained good friends with members of the Procurement and Assignment Committee, but they never conceded the fact that a research oriented teacher, living in Grady Hospital, could inspire students to see beyond the immediate needs of good medical practice.[7]

Stead's Achievements at Emory

Stead wrote Mark Silverman on November 26, 1990, the following statements about his effort to improve the library at Grady, where almost all the clinical teaching and research was conducted.

> In 1942 Elizabeth Weiss gave the medical library of Soma Weiss to my embryonic library at Grady. I noted that Paullin had a bound, complete and up to date set of the Journal of Biochemistry. Paullin asked me to apply for membership in the American College of Physicians. I replied that I would send in my application on the date that he contributed his set of the Journal of Biochemistry to the growing Grady library. The following week a truck delivered the volumes and I became a fellow of the college.[8]

Others joined Stead's department, including Jack Myers, Arthur Merrill, Phil Bondy, and Bruce Logue. The excellence of the teaching and research became nationally and internationally known.

The recruitment of Jack Myers should be emphasized because he became the first Chief of Medicine at the Lawson Veterans Hospital. The details of the complex metamorphosis of the Veterans Hospital is discussed on page 355. Lawson General Army Hospital was, at the end of World War II, converted to the Lawson Veterans Hospital. Also, in 1946, the national plan to have certain veterans hospitals become associated

---

[7] J. W. Hurst, "Soma Weiss' Contribution to Emory's Department of Medicine," *Emory University Journal of Medicine* 4, no. 1 (1990): 63–64. Reproduced by permission.

[8] Private correspondence shared with me by Mark Silverman. Reproduced by permission.

with medical schools was being implemented. Eugene Stead replaced Oppenheimer as dean of the School of Medicine in 1945 but continued to serve as chairman of the Department of Medicine. Stead was asked to select a Chief of Medicine for Lawson Veterans Hospital. Dr. Jack Myers was then a research fellow with Dr. Robert Wilkins at Boston City Hospital. He wanted to join Stead at Emory. Stead warned Myers that he might leave Emory for Duke, but that Myers could either join him or remain at Emory. Stead appointed Myers as Chief of Medicine at Lawson Veterans Hospital and associate professor of medicine at Emory University School of Medicine. Myers worked half-time there and the rest of his time at Grady Hospital. Myers remembers that many young doctors were returning from the service, and that he and Stead tried to accommodate them in the house-staff program at Grady and Lawson Veterans Hospital. After several months Stead moved to Duke, and Myers followed two months later. Jack Myers was destined to go down in history as one of the smartest doctors in the nation. In 1955 he became professor and chairman of the Department of Medicine at the University of Pittsburgh.

Stead's influence on students and house staff—especially the latter—was like magic. His comments about medical problems and the learning patterns of trainees were so colorful and meaningful that they rivaled those of Osler. His utterances were seldom forgotten. His "Sunday school" became famous. He and his associates offered a teaching session to the physicians of the area on Sunday morning. The sessions were held from 9:30 to 10:30 a.m. in order not to interfere with church service. Atlanta physicians and physicians who were serving in the army at nearby Lawson General Hospital and Fort McPherson attended the sessions. By every measurement he had created a great department of medicine using nothing but himself.

In those days there were three cardiac catheterization laboratories in the world: in London, New York, and at the Emory Division of Grady Memorial Hospital in Atlanta. Stead and his associates Warren, Brannon, Merrill, Myers, Weens, and Hickam used the cardiac catheter to study many physiologic problems related to the heart and circulation. Numerous first-rate research papers were published in superior, peer-review journals. Noteworthy was the paper on "Fluid Dynamics in Chronic Congestive Heart Failure," written with James V. Warren and published in the *Archives of Internal Medicine*.[9] This publication caused a great deal of controversy and wholesome debate.

---

[9] J. V. Warren and E. A. Stead, "Fluid Dynamics in Chronic Congestive Heart Failure," *Archives of Internal Medicine* 73 (1944): 138.

It should also be noted that the first diagnostic use of the cardiac catheter took place in Stead's cardiac catheterization laboratory at Grady. Dr. Joseph Massee had a patient who he believed might have an atrial septal defect. Jim Warren reasoned that if that were true there should be a step-up in the oxygen saturation of the blood in the right atrium of the patient. This turned out to be the case. Dr. H. S. Weens, professor and chairman of the Department of Radiology, was of great assistance. This diagnostic first was reported in 1945 in the *American Journal of Medical Science*.[10] It is highly likely that others in other laboratories had done the same, but Cournand, of Bellvue, credited the Emory experience as the first published report of the use of the cardiac catheter as a *diagnostic* tool.

Controversies During Stead's Chairmanship

The School of Medicine had to deal with two serious controversial problems in 1943. The first was the threat of Oglethorpe University to use the clinical facilities at Grady Hospital. Oglethorpe created a medical department in 1941, and its President, Thornwell Jacobs, demanded that the State Board of Medical Examiners permit Oglethorpe graduates to take the examination for licensing. Jacob's request was turned down because his school had not been accredited. Although Jacobs did not believe in the accreditation process, he applied for use of Grady Memorial Hospital for clinical training in order to improve the credentials of the Oglethorpe school. Emory opposed this because the addition of an unaccredited school would jeopardize Emory's standing. In addition, Emory had spent several hundred thousand dollars improving the facilities for the staff that worked at the Emory Division of Grady Memorial Hospital. Accordingly, Emory could not simply turn the facilities over to another school. The officials of Grady Memorial Hospital turned down Oglethorpe's request by only one vote.

The second controversy was just as irritating to Emory officials. The Emory faculty was accused by the dissidents of the Oglethorpe debacle of failing too many students and passing only those students who "toadied" to the professors. The standard of education was, according to the accusers, too high, and they claimed the professors passed their favorite students. These scandalous accusations were successfully rebutted by Emory President Goodrich White on November 3, 1943, at a large meeting on the campus, and the bitter accusations died down.

---

[10] E. S. Brannon, H. S. Weens, and J. V. Warren, "Atrial Septal Defect: Study of Hemodynamics by the Technique of Right Heart Catheterization," *American Journal of Medical Science* 210 (1945): 480.

The August 26, 1945, issue of the *Atlanta Constitution* carried an interesting story. Dr. G. Lombard Kelly, the dean of the University of Georgia School of Medicine, inquired whether Dean Eugene Stead and President Goodrich White of Emory, and T. K. Glenn of the Atlanta Hospital Authority, would permit him to move the University of Georgia School of Medicine from Augusta to Grady Memorial Hospital in Atlanta. Dean Kelly was extremely disturbed that the Cracker political party was interfering with the daily operation of the School of Medicine in Augusta. Kelly was exploring the feasibility of moving the first two years of the school to Athens and the last two years of the school to Grady Memorial Hospital.

Dean Stead wrote Dean Kelly the following letter.

> Speaking for the faculty, I can assure you we would be glad to divide the responsibility at Grady Hospital with you. While both schools would be crowded and considerable rearranging would be necessary in the teaching schedule, the advantages of having your school in Atlanta would far outweigh the disadvantages.
>
> When the new 1,000-bed hospital, which the hospital authority plans to build, is completed, there will be adequate space for two schools, if each student body is small and if the schools have the same standards and ideals and are able to work together, as would the University of Georgia and Emory, for the betterment of the health of the people.

President White said:

> While Emory, of course, has no part in the decision, if the University of Georgia Medical School is moved to Atlanta, we at Emory will be glad to welcome it and to establish an entirely co-operative relationship with its administration and its faculty.

Apparently Dean Kelly's threat to move the school and Emory's warm welcome calmed the turbulent water. The members of the Cracker political party mended their ways, and the University of Georgia School of Medicine remained in Augusta and continued to use the University Hospital there.

The 1944 Report of the Planning Committee

The opinions expressed by the 1944 Planning Committee of the School of Medicine were reversed by the 1946 Planning Committee. Despite this, the 1944 report is important because it highlights the thinking of the medical school leaders at that point in time. I have highlighted in italics certain important sentences.

> In January 1944, Dr. Goodrich C. White requested the Planning committee of the School of Medicine to reinvestigate the present needs and future

requirements for a program of continued progress in the development of the Medical School of Emory University. This committee consisted of Dean Oppenheimer, Drs. Paullin, Lewis, Calhoun, McCord, Paty, Stead, Kracke and Giddings. This committee has held twelve meetings and has contacted and consulted with all of the departments of the Medical School, and as the result of these deliberations we submit the following report.

We wish to reaffirm that Atlanta is an ideal place for the location and development of a medical center for the entire Southeast. Emory University has the opportunity to assume its rightful leadership in medical education and research to such an extent that Southern boys can be afforded advantages comparable to the best obtainable in any part of the country. Emory University Medical School should become a focus of original thought for the community and the nation, and through its faculty and the achievements of research assume the position of leadership. In order to accomplish this, it seems wise that every effort should be made to see that each member of the faculty receiving a salary from the University should not only do good teaching but should also engage in some form of scientific investigation. It is our belief that a successful teacher must continually strive for newer knowledge and unless he does this he loses his effectiveness and ceases to stimulate interest among his students. In filling new positions on the faculty the administration must strive to obtain the best men in the medical profession. It must not be content with merely satisfactory men. Plans must be made to replace members of the present medical faculty as well as future appointees who do not measure up to this standard. It is only by adherence to this line of thought that Emory University will continue to progress.

Because of the remoteness of Emory University from other large medical centers it is necessary that the number of men engaged in teaching and research be increased until the group is large enough to furnish its own momentum. Under present conditions it is desirable to select the departments which need immediate strengthening and to bring groups of well trained men into these departments, rather than to attempt to bolster up several departments by the addition of one man to each of several departments.

The great medical schools of the United States are dependent upon a large amount of clinical material for their successful operation. The Medical Department of Emory University is fortunate in having the satisfactory connection with Grady Memorial Hospital which allows the use of its material for teaching purposes. The future progress of the Medical School must be based on a continuation of this relationship, and we must look forward to strengthening this in every possible way. Much can be accomplished in this respect by the creation of more full time clinical teachers. *It is our belief that future plans for the development of the Medical School should envision no further building program for undergraduate teaching on the campus.*

In keeping with plans of well organized medical schools it will be necessary as time passes to move all of the preclinical departments from the campus to Grady Hospital. It is improbable that Emory University Hospital will be used extensively for undergraduate teaching. It should serve the Medical School by furnishing faculty members with facilities to carry on medical practice under favorable conditions, and an effort should be made now to eliminate from the Staff of the University Hospital all of those physicians who are not actively concerned with the teaching program of the School.

Post-graduate medical education and facilities for graduate teaching is another of the objectives of Emory University Medical School. The development of programs for these purposes is all the more necessary for several reasons. On account of the present emergency we have been compelled to reduce the number of internships and to give less training to the interns, residents and assistant residents than in normal times. Furthermore, because of the war we have been unable to give adequate training in the specialties. A satisfactory program of post-graduate teaching can be developed by utilizing the facilities of Emory University Hospital and other hospitals affiliated with the Medical School. Post-graduate medical education for those physicians already in the practice of medicine is a very desirable activity for the Medical School.

There are at the present time several Departments of the School which must receive immediate attention in order to place the under-graduate teaching program on a sound basis. Those that need immediate attention are the Department of Pathology and Bacteriology, Psychiatry, Pediatrics, Obstetrics and Gynecology. Suggestions can also be made which would greatly improve teaching in other Departments.

Steps are already being taken to procure a chairman for the Department of Pathology and it is the feeling of this committee that a separate Department of Bacteriology should be created. Funds for strengthening the Pathology and Bacteriology Departments constitute one of the immediate needs of the school.

The war has demonstrated that the average physician is unaware of the sequences of normal emotional development and that he has no under-standing of the causation or treatment of symptoms produced by emotional factors. The impact of emotional and psychic factors colors all aspects of illness. For this reason training in psychiatry is one of the School's most pressing needs.

A full time professor of Pediatrics is essential for organizing the teaching and ward work at Grady Hospital. The Department of Obstetrics and Gynecology, while already operating efficiently, will be greatly improved by the addition of personnel. The Department of Surgery needs more full time and part time teachers. Other departments in the school are in immediate need of additional personnel and equipment. Specific recommendations to cover these pressing requirements are listed in the attached budget. As we move forward in our development program it is of paramount importance that plans be made for the early establishment of a Department of Public Health and Preventive Medicine, a Department of Physical Medicine, as well as Departments of Anesthesiology and of Medical Arts and Illustration. Furthermore, in view of the present inadequate facilities at Grady Hospital for the diagnosing and teaching of neoplastic diseases, it is recommended that the Department of Surgery consider the establishment of a clinic at Grady to further the instruction of students and interns in these diseases.

We have given consideration to the budget as submitted by the Dean. Attention is directed to the present budget for operating the Medical School and also the proposed budget which contemplates the future development of the Medical School which we hope to attain in the not too distant future. It is realized that even if the money in the proposed budget could become immediately available it would be impossible because of the present emergency to fill many of the teaching positions recommended in this program. Future development of the University will be contingent upon the fulfillment of this ideal set up. At the present time we wish to stress the necessity of providing immediately an additional $100,000 to be expended for the development of the Departments to which attention has already been directed as being the urgent needs of the Medical School.

Because of the uncertainty of obtaining teachers to fill the vacancies it will be difficult to allot this appropriation to these departments so that they will share and share alike. The funds should be spent in those departments where it is possible to obtain the desired personnel. Until funds are appropriated, it is impossible to determine accurately the availability of a number of men who would make ideal additions to the medical faculty.

In conclusion, it is the desire of this Committee to express our thanks to all officials of the University and to all members of the faculty for their interest in the planning of this program, for their sympathetic understanding and for their hearty cooperation.

Dr. Stead does not remember being asked to attend any of the meetings of this committee. When be became dean of the School of Medicine he participated in the creation of the 1946 planning report, which contradicts the 1944 report(see page 90).

Stead as Chairman of the Department of Medicine and Dean

Stead was asked to become the dean of Emory University School of Medicine in 1945, when Russell Oppenheimer resigned. Stead accepted because there was no one else on the scene to do the job, and Emory had inadequate money to engage in a national search. Stead continued as chairman of the Department of Medicine and dean of the School of Medicine. He disliked the arrangement. Once again, Emory would not have a full-time chairman of the Department of Medicine, because it was hardly possible to fulfill both positions simultaneously.

Special Report of President White on the School of Medicine to the Executive Committee of the Board of Trustees

The last year of World War II brought many pressing difficulties to the School of Medicine. The trustees of the University weighed the severity of the school's needs in the last month of the war.

August 8, 1945

Gentlemen:

In the report submitted by the President to the Board of Trustees on November 10, 1944 the following statements were made:

The most urgent and the greatest financial needs of the University are for funds for the support of the program of the School of Medicine. The minimum goal we should set for ourselves is $10,000,000. It should be approached as rapidly as possible. There is no probability of providing for increased enrollment in the School of Medicine. But we must commit ourselves to a program of development such as I have presented above; and such a program will cost money. Endowment of $1,000,000 might wisely be sought for each of four or five of the major departments. But I cannot urge too strongly that at least half of the suggested $10,000,000 for the School of Medicine should be unallocated departmentally, thus to be available for the support of the program as a whole under the direction of the administrative officers and the Executive Committee of this Board. General endowment for the School of Medicine is our most vital need if we are to discharge the responsibility that is inescapably ours and make our contribution to the meeting of the needs of this metropolitan area and the region of which it is the capital.

I bring this statement anew to the attention of the Executive Committee, with the additional emphasis warranted by the developments of the intervening months.

I attach a statement summarizing the financial operations of the School of Medicine during the past ten years.

The initial steps in the development of a full time, salaried clinical staff were taken with the provision of special support for the Departments of Medicine and of Surgery and the appointment of Dr. Eugene A. Stead, Jr., as Professor of Medicine in 1942. Prior to that time the only full time member of the clinical faculty was Dr. J. R. McCord, who became Professor of Obstetrics and Gynecology in 1936, after having served in the Department since 1911. Dr. Daniel C. Elkin has been Professor of Surgery on a part time salaried basis since 1930.

I have felt myself under at least an implicit mandate to go forward with this program of development. No steps have been taken without approval of the Executive Committee. These steps have, however, involved commitments which cannot be met without greatly increased operating income.

I am unwilling to go further without explicit instruction from this committee. I am sure that we *must* go forward, and that fairly rapidly, or begin to lose some of the ground already gained. We cannot stand still. Some of the promising men recently added to our faculty have been secured only with great difficulty. They have been and are still being sought by other institutions. They are here now, eager to participate in the development of a great medical school as a part of a great medical center. We cannot hold them unless we add others to their number and unless we provide adequate facilities and equipment for their work. Not only must the development of the clinical departments continue, but the basic science departments must be greatly strengthened if they are to keep pace.

In addition to the basic need of funds for the operating budget there will be special needs for equipment as new full time departmental staffs are added. There will be need, too, for the reconstruction for teaching and laboratory purposes of the buildings owned by the University and now used by Grady Hospital, and for some additional building for the Medical School. This building program is now under study in connection with the plans for the new hospital building at Grady.

At the present time reconstruction work is under way on the present Medical School buildings at Grady, the cost of which totals about $70,000.00; and there are pending requests for some $17,500 of equipment for which special funds *must* be found if newly staffed departments are to operate effectively. The proposed budget for the School of Medicine for 1945–46, together with Dean Stead's comments, are submitted herewith for your consideration.

Respectfully,

Goodrich C. White
President

This message by Dr. White indicates the degree of poverty that prevailed at Emory University School of Medicine at a pivotal time in the history of the school. Elaborating on the school's urgent needs, Dean Stead submitted the following report to President White.

Report of Dean Stead to President White for the Period Beginning June 1, 1944 and Ending September 1, 1945

October 1, 1945

Dr. Goodrich C. White
President Emory University,
Georgia

Dear Dr. White:

This report covers three major subjects: (1) Progress during the last year; (2) Consideration of the location of the medical school; (3) The financial needs of the school.

Progress during the last year.

The faculty of the school has continued to grow in strength and cohesiveness during the last year. There are now fourteen full-time faculty members on the clinical staff. These men have had free time to consider the problems of the school and to plan for its future development.

Dr. Sidney Madden has made great progress in the reorganization of the pathology department. The physical facilities necessary to its successful operation at Grady Hospital will soon be available.

Dr. William Friedewald, the incoming professor of bacteriology, arrived September 1st. The remodeling to supply the necessary office and laboratory space for his department is nearing completion.

The teaching of bacteriology and pathology at Grady Hospital in the last half of the second year has required certain shifts in the curriculum of the first and second years. Physiology will now be taught in the last quarter of the first year in the time previously used by bacteriology and will continue through the first quarter of the second year. The schedules of the departments of biochemistry, anatomy, and pharmacology were not changed.

Dr. Blincoe resigned as chairman of the department of anatomy and Dr. Venable was appointed acting chairman of the department. With his cooperation the course in gross anatomy was shortened so that the freshmen now have one free afternoon in the middle of each week.

The integration of Emory University Hospital into the teaching program of the medical school has continued. Mr. Robert Whitaker, Superintendent of the hospital, has been very cooperative and has contributed many useful ideas. The appointment of Dr. Hugh Wood as physician-in-chief to Emory Hospital and Associate Professor of Clinical Medicine has greatly strengthened the resident training program in the University Hospital and has widened its opportunities for graduate and postgraduate teaching.

The department of surgery was reorganized with the appointment of Dr. Morris Paty as acting chairman of the department. The arrival of Dr. Osler Abbott on September 1st as the second full-time member of that department has lightened the load somewhat on Dr. Paty. Dr. Robert Brown has been added to the staff of the Winship Clinic. Further additions to the department will have to await the return of Dr. Elkin, which is expected on January 1, 1946.

The library at Grady is being remodeled and air conditioned. The large class room at Grady is also being air conditioned.

The research programs of the various departments have continued to grow. Substantial sums of money for research from sources outside of the University have been received by the departments of internal medicine, physiology, chemistry, neuroanatomy, and pharmacology.

Emory University, as a responsible leader of medical education in the South, must consider the problem of medical care for Negro patients and take steps to provide opportunity for training interns and for continuing the education of Negro physicians in the community. We have not yet begun to meet this challenge.

The school has made great progress during the last year. Further progress depends on the final decision as to the location of the school and on the finding of a way to finance the school on a more adequate and permanent basis.

Location of the school.

There is general agreement that the entire four years of medicine should be taught either on the University campus or at Grady Hospital. The question to be decided is: At which of these two places is it more desirable to develop the school?

In favor of Grady is the fact that the cost of hospitalization of the patients is borne by the city and county. However, the aims of the University and of a tax supported hospital are not always identical. The University is interested in providing the best medical care as the basis of its educational and research program. The hospital is satisfied with care that is adequate, as judged by the usual level of service given by the average city hospital throughout the country. This divergence of ideals makes difficult the complete integration of the work of the University and Hospital.

There are further reasons for hesitating to continue development at Grady Hospital: (1) The section of the community cared for; (2) The fact that medical services provided by the University return no income; (3) The heavy patient load.

(1) *The section of the community cared for.*

As the medical school develops it must give the best medical service of which the science of medicine is capable. This means that a large quantity of highly skilled medical services reaches only the section of our community which is socially and economically the least productive. Whether this is a wise course to follow indefinitely is a question of concern to the University and to the members of the medical profession who feel the responsibility of the University for the progress of medicine in the Southeast.

(2) *Medical services provided by the University return no income.*

Every year new developments in medicine and surgery make diagnostic and therapeutic procedures more expensive. It is estimated that the annual budget of the medical school at present should be $750,000. In the future it will unquestionably be more. Every step forward at Grady Hospital means more cost without additional income. Would it not be logical for the University to receive recompense for the large quantity of medical services which its staff gives to thousands of patients in the public hospital?

(3) *The heavy patient load.*

The staffing of the 1,000-bed hospital projected by the Hospital Authority will be a considerable burden to the University budget. A smaller, well run hospital would better serve the purposes of the medical school. One of the functions of the University is to give service to the community. Treatment of charity patients is one form of this service, but the University is not merely a service institution. Responsibility for too many patients may destroy the great opportunity of the school to function as a center of original thought for the Southeast.

Before committing itself to the responsibility of serving the new and larger Grady Hospital, Emory should review all of the considerations relating to such a commitment.

1. Proper treatment of a greater number of patients will require a larger staff than is necessary for demonstrating medical care to students and interns. This, in the long run, would increase the cost of the medical school without providing any additional income unless the members of the medical staff were permitted to operate a pay clinic. This is unlikely.

2. If the Emory school is located at Grady Hospital and serves patients in the hospital, it is clear that in the public mind responsibility for all the patients treated there will rest upon Emory. Emory must not be placed in that position unless it has the right to select all of the doctors through whom the patients will be served. It is doubtful that assurance can be given in any public hospital that political considerations will not dictate some of the staff appointments.

3. In order to demonstrate good medical care the hospital must have high standards of service. In the future, political interference and budgeting considerations may prevent the hospital administrator from maintaining these high standards of service.

4. Whether a hospital can be operated with reasonable economy depends to a great extent on the physical facilities available. The plans for the new Grady have not yet taken final form. If it should happen that the operating cost of the hospital is very expensive and if Emory is working there, Emory would be blamed by the public for the high cost of operation. Therefore, Emory should not enter into any agreement that will bind it to continue there until it has opportunity to inspect all of the projected plans.

5. If Emory is going to work at Grady Hospital it will be necessary to build a medical school building and to make other expensive capital outlays. Emory should not commit itself to do that until proper assurance can be given that politics will not make the Grady Hospital at some time in the future an undesirable place to conduct an educational program.

If it be decided that it is too hazardous for the University to project the development of the medical school at Grady Hospital, I am convinced that the development of the school on the Emory campus is now possible because of two new factors which have entered the picture during the last few years. They are: (1) hospital insurance; (2) the group practice of medicine.

In former years a school could not teach medicine satisfactorily in its own hospital because too much of the income of the school had to be directed to covering the basic cost of hospitalization. This difficulty has been removed by the rapid growth of hospital insurance. The expense of hospitalization for nearly all income groups will be covered by insurance either by voluntary payment, by industry, or by government.

The group practice of medicine has gradually become acceptable to the medical profession and to the community. It is now possible to establish a university clinic and to demonstrate there to students the proper practice of medicine.

Regardless of the decision, development of the undergraduate teaching program at Emory Hospital should be begun immediately. This program can readily be inaugurated in surgery because of the early completion of the surgical annex.

The concentration of all of the undergraduate teaching facilities on the campus would require the following:

1. A building to house the clinic.
2. A gradually increasing use of the beds in Emory Hospital by members of the staff of the University Clinic.
3. A gradually increasing utilization of Crawford Long Hospital.
4. Enlargement of the hospital to provide a psychiatric unit.
5. Provision for beds for children either by additions at Emory Hospital or by closer affiliation with Egleston.
6. Use of space in sub basement in University Hospital for clinic offices until clinic building is available.

Financial needs.

The opportunities for developing the school at Grady Hospital or on the campus must be presented to the Executive Committee of the Board of Trustees. If the Board decides that the school should remain at Grady Hospital, a large permanent endowment must be secured immediately. Unless a proper endowment is obtained in the very near future the development of the School will be greatly handicapped because of the difficulty in attracting a strong faculty.

If the decision is made to develop the school on the campus, the problem of immediate endowment may become less acute. The clinic should earn money after its first two years. If this money is contributed to medical education it will enable the last two years of the school to become more nearly self-supporting.

Appended to this report are certain statistical data relating to the enrollment and graduation of students.

Sincerely yours,

Eugene A. Stead, Jr., M.D.
Dean

This annual report reveals Stead "thinking it through." One can almost predict that the Planning Committee will be reconvened and that the next report would be vastly different from the 1944 report.

The 1946 Report of the Planning Committee of Emory Medical School (The Defining Moment)

The Planning Committee of Emory Medical School met weekly during the months of December and January at the request of Dr. White to consider the question of whether the School should be consolidated at Butler Street or on the Campus. The Committee was composed of Doctors Calhoun, Paullin, Elkin, Friedewald, Giddings, Lewis, Madden, Scarborough, Sauls and Stead. Dr. Sauls was absent because of illness.

It was agreed that the University was fortunate in having a choice of two locations for the development of the Medical School. If the school were located permanently on the campus, only the enlargement of present facilities would be needed; if located on Butler Street a new project would have to be undertaken.

The desirability of each location was viewed from many angles and discussed in detail. The advantages of the Butler Street location were summarized as follows:

1. There is a large source of varied clinical material which is available to the University for the present.

2. Butler Street is fairly centrally located and the services of physicians in other hospitals can be obtained easily.

3. Grady Hospital serves as a common meeting place for members of various hospital staffs.

4. The buildings now used for the colored hospital and clinic could be converted to Medical School buildings when the new hospital is completed. This would be expensive, but would give adequate housing space.

The disadvantages of the Butler Street location are:

1. The projected new hospital will be too large to be serviced by the Medical School.

2. The teaching staff of the University must be of its own selection. If Grady staff appointments were to be made by Emory, the charge would be made that Emory is benefitting too greatly from public funds.

3. A grade B medical school may be admitted to Grady at any time by the action of the Hospital Authority.

4. The aims of a university and a public hospital are different. A university in its teaching is interested in the best medical care. A public hospital in its economy can seldom afford the best medical care.

5. The patient load is so great that adequate time for teaching and research is lacking.

6. Too many of the patients admitted to the hospital show advanced pathology. They are not representative of the patients seen in private practice.

7. Pressure will be exerted to allow negro physicians and interns to care for the colored patients. If our entire Medical School is centered at Grady, the University will be accused of blocking this move for selfish ends.

8. The physical location is less desirable than on the campus. Easy access to the other schools of the University is lost.

9. It will be difficult to obtain the money to develop at Grady. We would have to give assurances that our position at Grady was completely stabilized and that Grady Hospital would always be a desirable place to carry on our main teaching program. This we are unable to do.

10. Every step forward at Grady requires additional endowment funds. The services of the staff create no income for the University.

Consideration of the development on the Campus revolved chiefly about the question of the source of patients to be used in teaching. If this could be solved, the Committee felt that the advantages of being on the Campus would be as follows;

1. The Medical School already has two large buildings and a large hospital.
2. The entire program would be under University control.
3. Close contact with other departments of the University could be maintained.
4. Private and semi-private patients would be used for teaching. The patient load would be regulated to allow time for research. The patients would be representative of those seen in private practice.
5. Teaching facilities should be maintained at Grady Hospital, thus obtaining for the Medical School and Grady Hospital the mutual advantages of the present cooperative program, without sacrificing our independence by being totally dependent on it.

The Committee believes that the establishment of an office building on the Campus would solve the problem of patients for teaching purposes. Such a building should house only faculty members who teach with their private patients. Each member of the faculty with offices at the campus would be engaged in the practice and teaching of medicine at the same time. Secretarial help and laboratory facilities would be supplied from a central source. Under this program the students would receive a greater degree of individual instruction than at present.

The program of primary development on the Campus with the use of Grady as a clinical teaching unit has only one major disadvantage. In time, the faculty members with offices on the campus would require most of the beds at Emory Hospital. This would mean that many faithful friends of the University, who have taken part in the Grady teaching program, but who do not desire to have office space on the Campus, would have difficulty in obtaining beds in Emory Hospital. To prevent the loss of this extremely valuable group of Emory faculty, it is suggested that either a new wing be built at Emory for this group, or that arrangements be made with Crawford Long Hospital to care for the patients of the members of the University faculty who are engaged in the teaching program at Grady. Such developments at Emory and Crawford Long Hospitals would in no wise conflict with the projected plans for a Greater Atlanta Medical Center.

Under the program projected here, the medical students would spend a large part of their third year at Grady Hospital, where they would benefit by the large quantity of walking pathology. In their fourth year at the University Hospital, they would apply what they had learned at Grady under conditions more nearly approaching those of private practice.

After careful consideration of the problem, the Planning Committee makes the following recommendations:
1. That the primary development of the Medical School should be on the Campus. Grady Hospital should be maintained as a clinical teaching unit.
2. An office building should be built on the campus with the understanding that each member having office space in this building will use his private patients for teaching.
3. A new wing at Emory University Hospital should be built, or arrangements should be made with Crawford Long for the patients of faculty members who

are engaged in the teaching at Grady and who do not have office space on the campus.

4. Two new buildings are greatly needed: one for office space, the other for library and laboratories. These needed additions are shown in the accompanying sketch.

5. To serve as a complete University Hospital, additional facilities for Pediatrics and Psychiatry will be needed.

The "defining moment" of Emory University School of Medicine was created when this report was completed. Stead's hand in the report is clearly seen.

Stead, in his November 26, 1990, letter to Mark Silverman, remembers the committee and its report as follows:

> I enjoyed Grady Hospital but believed that it would be in Emory's best interest to develop Emory Hospital and to establish a clinical faculty who practiced on the Emory campus. In 1946 Phinizy Calhoun, James Paullin, Russell Oppenheimer and I served as an Emory Planning Committee meeting frequently at Paullin's home. I presented the arguments in favor of making the Emory Campus the center of Emory's educational efforts with Grady Hospital and other Atlanta hospitals as satellites. This would keep Piedmont Hospital, Paullin's home base, as an important, but no longer the dominant player. The development of private practice on the Emory campus would cause concern among many Atlanta doctors. Paullin listened carefully, asked many questions and after several months endorsed the plan. As a man of great stature he put Emory's future before his personal ambitions.[11]

Stead remembers two additional points about the report that are worth recording. He recalls that Dr. Phinizy Calhoun called him at Duke University about six months after he had left Emory. Calhoun wanted to know if Stead still agreed with the report. Stead responded that he did. Stead also recalls that the report was not widely distributed. Apparently, other Emory officials did not believe the report would be accepted by the faculty and donors. Perhaps this is why I had a difficult time locating a copy of the report.

Stead's leadership reminds one of the stand Asa Candler took when he insisted that Wesley Memorial Hospital, later renamed the Emory University Hospital, should be built on the Emory campus rather than being built in the Grady area.

Why Stead Left Emory

Stead was offered the position of chairman of the Department of Medicine at Duke University and began work in Durham on January 1,

---

[11] Letter to Mark Silverman (Nov. 26, 1990). Reproduced with permission.

1947. Why did he leave Emory, which he loved? He had gathered around him a group of brilliant teachers and investigators. He had become a legend in the four and a half years he had worked at Emory. But he did not enjoy being dean as well as being chairman of the Department of Medicine. He wanted to focus on the education of trainees. While he did not object to the administrative duties that allowed him to deal personally with the trainees, as dean he was forced to deal with the non-teaching administrative problems of the entire School of Medicine, and there was less and less time to develop his teaching and research. He also believed, as the 1946 planning report emphasized, that the future development of the School of Medicine should be on the Emory campus, which he believed should be the hub of a system of satellites. The satellites could be further developed, but not at the expense of the campus. Finally, he believed that a private clinic should be developed on the Emory campus in order to support an increasing number of faculty members and to expose trainees to private medical practice. Duke had already developed a private diagnostic clinic and used the Duke University Hospital for the clinical training of students and house officers. Stead therefore accepted the Duke offer and, during the next few years, moved a large number of his Emory staff to Duke. Paul Beeson remained to become Emory's new chairman of the Department of Medicine. Stead wrote Mark Silverman on November 26, 1990, the following:

> Paullin did not approve of my decision to go to Duke. He did not approve of the Duke practice plans and did not believe that I could mount an active academic program in a place previously dominated by practice. I replied that in 75 years Emory would be the dominant southern school but that in my lifetime Duke would lead the way. This is the only time that I was wiser than Paullin.[12]

Brief Comments About Stead's Later Years

As years passed, Stead revolutionized the Department of Medicine at Duke. His excellent ideas continued to flow from his fertile mind as he built a world-class department. While Stead was leading Duke's Department of Medicine into new and unexplored waters, Evelyn Stead was writing a book with Gloria Warren. Gloria, a dietitian, was Jim Warren's wife. The book *Low Fat Cookery* was one of the first "low-fat" cookbooks. It was very popular and served a great need.

Stead always intended to resign from the chairmanship at Duke when he was fifty-nine years old. With Stead-like insight he said, "I do not

---

[12] Ibid. Used by permission.

believe a chairman can direct as good a department after he or she is sixty years of age as he or she did before the age of sixty." James Wyngaarden followed him as chairman of the Department of Medicine at Duke.

After resigning, Stead moved to New York so he would be out of the way of the new chairman. He spent 1968 teaching at Cornell. He also worked with the Commonwealth Foundation. When he returned to Duke, he resumed his active teaching role on the Osler Ward and, with Evelyn, edited the *Medical Times*. He then edited *Circulation* for five years and assumed the editorship of the *North Carolina Medical Journal*. At age seventy he became a distinguished physician of the Veterans Administration at the Durham Veterans Administration Hospital.

He built a home with his own hands on acreage he owned on Lake Ker near Bullock, North Carolina. This home, called Hanah Lee, is fifty miles from Durham.

When this page was written, Stead was eighty-seven years old. He ended one of our long telephone conversations by saying, "I would like to organize a medical school with only 24 faculty members." His vision and predictive ability were obviously intact.

Stead's Honors and Awards

Stead's career was literally studded with success. His many awards included:

> Phi Beta Kappa, Alpha Omega Alpha, the Abraham Flexner Award for outstanding contribution to medical education, president of the Associations of American Physicians, Distinguished Physician of the Veterans Administration, the Kober Medal of the Association of American Physicians for a distinguished career in academic medicine, president of the American Society of Clinical Investigation, Master of the American College of Physicians, founding member of the Institute of Medicine National Academy of Science, editor of *Circulation*, Distinguished Professor of Duke University, the John M. Russell Award of the Markle Foundation, the Robert Williams Award of the Association of Professors of Medicine, the Distinguished Teacher Award of the American College of Physicians, the James Herrick Award of the American Heart Association, the honorary Doctor of Science degree from Emory University, the Gold Heart Award of the American Heart Association, the Distinguished Teacher Award of the Duke Medical Alumni Association, an honorary doctorate from Yale University, and the Georgia Heart Association's Symposium in honor of Eugene Stead.

Stead's Associates and House Staff

Stead trained thirty-three department chairmen at Emory and Duke. He influenced many other individuals who assumed major clinical and administrative roles in numerous medical schools and hospitals. Of course he was equally proud of the trainees who entered the private practice of medicine. The members of the house staff and some of the faculty who worked under Stead at Emory are shown in the photographs in Figures 2-2 through 2-5. The names of faculty members for the years 1942 through 1946 were listed in the Emory University bulletins. These lists are reproduced in Appendixes 4 through 7. Many of the great teachers are not listed in the bulletin because they were not faculty members; they were medical residents or research fellows at Grady.

Paul Beeson remained at Emory to become professor and chairman of the Department of Medicine. Ivan Bennett later worked with Beeson at Yale and became professor and chairman of the Department of Pathology at Johns Hopkins and later vice president of New York University Medical School. Philip Bondy stayed at Emory with Beeson, later joined Beeson at Yale, and then became professor of medicine and chairman of the department at Yale. E. Harvey Estes became professor and chairman of the Department of Family Medicine at Duke. Abner Golden, who later trained in pathology, became professor of pathology at Emory and later became professor and chairman of the Department of Pathology at Georgetown, then chairman of the Department of Pathology at the University of Kentucky. John Hickam moved to Duke with Stead before becoming professor and chairman of the Department of Medicine at Indiana University. Bernard Holland followed Stead to Duke and became chief resident in medicine; he then trained in psychiatry and later became professor and chairman of the Department of Psychiatry at Emory. Jack Myers moved from Emory to Duke, finally becoming professor and chairman of the Department of Medicine at the University of Pittsburgh. James V. Warren remained at Emory, then moved to Duke and later became, first, professor and chairman of the Department of Medicine at the University of Texas in Galveston, then chairman of the Department of Medicine at Ohio State.

Others who worked with Stead at Emory achieved their own distinction:

Gordon Barrow later became the first cardiology trainee at Grady Hospital. He entered practice but continued his teaching in the cardiac clinic at Grady and later helped the department when he became involved with the Crippled Children Service of the state and was director of the Regional Medical Program.

Eugene Brown joined the Emory faculty in the Emory University Clinic.

Walter Cargill joined the Emory faculty and worked at the Atlanta Veterans Hospital.

William Friedewald remained in the department as a professor of medicine and chairman of the Department of Bacteriology. He later entered practice at St. Joseph's Hospital in Atlanta, and still later became medical director of that hospital.

Bernard Hallman remained at Emory and developed the area of endocrinology in the Emory University Clinic. He became Associate Dean for Grady Hospital when the clinical departments of Emory were reorganized in 1957.

Al Heyman remained on the Emory faculty but later joined Stead at Duke and became head of neurology.

Charles Huguley completed his training in hematology and oncology at Washington University under Carl Moore. He joined the Winship Clinic at Emory University Hospital and, in 1957, became director of the Division of Hematology in the newly organized Department of Medicine at Emory.

David James continued on the house staff with Paul Beeson and joined the Emory faculty as a member of the newly-formed Private Diagnostic Clinic.

Bruce Logue remained on the Emory faculty; he was assigned to Emory University Hospital in January 1946 and helped develop the medical training program there. Dr. Logue also started the Emory University Cardiology Training Program at Grady and Emory University Hospital. He was a major mover in the development of the Private Diagnostic Clinic which, along with two other groups, evolved into the Emory Clinic.

Arthur Merrill Sr. continued his work on kidney diseases as a highly effective part-time professor in the Department of Medicine at Emory. He eventually entered full-time private practice.

Max Michael remained on the Emory faculty as Chief of the Medical Service at the Veterans Hospital for several years and then accepted a position at the Maimonides Hospital in New York. He later coordinated the University of Florida's activities in Jacksonville.

William Stead, Eugene's brother, became nationally known in the field of tuberculosis. He was a professor in the Department of Medicine at the University of Minnesota and later at the University of Arkansas.

Calhoun Witham later became professor of medicine at the Medical College of Georgia, where he was Director of the Division of Cardiology.

A Final Note About the Stead Era

Whereas Stead physically left Emory in late 1946, his spirit did not—as Chapter 5 of this book will attest. Like tagging a chemical with an isotope, one can identify Stead's influence at Emory, Duke, and at numerous other schools. Stead's numerous publications reveal the quality of his research and give the reader some insight into his creative mind. A complete listing of his published papers can be found in William Hollingsworth's excellent book *Taking Care: The Legacy of Soma Weiss, Eugene Stead, and Paul Beeson.*[13]

The Governance and Financial Support of Grady Hospital

In 1946 Fulton and DeKalb Counties became responsible for the financial support of Grady Hospital. The commissioners of the two counties nominated the members of the Fulton-DeKalb Hospital Authority, who were to serve for four years. Leading citizens of the two counties were chosen to be members of the authority and served with great distinction.

The hospital authority provided the nonpolitical governance of the Grady Memorial Hospital; Fulton and DeKalb Counties provided the funds to run the hospital; and Emory University School of Medicine, by contractual arrangement with Grady, provided the professional supervision for the care of the patients. Despite this arrangement, certain day-to-day problems continued to plague the relationship of Grady Hospital to Emory University School of Medicine. Which institution was supposed to repair a broken window in a portion of the facility used by Emory faculty? Which institution should provide the reagents used in a student-house officer laboratory designed to assist in the care of patients?

Stead Selects Logue to Develop the Teaching Program at Emory University Hospital

The views of Eugene Stead were incorporated in the 1946 Planning Report (see discussion on page 90). One important aspect of the plan was that Emory University Hospital should become a major teaching facility. To accomplish this goal, Dr. Stead asked Dr. R. Bruce Logue, who had just been discharged from the army, to develop the teaching program at Emory University Hospital. Dr. Logue began work at Emory University

---

[13] W. Hollingsworth, *Taking Care: The Legacy of Soma Weiss, Eugene Stead, and Paul Beeson* (Chapel Hill, N.C.: Professional Press, 1994).

Hospital on January 1, 1946, and became a major force in the successful development of Emory University Hospital as an educational facility and in the creation of the Emory Clinic. The complete biography of Dr. Logue is presented in Chapter 5 of this book.

Emory's Moves After Stead's Departure

With Stead's departure, Emory had to fill two positions. Emory was fortunate in having two individuals on the Emory faculty who were held in high esteem nationally. Dr. Hugh Wood was chosen to follow Stead as dean, and Paul Beeson was chosen to follow Stead as chairman of the Department of Medicine.

The biography of Dr. Hugh Wood, an internist, is presented below, and the biography of Dr. Paul Beeson is discussed at the beginning of Chapter 3.

The Biography of R. Hugh Wood, M.D.

Dr. Hugh Wood followed Eugene Stead as dean of the School of Medicine in 1946 (see Figure 2-6). He was an active member of the Department of Medicine and Chief of Medicine at Emory University Hospital when the appointment was made. He remained dean until 1956.

Hugh Wood was born October 22, 1896, in Floyd County, Virginia, and attended Hampden-Sydney College in Virginia before entering the Medical College of Virginia in Richmond. He interned at St. Elizabeth Hospital in Richmond and became a resident in pathology at Memorial Hospital (affiliated with the Medical College of Virginia). In 1923–1924 he was a house officer at the Peter Bent Brigham Hospital in Boston. Dr. Dan Elkin, later chairman of the Department of Surgery at Emory, was at the Brigham at the same time and urged Dr. Wood to move to Atlanta in 1924. Wood served as a resident in medicine at the Emory Division of Grady Hospital for two years, then entered the practice of medicine with Dr. Paullin. He taught Emory medical students and had contact with a student named Stead. Stead was impressed with Wood's ability and wanted to train where Wood trained—the Brigham in Boston.

After 10 years, Dr. Wood began an independent practice of medicine. He served with distinction in the medical corps in North Africa during World War II and, on returning to the States, worked at Fort McPherson and later became Chief of Medicine at Lawson General Hospital. During that time, he undoubtedly attended the "Sunday school" taught at Grady Memorial Hospital by his former student, Eugene Stead. After release from the army in 1945, Wood became Chief of Medicine at Emory University Hospital. When Stead left Emory for Duke, Wood was appointed dean of the School of Medicine. During the early part of his deanship, his major office was located at Grady Memorial Hospital. He subsequently had a small office in the Physiology Building on the Emory campus. In 1954, he moved the dean's office to the newly completed Ernest Woodruff Memorial Research Building. He spent less time at Grady, although new offices became available for the dean in the new Glenn Memorial Building there. He was a gentle man, but his impact on the School of Medicine was enormous. The following quotes tell us a great deal about him, Emory, and Atlanta.

Dr. Wood's view of the medical school curriculum was expressed when he repeated the words of a Harvard physiologist, who said:

> I've listened to this discussion of the medical school curriculum this morning. I've listened to similar discussions for 40 years. It doesn't mean anything. If some teacher gets under the student's hide and wakes him up, he will educate himself in spite of the curriculum.[14]

His love of the profession of medicine is clearly seen in his exclamation, "I don't know whether I like students best—or patients!"[15]

He could be forthright. His speech to the Atlanta Council of Church Women on January 28, 1948, is an example of his toughness. The following comments appeared in several newspapers.

> "You go crazy in Atlanta and you go to jail," said Dr. Hugh Wood, dean of the Emory University School of Medicine. "It's horrible. It's unthinkable."

Dr. Wood directed his criticism at lack of hospital beds for mental patients, and at what he called the practice of sending such patients to jail in Atlanta.

> "There is not a hospital bed in Atlanta designated for care of psychiatric patients," he told the Atlanta Council of Church Women. "You have to go to Stone Mountain or Smyrna before you can find one." He blamed lack of public interest.

Dr. Wood also criticized the shortage of beds in Grady Hospital, a city institution. He said Grady was too small to serve Atlanta 20 years ago, and was only slightly larger now.

> "It's gotten so one virtually has to be in extremis (near death) to be admitted to Grady," he said.

The following notes illustrate how tight the budget was in 1946 and 1947:

---

[14] M. R. Duncan, "Hugh Wood, M.D.," *The Emory Magazine*, September 1965, 26-29.
[15] Ibid.

August 19, 1946

Dr. R. Hugh Wood
Emory University Hospital
Emory University, Ga.

Dear Dr. Wood:

I am pleased to notify you that at the meeting of the Executive Committee of the Board of Trustees on August 14 formal confirmation was given to your appointment, effective immediately, as Dean of the School of Medicine, at an annual salary of $10,000.

Please indicate your acceptance of this appointment on the attached copy.

I hope that you may find genuine satisfaction in this relationship to Emory.

Sincerely yours,

Goodrich C. White
President

* * *

To: Mr. Boisfeuillet Jones   September 5, 1947
     Assistant to the President   Travel Arrangements
                                     for Dr. Hugh Wood

From: Mrs. Hal Drake

This will confirm our telephone conversation regarding travel arrangements for Dr. Hugh Wood, Dean.

With Dr. Wood's work divided among Grady, Emory, and Lawson Hospital, his car is in constant use on medical school business. Would it be logical for him to receive $50.00 a month as reimbursement from the Travel Fund, Budget #10.50? This should be made a separate payment and not as a part of his salary.

* * *

TO: Mrs. Hal Drake   September 15, 1947
     Administrative Assistant
     Medical School

FROM: Assistant to the President, Boisfeuillet Jones

With reference to your memorandum of September 5, it is quite in order for Dr. R. Hugh Wood to receive reimbursement of $50. a month from the travel item in the Medical School budget for necessary travel in the city in connection with his position as Dean of the School of Medicine.

It might be pointed out also, that it is permissible for Dr. Wood to receive reimbursement of five cents per mile for official travel away from Atlanta.

Dr. Hugh Wood received the Gold-Headed Cane in 1962. The following comment appeared in *The Campus Report*.[16]

DR. R. HUGH WOOD, Dean of Emory's School of Medicine from 1946 to 1956 and currently Professor of Medicine, was recently awarded a gold-headed cane by the Department of Medicine and the administrative staff of the School of Medicine.

The Gold-Headed Cane is an "emblem of the attributes of mind and heart of the true physician," Dr. J. Willis Hurst, Chairman of the Department of Medicine says.

The tradition of the Gold-Headed Cane had its beginning with an outstanding British physician who lived from 1650 to 1729. His cane was passed to five successors and finally deposited in the Royal College of Physicians in the early 19th century.

The custom has been resumed primarily on the west coast of the U.S. in this century. Dr. Hurst believes that Dr. Wood's cane is the first given in the South.[17]

The photograph shown in Figure 2-6 was made at the request of the Communicable Disease Center (later named Centers for Disease Control and Prevention) to illustrate the advantages of immunization. It was shown at the New York World Fair. The exhibit was labeled The Human Approach. The photograph of Dr. Wood prompted me to state the following at a testimonial dinner for Dr. Wood in August 1965:

There Once was a Photograph

There once was a photograph of kindness, compassion, understanding, wisdom and humility.

There once was a photograph of humor, happiness and a touch of sadness.

There once was a photograph of love—real love.

These emotions cannot be photographed in the abstract. They come to life— they become tangible—they become a moving force in people. They all can be clearly seen in the face of our beloved Hugh Wood. His wonderful face looks that way because he is that way.

President Kennedy once said of Winston Churchill, "He mobilized the English language and sent it into battle." Dr. Wood possesses the finest of human qualities and sends them into battle for the medical profession. [18]

Toward the end of his ten-year tenure as dean, he also became the first director of the Emory University Clinic. Following a heart attack, he resigned from both positions in 1956. He continued to teach in the

---

[16] "Dr. Wood Gets Gold-Headed Cane," *Emory Campus Report*, 28 May 1962.

[17] M. R. Duncan, "Hugh Wood, M.D.," *The Emory Magazine*, September 1965, 26–29.

[18] J. W. Hurst, "There Once Was a Photograph: A Tribute to Dr. Hugh Wood," in *Four Hats* (Chicago: Year Book Medical Publishers, 1970).

Department of Medicine by attending in the medical clinic at Grady and working at the Georgia Mental Health Clinic. He then became Medical Director of the relatively new Wesley Woods geriatric facility. He retired from that position at the age of eighty-one to enter private practice with Dr. Denny Hall in Griffin, Georgia. Dr. Wood died in 1984.

Report of Dean Hugh Wood to President Goodrich White for the Year Beginning September 1, 1945 and Ending September 1, 1946

Dear Dr. White,

This report was prepared jointly by Dr. Eugene A. Stead, Jr. and the undersigned. It covers four major subjects: (1) Progress during the last year; (2) Relation of the University to other hospitals in the community; (3) Immediate needs of the School; (4) The financial needs of the school.

Progress During the Last Year

The last report of the Dean of the Medical School emphasized the importance of reaching a decision as to the location of the school. At the request of the Board of Trustees the Planning Committee of the Medical School considered this matter. It unanimously recommended that the major building program of the Medical School take place on the University Campus. This report was acted on favorably by the Executive Committee. This crystallization of thoughts as to the location of the school has made long range planning possible to a greater degree than heretofore.[19]

Graduate and Undergraduate teaching programs at Emory Hospital were greatly enlarged during the last year. For the first time fourth year students were taught medicine and surgery, neoplastic diseases and roentgenology at the University Hospital.

The return of Dr. Daniel C. Elkin from Ashford General Hospital, the Vascular Center of the Army, has allowed rapid progress to be made in the Department of Surgery. The offices of this department are now located in the Whitehead Surgical Pavilion. Three full time men have been added to the Staff of the Surgical Department; Dr. Robert Kelly in Orthopedic Surgery; Dr. William H. Galvin in Anesthesiology; and Dr. Fred Cooper in General Surgery. Dr. J. D. Martin, Dr. Paul Reith and Dr. William C. Ward are serving in a part time capacity. Dr. M. H. Harris, Assistant Professor of Clinical Surgery, is Chief of the Surgical Service at Lawson Veterans Administration Hospital. Dr. Louis W. Rosati, Associate in Surgery and Surgical Anatomy, is serving in a part time capacity. A number of young surgeons returning from the Army are working in the department on a voluntary basis. The experimental laboratories of the department are being reorganized in the Physiology Building. A grant of $28,000 from the Army and the award of a fellowship by the Life Insurance Medical Research Fund have speeded the development of these laboratories.

---

[19] Italics added by J.W.H. for emphasis.

Dr. Roy Robertson has been appointed as Instructor in the Department of Surgery and will spend full time in cardiovascular research. Other personnel to work on this program are now being sought.

The Department of Physical Medicine is now ready to occupy its quarters in the Whitehead Pavilion. The development of this department was made possible by a grant from the National Foundation for Infantile Paralysis. Dr. Robert Bennett, the Professor of Physical Medicine is now spending half time at the University Hospital. Dr. George C. Knowlton, the Assistant Professor of Physical Medicine in charge of physiological research, will be in his new laboratory in the Physiology Building by October first of this year.

In proximity to the Department of Physical Medicine, adequate quarters for Occupational Therapy have been secured. This project will be under the supervision and direction of Dr. Bennett. It is sponsored and financed by the Service Guild of Atlanta.

The graduate program at Emory Hospital was greatly strengthened by a $10,000 gift from the Kellogg Foundation. This was used to pay one-half the salary of the Physician-in-Chief and one-half the salary of the Roentogen-ologist-in-Chief of the hospital. The Kellogg Foundation has given an additional $15,000 this year to enlarge the graduate program.

The Faculty of the Medical School agreed to assume responsibility for a portion of the professional services at the Veterans Hospital, now located on the old site of Lawson General Hospital. It will now bear the name of Lawson Veterans Administration Hospital and will consist of a 750 bed general hospital. Resident training programs in Medicine and Surgery are now under way and appear to be of mutual benefit to the Veterans Hospital and the University. While part time services of new professional personnel are made available to the Medical School by this cooperative plan, it should be pointed out that the clinical teaching staff is spread thinly since both consultants and attending physicians must be kept in continuous attendance at the Veterans Hospital. The resident staff at Lawson must also be taught the basic sciences on a graduate level, and this further taxes the capacity of these departments.

The investigative programs of the faculty have increased in scope and size. The Departments of Anatomy, Physiology, Surgery, Medicine, Pathology, Biochemistry and Bacteriology have received grants-in-aid from sources outside the University.

Dr. John Venable, Acting Chairman of the Department of Anatomy, resigned to enter the Public Health Service. This department is at present headed by Dr. Harlow Ades. Dr. Stephen Gray and Dr. Robert Galambos have been added to the full time staff of the Department of Anatomy. Dr. John Akin and Dr. Rafe Banks have been appointed in a part time capacity.

Dr. Eugene Jackson, Chairman of the Pharmacology Department, resigned September first of this year. The Pharmacology course is being covered this year by Doctors Oppenheimer and Morrison.

Dr. Francis Parker left us in July to become Associate Professor of Pathology at the University of Virginia.

Dr. Morris Paty resigned his position as Associate Dean on January 1, 1946, and returned to work in China.

Dr. Eugene A. Stead, Jr. has resigned and will assume his duties as Professor of Medicine at Duke University School of Medicine on January 1, 1947. Dr. Paul Beeson, Professor of Medicine, has been named Chairman of this department. Dr. R. Hugh Wood was appointed Dean of the School of Medicine.

The Administrative Officers of the Medical School have been moved to the Physiology Building. Dr. Trawick Stubbs began his duties as Assistant Dean of the Medical School on July 1, 1946. Personnel of the Advisory Council of the Medical School are being selected with the advice of the President. It is thought that this committee will meet once every two months to pass on all matters concerning policy and planning. It will also concern itself with appointments of heads of departments and other key personnel. This committee will include all department heads and others whose advice and council are important in determining the scope of activities of the school and the relationship to other medical facilities in the community.

Relation of the University to Other Hospitals in the Community

The decision to increase the teaching of medicine in Emory University Hospital in no way curtails the activities of the Medical School at Grady Hospital in the clinical years. Grady Hospital is now and probably always will be of major importance in the teaching and research program of the Medical School. This relationship needs clarification in two important aspects. The first concerns financial equity and the second selection of hospital staff members. Accurate cost accounting studies are now being started to determine insofar as possible what activities should properly be paid for by Grady Hospital and what part by the Medical School. It seems clear that all costs of good patient care with adequate services, such as, laboratory, pathology and roentgenology, bacteriology, pharmacy and out-patient facilities should be paid by the hospital. It is also evident that costs of teaching and research should be borne principally by the Medical School. The only point of difference so far between the representatives of the two institutions is the definition of what constitutes an adequate professional service department and hence the cost of it. It is also not unreasonable to expect that the opinion of the Medical School should be considered in this regard. The second point upon which one might anticipate a divergence of opinion is in the appointment of department heads and staff members of Grady Hospital. So far there has been splendid cooperation in this respect. To prevent such differences in the future it is only necessary to abide by the accepted practices in the best hospitals of the country. That is to have all staff members and department heads nominated by the staff and appointed by the superintendent. He represents the Hospital Authority and it must have absolute veto power. This leaves professional people free to select doctors, which obviously cannot be done so well by laymen. On the other hand, the hospital is not forced to accept anyone who is objectionable for good cause.

Further study should be given to the various aspects of Emory Hospital's relationship to the Medical School. As the amount of teaching there increases, operating costs will increase hence it will be necessary to determine what portion of this cost may properly be borne by the Medical School. In this connection, it should be pointed out that a number of income-producing beds have already been taken over for doctors' offices and laboratories.

The private hospitals in the community are also interested in medical education and progress. These hospitals will gradually turn to the University for guidance and help in their educational programs. The University should consider the advisability of establishing departments in any hospital which desires to undertake an educational program, if the hospital is willing to furnish office and laboratory space and a part of the salaries of the full time staff. Such requests will come to the University in the future and are an essential part of the development of Atlanta as a Medical Center. The various specialty boards are requiring courses for accreditation which cannot be given by an individual hospital, but must be obtained through university affiliation.

As a corollary of the policy of broadening its interests to include whatever hospitals seek its cooperation, the University must become increasingly wary of investing its funds in the teaching program of any hospital which does not furnish laboratory facilities and part of the salaries of the men working full time in the hospital.

Immediate Needs of the School

The growth of the faculty and the enlargement of the teaching and research programs on the campus emphasize anew the need for immediate construction on the Emory campus. Space to house the laboratories of the Departments of Medicine, Pathology and Bacteriology must be obtained at once. This construction could serve as the initial unit of the laboratory building, which was proposed in the report of the Planning Committee.

The development of a Department of Pediatrics at Emory Hospital is needed to make it a general hospital. This must be done either by creating this department or by establishing an affiliation with some other pediatric facility in the community.

The equivalent of two wards at the University Hospital should be devoted exclusively to Medical School teaching. One of these wards can be obtained by moving the Calhoun Medical Library to the former internee' quarters on the first floor of the Obstetrical Pavilion. The second one will have to be taken from facilities already in operation. Financial arrangements will have to be made so that laboratory and x-ray studies may be freely obtained on the patients on these wards without additional cost to the patient.

Buildings to house the library and the offices of the men engaged in teaching in Emory Hospital are greatly needed.

Financial Needs

At the present time, nine physicians active in teaching in the clinical departments have their offices in Emory Hospital. Most of them carry on active private practice in these offices. The Chairman of the Department of Surgery and six members of his department are so located. The Cardiologist and the Physician-in-Chief are the only members of the Department of Medicine so far but it is anticipated that the Chairman of the Department of Medicine and at least one other on his staff will be located at Emory Hospital. The early adoption of a more definitive policy on financial arrangements of the hospital and school with these doctors is desirable. Tentative proposals have already been thoroughly discussed and documented but not finally accepted and openly stated.

The need for permanent endowment for the Medical School was stressed in the last report. I can only re-emphasize it here.

The operating budget of the Medical School is not sufficient to cover the development of the teaching services at Emory Hospital. A minimal sum of $100,000 a year should be set aside to defray the expense of establishing seventy teaching beds at Emory Hospital. At the end of two years this project will be partially self-supporting. The development of these teaching beds is the key to the successful implementation of the report of the Planning Committee. This development should not be handicapped by the lack of funds. Eventually one might envision the use of all five wards of the West Wing of the hospital as teaching beds. This would necessitate the spending of additional funds in the beginning but later would probably be largely self-supporting.

Progress toward reconversion from the accelerated program has been made. The present sophomore and freshman classes are already on a Fall to Spring basis. The present junior and senior classes are still on an irregular basis.

A tabulated list of statistical data regarding enrollment and graduation of students and their placement in accredited hospitals for internship is attached to this report.

Respectfully submitted,

R. Hugh Wood, M.D.

Dean

Acknowledgments

General References

English, Thomas H. *Emory University 1915–1965 A Semicentennial History*. Atlanta: Emory University (Higgins-McArthur), 1966.

This excellent book reveals the development of Emory University. Emory holds the copyright.

Hollingsworth, W. *Taking Care: The Legacy of Soma Weiss, Eugene Stead, and Paul Beeson*. Chapel Hill, N.C.: Professional Press (© Dr. J. W. Hollingsworth), 1994. Distributed by Medical Education and Research FDN, P.O. Box 81344, San Diego, CA 92138.

This magnificent book, written by William Hollingsworth, who trained under Stead and Beeson, presents a detailed story of Soma Weiss, Stead and Beeson.

Martin, John D., Jr., in collaboration with Garland D. Perdue. *The History of Surgery at Emory University School of Medicine.* Atlanta: Emory University (Fulton, Mo.: Ovid Bell Press), 1979.

J. D. Martin and Garland Perdue present a detailed account of the development of Emory University School of Medicine and its Department of Surgery. Some of the discussions in their book are germane to the development of the Department of Medicine.

Warren, James V. "Eugene A. Stead, Jr." *Clin Cardiol* 9 (1986): 233.

In this profile, Jim Warren, a life-long friend of Eugene Stead, characterizes the magic of the master teacher at work.

The quotations from the Stead 1990 letter to Dr. Mark Silverman are used with Dr. Silverman's permission.

The quotations from Stead's 1989 letter to me were published with his permission in the *Emory University Journal of Medicine* 4, no. 1 (1990): 63–64.

The information used to write Dr. Hugh Wood's biography, as well as Dr. Wood's letters used in this section of the book, came from Emory sources located in the Dean's office of Emory University School of Medicine.

The Help of Others

I wish to thank Dr. Paul B. Beeson, Dr. Joseph E. Hardison, Dr. Charles R. Hatcher Jr., Dr. Gary S. Hauk, Dr. William Hollingsworth, Dr. R. Bruce Logue, Dr. Jack Myers, Mr. J. W. Pinkston Jr., Dr. Thomas F. Sellers Jr., Dr. Mark E. Silverman, Dr. Eugene A. Stead Jr., and Dr. Judson C. Ward Jr., for their review of Chapter 2 of this book.

I especially thank Dr. Evangeline Papageorge for reviewing this chapter as well as Chapter 1.

Figure 2-1
Eugene Stead was the first full-time professor and chairman of the Department of Medicine of Emory University School of Medicine. He held this position from 1942 through 1946. During his last year at Emory he also served as Dean of the School of Medicine.

Figure 2-2
Grady Memorial Hospital, Department of Medicine, 1942–43
Row 1: Harris, Lentz, Cargill, Hickman, Stead, Beeson, Freedman, Brannon, Warren
Row 2: Miller, Paullin, Kern, Golden, Armour, Holland, Rodgers
Row 3: Brown, Haltom, Preseley, Hooten, Burge, Mays, McMath, Cook, Stanley

Figure 2-3
Grady Memorial Hospital, Department of Medicine, 1943–44
Row 1: Heyman, Oppenheimer, Massee, Byrd, Martin, Stead, Merrill, Brannon
Row 2: Barrow, Brown, Powell, Rodgers, Holland, Miller, Warren, Armstrong, Leadingham
Row 3: Stegeman, Hooten, Burge, Glover, W. Stead, Prive, Parks, Irwin, Beeson

Figure 2-4
Grady Memorial Hospital, Department of Medicine, 1945–46:
Row 1: James, Bandy, Engel, Anthony, Logue, Heyman; Row 2: Huguley, Beeson, Oppenheimer, Stead, Friedewald; Row 3: Michael, Warren, Cargill, Marshall, Boger; Row 4: Benton, Schroeder, Witham, Key, Craig; Morse; Row 5: Lentz, Fitzpatrick, Felden; Row 6: Jordan, Easley, Hodges, Giddings

Figure 2-5
Grady Memorial Hospital, Department of Medicine, 1946–47
Row 1: Engel, Miller, Michael, Stead, Heyman; Row 2: Merrill, Myers, James, Beeson; Row 3: Bondy, Paullin, Morse, Freedman, Stillerman, Bennett; Row 4: Senter, Nelson, Haltum, Lathem, Golden; Row 5: Hallman, Scheinberg, Withington, Buchanan, Butler, Brown, Lentz, Turner

Figure 2-6

Dr. Hugh Wood was Professor of Medicine at Emory University School of Medicine in 1945. He was Chief of Medicine at Emory University Hospital when he was appointed Dean of the School of Medicine, a position he held from 1946 to 1956.

This photograph was made at the request of the Communicable Disease Center (now named Centers for Disease Control and Prevention) to illustrate the advantages of immunization. It was shown at the New York World Fair, where it was part of the exhibit labeled "The Human Approach."

CHAPTER 3
The Pursuit of Excellence and Plans for the Future 1946–1952

Paul Beeson had become internationally known by the time Eugene Stead left Emory to become chairman of the Department of Medicine at Duke. Beeson was the first and only choice to become Emory's second full-time chairman of the Department of Medicine. His starting income as Chairman of the Department of Medicine in 1946 was $10,000; six years later it was $17,000.

The Biography of Paul Beeson, M.D.

Beeson's Early Years

Paul Beeson was born in Livingston, Montana, on October 18, 1908 (Figure 3-1). His father, Dr. John Beeson, was a general practitioner of medicine. Paul's brother, Harold, born some eight years earlier, also became a physician.

The Beesons moved to Seattle, Washington, in 1913, where Paul's father started a new practice. A little later Dr. John Beeson became an Assistant Surgeon for the railway that ran from Fairbanks to Anchorage and Seward in Alaska. The family moved to Anchorage and lived there from 1916 to 1926, during which time Paul's father was the chief surgeon for the Alaska Railway.

Paul Beeson did extremely well in the Anchorage schools and entered the University of Washington in Seattle at the age of 16. After college, he entered medical school at McGill University in Montreal, Canada.

Internship and Residency

Paul Beeson spent two years as an intern at the University of Pennsylvania from 1933 to 1935. The program at Penn was considered one of the best in the country. The first year was spent rotating through the specialties, and the second year was divided between medicine and surgery. The program prepared trainees for the general practice of medicine. The great teachers there had a profound influence on Paul Beeson, and the training undoubtedly influenced him, in his later years, to encourage the development of more primary care physicians.

Paul Beeson's Experience as a General Practitioner

Following his house-staff training at the University of Pennsylvania, Beeson joined his father and brother in Wooster, Ohio, where they had bought a practice. He decided after two years of general practice that he was not suited for the surgical aspects of the work, and he accepted a residency in medicine at Cornell in 1937. Following Cornell, he accepted a residency in medicine at the Rockefeller Institute Hospital, where he was assigned to the pneumonia service. The service was developing a type-specific rabbit serum for the treatment of pneumococcal pneumonia. He worked and rubbed shoulders with the infectious disease giants of the day who worked at Rockefeller Institute Hospital.

Beeson wrote several important research papers while working at the Rockefeller Institute Hospital, and the experience there influenced him throughout his subsequent career. He did not, however, view himself as a researcher.

Chief Resident Under Soma Weiss

Soma Weiss had just begun his work at the Peter Bent Brigham Hospital in Boston and needed a chief medical resident. He heard about a bright young man named Beeson working at the Rockefeller Institute Hospital, and while on a trip to New York he asked Paul Beeson to come to his hotel room for a talk. So, in 1939, at the age of 31, Paul Beeson became the chief resident in medicine at the Brigham. The house staff included Jack Myers, Gustave Dammin, and Richard Ebert. Weiss' research fellows included Eugene Stead, Charles Janeway, and John Romano. These were all bright people who later became famous chairmen of departments. Beeson and Myers later joined Stead's Department of Medicine at Emory.

Soma Weiss respected his house staff, viewing them as colleagues who would perhaps join him or assume a leadership role at some other institution. The same attitude in Beeson contributed to his success as a chairman of medicine.

Beeson's First Sojourn to England

In 1940 Paul Beeson was made chief of the Harvard Field Hospital, which was associated with the American Red Cross and was located in Salisbury, England. Beeson met his future wife, Barbara, there. Beeson was not drafted into the armed forces of the United States because of a congenital problem that connected his bladder to his rectum. The hospital served the needs of the military personnel and civilians in the area. The major problem was infectious diseases. Beeson remained there until 1942, making important medical contributions to the treatment of meningitis, serum hepatitis, and trichinosis.

Why Beeson Came to Emory

The story of Beeson's recruitment by Stead to join him at Emory is told on pages 76–77. Soma Weiss's letter to Beeson undoubtedly led Beeson to decide to join the faculty at Emory rather than return to the Brigham or to Cornell. Beeson's story of the event is told in the following pages.

Beeson's Own Story

Beeson tells his own story in Sharon R. Kaufman's 1993 book, *The Healer's Tale: Transforming Medicine and Culture.*[1] Kaufman's interview was evidently accomplished with the use of a tape recorder, and it reveals, parenthetically, that even among experts the spoken word is very different from the written word:

> While I was in Britain I had wanted to return to the Brigham. After Soma Weiss died, Eugene Stead, who had also been at the Brigham as an attending physician, was offered the chairmanship of the Department of Medicine at Emory in Atlanta. He wrote to me in Britain and said, "I could give you an offer of an assistant professorship, and you would be the infectious disease man." Stead was to be the first full-time chairman of the clinical department at Emory. At the same time, I had been corresponding through a Rockefeller friend with David Barr about going to the New York Hospital. It had a greater name. I had known it from my previous experience. And the Rockefeller group was next to it. Stead had to have my answer by a certain date. I sent him a cable accepting his offer. The next day I received the formal offer from Barr, but of course it was too late.
>
> So, I went off to Emory. It turned out to be the luckiest thing in the world for me. I was better able to function—and had much more visibility as practically the only infectious disease person in the Southeast of the United States—than I would have been in New York with that whole crew from Rockefeller and the New York Hospital. Fortune was again working on my side when I took that opportunity. I was there ten years, from 1942 to 1952.
>
> I met my wife, Barbara, in Britain. She was a nurse in the same unit in 1941–1942. We did all of our courting in Salisbury, where our hospital was located. We came back to the U.S. together in a convoy during the height of the submarine activity, although we didn't see any submarine action. She went to her home in Buffalo, and I went to visit my family in Ohio. A couple of

[1] Sharon R. Kaufman, *The Healer's Tale: Transforming Medicine and Culture* (Madison: University of Wisconsin Press, 1993). The following long excerpt is reproduced with the permission of the University of Wisconsin Press and the author.

weeks later we were married in Buffalo. We drove from there down to Atlanta to start the job at Emory.

When Barbara and I got down there we went and had dinner with the Steads. Gene remarked in the evening after dinner, 'Paul, I've got a lab for you and a technician.' I was so naive. I hope I didn't show it too much, but I was flabbergasted with the thought that I would be expected to do research. I could see myself teaching and taking care of patients, but it never occurred to me that I would be expected to do research also. Still, I had done some at Rockefeller and had done some more in the course of my residency at Brigham. I knew some of the techniques of bacteriology.

A few weeks later, there was no one to run the bacteriology lab of Grady Hospital, our teaching hospital, because someone there had quit. It was a big city hospital, completely divided into two parts—the black wards and the white wards. Our offices and labs were in the basement of what was then called the old colored nurses home. In fact, some earth had to be dug out in order to make ceiling room, but we had offices and labs down there and you could walk into it. It was a wonderful experience for me day after day to see the bacteriology. I was going to be an infectious disease expert. To see all the cultures that came into the lab and become a lot more familiar with general bacteriology, which I had to read about and teach myself, was a precious experience. And I found where the interesting infections were: around the orthopedic service, or the urology service, or obstetrics. It was perfectly all right for me to go see those patients, and I did. By giving me a research lab, and letting it be understood that I was expected to do research, Stead put me in a very favorable position. Infectious disease was not much of a recognized specialty, and I was virtually the only one in the southeastern United States who professed to have a special expertise in infectious diseases.

Stead had a tiny department with two or three other full-time people. I was an assistant professor. It was war time. Many of the best teachers and practicing physicians in the town had gone away to war. We were exempt because we were in medical education. We had a busy time of teaching and investigating. I owe an enormous debt to Stead for taking me and giving me my first academic job and for setting the conditions under which I could work and work productively. Eugene Stead was, in his own way, just as much of a leader and exciting teacher as Soma Weiss had been. Being in his department for four years taught me a great deal. I saw the way his students reacted to him, how he could make the dullest case seem interesting. He could always find something to talk about at the bedside.

I wanted a lot more clinical experience in a variety of kinds of infection. Instead of concentrating on one or two diseases, I deliberately tried to study fairly intensively a wide variety of conditions and to write articles about them. My first publications show a great range of interests. I have always been glad I did that. I didn't set myself up as a pneumonia expert and nothing else at that time. The research I did involved a variety of infectious diseases, doing special cultures, serologic tests, and so on. The important questions for me at the time came out of bedside discussions, arguments that arose there, wondering how something happens. Then I would go and try some experimental infections to see what I could learn about them. By that time, I did want to stay in academic medicine, and I did want to become chairman of a department. That's what everyone wanted then.

My first real hit was in terms of serum jaundice, or hepatitis. While we were in England we had gotten the idea of trying to protect some young British soldiers from an epidemic of mumps that was springing up in a training camp near us in Salisbury. So we got the idea that, since we had some mumps patients in our hospital, we would bleed them, collect their serum, and give it to a bunch of new trainees, and they would therefore have antibodies against mumps. This had been done in the case of measles already. Nothing was known about the danger of transmitting hepatitis. We managed to transmit hepatitis through the mumps serum, and this produced an epidemic of jaundice in those trainees.

Soon after I got to Emory, I was having lunch in a little cafe across from the hospital with a junior medical student who said he had an interesting patient with what was called toxic hepatitis. The patient had been in the hospital three months before with burns, and they had treated him with tannic acid, the standard treatment for burns. They thought a late tannic acid poisoning had given him the jaundice. With my guilty feeling of having produced hepatitis in those soldiers in England, I asked him, "Did he get transfusions?" The medical student said, "Oh yes, he did get transfusions." Well, transfusions were new at the time. Blood banks were developed during the war, and they were only one or two years old. I looked up the patient's record and, yes, he did get transfusions. Then I rushed to the record room and looked up all the recent cases of jaundice and toxic hepatitis and found six more. They all had this peculiar, long incubation period—two to four months between the time of the transfusion and the time of the clinical hepatitis. I wrote a paper on the transmission of hepatitis by blood transfusions. Stead helped me again. The president of the AMA was an Atlanta physician, Dr. James E. Paullin, who had been Franklin Roosevelt's physician. Stead spoke to Paullin and Paullin spoke to Morris Fishbein, who was the editor of the JAMA, and they got the paper I wrote on the subject published in no time. That caused quite an uproar: the transmission of hepatitis by blood transfusion. That paper gave me a lot of notoriety.[2]

I got into other things as well. In the prepenicillin days, the best treatment for syphilitic paresis, or general paralysis of the insane, was fever therapy. General paresis and tabes were the late forms of central nervous system syphilis, and they were very common. You could walk down the streets of Atlanta and see somebody shuffling along with the typical gait of tabes. We always had on our wards two to three patients, white or black, with general paresis who were getting fever therapy.

To give fever therapy we used typhoid vaccine intravenously. The interesting thing is that you start with a given number of organisms, and you

---

[2] The paper to which Beeson refers is "Jaundice Occurring One to Four Months After Transfusion of Blood or Plasma: Report of Seven Cases," *Journal of the American Medical Association* 121 (1943): 1332.

get a chill and fever. It will go up and stay up at 103–104 degrees (Fahrenheit) for some hours and then come back down. In order to get that much fever with the next treatment, you have to give at least double the dose. You keep giving double and double the dose in order to get a total of forty hours of fever over 104 degrees. This worked. This was effective. It began with the use of malaria. A physician in Europe, Julius Wagner-Jauregg, got the Nobel Prize for thinking of deliberately inoculating syphilitic patients with malaria and curing or greatly improving some of them. It worked with the typhoid vaccine therapy as well. I got fascinated when I saw the amount of typhoid vaccine we were giving. I remember so well one patient whose last course involved 200 cc's of undiluted typhoid vaccine intravenously. For an immunizing dose, you usually give 1/8 of a cc. We injected bottle after bottle of this awful-looking material right into this man, and he got the usual fever but no worse. So I took that into the lab and started giving rabbits the same dose of typhoid vaccine in daily injections and following their temperatures.

Then I read something about reticuloendothelial blockade. The reticulo-endothelia system of the body is the one that removes foreign particles from the circulating blood, dead blood cells, bacteria, or whatever. You can block it by giving certain agents such as Thorotrast. When I gave my rabbits Thorotrast and then typhoid vaccine, they got big fevers. What this seemed to demonstrate was that the tolerance to the endotoxin in the bacteria was not an immune phenomenon due to antibodies. It was a phenomenon of the reticuloendothelia system enhancing its ability to remove these foreign particles. I published several articles on various aspects of that phenomenon.

Another thing that worked out well for me was studying the bacteremia of patients with bacterial endocarditis. Bacterial endocarditis is an infection on a heart valve which is usually caused by a simple streptococcus, the kind that you carry in your mouth. These are harmless elsewhere, but if they can lodge in a little collection of platelets on a heart valve they can survive there, because white blood cells can't get at them, as there is no circulation in there. They grow and eventually the valve gets destroyed; emboli break off and damage the brain and the kidneys and so on. Over a period of months the patient dies. As I saw it in my internship, this was a uniformly fatal disease before penicillin.

I had an argument with one of my friends there about whether we would do any better to take arterial cultures rather than venous cultures in order to demonstrate the bacteria in the blood. I happened to be on the right side in that argument, but it didn't make any difference. By that time Stead, who was a cardiologist, and his colleague Jim Warren were using cardiac catheterization in their studies of the circulation. They used the procedure in the study of congenital heart disease, and showed its value in diagnosis of patent atrial septum. I went to them and said, "Could we take a patient with bacterial endocarditis and put in a catheter and get samples of arterial blood—which we could do with a needle in the femoral artery—and at the same time take the samples from different parts of the venous circulation and see whether there is any difference in the number of bacteria?" In particular, I wanted to go down into the inferior vena cava, go right on through the heart and get some blood samples from there. I also wanted to get some samples from the superior vena cava, which was draining the head mostly. Stead and Warren said, "Sure, go ahead."

The patient would be taken into this special study room which had a fluoroscope and put on an X-ray table. It was well-padded with pillows and so on. Putting a needle in the femoral artery is not very painful; they put novocaine in first. You get a needle in there with a canula inside it, pull the canula out, take your sample, and put it back in. Threading the catheter in through an arm vein sounds bad, but many people have had it done. Everybody who has coronary bypass surgery goes through that, and you don't hear much complaining about the arteriograms. So it wasn't really so bad, except that the patient had to lie on the table for one to two hours. However, they didn't seem to complain. They were all awfully sick. They had been ill for months, and what we hoped was that they felt that someone was trying to do something for them.

Stead and Warren and a fellow there named Emmett Brannon did the catheterizations. I was in the room the whole time, taking all the samples and timing them. I would put each one in a separate test tube and in an ice bath to keep any bacteria from growing until we could take them back to the lab. There we would pour agar plates, exactly 1 cc of blood from each specimen, and incubate them overnight to see how many colonies we could count on the plate the next day.

The results were simply spectacular. The blood coming through the liver had virtually no bacteria as compared with the arterial blood that was leaving the heart. The thing we lucked into by trying to go down into the vena cava was that we found we could get into the liver. That discovery opened up a whole field of liver metabolism, because we could get samples from there. By angling the tip of the catheter a few weeks later, Stead and Warren found they could get into the renal vein. Kidney physiology could be studied that way. It turned out to be a very useful technique.

It was just a little window of opportunity. The technique was there, but penicillin wasn't there. We would never have done those experiments then if we had had penicillin for these patients. I didn't know that penicillin was coming.

Some of the ethical problems about that sort of investigation that trouble us now never dawned on us then. There wasn't much clinical investigation as such in the early 1940s. There were very few people engaged in full-time clinical research anywhere. We never asked the permission of these patients to go through this procedure. We certainly never explained it. We never told them, "This isn't going to help you a bit, but it may give us a better understanding." No patient ever refused to participate. It wouldn't have occurred to them. We would go by the night before and say, "We are going to do a special study on you in the X-ray department tomorrow," and they would say, "All right." In that way they were like the British. British patients are completely complacent. They never challenge what a doctor is going to do. We had grown up in a tradition of charity hospitals and felt we were giving these patients our time and our skills. They were not paying anything for it. And, there was a social gulf between us. This was part of the reason that we felt we could study them.

As I look back on it, I think we did more of our studies on the black wards. There were more patients and they were closer to us. Atlanta was a segregated city. Our hospital was segregated. One of the things that annoyed all of us who had come from Boston was that the black patients always had to be called by their first names. It didn't matter how old they were. "This is Sarah and she is complaining of shortness of breath." On the other side of the hospital, "This is Mrs. Jones and she is complaining of shortness of breath." They had to be kept separate. They had separate nursing staffs and really separate nursing schools. The facilities in the black wards were not as good as those in the white wards. In our relationships with other doctors and with social acquaintances in Atlanta, we had to learn not to let the race problem get into the conversation or it would get us nowhere. We were completely outnumbered, and there was nothing we could do about it. There were no black medical students. Grady Hospital is no longer a segregated hospital. They have black and white patients on the same wards.

When penicillin was becoming available and small amounts were being allocated for civilian use, Stead did another thing for me. Most penicillin was allocated to the military, but Stead, through a contact in Washington, D.C., made an arrangement for me to be the "czar" of penicillin in the southeastern states. I was the first person to use penicillin at Grady Hospital. I also was allocating its use elsewhere in the area and talking to doctors on the phone, saying, "We haven't got any, and we aren't allowed to use it for this disease or for that." It was used for pneumonia, hemolytic streptococcal infections, and for staphylococcal infections. An episode I remember with clarity is that of a practitioner in another town calling me and saying he had a patient with syphilis and wanted to use penicillin for that, and I said, "No way. This drug is not to be used for syphilis because it has not been proved that it would be any good." My goodness, it just revolutionized the treatment of syphilis. Syphilis clinics had been places where patients would come back week after week for intravenous arsenic over periods of a year or a year and a half. It was a tedious and not very successful therapy. To be able to clear it within five days or so with penicillin was just stupefying. Being the penicillin czar certainly gave me a lot of exposure to the medical public and was a wonderful opportunity to know what this amazing drug was to going to do. It was a very heady thing for a few months.

Then, in 1943, supplies became bigger. By late 1943, penicillin was in general civilian use. There wasn't any Food and Drug trial of penicillin. It was so harmless and so good that you didn't need to do controlled, clinical trials. It was such a thrill to be able to save the life of someone with meningitis or bacterial endocarditis and to bring syphilis to a halt in a few days. I think we realized that this was a tremendously exciting new development. When it was followed by streptomycin, and then the tetracyclines came along in another year, we realized that we were going into a whole new era. The treatment of infections up to that time had been almost nil: bed rest, nutritious diet, and quiet. Sometimes attempts were made with antiserum, but they were only effective in a few things such as pneumococcal pneumonia. The use of antiserum against most things turned out to be a great disappointment. So there wasn't a lot of drug therapy until all of a sudden we realized that we were going to be able to treat so many things.

We were beginning to take things away from the surgeons. We treated empyemas ourselves, putting penicillin by needle into the pleural cavity. Before that, treating empyema, carbuncle, or abdominal abscesses had required surgical drainage. The only thing they could do was drain the pus and hope that the natural defense mechanisms would take over. There were these debates going on between the medical people and the surgeons about who ought to treat this or that.

During the Second World War, there wasn't a push to make medical schools enlarge their classes. The period of medical training was shortened by what they called the nine-nine-nine program, nine months internship, nine months assistant residency, and nine months of senior residency. At the end of twenty-seven months you were eligible for military service. Everyone, except those with physical handicaps or those with full-time teaching jobs, did have to go into the military. Things did change during the war in that some of the full-time and many of the voluntary faculty went into the service. A lot of research programs had to be put aside and halted. But at the same time there was money available, and the government was asking for the investigation of certain things, for example, treatment of infection and treatment of shock. That's why Stead and Warren got their catheter research going, to study patients in shock. They were chosen to do that research because Grady Hospital saw a lot of trauma; there were a lot of stabbings on Saturday night. The emergency room at Grady was like a wartime casualty department. So the shock team was always there. They spent Saturday nights there and studied patients in shock with cardiac catheterization to see what was going on with the circulation. Later they used the technique for other kinds of investigation.

It was abundantly demonstrated during the war that if you put enough money into a big problem, you could solve it: radar, jet propulsion, penicillin. Government researchers developed a good treatment for malaria, because our troops were going into malaria area. In war ads in the magazines, General Motors would say they were making tanks now, but just wait 'til after the war and see what our new automobiles are going to be like. The whole country was anxious to channel money out of wartime expenditures and into good living. There were a lot of influential people in Congress who saw that things could be done to improve the nation's health if enough federal funds were put into it. The NIH (National Institutes of Health), a branch of the public health service, began to give out large grants to the universities of the country. All of a sudden we had this big explosion of academic medicine—in surgery, medicine, whatever—with full-time departments growing.

There was federal financial support for people who were working on infectious problems and testing penicillin and the new antibiotics that began to arrive. The government was a source of research support for my work. We had a very small number of clinical teachers. We all carried a heavy teaching load, just because there were so few full-time people in the department. While

Stead was there, until 1946, our full-time department was six people. Stead surprised us all by accepting an offer to go to Duke in 1946. He had put so much into Emory and had just revolutionized the place that we couldn't imagine him leaving. When he left for Duke, he took three people with him. That left me and one other full-time person. I was made chairman of the department at that time (1946), and remained chairman for the six years until I went to Yale in 1952. In the Soma Weiss tradition, we used our senior residents as assistant professors, and they taught and helped conduct research as well as care for patients. I was forced to rely heavily on young people, on the resident staff, and some research fellows that I was able to recruit to do a lot of the academic work. I was lucky in getting a couple of very good ones to work with me.

Since the war was over, the practitioners—internists—in Atlanta came back and reopened their offices. They wanted to teach and they were an exceptionally good, well-trained bunch of people. With the aid of these volunteer clinical instructors, it went very satisfactorily. I went on with the same kinds of research that I had been engaged in before. The department was small enough so that I wasn't seeing people and sitting on committees all the time. My life didn't change greatly after Stead left. I got elected to the two societies in academic medicine that everyone wants to be elected to, the American Society for Clinical Investigation and the Association of American Physicians. I gave a couple of papers before the Association, which went well. I am sure that as a result of that I was approached by Yale.

Beeson at Emory

When Beeson became chairman of the Department of Medicine in 1946, his senior staff at Grady included: Dr. James Warren, who was professor and chairman of the Department of Physiology and held a joint appointment in the Department of Medicine; Dr. Phil Bondy in endocrinology; Dr. Al Heyman in venereal diseases; Dr. Robert Grant in cardiology and electrocardiography; Dr. David James, who had been chief resident in medicine at Grady; Dr. Walter Bloom in metabolism; and Dr. Ivan Bennett. Bennett was Beeson's last chief resident at Grady. He was a superb teacher and investigator and should be counted as a faculty member. The distinguished group also included Dr. John Patterson in pulmonary medicine, Dr. Arthur Merrill Sr., who was part-time and was later viewed as the local expert in kidney disease, and Dr. William Friedewald, professor and chairman of the Department of Microbiology and an associate professor in the Department of Medicine.

Dr. Bruce Logue, in cardiology, was located at Emory University Hospital, as was Dr. Spalding Schroder a gastroenterologist. Dr. Logue was chief of medicine there, and Dr. Schroder was in charge of the house-staff program, which was separate from the programs at Grady and Lawson Veterans Hospital. Dr. Charles Huguley, a hematologist, had joined the Winship Clinic at Emory Hospital. In 1950, I joined Dr. Logue in cardiology at Emory University Hospital. By then, Beeson and others had organized the Private Diagnostic Clinic of the department members at Emory University Hospital. Later Dr. Bernard Hallman, an endocrinologist, joined the group. Beeson was Director of the Private Diagnostic Clinic and spent some time each week seeing outpatients in the facility located on the first floor of the Lucy Elizabeth Pavilion of Emory University Hospital. This facility was built by the children of Asa Candler to honor their mother.

The faculty members located at the Lawson Veterans Administration Hospital included Dr. Max Michael, chief of medicine there, Dr. Walter Bloom, Dr. Martin Cummings, and Dr. Harry Price.

Important Events of Beeson's Years as Chairman

Beeson continued his research. His teaching on ward rounds and conferences was masterful and gentle, his style more reserved than Stead's. He was, we suspected, a bit shy. He was never intimidating and gained the immediate respect of the students, house staff, and colleagues. His immense knowledge was always evident. His house staff was excellent, and therefore the student program was very successful. Information about the separate house-staff programs—at Grady, Lawson Veterans Hospital, and Emory University Hospital—could not be found. Some former house officers remember them as completely separate; others remember some interchange of house officers among the three institutions.

Relationship to Lawson General Hospital and "Old 48"

Lawson General Hospital was located in temporary facilities in Chamblee, Georgia, in the suburb of Atlanta where old Camp Gordon had been located during World War I. The temporary hospital was deactivated at the end of World War II and was then used as a Veterans Hospital from 1946 until October 1952, when the facility was abandoned and the veteran patients were moved to the newly renovated "old 48" hospital. "Old 48" was the nickname for the United States Public Health Service Hospital for the Veterans of World War I and the Spanish American War.

The very effective partnership of medical schools and veterans hospitals was established by Congress in 1946. The administrative arrangement included the dean's committee to oversee the relationship and guide the arrangement to the benefit of both partners. Eugene Stead appointed Dr. Jack Myers to be the first chief of medicine at the Veterans

Hospital when it was housed in the deactivated Lawson General Hospital. Myers spent half his time at Lawson Veterans Hospital, as it was then called, and half at Grady Memorial Hospital. Beeson appointed Dr. Max Michael as chief of medicine at Lawson Veterans Hospital when Myers left to join Stead at Duke.

When "Old 48" on Peachtree Street was designated as the Veterans Hospital in 1952, the patients in the Veterans Hospital at Lawson General Hospital were moved to that facility. The house-staff program in medicine at the Veterans Hospital and the house-staff program in medicine at Emory University Hospital were joined together that year. It became known as the Emory-VA program. Although there are no documents that state with certainty who spearheaded this important development, Dr. Beeson believes that Dr. Michael developed the new program, which was started in July 1952, three months after Beeson moved to Yale.

The Organization of the Private Diagnostic Clinic at Emory University Hospital

In 1948 several members of the Department of Medicine appealed to President Goodrich White to permit them to organize a clinic, which would enable the Department of Medicine to recruit and support more teachers, researchers, and clinicians. President White agreed with their plan. The original group included Paul Beeson, who was to become director of the clinic, Dean Wood, Bruce Logue, Charles Huguley, and Spalding Schroder. Later, David James also participated in the Private Diagnostic Clinic, and I joined Dr. Logue there in cardiology in July 1950. The Private Diagnostic Clinic was one of the three organizations that eventually coalesced to form the Emory University Clinic (see discussion in Chapter 4 of this book).

Beeson's Contribution to Famous Textbooks

In addition to his research and teaching, Beeson became one of the editors of *Harrison's Textbook of Medicine*. One day he wandered into my office when I was not there. *Cecil Textbook of Medicine* was on my desk. Beeson wrote me a note on a prescription pad. He did not sign his name, but I recognized his handwriting. He wrote, "Anyone who displays this book prominently is just a damn traitor." I carried the note in my wallet for years and planned to show it to him when the time was right. The plan evaporated when the piece of paper eventually deteriorated.

Beeson later joined Walsh McDermott as co-editor of *Cecil Textbook of Medicine* and became even more famous.

Beeson's First Knowledge of Yale's Interest in Him

Paul and Barbara had two children during the time they lived in Atlanta. Their growing family needed a new home, so Barbara designed one. They were ready to build their new house when Paul received an odd hint of things to come. William Hollingsworth tells the story in his book *Taking Care*:

> Beeson was on one of those annual pilgrimages to the clinical research meetings in Atlantic City, quietly sitting in a stall in the men's room in Hadden Hall Hotel, when he heard two gentlemen walk in, chatting together as they emptied their bladders in a nearby urinal. One, forever unidentified by Beeson, said to the other, "Oh, we (at Yale) will go down to Emory and get Paul Beeson to replace Frances Blake."[3]

Beeson heard nothing from Yale, however, so he and Barbara built their dream house.

The Yale Offer and Afterwards

Officials at Yale contacted Beeson in 1952, and he accepted their offer to become professor and chairman of the Department of Medicine at that distinguished university. Beeson had been at Emory for ten years and had been chairman of the Department of Medicine for six. Although he and Barbara loved Emory and Atlanta, Yale's offer was impossible for him to turn down.

Beeson had some difficulty during his early years at Yale. Some of the old guard resented his appointment. But Beeson, always a great and practical poker player, played his best card. He simply waited a while to make his move, and when the time was right he took over the area of the department that had previously been autonomous.

In addition to the excellent faculty members who cooperated with him on his arrival, he added Dr. Phil Bondy and Dr. Ivan Bennett from Emory, and gradually other nationally-known experts to his department. He thrived at Yale.

Beeson's Second Sojourn to England

After thirteen years as chairman of the Department of Medicine at Yale, Beeson accepted the position as Nuffield Professor of Medicine at Oxford, England. He and Barbara had met in England during World War II and loved England. He and Stead visited Emory in 1965 just prior to

---

[3] W. Hollingsworth, *Taking Care: The Legacy of Soma Weiss, Eugene Stead, and Paul Beeson* (Chapel Hill, N.C.: Professional Press, 1994), 161. The passage is reproduced with Hollingsworth's permission.

his move to Oxford. In fact, the first public announcement of his move to Oxford occurred at a gathering I organized for him and Stead at Emory (see page 322). He spent ten very productive years, from 1965 to 1974, at Oxford, where he continued his research and teaching.

Beeson then moved to Redmond, Washington, near Seattle, to become a distinguished physician of the Veterans Administration at the University of Washington. Teaching at the University of Washington, he continued his friendship with one of his old pupils, Dr. Robert Petersdorf, who was professor and chairman of the Department of Medicine at the University of Washington.

Beeson's Honors and Awards

Like Stead, Beeson received numerous honors and awards. Beeson was a reserved, highly intelligent, gentle man who earned his awards by hard work and brilliant research. He was a member of the American Academy of Arts and Sciences; co-editor of the *Cecil Textbook of Medicine* from 1963 to 1979; fellow in the Royal College of Physicians; president of the Association of American Physicians; alumnus *Summa Laude Dignatus* of the University of Washington; member of the National Academy of Sciences; master in the American College of Physicians; Honorary Knight Commander of the British Empire; honorary fellow of the Royal Society of Medicine; honorary fellow, Magdalen College, Oxford; honorary member, Reticuloendothial Society; honorary fellow at Green College, Oxford; honorary member, Canadian Society of Internal Medicine; and co-editor of the Oxford *Companion to Medicine.* He received: the 1963 Gold Medal Award from the Brigham Hospital; the Bristol Award, Infectious Diseases Society of America; the Kober Medal, Association of American Physicians; the Phillips Award, American College of Physicians; the Flexner Award, Association of American Medical Colleges; the Gold Headed Cane Award, University of California, San Francisco; the Founders Award, Southern Society for Clinical Research; the William Thompson Award, American Geriatric Society; the Distinguished Teacher Award, American College of Physicians; and a 1968 honorary Doctor of Science Degree at Emory University. The Paul Beeson Professorship was established to honor him at Yale in 1981.

Beeson's Associates and House Staff

The members of the faculty and Grady Memorial Hospital house staff who worked under Beeson at Emory are shown in the photographs in Figures 3-2 through 3-7.

Beeson made ward rounds at Lawson Veterans Hospital once a week. The senior staff and house staff at Lawson are shown in Figure 3-7.

While at Emory and Yale, Beeson trained more than fifty individuals who either became chairmen of departments, deans, or held other important administrative offices.

The following people served in the Emory Department of Medicine under Beeson's leadership:

Dr. Waddell Barnes became the first professor and chairman of the Department of Medicine at Mercer's new medical school in Macon, Georgia.

Dr. Ivan Bennett moved from Emory to Yale. He became professor and chairman of the Department of Pathology at Johns Hopkins and later became dean and then vice chancellor at New York University.

Dr. Linton Bishop became an effective volunteer faculty member and played a major role in developing Emory-owned Crawford W. Long Hospital. He also became a member of the Emory University Board of Trustees.

Dr. Philip Bondy moved from Emory to Yale and later followed Beeson as professor and chairman of the Department of Medicine at Yale.

Dr. Walter Cargill joined the Emory faculty at the Veteran's Hospital.

Dr. Freeman Cary became physician to the United States Congress.

Dr. James Coberly joined the Emory faculty at the Veterans Administration Hospital.

Dr. James Crutcher became chief of medicine at the Veterans Administration Hospital in Atlanta and later became national director of the Veterans Administration.

Dr. John K. Davidson became an expert in diabetes mellitus and later, after intensive study in Toronto, returned to Emory as a professor in the Endocrine Division of the Department of Medicine.

Dr. Joe Doyle became head of the Division of Cardiology at the University of Albany in New York.

Dr. Harvey Estes became professor and chairman of the Department of Family Practice at Duke.

Dr. Abner Golden, who also trained in pathology, became professor and chairman of the Department of Pathology at Georgetown and later at the University of Kentucky.

Dr. Robert Grant held many important positions in the Public Health Service and became the director of the National Heart Institute.

Dr. Bernard Hallman was a founding member of the Emory Clinic. He later became associate dean at Emory University School of Medicine and was a major administrative force at Grady Hospital.

Dr. Al Heyman became head of neurology at Duke.

Dr. Edward Hook became professor and chairman of the Department of Medicine at the University of Virginia.

Dr. Charles Huguley, one of the founding members of the Emory Clinic, became director of the Division of Hematology and Oncology of the Department of Medicine at Emory University.

Dr. J. Willis Hurst became professor and chairman of the Department of Medicine at Emory and a founding member of the Emory Clinic.

Dr. David James remained on the faculty at Emory but later entered private practice in Atlanta.

Dr. Herbert Karp became director of the Division of Neurology in the Department of Medicine at Emory and later the first chairman of the new Department of Neurology at Emory. Still later, he became director of the Division of Geriatrics in the Department of Medicine.

Dr. Bruce Logue, was chief of medicine at Emory University Hospital and a founding member of the Emory Clinic.

Dr. John Patterson became the head of pulmonary medicine at the Medical College of Virginia.

Dr. Spalding Schroder, a gastroenterologist, remained on the faculty at Emory and was a founding member of the Emory Clinic.

Dr. Thomas F. Sellers Jr. became director of the Division of Infectious Disease of the Department of Medicine at Emory and later the second chairman of the Department of Preventive Medicine and Community Health.

Dr. John Sessions became professor and chairman of the Division of Gastroenterology of the Department of Medicine at the University of North Carolina.

Dr. James Warren later joined Stead at Duke, where he became Chief of Medicine at the Veterans Administration Hospital. He later became professor and chairman of the Department of Medicine at the University of Texas in Galveston and still later professor and chairman of the Department of Medicine at Ohio State University.

Beeson's publications attest to his clear thinking and writing. A complete listing of his publications can be found in William Hollingsworth's book *Taking Care: A Legacy of Soma Weiss, Eugene Stead, and Paul Beeson.*[4]

Interesting Notes in the Dean's File

The following letters were found in the Emory files of Dean Hugh Wood. They are reproduced here because they highlight some of the mores of the Emory University School of Medicine during the mid-twentieth century.

---

[4] Ibid.

February 13, 1942

Dr. H. W. Cox, President
Emory University, Georgia

Dear Dr. Cox:

I heard from Dr. Stead saying that Dr. Beeson, whom he wishes to bring with him as an assistant professor, full-time, will probably be available. He has some physical handicaps which will disqualify him for military service, but which will not affect his teaching or professional ability.

I would like to ask authority to proceed with negotiations with him on the basis of $4,000 a year salary.

Sincerely yours,

Russell H. Oppenheimer, M.D.
Dean

* * *

February 20, 1942

Dr. H. W. Cox, President
Emory University, Georgia

Dear Dr. Cox:

I am enclosing information concerning the preparation and work of Dr. Paul B. Beeson, whom Dr. Eugene Stead has recommended for appointment as assistant professor of medicine, full-time. The recommended salary is $4,000 per year.

Dr. Beeson, because of physical defect, is ineligible for military service. This defect, however, does not interfere with his work as a physician.

Dr. Stead is interested in having Dr. Beeson with us, not only because of his splendid training, but because of the fact that Dr. Beeson is greatly interested in infectious diseases including pneumonia. Dr. Stead feels that it is desirable that members of the department not be all interested in the same field. Dr. Stead himself is doing research work on the heart and circulatory system.

Sincerely yours,

Russell H. Oppenheimer, M.D.
Dean

September 6, 1944

Mr. G. H. Mew, Treasurer
Emory University
Emory University, Georgia

Dear Mr. Mew:

In accordance with my conversation with Dr. Oppenheimer, *Dr. Paul Beeson* is being made an Associate Professor of Medicine on September first, 1944.

This position carries with it additional responsibilities of administrative nature connected with the Department of Medicine and Grady Hospital. For these reasons we have agreed to increase Dr. Beeson's salary *to $6,500.00* per year, beginning September first, 1944.

I shall be glad to furnish you any further information concerning Dr. Beeson's duties.

Sincerely yours,

Eugene A. Stead, Jr., M.D.

* * *

September 13, 1946

Dr. Goodrich C. White, President
Emory University
Emory University, Georgia

Dear Dr. White,

Dr. Wood suggests that Dr. Beeson's appointment as Chairman of the Department of Medicine be made effective on Monday, September 16. It is felt that an announcement of the official change at the earliest possible time would be desirable.

My impression is that the official recommendation has been made by Dr. Wood, and that the announcement will come from your office. If there are other steps which should be taken in this office, please let me know.

Respectfully,

Trawick H. Stubbs, M.D.
Assistant Dean

July 12, 1950

Dr. Goodrich White
President
Emory University
Emory University, Georgia

Dear Dr. White:

I should like to recommend that Dr. Paul Beeson be appointed as Associate Dean. He would represent the clinical departments and be available at Grady Hospital for various routine matters which could be taken up during the hours when I would not be there, as well as during my absence from the city.

I should like ultimately for the Associate Dean located at Grady to be able to be in a position to handle the greater part of the administrative work as concerns Grady Hospital. However, this is not possible at the present time. The Superintendent of the hospital prefers to deal with the Dean of the Medical School, and we are proceeding in making some progress on that basis. Later, when the entire Grady-Emory relationship is clarified, it may be possible to delegate some of these duties to an Associate Dean.

The matter of Dr. Beeson's appointment has been discussed fully with the department heads and they all approve. The only reservation that we have is the question of whether Dr. Beeson should take the time from his other duties. I have discussed this with Dr. Beeson today and he is happy and even anxious to undertake it with the full understanding that the administrative load will not become too heavy. It should serve a useful purpose until such time as another suitable person can be found. This appointment will carry no additional salary.

Your action in this matter is respectfully requested. I shall be glad to discuss it with you if you so desire.

Sincerely yours,

R. Hugh Wood, M.D.
Dean

December 15, 1951

Dr. R. Hugh Wood
104 Physiology Building
Emory University, Georgia

Dear Dr. Wood:

We have already discussed the matter of my leaving Emory to accept the chairmanship of the Department of Medicine in Yale Medical School. This letter is simply a formal statement of my intention to make the change. The administrative officers at Yale have suggested that I begin work there on April 1, but that I go on salary there as of March 1. This would make up for some of the time which will have been lost in my trips to New Haven while still a member of the Emory Medical School. I should like to suggest, therefore, that my services here continue through most of March, but that my salary cease as of the end of February.

I shall be very sorry to leave Emory and friends here in Atlanta. I want to say in particular that I have enjoyed knowing you and working with you.

Sincerely yours,

Paul B. Beeson, M.D.

January 8, 1952

Dr. Paul B. Beeson
Grady Memorial Hospital

Dear Paul:

I feel depressed on turning to the dictaphone to acknowledge your letter of December 15, which was a formal statement of your intention to accept the chairmanship of the department of medicine at Yale Medical School. Your achievements here have been of such a superb nature and we have so long looked to you as the captain of the medical team and relied on your sound judgment in the planning for the entire school that one doesn't readily adjust to getting along without this tremendous asset.

I simply want to record here what I have told you in person. Everyone from the President to the last non-faculty employee deeply regrets your leaving. Also, I hasten to record my sincere wish that you will be most happy in your new assignment and that you will be able to go about your work without some of the annoyances, interruptions, and frustrations which you have encountered here. I congratulate you and feel that Yale is to be congratulated even more.

I shall forward your resignation through the regular channels in formal fashion, and I agree with your statement that your salary will continue here through the month of February and that you will remain here until approximately April 1.

I close with deep regret at your leaving and congratulations on your new appointment and with every good wish for the continued success which you so richly deserve.

Sincerely yours,

R. Hugh Wood, M.D.
Dean

* * *

January 7, 1953

Doctor Paul Beeson, Chairman
Department of Medicine
Yale University School of Medicine
New Haven, Connecticut

Dear Paul:

Plans for the Diagnostic Clinic have been slow, but have progressed fairly well. I thought you might be interested in reading the attached letter and statement which was mailed to members of the faculty prior to a discussion in Sunday's Journal.

With kindest regards to you, Barbara, and the children.

Sincerely,

R. Hugh Wood, M.D.
Dean

December 21, 1953

Dr. Paul Beeson
Department of Medicine
Yale University School of Medicine
New Haven, Conn.

Dear Dr. Beeson:

Emory University has done an "about face!" About a year ago when we moved out here we bought a coffee pot, coffee, etc. with some very special money and with the approval and blessings of the controller's office, not only did the Dean's office have coffee, but provisions were made for the departments of medicine, obstetrics, pediatrics, and others. This week our private source of money gave out, and we were told that it might be charged to the medical school budget. I believe that this is the first such charge to the University, but as Mr. Bessent said, "It's coming, just as electric fans and air conditioning came, and we may as well face it."

Things have moved along fairly rapidly in the Medical School since you left, but needless to say we miss you terribly. I have enjoyed being on the campus since it is close to my home, but Grady is still "home." The Glenn Building is perfectly lovely and has served a wonderful purpose in pulling medical school personnel together. The laboratories are not yet completed, so there is little research going on there. Mrs. Howard Candler furnished the student lounge, and it is magnificent.

You may have heard that Dr. Richardson was considering a position as director of research at Squibb. However, he has decided to stay at Emory.

You know that Dr. Harry Walker died in October. He continued to lecture to his classes until a week before he died. My mother had a coronary occlusion in November and lived only eight hours afterward. She had pulled through a long illness this summer with complications from ruptured appendix and diabetes, and had been doing fine.

Please give our regards to Barbara and all the boys, to Betty, Elizabeth, and the rest of the Emory family at Yale. Hal joins me in cordial wishes for a happy Christmas season.

Sincerely,

Mrs. Hal Drake
Administrative Assistant

I recall a minor flap that was precipitated because Dr. Beeson became annoyed that there was no approved money available for the purchase of a coffee pot. Paul pointed out the educational value of a coffee pot that attracted a group of debating faculty members. The letter reproduced above from Mrs. Drake to Beeson indicates that Beeson won his argument. The letter also indicates when Dean Wood moved his major office from Grady to the Ernest Woodruff Memorial Research building on the Emory campus.

August 18, 1954

Dear Doctor Beeson:

We hear that you have been in the hands of the surgeons recently and hope that you are improving daily. If your hospital is as hot as Atlanta, I feel sure that you have been in an air-conditioned room. This has been a record breaker here; temperature was 102 Monday. I do not know how we would have survived in the Glenn Building and the Woodruff Building without some relief.

You will be interested to know that the summer vacation for juniors and seniors has been extended to September 1, and the sophomores return on September 21. The extra month to get ready has certainly been welcome. You probably know that the Department of Pathology has moved to the campus and that Dr. Hausman, who worked with Dr. Sheldon, is now the Grady Hospital pathologist. The Department of Bacteriology will move the first of September to the fifth floor of the Woodruff Building, which is being completed. They will share the floor with Pathology.

The big news at Emory is the Centennial and all the history which is being dug up about the School of Medicine. I don't believe there has ever been a year when money wasn't the most important thing in the records. Some of the notes read as follows:

1866 – "Dr. Hill moved that the horse which was turned over to the dean in payment of a note given to the faculty for tuition be sold by him and the proceeds paid upon the debt of Hunnicutt and Taylor. Several months later the dean reported that the horse had taken sick about the time he was directed to sell him but that he was now getting better."

1867 – "The amount of sale of horse after expenses was $35."

1869 – "The faculty had another horse to sell. The commission for selling the horse was $4.37."

1943 – "The Department of Internal Medicine was re-organized and has been fortunate in having the services of Dr. Eugene Stead and Dr. Paul Beeson, both full-time."

You probably know that Dr. Oppenheimer has resigned, actually voluntary retirement, as of the end of this month. The Conference Room on the first floor has been beautifully furnished by him with postgraduate funds with theatre seats, mahogany tables, and gold blackout draperies. We have a marvelous photograph to hang when he leaves, and the room will be known as the "Oppenheimer Room." We shall miss him more than anyone who has ever been here. Dr. Paul Teplis is taking over his Battle Hill Haven job, but the postgraduate director's place has not been filled.

Hal joins me in best wishes to you, Barbara, and the children.

Sincerely,

Mrs. Hal Drake
Administrative Assistant

The Campus Development Committee

No new facilities were added to Emory University School of Medicine from 1946 to 1952. This was a period of important planning. Dr. Beeson was a member of the Campus Development Committee that developed the plans for the creation of the Emory Clinic. This important committee, composed of all of the department chairmen of the School of Medicine, met frequently from 1948 until the plans for the Emory Clinic were completed. The final plans for the clinic were sent to President Goodrich White in October 1952, only a few months after Dr. Beeson had assumed his position at Yale, and the plans were approved in 1953. The uninterrupted presentation of the details of the genesis and evolution of the Emory University Clinic is told in Chapter 4 of this book. Such an account of the story seems appropriate because it actually began in 1937.

The Hughes Spalding Pavilion
of Grady Memorial Hospital

The Hughes Spalding Pavilion of Grady Memorial Hospital was dedicated in 1952. The highly respected Grace Towns Hamilton had pointed out in 1947 that many private Negro patients had no place to go because they had sufficient resources to make them ineligible for admission to Grady Hospital.

The Hughes Spalding Pavilion was built to meet the needs of such patients. The 130-bed hospital was not utilized by the medical service at Grady, but Dr. Asa Yancey, chief of surgery there, developed an accredited program for surgical residents who rotated through the surgical service at Hughes Spalding Hospital.

When hospital desegregation became the law of the land the original purpose of the hospital was no longer operative. Affluent black patients could go to any of the Atlanta hospitals, so the Hughes Spalding Pavilion had fewer and fewer patients. By 1988 the Hughes Spalding Hospital was considered to be an integral part of Grady Memorial Hospital, and it became the pediatric "wing" of Grady Hospital in 1990–1992.

Emory's Next Move

Having lost Beeson to Yale, Dean Wood appointed a search committee to find a replacement. Dr. Wood served as the interim chairman of the Department of Medicine. In due time Dr. Eugene Ferris of the University of Cincinnati, another Soma Weiss-trained physician, was selected. His biography is included in the next chapter.

Acknowledgments

General References

Hollingsworth, W. *Taking Care: The Legacy of Soma Weiss, Eugene Stead, and Paul Beeson.* Chapel Hill, N.C.: Professional Press, 1994. Distributed by Medical Education and Research FDN, P.O. Box 81344, San Diego, CA 92138. © Dr. J. W. Hollingsworth, 1994.

This excellent book served, along with material found in the Dean's office, as the source of the information used to write the biography of Dr. Paul Beeson. The quotation on page 127 was used with permission of the author, who holds the copyright.

Kaufman, Sharon R. *The Healer's Tale: Transforming Medicine and Culture.* Madison: University of Wisconsin Press, 1993.

The long passage attributed to Dr. Paul Beeson himself is from this book. It was used with the permission of the University of Wisconsin Press and the author.

The letters reproduced in this part of the book came from Emory sources located in the Dean's office of Emory University.

The Help of Others

I wish to thank Dr. Paul B. Beeson, Dr. Joseph E. Hardison, Dr. Charles R. Hatcher Jr., Dr. Gary S. Hauk, Dr. William Hollingsworth, Dr. R. Bruce Logue, Mr. J. W. Pinkston Jr., Dr. Thomas F. Sellers Jr., Dr. Mark E. Silverman, Dr. Eugene A. Stead Jr., and Dr. Judson C. Ward Jr. for their review of Chapter 3.

Figure 3-1

Dr. Paul Beeson at his desk in 1950. He was Chairman of the Department of Medicine from 1946 until 1952. Dr. Beeson wrote on the back of the photograph, "this was quite an office in the basement of the old Grady Memorial Hospital (the Emory Division of Grady Memorial Hospital). Anytime it rained the place flooded and the rug all but floated out the door!"

Figure 3-2
Grady Memorial Hospital, Department of Medicine, 1947–48

Row 1: Ambrister, Hughes, Bondy, Beeson, James, Slade, Nichols, Geiser
Row 2: Gambrell, Grant, Patterson, Heyman, Jennings, W. H. Dean
Row 3: Butler, Hilsman, Moseley, Codington, Callaway, Kaufmann, Fitzhugh, Wilson
Row 4: Estes, McWhorter, Turner, Johnson, Dennison

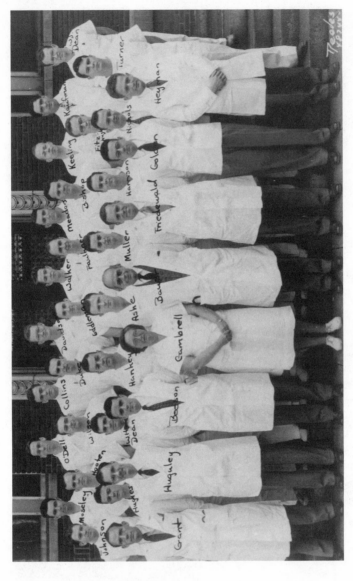

Figure 3-3
Grady Memorial Hospital, Department of Medicine, 1948–49
Row 1:   Grant, Huguley, Beeson, Gambrell, Bauer, Friedewald, Golden, Heyman
Row 2:   Hughes, W. H. Dean, Hankey, Ashe, Muller, Harrison, Nichols, Turner
Row 3:   Johnson, Hooten, Wilson, Duke, Eddleman, Faulkner, Bishop, Fitzhugh
Row 4:   Moseley, O'Dell, Collins, Davidson, Walker, Meadors, Keeling, Kaufmann, W. J. Dean

Figure 3-4
Grady Memorial Hospital, Department of Medicine, 1949–50
Row 1: Sessions, L. Felder, Huie, Dean, Sarrell, Logue, Reynolds, Hollis
Row 2: Heyman, Ginder, Warren, Friedewald, Doyle, Beeson, Bondy
Row 3: Grant, Estes, Mankikn, Moseley, Campbell, Mullen, King, Dees
Row 4: Hughes, Wilson, Crutcher, Jones, Coberly, Bishopie
Row 5: B. Felder, Sikes, McWhorter, DuBose, Milam, Alexander, Barnes

Figure 3-5
Grady Memorial Hospital, Department of Medicine, 1950–51

Row 1: Bondy, Doyle, Warren Beeson, Patterson, Merrill, Heyman

Row 2: Poole, Hodgins, Inman, Brown, Murdaugh, Johnston, Huie

Row 3: Whatley, Sarrell, Hook, Bennett, White, Milam, Hankey

Row 4: Donovan, Mitchell, Duke, Huff, Russell, Fitzhugh

Row 5: McGrath, Hallman, Mitchell, Vogel, Evans

Figure 3-6
Grady Memorial Hospital, Department of Medicine, 1951–52

Row 1: Bloom, Heyman, Oppenheimer, Bondy, Merrill, Beeson, Patterson, Warren, Felder
Row 2: Johnston, Evans, Melton, Bennett, Huie, Tokuyama, Walker, White
Row 3: Wall, Johnson, Cooper, Coggins, Dean, Inman
Row 4: Battey, Guze, Russell, Nation, Derivaux
Row 5: Freeman, Karp, Mitchell, Bauer, Fitzhugh, Suhrer, Cary
Row 6: Burgers, Dorsett, Gorsuch, Gibbs, Brewer, Murray, Ferguson

Figure 3-7
    Medical Staff 1950–51 at Lawson Veterans Hospital. Dr. Max Michael (7th from the left) was Chief of the Medical Service. Dr. Paul Beeson (5th from right) who was professor and chairman of the Department of Medicine made ward rounds at that institution once a week.

CHAPTER 4
Troubled Times 1952–1957

Paul Beeson's work at Emory ended on April 1, 1952. Dean Hugh Wood proclaimed himself the interim chairman of the Department of Medicine until a replacement for Beeson was found. The search committee interviewed several nationally known individuals and selected Dr. Eugene Ferris from among them. His chairmanship began September 1, 1952, and ended in November 1956.

The Biography of Eugene Ferris, M.D.

Eugene Ferris (see Figure 4-1) was born June 24, 1905, in McNeill, Mississippi. He earned a Bachelor of Science degree at the University of Mississippi in 1925 and graduated in 1931 from the University of Virginia School of Medicine, where he had been a Dupont fellow in biochemistry and internal medicine in 1930–31. Ferris was a medical house officer on the second medical service (Harvard) at Boston City Hospital from July 1931 to January 1933, then he became a resident on the chest service of the University of Michigan Hospital from January to July 1933. He then became an assistant resident in medicine at the Thorndike Memorial Laboratory at the Boston City Hospital and a research fellow at Harvard Medical School under Dr. Soma Weiss from September 1933 to September 1935.

Faculty Positions Prior to Coming to Emory

Ferris joined the faculty of the University of Cincinnati in 1936 as an assistant professor of medicine. He was promoted to associate professor of medicine in 1940 and to professor in 1951.

During his tenure at the University of Cincinnati, he had many clinical and administrative duties, including service as associate director of the Department of Medicine and director of Psychosomatic Teaching and the Commonwealth Fund Project. He was also on the directing staff of the Cincinnati General Hospital.

During World War II, Eugene Ferris remained a civilian and contributed significantly to the war effort. He was the responsible investigator and active director of the OSRD Project on Aviation Medicine from January 1942 until November 1945. He also served with

147

Carl Schmidt and Alvin Barach on a special committee to report on the "present status of pressure breathing."

Honors and Professional Activities

Dr. Ferris was a member of Phi Beta Kappa and of Alpha Omega Alpha. He was a member of Sigma Xi and was awarded the Horsely Prize for Research at the University of Virginia. He was listed in *Who's Who in America, American Men of Science,* and *Who's Who in Education.*

Ferris was editor-in-chief of the *Cincinnati Journal of Medicine* from 1945 to 1947 and was editor-in-chief of the *American Journal of Clinical Investigation* from 1947 to 1952. He served on the editorial boards of several journals, including the *American Journal of Clinical Investigation, Annals of Internal Medicine, American Journal of Psychosomatic Medicine,* and the *Journal of Laboratory and Clinical Medicine.*

A member of the Mental Health Study Section of the United States Public Health Service from 1946 until 1951, Ferris was also a member of the Cardiovascular Study Section of the U.S.P.S. He was consultant to the surgeon general of the United States Army from 1949 to 1953. He held many other important posts dealing with high blood pressure, mental health, and education and was an active member of numerous medical organizations.

Ferris became Professor of Medicine and Chairman of the Department of Medicine at Emory University School of Medicine on September 1, 1952, and served in that capacity until he accepted the position of medical director of the American Heart Association in February 1957. Dr. Al Bennett, who assisted him at Emory, joined him at the American Heart Association as Medical Associate for the Division of Rheumatic Fever and Congenital Heart Disease. Dr. John Peters also resigned from the Emory faculty and the Veterans Hospital in Atlanta, where he had been acting Chief of Medicine, and joined Dr. Ferris at the A.H.A. on May 20, 1957, as Assistant Medical Director of Research.

Ferris was well underway with his work at the A.H.A. when, in September 1957, he died suddenly at his desk as the result of an acute coronary event.

Rome Betts presented the following memorial tribute to Eugene Ferris at a meeting of the Executive Committee of the American Heart Association in New York City on October 5, 1957.

> Although Dr. Ferris has been with us only since last February 1st, his accomplishments in that all-too-brief time and the firm groundwork that he has laid will make it possible for us to continue surely along the path that has been indicated. Dr. Ferris died at his desk of a heart attack, while working with all his energy, experience, and skill toward the conquest of the very disease

that struck him down. This tragic irony makes all the more emphatic the urgency and seriousness of our task.

Dr. Ferris' achievements in the field of scientific research, medical education and practice have been well and widely known. Before joining our national staff he was Professor of Medicine and Chairman of the Department of Medicine at Emory University School of Medicine, Atlanta, Georgia. He had also served as a Vice President of the American Heart Association, Chairman of the Medical Advisory Board of the Council for High Blood Pressure Research, and as a member of the Executive Committee of the Scientific Council.

We mourn the loss of a most valued leader, friend and co-worker in the heart cause.[1]

Publications of Dr. Eugene Ferris

Ferris wrote over seventy scientific papers, many of them with Soma Weiss. Many of the papers dealt with the cardiovascular system and psychosomatic medicine.

Developments in the Department of Medicine

Eugene Ferris trained with Soma Weiss before Stead and Beeson. So the first three full-time chairmen of the Department of Medicine carried with them a great deal of the remarkable Soma Weiss. Remember, too, that Soma Weiss visited Ferris at the University of Cincinnati when Stead was chief resident in medicine there, beginning the Weiss-Stead connection.

Ferris brought Dr. Al Brust with him to Emory. Brust was to play a major role in the reorganization of the Department of Medicine. Ferris also recruited Dr. Noble Fowler in cardiology, who was to direct the famous Stead-Warren cardiac laboratory, then located in the Steiner building in the Grady Memorial Hospital area. Ferris recruited Dr. Charles LeMaistre in infectious diseases. Dr. Walter Bloom remained in the department when Beeson left for Yale. Dr. Al Heyman also remained on the staff but later joined Stead at Duke. All of these were stationed at Grady Memorial Hospital. Drs. Arthur Merrill Sr. and David James likewise continued to work in the Department of Medicine at Grady, although they were in private practice in Atlanta. Dr. Ferris appointed Dr. Al Bennett to assist him in student affairs.

Dr. Max Michael remained as chief of medicine at Lawson's Veterans Hospital. He had created a national reputation for his work there and was offered the position of chief of medicine at Maimonides Hospital in New

---

[1] The text of Rome Betts's tribute to Eugene Ferris was provided by the American Heart Association.

York in 1954. Ferris selected Dr. John Peters, one of his new appointees, as the interim chief of medicine at the Veterans Administration Hospital. Later, in 1955, he appointed Dr. Benjamin Gendel chief of medicine. The other members of the medical staff at the Veterans Hospital included Drs. James Crutcher and Walter Cargill.

The faculty located at Emory University Hospital were in the Private Diagnostic Clinic, which later joined two other groups of physicians to form the Emory University Clinic. They were R. Bruce Logue and myself in cardiology, Spalding Schroder in gastroenterology, Bernard Hallman in endocrinology, and Henry Jennings in general medicine. Charles Huguley in hematology was assigned to the Winship Clinic.

Junior medical students allocated to medicine were assigned to Emory University Hospital, where Ferris appointed me to be in charge of this student rotation. This duty was given to others when I was recalled to serve in the armed forces in 1954.

Some of the Grady Memorial Hospital faculty members and house staff are shown in Figures 4-2 through 4-6. The faculty members and house staff located at Lawson Veterans Hospital are shown in Figure 4-7.

Much of Ferris's four and one-half years as chairman of the Department of Medicine were consumed with the numerous meetings that dealt with the creation of the Emory University Clinic. As will be seen in the discussion that follows, Ferris initially supported and helped develop the Emory University Clinic. As time passed, he became increasingly unhappy with the policy of the university and the fledgling clinic (see discussion on page 161). This culminated in an administrative arrangement that would not work, so in November 1956, he was asked to give up the chairmanship of the Department of Medicine. He of course could have remained as a tenured professor but decided instead to accept the excellent position at the American Heart Association, which at that time had its headquarters in New York.

Dr. John Howard, chairman of the Department of Surgery, and Dr. William Caton, chairman of the Department of Obstetrics and Gynecology, were not reappointed as chairmen because they did not agree with the university and clinic policy and had strongly supported Ferris's point of view (see discussion on page 161).

The Department of Medicine was in a disorganized state following this upheaval. Dr. Al Bennett accompanied Dr. Ferris to the American Heart Association headquarters in New York. Dr. Walter Bloom resigned and became director of medical education at Piedmont Hospital in Atlanta. He later joined the faculty at Georgia Tech as vice president of biophysics. Dr. Brust also resigned. Dr. John Peters remained for a short while and then joined Ferris at the American Heart Association headquarters in New York. Dr. Noble Fowler remained in the department until the summer of 1957 when he became chief of medicine at the Veterans Administration Hospital in Cincinnati and, still later, director of the Division of Cardiology at the University of Cincinnati. Dr. Charles LeMaistre, an expert in infectious diseases, remained in the department until August 1959. He continued to be director of the Division of Infectious Diseases and also became the first chairman of the Department of Preventive Medicine at Emory University School of Medicine. He later accepted a position as professor of medicine at Southwestern University and director of the Woodlawn Hospital in Dallas. Still later he became chancellor of the Medical Division of the University of Texas and then medical director of the famous M. D. Anderson Hospital in Houston. Drs. Benjamin Gendel and James Crutcher remained on the faculty at the Veterans Hospital. Logue, Dorney, Schroder, Huguley, Hallman, Jennings, and I remained on the faculty at Emory University Hospital and Clinic.

Follow-up On a Few Grady House Officers and Faculty Members

Some years later the following Grady house officers and fellows became faculty members in the Department of Medicine at Emory: Drs. Herbert Karp, James Lea, Sam Poole, Charles Corley, Paul Seavey, Grigg Churchwell, Thomas Sellers, John Galambos, Elbert Tuttle Jr., and Robert Franch.

Dr. Ed Hook, who had been the chief resident in medicine at Grady Memorial Hospital, later became professor and chairman of the Department of Medicine at the University of Virginia, and Dr. Waddell Barnes became the first chairman of the Department of Medicine at the new Mercer School of Medicine in Macon, Georgia. After serving as Chief of Medicine at Maimonides Hospital in New York, Dr. Max Michael became professor of medicine at the University of Florida School of Medicine and coordinated the school's activity in Jacksonville, Florida. Dr. Linton Bishop later became a major force in the development of Emory-owned Crawford W. Long Hospital and a member of the board of trustees of Emory University.

New Buildings

The Glenn Building at Grady

The Glenn Memorial Building was completed and turned over to the Fulton-DeKalb Hospital Authority on July 21, 1953 (see Figure 4-8). Dr.

Wadley Glenn and Mr. Wilbur Glenn financed the five-story structure, which was named for their father, Mr. Thomas K. Glenn, a former member of the board of trustees of Emory University and the first chairman of the Fulton-DeKalb Hospital Authority. The new building was located at 69 Butler Street, across the street from the new Grady Memorial Hospital. Intended for use by the faculty of Emory University School of Medicine, the building housed a branch of the Emory Medical School Library on the first floor, along with the Oppenheimer classroom and the administrative offices of the dean of the School of Medicine. The basement housed the student lounge, the furniture for which was given by Mrs. Howard Candler. Some years later the lounge was converted into an additional, greatly needed classroom. The second floor was occupied by the Department of Medicine. The administrative offices of the chairman of the Department of Medicine were located there, along with a classroom and office and research space for several members of the department. This pattern was duplicated on the third floor for the Department of Surgery. The Departments of Pediatrics and Gynecology and Obstetrics shared the fourth floor of the building. The fifth floor, or penthouse, was used for animal research, especially by the Departments of Surgery and Medicine.

This structure was substantial evidence that facilities would be provided for the Emory faculty members who were primarily located in the Grady area. The building was owned by Grady but was to be used by Emory faculty. The timing of the construction was excellent because, at that time, two important buildings were being constructed on the Emory campus in keeping with the 1946 plan to develop the medical school on the Emory campus.

The Ernest Woodruff Memorial Research Building on the Emory Campus

The Ernest Woodruff Memorial Research Building was completed in 1954 (see Figure 4-9). Given to the university by the Woodruff Foundation, this building was located adjacent to, and was later connected to, Emory University Hospital. This important five-story building provided space for the dean's offices, classrooms, the A. W. Calhoun medical library, medical illustrations, and research space for the Departments of Pharmacology, Biochemistry, Microbiology, Pathology, Psychiatry, Surgery, and Medicine. A new wing and two additional floors were added later so that the building became seven-stories high. Still later, another "wing" was added to the building. This development permitted a shift of personnel so that the Departments of Anatomy and Physiology could each occupy entire, separate buildings.

The Ernest Woodruff Memorial Research Building provided the office space for the dean of the School of Medicine who would, from that time on, spend most of his time on the Emory campus (see letter on page 136). The dean retained his office space in the new Glenn Memorial Building at Grady and used it for the administrative meetings involving the chiefs of service at Grady Hospital.

The Emory University Clinic Building on the Emory Campus

The first stage of the Emory University Clinic building was completed in 1956 (see Figure 4-10A). Robert W. Woodruff financed the $1,000,000 cost of the building. The first half of the building looked awkward, so Woodruff insisted that the remaining part of the building should be added, although, in the beginning, it was only a shell (see Figure 4-10B). The inside of the southern portion of the building was not completed until later. The five-story building, located on Clifton Road across the street from Emory University Hospital, was connected to the hospital by a tunnel. The photograph shown in Figure 4-11 shows three of the people who worked together to develop the Emory University Clinic: Robert W. Woodruff, Dr. Elliott Scarborough Jr., and Dean Hugh Wood. Seventeen physicians occupied the building in 1956, including five members of the Department of Medicine. Other additions to the original central building were destined to be built, as were many other Emory University clinic buildings. This building was confirmation that a major multidisciplinary private clinic was to be developed on the Emory campus.

Changes at the Atlanta Veterans Hospital

The complex story describing the evolution of the relationship of Lawson General Hospital, Lawson Veterans Hospital, "old 48" Veterans Hospital, the new Veterans Hospital, and Emory University School of Medicine is discussed on page 125.

Lawson's Veterans Administration Hospital was housed in the old deactivated Lawson Army Hospital in Chamblee, Georgia, until 1952. At that time the patients were moved to the "old 48" Hospital on Peachtree Road near Oglethorpe University (see Figure 4-12). The hospital had previously been designated as a dean's committee hospital and had become closely affiliated with the School of Medicine. Dr. Ferris, as chairman of the Department of Medicine, had the authority to appoint faculty and house staff at the Atlanta Veterans Administration Hospital. The Emory Hospital-Veterans Hospital program for medical house officers was developed by Dr. Max Michael in 1952, while Dr. Beeson was chairman of the Department of Medicine. Apparently the first house officers to participate in the program were those recruited for the academic year beginning in 1953. The program was usually referred to as the Emory-VA program and was the successor to separate programs at Grady Memorial Hospital, Emory University Hospital, and the Veterans Hospital. With this development there were only two house-staff programs—the Grady program and the Emory-VA program. Dr. Ferris appointed Dr. John Peters as the temporary chief of medicine at the Veterans Hospital when Max Michael resigned to take a position at Maimonides Hospital in New York. Later, in 1955, he appointed Dr. Benjamin Gendel as chief of medicine at the Veterans Hospital.

From the beginning, the Atlanta Veterans Administration Hospital has been a valuable asset to the Department of Medicine and vice versa.

The Appointment of Dr. Arthur Richardson as Dean

Dr. Arthur Richardson was appointed dean when Dr. Wood resigned in 1956.

Arthur Richardson was born in Longmont, Colorado, on August 2, 1911 (see Figure 4-13). The family moved to Hawaii, where young Arthur attended school in Honolulu and Maui.

Richardson earned an A.B. degree at Stanford University in 1932 and an M.D. degree from Stanford in 1937. After serving his internship in medicine at Stanford Hospital in 1936, he was an assistant in research in the pharmacology department at Stanford from 1933 to 1936. He served as an instructor in the Department of Pharmacology for one year and in 1938 became a National Research Council fellow at Johns Hopkins. He then returned to Stanford as an assistant professor of pharmacology, continuing his work in the Departments of Pharmacology and Medicine at Stanford from 1940 to 1941. In 1941 he moved to the University of Tennessee as associate professor of pharmacology and became chairman of the Department of Pharmacology in 1943.

He became a member of the Squibb Institute for Medical Research in charge of medical research from 1944 to 1947, and simultaneously was a consultant to the Bureau of Biological Research at Rutgers University.

Richardson became professor and chairman of the Department of Pharmacology at Emory University in 1947, remaining in that position until 1954. He was associate dean at Emory University School of Medicine from 1950 to 1952 and was director of the Division of Basic Health Sciences from 1952 to 1956. This administrative structure was devised to coordinate the contribution of the basic science departments to the School of Medicine, the School of Dentistry, and the School of Nursing. Following a four-month period as acting dean, Richardson became dean of the School of Medicine on July 1, 1956, a position he retained until 1979.

Through the years Arthur Richardson served on numerous advisory councils at the national and state level. He wrote sixty-four scientific papers and several papers dealing with the problems of medical schools and medical staffing.

Elsewhere in the nation, the deans of medical schools would come and go in about three to four years. Richardson remained dean for twenty-three years.

He received many awards for his leadership, including: the Award of Honor of the Medical Alumni Association of Emory University; presentation of a portrait to Emory University by the faculty of the School of Medicine; Commencement Address, Emory University; the Thomas Jefferson Award for service to Emory University; Certificate of Distinguished Service for Special Recognition of Services Rendered, Medical Association of Atlanta; special consultant to the development of a private medical school in Bonn, Germany; dedication of the Statue of Hippocrates for Devoted Service and Outstanding Leadership as Dean of the School of Medicine; proclamation of the State of Georgia, by Governor George Busbee; resolution of the board of trustees of the Fulton-DeKalb Hospital Authority; Commendation of the Veterans Administration Medical Center (Atlanta); and emeritus membership in the Association of American Medical Colleges. He was a consultant to the University of South Alabama and spearheaded the development of the medical school in Mobile.

A description of Arthur Richardson must include the quickness of his mind. He saw answers while everyone else was contemplating the problem. This innate ability would at times make him appear to be abrupt in his actions. He knew this, and with conscious effort learned to listen and wait until others caught up with him. Although he spoke clearly and somewhat more loudly than most people, he was basically a gentle man who liked wood carving and doodling. He could have been a sculptor, and his doodles were so interesting that some of them were published.

His administrative style was varied and ranged from loose to strict. His Friday noon meeting with the chiefs of service at Grady had no agenda. The chiefs met with him at lunch and discussed any problems that seemed worthy of discussion. Accordingly, the subjects included new educational activities, improvement of services, and the search for space and money. Despite the lack of orderliness, the meetings were productive and created a sense of comradeship.

Richardson chaired the Monday afternoon meeting of the Advisory Faculty Council, which was made up of all department chairmen and assistant and associate deans. The initial meetings, after Richardson became dean, were held in the dean's conference room next to his office in the Ernest Woodruff Memorial Research Building. Later, as the size of the group grew, the meeting was held in a room down the hall. Still later, when the new Robert W. Woodruff Health Sciences Center Building was completed, the dean's meeting was held in an elegant conference room in that facility. Dr. Evangeline Papageorge (see Figure 4-14), the associate dean in charge of students, was always there. She had a magnificent stabilizing influence on the entire School of Medicine. The students adored her, and she adored them. Later, the medical school alumni created the Evangeline Papageorge Teaching Award in her honor. Some years later, Mike Aycock, an excellent member of the support staff and an associate dean, arranged the agenda for the Advisory Faculty Council meeting of the department chairs. The discussions included all matters germane to the running of the medical school. Richardson ran these meetings in an organized manner, in that respect making them different from the more informal chiefs of service meetings at Grady.

Richardson believed in making an appointment and allowing the new appointee free rein for development. He believed that a new appointee had to earn his or her position of leadership.

During most of his twenty-three years as dean, the School of Medicine progressed in a smooth and orderly manner. The chairmen respected him. Once, when he considered becoming dean at the University of South Alabama School of Medicine, the chairmen went in a group to his office and insisted he remain at Emory. Still, there were times when he and a chairman or two disagreed. With rare exceptions, these disagreements were transient, and the disagreements were settled because he and the arguing chairmen loved Emory.

Richardson had the unpleasant task of relieving three department chairmen of their positions soon after he was appointed dean in 1956 (see below, page 164). Following this the school grew in size and quality. He deserves much credit, because the School of Medicine was very different in 1979, at the end of his deanship, than when he became dean.

After Arthur retired from the deanship, he and his wife, Marion, lived in their Japanese-type home for a few years and then moved to Linbrook retirement home. He died in Piedmont Hospital on January 25, 1993, following a myocardial infarction.

He will be remembered as a survivor who led Emory University School of Medicine through some turbulent years to a period of stability and growth. He became the envy of his peers.

Postgraduate Course

Dean Richardson's influence extended to postgraduate education. Dr. Bruce Logue and I organized a postgraduate course on electrocardiography in 1954 and invited Dr. Robert Grant to participate (see Figures 4-15 A, B, and C). Dr. Grant had developed the vector method of interpreting electrocardiograms while at Emory. The course was given in a classroom of the Ernest Woodruff Memorial Research Building.

When Dr. Arthur Richardson became dean in 1956, he appointed me director of postgraduate education in the School of Medicine. (See discussion on page 233). Plans were made for the presentation of several courses for the year 1957.

The Genesis and Evolution of the Emory University Clinic

Dr. Ferris arrived at the School of Medicine when great changes were under way. The 1946 planning report was set in concrete as university policy, and the planning for the development of the Emory University Clinic by the Campus Development Committee was moving forward. Ferris was swept up in a rapidly moving sequence of administrative changes, and this undoubtedly influenced his actions. Therefore, it seems appropriate to discuss the genesis and evolution of the Emory University Clinic.

The 1946 planning report, written and approved during Eugene Stead's last year as chairman of the Department of Medicine and dean of the School of Medicine (see page 90), stated that the future development of the School of Medicine would be on the Emory campus. This development would include a private clinic, which would be used to support the faculty of the school and provide the patients for clinical teaching. The report also recommended that the facilities at Grady Memorial Hospital be used for clinical teaching, and that the faculty assigned there be supported. When Dr. Ferris arrived at Emory, these developments were moving forward at a rapid pace.

The Coalescence of Three Groups of Faculty Members to Form the Emory University Clinic

The Robert Winship Memorial Clinic

The Robert Winship Memorial Clinic was organized within Emory University Hospital in 1937 (see Chapter 1). The purpose of the clinic was to diagnose, treat, and engage in the research of neoplastic diseases.

Dr. Elliott Scarborough Jr. became the first director of the clinic, and Robert Woodruff was its benefactor. Originally, the Robert Winship Memorial Clinic was only loosely related to the Emory School of Medicine. Dr. Scarborough, a wise man, realized what had happened to the Steiner Clinic at Grady and began to develop a strong relationship with
the medical school. The clinic was eventually composed of full-time faculty members, including surgeons, hematologists, oncologists, and radiologists.

Physicians Whose Offices Were in Emory University Hospital

Prior to 1953 Emory University Hospital was an "open" hospital, permitting community physicians as well as Emory faculty members to admit patients. Some of the partially-salaried faculty members, mostly surgeons, rented office space in the hospital. They used the facilities of the hospital and agreed to teach as directed by the chairman of the Department of Surgery and the dean of the School of Medicine. Each individual in this group, it seems, developed his own individual relationship with the medical school.

The Private Diagnostic Clinic

The Private Diagnostic Clinic was organized in 1948, when members of the Department of Medicine asked President Goodrich White for permission to organize a clinic within Emory University Hospital devoted to medical school teaching, excellent patient care, and research. The group included Dean Hugh Wood, Dr. Paul Beeson, Dr. Bruce Logue, and Dr. Spalding Schroder. Dr. Charles Huguley was actually assigned to the Winship Clinic but was closely related to the group in the Private Diagnostic Clinic. The plan was accepted by the President, and space was allocated for its development on the first floor of the Lucy Elizabeth Pavilion of the hospital. Business matters were managed by Mrs. Lois Stephenson, who was already in place as the business manager of the Winship Clinic.

The Joining of the Three Groups

It became increasingly evident that it would be more efficient if the three groups described above worked in the same system. Accordingly, the Campus Development Committee began to hold hearings in 1948. The committee was composed of Dean Hugh Wood; Dr. Paul Beeson, professor and chairman of the Department of Medicine; Dr. Dan Elkin, professor and chairman of the Department of Surgery; Dr. William Friedewald, associate professor of medicine and professor and chairman of the Department of Microbiology; Dr. James Warren, professor of medicine and professor and chairman of the Department of Physiology; Dr. Walter Sheldon, professor and chairman of the Department of Pathology; Dr. Heinz Weens, professor and chairman of the Department of Radiology; Dr. Arthur Richardson, professor and chairman of the Department of Pharmacology; Dr. Harlow Ades, professor and chairman of the Department of Anatomy; Dr. Carl Whitaker, professor and chairman of the Department of Psychiatry; Mr. Robert Mizell, director of development; Mr. Robert Whitaker, who represented the university administration; and Dr. Elliott Scarborough Jr., director of the Robert Winship Memorial Clinic. The hearings were held in the offices of Scarborough, and Friedewald was the presiding officer.

After several meetings, the committee reaffirmed the 1946 planning report, and, as Dr. J. D. Martin Jr. later reported it,

> . . . Mr. Robert C. Mizell, director of development, addressed the group. Mr. Mizell pointed out that many people in this area had been talking for several years about a great medical development in Atlanta. He stated that the community expected the university to take the leadership, but that in his opinion the responsibility for development of leadership must be assumed by the people comprising the faculty of the School of Medicine. He reported that it was possible for the university to secure sufficient financial support to make possible a development of an integrated full-service medical center. He challenged the physicians to have the vision and to pay the price of responsibility and leadership to create a practical plan for such an enterprise.[2]

The published report that followed caused considerable discussion in and out of the school. During this period the school had an average annual deficit of $250,000. Each year Robert Woodruff, the Whitehead Foundation, and others would give them financial support to eliminate the debt. This annual financial deficit stimulated the development of a clinic, such as the Duke Private Diagnostic Clinic, that would support excellent faculty members in the School of Medicine. Martin continues:

> Therefore, discussions of the faculty components of various groups of teacher-practitioners around the hospital often centered on economic considerations such as fair income to the teachers without excessive diminution of income in relationship to that available in private practice and at the same time a fair reimbursement to the university for use of facilities. It was recognized that individual faculty members were unlikely to be capable of effectively meeting in a superior fashion all three major activities of the medical school: teaching, research, and patient care. It was emphasized that each member would be a member of a coordinated team organized to carry out all of these functions

---

[2] J. D. Martin Jr., *The History of Surgery at Emory University School of Medicine* (Fulton, MO: Ovid Bell Press, 1979), 215.

effectively. It was stressed that the activities of this group must be carried on in the existing framework of various departments, under the direction of their departmental chairmen, and responsible ultimately to the board of trustees of the university. Thus, the following considerations governed most of the planning:

• Individuals appointed must be needed to achieve balance.
• They must be professionally competent teachers with a primary commitment to medical education.
• They must be willing to abide by the administrative policy of the medical school.
• Their patients shall be a part of the teaching and investigative program of the medical school.
• Some portion of the income received should be submitted to the university for use in the medical school.

In these discussions it was stressed that the university should not be directly in the business of providing patient care, but it was recognized that a legitimate purpose of the School of Medicine is improvement in health and welfare of the people. The school could accomplish this best by providing an appropriate faculty and facilities with adequate financial resources. It was stressed that the hospital's primary purpose is to further the educational program of the School of Medicine. Formation of a clinic was considered essential to create new sources of support for the enlarged faculty necessary to meet the needs for teaching and to participate and keep abreast of advances in medical education. Organization of such a clinic must be within the existing framework of organization in the university.[3]

In October 1952 Hugh Wood, Eugene Ferris, and Dan Elkin petitioned President White for permission to organize the Emory University Clinic. President White agreed. The final plan, signed by the same individuals, was presented to President White on January 1, 1953.

There were eighteen founding partners of the Emory Clinic. They were:

Drs. Osler A. Abbott (surgery), Robert L. Brown (surgery), Frederick W. Cooper Jr. (surgery), Daniel C. Elkin (surgery), Eugene B. Ferris (medicine), Bernard L. Hallman (medicine), Albert Heyman (medicine), William A. Hopkins (surgery), Charles M. Huguley Jr. (medicine), J. Willis Hurst (medicine), Henry S. Jennings Jr. (medicine), Robert P. Kelly (surgery), R. Bruce Logue (medicine), William C. McGarity (surgery), J. Elliott Scarborough Jr. (surgery), J. Spalding Schroder (medicine), Samuel A. Wilkins Jr. (surgery), and R. Hugh Wood (dean of the medical school).[4]

---

[3] Ibid., 215–16.
[4] Ibid., 223.

The Turmoil Associated with the Early Development of the Emory University Clinic

The first medical director of the Emory University Clinic was Dean Hugh Wood, and he very early faced controversy. Several faculty members left the school. Others remained but did not immediately sign the clinic partnership agreement, and some of the original partners resigned within a few months. The exact reason for their departure is not known, but many physicians in the 1950s did not like clinics of any type; individualism dominated the profession.

Emory University Hospital became a "closed hospital" in 1953. This represented a giant step toward making Emory University Hospital a real University Hospital. The move was necessary because the plan for an increasing number of full-time faculty members who would be members of the Emory University Clinic called for an increase in access to beds in Emory University Hospital. A few volunteer faculty members on the hospital staff were permitted to continue to admit patients, but the majority of community physicians were to take their patients elsewhere. At that time, there was no other hospital in the Decatur area, and this move, although necessary, created a reservoir of ill feeling in the physicians who were inconvenienced. This, of course, hastened the day when an excellent hospital and other medical facilities would be built in DeKalb County.

In 1956, the members of the Clinic moved into the new Emory University Clinic building located across the street from Emory University Hospital.

In 1956, Wood resigned as dean of the School of Medicine and director of the clinic because of poor health. Arthur Richardson became dean, and Elliott Scarborough became director of the Emory University Clinic. Eugene Ferris became increasingly vocal about his disagreement with the policies of the university and the clinic. *He wanted to control the medical section of the clinic at a time when it was against the law for an institution to engage in the corporate practice of medicine.* Because of this, his day-to-day working relationship with Dean Richardson and other faculty members deteriorated. Ferris was relieved of his chairmanship in 1956 but remained on the faculty until resigning to become medical director of the American Heart Association on February 1, 1957. Dr. John Howard, chairman of the Department of Surgery and Dr. William Caton, chairman of the Department of Obstetrics and Gynecology, were sympathetic with the rebellion of Dr. Ferris, so they were relieved of their positions as chairmen of their respective departments. Dr. Walter Bloom was also seriously concerned about the events and resigned.

Needless to say, these events caused considerable turmoil within and without the School of Medicine. President White allegedly said, "Emory does not need a football team to create controversy; we have a School of Medicine." The newspapers were filled with detailed discussions about the matter. Students, members of the house staff, and members of the faculty of the entire School of Medicine were greatly concerned and disturbed.

Details of the Medical School Ruckus of 1956

The word ruckus was used to describe the ugly debate that erupted in 1956. In order to understand the ruckus, it is important to recall the 1946 planning report (see page 90), to remember that the corporate practice of medicine was unacceptable at that time, and to realize that Grady Hospital and Emory University School of Medicine were both poverty-stricken. The following article appeared anonymously in the March 1957 issue of the *Emory Alumnus*. It was undoubtedly written by several top Emory officials.

> Wherever education for the medical profession has been attempted or carried on, its history usually has been a series of explosions interspersed with longer or shorter periods of comparative peace. That certainly has been the pattern of medical education in Atlanta since its formal beginnings more than a century ago. And it has been the case at Emory since 1915, when the University, then one year old, entered the field of medical education.
>
> Emory's medical school has just experienced—and emerged from, in better health than ever—such a row, one of the most serious it has known. There can be no doubt that the commotion hurt the University to a degree which is indeterminable. But it is equally true that the trouble has given the faculty in medicine a unity and a oneness of purpose it had not previously known and brought the medical school into closer relationship with the rest of the University than it had been before.
>
> What the University considered a problem of internal administration but what the press labeled a controversy brought Emory publicity largely unwelcome, of course—such as it has not known in a long time. The two Atlanta daily newspapers alone carried, in a span of just over three months, nearly 50 news stories, editorials and cartoons. To a degree, news of the disturbance spread far beyond the boundaries of Georgia, especially in medical circles. Oddly, though, through the entire trial-by-newspaper the press printed only one letter-to-the-editor, it from a lady who defended Emory.
>
> For most of the period of three-plus months University officials, though inwardly burning, displayed outward and remarkable patience. As charges were voiced and published they were answered in statements to the press by Emory administrators, usually by Dr. Arthur P. Richardson, dean of the School of Medicine and the man on the hottest seat.

But finally the accusations became so strong that the University's frustrated public relations people, who had been champing at the bit, persuaded Emory officials in the last 10 days of the period to launch a counteroffensive which, to all appearances, has enlightened the public and carried the day.

As part of the counterattack Dr. Goodrich C. White, now serving his 15th and last year as Emory's president, used the strongest language he has ever uttered publicly in a speech and statement which included such words as "malicious," "unethical," "sabotage," "harassment," "malcontents," "distortion" and "sniping." His closing words were, "We do not have to submit to being pushed around, pulled and hauled now in this direction, now in that, knifed in the back, and falsely and misleadingly accused—by anybody."

A few days later the University took the dramatic step of placing a full-page advertisement in both Atlanta dailies to present to the public in full and for the first time its policies and programs for medical education. This ad was published in the newspapers of February 6. Since that time—at least until this issue of The Alumnus went to the printer on February 28—no more adverse criticism of the Emory medical school has been published.

Though several other individuals were at work who did not come out into the open but who are well known to the University, the medical school row stemmed directly from the demotion, discharge or resignation of four men, all of whom were comparative newcomers as full-time members of its clinical faculty. They were:

Dr. Eugene B. Ferris, Jr., who came to Emory in 1952 as professor of medicine and chairman of the department of medicine. At the same time Dr. Ferris was chief of the medical service at Atlanta's Grady Memorial Hospital, where most of the clinical teaching of Emory's upperclassmen in medicine is done. He spent nearly all his time at Grady and had his main office there in the Glenn Building, which is assigned to Emory. But he also was a part-time member of the Emory University Clinic and was assigned a second office in the Clinic Building on the main campus.

Dr. John M. Howard, who came to Emory in 1955 as Joseph B. Whitehead professor of surgery and chairman of the department of surgery. Dr. Howard, the only one of the four men who still remains (until August 31) on the Emory faculty, is also chief of the surgical service at Grady Hospital, where he spends most of his time. He has offices both in the downtown Glenn Building and in Emory University Hospital, and is a part-time member of the Emory Clinic.

Dr. William L. Caton, who came to Emory in 1953 as professor of obstetrics and gynecology and chairman of that department. Dr. Caton also was chief of the obstetrics-gynecology service at Grady and a part-time member of the Emory Clinic. He had his main office in the Glenn Building and was assigned another in the Clinic Building.

Dr. Walter L. Bloom, who came to Emory in 1947 but who has been a full-time clinical teacher (in the department of medicine) only since 1952, the year of Dr. Ferris' arrival. Since joining the faculty he has had titles in both the biochemistry and medicine departments his latest, associate professor of medicine and assistant professor of biochemistry—but before 1952 he did much of his work in the basic-science department of biochemistry. He had his office in the Glenn Building and, by choice, was not a member of the Emory Clinic.

The medical school blow-up fell chronologically into two phases, the first of which concerned—at least on the surface—Dr. Ferris alone. On Wednesday, October 31, Dr. Richardson, who has been dean of the school since last July 1 and was its acting dean for four months before that, informed the medical professor in a conference that he planned to recommend that Dr. Ferris be relieved of his departmental chairmanship because of his failure to cooperate in carrying out some of the school's "basic policies." The recommendation in no wise questioned Dr. Ferris' professional competence, nor did it suggest that he be dismissed as professor of medicine or that his salary be reduced.

The following day the dean went to Grady Hospital and told the other members of the department of medicine faculty of his intentions, and the day after that he so informed the Fulton-DeKalb (Counties) Hospital Authority, which has charge of operating Grady. On that day (Friday, November 2) he also made the formal recommendation to Boisfeuillet Jones '34–'37, Emory vice-president and administrator of health sciences, and to President White.

Dean Richardson, Mr. Jones and Dr. White thought that the matter of the removal of Dr. Ferris was a matter of Emory's internal administration alone, but others thought otherwise. On Sunday evening, November 4, the board of trustees of the Fulton County (Atlanta) Medical Society, having learned in some manner of the removal recommendation, met and voted to call a special meeting of the full society for Tuesday evening, November 6, which also was Election Day. The medical society trustees moved so rapidly in calling the special meeting that within four to six hours after their Sunday night session notices to members were printed, addressed and mailed in time to be postmarked 2 a.m. Monday, the 5th.

The society met on Tuesday to consider what the press called charges that Dr. Ferris was being relieved "without good reason." The *Journal of the Medical Association of Georgia* later said in an editorial, "Because of the fact that more than 200 of the society's members serve on the volunteer faculty of the medical school it was reasoned that medical school policies are a matter of special interest to the society."

The November 6 meeting was a closed one, attended by a large number of physicians, variously estimated at from 250 to 300. Fulton County Society officers later told the press that the session was "unbelievably harmonious and temperate." Among the speakers there were Dr. Ferris, Dr. Richardson, and Dr. R. Hugh Wood, whom Dr. Richardson succeeded as dean. The outcome of the meeting was that the society voted to ask the University's Health Services Board to "restudy its basic policies" in view of past "difficulties" in the administration of the medical school and the Grady Hospital medical care program.

The next day Dean Richardson issued a statement saying, "In the present instance in which question has been raised about the internal administration of the school, Emory will be glad to confer with a properly designated committee of the society in the interest of mutual information and understanding."

(Later on, in his statement of February 1, President White said, "We are perfectly willing to 're-examine' policies or to have them re-examined by competent and objective people. But such re-examination should not start with the assumption that the policies are wrong and should be radically altered.")

Two days later it was announced that Dr. Ferris would go before the Emory Health Sciences Board at its next meeting, scheduled for Tuesday, November 13. This board is a unit of the University's Board of Trustees specifically delegated responsibility for the health science functions of the University. It is headed by Trustee James D. Robinson, Jr. '25 and has as its other members Trustees W. N. Banks '03, Dr. F. Phinizy Calhoun '04M–'54H, F. M. Bird, C. H. Candler, Jr. '26 and George W. Woodruff.

The day before the Emory health board met, Hughes Spalding, chairman of the Fulton-DeKalb Hospital Authority, made an address before the Atlanta Rotary Club in which, the press quoted him as saying, he aimed to "throw oil on the waters" in the developing controversy. In his address he stated that the medical care being given at Grady under Emory's supervision "is better than at any time since I've been on the (Authority's) board." He specifically praised Drs. Ferris, Howard and Caton, as well as Dr. Richard W. Blumberg '35–'38M, acting chairman of Emory's department of pediatrics, whose name was never brought into the discussions before or afterwards.

The Health Services Board met on the 13th and heard Dr. Ferris. Two days later it met again and heard Dr. Richardson, then announced its unanimous decision: It felt "the dean's recommendation was justified" and authorized him to "bring the matter to a conclusion."

At the same time, the board pointed out that Dr. Ferris' removal from the chairmanship of the department of medicine did not affect his academic position as professor of medicine nor his salary and that it did not question his "professional competence."

Dr. Ferris' comment, when being informed of the board's action was, "I'm sorry about the decision, but I sincerely hope it works for the best interest of the medical school."

Up until that time, no one had publicly stated any of the points at issue. But when the board backed Dr. Richardson in his action to relieve the medical chairman, Dr. White listed the two "critical" points in dispute as the organization of the Emory University Clinic and the decision, made 10 years before in 1946, to "center" its medical school administration in facilities on the main University campus rather than at or near Grady Hospital. Later, after serious accusations had been made and other events had taken place, the president became more specific. He said in his February 1, statement:

"Initially the issue had to do with the question of whether Dr. Ferris (and by implication other full-time salaried members of the faculty) should control the Clinic and dictate its procedures in the private practice of medicine by its members. This could not be permitted by the University or the Clinic without violation of the legal prohibition of the corporate practice of medicine. To the corporate practice of medicine the University is definitely opposed.

"The University fully recognizes the prerogatives of a department chairman in the areas of teaching and research and in the related area of care for other than private patients. But authority over the private practice of members of the Clinic could not be given to Dr. Ferris. (He) and some of his immediate associates were unwilling to accept this policy decision and it became clear that because of his continuing attitude Dr. Ferris would have to be relieved of his chairmanship.

"Dr. Ferris and others directly concerned were so informed. Dr. Ferris appealed to our Health Services Board and was given a hearing. The recommendation of the dean was approved."

The organization in 1953 of the Emory University Clinic, which grew out of the earlier Winship Clinic for Neoplastic Diseases and Private Diagnostic Clinic, is a point of contention in Atlanta-area medical circles. Some physicians fear the Clinic is offering them "unfair competition" for private patients and raise the question of whether its members are engaging in the corporate practice of medicine. The University maintains that this is not true.

Its answer is that its medical school must have a large roster of capable teachers and that it is financially capable of employing only a limited number of them, since salaries in medicine are extremely high as compared with those in other divisions of the University. A great deal of assistance is obtained from "volunteer" faculty members: outstanding private physicians who give up part of their time, without pay, to teach medical students and at the same time care for patients at Grady and other hospitals. But even these two groups of teachers—full-time and volunteer—do not supply enough manpower for the instructional needs. The Clinic was organized to fill the gap.

It was formed as a partnership by a group of doctors, now numbering about 30 but eventually to be increased to twice that figure, who are interested in teaching while earning their livelihoods in private practice. They give at least 25 per cent of their time to the medical school. And because they are "geographically full-time" members of the faculty—by virtue of their location in the new Clinic Building on the main University campus—they are subject to the school's call at other hours. They pay for the space and facilities which Emory provides for them, and Emory makes beds in the University Hospital available for their patients.

Almost every medical school in the country has some sort of similar clinic arrangement, conceived of necessity. At its future peak of membership the Clinic will embrace fewer than 7 per cent of the physicians in the Atlanta area.

If the medical school should exert any authority over patient care in the Clinic, the University—and it has carefully investigated the applicable laws—would lay itself open to the charge of engaging in the corporate practice of medicine. Thus the authority of medical school department heads as regards the Clinic must be limited to the teaching done and research carried on by its members.

Full-time medical school faculty members are permitted, however, to join the Clinic as limited partners and supplement their medical school salaries by 25 per cent by conducting private practice there. Drs. Ferris, Howard and Caton so elected, and all have been receiving income from the Clinic.

To guard further against the charge of corporate practice, the members organized the Clinic as a referral basis. This means that patients from the

Atlanta area are admitted only if they are sent there by their own physicians; actually, a majority of its patients are referred by doctors from outside the area.

At any rate, after the November 15 action of the Emory Health Services Board in sustaining Dean Richardson in the Ferris removal, the first phase of the ruckus was all but over. Nothing about the Emory medical school controversy appeared in the Atlanta newspapers through the last half of November and all of December.

On January 4 Dr. Ferris, who could have remained on with the University in the capacity of professor of medicine, announced he would resign from that post effective February 1. Three days later it was reported that he had been appointed medical director of the American Heart Association. He has now taken over that office and has his headquarters in New York City. . . .

On January 4, 1957, Dr. Richardson announced my appointment as chairman of the Department of Medicine. I was promoted from assistant professor of medicine to professor of medicine. Within the month, the Fulton-DeKalb Hospital Authority also approved my appointment as chief of medicine at Grady Hospital. I began work on February 1, 1957.

The second phase of the ruckus developed rather quickly. Emory was accused by Drs. Caton and Bloom of jeopardizing the patient care and educational programs at Grady Hospital.

Dean Richardson denied that patient care and educational activity at Grady would suffer.

. . . At that time, continued Dr. Richardson, there were no vacancies on Emory's clinical staff at Grady, since Dr. Hurst already had been appointed to succeed Dr. Ferris, the only man who would depart immediately. The remaining three doctors who were to leave would, he said, "be replaced by men of equal or greater ability." He denied that Grady would encounter difficulties in engaging interns and residents at the close of the school year.

The written agreement between Emory and Grady, Dr. Richardson pointed out, specifies that the University's sole obligation is to provide one full-time physician or the equivalent in part-time doctors in each of four departments: medicine, surgery, obstetrics-gynecology and pediatrics. As of that date, he continued, Emory was providing the full-time equivalents of five men in medicine, four in surgery, two in obstetrics and three in pediatrics.

He went on to say that the amount of money Emory spends at Grady has grown from $65,000 in 1942 to $356,000 this year, plus about $100,000 in teaching grants and $250,000 in research grants.

(The University in its subsequent February 6 advertisement reported that last year a survey team from the American Medical Association and the Association of American Medical Colleges had informed the medical school that it already was spending more money and giving more patient care at Grady than it was justified in doing with its financial and faculty resources. The University's budget for clinical teaching is five times what it was 10 years ago and ten times what is called for by its contract with Grady.)

Even though Emory is far more than filling its Grady commitments, Dr. Richardson said, it recognizes that the medical staff at the hospital is inadequate in size and hopes to enlarge the staff as soon as money becomes available.

He denied emphatically rumors that the medical school was going to "pull out of Grady," where its upperclassmen have received the bulk of their clinical training since 1915 and where the University now spends 98 percent of its clinical teaching budget. Even though an Emory planning-committee report of 1946 stated that the major development of the medical school would take place on the main campus, the dean said, the same report specified that its program at Grady also should be developed.

. . . "If there is any falling off of patient care at Grady," said the dean, "it will be due to the individuals who are leaving between now and August 31. . . ."

. . . About this time the Atlanta press began to realize that the people of Atlanta had some responsibility for the medical care of its indigent and that this responsibility was not solely that of a private university which receives no public funds for such purposes. The Constitution of January 31 ran a front-page story calling attention to the fact that the per-diem patient-care expenditures ($14.60 in 1955) at Grady were far below the national average for nonfederal government hospitals ($20.62) and all general hospitals ($24.15).

The Constitution reporter checked Grady records and found that Emory was meeting its obligations in staffing the departments assigned to it but that most non-Emory departments at the hospital had no full-time chiefs or were otherwise understaffed.

In its newspaper advertisement of the following week Emory made this comment: "There is a limit to how much free medical care the school can give to the community at Grady. There are two stop signs: One, the amount of money the University has to spend on this part of its teaching, and two, the amount of this kind of work that teachers and students can do.

"When the need for medical care becomes greater than the school and the community doctors working with the school can give, something has to happen. Either the hospital must secure funds to help the school meet the cost of giving the extra care—and this is probably the most efficient and economical answer—or some other way must be found to provide it."

Commented the Constitutional editorially: "Our own city has grown so we do not realize what we have in Grady Hospital, or what the future will demand of us and the hospital authority. Money is the continuing problem. The 'either' in Emory's statement is inescapable. . . ."

. . . Up to that week Dean Richardson had borne the brunt of the accusations. He had appeared before the Fulton County Medical Society meeting of November 6. With Vice-President Jones he had met on January 24 with leaders of the Fulton County Medical Society and the Medical Association of Georgia and answered in great detail their questions about his school's policies and practices. He had met the press time and again.

Now, on January 30, he went before the entire medical faculty in a called meeting and presented the administration's case in the dispute. The faculty responded with a vote of confidence, given the dean in the form of a standing ovation. The same week he addressed the freshmen and sophomore medical classes in a joint meeting, and the following week he addressed the junior and senior classes at Grady in separate meetings.

On Friday, February 1, those who questioned the permanence and effectiveness of the Emory-Grady Hospital arrangement and who implied that a split between the two might develop had their props knocked from under them. On that day the Fulton-DeKalb Hospital Authority and the University issued a joint statement, signed by Mr. Spalding, Authority chairman; Frank Wilson, Grady Hospital administrator; Emory Health Services Board Chairman Robinson; President White, and Medical Dean Richardson.

"(We) are firmly convinced," it read, "that the interests of the Atlanta community, of Grady Memorial Hospital and of the Emory medical school will best be served by continuing the joint operation of Grady Hospital. Officials of the two institutions have reconfirmed their commitment to the relationship as defined in a contract dated September 1, 1951 and wish to assure the community that no basic differences exist between them in implementing it.

"The Hospital Authority, having the ultimate responsibility for the care of the eligible patients of the community, reiterates its confidence in the leadership of the medical school and in the school's ability, supported by the medical profession in Atlanta, effectively to supervise and direct the care of patients, as delegated to it. . . .

"While now, as in the past, there is room for improvement and expansion in the medical care program at Grady, the fact remains that the quality of this care has never been higher. . . .

"The relationship between Emory and Grady is spelled out in the contract which has already been mentioned, in which the responsibilities of each are detailed. Obviously, situations will arise which must be worked out by negotiation between the parties to the contract. Perfectly adequate machinery is provided for this purpose, and it is being used. . . .

"Emory University has stated repeatedly its intention to continue its teaching program at Grady and, within the limits of the resources available for that program, to help meet the community's patient care needs. For its part, Grady Hospital is even now in the midst of a tremendous expansion program to improve its facilities and services. Both will need increased financial support in the years ahead to make their work more effective."

That same day—Friday, February 1—President White called a meeting of all the University faculties, invited the press, and delivered the fighting statement which already has been quoted.

After telling of past disagreements concerning the medical school he said he had "complete confidence" in Dean Richardson and Vice-President Jones, and added, "Nothing has been done in the present situation without my knowledge and approval; I have been kept fully informed over a period of months while efforts were being made to reach agreement with and secure cooperation from the departmental chairman initially involved."

Dr. White said responsible University administrative officers always had been willing to discuss policies, explain them, and listen to questions and objections. "But agreements on the part of all concerned have been hard to get," he continued, "and when decisions of necessity have been made, those in disagreement have at times resorted to procedures that I consider both reprehensible and intolerable.

"As a matter of fact," he went on, "I think we may have been too patient and too much concerned to listen to every dissenting opinion. Instead of being inclined to dictatorial methods, we have been perhaps too tolerant of those who themselves wished to be dictators; sometimes these have been men within our organization, more often outsiders. . . ."

Two charges made against the medical school by departing professors will be answered in tangible form in the near future. One was that the school had an inadequate program in the field of psychiatry. The answer is that the school for the first time now has a stable budget for education in psychiatry. It plans both to improve that department and to make provision for the care of psychiatric patients at Emory Hospital.

The erstwhile faculty members also criticized the school for not having a full-time professor of pediatrics. The fact is that the school has never had a full-time chairman in this department. It soon should have, however, not only such a chairman but an enviable program in pediatrics training, for its program in this specialty will be integrated with that of Egleston Hospital for Children, which will begin this year construction of a fine new $2,000,000 plant at Emory.

The article concluded by stating that Richardson appointed Dr. John Cross to replace Caton as professor and chairman of the Department of Gynecology and Obstetrics. Richardson indicated that a chairman of surgery would be appointed when the present one left and that Bernard Hallman would replace Bloom.

Public Statement of University Policy

Because much of the trouble had been caused when a few faculty members disagreed with the policy of Emory University, there was a clamor for public dissemination of the policy. Although the policy had been stated publicly before, the president reformulated it into the following nine objectives and policies regarding medical education:

1. Development of the School of Medicine on the University campus as a part of the University community, while at the same time maintaining and strengthening its clinical teaching program at Grady Hospital.
2. Recognition of the Emory University Clinic as a means of securing part of the teaching service the school must have from doctors who earn their own incomes.
3. The privilege of limited private practice of medicine by full-time salaried members of the clinical faculty.
4. The operation of Emory University Hospital as a teaching hospital serving only patients of doctors participating actively in the educational program.

5. The operation of Crawford Long Hospital as a facility primarily for graduate medical education and to serve the private patients of volunteer members of the medical faculty and other physicians of the community.

6. Responsibility of the school for supervision of medical care programs at the Atlanta Veterans Hospital and affiliation with that hospital for teaching purposes.

7. Affiliation with the Henrietta Egleston Hospital for Children and with Aidmore Convalescent Hospital for Crippled Children for teaching purposes, those institutions maintaining their identities and independence of operation.

8. Affiliation with independent health agencies of the community, where there is mutual advantage in such affiliation for the purpose of supporting medical education.

9. Limitation of the University's commitments for direct patient care to those which can be justified as in support of medical education.

Annual Report of Dean Arthur Richardson to President White for the Academic Year 1956–57

An annual report should reflect a fairly complete picture of the year's events. To do that for the School of Medicine this year, would require several volumes and even then there would be much which can not now be written and may never be made part of the official record. My feelings regarding the past twelve months are perhaps best summarized by some remarks which I recently made at a meeting of the staff of the Department of Surgery:

> If it were our custom, as it is with the Chinese, of labeling each year with a descriptive title rather than a number, I am sure that 1956–57 for Emory University School of Medicine would be known as the "Year of Fire." Certainly it has been a period of great significance which will long be remembered. Fire is usually regarded as a destructive force, but I should point out that without it man could not mold iron into structures which have become so essential to our modern civilization. I sincerely believe that out of our ordeal of fire we have erected a framework of steel on which we are now building the kind of school of which we have all dreamed.

None of our problems have been unique. Similar "controversies" have rocked Stanford, University of Miami, Baylor, Medical College of Virginia, the medical schools of New York and others within the same space of time. In large measure they are based on: (a) changes in the nature of medical education; (b) increase in the responsibility of modern medical schools for research and public service; and (c) deep-seated changes in the pattern of the private practice of medicine.

Medical education was once a simple process involving a limited series of didactic lectures followed by an apprenticeship with established practitioners. By the time a student had completed his work with a medical school he had a fairly intimate acquaintance with the total "science" of his profession. The license which was granted entitled him to practice all branches of medicine. In recent decades the science of medicine has expanded at an almost fantastic rate so that today the degree of Doctor of Medicine entitles him to little more than the right of beginning to learn. Undergraduate education today, of necessity, must confine its attention largely to principles. The changing nature of medical education now requires the services of specialists who are first teachers and secondarily practitioners. The modern medical school must build its organization around a full-time staff whose first loyalty and interest is to the University. This is a change which has been taking place for over a half a century in American medical schools, but at Emory the change did not begin until the early 1940's. We have had to accomplish in less than fifteen years what has taken fifty years in other comparable institutions. Many of our recent problems can be traced back directly to the fact that the local community has not been aware of this changing emphasis. The volunteer faculty no longer has the time or background to dominate the medical educational program of this University as was once the case.

To many people a medical school is an institution which can accept unlimited responsibility for the care of the indigent sick, exercise leadership in the development of community health programs, and perform miracles in research on the unsolved problems of medicine. All of these things have had a marked effect on the activities of a faculty member in addition to his first responsibility which is the teaching of students. Research is a case in point. In 1940 research funds of this school approximated $5,000. For the coming year the total will approach $1,000,000. Whereas in 1940 research made up about 5% of the resources it is now about 40% of our total expenditures. The question must sooner or later be asked as to whether there is a point beyond which research can go without jeopardizing our educational commitments. A heavy dependence on research funds carries certain hazards. Such funds are seldom assured for more than a few years and are usually committed to specific fields which may not satisfy our most pressing needs. Few granting agencies have the foresight to make unrestricted grants to Universities.

The medical school's responsibility in the area of the care of indigent sick has also been undergoing a marked change. It is an accepted concept that every citizen, regardless of his means, has a right to a minimal program of health care. In recent years this minimal level has been greatly raised. What was once considered acceptable at Grady Hospital would now be regarded as scandalous. The unfortunate fact is that all too frequently funds and facilities are not made available to do the job required of us and as a result medical education is saddled with a burden which it cannot bear. One of our greatest problems has been and will continue to be that of convincing the community that we must have a great deal of financial help if we are to adequately discharge our *service* responsibilities at Grady Hospital. There seems to be no other source for these funds than from local tax sources.

The private practice of medicine is now in the midst of a great struggle. It is beset with problems growing out of the expansion of medical knowledge and the changing economic structure of our society. The individual doctor is no longer an island unto himself. He can become competent in only a limited field; therefore he can offer complete care if he has a close relationship to colleagues who are specialists in other fields. His position as a private citizen is changing because the public is coming to look on him as a quasi-public servant and as such he feels he is in danger of coming under public control in ways which he believes are contrary to the best interests of his profession. All of these factors have created a ferment in those institutions representing "Organized Medicine." Unfortunately and all too frequently organized medicine has looked on the medical schools as the source of their troubles. They are inclined to look on things a medical school does with suspicion and distrust.

All of the factors mentioned played a role in the "Emory controversy." Tension built up over at least ten years had reached a point where the only course left was for the medical school to state its position in a clear manner and to take forthright action. As I review the past year I firmly believe we made the right decisions and not only weathered the storm but came out of our difficulties much stronger. On the positive side all faculty members separated from the University have been replaced with competent people. We have immeasurably strengthened the full time staff with people who understand and endorse our policies; we have a clearer view of what our relations with the Fulton-DeKalb Hospital Authority must be; we have now come to a better understanding with organized medicine as evidenced by the endorsement by the Medical Association of Georgia of the plan of operation of the Emory University Clinic. Many physicians have been enthusiastic in praise of the changes taking place in the teaching program and we have every reason to view the future with optimism.

With these general remarks I transmit to you reports from individual departments which describe details of their work during the past year.

Dean Richardson Comments in 1982 Regarding the Ruckus

Arthur Richardson left the deanship in 1979, but was invited by Dr. Mark Silverman to present a lecture on the history of Emory University School of Medicine to the Atlanta Medical Historical Society on July 13, 1982. An audiotape was made of his lecture, and a part of it is summarized below.

Dr. Richardson stated that there were several individuals grouped around Eugene Ferris who were new and impatient and wanted money immediately. They did not like the plan of 1946 and wanted to control the Emory University Clinic. They believed the basic science departments should be moved to Grady, and they tried to work out a separate arrangement with the Fulton-DeKalb Hospital Authority to set up a research foundation at Grady that was unrelated to Emory University School of Medicine. They took their case to the Fulton County Medical Society. They were relieved of their administrative position.

It was not until early 1982, a few months before his talk, that Dean Richardson learned that Eugene Ferris was a candidate for the chairmanship of pharmacology at Emory and was passed over for him.

The Clinic Success Story

As will be discussed later in Chapter 5, the Emory University Clinic thrived. The clinic members were appointed by the department chairmen. The members of the clinic were expected to teach at Emory University Hospital and Grady Memorial Hospital. They were also expected to engage in all of the other academic affairs of the medical school. They earned their salary, paid the university rent for the use of the building and facilities, gave a specified amount of money to the dean for general use, and created a clinic research fund. In the following years, the building that housed the Emory University Clinic was enlarged many times and new clinic buildings were added, thanks to Robert Woodruff. Some years later the clinic also expanded to include facilities and faculty members at Crawford W. Long Hospital.

The clinic success story should not be closed without pointing out the contribution made by Barney Chisholm, the business manager of the Emory Clinic. His careful management of the financial aspects of the clinic was essential for the clinic's success. Roy Townsend followed Barney Chisholm as business manager and continues to be an excellent and highly respected administrator.

The Development of Emory University Clinic as Viewed from a Different Vantage Point

The story just presented outlining the need for, and the creation of, the Emory University Clinic relates the development as it was seen from the vantage of the medical school faculty. The following account of the development, written by Charles Elliott in his book *Robert Winship Woodruff: A Biography of the Boss*, says more about the context in which the clinic was formed. The story also pays homage to Boisfeuillet Jones (see Figure 4-16), a major mover in the development of the medical school, its Department of Medicine, and the Emory University Clinic.

> Some of those who feel that they are well acquainted with Robert W. Woodruff say that . . . his interest in helping people who are sick or in need began soon after he bought Ichauway Plantation and met the old Negro with malaria.
>
> Not so, say others; he was born with his special star in his crown. He has always been drawn to people in need.
>
> The malaria epidemic, however, could have been one of the highlights and the beginning of his interest in Emory University School of Medicine, for in a way it was his first collaboration with the medical school on a rather extensive scale. The story is now well known how a malaria control program was established on the plantation through the medical school and the U. S. Public

Health Service, and in a few years the trained staff had eliminated this and other crippling diseases in Baker and surrounding counties.

Throughout his life any person in distress and even in need appealed to him, and the pattern of his existence included a perennial crusade to ease the suffering or burdens of others. Had he been a small-town merchant, his principles of dedicating himself to other people would have followed the same inclination, for this has been one of the basics of his character. The large fortune he accumulated by his own efforts only allowed him to expand those horizons. The Reverend Gresham spelled this out when he said, "Through you, whether you know it or not, our Father in Heaven is continually pouring the stream that makes glad all that it touches."

The malaria episode may have started it, but what really triggered the gigantic development through which Emory went over the next decades under the tall shadow of Woodruff were two tragedies in his life. His maternal grandfather, Robert Winship, to whom he had been very close in his earliest years, had died of cancer at the age of sixty-five.

In 1937, Woodruff's mother was sick. It was diagnosed as cancer. There was no place in the Southeast that specialized in cancer except the Steiner Clinic at Grady Hospital, which had been established for charity patients. This was woefully inadequate.

Woodruff had already put the wheels in motion for the establishment of the Robert Winship Memorial Clinic in Emory University Hospital as a part of the medical school operation. The new format called for specialty treatment and for a research and teaching center, specializing in cancer and benign tumors. The objective of the clinic was then, and still is, to treat patients, and in the process to educate young medical graduates as well as undergraduates in the latest techniques of cancer diagnosis and treatment, so that professional service could be available wherever these young doctors established practice.

Woodruff always felt that if these facilities had been available soon enough, his mother's affliction might have been properly diagnosed in time.

With the Robert Winship Memorial Clinic underway, Woodruff and Bob Mizell went to Memorial Hospital in New York and employed J. Elliott Scarborough, Jr., who had just completed his advance training in cancer at the hospital there.

Those were the opening guns of a long campaign which created Woodruff Medical Center—its eventual name—as one of the finest establishments of its kind in the nation.

Woodruff passes most of the credit for this on to others. Among these key men were doctors, administrators and businessmen, and they worked long hours to accomplish remarkable results. Woodruff was always in the background. Few important moves were made without his approval. In a sense he was the power behind the growth of Emory's medical excellence, just as he was the power behind the expanding empire of Coca-Cola. In both, his lieutenants were prominent wheels in the machinery.

When, in 1935, Woodruff was elected to the board of trustees of Emory University, one of the university representatives who impressed him greatly was Robert C. Mizell, development officer at Emory, where his main duties also included raising funds for the expansion of the Emory complex. Mizell quickly became Woodruff's main contact with Emory. Woodruff recognized the depth and quality of his business judgment and discussed with him many of his personal business affairs. Mizell was the man who had helped organize the battle against malaria in Baker County and had brought in the resources of both Emory University and the U. S. Public Health Service. Close personal friends as well as business associates, Woodruff and Mizell spent many pleasant hours together planning ahead for the future of Emory.

Woodruff relied on him when, in 1944, Emory University was asked to assume responsibility for the Atlanta Southern Dental College and to make it Emory's school of dentistry, along with the existing school of medicine and school of nursing. It was reported that considerable indecision existed in the board of trustees, until Woodruff, who had given much study to the facts gathered for him by Mizell, gave a nod of approval. The vote was unanimous to establish the school of dentistry.

The school of medicine was having its problems. It had depended largely on practicing doctors who volunteered their services for lectures and teaching. The time had come for a full-time, paid faculty, especially for the basic sciences, instead of having to rely solely on volunteer teachers. Three trustees, one of them Woodruff, agreed to underwrite the anticipated deficit. The report is that after a year or two, the other trustees dropped out of this arrangement, leaving on Woodruff's shoulders the burden of making up this deficit, which ranged annually from one hundred fifty thousand dollars to four hundred thousand dollars.

This was unsatisfactory to both Woodruff, who felt obligated to meet this deficit, and the school of medicine, which was never quite sure that the deficit would or could be met. In 1952, Woodruff advised Dr. Goodrich C. White, president of Emory, and Robert Mizell that they should draw a blueprint for Emory's future plans that would put its school of medicine, dentistry and nursing, its hospitals and its other related services on a firm business foundation. Should the plan commend itself, he said, the Emily and Ernest Woodruff Foundation would consider underwriting it.

Dr. White turned the memorandum from Woodruff over to Boisfeuillet Jones (see Figure 4-16), who had received both his undergraduate and law degrees from Emory and had considerable experience as dean of administration for the university. After several months of consultation with the respective deans and key faculty members, Boisfeuillet Jones came up with a plan for organization and development which would provide for balanced budgets in the health sciences while supporting needed faculty and staff and related expenses. The plan would require five million dollars of capital from the Emily and Ernest Woodruff Foundation, four million for endowment to offset the continuing deficit anticipated and one million for construction of an office building to house a projected Emory University Clinic.

The key to the plan for financing the school of medicine was organization of the full-time clinical faculty into a partnership for the private group practice of medicine and a contract between the partnership and the university. The partnership would pay reasonable costs for facilities provided by the university, and the physicians would support themselves, pay all costs of their private practice, teach in the medical school program directly for about one-fourth of their time, and make reasonable contributions to the general teaching and research budgets of the medical school.

The partnership was designated as the Emory University Clinic and, as of this writing (1979), has had twenty-five years of highly successful operation and growth. It has some two hundred sixty physicians participating and contributes substantially each year to the operating budget of the school of medicine in addition to direct contribution of physician services as faculty members. Woodruff takes special pride in the Emory Clinic and in his essential role in its conception and development.

Emory trustees approved the plan for development of the health services in late 1952, and the university put it into effect in January, 1953, under direction of Boisfeuillet Jones, who was later named vice president and administrator of health services. The plan was presented to Woodruff for consideration of the foundation support requested immediately after approval by Emory. Dr. Philip Weltner was asked, as a consultant to the foundation, to study the plan in detail and make recommendations. After several months of intensive consideration, Woodruff advised Emory that the foundation would provide the five million dollars requested.

. . . Jones did such an outstanding job that he was appointed to many national health advisory groups. President Kennedy appointed him in 1961 as Special Assistant to the Secretary for Health and Medical Affairs, Department of Health, Education and Welfare the nation's top health policy position where he served for nearly four years. Woodruff brought him back to Atlanta in 1964 as president of the Emily and Ernest Woodruff Foundation, which had grown into one of the largest foundations in the nation.[5]

Future Development of the Emory University Clinic

The growth of the Emory University Clinic and the contributions made by its members will be further discussed in Chapter 5 of this book. Here, however, it should be pointed out that the faculty members who work in the Emory University Clinic have played a major role in the creation of the Robert W. Woodruff Health Sciences Center and the development of Atlanta into a medical center that is second to no other.

---

[5] Charles Elliott, *Robert Winship Woodruff: A Biography of the "Boss"* (N.p.: n.p. [R. W. Woodruff], 1979), 255–59. Emory University now holds the copyright.

Acknowledgments

General References

American Heart Association. Letter regarding the death of Dr. Eugene Ferris.

Elliott, Charles. *A Biography of the "Boss": Robert Winship Woodruff*. N.p.: R. W. Woodruff, 1979.

This remarkable book is entertaining and beautifully written. It was published privately and the copyright was held by Mr. Woodruff. The copyright is now owned by Emory University.

Martin, John D., Jr., in collaboration with Garland D. Perdue. *The History of Surgery at Emory University School of Medicine*. Atlanta: Emory University (Fulton, Mo.: Ovid Bell Press), 1979.

J. D. Martin and Garland Perdue present a detailed account of the development of Emory University School of Medicine and its Department of Surgery. Some of the discussions in their book are germane to the development of the Department of Medicine.

Mizell, Robert. Private papers located in Special Collections housed in the Robert W. Woodruff Library of Emory University.

Richardson, Arthur. Audiotape made of a lecture given to the Atlanta Medical Historical Society, July 13, 1982.

Woodruff, Robert. Private papers located in Special Collections housed in the Robert W. Woodruff Library of Emory University.

"The Medical Ruckus" was reprinted from the March 1957 issue of the *Emory Alumnus*. The copyright is held by Emory University.

The Help of Others

I wish to thank Dr. Paul B. Beeson, Dr. Joseph E. Hardison, Dr. Charles R. Hatcher Jr., Dr. Gary S. Hauk, Dr. William Hollingsworth, Dr. Charles M. Huguley Jr., Dr. R. Bruce Logue, Mr. J. W. Pinkston Jr., Dr. Thomas F. Sellers Jr., Dr. Mark E. Silverman, Dr. Eugene A. Stead Jr., and Dr. Judson C. Ward Jr., for their review of Chapter 4.

Figure 4-1
  Dr. Eugene Ferris was professor and chairman of the Department of Medicine, Emory University School of Medicine from September 1, 1952, until February 1, 1957.

Figure 4-2
Grady Memorial Hospital, Department of Medicine, 1952–53
Row 1: Spivey, Karp, Cary, Barnes, Mortimore, Young, C. T. Smith, Williams, Watson
Row 2: Heyman, Hamff, Friedewald, Bishop, Ferris, Oppenheimer, Merrill, Fitzhugh, James
Row 3: McLeod, Davidson, McCall, J. L. Smith, Hudgins, Varese, Johnson, Russell, Hein, Vaughan, Melton
Row 4: DiSalvo, Brust, Dunbar, Warren, Knight, David, McDonald
Row 5: Lea, Ferguson, Mitchell, Freeman, Baldwin, Barrineau, Felder

Figure 4-3
Grady Memorial Hospital, Department of Medicine, 1953–54
Row 1: Hankey, Bishop, Brust, Oppenheimer, Ferris, Hein, Hamff, McGinty
Row 2: Melton, White, Woodson, Grey, Saffan, Poole, Corley
Row 3: Hook, Krainin, Kenley, Pace, Fortson, Vetter, Watson
Row 4: Karp, Freeman, Cary, Johnson, Bolton, Lane, Churchwell
Row 5: Lea, DiSalve, Wilson

Figure 4-4
Grady Memorial Hospital, Department of Medicine, 1954–55
Row 1: Yount, Herman, Sharp, Hudgins, Hook, Ferris, Yauger, Fortson, Churchwell, Seavey, Cantrell
Row 2: Weeks, Webster, Hill, Larach, Major, Thomas, Adams, Smith, Ledbetter, Hilton, Crawford, Haseltine, Wright
Row 3: Blackford, Cooper, James, Saade, Tsagaris, Wainer, Findlay, King, Globus, Cheney
Row 4: C. Jones, Kaufmann, Woodson, Massee, Murphy, Claiborne, Brust, Woody, Hagans, Poole
Row 5: Hamff, Hein, Wells, Nardin, Bloom, Mills, Beasley, Cline
Row 6: Bennett, Candler, Fowler, Burson, Weinberg, Freedman, Barrow, Wilson, Wilber, Krainin, Whisnant

Figure 4-5
Grady Memorial Hospital, Department of Medicine, 1955–56
Row 1: Herman, Cooper, Johnson, Burns, Gaston, Furr, Yount, Tillman, Ross, Lane, Anderson
Row 2: Mostellar, Woody, Bloom, Gendel, Brust, E. Ferris, Yauger, Teplis, Kaufmann, Hamff, Evans
Row 3: Lipmann, McLoughlin, Lowance, Stone, Covall, Bennett, Pace, LeMaistre, H. Ferris, Hill
Row 4: Blackford, Cargill, Dunbar, Moscovitz, Cheney, Barr, Williams, Redfern, Guillebeau, Woolley
Row 5: E. Brown, Sellers, Candler, Franch, Davies, Wynne, Cantrell, Weigel
Row 6: Crutcher, Hudgins, Hook, Station, Bowen, Duggan
Row 7: Minor, Neill, Geiger, Galambos, Churchwell, Dunaway, Bennett, Andrews
Row 8: Ward, Dozier, Peters, Fowler

Figure 4-6
Grady Memorial Hospital, Department of Medicine, 1956–57

Row 1: G. Cooper, Blackford, Fowler, Bloom, Nardin, E. Ferris, Cantrell, C. Smith, H. Ferris
Row 2: Jones, J. Wilson, Galambos, Hein, Candler, Cummings, McCall, Everitt
Row 3: Peters, Crutcher, Williams, Leonardy, Tuttle, Sellers, Griffin, Epes
Row 4: Wilber, Hailey, Daniel, Holmes, McCann, Blackard, Foster, Rucker
Row 5: Boyd, Rhodes, Barrow, Wallace, Robertson, Krueger, S. Jones, Bewick, Franch

Figure 4-7
Lawson Veterans Hospital, Medical Staff, 1952–53. Dr. Max Michael (6th from the left) was chief of the medical service.

Figure 4-8
    Glenn Memorial Building—69 Butler Street. This building, located across the street from Grady Memorial Hospital, was completed and turned over to the Fulton-DeKalb Hospital Authority on June 1, 1953. The building was to be used by Emory University School of Medicine.

Figure 4-9
    The Ernest Woodruff Memorial Research Building on the Emory campus was completed in 1954. The building was later connected to Emory University Hospital, located to the left in the photograph.

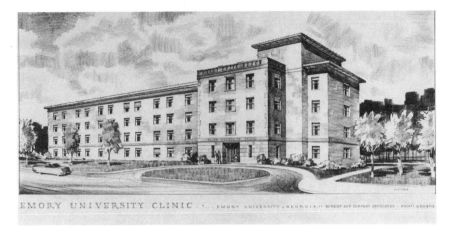

Figure 4-10A
The first stage of the Emory University Clinic building in 1956.

Figure 4-10B
Mr. Woodruff did not like the awkward appearance of half a building (see Figure 4-9A). Therefore, the *shell* of the south wing was completed in July 1956. The inside of the south wing was completed later.

Figure 4-11

Mr. Robert Woodruff, Dr. Elliott Scarbrough Jr., and Dean Hugh Wood standing in front of the Robert W. Winship Memorial Clinic. They were probably discussing the creation of the Emory University Clinic.

Figure 4-12

Atlanta Veterans Hospital ("old 48"). Patients were moved from the

Lawson's VA Hospital to the "Old 48" in 1952. "Old 48" was located on Peachtree Road near Oglethorpe University.

Figure 4-13
Dr. Arthur Richardson, dean of the School of Medicine from 1956 to 1979. He was a strong, effective dean who led the school of medicine through turmoil to a position of greatness.

Figure 4-14
Dr. Evangeline T. Papageorge, associate dean, was a highly respected, major contributor to the development of Emory University School of Medicine.

Figure 4-15A

Dr. Robert Grant talking at a course on electrocardiography in 1954. He emphasized the use of the vector concepts in the interpretation of electrocardiograms. (Photograph supplied by Dr. Leslie Franch, a participant at the course.)

Figure 4-15B

Dr. Bruce Logue lecturing at a postgraduate course on electrocardiography in 1954. (Photograph supplied by Dr. Leslie Franch, a participant at the course.)

Figure 4-15C
Dr. Willis Hurst lecturing at a postgraduate course on electrocardiography in 1954. (Photograph supplied by Dr. Leslie Franch, a participant at the course.)

Figure 4-16
Boisfeuillet Jones was vice president for health affairs of Emory University from 1955 to 1961. He later became president of the Woodruff Foundation. He was a major mover in the development of the Emory University School of Medicine, the Emory University Clinic, and the Department of Medicine.

CHAPTER 5
The Phoenix 1957–1986 (and a Little Later)

As described in the Prologue, I approached this portion of the story with considerable trepidation, aware that my personal involvement in the metamorphosis of the Department of Medicine threatened to shape any narrative with a distasteful number of first person singular pronouns. So, at the outset, I wish to stress that literally hundreds of people contributed to the *quest for excellence* in the Department of Medicine from 1957 through 1986. The individuals not only were inherently capable but also loved Emory. Accordingly, the pages that follow detail their contributions, and I am simply the one who tells the story. As chairman of the department, I appointed hundreds of house officers and fellows, numerous faculty members, and had an open door policy for the medical students. It is they, along with generous benefactors, who deserve the credit for the successful adventure in patient care, teaching, and research that occurred from 1957 through 1986. So please forgive me if, in the name of good grammatical syntax, the word *I* recurs frequently in this part of the book.

Refusing to write my own biography, to comment on my own bibliography, or to list the honors and awards that came my way, I asked Dr. Mark E. Silverman, a former cardiology fellow and a current member of the faculty, to do so.

The phoenix, the mythical bird of the Arabian desert, rose from its own ashes to live again. Atlanta did that. The Department of Medicine at Emory did it too. Here is the story.

The Biography of John Willis Hurst, M.D.[1]
by Dr. Mark E. Silverman

John Willis Hurst was born on October 21, 1920, in Cooper, Kentucky. The little village later became part of Monticello, Kentucky. He was the only child of John Millet and Verna Bell Hurst. When he was eleven months old, the family moved to Carroll County, Georgia, where his

---

[1] A portion of this biography has been reproduced from M. E. Silverman, "J. Willis Hurst— A Man of Achievement," *Clinical Cardiology* 20 (1997): 584–86. It is reprinted with permission of Clinical Cardiology Publishing Company, Inc., Mahwah, NJ 07430-0832, USA.

father became principal of a small school. The family lived in a large two-story house. His aunt, who taught the first three grades, and another teacher, who taught the fourth through the sixth grades, lived in the same house. In this concentrated atmosphere of schooling, young Hurst was taught to read by his aunt before he entered school. His second teacher insisted that he memorize poems and quotations that he still remembers today. He was profoundly influenced by the teaching methods of his father, whose Socratic style was to encourage students to seek the answers to their own questions. Hurst remembers, "When I had no questions, he would, in a gentle way, raise a few of his own and insist I look up the answers." Young Hurst lived in their encyclopedia, *The World Book*. He also observed his father's compassionate efforts to teach illiterate older people to read and write during the summer months when regular school was not in session. He learned, too, about the turmoil that can occasionally develop in a school, because his father met many obstacles when he spearheaded the creation and construction of a new school building.

The family moved to Carrollton, Georgia, when Willis was twelve years of age. The teachers at the high school were excellent. His interest in biology and psychology at age fourteen determined that he would become a physician. At age sixteen he entered West Georgia College in Carrollton, where he met his future wife, Nelie. After two years at that small college, he followed Nelie to the University of Georgia in Athens, where he graduated with a double bachelor of science degree in chemistry and zoology.

He entered the University of Georgia School of Medicine (now the Medical College of Georgia), located in Augusta, in 1941, where he soon realized that he admired the teachers who taught him how to learn as opposed to those who required rote memorization. In medical school, he began his lifelong habit of beginning the day at 4 a.m. in order to think and·write without interruption. He credits this early jump on the day as contributing in large measure to his success. Prior to his marriage to Nelie on December 20, 1942, he roomed with Eldrid Bass, a friend from his hometown. Two other medical students lived in the adjacent room. As time passed, the three medical students and others would go to Hurst's room with the request for a teaching session. Because of this, some of his classmates believed he was destined to be a "chief" of medicine.

Hurst was influenced by: Dr. V. P. Sydenstricker, the chairman of the Department of Medicine and a keen diagnostician; Dr. William Hamilton, the famous cardiovascular physiologist who was chairman of the Department of Physiology; Dr. Perry Volpitto, the respected chairman of the Department of Anesthesiology; and Dr. Harry Harper, who first interested Hurst in cardiology. During his senior year, he was impressed by the pioneering catheterization work of Dr. André Cournand, the Nobelist, who was a visiting professor. Hurst was elected to Alpha Omega Alpha as a junior student and served as president of the local chapter as a senior. He graduated first in his class in 1944.

Hurst served his internship and residency under Sydenstricker at the University Hospital in Augusta. Dr. Paul Dudley White was a visiting professor there in 1946. Dr. Harry Harper asked Hurst if he would like to have a fellowship with Dr. White at the Massachusetts General Hospital. Hurst made up his mind in a hurry. He said, "Yes." Harper arranged the fellowship with Dr. White; it was to begin in July 1948, after Hurst's military obligation. Hurst was assigned to the army and became a ward officer at Fitzsimons General Hospital in Denver, Colorado. He received board credit for the time he spent there. His tour of duty was cut short because his wife's mother and one child were killed, and his wife's sister severely injured, in an automobile accident. This led to his release from the army to assist in the prolonged care of the family. Weeks later, when his sister-in-law's long hospitalization was over and arrangements had been made for her rehabilitation, Hurst called Dr. White, who invited him to become a graduate student for six months prior to becoming a cardiac fellow at the Massachusetts General Hospital in July 1948 (see Figure 5-1).

The period as a graduate student was a time of intensive study. Dr. White was the foremost cardiologist in America, and his example of observing at the bedside, teaching, writing, and clinical research profoundly influenced Hurst in his future career. At Massachusetts General, Hurst was also influenced by the cardiologists who worked with White, including Drs. Howard Sprague, Ed Bland, Conger Williams, Oglesby Paul, Ed Wheeler, Gordon Myers, and Mandel Cohen, a psychiatrist. Hurst was also influenced by Drs. Fuller Albright, Howard Means, Chester Jones, Walter Bauer, and Joseph Aub, many of whose offices were just down the hall from White's. Hurst viewed them all as great teachers and scientists. He also developed lifelong friendships with some of the future leaders of American medicine on the house staff, including Lloyd Smith, James Wyngaarden, and Ernest Craige, as well as Grey Dimond, a cardiology trainee. During this period as a graduate student and cardiac fellow in Boston, Hurst was one of the authors on five scientific articles.

In July 1949, he said farewell to Boston and moved to Atlanta, where he entered private practice and developed a reputation by speaking to medical groups and teaching at Grady Memorial Hospital in his spare time. Along with Dr. Gordon Barrow, he also started the Heart Station at

Georgia Baptist Hospital. At that time, there were only a half dozen cardiologists in the city of Atlanta.

As the year passed, it became increasingly clear to him that his teaching, writing, and clinical research could best be done in a university setting. An offer was made by Dr. Paul Beeson, the chairman of the Department of Medicine at Emory, to join the Emory faculty to work with Dr. Bruce Logue in the newly developed Private Diagnostic Clinic at Emory University Hospital. Hurst gratefully accepted the offer and joined the full-time faculty at Emory in July 1950. An interest in teaching electrocardiography was abetted by Dr. Robert Grant, a leader in the vector approach to interpreting the scalar electrocardiogram.

With Grattan Woodson, a trainee, Hurst wrote his first book, *Atlas of Spatial Vector Electrocardiography*. Many books were to follow, including seven editions of the book *The Heart*. It became obvious to him that his writing interacted with his teaching; by writing he could clarify his ideas, which led to better oral communication. He would write as if he were the reader. He would discuss matters as if he were the listener. He became increasingly interested in whether facts were used by a trainee or simply memorized as abstract items.

Over the next four years, Hurst worked closely with Logue, helping him develop the reputation of Emory as a referral center, by giving talks throughout the state and working with trainees and students. Just as his academic career began to flourish, it was abruptly curtailed by the Korean conflict. Because of the automobile accident involving his wife's family, and the downsizing of the post-World War II army, he had been allowed to leave the military in 1947, short of completing his two-year obligation. Now he was recalled into military service and assigned to the U.S. Naval Hospital in Bethesda, Maryland. Later, when the very capable Dr. Henry Cooper left the military service, Hurst became chief of cardiology there. The hospital was located across the campus from the National Institutes of Health, which included the National Heart Institute. Dr. Robert Grant, formerly of Emory, and Dr. Harold Dodge, a former Emory cardiac fellow, were working there. Hurst attended teaching sessions at the NIH, and his friends attended sessions at the Naval Hospital. Hurst also developed a close relationship with Drs. Proctor Harvey and Joseph Perloff at Georgetown University and attended the cardiac clinic at the Children's Hospital. Hurst also worked closely with Dr. Ray Gifford, from Mayo Clinic, who was then one of the physicians to the United States Congress. During his tour of active duty at the Bethesda Naval Hospital, Hurst published four scientific papers and worked with Norman Barr to create a radio-transmitted electrocardiograph machine. Barr did the technical work, and Hurst did the clinical work. Although Hurst was never told the purpose of the work with Barr, he assumed the instrument was to be used in the space program that was just beginning.

When Lyndon Johnson, then majority leader of the Senate, suffered a heart attack on July 2, 1955, Hurst became his cardiologist. This led to an enduring relationship and close friendship of 18 years. A few years later Hurst traveled with Vice President Johnson to fifteen foreign countries. On the day of President John Kennedy's assassination, Hurst was called to Washington to be with Lyndon Johnson, because of the report that Johnson had experienced some pain in his arm. Hurst was with Johnson during each major illness and surgery. Hurst tactfully declined an offer by the thirty-sixth president to become White House physician, saying, "A patient doing well does not need a physician every day, and a physician needs more than one patient to retain his skills. I can serve you best as a consultant."

The experience at Bethesda Naval Hospital as chief of cardiology in 1955 honed his administrative and teaching skills and gave him added confidence that would soon be handy. He was given a commendation and discharged from the navy with the rank of commander.

In November 1955, Hurst rejoined Dr. Logue at Emory University Hospital and Clinic, where he resumed teaching auscultation and electrocardiography and practicing consultative cardiology. Considerable turbulence existed between the medical school administration and the chairmen of the various clinical departments. The trouble deepened as the months passed. In 1956, Hurst considered leaving Emory because of the turmoil, and because Dr. Howard Burchell, a highly respected scholar, tried to entice him to join the cardiology group at Mayo Clinic. Hurst made one trip to visit the Mayo Clinic as part of the negotiation process. As he was considering the possibility of leaving, the chairmen of the Departments of Medicine, Surgery, and Obstetrics at Emory were relieved of their administrative posts, leaving Emory rudderless. Dean Arthur Richardson chose Hurst as chairman of the Department of Medicine. Later, a search committee of Bruce Logue, Carter Smith Sr., and Arthur Merrill Sr. met and agreed; Hurst was unanimously selected to be the new chairman.

Hurst visited Gene Stead at Duke and Paul Beeson at Yale for advice. Each had been chairman of the Department of Medicine. Stead gave Hurst the same advice that he had been given by the great Soma Weiss, chief at Peter Bent Brigham, when Stead was asked to come to Emory in 1942: "So far you have proved to be a man of promise; if you succeed at Emory, you will also be a man of achievement."

In February 1957, at the youthful age of thirty-six, Hurst assumed the mantle of chairman of the Department of Medicine at Emory (see Figure

5-2). His daunting task was to rebuild a department that had been one of the finest in the country in the 1940s but had been decimated and demoralized from top to bottom. Town-gown problems were rampant. Like Soma Weiss and Eugene Stead, Hurst selected a young faculty with great promise who had not yet achieved national recognition. From this nucleus of a few, the faculty grew to 147 over the next thirty years. The teaching programs for students, house staff, and fellows became recognized as among the best in the nation, and patient care became excellent. Space gradually became available for research. As time passed, the town-gown problems all but disappeared.

The following quotes from Hurst's friends say much about his personality and interests.

Dr. Eugene Stead said, "Emory needed someone who loved Emory. He was the only one who could have utilized all the hospitals for clinical research. He gave his all to Emory in a time of great need. He saved the medical school.[2]

Dr. Bruce Logue said, "I think Willis is the greatest teacher of cardiology in the world in the last thirty years. I don't know anyone who has equaled his teaching ability. He has total recall. He is totally interested in medicine, patients, and patient care."[3]

Dr. Robert Schlant said, "Dr. Hurst was like a bulldog with his teeth set on his aspirations for the Department of Medicine. He'd get on causes and support them twenty-four hours a day. New people were coming in, and new ideas. He was a champion of high-quality teaching, of establishing standards for certification in cardiology, of the problem-oriented records system, and of the Emory Medical Television Network.

He appreciated the problems of being an academic physician—the perpetual juggling of clinical teaching, research, and administrative responsibilities—but he appreciated perhaps even more the problems of being a practicing physician full time."[4]

Bibliography

Hurst edited fifty-seven books. The best known are *The Heart* (seven editions) and *Medicine for the Practicing Physician* (four editions). He wrote three books on teaching and education, the best known being *The Bench and Me (Teaching and Learning Medicine)*.[5] He wrote one nonscientific

---

[2] E. A. Stead Jr., Personal communication, April 1996.

[3] R. B. Logue, Personal communication, 31 March 1996.

[4] S. Wrobel, "A Mid-life Career Change," *Medicine at Emory* (spring 1986): 38–39.

[5] J. W. Hurst, *The Bench and Me: Teaching and Learning Medicine* (New York: Igaku-Shoin, 1992).

book, titled *Essays from the Heart*. He wrote over 300 scientific articles and was on the editorial board for twenty-one scientific journals.

Post-Chairmanship

Hurst gave up the chairmanship of medicine on September 1, 1986. He had been chairman 14.3 percent of the time the United States had been a nation and that, he said, was long enough. He was given a small office suite in the Robert W. Woodruff Health Sciences Library, where he continued to write. He was also given an office in the Emory Clinic, where he continued to see patients in consultation. He increased his teaching and writing activity during this period. Now, in 1997, he continues to teach at Emory University Hospital, Grady Memorial Hospital, Crawford Long Hospital, and the Atlanta Veterans Administration Hospital. He writes more than ever. His latest book, the fourth edition of *Medicine for the Practicing Physician*, was published in July 1996.

Hurst received many honors and awards; some of these are listed below.

Honors and Awards

Member, Alpha Omega Medical Honorary Fraternity 1943; president, AOA 1944; top of class, School of Medicine, Medical College of Georgia 1944; selected as one of Atlanta's 100 young men by Time Magazine and the Atlanta Chamber of Commerce 1952; letter of commendation from U.S. Navy for cardiovascular teaching program at the U.S. Navy Hospital, Bethesda 1955; cardiologist to the 36th president of the United States (Lyndon B. Johnson) 1955–73; recognition as honorary member of senior class, Emory University School of Medicine 1957; honored by medical house staff, Grady Memorial Hospital 1961–62; president of Georgia Heart Association 1963–64; member, President's Commission on Heart Disease, Cancer, and Stroke 1964–65; member, National Advisory Council on Regional Medical Programs 1965–66; member, Subspecialty Board of Cardiovascular Diseases 1965–70; chairman, Subspecialty Board of Cardiovascular Diseases, American Board of Internal Medicine 1967–70; certificate of appreciation, medical house staff, Grady Memorial Hospital 1970; member, National Advisory Heart, Lung and Blood Council 1967–71; member, President's Commission for the Observation of Human Rights 1968; Hardman Award, presented by the Medical Association of Georgia for contributions to Medicine in Georgia 1968; honored by medical house staff, Grady Memorial Hospital 1969–70; "Master Teacher" Award, American College of Cardiology 1970; president, American Heart Association 1971–72; honored by medical house staff, Emory University School of Medicine 1971–72; Emory University Medical Alumni Association Award of Honor 1973; president, Paul Dudley White Society 1974; "Master Teacher" Award, American College of Cardiology 1974; Gifted Teacher Award, American College of Cardiology 1974; Gold Heart Award, American Heart Association 1974; plaque of appreciation for "A Year of Growth" by the interns in the Emory University Affiliated Hospitals Program 1976; selected as master by American College of Physicians 1978; Distinguished Physician's Award, *Modern Medicine* 1978; Distinguished Alumnus Award, Medical College of Georgia 1978; Herrick Award, American Heart Association 1980; Candler Professorship, Emory University School of Medicine 1980; Distinguished Alumnus Award, Medical College of Georgia 1984; president, Association of Professors of Medicine 1984–85; Distinguished Teacher Award, American College of Physicians 1985; Leaders in American Medicine, videotape at National Library of Medicine, selected by American College of Physicians 1985; Physician's Physician Award, Atlanta Region Medical Alumni Medical College of Georgia 1985; Williams Award, "The Distinguished Chairman of Medicine Award," presented by the Association of Professors of Medicine 1986; Theodore E. Cummings Award, Cedars Sinai Medical Center (presented by President Reagan and Mrs. Cummings 1989); J. Willis Hurst Award for Excellence in Teaching, to be given annually to the faculty members who are selected by the Cardiac Fellows 1990; J. Willis Hurst Outstanding Bedside Teacher Award established by the Georgia Chapter of the American College of Physicians 1992; establishment by Emory University of the J. Willis Hurst Chair of Cardiology 1992; Hurst Cardiology Service established at Emory University Hospital along with the Logue and Gruentzig Services 1993; Evangeline T. Papageorge Teaching Award for excellence in teaching, Emory University School of Medicine 1995; Leaders in American Medicine Series, selected by Alpha Omega Alpha 1995; the Laennec Award, presented by the American Heart Association 1995; and the Lifetime Teaching Achievement Award for Excellence in Internal Medicine, presented by the 1996–1997 Medical House Staff of Emory University School of Medicine 1997.

The Beginning: A Personal Account

Prior to Chairmanship

I left the Massachusetts General Hospital in Boston in July 1949 and joined Dr. Hal Davison's group in Atlanta. Although I considered offers to remain in Boston, I felt I should return home.

I learned a great deal about myself in the year I spent in practice. I liked private practice but missed the challenges and associations offered by academic medicine. During that year in practice I spent every spare minute at Grady Memorial Hospital, where most of the Emory medical students and house officers were located. I spent considerable time with Dr. Robert Grant, whose work in electrocardiography excited me.

Dr. Paul Beeson, professor and chairman of the Department of Medicine, appointed me to the faculty at Emory University School of Medicine on July 1, 1950. I was to work with the master cardiologist Bruce Logue. I was expected to earn my annual income of $7,200 working in the Private Diagnostic Clinic in Emory University Hospital (the Private

Diagnostic Clinic was one of the three groups of physicians that eventually coalesced to form the Emory University Clinic). This began my long association with Dr. Logue. Bruce and I had a great time developing cardiology at Emory University Hospital. He taught me a lot about a lot of things.

Beeson left Emory for Yale in 1952, and Eugene Ferris became chairman of the Department of Medicine. He was the third chairman of medicine who had been taught by Soma Weiss. Ferris came to Emory at a time of great change. The plans for the Emory University Clinic were well underway, and Ferris initially supported the development. By 1954, however, he had become unhappy about the plans for the governance of the clinic and disagreed publicly with the 1946 medical school planning report (see discussions in Chapters 2 and 4).

Although I had served in the army at Fitzsimons General Hospital in Denver in 1946 and 1947, I was recalled to serve in the navy in 1954 because of the Korean conflict. I was vulnerable because I had been a member of the group of medical students inducted into the army during my sophomore year of medical school. The army had paid for more than two years of my medical education. I was drafted a second time because I had been released from the army earlier than usual. The early release in 1947 had been necessary because of family hardship owing to an automobile wreck that killed my wife's mother and my wife's sister's child. Her sister had severe brain damage and remained in Crawford Long Hospital for several weeks. I lived in her hospital room during her hospitalization. I used up all of my official leave time and requested additional leave. I was told that it would be simpler to be released from the army, because the war was over and many physicians were being discharged earlier than usual. Senator Richard Russell helped achieve my emergency release from the army, and my wife and I moved into her sister's home to help with her rehabilitation. After supervising her gradual physical and mental rehabilitation, I called Dr. White, who arranged for me to become a graduate student in cardiology at the Massachusetts General Hospital in January 1948, prior to beginning my fellowship in July of the same year.

When I was recalled to the service in 1954, I was assigned to the United States Naval Hospital in Bethesda, Maryland, thus becoming one of the few physicians to serve in both the army and the navy. Dr. Henry Cooper was chief of cardiology there. One of the best cardiologists I have ever encountered, he was also a great teacher and friend. When he later resigned from the navy, I became chief of cardiology there.

My experience at the United States Naval Hospital in Bethesda was a very important one. My associates were excellent—three of us became departmental chairmen at various medical schools, and one became a dean.

In July 1955, I attended Majority Leader Lyndon B. Johnson, when he had his first heart attack. This began my long friendship with him and his family. I was discharged as a commander and awarded a commendation for my teaching sessions with the house staff and senior physicians. I returned to Emory in November 1955.

When I returned to Emory, the medical school was in turmoil (see discussion in Chapter 4). Dr. Ferris, apparently, disagreed with certain aspects of the policy of the university and Emory University Clinic. An administrative stalemate had developed among him, Dean Richardson, and the vice president for health affairs, Boisfeuillet Jones. The chairman of the Department of Surgery and the chairman of the Department of Obstetrics supported Ferris. Several members of the faculty, including me, were considering leaving Emory. I was receiving calls from friends of my alma mater regarding the possibility of my returning there. Dr. Howard Burchell, of the Mayo Clinic, was trying to entice me to move to Rochester, Minnesota. Plans for a new Mayo School of Medicine were being considered, and they were planning to recruit some additional physicians who aspired to academic careers. I made one visit to Mayo Clinic as part of the early negotiations. A little later, Emory made me an offer.

The Offer to Be the Chairman of the Department of Medicine

Some time in the late summer or early fall of 1956, Dean Richardson stopped me in the hallway of the Woodruff Memorial Research Building and asked me if I would consider becoming chairman of the Department of Medicine. I was shocked at the question. I muttered something like, "That depends on my colleagues—especially Dr. Logue; would they want me to do that?"

I realized that I could say nothing to anyone about Richardson's inquiry. Later, both Richardson and I considered this conversation as the beginning of my chairmanship of the Department of Medicine. I was thirty-five years old at the time. I later learned that Richardson had already asked Logue to consider the chairmanship, but Logue was not interested. He wanted to devote his time to the creation of the medical section of the new Emory University Clinic, and he supported me for the position of chairman.

Later Richardson, with the support of Vice President Jones, relieved Ferris, Howard, and Caton of their chairmanships (see discussion in Chapter 4).

In the midst of this confusion, the search committee, consisting of Drs. Logue, Carter Smith Sr., Arthur Merrill Sr., and others, formally recommended to Richardson that I be named the fourth full-time chairman of Emory's Department of Medicine. Richardson said to me, "The board of trustees has approved your appointment as chairman of the Department of Medicine. Whether or not you can be the chairman is up to you." This, I learned later, was his view of leadership. He believed that an appointment only gave an individual the authority to act, but that acceptance as a leader had to be earned by the appointee's acting responsibly. In effect, I was shown the track on which I was to run; the way I ran was up to me.

Advice from Stead and Beeson

I made a trip to Durham in November 1956 to visit Eugene Stead. He and Evelyn invited me to spend the night with them in their home, and Stead and I talked far into the night. He discussed his tenure at Emory. He obviously loved Emory. He indicated what he thought about Emory's future. He thought, in the long haul, Emory would outdistance Duke. He told me I should remember four things. First, I should go where I was needed. Second, he said to me what Soma Weiss had said to him, namely, that, "it was time to find out if I were a man of promise or a man of achievement." Then he emphasized that "the most important authority of a chairman is the power to make appointments." Finally, he pointed out that I "should dream many goals. Some goals could be reached quickly without offending others, while other goals might upset them. I must sense," he said, "when my effort to achieve a goal was upsetting others and temporarily back away, but *not lose sight* of the goal."

I spent the next day watching how he interacted with house staff at morning report, with a nurse with whom we had lunch, and with colleagues. He was masterful. I also talked to John Hickman, my old friend James Warren, and Jack Myers, who had previously been on the faculty at Emory.

I left Eugene Stead and traveled to New Haven and spent the night at the home of Paul and Barbara Beeson. Paul remembers it as a "pleasant visit." I remember it as a lesson from a wise and respected mentor.

Many people have asked me what President Lyndon Johnson taught me during my eighteen-year association with him, about guiding a large ship. He was a master psychologist and innovator who rarely failed in an effort he initiated. I respond that he taught me two things. First, "the best fertilizer for any man's ranch is the footprints of the owner"; and, second, "having a good idea is not enough, you must be able to sense the *time* the idea can be successfully implemented."

Ferris became medical director of the American Heart Association on February 1, 1957. Although I had been appointed chairman of the department several months earlier, I began work at the age of thirty-six as professor and chairman of the Department of Medicine and chief of the Medical Service at Grady Memorial Hospital on February 1, 1957.

Why I Accepted the Position

I had enjoyed my work at Emory from 1950 to 1954. I had come to love the place and recognized that Emory and Atlanta would rise hand-in-hand to greatness. In addition, and perhaps more importantly, *the legacy of excellence created by Stead and Beeson intrigued me.* I am sure their legacy stimulated me to step into the chaos that existed at the time. I must add that, although I do not understand it, I never considered the prospect of rebuilding the Department of Medicine as a difficult or impossible task. I viewed each day as an exciting adventure. I sensed that many individuals were willing to help. I suppose I can chalk that up to the naïveté of youth.

The Status of Emory University School of Medicine and Its Department of Medicine on February 1, 1957

When I became chairman of the Department of Medicine, there was no chairman of the Department of Surgery and no chairman of the Department of Obstetrics, and Dr. Richard Blumberg was the part-time chairman of pediatrics. There was no Department of Preventive Medicine or Department of Rehabilitation. In addition, the Departments of Psychiatry and Pathology were having enormous difficulties and were barely viable.

The faculty in the Department of Medicine at Grady was depleted. Drs. Al Brust and Walter Bloom left. Dr. Al Bennett joined Dr. Ferris at the American Heart Association office in New York. Dr. Noble Fowler remained in the Department of Medicine until the summer of 1957, when he became the chief of medicine at the Veterans Hospital associated with the University of Cincinnati. In 1970 he became professor of medicine and director of the Division of Cardiology at the University of Cincinnati, continuing in that position until 1986. We have remained lifelong friends. Dr. Charles LeMaistre remained in the Department of Medicine until August 1959. He continued to work in infectious diseases but became Emory's first chairman of the Department of Preventive Medicine and Community Health. He later became professor of medicine at Southwestern Medical School in Dallas and medical director of the Woodlawn Hospital. He then became chancellor of the University of Texas and still later, president of the M. D. Anderson Hospital in

Houston. Drs. Jerry Cooper and John Galambos were in the United States Public Health Service and were stationed at Grady Memorial Hospital. Cooper had a faculty appointment, and Galambos was considered to be a fellow.

The Emory Hospital and Clinic faculty included Drs. Bruce Logue (see Figure 5-3), Charles Huguley (see Figure 5-4), Spalding Schroder (see Figure 5-5), Ed Dorney (see Figure 5-6), Bernard Hallman (see Figure 5-7) and myself.

The Emory faculty at the Veterans Administration Hospital included Drs. Ben Gendel, chief of medicine (see Figure 5-8), James Crutcher (see Figure 4-6; Dr. Crutcher is second from the left in the third row), Julius Wenger (see Figure 5-9), and Walter Cargill (see Figure 2-2; Dr. Cargill is third from the left on the front row). Dr. John Peters remained a short time but soon joined Ferris at the American Heart Association (see Figure 4-6; Dr. Peters is located on the left end in the third row.)

The total full-time faculty for Grady Memorial Hospital, Emory University Hospital and the Veterans Administration Hospital numbered fourteen (including me).

The junior and senior students were extremely disturbed. To them, their medical future looked doubtful. The members of the medical house staff at Grady were also very disturbed. They had not decided what they would do. No house-staff appointments at the residency level had been made for the year beginning July 1957.

The Relationship of Emory University School of Medicine and Its Department of Medicine to the Community at Large in 1957

The town-gown problems that plague many medical schools and cities had grown progressively worse at Emory during the fifties. The creation of the Emory University Clinic had not been accepted by all physicians inside and outside the university, and the loss of three department chairmen had sparked another community controversy. The schism between the town and the academic community had widened to an alarming degree. Emory's national reputation was damaged considerably because the details of the ruckus had been widely reported in the newspapers throughout the nation (see Chapter 4).

Financial Support

My income as chairman of the Department of Medicine was $17,000. That did not trouble me because it was more than I had been making. I was permitted to continue my consultative work in cardiology at Emory University Hospital and Clinic.

In the beginning I had no departmental budget. This, too, did not trouble me. I believed I could successfully make my case to Dean Richardson for funds to recruit specific individuals. I preferred to do that rather than live within a fixed budget.

The department had been awarded two training grants: $25,500 from the National Institute of Neurologic Disease and Blindness, and a teaching grant of $25,000 from the National Heart Institute for the support of cardiology.

Buildings That Influenced Our Actions

Stead and Beeson had had no facilities except old Grady Memorial Hospital. Their offices were in the basement of the "colored hospital," which was the Emory Division of Grady Memorial Hospital. In that regard, I was comparatively lucky. The relatively new Glenn Memorial Building in the Grady area provided space for the dean's office as well as offices for four clinical chairmen. Although this building was owned by Grady, it had been built with the understanding that it would house Emory faculty. The new magnificent Grady Memorial Hospital was in the last phase of completion (see later discussion). It stood as a signal that things would be better than they had been.

In addition, the relatively new Ernest W. Woodruff Memorial Research Building located on the Emory campus was occupied with productive people.

The first phase of the Emory University Clinic building program had been completed. This was the signal that the medical school planning report of 1946 was being fulfilled.

The old Veterans Administration Hospital was functioning well, and plans for a new Veterans Hospital were being discussed.

Thoughts in Early 1957

It was clear: Emory needed to rebuild all of its clinical departments and required several decades of stability. Time was needed for wounds to heal. The confidence of the students and house staff had to be restored, and the town-gown breach had to be closed. An excellent national and international reputation had to be earned. Patient care, teaching, and research goals had to be developed and implemented. At that time, Emory University School of Medicine, including its Department of Medicine, as well as Grady Memorial Hospital and Emory University Hospital, were still poverty-stricken, and financial resources had to be found. Because there were no other clinical chairmen in place, I was not only charged with the responsibility of rebuilding the Department of Medicine but was also involved with rebuilding all the clinical departments. Fortunately, Dean Richardson was a quick thinker and decisive administrator. Accordingly, he moved swiftly to stabilize the other clinical departments.

Early Actions in 1957 and 1958

I moved most of my activities from the Emory University Clinic to the second floor of the Glenn Memorial Building in the Grady Memorial Hospital area on February 1, 1957. I retained an office in the Emory University Clinic because I intended to continue my consultative practice in cardiology at Emory University Hospital and Clinic.

Mrs. Ruth Strange, my secretary in the Emory University Clinic, agreed to become the senior secretary in the Department of Medicine office in the Glenn Memorial Building (see Figure 5-10). She deserves enormous credit for the success of the fledgling department, because she was older and wiser than her "boss." She was brilliant, competent, and mature. Were she living today, she could easily be the chief executive officer of a large company. She managed the department, including its business affairs. Mrs. Anne Webb, who had worked in the Department of Obstetrics, joined her in 1958 (see Figure 5-11). Anne was destined to play a major role in the Department in the years that followed (see page 325).

Dr. Bernard Hallman, an endocrinologist in the medical section of the Emory University Clinic, agreed to be assistant dean of professional services at Grady Memorial Hospital (see Figure 5-7). He moved his office into Grady Memorial Hospital. This unique individual was perfectly suited for the job. We soon named him "iron pants," because he would listen to disgruntled and anxious individuals for hours on end. He made reasonable recommendations to Frank Wilson Sr., the superintendent of Grady Memorial Hospital. He gained Wilson's confidence, which was vital for the future development of the clinical departments. My weekly discussions with Hallman by phone and in person helped me make many difficult decisions. He was an effective counselor and the invisible and silent force that calmed the turbulent water.

Dr. Ben Gendel, chief of medicine at the Veterans Administration Hospital, wanted to be more closely related to the medical students (see Figure 5-8). Accordingly, I asked him to move from the Veterans Administration Hospital to the Glenn Memorial Building. He organized and supervised the junior and senior student programs. A superb teacher-lecturer, he deserves a very special place in the history of the Department of Medicine.

I appointed Dr. James Crutcher, an excellent teacher and strong leader, to replace Gendel as chief of medicine at the Veterans

Administration Hospital (see Figure 4-6; Dr. Crutcher is second from the left in the third row).

I met often with John Dodd, the respected leader of the senior students. We talked at leisure. He helped plan the approach to the concerned junior and senior medical students. This is when I learned that good teaching calms the troubled feelings of bright medical students. So I spent an increasing amount of time with the students on the wards, in conference rooms, and in the dining room. I was rewarded at their graduation, when they made me an honorary member of their class.

In the beginning, there were two house-staff programs: the Grady Memorial Hospital program and the Emory-Veterans Administration Hospital program. The appointments of the 1957 house staff in the Emory-VA program were not a problem. But the appointments of the residents in the Grady program had not been made, and that was a problem.

Dr. Craig Cantrell was the chief resident in medicine at Grady when I began my work as chairman. Appointed by Ferris, he was an excellent and mature chief resident. We worked well together. I worked with him to improve the teaching of the house staff. One day I asked fourteen of the medical house officers to meet me in my office. I discussed with them what I hoped to do. I made it clear that I could not guarantee that my plans would come to fruition but I pledged to work with them and hoped they would remain. They left my office. Alone, I thought—if they don't sign up, my days are numbered. In a few minutes their spokesman opened the door and said they would all stay. I was saved.

I selected Dr. Huddie Cheney as my first chief resident at Grady Memorial Hospital (see Figure 4-5; Dr. Cheney is fifth from the left on the fourth row). He was highly respected by the house staff. He, too, deserves a special place in the history of the Department of Medicine, because he knew we had very little except plenty of patients and an intense desire to develop a world-class patient care and educational system. I cherish the book, *The Life of Sir William Osler*, that he and the house staff gave me at Christmas 1957.

Cheney assisted me in recruiting house officers. His leadership, beginning in July 1957 and ending in July 1958, set the stage; there was never a time during the next thirty years that we did not fill our house-staff quota with excellent young trainees.

The members of the volunteer faculty were wonderful. Many of the friends I had made during the year of practice helped with the teaching program at Grady Memorial Hospital.

By July 1957 the confusion was settling down in the Department of Medicine. Everyone could see an organizational structure beginning to take shape.

I appointed Dr. Elbert Tuttle Jr. to the faculty (see Figure 5-12). He was interested in renal disease and had completed his fellowship in renal medicine under Alexander Leaf at Massachusetts General Hospital. Elbert, who was obviously brilliant, wanted to join the Emory faculty in 1956, but there was no money. He came as a senior resident in medicine at Grady Memorial Hospital, and I appointed him to the faculty in 1957, using money supplied by the Georgia Heart Association.

I appointed Dr. Grigg Churchwell to the faculty in 1957 (see Figure 4-3; Dr. Churchwell is on the extreme right in the fourth row). He had been a member of the house staff and was interested in pulmonary disease.

Dr. Ross L. McLean (see Figure 5-13) was recruited in July 1957 to develop pulmonary medicine. He had been on the staff of the Baltimore Veterans Hospital.

Dr. Robert Franch, a fellow with Dr. Noble Fowler at Grady Memorial Hospital, was recruited in July 1957 to direct the cardiac catheterization laboratory located in the Woodruff Memorial Research Building on the Emory campus (see Figure 5-14). As will be seen later, he was an excellent choice. Dr. Gordon Barrow, working with the Crippled Children Service of the State of Georgia, supplied the equipment for the laboratory. This was the first cardiac catheterization laboratory on the Emory campus and the only cardiac catheterization laboratory in Atlanta at a private hospital.

Dr. John Galambos joined the Department of Medicine in July 1957 (see Figure 5-15). Trained in gastroenterology at the University of Chicago, he was interested in research related to the liver.

Bruce Logue was chief of medicine at Emory University Hospital and head of the Medical Section of the Emory University Clinic (see Figure 5-3). His excellent leadership and experience were recognized in Atlanta and at the national level. My first appointment to the Emory University Clinic in 1957 was Dr. Charles Corley (see Figure 5-16), who was to work with Dr. Charles Huguley in hematology. Corley had been an outstanding fellow in hematology. I also appointed Dr. Sam Poole in cardiology. He was assigned to work in the Emory University Clinic and was asked to direct the course in physical diagnosis for sophomore medical students. Poole entered private practice in Gainesville, Georgia, one year later.

Most of these early actions and appointments took place in 1957. At that time there were no formalized divisions in the Department of Medicine. There could be no divisions until there was a critical mass of people to divide.

Other Important Appointments in the Department of Medicine

Dr. Herbert Karp, a brilliant teacher, joined the Department of Medicine in January 1958 (see Figure 5-17). He had been a member of Beeson's house staff and later trained in neurology at Duke and the Massachusetts General Hospital.

Dr. John Preedy joined the department in 1958 (see Figure 5-18). He was an excellent researcher in endocrinology. I had asked Dr. Alfred Wilhelmi, the chairman of the Department of Biochemistry, to recommend the best person he knew who could develop a research-oriented Division of Endocrinology. He recommended John Preedy, who, at that time, lived in London, England.

Dr. Robert C. Schlant joined the department in cardiology in July 1958 (see Figure 5-19). He had trained with Lewis Dexter at the Peter Bent Brigham Hospital in Boston and was recruited to direct the Stead-Warren Cardiovascular Laboratory in the Steiner Building in the Grady area. Dexter reported that he was one of his best trainees.

Dr. Thomas F. Sellers Jr. joined the department in 1958 and became director of the Division of Infectious Diseases (see Figure 5-20). Sellers had graduated from Emory and had received his infectious disease training at Emory under LeMaistre and at Cornell under Walsh McDermott.

Dr. B. Woodfin Cobbs Jr. (see Figure 5-21), who trained with Dr. Ed Bland at the Massachusetts General Hospital, was added to the cardiology staff at Emory University Hospital and Clinic in 1958. He was fresh from his work with Dr. John Goodwin at Hammersmith in London and was an excellent addition to the group.

These were the early appointees. They were young, brilliant, and devoted to building an excellent Department of Medicine. The department was eventually organized into divisions. The story of the development of each division is told later in this chapter (see pages 240–89).

New Appointments in Other Clinical Departments

I served on the search committees to select Dr. J. D. Martin as the new chairman of the Department of Surgery and Dr. Richard Blumberg, who had been the effective part-time chairman of the Department of Pediatrics, as the full-time chairman of that department. Dr. John Cross served as acting chairman of the Department of Gynecology and Obstetrics until Dr. J. Dan Thompson was appointed to the position. Dr. Bernard Holland was selected to be chairman of the Department of Psychiatry in 1959. Holland was a Stead-trained internist who also trained in psychiatry. He was a superb choice. Dr. Hugh R. Dudley, who trained at the Massachusetts General Hospital, was appointed chairman of the Department of Pathology in 1961, after Dr. Walter Sheldon moved to John Hopkins.

Unfortunately, soon after Dudley arrived to chair the department of pathology, he died of a ruptured berry aneurysm. His future was bright, and the loss was enormous. He was replaced by Dr. John Ellis of Cornell in 1962.

Relationship to Basic Science Departments

I established a working relationship with the basic science departments by organizing teaching sessions in the basement of my home. Several members of the basic science departments would report on their research, and we would discuss teaching activities.

Building Bridges to the Community

My friends at Piedmont Hospital and Georgia Baptist Hospital asked me to present teaching sessions at each of the hospitals. I would discuss interesting patients but, in addition, when asked, said that I thought the time had come when hospitals should do two things. They should build an office building to house the physicians that used the hospital (when possible, the building should be attached to the hospital) and, because medicine was becoming more complex, they should have a teaching program for physicians, nurses, and all the people who worked in the hospital. I knew that such a development would eventually decrease the number of practicing physicians who came to medical grand rounds at Grady Memorial Hospital, but I also knew that with the passage of time, each hospital would create its own educational activities. In the years that followed, these two developments did take place, not because I urged them, but because it was part of the evolutionary growth of medicine in Atlanta. My visits to the hospitals and my pleas to the volunteer physicians to help in our teaching programs decreased the town-gown problem. In subsequent years, the schism disappeared, because an increasing number of our medical house officers began to practice in Atlanta. The ugly schism of the late fifties was replaced by a warm and comfortable feeling, and the town-gown problem vanished.

Invitations to visit and teach at other medical schools began to increase. Wherever I went, I insisted on meeting with junior and senior medical students, because I hoped some of them would apply for our internship. They did. When teaching at another institution, I always considered that I represented Emory, and that I must not let Emory down.

The Department of Medicine sponsored postgraduate courses in many subjects (see page 233). Postgraduate courses in electrolytes, hematology, cardiac arrhythmias, and liver disease were presented in 1957 (see Figures 5-22A, B, C, and D). These courses were given in a classroom located in the Physiology Building on the Emory campus. Later, when the new Grady Memorial Hospital was completed, the courses were presented in the Grady Memorial Hospital Auditorium. Through this effort, the visiting faculty from the United States and abroad, as well as the participants that came from all over the country, learned about Emory and what was happening in the Department of Medicine. The excellent work of the members of the Department of Medicine soon became recognized internationally. Dean Richardson credited the postgraduate courses as the major reason Emory alumni regained their respect for Emory following the ruckus of 1956.

The teaching activity in the department was also recognized by medical students everywhere. Accordingly, the recruitment of excellent house staff was becoming routine. At Emory University School of Medicine, 50 percent of the senior class planned to enter internal medicine or its subspecialties. Half of them applied to our programs. Of these, I would select about seventeen to twenty as interns in the internal medicine programs of Emory University. The remaining first-year appointees were selected from the superb applicants from many excellent medical schools. Also, Emory students themselves created their own excellent reputation. Accordingly, the departments of medicine at other schools wanted to recruit Emory students into their house-staff programs.

During the early years of the new department, I presided over a weekly teaching session at Emory University Hospital and Clinic and the Veterans Administration Hospital. I took morning report on every new admission to Grady Memorial Hospital each day and organized many teaching conferences. Phone calls to house officers at night and late-night visits to the wards set the tone for excellent patient care.

Patient care was visibly improved as the teaching programs improved. This is why all hospitals should be teaching hospitals. Hospitals should not require the presence of students and house officers to establish an educational program; anyone and everyone who works at the hospital should be involved with teaching.

Questions and Answers in the Early Months

As the faculty grew in number at Grady Memorial Hospital, Emory University Hospital and Clinic, and the Veterans Administration Hospital, it was necessary for me to answer the following questions:

• Would I, as chairman, run the department as a dean runs a medical school?

I did not choose to do that. I did not aspire to be a dean or a mini-dean who ran a department. I preferred to work in the trenches. I wanted to continue personally to teach, to see patients in consultation, and to engage in clinical research and write.

• Should the department be organized like Harvard's, where each hospital in the system is virtually autonomous?

I thought not. In time there would be divisions in the department, and each division director would be responsible for coordinating the educational and research actions of the faculty members located in the various hospitals where the Department of Medicine was responsible.

• What type of faculty members would be needed in the Department of Medicine?

The department needed several different type of faculty members in order to deliver excellent patient care, teach medicine, and create new knowledge by research. It was obvious: Emory was going to become a large medical center, and such a center would require the appointment of many different types of people.

The clinicians, teachers, and researchers who were appointed would be equally respected. Each would be judged only by his or her performance. I was familiar with the metaphor of the three-legged stool that characterized the function of a medical center. One leg was named *patient care*, another leg *teaching*, and the remaining leg *research*. The objective was to maintain a *level seat*. I believed we would need all three types of faculty members in the Department of Medicine.

• How were faculty members to be supported financially?

There were only three sources of financial support. The money could come from the university endowment that became part of the department budget, from government sources, or from patient fees. Accordingly, I set about developing these sources of financial support. This approach, I reasoned, would give the flexibility needed for the varied tasks required to develop an excellent department of medicine. I envisioned excellent teachers who earned *some* of their income in the Emory University Clinic, excellent clinicians who earned *all* of their income in the Emory University Clinic but taught one quarter of their time, and excellent researchers who obtained government grants for research and earned *some* additional income in the Emory University Clinic.

This approach was successful for many years, but trouble eventually came when promotions to tenured positions, which had to be approved by the Advisory Faculty Council, were permitted only for those members engaged in research. The basic science faculty members on the Advisory Faculty Council gave little credit for excellent teaching and excellent patient care (until they had a daughter or son in medical school or became ill themselves). So despite my own belief that all faculty members should be treated equally, our system of promotion could checkmate such a belief. This reality, of course, was no different from that of other schools. I viewed such a policy as a vestige of a time that had passed. It was just as clear to me in 1957 as it is in 1997 that all types of faculty members are needed to run a medical center, and that each faculty member should be judged by his or her performance.

In later years, after observing many troubled medical centers, I changed the metaphor. Rather than consider the function of a medical center to be like a three-legged stool, I believed it was wise to consider it to be like a parent with three children. The children are named *patient care, teaching,* and *research.* Trouble was certain to come should the parent show favoritism for one of the "children" but neglect the other two. Should one child be favored over the others, then the two unfavored children would tell the world about it (loudly).

• How could we as a faculty communicate the pleasures that come from the pursuit of excellence?

The students and house officers needed to live in an environment of excellent patient care, excellent teaching, and excellent research. They needed to feel the excitement associated with the pursuit of excellence. We, as a faculty, had to communicate to our trainees the excitement we felt about the opportunities that surrounded us to learn, to teach, to discover, and to be of service.

• What was a professional?

This question bothered me until I heard Judge Elbert Tuttle's graduation address at Emory in the summer of 1957. Since then, I have quoted his definition of professionalism to students, house officers, and fellows whenever the occasion was right. The Tuttle quotation did a lot to guide the developing department, because it states clearly the purpose of the effort.

> The professional man is in essence one who provides services. But the service he renders is something more than that of the laborer, even the skilled laborer. It is a service that wells up from the entire complex of his personality. True, some specialized and highly developed techniques may be included, but their mode of expression is given its deepest meaning by the personality of the practitioner. In a very real sense his professional service cannot be separate from his personal being. He has no goods to sell, no land to till; his only asset is himself. It turns out that there is no right price for service, for what is a share

of a man worth? If he does not contain the quality of integrity, he is worthless. If he does, he is priceless. The value is either nothing or it is infinite.

So do not try to set a price on yourselves. Do not measure out your professional services on an apothecary's scale and say, "Only this much for so much." Do not debase yourselves by equating your souls to what they will bring in the market. Do not be a miser, hoarding your talents and abilities and knowledge, either among yourselves or in your dealings with your clients, patients, or flock. Rather be reckless and spendthrift, pouring out your talent to all to whom it can be of service! Throw it away, waste it; and in the spending it can be of service. Do not keep a watchful eye lest you slip, and give away a little bit of what you might have sold. Do not censor your thoughts to gain a wider audience. Like love, talent is useful only in its expenditure, and it is never exhausted. Certain it is that man must eat, so set what price you must on your service. But never confuse the performance, which is great, with the compensation, be it money, power or fame, which is trivial.[6]

The New Grady Memorial Hospital and the End of an Era

The last ward rounds in old Grady Memorial Hospital were made on January 27, 1958. This is the day the patients were moved to the new, but still segregated, Grady Memorial Hospital. The last patient seen on medical ward rounds is shown in Figure 5-23.

The move from the old "Gradys" to the new Grady Memorial Hospital in 1958 marked the end of an era. The old "Gradys" had served the community well for half a century, but the hospitals were worn out. Worn out from use by millions of very sick patients. No one who entered the hospitals would ever forget the distinct odor produced by the combination of sick patients and the pungent disinfectant used to clean the floors. The walls of the ward offices were lined with slides that had been taped there for "safekeeping" by the house officers. The slides were testimony to the types of diseases seen there. Not only had "the Gradys" served the sick, but they had become the site of excellent medical teaching and research by devoted volunteer and full-time Emory faculty members. During the first half of the twentieth century, there would have been no Emory School of Medicine had there been no "Gradys."

The plans for the new Grady Memorial Hospital began in the late forties and were spearheaded by Frank Wilson, the administrator of the hospital, and T. K. Glenn, chairman of Fulton-DeKalb Hospital Authority. The community agreed to finance the twenty-one story building that was

---

[6] E. P. Tuttle Sr., "Heroism in War and Peace," address given at the commencement exercises of the professional and graduate schools of Emory University, 7 June 1957, *The Emory University Quarterly* 13, no. 3 (October 1957): 129–30.

to contain 1,100 beds and numerous outpatient facilities, including an enormous emergency clinic. The building was located across the street from the Glenn Memorial Building, which housed the Emory faculty. It is interesting to note that the new Grady Memorial Hospital was to be built on land formerly owned by Emory University. The new hospital would occupy a full block (see Figure 5-24). It was built in the fifties at a cost of $22,000,000. The patients who were in the old Gradys were moved to the magnificent new hospital on January 27, 1958 (see Figure 5-23).

African-American patients were admitted to the C-D side of the new hospital, and white patients were admitted to the A-B side of the hospital. More time would pass before all parts of the hospital could be integrated (see page 218). The medical service was located on the sixth floor of the hospital. Each of the four medical wards had an office and treatment room. A conference room for teaching was located in the connector between the A-B and C-D side of the hospital. A small teaching laboratory was also located in the connector. A large auditorium was located on the ground floor of the hospital.

The move to the new hospital was accomplished without a major incident. Wilson, the powerful superintendent of Grady Memorial Hospital, did not initially permit the medical school to use the new hospital auditorium. The medical school was forced to continue to use the old auditorium in the lower part of the old "colored" hospital. The point Wilson was trying to make was never announced, but one can guess that he was trying to establish the importance of Grady in the Emory-Grady setup.

There were three dining rooms in the new hospital: one for white people, one for "professional" black people, and one for the "nonprofessional" black people. There was segregation not only according to race but also according to occupation.

The move to the new Grady Memorial Hospital was an important event. The inpatient services were greatly improved. The services in the outpatient clinics were also improved, as was the service in the busy emergency clinic. There was one major problem; the hospital was not air-conditioned. The Grady administrators believed it would not be wise to spend the public's money to air-condition Grady Memorial Hospital when no private hospital in Atlanta was air-conditioned. Some years later, at great expense, Grady was air-conditioned, when it was pointed out that the physicians had to close the windows on the side of the hospital near the new noisy expressway in order to talk to patients, or to listen to their hearts and lungs with a stethoscope. Closing the windows to perform these acts made the heat unbearable. Therefore, it was concluded that it was *medically necessary* to air-condition the hospital.

Office space for certain members of the Emory faculty was made available in Grady Memorial Hospital. Through the help of Emory's Boisfeuillet Jones and the Woodruff Foundation, a new cardiac catheterization laboratory and facilities for renal medicine were built in the new hospital. The old cardiac catheterization laboratory located in the Steiner Building was closed.

House-staff quarters were located on the top floor of the new hospital. Many, if not most, of the house officers in 1958 stayed in the house-staff quarters provided by the hospital. An intern was paid $75 a month.

Frank Wilson died in 1964, and William Pinkston became the hospital administrator. Pinkston worked closely with Dean Richardson to create a cooperative environment. Pinkston was excellent. He could not always do what others wanted him to do, but his honesty was always evident. Emory University and the citizens of Fulton and DeKalb Counties owe him a strong vote of gratitude.

By 1982 the new hospital was no longer new but had worn out in twenty-five years of intense use. More rooms and new types of facilities were needed. Plans were discussed to renovate the hospital and to add a new outpatient facility.

As chairman of the Department of Medicine, I was also chief of the medical service at Grady Memorial Hospital from 1957 to 1986. Dr. Ken Walker, who replaced Ben Gendel on July 1, 1971, assisted me in the day-to-day running of the medical service (see Figure 5-25). We often took morning report together. He was an excellent recruiter for house staff, the organizer for the sophomore, junior, and senior student programs, a listener to students and house staff, and an advisor. We talked daily with each other and then summarized our progress by talking together each Sunday morning. He and I edited two books on the problem-oriented record. He, Dr. Dallas Hall, and I, edited the large book *Clinical Methods*, dedicated to William Pinkston (see Figure 5-26). Walker was a capable, creative, individual who after 1986 was destined to be a major mover in the creation of the Emory-sponsored medical school in the Republic of Georgia and chairman of the advisory committee of the National Library of Medicine.

The Desegregation of the New Grady Memorial Hospital

According to the custom of the day, the original Grady Memorial Hospital was segregated according to race.

The entire Emory University School of Medicine was located in the old Atlanta Medical College building until 1917, when the Anatomy and Physiology Buildings were completed on the Emory campus. The clinical departments of Emory used the entire Atlanta Medical College building until 1921, when most of the building was converted into a hospital for African-American patients. This, of course, meant even more segregation of the races. From then until 1958, when the patients were moved to the new Grady Memorial Hospital, the facility was designated as the Emory Division of Grady Memorial Hospital.

The new Grady Memorial Hospital opened in 1958, still segregated. The hospital was desegregated by federal law on June 1, 1965. I personally pushed a bed from the C-D side of the sixth floor of the hospital to the A-B side of the hospital. Dallas Hall, a resident in medicine, accompanied me on the "trip." I sensed that history was being made, but no photograph was taken. Despite the dire predictions of some, the desegregation of the hospital created no problems. The patients accepted the change without complaint.

Modus Operandi

Teaching and Learning (1957–1986)

Freshmen and Sophomore Students

Members of the Department of Medicine were invited to give several lectures to the freshmen. The goal was to introduce them to clinicians.

The Department of Medicine was responsible for the organization of the course in "physical diagnosis" for sophomore medical students. The course actually dealt with matters in addition to physical diagnosis and, in later years, was referred to as "clinical methods" because it included history-taking, physical diagnosis, clinical laboratory procedures, and sessions on the use of statistics labeled "analytical medicine."

Presented two afternoons each week for six months, the course focused on patients in Grady Memorial Hospital, Emory University Hospital, and the Atlanta Veterans Administration Hospital. Later, when Crawford Long Hospital was added to the Emory system, its patients were also included in the course, as were patients admitted to Piedmont Hospital, DeKalb Medical Center, and West Paces Ferry Hospital. Numerous faculty members from several departments met the students and guided their work. More than fifty members of the faculty were involved each afternoon, and many capable volunteer faculty members also took part in it. The course was extremely important because *a major goal of every medical school should be to make certain every graduate can examine patients.*

In 1957, Sam Poole organized the course. Herbert Karp, an excellent teacher, organized the course from 1958 until 1960. Robert Franch organized the course until 1977, Ken Walker and I organized it from

1977 to 1986. The principles of the problem-oriented approach were emphasized during the seventies and eighties (see page 237). The book *Clinical Methods*, which I edited with Walker and Hall in 1976, emphasized the problem-oriented record and was a major resource for the course.

Junior Students, Senior Students, House Staff, and Fellows

I believed that a teaching hospital should be defined as a hospital where everyone taught. So, in 1957, I established a rule: everyone assigned to the medical service at Grady Memorial Hospital, Emory University Hospital, and the Veterans Administration Hospital was expected to teach. Teaching was defined as more than dispensing *facts*. The teacher was expected to determine whether the trainees incorporated the facts into a *thought process* and *used* the newfound knowledge in their work. Fellows were expected to teach residents. Residents were expected to teach interns. Interns were expected to teach medical students. Students were expected to teach each other as well as the patients. Senior staff guided the system and learned from each other as well as from the house staff, fellows, and students. Young trainees observed older senior staff members trying to learn. I believed that a senior faculty member who did not attend teaching sessions involving young trainees sent the wrong signal. The students and members of the house staff believed that such faculty members were too wrapped up in themselves to care about students. Accordingly, members of the senior staff attended certain designated teaching sessions that involved students and house staff.

To create a cohesive Department of Medicine, we had a patient-based noon conference five days each week at Grady Memorial Hospital. As divisions were formed, we had enough people to present two 30-minute discussions on Monday, Tuesday, Wednesday, and Friday. Thursday was reserved for grand rounds. Everyone attended the teaching conferences, including the senior staff, interns and residents, fellows, and students assigned to medicine. Many nurses also attended. In addition, the Division of Cardiology had a 5:30 to 7:00 p.m. conference in the Grady auditorium on Wednesdays. Volunteer faculty commonly attended these conferences, and the Grady Memorial Hospital auditorium was often filled with enthusiastic people. The conferences were not mere lectures where the speaker announced information. Rather patients were presented by house officers, and patient-based teaching was emphasized.

One of the finest teaching sessions was held on Saturday mornings in the Oppenheimer Room in the Glenn Memorial Building. Those interested in cardiology met from 10:00 a.m. to noon. This uninterrupted teaching session involved the cardiology fellows, members of the house staff, members of the full-time senior staff, and volunteer faculty members. This teaching session was comparable to Stead's "Sunday school" of the forties.

Some interesting things happened along the way. In 1958, when the new Grady Memorial Hospital opened, there was no microscope on the medical floor of the hospital. My next-door neighbor, Mr. Roy Warren, supplied the money in honor of his physician, Dr. Clarence Mills, another one of my neighbors. The teaching microscope was used to teach the house staff and students how to examine sputum, urine, blood, etc. There was a problem; was Emory or Grady to supply the reagents needed for the laboratory? After much negotiation, Grady supplied the badly needed reagents.

Robert Woodruff marketed Coca-Cola by placing the drink with the secret formula "within arm's reach of desire." I applied the same philosophy to "marketing" information. Roy Warren supplied a sum of money annually to purchase books. Although an adequate branch of the Emory medical library was located in the Glenn Memorial Building, across the street from Grady Memorial Hospital, I wanted the books to be "within arm's reach" of those who needed to look up information. Accordingly, I designed a book rack for each of the four Grady medical wards. The books were then chained to the racks. Before long, the attending physicians, as well as the students and members of the house staff, were looking up needed information when they made ward rounds. The first step in the learning process was easily accomplished. The *true teacher* could then demonstrate how the information was used.

Walter Sheldon, chairman of the Department of Pathology, had moved his operation from Grady Memorial Hospital to Emory University Hospital. He resigned in 1961 to join Ivan Bennett, chairman of the Department of Pathology at Johns Hopkins. This move had a profound effect on the pathology service at Grady Memorial Hospital. For a while, Grady Memorial Hospital attempted to support a pathology service that was separate from the department at Emory. This practice led to an inadequate number of house officers in the Department of Pathology at Grady. This had a negative impact on the medical service because the accreditation process required that we obtain autopsies on at least half the patients who died on the medical service. The requirement was justified, because the autopsy was an excellent audit system and a fine teaching device. We all stopped what we were doing and went to the autopsy room when the proper announcement was made on the loud speaker. The pathology service offered by Grady Memorial Hospital was inadequate, because there was an insufficient number of pathology house officers to perform the autopsies. There was an adequate number of senior pathologists to process and interpret the material, but they needed help with the autopsies. So I rotated medical house officers through the pathology service, and they did the autopsies. The medical house officers learned a great deal, and one of them decided to spend a year in pathology before continuing his training as a medical house officer. The actions of these medical house officers demonstrated their determination to learn medicine.

Eventually, the pathology service at Grady Memorial Hospital returned to its former status when it became, once again, part of the Department of Pathology of the university. Dr. Hugh R. Dudley, a Harvard faculty member at the Massachusetts General Hospital, became chairman of the Department of Pathology in 1961. Unfortunately, he died of a ruptured berry aneurysm in the brain on September 10, 1961, and Dr. John Ellis, from the faculty at Cornell, became the new chairman on July 1, 1962.

The Division of Cardiology, in cooperation with Dr. Michael Gravanis, of the Department of Pathology, brought Dr. Reginald Hudson, of the National Heart Hospital in London, to Emory for several weeks each year for several years. He was a true teacher. A gentle man who compelled trainees to listen and think, he profoundly influenced the students, house officers, fellows, and members of the senior staff.

Later, Dr. Michael Gravanis, became chairman of the Department of Pathology. He was greatly interested in teaching and contributed enormously to the teaching program in medicine. He became nationally known as an expert in cardiac pathology.

I discovered that the usual house officer had little instruction during medical school in the examination of the eye. Accordingly, I asked a member of the ophthalmology service to visit the Grady medical wards once a week and, along with the medical house officers, examine the eyes of selected patients. Regrettably, as time passed, the ophthalmologist became so busy that the sessions on the medical service could not be continued.

I recognized that all patients, all house officers, and all physicians, would, sooner or later, have emotional problems. When Dr. Bernard Holland became professor and chairman of the Department of Psychiatry in 1959, I asked him to visit on a medical ward and discuss psychiatric problems with members of the house staff. He had trained at Grady Memorial Hospital under Stead and later became Stead's chief resident in medicine at Duke. He then trained in psychiatry. His weekly sessions were magnificent. Regrettably, he could not continue this activity indefinitely because of the pressure of other duties.

For many years the medical house officers and fellows participated in House Staff Research Day. Every member of the medical house staff was expected to work on a research project. The only rule was that each house officer was to pursue, in-depth, the answer to a question about a patient he or she had attended. The house officers and fellows could team up with faculty members, but the ideas had to originate with the house officers and fellows. Initially, every house officer and fellow was asked to present his or her work at the Annual House Officer Research Day. As the number of trainees increased, it became impossible for every house officer and fellow to present. Accordingly, a committee of faculty members selected the scientific papers to be presented. A nationally known expert was invited to visit the Department of Medicine and judge the presentations of the house officers and fellows (see Figure 5-27). The visitor delivered a speech at the dinner that followed the day of presentations. It was an exciting·educational activity.

We secured Harvey. Harvey was a mannequin that was created by Dr. Michael Gordon at the University of Miami. The mannequin was named for Dr. Proctor Harvey, of auscultation fame. Dr. Garland Herndon and Boisfeuillet Jones obtained the funds from the Woodruff Foundation to purchase the teaching mannequin. Dr. Joel Felner, a member of the Division of Cardiology at Emory, helped create the programs for the mannequin. Because the physical findings of various cardiac diseases could be displayed by the mannequin, it was and is an excellent teaching device.

The electronic equipment needed to teach auscultation of the heart was obtained for Emory University Hospital, Grady Memorial Hospital and the Veterans Administration Hospital. The equipment for Emory University Hospital was bought by money given as a prize at a golf tournament. This equipment was used in sessions to teach basic skills to students and house staff.

Prior to 1957, junior students allocated to medicine were assigned to Emory University Hospital and the Veterans Administration Hospital. I was in charge of the program at Emory University Hospital in the early fifties. In 1957, the junior students assigned to medicine were placed at Grady Memorial Hospital and the senior students were placed at Emory University Hospital and the Veterans Administration Hospital. This permitted the development of a junior curriculum implemented completely in one place under very close supervision. The residents and fellows were expected to teach the students; the faculty guided the system. This change was very successful, because the senior students assigned to the other two hospitals had a good knowledge base that permitted them to learn from the excellent faculty at Emory University Hospital and the Veterans Administration Hospital.

Early in my chairmanship, I arranged for excellent senior students to take electives in medicine at other institutions. Several students, for example, participated in programs at the Massachusetts General Hospital. We also encouraged senior students at other schools to spend their elective time with us. Many did, and this spread the word about our teaching program. Many of them applied to be interns in our program.

In 1957 there was a Grady Memorial Hospital house-staff program and a separate Emory University Hospital-Veterans Administration Hospital program. In 1973 these two programs were combined into the Emory University Affiliated Hospitals Program in Medicine. A little later the Crawford Long Hospital medical house-staff program joined the University Affiliated Hospitals Program (see page 351), creating the unified training program that has continued to the present time.

After the Clinical Research Facility was developed at Emory University Hospital, arrangements were made for students and house officers to rotate through that facility. Drs. Garland Herndon, Dan Rudman, and Herbert Bonkovsky, who, over the years, directed the facilities, profoundly influenced many of the students (see page 228).

I took morning report at Grady Memorial Hospital. Every admission to the medical service was reviewed in the ward offices on Wards 6A, B, C and D until about 1973 when we introduced the problem-oriented record. After that time, morning report was held in the conference room on the sixth floor of Grady. The charts of all new admissions were reviewed with the house staff (see discussion on page 239). Morning report was held by various members of the faculty at Emory University Hospital, the Veterans Administration Hospital, and Crawford Long Hospital. Drs. Logue, Crutcher, Hardison, Ramos, Shulman, and others contributed to this important teaching exercise.

As years passed I had several teaching sessions each week at Grady Memorial Hospital and one teaching session each week at each of the other three hospitals. The goal of these sessions was to demonstrate the collection, analysis, and use of medical data. The question "why" was stressed as much as the act of discovery. Although Emory had always had excellent medical students, it became clear to me that the better the house staff, the better the excellent Emory students performed. The resident who teaches night and day profits enormously from the effort, as do the students he or she teaches.

We were interested in the overall development of the student and house officer. The trainees, I believed, should observe senior physicians at Emory University Hospital and Crawford Long Hospital diagnose, manage, and serve private patients. This is why I continued to see private patients at Emory University Hospital and Clinic during my entire chairmanship. As the saying goes, I believed I should "walk the walk" and not simply "talk the talk." Faculty members in the Department of Medicine could arrange to see private patients at Emory University Hospital and Clinic and, later, at Crawford Long Hospital as well. In addition, and very importantly, the faculty members appointed to the medical section of the Emory Clinic, at Crawford Long Hospital, and at the Veterans Administration Hospital made attending rounds at Grady Memorial Hospital. They were skilled at emphasizing the relationship of the physician to the patient.

The volunteer faculty members were excellent. They made scheduled ward rounds at Grady Memorial Hospital, worked in some of the Grady outpatient clinics, and contributed significantly to the education of the house officers and students. Dr. Arthur Merrill Sr., who had been on the faculty with Stead, continued to meet the trainees once a week for many years. Eventually, however, it became more difficult for the volunteer faculty to contribute. The overhead cost of running their private offices made it difficult for them to leave their offices.

Numerous visiting professors passed through the Department of Medicine during the thirty years under discussion. Dr. Lewis Thomas was I believe, the first of our visitors. He later became world famous. I recall going with him at night to one of the fraternity houses where a number of medical students had gathered to meet him informally. The visitors not only presented at grand rounds but also made ward rounds with the house staff and students. Emory faculty members were not permitted to attend the ward rounds because we wanted the house officers, especially the chief resident, to be responsible for the success or failure of the activity. This approach to the development of leadership was implemented in many other ways, because we wanted the house officers and fellows to become the future leaders in the hospitals where they would eventually practice.

Many postgraduate courses were held in the Grady Memorial Hospital auditorium. The experts of the nation, and from abroad, came to present their work. The students, house staff, and fellows were influenced profoundly by these experts.

We added the television system to the teaching program in 1967 (see page 235). Teaching conferences were then televised from the Grady Memorial Hospital auditorium to Emory University Hospital, the Veterans Administration Hospital, Crawford Long Hospital, and numerous hospitals within a twenty mile radius. A physician could call in and ask questions of the speaker or add to the discussion. Videotapes were made and marketed. This effort is described on page 235. I always pointed out that audiotapes, live television, and television tapes are merely modern methods of transmitting a lecture (see page 236). Such methods can transmit information, but we should never forget that the transmission of information is not teaching or learning. *Information gathering* is only the first step in learning. The other two steps entail the rearrangement of the facts into a new perception—this is known as *thinking*—and the *use* of the new perception—which is *learning*.

In 1986, the editor of the *Journal of the American Medical Association* requested that I write a short piece on the goals of house-staff training. The piece indicates how I viewed the goals of house-staff training after working thirty years in the trenches with the house staff and fellows:

> Having observed the exciting scene known as house staff training for 30 years, I believe the following. The objective of any educational system is to encourage those who are participating in the effort to learn how to learn and to be sensitive to interpersonal relationships.
>
> House officers must learn how to learn medicine, and they must also learn how to deliver what they know to the satisfaction of their patients, colleagues, the public, and themselves. Furthermore, they must maintain these goals in the context of a changing environment for the next 40 to 50 years. So, house staff training is a bridge between medical student activity and postgraduate activity, which may include practice or academic medicine.
>
> House staff training is implemented in a teaching hospital. A teaching hospital is a place where everyone teaches. If everyone is committed to teaching, one must then define the characteristics of a good teacher. A good teacher has the ability to stimulate medical students, house officers, seasoned physicians, and others to think about problems they have not previously considered. The good teacher encourages self-learning and makes the pursuit of knowledge exciting. The good teacher emphasizes the difference between memorizing facts and using the facts in a thought process. The teacher of medical students and house staff must also show them, by example, that there are certain important nonmedical and nonintellectual activities that must also be learned. These include the ability to determine if patients are satisfied with their service and to correct the situation if they are not and the ability to communicate properly to their patients and their families and to correct the problem if they do not. They also include the ability to assess whether their colleagues are pleased with their relationship with them and to correct the situation if they are not and to learn how to develop a proper relationship with co-workers, including nurses, technicians, and administrators, and to correct any problems they might have with this relationship.
>
> A department head is responsible for creating the environment where all of these elements are emphasized. The task is large, and trainees have different interests and different talents. The department head must create the interface between patients, trainees, and senior physicians and must constantly assess the value of the effort. It is not a matter of who knows the most because all of us are relatively ignorant. It is the environment that is crucial. It must be one wherein everyone is struggling to learn medicine and everyone is sensitive to

the elements that patients care about, namely, kindness, trustworthiness, thoughtfulness, humaneness, and excellence in all that is done.

The organization of time periods in which to emphasize all of the elements I have discussed previously should vary from institution to institution. The value of most of the sessions is that there must be a starting time and a designated meeting place for intellectual, practical, and social interplay. The content of the activity will vary with the personality and belief of the member of the group who is designated to be in "charge." The one feature of the activity that must be clearly visible is that there is a standard of excellence that everyone must struggle to attain.

One may call the various activities by many names, but it is probably not useful to divide them into educational and noneducational functions. The point is, no activity should be encouraged unless it is useful either for education or for the provision of patient care. It is wise to establish one or two objectives for each of the sessions currently identified as morning report, ward rounds, teaching rounds, attending rounds, conferences, and medical grand rounds. For example, morning report is an excellent place to learn about new admissions, hear about patients whose conditions are deteriorating, and discuss complications of therapy. It is where the leader listens to the house officer and students and hears and solves the problems associated with running the medical service. Teaching sessions might be devoted to patient-centered pathophysiology. Attending rounds should always be made at the bedside because this is the time the senior physician discusses the patient's problem with the patient. Important points in the history and physical examination should be emphasized. This is where the attending physician "pulls" the entire endeavor together for the patient. The x-ray films, electrocardiograms, and other laboratory data are reviewed in a nearby conference room. To reemphasize, the effort within the established goals will vary according to the beliefs and personality of the leader of the group. When similar activities are duplicated in the different sessions, it is time to eliminate some of the sessions.

The best of teaching systems encourage thinking, discussion, and action by trainees. The leader arranges, keeps reasonable order, and guides. When house officers leave an institution, they should have learned how to learn and should be able to deliver what they know in a humane manner. The success of the training period in achieving these goals cannot be determined for many years after the training period is over.[7]

As the years passed it was possible to recruit better and better qualified house officers and fellows. It thus became increasingly difficult to assess the contribution of the members of the senior staff to the development of the excellent trainees. *This being true, I can say with certainty that the more a house officer teaches, the better he or she becomes.* The chief residents at all of

---

[7] J. W. Hurst, "Learning How to Learn: The Goals of House Staff Training," *Journal of the American Medical Association* 256, no. 6 (1986): 756 (Editorial). Reproduced with the permission of the *J.A.M.A.*

the hospitals deserve much credit for the minute-to-minute success of the house-staff program. The chief residents at all four of our teaching hospitals were superb. This led the house staff to appreciate excellence.

Huddie Cheney joined me at Grady Memorial Hospital as the first chief resident I appointed in 1957 (see Figure 4-5; Cheney is fifth from the left on the fourth row). I highlight him because, when he accepted the offer, we knew for sure only that we—he and I—would be there.

The last two chief residents I appointed at Emory University Hospital also deserve special emphasis, because in November 1986 a new chairman was coming. I knew the value of a superb chief resident. So, in an effort to make the new chairman's entry as easy as possible, I arranged a split schedule for the last two chief residents at Emory University Hospital. Dr. Scott Pollak served from July 1 to December 31, 1985, and from January 1 to June 30, 1987. Dr. David Talley served January 1 to December 31, 1986. Each of them served six months with me and six months with the new chairman, Dr. Juha Kokko. This permitted a knowledgeable chief resident to be in place at Emory University Hospital when the new chairman arrived.

Over the years, we trained approximately 5,000 house officers and fellows and 3,600 students in medicine. Many house officers and fellows eventually became department chairmen, division directors, deans or associate deans, or attained leadership positions in other areas of medicine. Their names are listed on page 316. Just as important, the house officers and fellows who chose to practice medicine became respected professionals who served the needs of their patients.

As I write this in 1997, I must say the letters I continue to receive from former house officers and fellows are among my most cherished possessions. The letters are testimony to the idea that the best teaching over the long haul is that which *creates an attitude that leads to an excellent performance.*

Research Activity

I have always believed that the research performed by faculty members and trainees was an essential element of a balanced department of medicine. Students, house officers, fellows, and colleagues are profoundly influenced by the faculty members engaged in research when they are a part of the research effort. Faculty members who engage in research but sequester themselves will have little impact on the other people working or training at the same institution. Knowing this, the students, house staff, and fellows in the Department of Medicine were encouraged to be active participants in the research of the faculty members.

Initially, in 1957, few faculty members had time for research and there was little space for it. There were patients to care for at Grady Memorial Hospital, Emory University Hospital, and the Veterans Administration Hospital, and the students, house officers, and fellows had to be taught. Sick people always deserve the best that can be offered, and trainees must be influenced by the best of true teachers. As time passed, everyone in the department contributed to the patient care and teaching activity. The quest for excellence in these areas became internationally known. Patients came from great distances to Emory University Hospital and Clinic, and the recruitment of excellent students, house staff, and fellows became the rule.

During those early years, house officers and fellows were encouraged to work on "research projects" with faculty members. As time passed, the divisions became better formed, and the members of the faculty increased their clinical and basic research efforts. At this time, the lack of research space greatly hampered the research effort.

A major development took place in 1960; Emory University School of Medicine was awarded a clinical research facility. It was later named the General Clinical Research Center (GCRC). The facility occupied the entire second floor of the part of Emory University Hospital known as the Lucy Elizabeth Pavilion (the LEP was named for the wife of Asa Griggs Candler; see Chapter 1). Operated under the aegis of the dean's office, the research facility was directed by Dr. Garland Herndon, professor of medicine (see Figure 5-28). He was a very effective director, and most of the research in the facility was done by members of the Department of Medicine. Students and house officers were encouraged to spend some time in the facility so that they would be influenced by Herndon and the work there. For example, student William Kelley, took advantage of this opportunity. Kelley later became professor and chairman of the Department of Medicine at the University of Michigan and, still later, dean and vice president for health affairs at the University of Pennsylvania. Herndon continued as director of the facility until 1968, when he became vice president for health affairs, medical director of Emory University Hospital, and personal physician to Robert Woodruff.

Dr. Dan Rudman, of Columbia University, was appointed professor of medicine and director of the General Clinical Research Center in 1968 and held the position until 1983. During his directorship, the facility was moved to new quarters in the new G-wing of Emory University Hospital. Dr. Dan Nixon, an oncologist in the Department of Medicine, held the position from 1983 until 1985. Dr. Herbert Bonkovsky, a gastro-enterologist from Dartmouth, was director of the General Clinical Research Center from 1985 until 1988. Dr. Dallas Hall, a former Emory student, house officer, chief resident at Grady Memorial Hospital, and director of the Division of Hypertension, became the director in 1988.

The General Clinical Research Center has had continuous funding since its beginning from the National Institutes of Health. Research grants are highly competitive, so this is a testimony to the excellent work that has been done in the Emory facility.

Other members of the Department of Medicine who had official positions, or roles, in the General Clinical Research Center were Dr. Steve Heymsfield, who emphasized nutrition; Drs. Charles Huguley, John Galambos, and Leon Goldberg of the Departments of Medicine and Pharmacology; and Drs. Michael Henderson and Dean Warren of the Department of Surgery. Dr. Warren, professor and chairman of the Department of Surgery, made important contributions to the development of surgically created shunts for the treatment of cirrhosis of the liver. The facility was later named for Dr. Warren.

By 1986, most divisions in the Department of Medicine were mounting successful research efforts. More details of the research activity of the divisions are discussed on pages 240–89.

Trainees were not "pushed" into research. Some departments of medicine did that, and the applicants soon learned to state that they were profoundly interested in research in order to obtain an appointment. During the 1960s and 1970s hundreds of eager, intelligent, young trainees from the nation's medical schools and hospitals attended the Atlantic City research meetings, where many of them presented their work. Only a few remained in research. Since many research trainees do not continue in research, how does one justify the time the trainee spends in research? A period of research, some say, makes a trainee a better thinker and a more critical reader. I learned that while research does undoubtedly stimulate some trainees to become better thinkers and more critical readers, it does not guarantee such thinking and reading. Then, too, trainees in an excellent clinical program should become better thinkers and more critical readers. In fact, that should be one of the goals of house-staff training. I always encouraged the trainees to spend one or more years in research if they had a problem they wished to solve. I was not too impressed with those who had a generic interest in research in order to obtain a sought-after position, but had no questions they wished to pursue.

The faculty members who were doing research were urged to avoid isolation. They were encouraged to rub shoulders with the students, house staff, and fellows. Arguments, bull sessions, lunching together, and any other teaching devices that ensured the development of an effective interface between new and old learners were encouraged.

Research space gradually became available. In the Grady Memorial Hospital area, research space was located in the hospital, the Steiner Building, the Glenn Memorial Building, and the renovated Gray Building (Henry Woodruff Research Building). Research space became available in the Ernest Woodruff Memorial Research Building on the Emory campus and at the Veterans Administration Hospital. The research and teaching funds awarded the department in 1957 amounted to less than $100,000. The peak funding for the department eventually reached the level of approximately $10 million.

The research activity moved from none in 1957 to considerable in 1986. By 1986, a new research building was planned on the Emory campus. This building, financed jointly by Emory, the State of Georgia, and philanthropist O. Wayne Rollins, would free space in the Ernest Woodruff Memorial Research Building for a major research effort by the Department of Medicine. A new research wing to the Ernest Woodruff Memorial Research Building was also planned. Since the dental school was destined to close, the medical library could move from the Ernest Woodruff Memorial Research Building to the old dental school building. This move permitted the development of even more research space for the Department of Medicine. Additionally, a new research building was planned for the Veterans Administration Hospital. By 1986, all of these developments set the stage for a major research effort. Such an effort would be possible, not simply because space was becoming available, but because the teaching and patient care responsibilities had become fully developed and highly respected. This being the case, more time and effort could be directed toward increasing the research productivity.

Patient Care

The key to running a medical service is to establish the doctrine that patients come first. Other activities, such as teaching and research, are needed to ensure excellent patient care, but the excellent and compassionate care of patients is the golden core of the profession of medicine. I strongly emphasized that the patient care at all of our facilities had to be excellent and as equal as we could make it.

The End of a Building—The End of an Era

I looked out the window of my office in the Glenn Memorial Building in 1962. A wrecking crew was demolishing the old "colored Grady Hospital." The old Atlanta Medical College building that had become Emory University School of Medicine was being torn down! The historic building was so dilapidated that it could not be restored for any purpose.

The wrecking crew left the first few feet of the building, because, not to do so, would require major excavation.

Some time later, in 1962, Marvin McCall, our chief resident in medicine at Grady Memorial Hospital invited me and my wife to dinner (see Figure 5-29). He surprised me with a gift. He had made a coffee table out of the discarded timbers of the old medical school building. So, all that is left of the old Atlanta Medical College and the original Emory University School of Medicine is shown in Figures 5-30A and 5-30B. Emory, however, still owns the land on the corner of Armstrong and Butler Streets.

The Physician Assistant Program

By 1965 the delivery of patient care in hospitals and physician's offices was becoming more complicated. This was occurring because the scientific developments in medicine needed to be translated into improved patient care. There seemed to be a need for a new type of person who would help physicians implement what was needed in the care of patients. Nurses were creating nurse clinician programs. Eugene Stead, at Duke, observed the work of former army corpsmen and reasoned that similar individuals could assist physicians. So in 1965, he developed a Physician Assistant Training Program.

I always observed Gene Stead's actions. He had been right more often than anyone else I knew. So, after discussing the matter with Dr. Gordon Barrow, the director of the Regional Medical Program in Georgia, who had access to funding, I started a Physician Assistant Training Program at Grady Memorial Hospital. At that time, the new program was officially sponsored by Grady Memorial Hospital and was known as the Medical Specialty Assistant Program.

Three trainees were assigned to the medical wards and coronary care units at Grady Memorial Hospital for one year. They participated in many of the educational activities attended by the interns and residents. I met them for breakfast and directed their reading. We were lucky, for they were serious-minded, hardworking, capable individuals. Looking back, they were a courageous group of trainees, because, at that time, we had no guarantee that they would be allowed to "practice their art" after they left the program; there were as yet no official requirements for training or accreditation. Physicians, who were legally responsible for the actions of the physician assistants, would have to be assured that the assistants could assist them only in the implementation of patient care plans created by physicians. The physician assistants were not to create new plans on their own.

The financial support for the three trainees came from the Regional Medical Program directed by Barrow. I was on President Johnson's Heart, Cancer and Stroke Commission and a member of the advisory board of the Regional Medical Program, one of the many programs developed after the Commission's report was accepted by President Johnson.

The first three students enrolled in the Medical Specialty Assistant Program at Grady Memorial Hospital were Donald Donavon, Bill Armstrong, and Jimmie Minor. They began the program in February 1967 and completed their training eighteen months later, in June 1968. The members of the next and subsequent classes were in training for twenty-four months. Robert Smith and Thomas Walker were members of the second class.

By 1971, Dean Arthur Richardson saw the value of the program and transferred it to the newly formed Division of Allied Health. Dr. Harry Williams was in charge of the division until poor health prevented him from functioning. At that time, Dr. Robert Jewett became the director of the division. Moving the program to the School of Medicine permitted each graduate to receive an academic degree. That first class of physician assistants yielded twenty-five graduates in December 1973. The Division of Allied Health was later discontinued and the Department of Preventive Medicine and Community Health became responsible for the Physician Assistant Program. By 1986 the large and competent staff was training thirty-five to forty physician assistants a year in a twenty-four month program.

The program continued its evolution and in 1988 offered the first master's degree program in the nation, extending to twenty-eight months in length. The first class graduated in 1990.

In 1993 the Department of Preventive Medicine and Community Health evolved into the Department of Family and Preventive Medicine. The Physician Assistant Program remained in the Department of Family and Preventive Medicine. Within this framework, the Physician Assistant Program has grown into one of the largest in the nation, graduating fifty master's degree physician assistants annually. In 1994, 80 percent of the graduating class went into primary care, and over half of that class was serving in medically underserved locations.

Soon after starting the program in 1967, I wrote Gene Stead that I had done so. He wrote a short Stead note stating, "Imitation is the best form of flattery." Stead believed that his reputation for developing a large number of department chairmen was unjustified, because he thought those bright people could have made it without him. On the other hand, he thought that the fledgling physician assistant programs needed his presence, prestige, and drive to succeed.

Postgraduate Education, Medical Television, and Medical Illustrations

Postgraduate Programs

Emory University School of Medicine has always recognized the importance of the continuing medical education of physicians. In 1922, Dean W. S. Elkin created the annual Emory Postgraduate "Clinic." He had two purposes in mind. He wanted to bring together all the alumni of the medical schools that had evolved to become Emory University School of Medicine, and to bring up-to-date information in medicine to those who attended. Although these "clinics" were initially successful in meeting Dean Elkin's goals, as time passed the initial enthusiasm and interest began to wane.

Dr. Russell Oppenheimer was appointed director of postgraduate education in 1947 and held that position until he retired in 1954. He obtained a grant from the Kellogg Foundation to support the implementation of the program. Although several successful postgraduate courses were offered, and visiting professors of national reputation were invited to participate, the courses were discontinued.

In 1950 the former house officers of Grady Memorial Hospital formed the Grady Clinical Society and organized an annual educational program. This organization then joined the group that planned the Emory postgraduate "clinics" and presented an annual course to the Emory medical alumni. This effort was abandoned as the nation's medical schools began to develop continuing educational departments with full-time staff in an effort to reach practicing physicians regardless of where they graduated.

Bruce Logue and I organized a course in electrocardiography in 1954. Robert Grant, who created the vector approach to electrocardiography while at Emory, was the star (see Figure 4-15A).

During 1950–1954, Dr. E. Grey Dimond, professor and chairman of the Department of Medicine at the University of Kansas, asked me to participate in some of their postgraduate courses. I was impressed with the interaction of the practicing physicians with the faculty members who participated in the courses. When I returned to Emory after my navy service, I pointed out to Dean Richardson in 1956 that little was being done in this field on the east coast except in Baltimore, New York, and Boston. He promptly made me the director of Emory's postgraduate education program.

The next step in the development of the postgraduate education program was unusual. I admitted a patient from Detroit to Emory

University Hospital in 1956. He had become ill in Atlanta. Before his discharge, he asked for my bill. I sent it to his hospital room. He became disturbed. He said, "This bill is ridiculous." I said, "I will be glad to change it; it is my usual bill." He said, to my surprise, "It is too little. What do you need around here?" I responded, "We need money to develop a continuing education program." He gave the medical school $2,000, which was a sizable amount of money in 1956.

I planned four postgraduate courses in medicine, which were implemented in 1957 after I became chairman of the Department of Medicine (see Figure 5-22A-D). I continued to be director of continuing medical education and gave one-fourth of the $2,000 to the Department of Pediatrics, the Department of Surgery, and the Department of Gynecology and Obstetrics, urging each of them to sponsor postgraduate courses.

As time passed, the courses offered by the Department of Medicine became increasingly popular. For several years they were given in the Grady Memorial Hospital auditorium. The students and house staff were encouraged to attend. These young trainees were impressed with the expertise of the invited guests. They met the leaders of medicine. They were stimulated to become as good as the experts they met. We gave the first postgraduate course for physicians sponsored by the American Heart Association (see Figure 5-31). With the important help of Mary Woody, the head nurse at Grady Memorial Hospital, we also gave the first postgraduate course for nurses sponsored by the American Heart Association.

The attendance at the courses offered by the Department of Medicine ranged from 100 to 600, depending on the subject. Eventually it was obvious to Dean James Glenn that the time had come to develop an office of continuing medical education that could assist all departments in the development and implementation of postgraduate courses. In addition, the newly developed national criteria required for accreditation of each program had to be met. Accordingly, the administrative requirements were becoming more complex and time-consuming. So, on July 1, 1981, the new Office of Continuing Medical Education was organized. Space for the growing department was made available on the ground floor of the Robert W. Woodruff Health Sciences Center Administration Building on the Emory campus. Dan Joiner became director of the facility and developed a very capable staff that served all departments in the School of Medicine.

By 1986, when I left the chairmanship of the Department of Medicine, the School of Medicine had sponsored and implemented 244 post-graduate courses. They were given in the auditorium of the Robert W.

Woodruff Health Sciences Center Building, in various hotels, in foreign countries, and on ships at sea. The annual Gruentzig course in angioplasty, organized by Drs. Andreas Gruentzig and Spencer King, would draw 500 or more attendees (see Figure 5-32). During 1986, 6,082 postgraduate "students" attended Emory postgraduate courses.

Since 1986, the Continuing Education Department has maintained its growth; by 1996 it produced over 100 programs annually, with registrants totaling more than 9,000 each year. The offices for the department were moved to the second floor of the old dental building in 1997.

Medical Television

The following passage is from the book *The Bench and Me.*

Television has replaced motion pictures in the medical arena. I became involved in exploring the use of television in medical education in 1965. Dr. James Leiberman was stationed at the Centers for Disease Control (CDC) in Atlanta, Georgia. He was greatly interested in medical education even though he was a veterinarian. The National Audiovisual Center was located at the CDC and he was its director. With the approval of Dean Arthur Richardson and with the help of Dr. Heinz Weens, Chairman of the Department of Radiology, we at Emory University joined with Dr. Leiberman to develop a pilot project in the use of television in medical teaching. Accordingly, the Emory Medical Television system was born; the first broadcast was in March 1967. The system would permit us to transmit live television teaching programs from Grady Memorial Hospital to Emory University Hospital, the Veterans Hospital, and Crawford Long Hospital. Any hospital within a radius of 15 to 20 miles could participate in the system. The excellent personnel of the audiovisual center helped us develop this pilot project in television teaching. Later, after the audiovisual center withdrew from the project, partial funding was supplied by the Regional Medical Program. Still later, the system became almost financially self-sufficient; the deficit was picked up by Emory University. . . .[8]

The system permitted viewers to call in by telephone and ask questions.

Medical Illustration

The Department of Medical Illustration was originally located in the Woodruff Memorial Research building, adjacent to and connected to Emory University Hospital. Kathleen Mackay was the medical artist, and Joe Jackson the photographer. Both were excellent professionals. Their salaries and facilities were originally supported by the Robert Winship Memorial Clinic. By 1968, the need for such services was increasing in the Grady Memorial Hospital area. New medical manuscripts were being

---

[8] J. W. Hurst, *The Bench and Me: Teaching and Learning Medicine* (New York: Igaku-Shoin 1992), 70. Reproduced with permission of the publisher.

written by an increasing number of Emory faculty members, and more convenient access to the Medical Illustrations Department was needed. The demand for such services by the Department of Medicine was particularly great. Accordingly, Dean Richardson supported the development of a branch of the Medical Illustration Department at Grady Memorial Hospital. Grady provided the space and Emory provided the professional staff. Grover Hogan became the illustrator, and Bob Beveridge the photographer. Patsy Bryan, an excellent medical artist, and Eddie Jackson, a capable photographer, joined the department at Grady in the spring of 1972.

Later, the Medical Illustrations Department on campus was moved from the Ernest Woodruff Memorial Research Building to the first floor of the new Robert W. Woodruff Health Sciences Administration Building. Hogan became director of the unit at Grady and the unit on the Emory campus. Patsy Bryan moved from Grady to the new facility on campus in August of 1981, and Eddie Jackson remained as the photographer at Grady.

Combining the Activities

As time passed, it became obvious that these three developments had much in common and could be combined under one administrator. A committee with a chairman was appointed by Dean Glenn to oversee the development. Still later—to move ahead of the story—in 1995 Dean Jeffrey Houpt appointed Dr. Marilynne McKay director of the Department of Continuing Medical Education and Biomedical Media, which includes postgraduate medical education, medical television, and medical illustration. Mr. Charles W. Bogle III is currently assistant director of biomedical media. As such, he oversees medical illustrations. He and his coworkers are excellent artists and medical photographers and work wonders with the crude drawings presented to them by the faculty.

A Word of Caution

As the postgraduate educational program and medical television system evolved, I constantly pointed out that these efforts were simply modern methods of transmitting medical information to those who listened. The transmission of information is only the first step in a learning process. True teachers do more than that. True teachers are obsessed with leading those who are trying to learn to organize the new information into a new thought process, and then to use the newly perceived thought in the daily practice of medicine. Only then can the activity be referred to as learning. Information alone is not the same as thinking, and thinking is not the same as learning. We will always need true teachers who do much more than dispense information.

During my chairmanship, I tried another method of postgraduate education. I invited a practicing physician to "join" the Department of Medicine for one or more weeks at the time. Several drove to Grady Memorial Hospital from neighboring towns, and one came from another state to participate in the informal program. These physicians attended ward rounds and conferences and read in the library. They paid no "course" fee. They restored their interest in pursuing the solutions to problems. This system is superior to lecture courses but works only for those who are highly motivated. Also, only a few "students" of this type can be accommodated at the time. The challenge to directors of postgraduate medical education is still to develop a system in which practicing physicians can "join" departments of medicine temporarily to learn new skills and to restore their excitement in learning.

Implementing the Problem-Oriented Record

By the early seventies, there was ample evidence that health care was becoming increasingly complex. Scientific advances were more common, and the delivery of medical care was changing. Group practice was becoming the rule. These changes were creating new problems. For example, communication between health professionals and patients was becoming more important and more difficult; teaching trainees to hone their analytical abilities was becoming more important than ever; and the need to create medical records that documented what physicians did was becoming a legal requirement.

Dr. Lawrence Weed, of the University of Vermont, created a solution to these problems (see Figure 5-33). He wrote a book and published articles on the problem-oriented system and problem-oriented record.[9] The words in his entertaining lectures disturbed many who heard him. He visited the Department of Medicine at Emory in the early seventies. He was clearly a genius with a mission. It seemed wise to listen to him, since he was smarter than the rest of us. So I ignored the statements that upset others and listened. Weed was right about many things. Following his visit, Ken Walker, Dallas Hall, and Steve Clements assisted me in implementing the use of the problem-oriented record.

The medical record was organized into a data base, problem list, initial plans, and follow-up. I was interested because it fit my approach to teaching. We had to decide what data to collect from the patients

---

[9] L. L. Weed, *Medical Records, Medical Education, and Patient Care* (Cleveland, OH: Case Western Reserve University Press, 1970).

admitted to the medical services at Grady Memorial Hospital and Emory University Hospital, and the house staff and students had to develop the skills to collect the data. This was called the *data base*. Furthermore, the trainees were expected to know the basic science background for normal and abnormal findings.

A *problem list* was created by analyzing all of the data. The problem list was placed at the front of the chart. Each problem was numbered. A true teacher could ask the trainee, "What data did you use to formulate this problem?" The true teacher could then determine whether the house officer had overstated or understated the problem based on the available data. This, of course, is the essence of analysis and synthesis. All the patient's problems were listed. This enabled the true teacher to determine whether the trainee had identified all the patient's problems and if his or her projected plans for one problem adversely affected another problem. This approach to the patient improved judgment. The true teacher could encourage the house officer to look up each of the patient's problems rather than read a journal just because it arrived in the mail. This approach guaranteed that the teaching on the wards was linked directly to the patients being managed. This increased the likelihood that the trainee could remember what he or she had read.

Plans, including orders, were written for each numbered problem. This permitted true teachers to identify the diagnostic work and treatment for each problem.

Follow-up notes, or *progress notes*, were written for each numbered problem. This permitted the true teacher to determine whether the correct items were being followed.

We had several postgraduate courses on the problem-oriented subject. Weed was always the star. Five hundred to 1,000 physicians participated in the courses.

The records on the medical services of Grady Memorial Hospital, Emory University Hospital, and the Veterans Administration Hospital became problem oriented. Physicians from foreign countries visited the Grady wards and went home to initiate the use of the problem-oriented record. Physicians from Japan were especially interested. We wrote and edited two books on the subject.[10]

Those faculty members who studied the principles of the problem-oriented record appreciated its use in teaching and communication. It highlighted the difference in the teaching goals for the sophomore and

---

[10] J. W. Hurst and H. K. Walker, eds., *The Problem-Oriented System* (New York: Medcom, 1972), and H. K. Walker, J. W. Hurst, and M. F. Woody, eds., *Applying the Problem-Oriented System* (New York: Medcom, 1973).

junior students compared to the teaching goals for the senior students and house officers. The difference is, the true teacher should emphasize the *collection* of data to the sophomore and junior students and should emphasize the *use* of data to the senior students and house officers. Perceptive faculty members saw the problem-oriented record as a way to teach what really matters when a physician "works up" a patient. They saw it as a way to determine if the trainee could use information in the data base to create a new thought process that was stated on the problem list. The exercise was utilized to discuss the steps that should be used to transfer medical knowledge to the care of a patient.

As expected, some faculty members did not appreciate the value of the problem-oriented record but went along with the approach. Also, as expected, some faculty members never understood it.

For many years at morning report I reviewed the problem-oriented record of every new patient admitted to the medical service at Grady Memorial Hospital. I also visited the wards and reviewed records. I would leave notes for the house officers to call me. I would state, "I could not find the data in the chart that supported your contention that the patient had so and so. Check that for me please."

One year I had the house officers at Grady send me a copy of each consultation note they wrote. It was amazing how the consultation notes improved.

I suggested to the house officers that I would like to send copies of the records they created on their patients in the letters of recommendation I wrote for them. I pointed out no one should buy a painting created by an artist without viewing the painting itself. Again the records improved. The pride of creation became the rule.

Our interest in the problem-oriented record and frequent contacts with Lawrence Weed prompted our interest in computerizing the medical records at Grady Memorial Hospital. Accordingly, by the late seventies and early eighties Ken Walker and Dallas Hall began to develop such a system. Although the system is not perfect, it is a giant step in the right direction.

As I write this in 1997, I still believe that the problem-oriented record enables a true teacher to function in a very specific way. Simply stated, when trainees commit themselves to the production of a carefully organized problem-oriented record, it permits a true teacher to look into their minds and determine how they arrived at their conclusions and what they plan to do about them. This is very different from giving a mini-lecture.

Parenthetically, the need for such a record is greater now than ever, because patients commonly shift from one group of physicians to another group of physicians. When the medical record is noncommunicative, the entire system of medical care is seriously injured.

Weed received the prestigious Lienhard Award on October 16, 1995, for his outstanding achievement in improving health care in the United States.

The Atlanta Medical History Society

An Emory Medical History Club was organized at Emory in 1924; Dr. Stewart Roberts was a founding member. Unfortunately, the Club was discontinued in 1928. I wrote Dr. Mark Silverman and Dr. John Stone on February 14, 1980, and urged them to create a Medical History Society. By 1980 a number of faculty members in the Department of Medicine and in the medical community at large were interested in medical history—an important subject for two reasons. First, it emphasizes that the profession is like a relay race in that one generation of physicians passes what it has learned to the next generation. Secondly, it is wise to trace the evolution of an idea that passes from one generation to the subsequent generation, because this type of information enables one to determine whether a new idea has a solid footing or is springing de novo from a creative mind.

The new Atlanta Medical History Society was formed on October 8, 1980 at a meeting attended by Dean James Glenn, Drs. Silverman and Stone, Dr. John Skandalakis, Dr. Crawford Barnett, Dr. Julius Wenger, Dr. Harvey Young and myself. Initially, Dean Glenn's office provided the financial needs of the society and served as the secretariat, but, as time passed, the Atlanta Medical Association assumed that role.

Drs. Silverman and Stone, Dr. Nicholas Davies, and Dr. Barry Silverman developed the society and have, as Mark Silverman said, "tried to foster a spirit of respect for our medical heritage in the community and medical school." A nationally known scholar is invited to dinner, after which he or she gives the annual oration to the membership of about 100. In many ways, this society signals that Atlanta has "come of age" as a medical community.

The Evolution of the Divisions

In 1957 there were only fourteen physicians in the entire Department of Medicine. Accordingly, there were no divisions as they are known today, although individuals specialized in certain areas.

In time a sufficient number of faculty members permitted development of divisions. At the outset, I called the leader of each division a "coordinator," who organized the division's teaching and research. The term was used to emphasize the teaching and research responsibilities of the divisions and to avoid the division members' thinking the director controlled any other areas of their work. After a few years, everyone was comfortable with the leadership of the divisions, and the leaders were then designated as directors.

The evolution of the divisions of the Department of Medicine is discussed below.

The Division of Cardiology

The cardiovascular heritage at Emory University School of Medicine began in 1915. Its roots are long and deep. This is why the discussion of the Division of Cardiology is longer than the discussion of other divisions. During my thirty years as chairman of the Department of Medicine, we trained about 200 cardiologists. We were fortunate in the early days to receive $25,000 annually from the National Heart Institute for cardiovascular teaching. Later, in the sixties and seventies, we were awarded a large clinical-training grant from the National Heart Institute (later called the National Heart, Lung, and Blood Institute).

I organized the annual meetings of the former cardiology fellows in the early sixties. Initially, we gathered in my hotel room in the city where the American Heart Association and the American College of Cardiology held their annual meetings. As time passed and the number of graduates increased, the gathering was moved to a large room in the hotel. These twice-a-year social meetings enabled all of us to keep up with each other. These two annual social activities still continue.

Dr. **Jean George Bachmann** in 1910, was professor and chairman of the Department of Physiology at the Atlanta Medical College. He became the first chairman of the Department of Physiology at Emory University School of Medicine when Emory University took over the Atlanta Medical College in 1915 (see Chapter 1). He remained in that position for thirty-seven years and retired in 1947. One of the first physicians to perform medical research in Atlanta, he became internationally known for his work in electrocardiography. Bachmann's bundle, located in the atria of the heart, was named for him.

Dr. **Stewart Roberts**, president of the American Heart Association in 1933 (see Figure 1-18), was considered by many to be the first cardiologist in Georgia.

Dr. **Carter Smith Sr.**, a loyal volunteer clinical faculty member, introduced the technique of electrocardiography at Grady Memorial Hospital in the late twenties. He became a dominant force in the development of Piedmont Hospital. The Carter Smith Professor of Medicine at Emory University was created in his honor.

Dr. **Dan Elkin**, in the Department of Surgery, became known for his interest in patients with traumatic arteriovenous fistula who were seen at Grady Memorial Hospital. This interest led to his World War II army experience with vascular disease. When he returned to Emory after the war, he and Dr. **Fredrick Cooper** became nationally known for their work on the peripheral arteries.

Drs. **Eugene Stead** and **James Warren** made Emory famous. Their use of the cardiac catheter at Grady Memorial Hospital from 1942 to 1946 catapulted Emory into the first ranks of American medicine (see discussion on pages 79–80; Stead and Warren were joined in their work by Merrill, Brannon, Weens, Hickam, Myers, and others). Warren moved briefly to Yale, where he intended to develop a cardiac catheterization laboratory, but was soon enticed to return to Emory as professor and chairman of the Department of Physiology. In his new Emory position, he retained an appointment in the Department of Medicine and continued his contributions to it until, in 1950, he joined Stead at Duke as chief of medicine at the Veterans Administration Hospital there.

Dr. **R. Bruce Logue** began to develop clinical cardiology at Emory University Hospital in 1946. He also became a major mover in the development of the Emory University Hospital and Clinic. Whereas his biography could be placed under many of the headings in this book it is arbitrarily placed in this section.[11]

Logue is an Emory legend (see Figure 5-34). He was born in Augusta, Georgia, on October 9, 1911. After schooling in Augusta, he entered Emory University in 1931 and remained at Emory for the next 55 years.

Logue obtained a Bachelor of Science degree from Emory University in 1934 and his medical degree in 1937, 1934 being simultaneously his last year of college and his first year in medical school. During that year, he also served as president of the university student body. He married Carolyne in 1938 and spent one year on the house staff at the Royal Victoria Hospital in Montreal, Canada, under the tutelage of Dr. Jonathan Meakins, who had worked with Sir Thomas Lewis. Logue returned to Grady Memorial Hospital to complete his residency training under Dr. J. Edgar Paullin.

Logue spent the years 1941 to 1946 in the Army Medical Corps. He was chief of cardiology at Lawson General Hospital for three years (see Chapter 2) and attended Eugene Stead's famous "Sunday school" at Grady. He then spent a year at Fort Bragg General Hospital, following

---

[11] J. W. Hurst, "Profiles in Cardiology: R. Bruce Logue," *Clin Cardiol* 15 (1992): 931–33.

which he became chief of medicine at the 248th General Hospital in the Philippines. He was discharged from the army as a lieutenant colonel.

When Logue returned to Atlanta in 1946, Stead offered him a position in the Department of Medicine at Emory. There were many bright young men in the department at that time, but Stead later said that appointing Bruce Logue to the faculty at Emory University Hospital was "one of the smartest things I ever did."

As history unfolds, it becomes clear that Stead saw in Logue those qualities that would enable him to begin utilizing Emory University Hospital as a major resource for the Department of Medicine. Accordingly, Logue was charged with the responsibility of organizing the training program for house officers at Emory University Hospital, although the program there was, at that time, separate from the training program at Grady Memorial Hospital.

Stead, with his vision, probably had another reason for assigning Logue to Emory University Hospital. I suspect Stead envisioned the beginning of a group of physicians who would earn their way, teach, and provide patients for the Department of Medicine.

As one of the first cardiologists in Georgia, Logue became a sought-after consultant. In 1949, Logue, along with the new chairman of medicine, Paul Beeson, and Charles Huguley, Spalding Schroder, and Dean Hugh Wood, advocated and developed the Private Diagnostic Clinic. This organization was destined to join the Robert Winship Memorial Clinic, and other physicians who had offices in Emory University Hospital, to become the Emory University Clinic. I was asked by Beeson and Logue to join the Department of Medicine and the Private Diagnostic Clinic group in 1950. Our offices were in the Lucy Elizabeth Pavilion of Emory University Hospital.

Logue became nationally known through his lecturing and writing. One of my first acts as chairman of the Department of Medicine was to recommend his promotion to full professor. He remained chief of medicine at Emory University Hospital from 1957 to 1980 and chief of the Medical Section of the Emory Clinic from 1955 to 1980. The medical service at Emory University Hospital and the medical section of Emory Clinic were enormously successful under his leadership.

When Logue retired from his duties on the Emory campus in 1980, he became director of the Carlyle Fraser Heart Center at Crawford Long Hospital. His leadership there was again evident.

Logue's accomplishments and honors include the following: certified by the American Board of Internal Medicine, 1940; fellow in the American College of Physicians, 1946; certified by the Subspecialty Board of Cardiovascular Diseases, 1947; developed the first cardiology fellowship program at Grady Hospital, 1948; developed the cardiology fellowship program at Emory University Hospital in 1948 (Dr. Linton Bishop was the first fellow); founding member of the Emory University Clinic; first chief of the Medical Section in the clinic in 1955; founding father and first president of the Georgia Heart Association; president of the American Federation of Clinical Research; vice president of the American Heart Association and member of its executive committee; chairman of the Subspecialty Board of Cardiovascular Diseases; Master Teacher Award of the American College of Cardiology, 1969; author of nearly 100 scientific papers. Logue and I worked together to create the book *The Heart.* We met each Thursday morning for more than a year planning and writing to create the first edition in 1966. We were lucky; the book was a great success. He also received the Award of Honor by Emory Medical Alumni, 1979; the R. Bruce Logue Professor of Medicine was created by patients and friends in 1981; and the Logue Service was established in Emory University Hospital along with the Hurst and Gruentzig Services in 1993.

A personal note

The preceding discussion does not do justice to R. Bruce Logue. He contributed greatly to Emory's growth and development. He was a brilliant clinician and, with it all, an extremely interesting person. For example, he was a fine cabinetmaker, an excellent dancer, a superb golfer, and a great cook. He made medicine fun. He was like a magnet in that students, house staff, and fellows rushed to attend his teaching sessions. He was entertaining. He, like Stead, expressed complex notions in an unforgettable way. He taught at Emory University Hospital and Grady Memorial Hospital for forty years. He also taught at the Veterans Administration Hospital and Crawford Long Hospital for many years. He avoided administrative duties and spent his time with patients and trainees. In 1957 he could have been chairman of the Department of Medicine but threw the ball to my court. So I am deeply indebted to him for my career at Emory.

Dr. **Robert Grant** (see Figure 4-15A) developed vector electrocardiography while at Emory University from 1947 to 1950. He and his work became known throughout the world. He later became director of the National Heart, Lung, and Blood Institute.

Dr. **J. Willis Hurst** joined Dr. Logue in Beeson's Department of Medicine in 1950. Our offices were located on the ground floor of the Lucy Elizabeth Pavilion of Emory University Hospital. We earned our income at the new Private Diagnostic Clinic (see page 126). Dr. Logue had previously started the fellowship programs in cardiology at Grady Memorial Hospital and Emory University Hospital (see Logue's biography). Accordingly, we both spent a great deal of time with fellows. Dr. Ferris, chairman of the Department of Medicine, asked me to be in charge of the junior medical students who were, at that time, all assigned to Emory University Hospital.

Dr. **Gordon Barrow**, an excellent part-time faculty member, was in charge of the cardiac clinics at Grady Memorial Hospital.

Dr. **Osler Abbott** was the leading cardiac surgeon in the Southeast. He operated on patients with patent ductus arteriosus, constrictive pericarditis, coarctation of the aorta, and tetralogy of Fallot. He operated on a patient of mine with mitral stenosis in 1951, the first intracardiac surgical procedure performed in the South. Following that procedure, many more were done, and Emory cardiac surgery flourished.

After I was drafted for the second time in 1954, Dr. **Clyde Tomlin**, a cardiology fellow planning to enter practice in New Mexico, agreed to join the faculty to help Logue cover our large and expanding cardiac consultative service. Dr. Tomlin entered private practice in New Mexico before I returned to Emory in November 1955.

While I was away in Washington, Dr. Ferris recruited Dr. **Noble Fowler** to be director of the Stead-Warren Cardiovascular Laboratory in the Steiner Building on the Grady Memorial Hospital campus. Fowler was a superb addition to the department. I urged him to remain at Emory after I became chairman, but he accepted an excellent offer at the University of Cincinnati (see page 204).

Dr. **Edward R. Dorney** (see Figure 5-6) had trained under Fowler in New York before Fowler came to Emory. I traveled from Washington to Philadelphia, where Dorney was attending a meeting of the American College of Physicians, to interview him. Logue and I both recommended his appointment by Ferris, and Dorney arrived at Emory in 1955, just as Tomlin was leaving to enter the practice he had delayed.

The Development of Cardiology at Grady Hospital

After I began work as chairman of the Department of Medicine, and Fowler left to become chief of medicine at the Veterans Administration Hospital in Cincinnati in 1957, the urgent need was to recruit someone to direct the famous Stead-Warren Cardiovascular Laboratory at Grady Memorial Hospital. **Robert Schlant**, who trained with Lewis Dexter at the Brigham, was appointed in 1958 (see Figure 5-19). He was reported to be one of Dexter's best fellows. Later, new modern laboratories were constructed within Grady Hospital using money obtained by Boisfeuillet

Jones from one of the Woodruff Foundations (see further discussion of Dr. Schlant on page 252).

I asked Dr. **Freeman Cary**, a former Emory student and house officer who had worked with me at the Naval Hospital in Bethesda, to be in charge of the Grady Cardiac Clinics. By then, he had moved to Atlanta. A loyal volunteer faculty member, he was an excellent cardiologist and was offered an excellent position at the Orange Memorial Hospital in Orlando, Florida. He later became physician to the United States Congress.

Dr. **Nanette Kass Wenger** (see Figure 5-35) completed her last year of house-staff training and cardiology fellowship in our program in 1959 and was appointed director of the Cardiac Clinics at Grady in 1960. She has remained in that position throughout her career, becoming a national leader in cardiac rehabilitation and in heart disease in women. She is an extremely active member of the American Heart Association and the American College of Cardiology. She was, and is, a master at the lectern and with the pen. Having presented her well-polished discussions throughout the world, she is internationally known and respected.

Over the years the following appointments were made in cardiology at Grady Hospital.

Dr. **Don O. Nutter**, one of our former fellows, was appointed to the faculty at Grady in 1968. An excellent teacher-researcher, he also became a very productive director of the Stead-Warren Cardiovascular Laboratory in 1973. In 1978 he received a Robert Wood Johnson fellowship and went to Washington, D.C., to work with Senator Richard Schweiker. When he returned to Emory in 1979, he became executive associate dean of the School of Medicine. He later left Emory to become senior associate dean of the medical school at Northwestern University.

Dr. **E. Alan Paulk Jr.**, a former resident and cardiology fellow in our program, was appointed in 1968. He assisted in the development of the coronary care units at Grady Memorial Hospital, then entered practice in 1973.

Dr. **Charles Gilbert** joined the staff at Grady in 1967 and developed stress testing. He entered private practice in 1979.

Dr. **Joel Felner** was appointed to the volunteer clinical faculty in 1969, when he was assigned to the Centers for Disease Control and Prevention. After completing his senior residency and cardiology fellowship at Grady Hospital, he was appointed Assistant Professor of Medicine in 1974. He received the American Heart Association Teaching Scholar Award (1978–1981). He developed echocardiography at Grady Memorial Hospital and was one of the first to use the mannequin to teach cardiovascular physical diagnosis. Felner was director of the coronary care unit at Grady from

1974 to 1985. He became associate dean in charge of junior and senior students and medical house staff in 1985 but retained his teaching and patient care duties. He was instrumental in developing and directing the pathophysiology course for sophomore medical students.

Dr. **Dan Arensberg**, a former cardiology fellow in our program, was appointed in 1977 and has remained on the faculty. He is an excellent clinician-teacher.

The following physicians joined the faculty in the Division of Cardiology and later entered private practice. They made a significant contribution to the teaching and research program, and their efforts were greatly appreciated.

Dr. **William J. Rawls**, appointed to the faculty on July 1, 1962, initially received support from the Georgia Heart Association. He worked in the Stead-Warren Cardiovascular Laboratory and made a significant contribution to the teaching program. He entered private practice in 1965 and created one of the first group practices in the Decatur, Georgia, area. Regrettably, he died in 1995.

Dr. **Dwight W. Clark**, appointed in 1972, was a member of the cardiac catheterization team. He entered private practice in Memphis, Tennessee, in 1974.

Dr. **D. Bruce McCraw** joined the staff in 1973 and participated in the catheterization laboratory and in the teaching program. He entered private practice in Pensacola, Florida, in 1976.

Dr. **Charles W. Wickliffe** joined the staff in 1975 and was a member of the cardiac catheterization team. He entered private practice in Atlanta in 1976.

Drs. **Benjamin Alimurung**, **William Lieppe**, **Azhar Faraqui**, **Brian Donahue**, and **Henry Smith III** joined the staff in the Division of Cardiology. Dr. Alimurung returned to the Philippines, his native country, and Dr. Lieppe entered private practice in Atlanta. Dr. Faruqui later returned to Pakistan and became one of the leading cardiologists there. Donahue and Smith entered private practice.

The Development of Cardiology at the Veterans Administration Hospital

The first full-time faculty member appointed in cardiology at the Atlanta Veterans Administration Hospital was one of our former cardiology fellows, Dr. **Joseph Lindsay Jr.** He was appointed in 1966. He was an excellent clinician-teacher and clinical researcher. Dr. Lindsay joined the faculty at George Washington School of Medicine in Washington in 1970. He later became director of the Division of Cardiology at the University of Louisiana in Shreveport. Later still, he became director of cardiology at the Washington Medical Center.

Dr. **I. Sylvia Crawley** joined the cardiology staff at the Veterans Hospital in 1967. She left for practice in 1968 but returned to the staff in 1970. Dr. Crawley became chief of cardiology at the Veterans Administration Hospital in 1970.

Dr. **Paul F. Walter,** one of our former cardiology fellows, joined the staff at the Veterans Administration Hospital in 1971. A brilliant observer, he became increasingly interested in cardiac arrhythmias and later moved to Emory University Hospital and Clinic to develop the electrophysiologic laboratory there.

Drs. **Paul D'Amato, Richard Coralli, Laurence Lesser, Gordon Brandeau,** and **Michael Sabom** joined the cardiology staff at the Veterans Administration Hospital. D'Amato later became a member of the cardiology faculty at Mercer University in Macon, Georgia. Coralli, Lesser, Brandeau, and Sabom later entered private practice in the Atlanta area.

The Development of Cardiology at Emory University Hospital and Clinic

In 1957, soon after I became chairman of the Department of Medicine, I appointed Dr. **Robert Franch,** who had worked with Fowler, to direct a new cardiac catheterization laboratory being constructed in the Ernest Woodruff Memorial Research Building on the Emory campus. Gordon Barrow had been able to obtain financial support from the State Department of Crippled Children. This was the first cardiac catheterization laboratory on the Emory campus, although the vascular surgeons had previously developed a peripheral vascular laboratory and had used the catheter in their studies. No other private hospital in Atlanta had a cardiac catheterization laboratory.

Several additional important appointments were made in 1957 and 1958. Dr. **Sam Poole** joined the faculty in cardiology in July 1957. He worked in the Emory University Clinic and supervised the course in physical diagnosis for sophomore medical students. He was superb but returned to practice in Gainesville, Georgia, in July 1958. Herb Karp assumed the responsibility of organizing the course when Poole left.

In 1958, Dr. **B. Woodfin Cobbs Jr.** (see Figure 5-21), who trained with Ed Bland at the Massachusetts General Hospital in Boston and Dr. John Goodwin at Hammersmith Hospital in London, was added to the cardiology staff at Emory University Hospital and Clinic. His major interest was in phonocardiography and auscultation. A creative person, he made significant contributions to the medical literature.

Dr. **Paul Robinson** joined the cardiology staff at Emory University Hospital and Clinic in 1967. He has remained in that position and is an excellent clinician-teacher.

Dr. **Stephen D. Clements Jr.** joined the Division of General Medicine at the Emory Clinic in 1973, then shifted to the Division of Cardiology in 1974. His house-staff and cardiology fellowship training had been with us. A superb clinician-teacher, he worked with Sonia Chang to develop an Echocardiography Laboratory at Emory University Hospital and Clinic. Chang had been Harvey Feigenbaum's chief technician and was a great asset to us in the early days of echocardiography. Clements also developed the Andreas Gruentzig Outpatient Cardiac Catheterization Laboratory in the Emory University Clinic.

Dr. **Spencer B. King III**, one of our former cardiac fellows, was making a name for himself in Denver. We enticed him to return to Emory University Hospital and Clinic in 1972 to develop the cardiovascular laboratories. At that time Franch was heavily involved in the catheterization of children with congenital heart disease, and a member of the Department of Radiology was performing coronary arteriography in a small room in the Radiology Department. King assumed the leadership position and developed coronary arteriography. In 1976, he designed four laboratories within the new construction in Emory University Hospital. He, along with Dr. John Douglas, developed coronary angioplasty at Emory Hospital after the unfortunate death of Dr. Andreas Gruentzig (see discussion below).

Dr. **John S. Douglas Jr.**, one of our former fellows, joined King in 1974, and they achieved national reputations for their work.

Dr. **John Stone** at Grady saw patients in the Emory University Clinic when time permitted. He became the excellent, unofficial "poet laureate" of the whole university.

In 1979 King indicated that a young man named Dr. **Andreas Gruentzig**, in Zurich, Switzerland, might move to the United States (see Figure 5-36). After years of laboratory research, Gruentzig had created a catheter with an inflatable balloon on its tip. The catheter could be inserted into the coronary arteries and, when blown up, would compress an obstructive atheromatous plaque. I first met Gruentzig in Cleveland when we were both on a medical program there. I later contacted him and invited him to come to Emory for a visit. By then, he was looking at several opportunities in the United States. We met with Emory President James T. Laney, who was at his recruitment best. Gruentzig also met with the Emory surgeons, who welcomed him.

Gruentzig told me he needed four things. He needed a Georgia license but did not want to take an examination. He wanted a permanent residence visa. He wanted adequate office space with an office window, and he wanted a full professorship with adequate income. After a few months, we were able to deliver on those requests. With the financial help of my friend and patient J. B. Fuqua, Gruentzig moved to Atlanta in 1980 and began his work at Emory University Hospital and at Crawford Long Hospital. The demand for his service was enormous. I initially gave him about half my office suite at Emory Hospital. He later was given the entire sixth floor in the connector between the E and G wing of the hospital. The most unusual problem I had in my effort to satisfy Gruentzig's needs was to obtain a permanent parking place for the motor scooter that he rode to work. His research was recognized worldwide, and he generated many important papers on angioplasty.

Gruentzig and his wife, Margaret Ann, were killed in a plane crash in 1985. He piloted his own plane, although I repeatedly begged him not to do so. A lovable, charismatic genius who had made his mark on the world at large and on Emory in particular, he was mourned all over the world. I wrote the following essay about Andreas Gruentzig a short time after he and his wife died. It was published in the March 1986 issue of *Circulation* and is reproduced here with the permission of the publisher.[12]

How to begin? How does one translate through paper the feelings generated by observing a great life? John F. Kennedy said this about Theodore Roosevelt:

The credit belongs to the man who is actually in the arena, whose face is marred by dust and sweat and blood, who knows the great enthusiasms, the great devotions, and spends himself in a worthy cause; who at best, if he wins, knows the thrills of high achievement, and, if he fails, at least fails daring greatly, so that his place shall never be with those cold and timid souls who know neither victory nor defeat.

I see Andreas Gruentzig in that quotation. He is standing there with the great adventurer Theodore Roosevelt, but, unlike Roosevelt, he has a novel, uniquely useful catheter in his hand.

This tribute, though not a diary, was written in diary-like fashion, *in reverse chronological order*, on St. Simons Island between November 28 and November 30, 1985. The lives of Andreas and Margaret Ann Gruentzig ended after they left the small airport at St. Simons, never to reach Atlanta.

November 28, 1985: The beautiful coastal islands Georgia are known as the Golden Isles. They are called by romantic names such as Blackbeard, Sapelo, Cumberland, St. Simons, Little St. Simons, Jekyll, Sea Island, among others. The Gruentzigs loved them. The Quale Indians were the islands' aborigines. The French arrived during the 1500s, the Spanish a century later, and the English, led by General James Edward Oglethorpe, settled in 1736.

Our place is on St. Simons. Theirs was on nearby Sea Island. Yesterday we drove by the St. Simons air strip where they began their last flight. Today we

---

[12] J. W. Hurst, "Tribute: Andreas Roland Gruentzig (1939–1985)," *Circulation* 73, no. 3 (March 1986): 606–10. The second paragraph, John F. Kennedy on Theodore Roosevelt, New York City, December 5, 1961, appears as quoted in the front matter of *The Last Lion*, a book on the life of Winston Churchill by William Manchester (Little, Brown and Co., 1983).

visited their beautiful, but empty, pale yellow home located on East Quale Street by the sea. The name Gruentzig was etched on the brass plate that was attached to the front door. How I wanted the door to open! He would have welcomed me with open arms and kissed my wife's hand. But such was not to be. . . .

November 16: Dr. Charles Hatcher, Dr. William Casarella, and I met to discuss how we could carry on after the loss and how we could honor Andreas in doing so. We embarked on creation of the Andreas Gruentzig Cardiovascular Center, knowing that it would require approval by the trustees. We all knew Gruentzig's long-term goal. It was far greater than angioplasty. We knew the family's wishes because Johannes, his brother, had discussed them with me on the third day of November and had reiterated them in a subsequent letter.

We agreed that, despite the great loss, we must proceed with a randomized study that matched bypass surgery against coronary angioplasty in patients with multivessel coronary disease. He had fought for such a study. We agreed that the angioplasty service would continue and that the Gruentzig angioplasty courses would continue under Dr. Spencer King's direction. We agreed that an Andreas Gruentzig Angioplasty Society should be created.

November 12: The American Heart Association (AMA) Meeting in Washington, DC, was attended by 7,198 physicians. It was not possible to walk more than a few feet in the Convention Center without being stopped by a friend or someone who knew of his work who would say, "I am so sorry. What a creative genius. What integrity. What a loss to cardiology and to the world."

A memorial service was organized by AHA President, Dr. Thomas Ryan. Drs. Myler, Hurst, Kaltenbach, and King presented tributes on November 12.

November 3: President James Laney of Emory University led the memorial service in Atlanta for Andreas Gruentzig and Margaret Ann Thornton Gruentzig. Drs. Hurst, Casarella, Kaltenbach, and King presented eulogies. The service was a University-wide one in the beautiful Glenn Memorial Church on the Emory campus.

November 1: We were in Macon, Georgia, the home of Margaret Ann Thornton Gruentzig. The church service was over. We were at the graveside. I was moved to write the following just after returning to Atlanta:

She stood up, with a son on her left and a friend on her right, and walked toward the *two* caskets. The smile on her face was sweet and her dark eyes were concentrating on the task she was about to perform. She opened the plastic bag she clutched in her hand. She reached inside of it and began to sprinkle soil on the top of *his* casket and when she was through there, she sprinkled soil on her casket. She and the soil were from Germany. She had come to bury her son Andreas and his wife Margaret Ann in the middle Georgia town of Macon. The date was November 1, 1985. The smile on her lovely face and her soft whispering of *auf Wiedersehen* as she slowly performed her task was simultaneously sad and beautiful, and the crowd wept. *Auf Wiedersehen* means more than goodbye. It means, until we see each other again.

October 28: The rumor surfaced at 8 a.m. Their plane was down. The feeling was one of helplessness, despair, nauseating sorrow, and shock. By midafternoon it was definite—they were gone.

As the news spread the telephone rang constantly. Telegrams came from Hong Kong, South America, everywhere. I called his brother Johannes in Düsseldorf, Germany. He was to tell his mother in Heidelberg. This was a sad, sad day. The circle of intense sadness spread quickly from a few to thousands, like a ripple produced by a pebble thrown in a lake.

October 27: Margaret Ann Thornton Gruentzig telephoned her mother in Macon, Georgia, and said they were leaving the coastal islands for Atlanta. Her mother exclaimed that the weather was bad. Her daughter said that Andreas had checked with the officials and it was all right. They boarded their own plane; Andreas was the pilot and she was the co-pilot. They flew despite my pleading with them not to do so. She flew with him because she loved him, not because she loved flying. He apparently radioed for help on two occasions—he said he had lost his way. Then a final statement that "it's all out." Hunters saw them circle twice and then crash in Monroe County, Georgia.

September 1980 to October 26, 1985: Who was Gruentzig? What did he do and why did he do it? He was with us at Emory for five years. He taught us daily and we studied not only what he said. We studied him. He was a caring genius.

He was tall and thin. His skin was dark as were his penetrating eyes. He sported a neatly trimmed mustache. You could sense his intelligence. His movements were quick but graceful. He and Margaret Ann were great dancers, and his superb coordination enabled him to ski with great skill. His hands appeared to be perfectly shaped. A broken thumb during a ski trip did not stop his elegant work. He could draw a single line and make it look beautiful. He spoke with a graceful German accent. He was gallant. He was charismatic. He was a gentleman. He was an adventurer—a swashbuckling adventurer—a Teddy Roosevelt. He was as persistent as Edison, as fearless as Churchill, and as courageous as young Charles Lindbergh. He drove his Porsche too fast and loved his airplane. He dashed into our early "morning report" with enthusiasm and added his thoughts to the discussion. He obviously enjoyed life.

To look a little deeper—he was intensely honest. He was kind. He never hurt anyone in his march toward his goals. He had an abundance of goodwill for people everywhere and learned from the experts from all countries. He was persistent. He was aggressive, but his approach was conservative.

He was creative. The world knows him as the person who invented percutaneous transluminal coronary angioplasty while working in Zurich. He and his colleagues performed almost 5000 coronary angioplasties during his five years at Emory. He designed several other catheters that enabled him to perform the procedure more perfectly. In my judgment, he was destined to move away from his daily work on angioplasty to research in other areas because his fertile mind was churning with so many ideas.

Why could he, and he alone, bring percutaneous transluminal angioplasty to its current popularity? The person who did it had to be intelligent, creative, critical, persistent, and adventurous. Two other qualities would be needed as well. He had them both. The first is an intense caring for patients. He really did not care if he harmed himself in an airplane. This was his free and adventurous spirit in full flight. He *did* care enormously about the welfare of his patients. This combination of the adventurer, who always placed the welfare of his patients first, was needed to develop the procedure. The second quality is that of the teacher. He taught his trainees at the catheterization table. He taught physicians in angioplasty courses he directed twice a year. The first course was given in Zurich. Twenty-eight people attended. After four courses there he gave 10 at Emory, with audiences ranging from 300 to 500 people. He taught while performing the procedure on patients under television lights with live transmission to the auditorium a block away. He was a master teacher. He wanted to share his knowledge with everyone. He taught all he knew. He wanted his method to be tested.

When he arrived we had two diagnostic catheterization laboratories at Emory Hospital. When he left us we had six. One is an animal research laboratory where members of his staff worked with laser. He was an excellent investigator. Each year, at the AHA Meeting and the American College of Cardiology Meeting he and his colleagues and trainees would present some new insight they had learned about coronary angioplasty. He moved the field forward in small and gentle steps.

The scientist in him made him cautious in exploring the use of angioplasty in multivessel coronary disease. He called for a randomized study to match angioplasty against bypass surgery. He believed that details should be worked out with single-vessel coronary angioplasty before multivessel angioplasty was used regularly. He reasoned that a "big operation seemed out of place when there was obstruction in only one coronary artery." He believed, too, that bypass surgery had been quite successful in the treatment of multivessel disease.

He often spoke of *new directions.* That is the way he referred to research. He would write notes to himself about *new directions.* In time, some will be published.

It is not generally appreciated that he was greatly interested in the prevention of coronary atherosclerosis. He believed that "risk factors" accelerated the disease process but did not cause it. He actually viewed his attack on single-vessel coronary disease as a preventive measure. Not only did the procedure relieve angina but he reasoned he was preventing multivessel disease. He knew a certain number of patients with triple-vessel disease must have started with single-vessel disease. Viewed in this manner, one could say that single-vessel coronary disease is a risk factor for the development of multivessel coronary disease. So, if he successfully overcame obstruction of single vessels he was preventing the appearance of triple-vessel disease.

During the last two years of his life he led me to believe that the time had come for outpatient cardiac catheterization. He believed that new catheters and new radiographic equipment would make the task easy and safe. To prove his point, in late 1984, he asked Dr. Hall Whitworth, one of our cardiology fellows, to perform coronary angioplasty on him. Gruentzig jumped on the catheterization table at about 5 p.m. The procedure was completed quickly. Gruentzig jumped off the table and went home to pick up Margaret Ann and

arrived at our Christmas party at 7 p.m. He had two thoughts in mind. He saw
the need for an outpatient catheterization laboratory to decrease the cost of
coronary arteriography in carefully selected patients thought to have angina.
But his goal was greater. He saw the day when asymptomatic subjects would
have this new simple type of coronary arteriography performed as part of a
screening procedure. Should severe single-vessel coronary obstruction be
found, it would be subjected to dilatation. In this way he might prevent sudden
death, infarction, and triple-vessel disease. He hoped to start the activity with a
carefully designed research protocol and move on, if warranted, to routine use.
Obviously, this approach would make it possible to design studies to test the
effect of medical measures on the speed of development of the disease process
in a small population of patients, whereas current studies require a huge
population of patients for their implementation.

January 1980 to September 1980: His name was already known in cardiology
circles. He had spent years improving the catheters used to dilate the arteries
in the legs. He had finally succeeded in miniaturizing the catheters so they
could be used in the coronary arteries. He performed the first percutaneous
transluminal coronary angioplasty in 1977 and reported results from five
patients in the *Lancet* in 1978. Word had been passed through the academic
grapevine, among the fastest of all communication systems, that Gruentzig was
considering moving from Zurich to the United States. I invited him to visit
Emory. He felt he could develop his ideas at our institution, and we met his
requirements. He came in September 1980. I gave him half of my office suite
at Emory Hospital. I was pleased to do so because I was placed in frequent
contact with him. His activity grew and grew, and I was able to provide him
with twice as much space two floors up. He had been in his new space for
about two months when the tragedy occurred.

1964 to 1980: Gruentzig graduated from the University of Heidelberg in
1964 and wrote his thesis the same year. His remarkable 15 years of
postgraduate training included the following: First- and second-year intern in
the Hospitals of Mannheim, Hannover, and Ludwigshafen, Germany, 1964–
1966; Research Fellow, Department of Physiology, Section of Social Medicine
and Epidemiology of Chronic Diseases, University of Heidelberg, German,
1966–1969; Research Fellow, Institute of Social Medicine and Epidemiology of
St. Thomas's Hospital, University of London, U.K., 1967; Postgraduate Course
in Medical Statistics and Epidemiology, London School of Hygiene and
Topical Medicine, University of London, U.K., 1968; Fellow, Internal
Medicine, Max-Ratschow Hospital, Darmstadt-Eberstadt, Germany (6 months),
1969; Fellow, Internal Medicine, Department of Angiology, Medical Policlinic,
University Hospital, Zurich, 1970; Resident, Internal Medicine, Department of
Medicine, University Hospital, Zurich (11 months), 1972; Fellow, Department
of Cardiology, Medical Policlinic, University Hospital, Zurich, 1973–1974;
Chief Fellow, Department of Cardiology, Medical Policlinic, University
Hospital, Zurich, 1974–1979.

He was made Physician-in-Chief, Department of Cardiology, Medical
Policlinic, University Hospital, Zurich, in 1979 and held that position until he
came to Emory University as Professor of Medicine (Cardiology) and

Radiology and Director of Interventional Cardiology at Emory University Hospital...

June 25, 1939: Andreas Roland Gruentzig was born in Dresden, Germany, on June 25, 1939.

His impact

Forssmann started it all when he pushed a urethral catheter into his own arm vein and inched it into the right atrium. This was followed by physiologic studies, diagnostic studies, left heart catheterization, and finally Mason Sones' catheterization of the coronary arteries. Andreas Gruentzig, standing on the shoulders of Sones, Dotter, and Judkins, was the first person to place a balloon-tipped catheter inside a coronary artery and dilate an obstruction located within it. He was successful. The world took notice. His unique personality made it possible for him to popularize the procedure.

His scientific achievements were obvious. His impact exceeded even them. He became known as a man of great integrity, and the medical community at large was proud of him.

As he viewed himself

The notes for the book he was preparing contain the following statement by him.

Whatever becomes of the method, I have left one mark on medicine. Forssmann demonstrated that man could place a catheter into his heart successfully. Mason Sones studied the coronary arteries selectively by angiography without significant mortality. I have shown that man can work therapeutically within the coronary arteries themselves in the face of an alert, comfortable patient.

The future

I cannot close this tribute without pointing out that he lived in the present as few have dared to live. He saw the future and, in fact, molded it to his liking. We are still grieving his loss but he would be impatient with us. He would say, "It is time to move on." And we shall try to do that.

His family

He is survived by his first wife, Michaela Gruentzig, and their daughter, Sonya, of Zurich, his mother Mrs. Charlotte Gruentzig of Heidelberg, and his brother, Johannes Gruentzig, of Düsseldorf, Germany.

Final comment

The following passage was written by Dr. Ignacio Chavez in his instructions to Diego Rivera when the latter was charged with painting the frescoes for the Instituto Nacional de Cardiologia in Mexico City:

The men who forged cardiology are of the most varied nationalities: Belgians and Frenchmen, Italians and Germans, Englishmen and Czechs, Spaniards and Americans—both of the Saxon and the Latin worlds—, Greco-Romans and Austrians, Dutchmen and Japanese. This single fact marks the spirit which should imprint itself upon the picture, which consists in emphasizing that scientific progress in our field, as in any other, has not been the patrimony of any race or of any tightly nationalistic culture. It is the genius of the man of every time and of every people which has developed universal culture. And it is this spirit of universality which you should embody in the two great frescoes.

Of course, Chavez and Gruentzig never met, but I believe Gruentzig exhibited what Chavez had in mind. Chavez might have said to Rivera, "He has what I am talking about. Capture Gruentzig's spirit in your frescoes."

Drs. King and Douglas picked up Gruentzig's mantle and carried on in a magnificent manner. The world at large soon recognized them as the leaders in the field of coronary angioplasty.

By 1985 the clinical research, spearheaded by King and Douglas and the cardiac surgeons, increased to the point that we needed to add a clinical-epidemiologist-statistician to the group. Dr. **William Weintraub** was selected and he and his staff have amply fulfilled the needs of the division.

Development of Cardiology at Crawford Long Hospital

Dr. **Linton Bishop**, a former cardiology fellow at Emory, was the major force in developing cardiology at Crawford Long Hospital. He was on the volunteer faculty and was later made a member of the Emory Board of Trustees. The development of Crawford Long Hospital became our responsibility in 1963 (see page 351). The Carlyle Fraser Heart Center was developed in 1973 (see page 352).

Dr. **Arthur Merrill Jr.** was appointed director of the cardiac laboratory, and was later joined by Dr. **John W. Hurst Jr**. Both later entered private practice at Piedmont Hospital, and Dr. **Douglas C. Morris**, one of our former fellows, was appointed to direct the cardiac laboratory at Crawford Long Hospital. Dr. **Byron Williams** joined the staff to develop nuclear cardiology. He had spent six months with Barry Zaret at Yale studying nuclear cardiology during his year of fellowship with us. Dr. **Henry Liberman** and Dr. **Louis Battey** also joined the cardiology staff at Crawford Long Hospital. They, too, had been cardiology fellows in our department. Dr. Williams left for private practice in 1983. He missed teaching and rejoined the faculty in 1994 (see discussion on page 353).

Dr. **Randolph Patterson**, an excellent researcher, joined the staff in 1984. He had become well known for his work at the National Institutes of Health. He further developed nuclear cardiology and stimulated more research activity.

Drs. **André Churchwell**, **Steven Eilen**, **Andrew Taussig**, and **Hall Whitworth** joined the staff but later entered practice. Churchwell developed a large practice in Nashville. Taussig and Whitworth joined Dr. Tommy Dickinson and several other former Emory cardiology fellows in

Orlando, Florida, to create one of the largest groups in Florida. Eilen entered practice in Atlanta.

Bruce Logue became Director of the Carlyle Fraser Heart Center in 1980, and Dr. Douglas Morris became the Director of the Center when Dr. Logue retired in 1986. In 1996, Morris became the J. Willis Hurst Professor of Medicine and director of the newly-created Emory Heart Center.

The Relationship of Cardiology to Piedmont, Georgia Baptist, and Northside Hospitals

The relationship of the Division of Cardiology to Piedmont Hospital, Georgia Baptist Hospital, and Northside Hospital is discussed on pages 293–95.

Schlant as Division Director

In the late fifties, I assumed the role of coordinator of the enlarging staff in cardiology. Later, when the official title of director was used, I assumed the role of director of the division until 1962. By 1962, Schlant was well on his way to becoming nationally known for his work in hemodynamics, and his administrative talent was evident. His excellent performance led me to appoint him as director of the Division of Cardiology. He received a US Public Health Service Career Development Award from 1961 to 1971. He performed the first coronary arteriogram in Georgia in the cardiac catheterization laboratory at Grady Memorial Hospital. He achieved national and international prominence as chairman of the Council on Clinical Cardiology of the American Heart Association. He received the Distinguished Service Award of the Council in 1990 and the Herrick Award from the American Heart Association in 1994. Most importantly, he handled the administrative aspects of the division that had more than twenty-nine faculty members and as many as thirty fellows annually. He remained director of the division until 1988. Cardiology at Emory would not be what it is today had it not been for the brilliant, well-focused leadership of Robert Schlant.

Excellent Nurses

An excellent cardiac service cannot be developed without the help of excellent nurses. We were blessed in this regard; the nurses at each of our hospitals were outstanding. I especially thank Julia Purcell at Emory University Hospital, who spearheaded a very successful teaching program for the nurses assigned to cardiology.

Excellent Cardiac Surgery

The cardiac surgeons included Dr. Charles Hatcher, director of the Division of Cardiac Surgery, Dr. Ellis Jones, Dr. Joe Craver, Dr. David Bone, and Dr. Douglas Murphy at Emory University Hospital, Drs. Robert Guyton and John Gott at Crawford Long Hospital, Drs. Willis Williams and Kirk Kanter at Egleston Hospital, and Dr. Peter Symbas at Grady Memorial Hospital and the Veterans Administration Hospital. They became nationally known for their superb surgical treatment of coronary disease, congenital heart disease, valve disease, traumatic heart disease, and cardiac transplantation.

Activities of the Division of Cardiology

The teaching of cardiovascular medicine to students, house officers, and fellows was intense. Modern teaching aids were obtained for use in the teaching program. Equipment was made available to teach auscultation to groups of trainees. The mannequin, Harvey, obtained with the help of the Woodruff Foundation, could display the physical findings of a number of cardiac diseases. Saturday morning teaching sessions in the Oppenheimer Conference Room in the Glenn Memorial Building on the Grady campus became well known. Those sessions rivaled the famous "Sunday school" sessions of Stead's era. The Wednesday evening televised conferences in the Grady auditorium were well received. Many physicians from the community at large attended these sessions. When a famous cardiologist, such as Paul White, presented at the Wednesday evening session, all of the seats in the Grady Auditorium were filled.

In order to strengthen the cardiology fellowship program, we arranged a rotation with Dr. Henry J. L. Marriott in St. Petersburg, Florida, one of the leading scholars in cardiac arrhythmia and an excellent teacher. The Rogers Heart Foundation in St. Petersburg supported the effort. We also arranged yearly visits of Dr. Reginald E. B. Hudson of the Heart Hospital in London. He was one of the world leaders in cardiac pathology and a superb teacher. He and his wife, Dorothy, stayed in Atlanta for several weeks at a time when he taught cardiac pathology to the students, house staff, and fellows. Later, Dr. Michael Gravanis assisted us a great deal as he became increasingly interested in cardiac pathology. As the years passed, Gravanis became nationally known as an excellent cardiac pathologist. He continues to contribute a great deal to our teaching program.

Annual postgraduate courses became nationally known. From the beginning in 1957, the courses were attended by 100–600 participants. Numerous world leaders presented at the courses. Beginning in 1981,

Gruentzig, and later King and Douglas, presented an annual course in angioplasty (see Figure 5-32). As many as 500 physicians attended each of these courses.

During the fifties and sixties, Logue and I were the pediatric consultants at Emory. We saw a large number of patients with congenital heart disease. The only preparation of digitalis available for children was the unreliable tincture of digitalis. I worked with Burroughs-Wellcome pharmaceutical house and one of our cardiology fellows, Dr. Larry Lamb, to develop the elixir of digoxin; this preparation of the drug is still used today.

Research activity increased over the years as space became available. The research was predominantly in the area of hemodynamics, cardiac rehabilitation, heart disease in women, and coronary angioplasty. My friend and patient Harold Brockey helped us gain the support of the Rich's Foundation to develop the Rich Vascular Laboratory in the Ernest Woodruff Research Building. In 1981 I suggested to Dr. Gerald Fletcher, then president of the Georgia Affiliate of the American Heart Association, that the time was right to initiate a Heart Ball in Atlanta to raise money for cardiovascular research. He did so. The first Heart Ball was sponsored in 1982. From then on the local funds for research increased, and Emory and all other Georgia institutions profited from it.

The patient care program was intensified at all facilities. The first mitral commissurotomy was performed at Emory University Hospital on a patient of mine in 1951. The value of cardiac defibrillation and pacemakers for the treatment of cardiac arrhythmias was demonstrated by the staff at Grady Memorial Hospital. In February 1967, Robert Franch and Sylvia Crawley, a cardiology fellow, used a catheter to perform an atrial septotomy. This was the first time the procedure had been done in the South. Patients came from other states and abroad to Emory University Hospital and Crawford Long Hospital. Diagnostic cardiac catheterization laboratories were busy in each of the four hospitals. The amount of teaching, service, and research provided by the activities in the four hospitals exceeded that of most medical centers in the nation. Emory University Hospital is often ranked in the top ten in national polls rating the quality of cardiology.

I became president of the American Heart Association in 1972. I was a member of the Subspecialty Board of Cardiovascular Disease from 1965 to 1970 and served as its chairman from 1967 to 1970. During that time, and for a number of years afterward, we often gave the oral cardiovascular examination at Grady Memorial Hospital.

The publications of the Division of Cardiology steadily increased over the years. Many books were written, including *The Heart*, created in 1966 and for three editions edited by Hurst and Logue (see page 244). Dr. Logue and I worked each Thursday morning to prepare the first edition of the book. Drs. Schlant and Wenger were superb associates in the production of the book and worked with me each Saturday morning for an extended period. They developed the index for the first edition. I was Editor-in-Chief for the fourth, fifth, sixth, and seventh editions. Many people contributed to the book, which became known throughout the world and was translated into five foreign languages. The eighth edition, known as *Hurst's The Heart*, was edited by Drs. Schlant and R. Wayne Alexander.

In 1980 I became chief of medicine and cardiology at Emory University Hospital and Clinic and head of the Medical Section and cardiology in the Emory Clinic. I relinquished the positions of Chief of Medicine at Emory University Hospital and head of the Medical Section of the Emory Clinic to Dr. Juha Kokko, the new chairman of the Department of Medicine, in the fall of 1986. I continued as chief of cardiology at Emory University Hospital and Clinic until Dr. Wayne Alexander arrived as the new director of the Division of Cardiology in 1988. He was a superb choice. He was already nationally known as an excellent researcher and clinician. The respect for him was immediate. Alexander promptly added several nationally known researchers to the division. Schlant continued his work as chief of cardiology at Grady Memorial Hospital. New research space had become available in the Ernest Woodruff Research Building on the Emory campus, and Emory became positioned to be one of the national leaders in cardiovascular molecular biology.

The Division of Dermatology

When I assumed the chairmanship of the Department of Medicine in 1957, there were no full-time dermatologists at Emory University Hospital and Clinic, Grady Memorial Hospital, or the Atlanta Veterans Administration Hospital. The patient care and teaching programs in dermatology were implemented by the volunteer clinical faculty.

In 1957 Dr. **Herbert Steed Alden**, a clinical professor and one of Atlanta's leading dermatologists, became incapacitated from the symptoms of a herniated intervertebral disk. He selected Dr. **Hiram Sturm**, a newcomer in Atlanta, to replace him in the Dermatology Clinic at Grady Memorial Hospital. Sturm saw patients and taught students in the outpatient clinic and made inpatient rounds in Grady Memorial Hospital. The volunteer dermatology staff included Drs. **Charles Adams, Phillip Nippert, William Dobes Sr., Harold Levin, Hugh Halley, Joseph Rankin**, and **David Hearin**.

The group of volunteer faculty members had an intense desire to raise the level of dermatology at Emory University School of Medicine and in Atlanta. They urged me to appoint a full-time faculty member to be their leader. Having no endowment money to do so, I appointed Dr. **Sidney Olansky** from Duke, to work in the Emory University Clinic and to develop dermatology within the Department of Medicine at Grady Memorial Hospital, Emory University Hospital and Clinic, and the Veterans Administration Hospital.

Olansky arrived at Emory in September 1959 and became the first full-time director of the Division of Dermatology at Emory University School of Medicine. The house-staff training program was approved about a year later. Olansky selected two members of the volunteer faculty, Drs. Sturm and **Robert Fine**, to assist him in his duties at Grady Memorial Hospital. Dr. **Glenn McCormick** joined Olansky in the Emory Clinic and remained for four to five years before entering private practice. Dr. **Mary Lou Applewhite** joined the group and later entered private practice in New Orleans. Drs. **Dan Whyte, A. C. Brown**, and **Don Pirozzi** joined Olansky before entering private practice in Atlanta, and Drs. **Fredrick Hardin** and **Chenault Hailey** joined the active volunteer faculty.

Dr. **A. C. Brown** was director of the Division of Dermatology from 1971 until 1974, when he entered private practice in the Atlanta area. He emphasized dermatopathology, and this contributed significantly to the patient care and teaching program. When Brown left, I again turned to Hiram Sturm for help. He then directed the dermatology patient care and teaching program as well as the house officer program for eight residents. Other volunteer faculty members joined in the effort, including Drs. **Harold Meltzer, John Broyles, Fred Hardin, Levore Hailey**, and capable individuals from the Centers for Disease Control and Prevention. Dr. **Issac Willis** joined the staff at the Veterans Administration Hospital and remained on the staff for a few years.

Sturm ran a good division with few resources. He again urged the appointment of a full-time Emory dermatologist to direct the program. Sturm chaired the search committee that led to the appointment of Dr. **Earl Jones**, from the University of Michigan, to be the director of the Division of Dermatology in the Department of Medicine.

Jones came to Emory in October 1976 as an associate professor of medicine and director of the Division of Dermatology in the Department of Medicine and Emory University Clinic. He was an effective leader, and the volunteer faculty supported his efforts.

By the late seventies the Division of Dermatology was sufficiently strong to stand on its own legs. Accordingly, I suggested the division become a separate department. This was accomplished in February 1977.

Jones, then an associate professor, was appointed acting chairman of the new department until August 1977, when he became professor and chairman. He entered private practice in Mobile, Alabama, in April 1984. Dr. **Robert Rietschel** became acting chairman for one year prior to joining the Oschner Clinic in New Orleans. Dr. **Marilynne McKay**, associate professor of dermatology, was acting chairman of the Department of Dermatology from May 1, 1985, to August 1, 1988.

Dr. **Richard Krause**, dean of the School of Medicine, enticed the nationally recognized Dr. **Thomas J. Lawley**, whom he had known at the National Institutes of Health, to become the next professor and chairman of the Department of Dermatology.

Lawley arrived on August 1, 1988, and rapidly recruited a number of research-oriented dermatologists. He spread out on all fronts. He improved patient care in Emory University Hospital and Clinic, Grady Memorial Hospital, and the Veterans Administration Hospital. The department improved its teaching of students and house officers. The research effort moved from none to become nationally recognized.

Now, in 1996, the Department of Dermatology ranks third in the nation in Federal research funding, which signifies the amount of creative work performed in the department.

Sturm wrote me the following note on May 8, 1996. It reveals the pride of the volunteer clinical faculty.

> The Department of Dermatology now prospers under the leadership of two nationally known research-oriented dermatologists from the National Institutes of Health, Dr. Thomas Lawley and Dr. Wright Caughman. The Atlanta Dermatological Society (and I) fought hard and long in an advisory capacity to the search committee to bring them to Emory. They have established a full-time staff of twelve physicians, with a residency staff of fourteen. The basic and clinical research emanating from the Department of Dermatology of Emory University is heralded and respected throughout the world by other departments of dermatology. Our training program positions are much sought after; Emory Dermatology is considered to be among the top five programs in the country.

Lawley became Interim Dean of the School of Medicine on May 14, 1996, and Dr. Caughman, professor of dermatology, became acting chairman of the Department of Dermatology on May 14, 1996. Lawley became dean of the School of Medicine on September 1, 1996.

This long story is told in some detail because, working with no financial support, the volunteer faculty and a few full-time faculty members, plus Lawley, literally willed themselves into one of the nation's best dermatology departments. The Department of Medicine is proud of its role as a facilitator of this development.

The Division of Digestive Diseases

In 1957 there were two faculty members who devoted their time and interest to digestive diseases: Dr. **Julius Wenger**, appointed by Eugene Ferris in 1956, was located at the Veterans Administration Hospital, and Dr. **Spalding Schroder**, appointed by Paul Beeson, who was located initially in the Private Diagnostic Clinic in Emory University Hospital.

When I started my work as chairman, I needed help. I was fortunate to discover Dr. **John Galambos** (see Figure 5-15) at Grady Memorial Hospital, completing his two-year stint in the United States Public Health Service. He was considered a fellow in the Department of Medicine. He worked with Dr. Jerry Cooper, also in the USPHS. Their laboratory and offices were located in the old Grady Clay Eye Clinic on the Grady campus. I appointed Galambos to the faculty on July 1, 1957. He later became the director of the Division of Digestive Diseases. He remained on the faculty until December 31, 1991. Galambos was deeply interested in research related to diseases of the liver. He had trained in gastroenterology with Dr. Walter Palmer and Dr. Joseph Kirsner at the University of Chicago. He developed a laboratory for his research in the Henry Woodruff Research Extension Building on the Grady campus, helped recruit new faculty members, and developed a training program in diseases of the liver and gastrointestinal tract.

One of Galambos's first fellows was Dr. **James Achord**, appointed to the faculty in 1960. His work was located, for the most part, at Emory University Hospital and Clinic. He remained a few years and then became director of the Division of Digestive Diseases at the University of Mississippi.

Dr. **Martin Teem** joined the faculty in the Emory University Clinic in 1971 and entered practice in Marietta, Georgia, in 1972.

Dr. **Theodore Hersh**, who trained at the Mayo Clinic and the Harvard Division at Boston City Hospital, joined the faculty in 1973. Located at Emory University Hospital and Clinic, he served as co-director of the division for two years. He also chaired the Human Investigations Committee of the medical school. He became emeritus in 1996.

Dr. **Scott Brooks**, a former fellow in the Division of Digestive Diseases, joined the staff in 1974, located at Emory University Hospital and Clinic. He developed endoscopy at the Emory University Clinic, then entered private practice at Piedmont Hospital in 1989.

Dr. **Jacinto Del Mazo** joined the faculty in 1974, working at the Atlanta Veterans Administration Hospital until he entered private practice in 1979.

Dr. **Horacio Jinich** joined the staff in 1975. He was located, for the most part, at Emory University Clinic and participated in the teaching program at Grady Memorial Hospital. He joined the faculty at the University of California in San Diego in 1978.

Dr. **Salah Nasrallah**, appointed to the faculty in 1976, was located, for the most part, at Grady Memorial Hospital but entered private practice in Baltimore in 1981.

Dr. **Michael Perkel**, a former fellow in the program at Emory, joined the faculty in 1976, then entered private practice in Atlanta in 1983.

Dr. **Stanley Riepe**, who graduated from Emory and trained at Barnes Hospital in St. Louis, Missouri, joined the faculty in 1978 and remains on the faculty as an excellent clinician in the Emory Clinic.

Dr. **Cynthia Rudert**, a former fellow in the Division of Digestive Diseases, joined the faculty in 1984 and was assigned to Grady Memorial Hospital. She entered private practice in Atlanta in 1992.

Dr. **Douglas C. Wolf** joined the faculty in 1984, assigned to the Veterans Administration Hospital. He entered private practice in 1992.

Dr. **Alice O. Johnson**, a former fellow in the Division of Digestive Diseases, joined the faculty in 1985, assigned to the Veterans Administration Hospital. She entered private practice in Atlanta in 1992.

Dr. **Herbert Bonkovsky** joined the faculty in 1985, coming to Emory from Dartmouth as director of the General Clinical Research Center, where he spearheaded an extensive research program (see page 228). He joined the faculty at the University of Massachusetts Medical Center in Worcester, Massachusetts, in 1990.

Dr. Dean Warren, professor and chairman of the Department of Surgery, was interested in the shunt procedure used to treat patients with bleeding varices due to cirrhosis of the liver as well as liver transplantation. Galambos and his colleagues worked closely with Warren and his colleagues in the research related to these procedures. The first liver transplant was done at Emory University Hospital on January 21, 1987.

The research in the division involved Hersh, Emory's director of the National Gallstone Study; Galambos, interested in all aspects of cirrhosis of the liver; and studies on gut adaptation of massive resection of the bowel, gastrointestinal motility, and malabsorption syndromes.

The Division of Endocrinology

Dr. **Phil Bondy**, who worked in Stead's department at Emory, achieved national recognition as an endocrinologist and remained at Emory during Beeson's time as professor and chairman of the Department of Medicine. He followed Beeson to Yale succeeding him later as chairman of the Department of Medicine.

Dr. **Bernard Hallman**, the only endocrinologist in the Department of Medicine at Emory in 1956, the next year became assistant dean of professional services at Grady Memorial Hospital and had no time to develop endocrinology. Alfred Wilhelmi, professor and chairman of the Department of Biochemistry, was nationally known for his work on growth hormone and was well informed on the research activity of investigators in endocrinology. I asked him in late 1957 to suggest the name of a research-oriented endocrinologist whom we might recruit to develop a Division of Endocrinology in the Department of Medicine. He suggested Dr. **John R. K. Preedy**, an Englishman, who resided in London. After appropriate letters back and forth and a phone call, Preedy came for an interview. He accepted my offer to join the department in 1958. Based primarily in the Glenn Memorial Building at Grady, where space was available for his research, he was an expert in estrogen metabolism and had developed new methods to measure the hormone. He was also an entertaining lecturer, and his English demeanor and accent interested his colleagues, students, and members of the house staff.

Drs. **Hrair Balikian** and **Victoria Musey** joined Preedy in the Grady area in 1968 and January 1977, respectively. Dr. **John Ward** was appointed to the Atlanta Veterans Administration Hospital in 1957, and Dr. **Khalid Siddiq** in 1978. Dr. **James Christy** was appointed to Emory University Clinic and Hospital in July 1964.

Dr. **Jack Davidson**, a nationally known expert in diabetes, was added to the staff at Grady in July 1968. A former Emory student and house officer, he had spent several years at the University of Toronto, where Best, the co-discoverer of insulin, worked. During his tenure at Emory, he wrote the book *Diabetes*, which became well known throughout the world.

In 1968, Dr. **Dan Rudman** was appointed director of the General Clinical Research Center in Emory University Hospital (see page 228), and Dr. **Mario DiGirolamo** joined the endocrine group at Grady. These two excellent researchers had been on the medical school faculty at Columbia University. **Delwood Collins**, Ph.D., was also added to the staff at Grady as were **Victoria Musey, E. Hobgood, Charles O'Neal, Robert Spanheimer**, and **Kristina Wright**.

In 1981, Dr. Preedy was offered the position of assistant chief of staff in research at the Atlanta Veterans Administration Hospital, a position he held until retiring in 1986. Preedy's move to the Veterans Administration Hospital stimulated more research there, and DiGirolamo was appointed interim director of the Division of Endocrinology, a position he held until 1983. Dr. DiGirolamo was an excellent interim director but preferred to be more intimately involved with research than was possible as director of a division. He also contributed chapters to the textbook,

Medicine for the Practicing Physician. Collins was offered a position at the Veterans Administration Hospital and was later appointed vice chancellor for research and graduate studies at the University of Kentucky Medical Center, in 1991.

Drs. **Nelson Watts** and **Suzanne Gebhart** were appointed to the Emory University Clinic in 1983 and 1984, respectively. They were excellent additions to the staff and edited the section on endocrinology in the textbook, *Medicine for the Practicing Physician*. Drs. **Richard Clark, R. K. Chawla**, and **Paul Davidson** were also added to the staff at Emory University Hospital and Clinic.

Drs. **Bayard Catherwood, Louisa Titus**, and **Rosemary Titus** were added to the staff at the Veterans Administration Hospital.

The clinical work was superb, and the group became recognized as experts in estrogen metabolism, diabetes mellitus, parathyroid disease, and pituitary tumors. They developed an excellent fellowship program that received financial support from the National Institutes of Health starting in 1978. They also worked with the basic science departments to develop an endocrine group capable of training individuals in a graduate program. They worked with neurosurgeons in the treatment of pituitary tumors and with general surgeons in the treatment of parathyroid tumors.

The research activity involved investigation of estrogen metabolism, fat cell metabolism, thyroid disease, parathyroid disease, growth hormone, and diabetes.

Dr. **Larry Phillips**, appointed director of the Division of Endocrinology in 1983, had previously been on the medical school faculty at Northwestern University.

The Division of General Medicine

By the early seventies, it was obvious that more generalists were needed in the department. Many patients at Grady Memorial Hospital, Emory University Hospital and Clinic, and the Veterans Administration Hospital needed comprehensive medical care. Students and house officers needed to be exposed to true teachers who were excellent role models in comprehensive care. There were also signs that the nation's medical schools and hospitals were training too many subspecialists and too few generalists.

My initial effort at creating a Division of General Medicine required that the first director become responsible for the General Medical Appointment Clinic at Grady, the "screening" clinic at Grady, and the busy Medical Emergency Clinic at Grady. The development of general medicine at Emory University Hospital, the Emory University Clinic, and the Veterans Administration Hospital was less difficult.

Dr. **John Stone**, a former chief resident in medicine at Grady, who had also trained in our cardiology program, was appointed the first director of the Division of General Medicine of the Department of Medicine in 1973. As such, he was also responsible for the Medical Emergency Clinic at Grady. He later became director of the Emergency Medicine residency training program at Grady. He was excellent but wanted to be more involved in student affairs. He moved to the dean's office in 1981 as professor of medicine (cardiology), associate dean, and director of admissions to Emory Medical School. He continued his work in cardiology and also became an excellent poet and orator of national reputation.

Dr. **Dallas Hall**, interim director of the division from 1982 to 1985, was followed by Dr. **Corey Slovis** and Dr. **Michael Lubin**. Slovis, an excellent, enthusiastic teacher, had been a member of our house staff from 1975 to 1978. He was a resident and then chief resident in the Emergency Medicine program from 1978 to 1980 and was in charge of the Medical Emergency Clinic from 1979 to 1989. He was the Program Director of the Emergency Medical Program from 1985 to 1989, then became co-director of the Division of General Medicine in 1985, a position he held until 1989. He subsequently became professor and chairman of the Department of Emergency Medicine at Vanderbilt.

Lubin, who became co-director of the division along with Slovis in 1985, was another former house officer. He had been awarded a Hartford Foundation Fellowship in Geriatrics and had special training in that field.

In 1985, most of the director's time was spent at Grady Memorial Hospital. Dr. **Paul Seavey** became the senior physician in general medicine at the Emory University Clinic. An excellent generalist, he assumed the medical care of former President Jimmy Carter and his family. Dr. **Joseph Hardison** was the senior physician in General Medicine at the Veterans Administration Hospital.

In 1963 Emory-owned Crawford Long Hospital began to be operated by Emory University. Accordingly, the volunteer faculty members at Crawford Long Hospital who were general internists were added to the list of volunteer faculty members in the Division of General Medicine. The same was done for all other volunteer faculty members in Atlanta who were internists.

Several faculty members appointed to Emory University Hospital and Clinic later entered practice, among them Drs. **Eugene Brown** and **Charles Brake.**

In 1986, the faculty members in the Division of General Medicine at Grady Memorial Hospital included: Drs. **Steve Brody, Tom Eglin, Barbara Greene-Plauth, Dick Hansen, Dorothy Karandanis, Sue Lee, Michael Lubin, Pat Meadors, David Simon** and **Corey Slovis.**

In 1986, the faculty members in the Division of General Medicine at Emory University Hospital included Drs. **S. Carter Davis, Donald Davis, Paul Seavey, Sally West,** and **Grattan Woodson.**

Drs. **William Budell** and **Miriam Gentry** were assigned to the Emory University Student Health Clinic. Dr. **Larry Kirkland** was assigned to the Emory University Hospital Employees Health Clinic.

The members of the Division of General Medicine assigned to the Veterans Administration Hospital included: Drs. **Ronald Gebhart, Joseph Hardison, Stephanie B. Johnson, Milford Rogers,** and **Susan Wodica.**

Dr. **Harold S. Ramos** in the Division of General Medicine was stationed at Crawford Long Hospital.

A postgraduate course in internal medicine was offered annually. First given in 1976, the course was very popular and was offered as an audio "textbook." Dr. Sidney Stein continues to organize the course under the direction of Dr. Kokko.

I perceived that a new and different type of medical textbook was needed. I became editor-in-chief of the textbook, *Medicine for the Practicing Physician.* The first edition was published by Butterworths in 1983. A great deal of the book was written by Emory faculty. This book was my signal that as a specialist, I believed it was wise to remain interested in general medicine. The new, fourth edition of the book was published by Appleton & Lange in July 1996.

By 1986, the organizational structure of the Division of General Medicine had not been fully formed, but the framework of the arrangement was clear. There was little time for the division director, who spent his time at Grady, to develop a cohesive group of faculty members that also involved the physicians at the Emory University Hospital and Clinic, the Veterans Administration Hospital, and Crawford Long Hospital. The next major activity would obviously be centered on the refinement of the duties to be performed by an increasing number of faculty members who would undoubtedly be recruited in the Division of General Medicine. This development would parallel the new emphasis on the training of larger numbers of primary care physicians.

Dr. Kokko appointed Dr. William Branch director of the Division of General Medicine in 1995. Branch was awarded the Carter Smith Sr. Professorship in Medicine.

The Division of Geriatrics

By the early eighties, the number of elderly patients in our hospitals and clinics was increasing. In addition, each elderly patient was prone to have more than one disease, more elderly patients were in nursing homes, and the cost of caring for the medical needs of such patients was far more than for younger patients. It was also apparent that trainees needed special training for the special medical needs of elderly patients.

The questions were: should there be a separate Department of Geriatrics, as there was a separate Department of Pediatrics; should there be a separate Division of Geriatrics within the existing Department of Medicine; or should geriatric training be emphasized within the Division of General Medicine of the Department of Medicine?

Eugene Stead had become an expert on the subject of geriatrics. After he relinquished the chairmanship of the Department of Medicine at Duke, he worked in a nursing home in Durham, North Carolina. In Stead-like fashion, he observed, he doctored, and he learned more about the problems of the elderly. Because of his knowledge, I asked him to visit Emory and advise us in our efforts to improve the educational opportunity we offered our students and medical house staff. He visited us in 1982. Following his visit, I decided to create a Division of Geriatrics within the Department of Medicine.

The Wesley Woods Geriatric Center, built in 1965 on Clifton Road, was a magnificent structure and had a loose arrangement with Emory. **Hugh Wood**, former dean at Emory, was appointed the first medical director of the facility in 1966. **Robert Brown**, former director of the Emory Clinic, became its second medical director in 1980. In 1983 **Herb Karp**, professor and chairman of the Department of Neurology, decided to relinquish the chairmanship of the Department of Neurology and become the medical director of Wesley Woods. He would simultaneously return to the Department of Medicine as the first director of the new Division of Geriatrics. Interested in Alzheimer's disease, and a magnificent teacher, he was a good colleague to have back in the Department of Medicine.

Initially, medical house officers were allowed to elect to rotate through the facility. In 1984, Dean James Glenn asked me to develop a document that described the use of Wesley Woods in our teaching program. The final document of official affiliations between Emory and Wesley Woods was signed in 1985.

A new nursing home for veterans was built in the early eighties and dedicated on October 26, 1982. The first patient was admitted to the facility on October 11, 1983. Dr. **Joseph Hardison**, chief of medicine at the Veterans Administration Hospital, was interested in developing a teaching program in geriatrics in that facility. He was highly respected by house staff and students, and his interest in the care of the elderly was a great stimulus to the trainees. The Veterans Administration began to support one house-officer position in geriatrics in 1988, and since then at least one house officer a month, and sometimes two, has learned about the care of the frail and the elderly at the Veterans Hospital.

Drs. Karp and Hardison were perfect leaders, because they understood the needs of patients and the educational needs of house officers. Because of them, the program flourished. The training program soon met all of the requirements established by the American Board of Internal Medicine. Therefore, some trainees participated in the program for an additional full year. The training fellowship at Wesley Woods Geriatric Center is officially called the Herbert Karp Fellowship in Geriatric Medicine.

Karp recognized the need for a geriatric hospital and helped the officials at Wesley Woods stimulate the appropriate donors for the creation of a new one-hundred-bed Wesley Woods Geriatric Research Hospital, which was completed in 1987. Emory University Hospital, Crawford Long Hospital, and other community health agencies provide additional facilities and expertise when needed.

This remarkable development was supported by the Woodruff Foundation in order to make the Emory-Wesley Woods connection as solid as possible.

When Karp retired from the medical school in 1990, Dr. Kokko named Mario DiGirolamo director of the Division of Geriatrics.

The Division of Hematology and Oncology

Dr. **Roy R. Kracke** joined the Department of Pathology at Emory following the first world war. He eventually became chairman of the Department of Pathology. His consuming interest and publications about the blood led to his national recognition, and his work helped make hematology a specialty. He and Dr. Jean George Bachmann, the first chairman of the Department of Physiology at Emory University School of Medicine, were the major researchers in the basic science departments of Emory University. Kracke became dean of the University of Alabama School of Medicine in Birmingham at the end of the second world war, when the School of Medicine there changed from a two-year school to a four-year school.

There were only two hematologists in the Department of Medicine in 1957, Dr. **Charles Huguley** and Dr. **Ben Gendel.** Huguley had trained under Stead at Emory and Carl Moore at Barnes Hospital in St. Louis. He was originally in the Robert Winship Clinic and Private Diagnostic Clinic at Emory Hospital and later in the Emory University Clinic. He could do it all, because he was a superb clinician, an excellent teacher, and researcher. He was a scholar's scholar.

Gendel was chief of medicine at the Veterans Administration Hospital. He wanted to be more closely related to the medical students, so I requested that he move to the Glenn Memorial Building on the Grady campus and supervise the junior and senior student programs in medicine. A great teacher, he was very popular with students and house staff. Those early days were wonderful, because during that period students and house staff used the teaching microscope in the student laboratory on the sixth floor of Grady Hospital. Gendel and his technician spent considerable time teaching them hematology. He rejoined the Veterans Administration Hospital in Memphis, Tennessee, in 1971 and died of complications of coronary atherosclerotic heart disease in 1977.

Dr. **Charles Corley**, my first appointee in hematology, joined the staff in July 1957. He was located at Emory University Hospital and Clinic, where the patient load was increasing. He was an excellent clinician-teacher and later became assistant director of the Emory Clinic until retiring in 1991.

Huguley and Corley also covered the pediatric hematology service at Egleston Hospital until a Division of Hematology evolved within the Department of Pediatrics.

Over the years, the following individuals were appointed to work at Emory Hospital and Clinic: Dr. **James Lea**, who also helped direct the medical house-staff program at Emory University Hospital, Dr. **E. V. Bruckner**, Dr. **L. T. Heffner**, Dr. **James Keller**, who later became an expert in radiation therapy, Dr. **Ralph Vogler**, Dr. **Elliott Winton**, and Dr. **David Gordon**. When the oncology subsection was added to the Winship Clinic within the Emory Clinic, Dr. **Daniel Nixon**, Dr. **Martin York**, and Dr. **David Lawson** were added to the staff.

Dr. **Julian Jacobs** and Dr. **Ravi Sarma** joined the staff at the Atlanta Veterans Administration Affairs Hospital.

The following faculty members were added to the hematology staff at Grady Memorial Hospital: Dr. **Herbert Kann**, Dr. **Melvin Moore**, Dr. **Sidney Stein**, Dr. **James Eckman**, and Dr. **Sam Newcom**.

As time passed, the medical treatment of cancer improved considerably. Hematologists, who formerly treated leukemia and other cancers of the blood, were beginning to treat other cancers. The Division of Hematology eventually became the Division of Hematology and

272 *The Quest for Excellence*

Oncology. Creative students called it Hemonc. In many schools oncology became a separate division of the Department of Medicine.

The Division of Hematology-Oncology thrived under Huguley's direction. He was also in charge of clinical pathology during my early years as chairman. As the curriculum changed, Huguley and his colleagues were always eager to contribute to the teaching program. Their research, heavily funded by the National Institutes of Health, involved clinical studies of chemotherapy for hematologic and nonhematologic malignancies. Eckman's research in sickle cell disease at Grady Memorial Hospital became nationally recognized.

The research space required for the research activity was located in Emory University Hospital, the Ernest Woodruff Memorial Research Building on the Emory University campus, and at Grady Memorial Hospital.

Huguley retired in 1988 after a very successful academic career.

The Division of Hypertension

General rules hold that it is not wise to create divisions that are devoted to specific diseases within a Department of Medicine. While this is generally true, exceptions should be made when there are faculty members on the scene capable of developing a program that focuses on a specific condition or disease to the degree that patient care, teaching, and research can be improved significantly. By 1976 Dr. **Dallas Hall**, in the Division of Renal Medicine, had developed a great interest in hypertension. In addition, Grady Memorial Hospital was filled with patients with hypertension. Federal funding was becoming available to mount a major research effort to learn more about this serious and common condition. Because of these opportunities, it seemed wise to break the general rule and create a Division of Hypertension. Accordingly, it was a near-unique move for a Department of Medicine to create a Division of Hypertension that was separate from the Divisions of Clinical Pharmacology, Nephrology, and Cardiology.

The development of the new division stimulated Hall to create a concentrated curriculum for medical students and house officers. Hall also provided a focus for large-scale NIH-funded clinical trials such as the Hypertension Detection and Follow-up Program (HDPF) and the Systolic Hypertension in the Elderly Program (SHEP).

The Division of Hypertension was organized in 1976 with only two faculty members, Hall and Dr. **Neil Shulman**. Later, Dr. **Gary Wollam** joined the Division. He had trained with the famous Dr. Ray Gifford at the Cleveland Clinic. Subsequently, **Zafar Israili**, Ph.D., and **Babatunde**

Olutade, M.D., joined the division. Almost all of the work of the division was centered at Grady Memorial Hospital.

The Division of Hypertension was awarded approximately $5-8 million dollars in research grant support, primarily from NHLBI (NIH). Important contributions, especially relevant to the inner-city population, resulted from the clinical trials such as HDFP and SHEP. The members of the division also conducted NIH-sponsored trials on church-based programs for Rural High Blood Pressure (HBP), and Statewide High Blood Pressure (HBP) Coordination Programs. These efforts, in part, led to the creation of the International Society of Hypertension in Blacks (ISHIB), currently a world-wide organization in its eleventh year.

The members of the division also created a Hypertension Research Clinic at Grady, which is currently entering its twentieth year of continuous, 100-percent research funding. Important contributions from this work have included many studies on echocardiographic regression of left ventricular hypertrophy following treatment, ambulatory blood pressure monitoring, and the mechanisms of hypertension in blacks.

Medical residents rotated through the hypertensive consultation service at Grady Memorial Hospital. Drs. Michael Monahan and Devon Lowdon trained in the division as fellows supported by the United States Public Health Service. Monahan is now practicing nephrology in Virginia, and Lowdon is practicing internal medicine at Piedmont Hospital in Atlanta. Wollam eventually began to practice medicine in Marietta, Georgia.

The Division of Infectious Diseases

The legacy of the Division of Infectious Diseases at Emory began with **Paul Beeson** (see Chapter 3). He and a few associates developed a worldwide reputation in the field, although in his day there were too few faculty members to justify the creation of a division of infectious diseases.

In 1957, I asked Dr. **Charles LeMaistre**, an expert in infectious diseases, to remain in the Department of Medicine. He later became the first chairman of Emory's Department of Preventive Medicine and Community Health but continued to be the director of the Division of Infectious Disease in the Department of Medicine. Dr. **Thomas F. Sellers Jr.** (see Figure 5-20), joined the faculty and replaced LeMaistre as director of the Division of Infectious Diseases. Sellers had trained under LeMaistre at Emory and at Cornell under Dr. Walsh McDermott.

LeMaistre left his post as professor and chairman of the Department of Preventive Medicine and Community Health in August, 1959, to become professor of medicine and director of Woodlawn Hospital Chest Division at the University of Texas in Dallas. He became associate dean at that institution in 1965 and chancellor of the University of Texas in 1971. He later became President of the M. D. Anderson Cancer Center in Houston.

When LeMaistre left for Texas, Sellers became professor and chairman of the Department of Preventive Medicine and Community Health, but continued as director of the Division of Infectious Diseases in the Department of Medicine. Sellers spent most of his time at Grady Memorial Hospital but also saw patients in consultation at Emory University Hospital.

The volunteer faculty included Drs. **Hyman Stillerman**, **Dan Hankey**, and **William Friedewald**. Friedewald had formerly been professor and chairman of the Department of Microbiology at Emory. During Beeson's chairmanship, he had a joint appointment in the Department of Medicine, and his office and laboratory were located at Grady Memorial Hospital. Regrettably, Dr. Friedewald died in 1996.

Dr. **William Marine**, who trained at Emory, Michigan, Cornell, and the Centers for Disease Control, joined the Division of Infectious Diseases at Emory in 1964, remaining until 1975, when he became professor and chairman of the Department of Community Health at the University of Colorado.

Dr. **Edmund Farrar** joined the Division of Infectious Diseases in 1965, after training at the Medical College of Georgia, Emory, and the Walter Reed Army Institute of Research.

In the late sixties, Sellers and his staff in the Department of Prevention Medicine and Community Health developed Grady's first satellite clinic, the Southside Clinic. The administrative and clinical load shouldered by Sellers was enormous, making it necessary for Sellers to devote full time to the further development of the Department of Preventive Medicine and Community Health. He gave up his role as director of the Division of Infectious Diseases in 1969, and in 1970 I appointed Dr. Edmund Farrar in his place. Before this discussion is closed, I wish to thank Tom Sellers. He was a solid, dependable, quiet, brilliant, and compassionate physician. Emory owes him much. Dean Richardson used to say, "Sellers was the Thomas Jefferson of the School of Medicine."

Farrar continued as director of the division until 1971, when he became director of the Division of Infectious Diseases at the Medical University of South Carolina. Two years later he was also appointed professor in the Department of Microbiology at the same institution. He remained in these positions until 1990, when he retired.

Dr. **John Boring** was appointed to the Division of Infectious Diseases in 1966. With a doctorate in bacteriology, he had worked at the Centers for Disease Control in Alex Langmuir's program. He wanted to teach, so

Sellers persuaded him to join the Emory faculty, where he became recognized as an excellent teacher. He later became professor and chairman of the Department of Epidemiology at Emory's new Rollins School of Public Health. Here it should be pointed out that Dr. Sellers was a major mover in the development of Emory's very successful School of Public Health. Sellers, Boring, and others in the Department of Preventive Medicine helped create the new school. So the Department of Medicine spawned the Department of Preventive Medicine and Community Health, which then played an indirect role in the development of the Rollins School of Public Health.

Sellers was the department's liaison with the Centers for Disease Control and Prevention. He became acquainted with Dr. **Jonas Shulman,** who was assigned to the centers but was permitted to spend a great deal of time at Grady Memorial Hospital. When Shulman's service time was completed, he returned to the University of Washington to complete his residency in medicine and training in infectious diseases with Dr. Robert Petersdorf, professor and chairman of the Department of Medicine there. Petersdorf had trained with Beeson at Yale. When I offered Shulman a position at Emory, he accepted and arrived on July 1, 1967. He was, and still is, a great teacher and excellent clinician. I selected him to be the director of the Division of Infectious Disease when Farrar left for the Medical University of South Carolina in 1971, Shulman recruited additional faculty and trained a number of excellent fellows. He enjoyed working with medical students to the point that the dean appointed him assistant dean of students for the clinical years in 1975. In 1985, I was asked to appoint a new chief of medicine at Crawford Long Hospital. Harold Ramos was moving up the ladder to become medical director of Crawford Long Hospital and was relinquishing the position as chief of medicine. Shulman was an ideal choice for the position, so I appointed him to fill the vacancy. He was magnificent in his new role and deserves the credit for catapulting the medical service there into its current, excellent position. During that time he continued his work in the dean's office.

By 1991, Shulman had to make a choice, because Dr. Dorothy Brinsfield was retiring from her position as associate dean of students, and that position had to be filled. Shulman accepted the offer by Dean Jeffrey Houpt to follow Brinsfield as associate dean. This meant that Shulman would have to relinquish his position as chief of medical service at Crawford Long Hospital. He performed beautifully in his new position and was presented the Thomas Jefferson Award by the University and the Evangeline Papageorge Teaching Award by Emory University School of Medicine.

Dr. **John McGowan** joined the Division of Infectious Diseases in 1973, assigned to Grady Memorial Hospital. He became increasingly interested in clinical microbiology through his role as hospital epidemiologist and was given a joint appointment in the Department of Pathology. He has performed remarkably well, developing a nationally recognized program in hospital epidemiology, and protecting the patients and staff at Grady Memorial Hospital from in-hospital infections. He also teaches in the School of Public Health.

Dr. **David Rimland**, an Emory graduate, joined the faculty in 1977, assigned to the Veterans Affairs Hospital. He continues his excellent work at that institution and directs the AIDS clinical research program there.

Dr. **Lee Hand** trained at Emory and was chief resident in medicine at Grady. He then trained in infectious diseases with Jay Sanford at Southwestern, returning in 1970 to the Emory faculty and the Veterans Administration Hospital. When Shulman gave up the directorship of the division in 1991, I appointed Lee Hand director. This was an important move because, for the first time, a division director within the Department of Medicine was physically located at the Veterans Administration Hospital. Hand remained at Emory until 1992, when he became professor and regional chairman of the Department of Medicine at Texas Tech University Health Center in El Paso, Texas.

Dr. **Sumner E. Thompson III**, a fellow in the Division of Infectious Diseases in 1973, joined the Centers for Disease Control and Prevention in 1975, where he was the chief of the Clinical Studies Section of the Venereal Disease Control Division (now the Division of Sexually Transmitted Diseases and HIV Prevention). While working at the Centers, he joined the Emory faculty and was permitted to spend much of his time at Grady Memorial Hospital. He became a full-time faculty member at Emory in 1987. He headed the Infectious Disease Clinic at Grady Memorial Hospital and became a national leader in the fight against AIDS. He was the major mover in creating the Ponce de Leon Center, which is recognized as an excellent facility for the care of AIDS patients. He died of a brain tumor on November 12, 1995. He was considered one of the best and is sorely missed by those who knew him.

From 1957 to 1986 the Division of Infectious Diseases trained a number of excellent fellows. Those who joined the Emory faculty are listed below. Others joined the faculty at other universities and are listed in the section dealing with *Leaders* on page 316.

Dr. **Steve Schwarzmann**, a fellow in the mid-sixties, was offered a faculty position to work in the Emory University Clinic. He has made an enormous contribution to Emory University Hospital and Clinic and is currently an associate professor in the Department of Medicine and a highly respected clinician. George Woodruff endowed a chair in infectious diseases in Schwarzmann's honor.

Dr. **Charles Hamilton**, a fellow for one year, accepted an appointment in Southside Clinic. He has spent the last twenty years in the Northwest Clinic, another Grady satellite clinic. He has performed well and continues to sing bass in Atlanta Symphony Chorus.

Dr. **Carl Perlino**, a fellow in the Division of Infectious Diseases in the late sixties, joined the Emory faculty in 1974. An excellent clinician, he works at Grady Memorial Hospital and Emory University Hospital, where he is a highly respected consultant and teacher.

Dr. **Phyllis Kozarsky** joined the faculty at Crawford Long Hospital and specialized in the infections of world travelers, and Dr. **Monica M. Farley** joined the Veterans Administration Hospital.

Dr. **David Stephens** joined the Emory faculty as an assistant professor of medicine in 1982 and was initially assigned to the Veterans Administration Hospital. Stephens graduated from Bowman Gray School of Medicine and was a house officer at Vanderbilt, where he also received his fellowship training in infectious diseases. He was appointed to the faculty at Vanderbilt in 1981. Stephens was a strong addition to the division at Emory because he was deeply interested in research and teaching as well as patient care.

Stephens was destined to become the director of the division when Lee Hand moved to the Texas Tech University Health Science Center in 1992. The Division of Infectious Diseases has continued to develop and is one of the largest divisions in the Department of Medicine. By 1996 there were twenty-three full-time faculty members.

The Division of Infectious Diseases conducts basic, clinical, and epidemiologic research. A strong clinical base (over 2000 beds), the excellent research commitments of Emory University, and collaborations with the Centers for Disease Control and Prevention, and other Atlanta-based agencies, provide the critical mass necessary for the creation of excellence in clinical care, research, and education in infectious diseases.

The Division of Nephrology and Inorganic Metabolism

Dr. **Arthur Merrill Sr.** rose to national prominence in nephrology during the Stead and Beeson periods (1942–1952). Merrill, a full-time faculty member during Stead's chairmanship, became a half-time faculty member during Beeson's. Merrill continued to teach one session each week for many years during my chairmanship. Merrill was joined in his academic work at Grady and in his practice by Dr. **Francis Fitzhugh** and later by Dr. **Joe Wilson**, who were both excellent. In 1951 Merrill and his associates were moving vigorously toward setting up a renal dialysis unit at Grady Memorial Hospital.

On November 15, 1951, I was asked to see a thirty-five-year-old woman who had developed shock during surgery for Crohn's disease. Her clinical course was complicated by the development of acute renal failure. She needed renal dialysis, but Arthur Merrill's order for the machine had not been filled. I transported the unconscious patient by Eastern Airlines to the Peter Bent Brigham Hospital in Boston for renal dialysis. She recovered. She is now 81 years of age. The publicity surrounding her case undoubtedly hastened the day when Emory developed a large renal dialysis program. Wilson, a part-time faculty member, and Fitzhugh were major advocates of such a development. Having had the experience, I resolved, when I became professor and chairman of the Department of Medicine, that one of my goals would be to develop patient care to the point that no patients need leave Atlanta for medical care unless they chose to. In fact, I reasoned, patients should eventually come from other states and abroad for medical care at Emory University Hospital and Clinic. The patients at Grady should, I insisted, have the same access to excellent medical care as those at Emory University Hospital.

In 1957, I recognized the extraordinary talent of a senior resident on the medical house staff, Dr. **Elbert Tuttle Jr**. He had completed his house-staff training at the Massachusetts General Hospital as well as a fellowship in nephrology under Dr. Alexander Leaf at the same institution. He wanted to join the faculty at Emory in 1956, but Dr. Ferris indicated there was no money for him. Not to be deterred, Tuttle accepted a position as senior resident in medicine. I appointed him to the faculty on July 1, 1957, using funds supplied by the Georgia Heart Association. Accordingly, he was the first director of the Division of Nephrology and remained director of the division until 1983. He was the most altruistic person I have ever known, an original thinker and questioner, who performed many experiments on himself.

Tuttle worked primarily at Grady Memorial Hospital in space he designed. Construction of the space was financed by the Woodruff Foundations. Over the years he was tireless in his efforts to create a first-rate patient care, education, and research program. He was joined at Grady Hospital by Drs. **Ed Macon**, **John Sadler**, **James Shinaberger**, **Jerry Cooper**, **Vardaman Buckalew**, **James Wells**, **Ronald Mars**, **Susan Fellner**, **Eda Hochlerent**, and **Lydia Whatley**, an excellent social worker. Tuttle helped develop a number of leaders in the field of nephrology, although he would say they did it themselves. Fellner joined the faculty at the University of Chicago. Buckalew became director of the Division of

Nephrology at Winston-Salem, and Sadler became director of the Division of Nephrology at the University of Maryland. Shinaberger became prominent in renal medicine at the Wadsworth Veterans Hospital in California, and Dr. **Robert McDonald**, who trained as a fellow under Tuttle and Goldberg, became director of the Division of Clinical Pharmacology at the University of Pittsburgh.

Within a few years Drs. Tuttle and Preedy indicated they needed a machinist to help them create their research work. Preedy then helped us locate a machinist in London named **Eric Penfold**, who was willing to join the Department of Medicine at Emory. His rather large shop was located in the basement of the Gray Building on the Grady campus. He contributed significantly to the research effort in the department.

Dr. **William Waters** was appointed in 1962 to develop the renal program at Emory University Hospital and Clinic. Waters had graduated from Emory Medical School and had been an outstanding house officer in our program. He specialized in renal medicine under Drs. William Schwartz and Arnold Relman at Tufts. In 1966 he spearheaded the first renal transplant in Georgia. Following the successful outcome in that patient at Emory University Hospital, a large number of transplants were performed at Grady Memorial Hospital. Dr. Waters entered private practice in 1970, rising in time to the top at Piedmont Hospital. Eventually, Emory surgeons performed renal transplantation at Piedmont Hospital as well as at Emory University Hospital.

Tuttle worked with Dr. James Bland in the Department of Pediatrics in the late sixties to develop peritoneal dialysis in children. Dr. **Robert C. McDonnell**, one of Tuttle's renal fellows, joined the faculty after completing a renal fellowship in pediatric nephrology at the University of California in San Francisco. He had a joint appointment in pediatrics and medicine. Of great assistance in developing pediatric nephrology, he joined the faculty at Vanderbilt in 1978.

Drs. Susan Fellner and Eda Hochlerent moved from Grady Memorial Hospital to Emory University Hospital and Clinic when Waters entered private practice.

Dr. **George Callaway** was appointed to develop the renal program at the Veterans Administration Hospital. Unfortunately, he died of rectal carcinoma in 1985. Dr. **Oved Soffer** joined the faculty at the Veterans Administration Hospital but later entered private practice in Columbus, Georgia. Dr. **Carl Oettinger** also joined the faculty at the Veterans Hospital and later moved to Crawford Long Hospital.

Dr. **Tuncer Someren** joined the faculty at Crawford Long Hospital and was later joined by Oettinger. Dr. **Ed Macon** moved from Grady Memorial Hospital to Crawford Long Hospital and then moved back to Grady.

Renal dialysis was performed at each of the four hospitals. In addition, in order to manage the large number of patients who needed dialysis, a separate dialysis center was developed on Piedmont Avenue. This clinic was part of Dialysis Clinics, Inc., whose home base was at Vanderbilt. Similar clinics were developed at Crawford Long Hospital and on West Peachtree Street.

Dr. **Edmund Bourke**, who trained with Dr. George Schreiner at Georgetown University, became director of the Division of Nephrology in 1983. His wife, Dr. **Vera Delaney**, joined the division at the same time and was stationed at Emory University Hospital and Clinic. Dr. **Jay Guntupalli** joined the division in 1984 and was assigned to the Veterans Administration Hospital. Dr. **Jantts Dass** joined the Division in 1984 and was assigned to Emory University Hospital.

Dr. **Ron Mars** joined the staff at Grady Memorial Hospital and later moved to the faculty at the University of Florida. Dr. **James Wells** joined the staff at Emory University Hospital and Clinic before entering private practice in Atlanta.

The research activity of the faculty members in the Division of Nephrology included vascular access for dialysis; acid-base balance with specific attention to pulmonary changes induced by dialysis; renal bone disease and its control with phosphate binders and vitamin D analogues; development of the dialyzer called the Emory Klung in collaboration with Dr. Converse Peirce of the Department of Surgery; and procurement of organs for transplantation. The procurement program became one of the most active programs in the country. Research activity also included organ preservation, perfusion, and transplantation; the development of more effective and efficient dialysis, including dialyzer development; the production and safety of bicarbonate dialysis; and adequate control of chronic acidosis in the treatment of renal failure.

In 1986 Dr. Bourke accepted a position as chief of the medical service at the Brooklyn Veterans Administration Hospital. He was appointed professor and vice chairman of the Department of Medicine at SUNY Health Science Center in Brooklyn. Dr. Delaney became associate professor of medicine and surgery at New York Medical College. They both achieved considerable national recognition.

The division was reorganized after Dr. Juha Kokko arrived as chairman of medicine at Emory in the fall of 1986. Dr. Kokko, a brilliant academician, had been director of the Division of Nephrology at Southwestern, a branch of the University of Texas in Dallas. He had graduated from Emory University School of Medicine and had his house officer training at Johns Hopkins. He continued his research at the National Institutes of Health. In 1987, he appointed Dr. William Mitch, a nationally known expert in nephrology, as the new director of the Division of Nephrology. Kokko and Mitch reorganized the division and recruited several additional faculty members. Their research became recognized throughout the nation and abroad.

The Division of Neurology

Prior to 1957, Emory University School of Medicine had no full-time neurologist. Two devoted volunteer clinical faculty members were responsible for the patient care and teaching in the Department of Medicine. They were Drs. **William Smith** and **Richard Wilson**. Emory University School of Medicine owes them a great deal for their effort and generosity.

In 1957 I discovered that an unused training grant of $25,000 had been awarded to the Department of Medicine by the National Institute of Neurologic Disease and Stroke. Apparently, the ruckus of 1956 and 1957 had prevented the implementation of a training program in neurology. Dr. Donald Warren, a former cardiology fellow during the early fifties, called my attention to a clinical pathologic conference that had just been published in *The New England Journal of Medicine*. The star discusser was **Herbert Karp**. I had known Karp as a house officer during the early Ferris days and recognized his unusual teaching ability. Don Warren had known Karp at Duke, where Karp began to specialize in neurology. Karp left Duke and continued his training in neurology with Dr. Raymond Adams at the Massachusetts General Hospital. I contacted Karp in 1957 and offered him the position as Director of the Division of Neurology in the Department of Medicine at Emory. Karp loved Emory and Atlanta and accepted the offer, knowing we had much building to do. Willing to help us build, he arrived in January 1958. Although initially he was stationed primarily at Grady Memorial Hospital, from the outset he made his presence known at Emory University Hospital, Egleston Hospital for Children, and the Atlanta Veterans Administration Hospital.

Over the years the following physicians joined the Neurology Division of the Department of Medicine: Drs. **John Ammons**, **Robert Kibler**, **Dale McFarland**, **Linton Hopkins**, **Alexander McPhedran**, **Sandy McKinney**, and **Charles Epstein**. With these additions, neurology was emphasized at Emory University Hospital and Clinic, Grady Memorial Hospital, and the Atlanta Veterans Administration Hospital. Later, Dr. **James Schwartz** became director of the Division of Neurology in the Department of Pediatrics. He and Karp worked well together, and the two separate divisions thrived. The teaching and patient care were superb. Both basic and clinical research increased as the years went by.

Karp was director of the Division of Neurology in the Department of Medicine from 1958 until 1976. By 1976 most medical schools had separate departments of neurology. The separateness seemed to improve the chances of obtaining research funds from the National Institute of Neurology and Stroke. I was concerned that the separation of neurology from medicine would decrease the exposure of the medical house staff and students to the excellent neurologic teaching provided by Karp and his associates. I was also concerned that I would personally learn less neurology if the division became a department. Stead was trying to entice Karp to return to Duke. Gene, who always acted "above-board," called me and said, "Herb Karp is up here paddling around, and we are considering him for a position." I responded, "Gene, not that!" I knew when Gene called that the time had come when neurology should be a separate department—no doubt about it. I wanted Karp to remain at Emory; a separate Department of Neurology would keep him here. Karp was professor and chairman of the new Department of Neurology from 1976 to 1983.

Dr. **Robert Kibler** followed Karp as professor and chairman of the Department of Neurology. He remained chairman of the department until 1990, when Dr. Mahlon Delong was appointed professor and chairman of the Department.

Delong and his group of excellent clinicians, teachers, and investigators became nationally known for their work on many neurologic problems, especially Parkinson's disease. The Department of Medicine is proud of its role as a facilitator in this development.

The Division of Pulmonary Medicine

Dr. **John Hickam**, a chief resident in medicine at Grady Memorial Hospital during Stead's chairmanship, was interested in research related to pulmonary disease (see Figure 2-2; Hickam is fourth from the left on the front row). He followed Stead to Duke in 1947 and later became professor and chairman of the Department of Medicine at the University of Indiana.

Dr. **John Patterson** was in Beeson's department in the late forties and early fifties (see Figure 3-5; Patterson is third from the right on the front row). He also had a joint appointment in the Department of Physiology. He was interested in pulmonary research, and his laboratory was in the Steiner Building at Grady Hospital. When Beeson left for Yale, Patterson joined the faculty at the Medical College of Virginia.

Dr. **Grigg Churchwell** (see Figure 4-3; Churchwell is third from the left on the front row) was a house officer at Grady Memorial Hospital when I became chairman of the department in 1957. He was interested in pulmonary medicine. I appointed him to the faculty in July 1957. His laboratory was in the Steiner Building in the Grady area. He eventually entered private practice.

Dr. **James Crutcher**, who was appointed chief of medicine at the Veterans Administration Hospital in 1957, was interested in pulmonary medicine and created an exciting environment for house officers (see Figure 4-6; Crutcher is second from the left in the third row).

Dr. **Ross McLean** (see Figure 5-13), formerly of the Baltimore Veterans Hospital, was appointed to the Department of Medicine in 1957. He became director of the division when there were sufficient faculty members to form a division, and he remained in that position until 1970, when he accepted a position to work with the Regional Medical Program in Texas.

Dr. **Arend Bouhuys** joined the faculty in pulmonary medicine in 1963, spearheading a research program in byssinosis. This effort attracted a great deal of national attention because of its relationship to industry. Dr. Bouhuys accepted a position at Yale in 1965.

Dr. **Roland Ingram** was appointed director of the Division of Pulmonary Medicine in 1969. A graduate of the Yale University School of Medicine, with pulmonary medicine training under Dr. Alfred Fishman at Columbia-Presbyterian Medical Center in New York, he was a brilliant researcher and teacher. He developed his research laboratory in Grady Memorial Hospital.

Ingram assisted in the recruitment of Dr. **Gilbert Grossman** to work at Grady and Dr. **Michael Duffell** to work at the Atlanta Veterans Administration Hospital. Grossman, who had trained at Georgetown and the University of San Diego, received the Pulmonary Academic Award from the National Institutes of Health. Duffell was one of our former fellows in the Emory program. **Alan Plummer**, who trained at the Mayo Clinic, was added to the Emory Clinic.

Ingram's work attracted the attention of Eugene Braunwald, chairman of the Department of Medicine at the Peter Bent Brigham Hospital in Boston. Braunwald offered Ingram the position as director of the Pulmonary/Critical Care Division at the Brigham, and Ingram left for Harvard in 1973, remaining there for sixteen years. He became the first incumbent of the Peter B. Francis Chair of Medicine at Harvard. He moved to Minneapolis, where he became chief of medicine at Hennepin County Hospital and vice chairman of the Department of Medicine at the University of Minnesota.

When Ingram left for Harvard, I asked Duffell and Grossman to be co-directors of the Division of Pulmonary Medicine. Grossman moved to Crawford Long Hospital in 1973 in order to develop pulmonary medicine in that facility, while Duffell moved to the Emory Clinic and became director of the division in 1976. He remained in that position until 1991 when Ingram returned to Emory.

Dr. **Gerald Staton** joined the faculty at Crawford Long Hospital in 1981. Dr. **Bailey Francis** joined the faculty at the Veterans Administration Hospital in 1974. Drs. **Eric Honig** and **Murray Gilman** joined the faculty at Grady in 1979 and 1980. Honig received the Young Faculty Academic Award and took additional training at Johns Hopkins School of Medicine and Hospital. Dr. **Jeffrey Pine** joined Duffell and Plummer at the Emory University Clinic in 1976.

Dr. **Ralph Haynes** joined the division in 1976 and was located at Grady Memorial Hospital. He entered practice in 1977.

Dr. **William Corwin** joined the staff in 1980. He was located at Crawford Long Hospital but entered practice in 1981.

The members of the Pulmonary Division expanded their teaching activities with the house staff and developed an excellent fellowship program. Their patient care activities expanded in all of the hospitals.

The research interests were mainly spearheaded by Ingram and included investigation into the presence of small airway disease in young cigarette smokers and its reversal following smoking cessation, factors that limit exercise performance in chronic obstructive pulmonary disease (COPD), the mechanism by which arterial PO_2 falls in asthmatics in response to bronchodilators, effect of hypocapnia and hypercapnia on airways (their caliber and regional gas exchange), mechanism of airway closure at low lung volumes, pulmonary arterial response to neuronally released versus blood-borne norepinephrine, and diminished ventilatory responsiveness to CO_2 as an aftermath of chronic upper airway obstruction.

In 1987 Dr. Kokko, chairman of medicine, enticed Roland Ingram to return to the Department of Medicine at Emory as director of the Division of Pulmonary Medicine and Critical Care and chief of medicine at Crawford Long Hospital. Ingram added several excellent faculty members to the division and spearheaded an excellent new research development. Ingram was named the Martha West Looney Professor of Medicine in 1994.

The Division of Rheumatology

Prior to 1966, rheumatology was taught by the volunteer clinical faculty. Dr. **Vernon Powell** was one of the leaders. I appointed Dr. **Colon Wilson** director of the new Division of Rheumatology in July 1966. Wilson had trained with Dr. Evan Calkins at the University of Buffalo. Wilson's academic office was in the Glenn Memorial Building at Grady. He quickly developed a teaching program and a referral practice in the Emory University Hospital and Clinic.

Dr. Colon Wilson did a lot with few resources. He built a good rheumatology training program and stimulated a great deal of interest in rheumatology. He was mainly responsible for developing the Emory Clinic as a referral center for patients with diseases of the joints. He also established a meaningful relationship with the Division of Orthopedics in the Department of Surgery. Wilson resigned to enter private practice in 1984 and died in 1995.

Dr. **John Goldman** joined the faculty at Emory Hospital and Clinic in July 1973. An excellent clinician, he chose to enter private practice in Atlanta in 1982.

Dr. **Stephen Miller** joined the faculty in 1977 after training at Rochester General, Montefiore, and New York University Medical Center at Bellevue. His office was located in the Emory Clinic.

Dr. **D. A. Rajapakse** was chosen to spearhead the research effort in the division in 1978. His new laboratories were located in the Woodruff Memorial Research-Henry Woodruff Extension Building at Grady. He continued his research efforts until 1985, when he entered private practice in Atlanta.

Dr. **Nicholas Tiliakos** joined the faculty in 1980 and was based at the Atlanta Veterans Administration Hospital. He entered private practice in 1986 but remains on the clinical faculty.

Dr. **Carol Aitcheson** joined the faculty at the Atlanta Veterans Hospital in 1982 but entered private practice in 1984.

Dr. **William Maier** joined the faculty at Emory University Hospital and Clinic in 1985 and entered private practice in Eugene, Oregon, in 1991.

Dr. **Sam Schatten** joined the faculty at Grady Memorial Hospital in 1985 but entered private practice in 1986.

Dr. Stephen Miller was named director of the Division of Rheumatology in 1984 and served in that capacity until he joined the faculty at Mercer University School of Medicine in Macon, Georgia, in March 1994, where he became associate dean and vice chairman of the Department of Medicine. He returned to the Emory Clinic in 1996.

The faculty of the Division of Rheumatology were involved in many clinical studies depending on their specific interests. These included observations in rheumatoid arthritis, juvenile rheumatoid arthritis, and systemic lupus erythematosus. The group participated in many pharmaceutical trials in a wide variety of diseases. New treatment strategies in rheumatoid arthritis were evaluated including the use of plasmapheresis and lasers. Investigation of disease activity in systemic lupus and its correlation with various testing modalities as well as studying patients with neonatal complete heart block were ongoing projects. In 1978, the State of Georgia awarded the Division of Rheumatology a yearly renewable grant to support basic research in the rheumatic diseases. The major projects were centered on studies of the regulation of lymphocyte function and association of activation antigens with inflammatory activity in patients with rheumatoid arthritis.

Experimental Divisions

Clinical Pharmacology

By the early sixties, "units" of clinical pharmacology were being developed in several medical schools in the United States. The impetus for such developments was the perception that the faculty teaching pharmacology in a basic science department had little opportunity to determine whether junior and senior students, house staff, and fellows used the lessons they were exposed to in pharmacology. The pharmaceutical industry also was developing many new drugs, and there was an inadequate number of trained personnel to conduct clinical trials to determine the usefulness and safety of the new preparations.

Dean Richardson, formerly professor and chairman of the Department of Pharmacology, was interested in developing a Division of Clinical Pharmacology in which the faculty members held joint appointments in the Departments of Medicine and Pharmacology. The Departments of Pediatrics and Anesthesiology were also involved in the development of Clinical Pharmacology. The Burroughs-Wellcome Pharmaceutical Company offered to give financial support to the development. Dr. James Bain, chairman of the Department of Pharmacology, and later Dr. Neil Moran, who became chairman of pharmacology in 1962, looked with favor on the idea. In fact Moran, who had often contributed his teaching talent to the medical conferences at Grady Memorial Hospital, was very enthusiastic about such a development.

Dr. **Leon Goldberg** was appointed to direct the new unit. His house-staff training had been in the Department of Medicine at the Massachusetts General Hospital, and he had earned a national reputation while working at the National Heart Institute.

Dr. **Menachem Wurzel** joined the group as a visiting professor from 1961 to 1962. Dr. **John McNay** was appointed to the faculty in 1965, Dr. **Peter Dayton** was appointed in 1967, and Dr. **Samuel Cucinell** joined the group in 1969.

The clinical pharmacologists spent time on the Grady Memorial Hospital wards teaching the nuances of the actions of drugs and performed bench research in the laboratories located in the Department of Pharmacology on the Emory campus. They became nationally known for their work that established dopamine's clinical value.

In 1974, Goldberg was offered an excellent opportunity to develop clinical pharmacology at the University of Chicago. There he would have more independence and could make his own appointments. He accepted the position but unfortunately died of lymphoma in 1989. McNay was offered a position as director of clinical pharmacology at the University of Texas in San Antonio in 1974. Dayton joined the faculty at Dartmouth, and Cucinell returned to the army in 1970.

Dr. **Robert McDonald** was a fellow in the Division of Clinical Pharmacology, where he worked with Leon Goldberg from 1961 to 1963. During that time, he also worked with Elbert Tuttle in the Division of Renal Disease and Inorganic Metabolism. McDonald spent two years at the National Institutes of Health working with Dr. Stanley Sarnoff. He then worked at University College, London, in the Department of Physiology, from 1965 to 1966. He joined the faculty at the University of Pittsburgh in 1966 and eventually became professor of medicine, pharmacology, and epidemiology, and director of the Division of Clinical Pharmacology from 1971 to 1991.

Dr. **Billy Yeh**, who trained with the group in 1967–1968, joined the faculty at the University of Miami.

Dr. **Robert Talley**, one of our cardiology fellows, trained with Goldberg's group in 1968–1969, joined the faculty at the University of Texas in San Antonio, and then became professor and chairman of the Department of Medicine at the University of South Dakota. Still later, he became dean at South Dakota.

During 1969–1970, Dr. **Perry Halushka** worked with Goldberg at Emory for three months as a senior-year medical student at the University of Chicago under the sponsorship of the Pharmaceutical Manufacturers' Association Foundation. Halushka served his internship and first-year residency in our program from 1970 to 1972. His work was always excellent. From 1972 to 1974 he received fellowship training at the National Institutes of Health, National Heart, Lung, and Blood Institute. Halushka joined the faculty in the Departments of Medicine and Pharmacology at the Medical University of South Carolina in 1974. He attained the rank of professor of medicine and pharmacology and was appointed director of the Division of Clinical Pharmacology in 1990.

Dr. **Keith McConnell**, a Canadian, joined the faculty at the medical school in Alberta. Dr. **Carl Hug** remained at Emory and became a leader in the Department of Anesthesiology. Dr. **Albert Pruitt**, who worked in Dayton's laboratory, became an important member of the Department of

Pediatrics at Emory and later became professor and chairman of the Department of Pediatrics at the Medical College of Georgia.

The effort to develop clinical pharmacology was successful, in that Leon Goldberg and his team demonstrated that it was educationally valuable to expose junior and senior medical students, medical house officers, and fellows to individuals who had considerable knowledge in the action of drugs. Unfortunately, such an effort is difficult to support without sufficient research grants. Because of this, the Division of Clinical Pharmacology was discontinued.

Clinical Physiology

By the late sixties many influential academicians in the country were becoming concerned that physiology, as taught in the basic science departments of medical schools, was misdirected. Departments of physiology were becoming departments of cellular biology, and the type of physiology used by thinking clinicians was not being emphasized. I decided, after observing the successes of our Division of Clinical Pharmacology, that it would be useful to create a Division of Clinical Physiology within the Department of Medicine. Roland Ingram, Director of our Division of Pulmonary Medicine, informed me that Dr. **Sheldon Skinner** was interested in the type of physiology used by clinicians. Skinner accepted my offer to become director of the Division of Clinical Physiology in the Department of Medicine. He received a Career Development Award and was given research space in the Henry Woodruff Research Building at Grady. He enjoyed teaching and was especially effective with house officers, whom he invited to his home for scientific "bull sessions." Skinner joined the faculty at Bowman Gray Medical School in 1973 and later became professor and chairman of the Department of Physiology there.

Dr. **Gerhart Brecher**, who was a leading investigator in venous physiology, joined the division when he retired from his position of professor and chairman of the Department of Physiology at Emory. He was given office space in the Glenn Building at Grady. Brecher later moved to the medical school at the University of Oklahoma before retiring from active work.

At one time, I tried to recruit the famous Dr. Richard Bing to join the division but could not muster the finances to do so. Bing, a friend of Charles Lindbergh and associate of Alexis Carrel, had made his reputation at Hopkins and Wayne State University. He was, and still is, a great scientific innovator and composer of music.

Although the clinical effort had been successful, no attempt was made to rejuvenate the division after Skinner left, because it was difficult to support the staff financially. Considerable endowment money would be needed to make such a division thrive.

Three New Departments Spawned by the Department of Medicine

The Department of Medicine spawned three other departments at Emory University School of Medicine: the Department of Preventive Medicine and Community Health, the Department of Neurology, and the Department of Dermatology. These developments were discussed earlier in this chapter of the book.

In 1986 the Department of Medicine also provided Dr. **Gerald Fletcher** to be the new chairman for the Department of Rehabilitation and supported the development of a training program in emergency medicine. Later the Department of Medicine supplied many of the faculty members for the new School of Public Health.

Relationship to Other Departments

The relationship of the Department of Medicine to the basic science departments was excellent. Interdepartmental "groups" were formed in the eighties to improve communication between the basic science departments and clinical departments. For example, the Division of Digestive Diseases joined interested members of the Department of Surgery and appropriate basic science departments to form the "Liver Group." The Division of Endocrinology joined the Departments of Surgery and Biochemistry to form the "Endocrinology Group," a graduate training program was created by the "Endocrinology Group." Whenever there was a need for interdepartmental cooperation in teaching, research, or patient care, this method was used to achieve the goal. This approach prevented the development of independent institutes that at times tend to go their separate ways.

The Department of Medicine worked closely with several divisions of the Department of Surgery. Liver transplantation was first carried out at Emory University Hospital in 1987. The team of liver experts consisted of faculty members of the Department of Surgery and members of the Department of Medicine. They created one of the best liver transplant programs in the country.

The faculty in the Division of Cardiology in the Department of Medicine worked closely with the faculty of the Division of Cardiovascular Surgery to create an excellent record in the surgical treatment of heart disease. Dr. **Osler Abbott** performed closed mitral commissurotomy on a patient of mine in 1951, the first such operation performed in the South.

Dr. **Charles Hatcher** became chief of the Division of Cardiothoracic Surgery in the Department of Surgery in 1971 (see Figure 5-37). A brilliant surgeon and superb leader, he had trained at Johns Hopkins with Alfred Blalock and at the Brigham with Francis Moore. His team included Drs. **Ellis Jones, Joe Craver**, and **Kamal Mansour** at Emory University Hospital; **Peter Symbas** at Grady and the Veterans Hospital; **Robert Guyton** at Crawford Long, Emory University, and Egleston Hospitals; **John Gott** and **Joseph Miller** at Crawford Long Hospital; and **Willis Williams** and **Kirk Kanter** at Egleston Hospital. Dr. **David Bone** was assigned to Crawford Long Hospital but later entered private practice. Dr. **Douglas Murphy** was assigned to Emory University Hospital but later entered private practice.

Under Hatcher's leadership, the team of surgeons excelled in every aspect of the surgical treatment of heart disease. They became national leaders in coronary bypass surgery, valve surgery, and surgery for congenital heart disease. Their record in cardiac transplantation in adults and children soon became one of the best in the nation. They also excelled in the transplantation of lungs. Hatcher became director of the Emory Clinic in 1976 and continued to direct the Division of Cardiac Surgery until 1990, when Guyton became director of the Division of Cardiothoracic Surgery. Hatcher became vice president for health affairs and director of the entire Robert W. Woodruff Health Sciences Center in 1984. A bold, effective leader, and he stimulated an enormous amount of growth at the medical center and helped make the Clifton Corridor a reality (see page 327).

Drs. **Robert Smith, Garland Perdue**, and **Thomas Dodson** developed a superb surgical program in peripheral vascular disease. They followed Drs. **Dan Elkin** and **Fred Cooper**, who were the nationally recognized early pioneers at Emory.

Dr. **Bruce Logue** and **I** served as the pediatric cardiologists for children with congenital heart disease, until Drs. **Kathryn Edwards** and **Dorothy Brinsfield** were added to the pediatric staff. There had been a cardiac catheterization laboratory at Grady Memorial Hospital since 1942, but there was no cardiac catheterization laboratory on the Emory campus until the Department of Medicine developed it in the Ernest Woodruff Memorial Research Building in 1957. Dr. **Robert Franch** was chosen to direct the laboratory, and Dr. **Gordon Barrow** was able to obtain support for the laboratory from the Crippled Children branch of the Georgia State government. Edwards became director of the Division of Pediatrics in 1960 and was given free access to the use of the laboratory. Later, when she gave up her position to become a pediatric radiologist, Brinsfield became director of the Division of Pediatrics. She was an excellent choice but eventually became associate dean in charge of students. Dr. **William Plauth** became the director of pediatric cardiology in 1971. He had trained with the famous Alexander Nadas in Boston, and his teaching and patient care became recognized at the national level as pediatric cardiology continued to blossom.

Logue and I cooperated fully as it became apparent that pediatric cardiology had come of age. The first cardiac catheterization laboratory in Egleston Hospital was developed in 1975. Under Plauth's direction, the Division of Pediatric Cardiology became one of the finest divisions in the nation. A downside of this development was that the trainees in cardiology in the Department of Medicine had less experience with patients with congenital heart disease. For a while, the cardiology fellows in medicine rotated through pediatric cardiology at Egleston Hospital. This eventually became financially difficult, and the trainees' experience with congenital heart disease was mainly limited to adult patients at Emory University Hospital, Grady Memorial Hospital, and Crawford Long Hospitals. The pediatric cardiologists continued to present conferences for the trainees in the Department of Medicine, but, excellent as the conferences were, they did not substitute for the hands-on experience previously attained. Plans were formulated to develop a clinic where adult patients who had had heart surgery in childhood could be followed by cardiologists from the Departments of Medicine and Pediatrics.

Dr. **John Preedy**, director of the Division of Endocrinology in the Department of Medicine, was called upon for consultation in selected children who had endocrine diseases. Dr. **John Parks**, an excellent pediatric endocrinologist, was added to the pediatric faculty in 1982 and developed pediatric endocrinology.

Drs. **Charles Huguley** and **Charles Corley** served as pediatric hematologists until the Department of Pediatrics recruited its own hematologists.

In the late sixties, Dr. **Elbert Tuttle**, director of the Division of Nephrology in the Department of Medicine, worked with the faculty members in the Department of Pediatrics to develop peritoneal dialysis in children. In the seventies, Dr. **Robert McDonnell**, a former renal fellow in the Department of Medicine, joined the faculty and was of further help to the Department of Pediatrics in developing a superb renal disease service.

Dr. **James Christy**, an endocrinologist in the Emory Clinic, worked closely with Dr. **William McGarity** of the Department of Surgery to identify and surgically treat numerous patients with hyperparathyroidism. Christy also worked closely with neurosurgeon Dr. **George Tindall** to identify and surgically treat patients with pituitary tumors.

There was also a close working relationship between the Division of Rheumatology of the Department of Medicine and the Division of Orthopedics in the Department of Surgery.

The Department of Medicine always supported the actions of the Department of Anesthesiology. Dr. **John Steinhaus** was an excellent chairman of anesthesiology and contributed to the teaching program in medicine. The support I, as chairman, offered the Department of Anesthesiology was stimulated by my medical school experience, because I served as an anesthesiologist during my senior year in medical school. I worked under the guidance of Dr. **Perry Volpitto**, one of the nation's pioneers in anesthesiology, who led me to appreciate the importance of anesthesiology.

Dr. **Bernard Holland**, professor and chairman of the Department of Psychiatry, was superb. Trained initially at Grady and then at Duke under Eugene Stead before he trained in psychiatry, he would visit the Grady wards and discuss psychiatric problems with the house staff (see page 221).

Dr. **Michael Gravanis**, chairman of the Department of Pathology for many years, was very cooperative and participated actively in the teaching program of the Department of Medicine. He rose to national prominence in the field of cardiac pathology.

The Department of Radiology was initially chaired by Dr. **Heinz Weens**, who worked alongside Stead and his group at Grady Memorial Hospital. Weens was one of the best radiologists in the nation. He participated with Warren and Brannon in the first diagnostic cardiac catheterization, reported in 1945. He was a pioneer in the development of angiography. The members of the Department of Radiology always worked closely with the members of the Department of Medicine. Dr. **Ted Leigh** was a major contributor to the development of radiology at Emory University Hospital. When Weens and Leigh retired, Dr. **William Casarella** became chairman of the Department of Radiology. He moved the department into the current era, and the members of the Department of Radiology participate actively in the teaching program of the Department of Medicine.

Dr. **Dan Thompson** was professor and chairman of the Department of Gynecology and Obstetrics. According to him, we competed to see who could develop the better department. As chairman of medicine I enjoyed and respected Dan Thompson. We had fun performing our "work," and our personal interplay was refreshing.

These stories of cooperation between the Department of Medicine and other departments serve to emphasize that a cooperative spirit prevailed, and this served as a platform from which excellent patient care, teaching, and research could be maintained and improved.

Relationship with Other Community Hospitals

Piedmont Hospital

Drs. Carter Smith, Arthur Merrill Sr., and Charles Stone of Piedmont Hospital visited me in my office in 1970. They were interested in developing a first-rate Department of Education at Piedmont Hospital. As discussed in Chapters 1 and 2 of this book, the Department of Medicine at Emory had always had a close relationship to Piedmont Hospital. Dr. J. Edgar Paullin had been an effective volunteer chairman of medicine prior to 1942 and helped recruit Gene Stead to be the first full-time chairman of the Department of Medicine. Since Paullin's time, numerous Piedmont physicians had given their services to the patient care and educational programs at Grady Memorial Hospital. The three who visited me knew, from my earlier discussions at Piedmont Hospital, that I believed every hospital should be a teaching hospital. So I responded to their request by suggesting that I recruit an individual acceptable to them and place him on the Emory faculty. He could, I suggested, develop the program at Piedmont and teach in the Department of Medicine at Emory. I would, of course, need to obtain the approval of Dean Richardson. The dean approved, and I recruited Dr. **Mark Silverman** for the position (see Figure 5-38). Silverman had been a cardiology fellow with us and was an outstanding teacher and leader. He accepted the position and began his work at Piedmont when he was released from the air force in 1970. He was an immediate success at Piedmont and at Emory.

We rotated cardiology fellows through Piedmont Hospital for twenty-five years. The experience they gained there was rewarding, as they learned a great deal from Silverman and other physicians. I never had a trainee who did not think more of the subject and the profession after working with Silverman. This achievement by Silverman was the highest accolade a teacher can receive.

Another group of physicians from Piedmont Hospital visited me in 1979 to express a need for medical house officers. The Department of Surgery at Emory was then rotating surgical residents through Piedmont Hospital, and the continued accreditation of the program required that the hospital have residents in medicine. I agreed and, because the recruitment of excellent medical house officers was not a problem, I deduced that this would enable us to enlarge our house officer program and bring more excellent doctors to Atlanta and Georgia. So from 1979 to 1990 we rotated three to five medical house officers through Piedmont Hospital each month. This would not have been possible except for the excellent performance of Silverman, who also taught freshman, sophomore, junior, and senior medical students on the Emory campus and at Grady Memorial Hospital.

I viewed the relationship of the Department of Medicine at Emory with Piedmont Hospital as the continuation of the warm relationship that had started with Paullin. The relationship was an important part of Emory's heritage, and numerous Piedmont physicians continued to serve on the volunteer clinical faculty at Emory.

Georgia Baptist Hospital

A somewhat similar relationship was established with Georgia Baptist Hospital. Dr. **Gerald Fletcher** was appointed to the Department of Medicine of Emory in 1969 and simultaneously became director of internal medicine at the Georgia Baptist Hospital. He developed an excellent cardiac rehabilitation program, and over the years we rotated about thirty cardiac fellows through his program. Dr. **John Cantwell**, a former cardiology fellow in the Department of Medicine at Emory and a member of the volunteer clinical faculty, was also a major mover in the development of a preventive cardiology program at Georgia Baptist Hospital.

Fletcher was successful in his efforts but, in 1983, moved to the Emory campus to direct the cardiac rehabilitation program and the Emory Health Enhancement Program at the new George Woodruff Physical Education Center. These developments were a great asset to the Department of Medicine. Later, in 1986, Fletcher became professor and chairman of the Department of Rehabilitation Medicine and chief at the Rehabilitation Hospital (see page 289).

The official relationship with Georgia Baptist Hospital ended when Fletcher moved to the Emory campus. Cantwell continued the work there, and he, too, was a successful leader. Many of the physicians at Georgia Baptist Hospital are on the volunteer clinical faculty at Emory.

Northside Hospital

I established a relationship with Northside Hospital somewhat similar to that with Piedmont and suggested that Dr. **Barry Silverman** be selected to lead the program. We rotated cardiology fellows through the program for a few months each year. The official relationship was discontinued after a few years because of financial restriction. Barry Silverman continues to direct the cardiology program there and remains an effective member of the volunteer clinical faculty. Many other physicians at Northside Hospital are also on the volunteer clinical faculty at Emory.

St. Joseph's Hospital

St. Joseph's Hospital had organized its staff and programs so that there was no need for new positions that would officially relate to Emory. Accordingly, I mounted no initiative to create any new relationship. Many of the physicians at St. Joseph's Hospital volunteered their time to the Department of Medicine at Emory and were on the clinical faculty.

A Note of Appreciation

The relationship of the Department of Medicine at Emory and the four Atlanta community hospitals mentioned above was excellent during the thirty years I was professor and chairman of the Department of Medicine at Emory. Many of the physicians who trained in Emory house-staff programs eventually practiced in one or more of the community hospitals. This, more than any other factor, virtually eliminated a town-gown problem in Atlanta. I am eternally grateful to those volunteer faculty members who came to my rescue in 1957 and continued to serve on the volunteer faculty during the thirty years I was professor and chairman of the Department of Medicine.

The Relationship with the Georgia Medical Center in Columbus, Georgia

Dean Richardson was not an enthusiastic supporter of a family practice program. He contended that graduates of such programs commonly limited their work to one or two areas because it was difficult to remain competent in all areas of medicine. Accordingly, he believed, family physicians did not continue to be family physicians. He had an interesting relationship with the leaders of official organizations that represented the family physicians: they disagreed violently with him, but they liked him immensely. When he was asked to present his views to them, he stated his views bluntly, as was his custom, and they liked to hear him.

By 1967, Richardson agreed to assist in the development of a family practice program at the Georgia Medical Center in Columbus, Georgia. Bernard Hallman was chosen to assist in the development of the program. The Department of Medicine, and all other departments, sent faculty members from Emory to Columbus to give lectures and teaching conferences. The physicians in Columbus who taught in the program had their Emory faculty appointments in the Department of Preventive

Medicine and Community Health. After several years, the relationship of Emory to the program was discontinued.

Dean Glenn tried to develop a family practice program in the mid-eighties but met obstacles and backed away. Dean Krause was not at Emory long enough to consider the problem. Dean Houpt initiated the family practice program at Emory in the early nineties. Dr. Lawrence Lutz was appointed professor and chairman of the Department of Family Medicine and Prevention in 1993.

The Relationship with the Nursing Services

It is not possible to have an excellent medical service without excellent nursing. In this regard we were always blessed. The capabilities of Grady Memorial Hospital nurses were recognized everywhere. The Nell Hodgson Woodruff School of Nursing on the Emory campus is a superb school where nurses participate in graduate education. Graduates of the Nell Hodgson Woodruff School of Nursing have become national leaders.

In 1957, **Frances Hammett** was director of the nursing service at Grady Hospital, and **Helen Graves** held a similar position at Emory University Hospital. **Mary Woody**, whose skill I recognized in the early fifties when she and I worked together at Emory University Hospital, became director of the nursing service and assistant hospital administrator at Grady Memorial Hospital in 1968 (see Figure 5-39). She was superb. She and William Pinkston, the Hospital Administrator, and I made occasional rounds together on the medical service, at which time we discussed ways to improve the medical services. A generous spirit of cooperation was always apparent. Woody and I organized the first postgraduate course for nurses sponsored by the American Heart Association. Together we implemented the problem-oriented system of medical records in the early seventies. In 1973 Medcom published the book *Applying the Problem-Oriented System*, edited by H. K. Walter, J. W. Hurst, and M. F. Woody.

When Woody left Grady to develop a school of nursing at Auburn University, **Betty Blake** became the director of the nursing service in 1979. She was an excellent choice. Despite many obstacles she maintained a high standard of nursing. In 1984, Miss Woody returned to become the director of the nursing service at Emory University Hospital. By then, I was spending most of my time at Emory University Hospital and worked closely with her in the continuing effort to improve patient care and teaching. We were able to implement the problem-oriented record on the medical service at Emory University Hospital,

As the Veterans Administration Hospital and Crawford Long Hospital became more involved with Emory, it became apparent that the nurses at these institutions played a major role in the care of patients on the medical service.

Pages could be written on the importance of skilled and compassionate nursing. This brief passage is an honest gesture of gratitude to all the nurses who contributed to the care of medical patients and who taught many "green" medical students and house officers what they needed to know about "hands-on" patient care.

My advice to medical students and medical house officers has always been, "Listen to the nurses. They will teach you a great deal."

The Relationship with the Morehouse School of Medicine

The Morehouse School of Medicine was officially founded in 1975. Arthur Richardson and Bernard Hallman of Emory University School of Medicine assisted Morehouse in every possible way, as the accreditation of Morehouse was contingent upon Emory support.

Initially, Morehouse was a two-year school. Emory University School of Medicine accepted about 50 percent of the Morehouse students into the 1980–81 junior class; the remaining students were accepted into the junior classes of several other medical schools. This method of operation continued until 1986, when a five-year plan was developed, by which Emory University would teach Morehouse junior students and Morehouse would teach its students the other three years. Since 1991–92, Morehouse has taught its own students the entire four years. Morehouse began awarding the M.D. degree in 1985.

Everyone recognized that Grady Memorial Hospital was essential for the development of the Morehouse School of Medicine. Accordingly, in 1984 Morehouse became officially associated with Grady Memorial Hospital when the Fulton-DeKalb Hospital Authority and Emory University agreed at a public news conference that Morehouse School of Medicine could use 50 percent of Grady Memorial Hospital for patient care and teaching activities. That same year, a thirty-year contract was signed between Emory and the Fulton-DeKalb Hospital Authority enabling the two institutions to continue their official relationship.

Charles Hatcher, then vice president for health affairs at Emory, established the very important "Liaison Committee" in 1985. The following account of the creation of the committee and its charge was written by Dr. **Asa Yancey**, who was the medical director at Grady Hospital.

In 1985 Charles R. Hatcher, M.D., appointed a "Liaison Committee" for Emory-Morehouse relationships at Grady Memorial Hospital. The committee consisted of the dean of Emory University School of Medicine, the dean of Morehouse School of Medicine, the medical director of Grady Memorial Hospital, and subsequently the Emory Executive Associate Dean for Clinical Affairs of Grady Memorial Hospital. This group met monthly and effectively proposed solutions to problems of two schools of medicine working in one hospital. It also discussed the needs Morehouse School of Medicine had for the use of Grady Memorial Hospital for the education of its students and for the developing graduate medical educational programs. The chairmen of Morehouse's Departments of Medicine, Surgery, and Psychiatry were appointed to serve, along with the dean of the Morehouse School of Medicine, on the Executive Committee of the Medical Staff, Grady Memorial Hospital. In this manner, the participation of the Morehouse School of Medicine in the activities of Grady Hospital was enhanced considerably.

Morehouse initiated a house-staff program in internal medicine at Grady Memorial Hospital on July 1, 1992, with thirteen residents.

The Winds of Change

Medicare and Medicaid became available in 1965, and some of the Grady Memorial Hospital patients became eligible for these types of government-financed medical care. In addition, some patients seen at Grady Memorial Hospital had private insurance that was financed by their employers. This, of course, increased the revenue that the hospital could collect on the patients who were seen there. At the same time, the volunteer faculty found it difficult to leave their offices to care for patients at Grady. This difficulty arose because the cost of running their offices had increased considerably. Also, the physicians began to see some of the patients who formerly went to Grady Memorial Hospital in their private offices, an action that decreased the stimulus for physicians to perform charity work declined.

When Dr. **Douglas Kendrick** became medical director at Grady Memorial Hospital and associate dean of Emory University School of Medicine in 1967, he saw an opportunity to solve an old and difficult problem. Kendrick was a very capable administrator. He had been the physician to General MacArthur during his long and distinguished army career. The old problem was that Grady Memorial Hospital contributed almost nothing to the income of Emory physicians who worked there. The physicians made enormous contributions to the care of Grady patients but received no recompense for it. The School of Medicine supplied the salary for the physicians but was obligated to support financially only the chiefs of services. The support for many faculty members came from research grants and Emory funds that could be justified by Dean Richardson. While the Department of Medicine received a good bit of the school's financial pool, the pool itself was too small. The physicians in the Department of Medicine who earned their incomes from private patients in the Emory Clinic continued to contribute to the teaching and patient care programs of the medical service of Grady Memorial Hospital, as did Emory physicians from the Veterans Administration Hospital and a number of community physicians. Had it not been for them, the Emory physicians located at Grady Memorial Hospital would have been overwhelmed by patient care responsibility.

Kendrick and others created the *Medical Fund* at Grady Memorial Hospital in October 1967. Faculty members who documented their professional contribution to the care of patients at Grady Memorial Hospital could make a legitimate claim to Medicare, Medicaid, and insurance companies. The money collected was to be used only to improve the patient care at Grady Memorial Hospital. The funds were assigned to the service that did the work, then distributed by the chief of the service with the approval of the dean of the School of Medicine and the medical director of Grady Memorial Hospital. This was a giant step forward. As expected, much time and effort were expended to create an efficient system of documenting, charging, billing, and collecting from the Grady Memorial Hospital patients. The system became increasingly efficient and served as an important source of income for the Emory physicians at Grady.

Dr. **Asa Yancey** followed Kendrick as medical director of Grady Memorial Hospital and associate dean of the School of Medicine, serving in these positions from 1972 to 1989. Yancey had previously served as chief of surgery at Tuskegee Veterans Administration Hospital in Tuskegee, Alabama, from 1948 to 1958. He also served as chief of surgery at Hughes Spalding Hospital on the Grady campus from 1958 to 1972. He was credited with the establishment of the first accredited training program in surgery for African Americans in Alabama and in Georgia. Yancey, in his quiet and effective way, continued the important work performed by Kendrick. This included developing the Grady Medical Fund. Both men were great assets to Grady Memorial Hospital and Emory University School of Medicine and assisted in the development of the Department of Medicine.

Sensing the winds of change in 1974, the editor of the Medical Association of Atlanta asked me to write about the profession of medicine as it might be in the year 2000. My article is reproduced here, with slight modification.

Medicine in the Year 2000 (as predicted in 1974)

The forces of change are all around us. Medicine will be different in the year 2000. We must contribute to the change and prepare for the change. By then:

Solo practice will be uncommon and group practice will be the rule.

Physician assistants and nurse clinicians will assist the physician. They will assist the physician in data gathering and in the execution of therapeutic and educational algorithms.

Patients will have a primary physician who will manage most of their problems. The primary physician will also be responsible for obtaining the specialty care their patients require.

Hospitals will not be built as independent units. The physician's office in a professional building will be attached to the hospital. This will increase the efficiency of the physician who cares for hospitalized patients and ambulatory patients.

Medical centers that are not physically attached to hospitals will be administratively associated with one or more hospitals in order to guarantee the proper flow of patients from one facility to another.

The physician's office and the hospital will become educational centers. Special teaching areas will be designed so that modern technology can be utilized by the physician and his assistants. General health information and problem-specific "education" will be delivered in these areas. The education of the patient will have a prominent place in the health care system of the year 2000.

Every hospital and office will become an educational center for patients, physicians, nurses, allied health workers, dietitians, and administrators. The physicians will set aside an afternoon each week for conducting their own educational program. The program will not be one where abstract subjects are discussed. The program will deal with the problems their patients have. From such a base a new method of continuing education will emerge. The new method will depend upon the ability of the physicians to assess the quality of care they are rendering their own patients and constantly to update their work. When this is done the physicians will learn more from what they do each day and their patients will be the beneficiaries.

House staff training is gradually changing. House staff training will be viewed as the bridge that spans the gap between medical school and practice. House staff training will be seen as group practice, and the principles learned during that period will be used in practice.

Patients will carry their health record with them. It will be miniaturized and set in a plastic card the size of one's driver's license. Privacy will be maintained since a special "reader" will be needed to access the material. Accordingly, only physicians or other authorized personnel (such as emergency room staff) will be able to "read" the record.

The common denominator for all of the above is the problem-oriented record and the system it helps to create. Communication between physicians, nurses, allied health personnel and to patients is becoming increasingly important. The problem-oriented record and system is a teachable and reproducible method of achieving the goal. Now, increasing numbers of physicians, nurses, etc. are using the problem-oriented record, and the system is implemented manually. This will lead to the proper use of computers to assist in patient care and education. By the year 2000 physicians will be utilizing the computerized problem-oriented record and system.

Students and house staff have never been more enthusiastic about our profession than they are now. The job at hand is to develop programs for the students and house staff that will prepare them for the future. We in the Department of Medicine of Emory University School of Medicine have considered the points mentioned in this communication in our efforts to create our programs.[13]

The Fleas Come with the Dog

The evolution of the Department of Medicine from 1957 to 1986 was smooth, orderly, and exciting 99 percent of the time. The department members were functioning well as a group: we were enjoying medicine; we were having fun; we were learning from each other. But as every adult knows, fleas come with the dog. Therefore, to make the story complete, I mention the following "fleas." Some are large, some small, and some, simply interesting.

An Administrative Blockade

In the late fifties, it was customary for the superintendent of Grady Memorial Hospital to mail contracts to the new house officers selected by the chief of medicine. The powerful superintendent was delaying the mailing of letters, and I was receiving calls from the appointees, to whom there had been an oral agreement, asking for their contract. I walked into the superintendent's office at Grady Memorial Hospital to discuss the matter. An unpleasant event occurred that will be kept secret. Suffice it to say that the letters were mailed promptly, and that administrative blocks of this sort were never again placed in the way of the Department of Medicine's development.

Problems with Faculty Appointments

On two occasions faculty appointments to the Department of Medicine were well under way before I was notified. Negotiations with the prospects had been carried out by powerful officials of the university. Following Stead's earlier advice to me, I stopped these appointments. Both of them required a threat on my part that a new chairman of the

---

[13] J. W. Hurst, "Medicine in the Year 2000," *Atlanta Medicine* (March 1974): 19–31. Reprinted, in altered form, with permission from the Medical Association of Atlanta

Department of Medicine would have to be found if the appointments proceeded. The negotiations with the individuals were discontinued. Whereas the potential appointees were probably excellent, the method of appointment was unacceptable.

Problems with Dismissals

On one occasion it was necessary to inform a faculty member that academic medicine was not for him. This led to a sticky investigation and a "hearing" before a committee composed of faculty members from the law school. The problem was resolved in favor of the Department of Medicine. On another occasion, a faculty member did not follow school policy regarding sick leave and Dean Glenn terminated the faculty member's role at Emory. This led to an investigation and lawsuit, which the school lost.

We declined to give one cardiology trainee a certificate, and he engaged a lawyer to fight his battle. Again we lost. Another time, when two cardiology fellows were not reappointed, one of them wrote hostile letters to me, the dean, the president of the university, and others. For years the letters came every few months. The other trainee accepted the decision without protest.

Obstacles to Change

Not all faculty members were pleased when the Emory-Veterans Hospital program was discontinued in 1973 and the new Emory University Affiliated Hospitals program in internal medicine was started. In a short time, however, the new program (which integrated the house-staff activity of Grady Memorial Hospital, Emory University Hospital, and the Atlanta Veterans Administration Hospital) was considered superior to the former system, which involved two separate programs.

Nor were all of the faculty members happy when, in 1965, the University Trustees requested that Dean Richardson bring Crawford Long Hospital into the overall activities of the various departments involved. I appointed a chief of medicine at Crawford Long Hospital and later, in 1974, incorporated the house-staff program into the Emory University Affiliated Hospitals program. Some members of the faculty located on the Emory campus and the community physicians at Crawford Long Hospital strongly opposed these moves (see page 351). The faculty members on the Emory campus were concerned that the effort made at Crawford Long would dilute the effort at the Emory campus. The community physicians at Crawford Long Hospital feared that Emory would squeeze them out of the hospital, as had happened at Emory University Hospital in the early fifties. I assured the community physicians that they could continue to use Crawford Long Hospital after Emory faculty members were appointed there. As time passed, the value of Crawford Long Hospital to the University and the Department of Medicine was recognized by all Emory faculty members. In addition, the community physicians soon saw that as the hospital improved, their patients received better care.

The Benefits of Obstacles

In 1958, soon after we moved into the new Grady Memorial Hospital, I received a phone call in my office in the Glenn Memorial Building. At that time we were still understaffed with secretaries. I answered the phone. The nice woman on the line said, "We are out of toilet paper in the renal laboratory." I obtained a roll of toilet tissue from the toilet near my office and walked across the street to the renal laboratory. I asked, "Who needed the toilet paper?" A lesson was taught: I was willing to do anything to maintain a happy group of faculty members, technicians, and secretaries.

The student laboratory on the sixth floor of Grady Memorial Hospital was often dirty and untidy. Despite my encouragement, the students and house officers would make a mess that they themselves did not clean up. The hospital personnel were reluctant to touch or move anything because they could not determine what was important. Therefore, one weekend I cleaned up the laboratory myself. For a while, this act had a salutary effect.

Parking behind the Glenn Building at Grady was a problem in 1957. It was necessary to park one car behind another in the small lot. I commonly helped move cars so that a blocked car could back out. Another lesson was taught: I would do all I could to make a place for volunteer faculty who worked to help us teach.

I commonly picked up paper that had been dropped on the floor at Grady Memorial Hospital and Emory University Hospital. The lesson was that everyone of us should help maintain the cleanliness of the hospitals. Nothing should be beneath any of us as we try to create a pleasant environment for our patients.

The Problems of a Former Trainee

The most serious problem, and hence the largest flea, that arose from 1957 to 1986 occurred in the early eighties. The difficulty involved a trainee who had left the Department of Medicine at Emory and was continuing his training at another excellent institution. The brilliant, creative, articulate, highly respected, very popular former trainee was discovered falsifying research data at another institution. This led to a review of the work he had done with some of the faculty members at Emory. Whereas some of the data used to write the papers were definitely falsified, an internal investigation by a committee of Emory faculty members and an external investigation by a committee from the National Institutes of Health, revealed that Emory faculty members themselves were not involved in the falsification of the data. They had trusted the brilliant trainee completely. This led to the development of the attitude that it is proper to trust, but it is necessary to verify every modicum of data used in a report of research activity.

The Problems Created by the Narrow Tenure Track

I viewed all faculty members as equally important to our effort. The superb clinician, superb teacher, and superb researcher were equally important and equally respected. However, my recommendations for the promotion of each of these devoted, capable individuals were not implemented as if they were equal. This obstacle was created by members of the Advisory Faculty Council, which was composed of all department chairmen and which had to approve *all* appointments and promotions. The basic science chairmen were reluctant to promote any faculty members who had chosen the tenure track unless they were successful researchers. Accordingly, certain council members could block my recommendations. They believed the only way to judge competence was to count the number of research papers published in excellent peer-review journals. They did not believe that good teaching and good patient care could be identified by a peer-review group. I disagreed. They did not appreciate that their own income depended, at times, on the funds supplied to the dean by the clinicians in the Emory Clinic. A humorous event occurred when one basic scientist informed me, "If you are not careful," he said, "you will fill up your department with good teachers."

Rare Disagreements

Dean Richardson was an excellent dean. I agreed with him and his actions almost all of the time. In the early sixties, I resigned for a few hours because the dean assigned research space promised to the Department of Medicine to another department. Wise colleagues counseled me not to resign. I heeded their advice and withdrew my resignation.

Later, in the early seventies, the dean suggested that I relinquish the chairmanship of the Department of Medicine. He implied that I had ruffled some feelings. I responded that I was carrying out his policy but would discontinue my efforts in that area. He withdrew his suggestion a few hours later after being counseled by some wise advisors that he should not pursue the idea.

My devotion to the dean continued throughout his deanship. Sometime later, when he considered leaving Emory to assume the deanship at the University of South Alabama, I, along with several other chairmen, cornered him in his office and urged him to remain at Emory. He did.

Illness

In 1977 I discovered that I had cancer of the colon (this was the cause of my absence from the 1977 annual photograph). I wrote the house staff and fellows the following letter on June 15, 1977. The lesson I was trying to convey was the value of the *trust* in the doctor-patient relationship.

> I am sorry I cannot be with you this year at the annual breakfast. Forces beyond my control prevent me from being there.
>
> I have had the opportunity to work with many problems during my career. Some were big and some were small. I want you to know that I face the problem I now have with considerable equanimity. My family history has been such that I have planned this battle for a long time. I may or may not win it but I can assure you I will handle whatever comes.
>
> I have every confidence and trust in my internist, surgeon, and anesthesiologist, which brings me to the real point of this letter. I wish for all of you that your patients will have complete confidence and trust in you as responsible, dependable, knowing, and caring physicians. If you achieve that, it will lead you to study, work, and pursue excellence in the field that we all love. You see, one of the greatest human qualities is the trust one person has in another person. Because your patients trust you, you must never let them down.
>
> Each year I give each of the four Chief Residents an Emory chair. We all owe Dr. Candace Miklozek, Dr. Jerre Lutz, Dr. Steve DeWees, and Dr. David Webb an enormous amount of gratitude for steering our ship through safe, exciting, and beautiful waters.
>
> I would like to see each of you. Please come by in a few days.
>
> For those of you who are leaving, may I say it has been a pleasure to have you here and I wish you well.

Surgery went well. Ken Walker, who had had a similar operation one year earlier, served as interim chairman of the Department of Medicine during my convalescence.

One year later, on routine follow-up examination, the CAT scan showed what was interpreted to be metastatic lesions in the liver. Later, however, in consultation with friends at the Mayo Clinic, I was given a clean bill of health. Prior to traveling to the Mayo Clinic I had told a group of the faculty good-bye and believed my days were numbered.

When the diagnosis was reversed at the Mayo Clinic, I called home and announced, "I am fine. Don't appoint a search committee!"

Now, in March 1997, at the time of this writing, Ken Walker and I are well. Dick Amerson, our surgeon, did a great job two decades ago.

Extortion

It was not uncommon for the chairman's name to appear in the newspaper. Sometimes, especially after my name appeared in relationship to President Johnson, I would receive crank mail and phone calls. One day I received a call from a nice-talking woman who said, after we had chatted a bit, that she wanted me to talk with someone else. She handed the phone to her male companion. The quick-talking male said that he wanted money and would call later and give me instructions. He then hung up. I alerted all the secretaries in the office that a call might come in. It did. The nice lady, who had first called me, again talked to me and turned the conversation over to her male friend. He pointed out that he knew where I lived and that I had children. He also noted that my mother lived in Carrollton, Georgia. He then said he would be back in touch with me to tell me where to meet him to give him money. At no time did he state the amount of money he wanted. The caller was now making threats against members of my family.

My wife, of course, was completely informed. I called Rader Thredgill in Carrollton, Georgia, the chief of police, who lived across the street from my mother. He was willing to keep watch on my mother. I then called my mother, who was not the least bit alarmed. Later, she did receive a collect call from Atlanta but refused to talk to the party. I then called my friend Tommy Haynes, who was my former college roommate and an excellent FBI agent. I called my friend Jerry Kevitt in nearby Marietta. He was a former secret service agent and had been assigned to Lady Bird Johnson. They advised me to call the Atlanta chief of police. Tommy asked me to recount the entire story to him. I remembered only one fact that he perceived as a clue: I had heard the nice lady use the word "Seville." The word meant nothing to me. Later in the day Tommy called, and I believe the Atlanta chief of police also called, to state that they had solved the case.

A man had forged my name to a check on a bank in Carrollton. He bought some expensive shoes at the Seville shop and was given cash for the remainder of the amount of money indicated on the check. The check "bounced," and the owner of the shop, not realizing my name had been forged, turned the problem over to what was apparently a ruthless collection agency. A member of the agency called me and chose to use Mafia tactics because they assumed I had written a "bad" check. Tommy pointed out to the owner of the Seville shop that my name had undoubtedly been forged. The man who forged the check was identified rather easily because his work was well known to the police.

Whereas this episode was only indirectly related to my position in the Department of Medicine, it did produce considerable turmoil for about forty-eight hours.

The Worrisome Reaction to a Speech

The entire medical staff at Grady Hospital met in the Grady Memorial Hospital Auditorium on October 11, 1985. Two of the leading politicians of the hospital's two authorizing counties were invited to attend. I was selected to speak to the staff and the politicians who attended the meeting. At that time there were rumblings suggesting that the political leadership was not leading the citizens to understand the amount of service Grady Memorial Hospital delivered to the community at large. There was talk of decreasing the financial support of Grady Memorial Hospital. Actually, more funds were desperately needed to maintain an excellent hospital.

I worked hard on the speech, and many people checked its content. The seats of the Grady auditorium were filled with members of the medical staff.

When I finished delivering the speech, my colleagues and friends applauded for several minutes. Then it happened. One of the politicians rose to condemn the speech. He was furious. He uttered a few distasteful comments and stalked out of the auditorium. The embarrassing scene was handled quite well by Charles Hatcher, who was chairing the session. Had it not been for his skill, an ugly scene could have developed. The other politician told me privately that he did not like the speech. In the speech, I had recognized and thanked the medical staff, which was made up of physicians and nonphysicians, for their love and support of the hospital. I had thanked the political leaders for their efforts to help and to lead. Why then, in 1985, did the two politicians react adversely to the speech?

I queried several people who might know the answer, but they could not explain the reaction. Some observers of the scene believe it was a planned performance by the politicians. As days passed, I began to realize why the politicians had not liked the speech that touched the hearts of the members of the audience. The politicians, I reasoned, had other plans for the hospital. A movement had already started in the community to decrease the funding for the hospital. The politicians were beginning to support that type of movement. My speech was an appeal to continue to support the hospital. The politicians were apparently moving away from the wonderful Grady spirit that had been the pride both of those who worked at the hospital and of the citizens who supported it.

The reaction of the politicians to that speech in 1985 taught me that Grady Memorial Hospital would change in the years ahead. I hoped, however, that the Grady spirit would continue.

These were the "fleas that came with the dog." They occupied only one percent of the time that elapsed during the three decades discussed in this chapter of the book. The other 99 percent of the time was filled with excitement and progress.

Humor Along the Way

The thirty years beginning on February 1, 1957, and ending November 1, 1986, were filled with intellectual adventures. We were deeply engaged in the serious business of patient care, teaching, research, organizing, and developing. Many humorous events also occurred along the way. In fact, an entire book could be written about the funny things that happened. The following five stories are told as examples of the humorous events that were, in fact, commonplace.

Early in my chairmanship, I decided to give the junior students an open-book examination in medicine. They would be allowed to bring any books they chose to the examination. Prior to that time, the junior students were given a lengthy, comprehensive, final examination without the aid of textbooks. When I made the announcement, the members of the class applauded. I was moving away from requiring that they know everything and moving toward an examination that tested their problem-solving skills.

I returned to my office feeling I had made a proper move. A few minutes later a pale, perspiring, junior student came to see me. He blurted out that my plan for the examination was very unfair. Taken by surprise, I asked, "What is wrong with it?" He responded, "Don't you see—the students who have been using the books all year will have an unfair advantage!"

I made arrangements to send excellent Emory senior students to other institutions for a one-month elective rotation on the medical service. I walked up to Tom (not his real name), who was then assigned to the medical service on the sixth floor of Grady Memorial Hospital. I said, "Tom, how would you like to spend a month on the medical service at the Massachusetts General Hospital?" Tom responded, "That would be great." Tom completed his rotation at the Massachusetts General Hospital. Years later he became director of the Division of Cardiology at a major medical school. More years later, he confessed to me: "When you asked me to go to the Massachusetts General Hospital, it meant nothing to me. I had never heard of the place."

I commonly called each of the four medical ward areas at Grady to ask about patients. I would also make unexpected ward rounds late at night when I returned to Atlanta from an out-of-town teaching assignment. One night, at the beginning of a new academic year, I called one of the medical wards at the hospital. The nurse answered the telephone. I said, "This is Dr. Hurst, may I speak with the intern?" She called the intern, but I assume she did not tell him who was calling. I asked the intern, "How is Mr. Brown?" The answer was a bit flippant. I spoke a little more firmly but his answer was even more flippant. I said, "Do you know whom you are talking to?" He said, "No." I answered, "This is Dr. Hurst." There was silence on the telephone. He then said, "Do you know who this is?" I said, "No." The next sound I heard was the click of the telephone as he hung up the instrument. Of course, you can be sure I never found out whom I was talking to!

The fourth story is about a resident on another service. It is an oxymoron in that, at the same time, it is humorous and sad. I was one of a "jury" of department chairmen selected to determine the innocence or guilt of a resident on the anesthesiology service. The hospital police suspected that someone was stealing gasoline out of the Grady bus. The police set a trap to catch the thief. To them, it was a "sting" operation. They left the bus in a location that would invite the thief to help himself. They watched the bus from the second floor of the hospital and, as they suspected, a person in a white suit began to siphon the gasoline from the tank of the bus. When caught in the act his excuse was, "My wife is acutely ill. I must get to her, and my car is out of gas."
We found the resident guilty and dismissed him from the program.

Dr. Proctor Harvey, of Georgetown University, was visiting us, as he often did. He had been teaching all day and he, the Hursts, and the Logues were relaxing at the home of the Schlants. Just as we were leaving to go to dinner, Dr. Harvey chose to visit the restroom. Robert Schlant was not aware of this. The Hursts and Logues left to go to the restaurant for dinner. Schlant, not seeing Dr. Harvey, assumed he had left with either the Hursts or Logues. Schlant then let his large dog into the house, and he and his wife left for the restaurant. When Dr. Harvey came out of the restroom, he was met by only a growling dog. At that point, he called his wife in Washington, who allegedly scolded him: "I told you not to go without me." The Schlants, Logues, and Hursts were by then seated at the restaurant. I asked, "Where is Dr. Harvey?" Schlant, without a word, left instantly and rushed to his home to rescue Dr. Harvey. The moral of this story is: being a visiting professor is no rose garden.

———

These stories should be viewed as signals that, even though the work was hard, we were a happy lot. Individuals that are emotionally healthy exhibit a full spectrum of emotions. So it is with a group of students, house officers, and faculty members.

Governance of the Department of Medicine

The governance of the Department of Medicine must be viewed in the context of a larger administrative structure. Accordingly, Appendix 4 lists the names of the chairmen of the board of trustees of Emory University; the presidents of Emory University; the vice presidents for health affairs of Emory University; the deans of Emory University School of Medicine; the administrators and medical directors of Emory University Hospital and of Crawford Long Hospital; the directors of the Emory Clinic; the chairmen of the Fulton-DeKalb Hospital Authority; the administrators and medical directors of Grady Memorial Hospital; and the directors and chiefs of staff of the Veterans Administration Hospital.

The photographs of the department chairmen of Emory University School of Medicine in the sixties, seventies, and eighties are shown in Appendixes 5 through 7.

Early in the development of the Department of Medicine when there were only fourteen members, I met the Grady staff at lunch once a week and met the group that worked in the Emory University Hospital and Clinic at grand rounds once a week. As a member of the Advisory Faculty Council, I met with the dean, along with the other department chairmen, once a month. I attended the chiefs luncheon with the dean at Grady once a month and the administrative meetings at Grady Memorial Hospital and Emory University Hospital once a month. I attended the administrative committee meeting of the Emory Clinic once a month. I attended the dean's committee meeting at the Veterans Administration Hospital every few months. I attended the cardiology luncheon each Friday. The meetings were arranged so that I attended no more than four committee meetings each week, two of them during lunch.

During the last decade of my chairmanship, I met with the division directors at breakfast on Friday morning every two weeks. The chiefs of medicine at Crawford Long Hospital and the Veterans Administration Hospital were invited to attend, as was the deputy chief of medicine at the

Emory Clinic and Ken Walker (see Appendix 8). New appointments, promotions, allocation of available research funds, and other matters were discussed.

Communication is the secret weapon used by successful leaders to run things. Accordingly, throughout my thirty years as chairman, I tried to communicate to the members of the Department of Medicine the information passed on to the department chairmen by the vice president of health affairs, who reported to the Dean's Advisory Faculty Council. This effort kept the department members in touch with the University as a whole. I communicated the other information presented at the Dean's Advisory Faculty Council meeting to members of the Department of Medicine. This kept the members of the department informed about the medical school itself.

I had a rule: when the dean called and requested an action that was not urgent, I would discuss it at the next appropriate meeting of the staff. If the dean needed an answer within a few hours, or a day or two, I would call the appropriate faculty members and discuss the matter. If the dean needed an answer immediately, I would answer him promptly and report my action at the next appropriate meeting of the faculty of the Department of Medicine.

I also learned that while some items could be discussed initially with the group as a whole, it was wise to discuss certain matters with individual members of the department prior to the discussion at a division meeting. Discerning the difference in these two types of subjects was the key to successful and productive meetings of division directors.

I learned that good governance of a department requires two equally important actions. Reasonable ideas must be heard and respected, and communication must be the watchword. Intelligent individuals do not like to work in a system without knowing what the system itself is doing. In fact, many individuals wish to contribute their ideas to the operation of the system. Without proper communication and input an individual cannot feel the joy of success or the pain of failure of the system as a whole. How can one love an institution if he or she knows little about the institution where he or she "works"? So communication is the key to success.

Some Annual Social Events

The Department of Medicine had a reception for all the new incoming interns in late June of each year at the Houston Mill House when it became available. An annual Christmas party was held in the same facility. Departing senior residents went to dinner with key faculty members.

Grady Memorial Hospital provided a barbecue for the entire faculty and house staff each August. The faculty worked the wards at Grady Memorial Hospital, while the house staff who were scheduled to work attended the barbecue. One year, I noted that the faculty did not work the wards because the house staff did not relinquish their duties in order to attend the barbecue. When I investigated, Ken Walker, one of the house officers at the time, said, "We didn't want the faculty messing up our wards." After that, I suggested to William Pinkston, superintendent of the hospital, that the barbecue be given on two consecutive Saturdays so that all the house staff could go to the magnificent feast the hospital provided.

The end-of-the-year house-staff and faculty breakfast was provided by Grady Memorial Hospital on the top floor of the hospital. This breakfast was given the last week of the academic year, when new interns had already arrived. It was our custom to have the new interns arrive a week early. The old interns could have the week off, and the new interns were indoctrinated by the residents. The incoming interns were invited to breakfast and were able to sense the esprit de corps of the house staff. The purpose of the breakfast was to honor the chief residents at each of the four hospitals. A house officer was chosen to "roast" each of the four chief residents. As expected, a few others—including me and other members of the faculty—were also roasted. An Emory chair was given to each chief resident as well as a photograph of the house staff with signatures of its members. One year I gave each of the four chief residents a leaf from the tree of Hippocrates. We had just returned from a trip to the Isle of Cos, where Hippocrates taught. I brought back several leaves from the famous tree.[14]

A photograph of the medical house staff, fellows, and faculty was made in front of the Glenn Memorial Building each year until the size of the house staff demanded the venue be moved (see Figures 5-40 through 5-69). Regrettably, we never found a proper location where all the faces could be seen. Many of the fellows and most of the faculty did not attend, because there was not enough space for them.

A few photographs were made annually in front of Emory University Hospital and at the Veterans Administration Hospital when there was a separate Emory-Veterans Hospital program (see Figures 5-70A and B). In

---

[14] To my great surprise, as this book was being finished, the 1996–1997 medical house staff awarded me the Lifetime Teaching Achievement Award for Excellence in Internal Medicine, for which I was most grateful.

addition to these photographs, many of the divisions had photographs made of their members and fellows.

I missed only one annual breakfast and annual house-staff photograph because of illness (see page 305).

The Changing World of House Staff and Fellows

A highly entertaining epic could be written about the changes that have occurred in house-staff training.

When I was a house officer in the forties, I made $25 a month during my internship. House officers of that era were relieved that they no longer had to pay tuition. I had no work schedule because World War II was raging, and the University Hospital in Augusta, Georgia, was understaffed. Because of this, we worked almost continuously. We wore "whites." As a medical resident I was in charge of the clinical laboratory at night and matched blood for all of the hospital services. I also performed the agglutinations needed to diagnose certain infectious diseases. Although marriage was frowned upon, I was married. I was permitted to live in a shack near the furnace of the hospital because it was no farther away from the hospital wards than the house officer quarters. It did cost me $8.00 a month. Vacations were rare. Nationally known visiting professors were rare, but when they came, it was not uncommon for every student and house officer to attend their lectures.

In 1957, house officers at Grady Memorial Hospital made $75 a month. Most were unmarried and lived in the house officer quarters. They worked every other night and every other weekend. Vacations were offered during holidays and once a year. They still wore "whites." I talked Mr. Wilson, the hospital superintendent, into a $50 raise for the house staff. When a house officer missed morning report, I would sometimes take the other house officers to his room for report. After offering to help the sleepy house officer get dressed, we would continue with morning report. It was a happy period. The house officers only occasionally left the hospital. I recall one house officer asking me the direction to town in November.

The arrangements for house officers at Emory University Hospital and the Veterans Administration Hospital were similar to those at Grady.

By the sixties and seventies, the house officer's world was changing. House officers believed they were underpaid (and they were). They wanted more money for the service they delivered. There were more visiting professors than ever, but the trainees expected that.

By 1997, the stipend for interns had increased to $33,000 per year. A one-month vacation was granted, and the interns worked every sixth night. Many were married, and virtually all lived in apartments or homes. The day of the white suit was almost over. Visiting professors were commonplace but rarely made ward rounds. They gave lectures. The working conditions for the house officers had gradually loosened up, so the house officers could participate in the cultural opportunities of the community.

During the eighties and nineties, the changes in working hours for the house staff led to a national debate regarding the role of patient care in the education of a house officer. Some national leaders believed the new system did not instill the sense of responsibility that the old system literally demanded. They believed that there was little evidence that the less-busy house officer studied more than the busy house officer, and that there was no evidence that the house officer who had little night duty took advantage of the cultural opportunities of the community. Others believed that the new system was more humane and that the house officers were less tired and therefore made fewer errors.

My own view was that both the old system and the new systems were wrong. Hospitals were becoming large intensive-care units, and more and more patient care was being performed in outpatient facilities. I believed there needed to be a period of training during which the house officer worked exclusively in an excellent outpatient department. During that time, he or she should have little night duty. Earlier, this could not be accomplished nationally because there were no excellent outpatient facilities that could be organized for first-rate education. The usual outpatient service was not supervised by a sufficient number of true teachers, and the logistics needed to workup patients were rarely available. This problem was gradually being solved.

I also believed there needed to be a period when house officers virtually lived in the hospital. This time is needed for house officers to learn how to take care of the numerous needs of seriously ill patients and to appreciate the responsibility that goes with doctoring. A house officer should not, and would not, leave a patient who is in shock, even when another house officer arrived to take over. The period of time allocated to this type of experience could be far less than it formerly was, but working every sixth night did not accomplish the educational goal for that type of service.

As I write this in 1997 the debate is still not settled. It is clear that house-staff training will never be as intense as it was prior to the sixties. But the debate continues. It will not be settled until the national leaders recognize that health care will be divided into outpatient service for ambulatory patients, with their particular needs, and a hospital service of

very sick patients, with their particular needs. The educational requirements and patient care needs of these two types of patients are different.

Emory, more than any place I know, has the opportunity and facilities
to organize a house-officer program that takes into account the factors
mentioned above.

The source of pay for house officers has become a national problem
now that there is a financial crisis in the health care "business" and now
that house officers make more than $30,000 a year. During the second
administration of President Ronald Reagan, there was a move to
discontinue all house-officer pay that was derived from federal sources,
such as Medicare. At the time, I was president of the Association of
Professors of Medicine. My year as president was devoted almost wholly to
working with other organizations in the effort to prevent the discontinu-
ance of the federal financing of house officers.

The movement to discontinue federal sources for house-staff pay
gradually died down. Now, in 1997, the problem is resurfacing. With all
of the discussion about the cost of health care, there is a chance that
house-staff pay will be "overlooked" because other, larger problems
receive all the attention. One can justly ask why "they" don't understand.
The decision makers, mainly nonphysicians and politicians, respond by
asking why the educators don't understand. Everyone, "they" say, must
understand that the government has already supported one-third or
more of the house officer's medical school education. "They" say that
government does not pay for the training of any other professionals.
"They" say that physicians make a lot of money. Doctors can borrow
money easily and pay it back quickly. Their mail, "they" say, is filled with
letters from unhappy patients. "They" also say we have too many
specialists now and don't need to train more.

The answer to all of this is that the education of physicians, including
the proper number of specialists, must be guaranteed. We must not leave
to chance that there will be a sufficient number of skilled physicians to
practice, teach, and engage in research. No other profession needs such a
guarantee.

I have dealt with this side issue in an effort to point out that the
people who control the current major source of house-staff pay do not
have the same view as the educators or the house officers. In 1997 it is
absolutely necessary for national medical leaders to watch the changes in
health care and not to allow the financial support of house staff to be
neglected. Clearly, as time passes, house-staff programs will again be
perceived as being part of the education of a physician, and the
"participant" in the program will not be perceived as receiving pay for
service. In a sense, it will be "back to the future." This time around,

however, there will be an adequate income for the house officer, whereas years ago it was $25 a month.

This is why, in 1997, I find myself saying to house officers, "We pay you to study. Your days as a house officer and fellow should be filled with the excitement of a grand adventure. You can make a new personal discovery every day. It is a time for intense study and thinking."

One of my great pleasures as chairman of the Department of Medicine was working with excellent house officers and fellows. The profiles of the interns appointed in the Department of Medicine in 1984, 1985, and 1986 were found among the annual reports I sent to the dean of the School of Medicine. They are discussed on page 359.

The photographs of the house staff, fellows, and faculty from 1957 to 1986 are shown in Figures 5-40 through 5-70. Not all house officers, fellows, and faculty could be present for the photographs, because they were busy taking care of patients. Even so, one can detect the group getting bigger. The steps in front of 69 Butler Street could not "hold" the enlarging group. We moved to the steps inside the entrance to Grady Memorial Hospital. Although the move accommodated a larger number of house officers, their faces became too small to recognize. So, I apologize to Dr. Juha Kokko for not finding a place to make the annual photograph of all members of the house staff, fellows, and faculty.

As I write this in 1997 I still have 6–9 teaching sessions each week with the students, house officers, and fellows. I still look forward to arriving each morning at Emory University Hospital at 6:30 a.m. I also review the work of the house officers as depicted in the records they create on their patients. I then congratulate, discuss, suggest, and challenge them on a point or two. I am likely to ask, "What data did you use to state the problems?"

Medical Leaders Trained During 1957–1986

More than 200 full-time faculty members, 5000 house officers and fellows, and 3600 students were involved in the activities of the Department of Medicine during the period 1957–1986. From the beginning, a conscious effort was made to create an environment that spawned the leaders of tomorrow. Accordingly, it is appropriate to mention the individuals who became department chairmen, vice chairmen, directors of divisions, deans, associate and assistant deans, and leaders of other areas of medicine. The list below includes the names of these individuals.

Department Chairmen and Vice Chairmen

Sixteen former faculty members or house officers became department chairmen, and three became vice chairmen:

• Dr. John Boring, professor and chairman of the Department of Epidemiology at the Emory School of Public Health;

• Dr. Edmund Bourke, professor and vice chairman of the Department of Medicine at State University of New York-Health Science Center at Brooklyn;

• Dr. Gerald Fletcher, professor and chairman of the Department of Rehabilitation Medicine at Emory;

• Dr. Lee Hand, professor and regional chairman of the Department of Medicine at Texas Tech University Health Center in El Paso, Texas;

• Dr. Marion Hargrove, professor and chairman of the Department of Medicine at Louisiana State University at Shreveport;

• Dr. Roland Ingram, professor and vice chairman of the Department of Medicine at the University of Minnesota;

• Dr. Earl Jones, first full-time professor and chairman of the Department of Dermatology at Emory;

• Dr. Herbert Karp, first full-time professor and chairman of the Department of Neurology at Emory;

• Dr. Robert Kibler, professor and chairman of the Department of Neurology at Emory;

• Dr. Charles LeMaistre, first full-time professor and chairman of the Department of Preventive Medicine and Community Health at Emory;

• Dr. Marvin M. McCall, chairman of the Department of Internal Medicine at Charlotte Memorial Hospital;

• Dr. William Marine, professor and chairman of the Department of Community Health at the University of Colorado;

• Dr. Stephen Miller, professor and vice chairman of the Department of Medicine at Mercer University School of Medicine in Macon, Georgia;

• Dr. Donald W. Paty, professor and head of neurology at the University of British Columbia and Vancouver General Hospital;

• Dr. Albert Pruitt, professor and chairman of the Department of Pediatrics at the Medical College of Georgia;

• Dr. Thomas Sellers, professor and chairman of the Department of Preventive Medicine and Community Health at Emory;

• Dr. Sheldon Skinner, professor and chairman of the Department of Physiology at Bowman Gray University;

• Dr. Corey Slovis, professor and chairman of the Department of Emergency Medicine at Vanderbilt; and

• Dr. Robert Talley, professor and chairman of the Department of Medicine at the University of South Dakota.

Directors of Divisions

Thirty-five former colleagues or trainees became directors of divisions at Emory or elsewhere.

• Dr. George Abela, director of the Division of Cardiology at the University of Michigan;

• Dr. James Achord, director of the Division of Gastroenterology at the University of Mississippi;

• Dr. Vardaman Buckalew, director of the Division of Nephrology at Bowman Gray School of Medicine;

• Dr. Dan Cabaniss, director of the Division of Cardiology at the University of South Alabama in Mobile;

• Dr. Robert Cantey, director of the Division of Infectious Diseases at the Medical University of South Carolina;

• Dr. Mario DiGirolamo, director of the Division of Endocrinology at Emory;

• Dr. Michael Duffell, director of the Division of Pulmonary Medicine at Emory;

• Dr. Edmund Farrar, director of the Division of Infectious Diseases at Emory and later at the Medical University of South Carolina;

• Dr. Noble Fowler, director of the Division of Cardiology at the University of Cincinnati;

• Dr. Luke Glancy, director of the Division of Cardiology at University of Louisiana in New Orleans;

• Dr. Leon Goldberg, director of clinical pharmacology at the University of Chicago;

• Dr. Dallas Hall, director of the Division of Hypertension at Emory;

• Dr. Lee Hand, director of the Division of Infectious Diseases at Emory;

• Dr. Henry Hanley, director of the Division of Cardiology at the Louisiana State University in Shreveport;

• Dr. Roland Ingram, director of the Division of Pulmonary Medicine and Critical Care at Harvard (Peter Bent Brigham Hospital) and later at Emory;

• Dr. Herbert Karp, first director of the Division of Geriatrics at Emory;

• Dr. Joseph Lindsay Jr., director of the Division of Cardiology at the Louisiana State University in Shreveport;

• Dr. George Litman, chief of the Department of Cardiology at the Akron General Hospital in Akron, Ohio, and professor of medicine at Northeast Ohio Universities College of Medicine;

• Dr. Marvin M. McCall, chief of cardiology and director of the residency program at Charlotte Memorial Hospital;

• Dr. John L. McCans, director of the Division of Cardiology at McGill University School of Medicine and Royal Victoria Hospital in Montreal, Quebec;

• Dr. Robert McDonald, head of clinical pharmacology at the University of Pittsburgh;

• Dr. John McNay, director of clinical pharmacology at the University of Texas in San Antonio;

• Dr. J. Ronald Mikolich, director of the Division of Cardiology at Northeastern Ohio Universities College of Medicine;

• Dr. Stephen B. Miller, director of the Division of Rheumatology at Emory;

• Dr. Robert J. Myerburg, director of the Division of Cardiology at the University of Miami;

• Dr. Robert C. Schlant, director of the Division of Cardiology at Emory;

• Dr. Jonas A. Shulman, director of the Division of Infectious Diseases at Emory;

• Dr. Mark Silverman, chief of cardiology at the Fuqua Heart Center at Piedmont Hospital.

• Dr. Edward Spoto, director of the Division of Cardiology at the University of South Alabama;

• Dr. David S. Stephens, director of the Division of Infectious Diseases at Emory;

• Dr. John H. Stone, director of the Division of General Medicine at Emory;

• Dr. J. David Talley, director of the Division of Cardiology at the University of Arkansas;

• Dr. Robert C. Talley, director of the Division of Cardiology at the University of Texas in San Antonio;

• Dr. Elbert Tuttle Jr., director of the Division of Nephrology at Emory; and

• Dr. David Waters, chief of cardiology at Hartford Hospital and director of the Division of Cardiology at the University of Connecticut.

Deans, Associate and Assistant Deans, and Leaders in Other Areas

• Dr. Delwood Collins, vice chancellor for research and graduate studies at the University of Kentucky Medical Center;

• Dr. James C. Crutcher, chief of medicine at the Atlanta Veterans Administration Hospital and later national medical director of the Veterans Administration;

• Dr. Victor Del Bene, medical director of the Medical University of South Carolina;

• Dr. Carlos Del Rio, director of CONASIDA, Mexico's National AIDS Commission;

• Dr. Morris Dillard, associate dean at Yale University School of Medicine;

• Dr. Joel M. Felner, associate dean of Emory University School of Medicine in charge of Emory students at Grady Memorial Hospital.

• Dr. J. Harper Gaston, physician-in-chief at Kaiser Permanente Hayward-Freemont Service Area in California and medical director of the Southeast Permanente Medical Group (Georgia and North Carolina);

• Dr. P. Bailey Francis, chief of staff at the Veterans Administration Hospital in Atlanta;

• Dr. Gilbert D. Grossman, associate clinic director in the Emory Clinic;

• Dr. W. Dallas Hall, director of the Clinical Research Facility at Emory University School of Medicine;

• Dr. Joseph E. Hardison, chief of medicine at the Atlanta Veterans Administration Hospital;

• Dr. E. Garland Herndon Jr., first director of the Clinical Research Facility in Emory University Hospital and later vice president for health affairs of Emory University, director of the Robert W. Woodruff Health Science Center, and medical director of Emory University Hospital (he was the personal physician to Mr. Robert W. Woodruff);

• Dr. Lyall A. J. Higginson, director of cardiology at the University of Ottawa Heart Institute in Ottawa, Ontario;

• Dr. Allen Johnson, head of the University Medical Associates at the Medical University of South Carolina;

• Dr. Talmage King, professor of medicine and vice chairman of clinical affairs at the University of Colorado in Denver;

• Dr. R. Bruce Logue, chief of medicine and cardiology at Emory University Hospital and head of internal medicine and cardiology at the Emory Clinic;

• Dr. D. Douglas Miller, professor of medicine and director of nuclear cardiology and cardiovascular biology, St. Louis University Medical Center, St. Louis;

• Dr. Douglas C. Morris, chief of cardiology at Crawford Long Hospital, then director of the Carlyle Fraser Heart Center at Crawford Long

Hospital, and later director of the Emory Heart Center and the J. Willis Hurst Professor of Medicine;
• Dr. Donald O. Nutter, vice dean at Northwestern University;
• Dr. John R. Preedy, director of research at the Atlanta Veterans Administration Hospital;
• Dr. Harold S. Ramos, chief of medicine at Crawford Long Hospital, then medical director of the hospital;
• Dr. Howard S. Rosman, associate chief of the Division of Cardiology at the Henry Ford Health Systems in Detroit, Michigan, and head of the Cardiology Fellowship Program and professor of medicine at the Case Western Reserve School of Medicine in Cleveland, Ohio;
• Dr. Paul Seavey, senior physician in internal medicine in the Emory Clinic and personal physician of former President Jimmy Carter;
• Dr. Jonas A. Shulman, chief of medicine at Crawford Long Hospital, and later associate dean in charge of students at Emory University School of Medicine;
• Dr. Mark E. Silverman, director of medical education and chief of cardiology at Piedmont Hospital in Atlanta;
• Dr. John H. Stone, associate dean in charge of admissions to Emory University School of Medicine;
• Dr. Larry Tierney, associate chief of medicine at the Veterans Administration Hospital and program director of the house staff at the University of California, San Francisco;
• Dr. H. Kenneth Walker, assistant to the chairman of the Department of Medicine at Emory University, later president of the Emory University Senate, still later Emory's major administrative force in developing a sister medical school in the Republic of Georgia, and chairman of the Board of Regents of the National Library of Medicine;
• Dr. William C. Waters III, chief of medicine at Piedmont Hospital, Atlanta.

Not mentioned, but not forgotten, are the colleagues and trainees who became effective faculty members at other medical schools and teachers at various hospitals all over the nation. Also not mentioned, but not forgotten, are the large number of colleagues and trainees who entered the noble practice of medicine. They are highly respected, and they, too, are viewed as leaders. As stated throughout this book, we need all types of people in the medical profession. The hope is that each individual will excel at what he or she does. Therefore, I state with some pride, that those colleagues and trainees who entered practice achieved a degree of competence that influenced the practice of medicine in a very positive way. Many of them who remained in the Atlanta area became excellent volunteer faculty members, and some of them became great teachers.

Further Contacts with Stead and Beeson

On one occasion, when Stead visited the Department of Medicine at Emory, I projected the picture shown in Figure 5-71 at Grand Rounds at Grady Memorial Hospital. The commentary that accompanied the picture was as follows:

> I discovered the shoes shown in this picture in Old Grady Hospital. Note they are a little large for the one who is wearing them. The shoes belong to Eugene Stead, Emory's first chairman of the Department of Medicine, and the little fellow trying to fit into them is me.

The photograph was actually made in Denver, Colorado, in 1946. The shoes are army boots, and the little fellow wearing the oversized boots is my son, John Hurst Jr. The boots were used to stabilize him in the snow. I was trying to show Stead, and others, how much he was respected, and that his shoes were too large for me.

Stead and Beeson visited Emory at the same time in 1965 (see Figure 5-72). Beeson had just finalized his acceptance to become the Nuffield Professor of Medicine at Oxford in England. He permitted me to make the first public announcement of his plans. After Beeson moved to Oxford, I continued to correspond with him. Knowing that he would not remain there indefinitely, or hoping he would return to the United States sooner than he had originally planned, I wrote him the following letter:

November 19, 1969

Paul B. Beeson, M.D.
Nuffield Professor of Medicine
Oxford, England

Dear Paul:

Would you consider moving back to the States? I would like to explore the possibility of your returning to join the Department of Medicine, Emory University School of Medicine in some capacity. I can't say much more than this at the moment because I would not wish to explore possibilities without your permission. It might just be possible to establish a Distinguished Professorship of some sort. Would you be interested?

As you know, the School has progressed nicely, the Department has grown to full flower and Atlanta is still charming. What are your wishes?

I will have the revised material for the new book in to you soon. The new edition of THE HEART has just come out and when copies are available, I will send you one.

Sincerely,

J. Willis Hurst, M.D.
Professor and Chairman

His response to the above letter is reprinted below.

Nuffield Department of Clinical Medicine,
Radcliffe Infirmary, Oxford

Dr. J. Willis Hurst, Chairman
Department of Medicine
Emory University
69 Butler Street, S.E.
Atlanta, Georgia 30303

November 24, 1969

Dear Willis

It was indeed a warming experience to receive your nice letter of November 19th. Certainly the opportunity to return to Emory and Atlanta has many attractions. The trouble is that I have been here only 4 years and that things move rather slowly in this old university. I have started a few things in the Department of Medicine and I feel committed now to seeing them get started. Barbara too feels that she has laboured hard to establish a home here and that she would like to spend a few years enjoying it. Life in Oxford is very pleasant for both of us. We are indeed grateful to you for the thought.

I'll be delighted to receive a copy of the new edition of "The Heart." I have made use of the first edition on many occasions and have usually been able to find what I wanted, which is my test of whether a book is good. Thank you again for everything.

Yours sincerely,

Paul B. Beeson

I talked often with Stead by telephone and have priceless letters from him. His last visit to the Department of Medicine was in 1982. We were developing geriatrics in the Department of Medicine and needed his advice. We discussed the matter in Charles Hatcher's office in the Emory University Clinic. Stead also talked at Grand Rounds at Grady (see Figure 5-73). We then had an informal luncheon with the house staff. He pointed out the wisdom of incorporating both private and public patients in our house-staff program. I walked with him to the old Grady Memorial Hospital. As we passed in front of the old building, I believe I saw a little moisture collect in his eyes. Later, he talked in the Emory University Hospital auditorium. His talk dealt with his experiences working with elderly patients. As usual, he saw things others had not seen. That night we had dinner with friends who knew him in his early days at Emory, when he was chairman of the Department of Medicine. These included Bruce Logue, Charles Huguley, and Spalding Schroder and our wives. He commented to Dean James Glenn, who was from Duke, that he was pleased to see the chairman of medicine spending so much of his time at Emory University Hospital.

The Last Hurrah

Gene and Evelyn Stead invited my wife, Nelie, and me to spend the weekend of October 5 and 6, 1996, with them in North Carolina. The date of the visit was fifty years after Stead and others wrote the 1946 planning report (see page 90) and forty years after I had spent a night with them in November 1956. At that time, I had needed advice from him as I assumed the chairmanship of the Department of Medicine. Our visit in 1996 coincided with Gene's birthday, the sixth of October. Nelie and I traveled by car from Atlanta to their home, Hanah Lee, on Lake Ker about fifty-five miles from Durham (see Figure 5-74). The Steads had built their home and most of the guest house with their own hands.

Stead and I talked from 2 p.m. to 11 p.m. on the fifth of October and continued the next morning (his eighty-eighth birthday). We talked about medical education, teaching, the delivery of health care, and his views about chemistry. We talked about the people who worked with him at Emory. Paul Beeson's name came up time and time again.

Henry Thoreau had his Walden Pond, but Gene and Evelyn have their Lake Ker. They are both wise and generous. When we parted, I thanked them with my limited vocabulary for all he and Evelyn had done for Emory, the Department of Medicine, and me.

Osler was the most influential American physician during the first half of the twentieth century. Osler, I believe, would pass the baton to Gene

Stead who, in my opinion, became the most influential physician of the second half of the twentieth century.

Secretaries and Business Managers: Without Them We Could Not Function

Every physician knows that he or she can implement very little without the help of dependable and loyal secretaries, administrators, and business managers. Running a developing, growing department of medicine requires the special talents of a large group of secretaries, administrative assistants, and business managers. I was fortunate at the outset. Ruth Strange, an extremely competent "jill-of-all-trades," became the first secretary–administrative assistant–business manager of the department (see page 207 and Figure 5-10). She did it all. Later, Ruth was assisted by Elizabeth Holmes and Kitsy Lester Mostellar. As time passed, many other secretaries assisted her and the faculty members at Grady, the Emory Clinic, and the Veterans Administration Hospital. Mrs. Strange retired in 1971 and died of leukemia in 1973.

Anne Webb joined the department in 1958 (see Figure 5-11). She had formerly worked in the Department of Gynecology and Obstetrics. When Ruth Strange retired in 1971, Anne, an administrative assistant, was placed in charge of the secretarial staff for the Department of Medicine. She knew everyone at Grady and Emory, and that helped enormously. She enjoyed people and kept up with former house officers. Anne remained in that position until 1974, when she retired for a short time. I urged her to return and run our new office in the connector (see page 334) in the new G wing of Emory University Hospital. She remained in that position until she retired in 1987. She was loved by all who knew her. She was of considerable help to Dr. Kokko during his first year as chairman.

When Ruth Strange retired in 1971, I recruited Alex Nelson as the business manager for the department (see Figure 5-75). Alex, a retired army colonel, had managed the logistics for the Third Army. I, therefore, believed he could manage the affairs of the growing Department of Medicine. He was very popular and served us well. Regrettably, he died in 1992 of complications from diabetes.

Ivan Hawkins joined the staff in 1980 (see Figure 5-76). He assisted Ken Walker and me in the administrative duties associated with students and house staff. He served well in this capacity and remained on the staff in the Department of Medicine until 1997.

Carol Miller joined the staff as a secretary in 1964 (see Figure 5-77). She became responsible for the preparation of manuscripts for the department chairman and, as will be seen later, became an essential member of the support staff.

Paula Noriega joined the staff in 1974 (see Figure 5-78). She remained with us for nine years and then returned to her hometown of Wisconsin Rapids. She was an excellent secretary.

The Division of Cardiology became sufficiently large that Jim Griffin was recruited to attend to the business of the division. Likewise, the Division of Hematology and Oncology became sufficiently large that David Bissett was recruited to handle the business of the division. When Alex Nelson retired in 1978 David replaced him (see Figure 5-79). Excellent at his work, he lifted an enormous administrative burden from all of us. Regrettably, he died of amyotrophic lateral sclerosis in 1987. Van Metcalfe was recruited to help Bruce Logue administer the medical section of the Emory Clinic.

Joyce Mundy (see Figure 5-80) joined the staff in 1981 and worked with Anne Webb in my Emory Hospital office. She remained on the staff until 1986.

Billie Hackemeyer joined the staff in 1983 at Grady (see Figure 5-81) and became Dr. Kokko's administrative assistant when he became chairman in 1986.

Over the years, many secretaries have assisted in the activities of the Department of Medicine. Of these, Penny Yeargan remained after 1986.

The secretaries of all the faculty members deserve our gratitude. My Emory Clinic secretaries, Dorothy Todd, Barbara Brown (see Figure 5-82A) and Joyce White (see Figure 5-82B) made my consultative activity a pleasure.

Carol Miller (see Figure 5-77) was the organizer behind the scenes for the manuscripts I produced during my chairmanship. She prepared most of the communication to faculty members, completed most of the forms required to run a department, and prepared manuscripts for my scientific articles and books. Ruth Strange helped with the first two editions of *The Heart*, but Carol was the secretary who helped me with the next five editions of the book. She has kept order and typed the manuscripts for most of the fifty-seven books I have edited and written, as well as most of the 300 articles I have written. She is a tireless worker who types rapidly and loves her work. She continues her typing, editorial, and scheduling role in my office suite on the third floor of the Robert Woodruff Health Sciences Center Library. Now classified as an editor, she has been greatly appreciated. Much that you see would not exist had it not been for her.

To emphasize, we physicians can't do much without competent secretaries and business managers. The department was lucky; there were many competent secretaries and administrative assistants in the department.

The Robert W. Woodruff Health Sciences Center and Its Affiliates

In 1966 the trustees of Emory University wished to honor the University's major benefactor. They assigned the name Woodruff Medical Center to the facilities and affiliated institutions concerned with patient care, education of health professionals, and biomedical research. In 1983, after considerable growth and development, the center was renamed the Robert W. Woodruff Health Sciences Center.

The Robert W. Woodruff Health Sciences Center consists of Emory University School of Medicine, the Nell Hodgson Woodruff School of Nursing, the Rollins School of Public Health, Emory University Hospital, Crawford Long Hospital, and Yerkes Regional Primate Center. The center is affiliated with the Emory Clinic and its numerous satellites, Egleston Children's Hospital at Emory University, Grady Memorial Hospital, Atlanta Veterans Affairs Medical Center, and Wesley Woods Geriatric Center and Research Hospital.

The Emory Campus and Clifton Corridor

This part of the discussion is designed to give the reader a view of the remarkable development on the Emory campus. Almost all of the buildings and developments directly or indirectly had an impact on the Department of Medicine. Further details of each facility are discussed on pages 331–57.

In 1915 the area now located between North Decatur Road and Briarcliff Road was a forest. The land was given to Emory University by Asa Griggs Candler, the first benefactor of the university (see Chapter 1). Suppose, in 1997, you travel east in a car on North Decatur Road until you reach Clifton Road. If you turn left at the traffic light on Clifton Road and drive north on Clifton Road, here is what you see:

The Goizueta Business School is rising on the left, and the Lamar School of Law is on the right. Next, a university residence hall is located on the left, and the Nell Hodgson Woodruff School of Nursing can be seen in the background.

The latest addition to the Emory Clinic is on the right. This new building houses a number of essential facilities (see page 331).

Next, Emory University Hospital is on the left. There have been numerous additions to this building (see page 331). The Ernest W. Woodruff Research Building is attached to Emory University Hospital.

There have also been several additions to this building, the latest completed in 1995 (see page 337).

The original Emory Clinic building, known as the Scarborough Memorial Building, is on the right (see page 338). There have been three additions to this building as well as new parking facilities.

Next on the left are the Anatomy and Physiology Buildings (see page 338). These buildings were completed in 1917. A large new connector joins the Physiology Building with the Anatomy Building and houses several modern classrooms.

On the right is the Psychoanalytic Institute. The building was formerly a dormitory. Next to that building is the Inpatient Psychiatric Center. The next building contains the Emory University Student Health Clinic.

Next on the left is the Robert W. Woodruff Health Sciences Center Administration Building (see page 338), one of the largest administration buildings devoted to the health sciences in the nation.

On the right is the Henrietta Egleston Hospital for Children. There have been two additions to this facility (see page 339). The Center for Rehabilitation Medicine is also located on the right, built where the old Emory University, Georgia, Post Office was located (see page 339).

Now cross the railroad. Passengers no longer stop at the old train station on the left. The station is now a sandwich shop.

Next on the left is the remodeled building that formerly housed the dental school (see page 340). The building is now filled with medical school activities and the Robert W. Woodruff Health Sciences Center Library. This building also houses the offices of Continuing Medical Education. My office suite is located on the third floor of this building.

Just behind the dental school building is the new O. Wayne Rollins Research Center (see page 341), completed in 1990. It houses the Departments of Pharmacology, Physiology, Microbiology, Physics, and Biology. The new facility for the Department of Biochemistry is located underground and was developed as part of the construction of the Grace Crum Rollins Building, which houses the Rollins School of Public Health.

On the right is a university residence hall. Should we turn to the right on Gatewood Road, just north of the student dormitory, and follow the winding road, we would encounter the Emory-Yerkes Primate Research Center, one of the few primate centers in the world (see page 343).

Next on the left (back on Clifton) is the new Rollins School of Public Health (see page 341).

On the right, at 1525 Clifton Road, is the current construction that, when completed, will house primary care physicians of the Emory Clinic. The building will also provide additional space for the Rollins School of

Public Health, the health enhancement program, and the cardiac rehabilitation program (see page 343).

Next on the left are former homes, now used by Emory while waiting for new buildings.

Next on the right is Houston Mill Road, which leads to the Houston Mill House, where faculty, staff, and many others gather for lunch, and where many social events are enjoyed (see page 344).

Next on the right is the building that houses the national offices of the American Cancer Society (see page 344).

Next on the left is the U. S. Centers for Disease Control and Prevention. A large new addition was completed in 1995. This is the largest government-operated health facility outside of Washington D.C. (see page 345).

To the right is the Emory Conference Center Hotel. This excellent facility provides hotel rooms and conference space for postgraduate courses (see page 346). Also to the right is the Emory Inn.

Down the hill on the left we can see several new buildings that house many of the support facilities of the university.

The Wesley Woods Geriatric Center and Wesley Woods Geriatric Research Hospital are on the right (see page 346).

Finally we arrive at Briarcliff Road, where Dusty's Barbecue is located on the left.

Clifton Corridor, one and one-half miles long, was named by President James Laney, who wanted to emphasize that it is a very special road. As time passed, the road became the center of Emory's accelerated forward movement in the health professions. Charles Hatcher, vice president for health affairs, spearheaded the addition of many of the buildings located on this street. As years pass, this road, with all that goes with it, will be a major national resource.

Other Facilities on the Emory Campus

The George S. Woodruff Physical Education Center facility is located in the center of the Emory campus. It houses the Emory cardiac rehabilitation program and health enhancement program which will eventually move to the new building being constructed at 1525 Clifton Road (see page 347).

The Nell Hodgson Woodruff School of Nursing is located west of the Emory University Hospital (see page 348).

Facilities Off the Emory Campus

This section is designed to give the reader a view of the extraordinary developments off the Emory campus. The details are discussed on pages 348–57.

Grady Memorial Hospital

Grady Memorial Hospital's renovation was completed in 1995 at a cost of $336 million (see page 348). William Pinkston began to formulate the plans for the renovation in 1983. The contractual relationship between Emory and Grady continues.

Crawford Long Hospital

Emory-owned Crawford Long Hospital has continued to develop (see page 349). It is now an equal partner to Emory University Hospital.

The Atlanta Veterans Affairs Hospital

By 1997, the Veterans Affairs Medical Center has expanded considerably (see page 355). The planning for the new addition, including the research facility and nursing home, began in the early 1980s. The facility is now one of the best in the nation.

Emory Clinic Satellites

In 1997, there are seventeen Emory Clinic health centers throughout Georgia, and more are planned.

Why These Facilities Are Discussed

One can properly ask why these facilities are discussed in a book that deals primarily with the Department of Medicine of Emory University School of Medicine. There are two reasons.

First, many of these buildings contain research or office space for members of the Department of Medicine. In addition, the people who work in the buildings serve as expert resources for members of the department. Whereas, in 400 B.C., Hippocrates could teach medicine under the plantene tree on the Isle of Cos, today even he would need research space and expert consultants in his effort to develop modern scientific medicine. No sensible department chairman will ever say he or she has adequate research space. I can say that the Department of Medicine, which had no research space on the Emory campus and very little space on the Grady campus in 1957, now has perhaps fifty times the research space it had at that time.

Secondly, this section has been included in the book to emphasize that, during 1957–1986, the Department of Medicine recognized its need to be part of the whole university. This is what Flexner meant in his report on medical schools in the early part of the century.

The developments described on these pages are the result of the 1946 planning report which was initiated by Eugene Stead. His dream has been fulfilled. In 1946 he had the wisdom to see fifty years into the future.

An In-Depth Look at the Facilities that Make Up the Robert W. Woodruff Health Sciences Center and Its Affiliates

Emory Clinic Building B

This building was constructed in 1985 (see Figure 5-83). It houses the Ambulatory Surgery Center, Plastic Surgery, Breast Center, Psychiatry, the Winship Cancer Center, the Emory Eye Center, Neurosurgery, Oral Surgery, and the Infusion Center. Many departments, including the Department of Medicine, supply the faculty for the Winship Cancer Center. Dr. Rein Saral, Director of the Emory Clinic, other administrators of the clinic, and clinic business managers have their offices in this building. Clair Harris and his wife, Reunette, supplied the money to build this addition to the Emory Clinic.

Emory University Hospital

Emory University Hospital was built in stages (see Figures 5-84 through 5-86). The original Wesley Memorial Hospital was located on Courtland Street and Auburn Avenue (see Figure 1-11). In 1915 the Medical College of Atlanta, located across Butler Street from Grady Memorial Hospital, became Emory University School of Medicine. A new Wesley Memorial Hospital was planned by the Emory trustees to be located in the Grady Memorial Hospital area. But Asa Griggs Candler insisted that the hospital should be on the Emory campus, where the Anatomy, Physiology, and Chemistry buildings were located. He provided the money to build the new Wesley Memorial Hospital, which was completed in 1922 and renamed Emory University Hospital in 1932. (See discussion on pages 14–15 and Figure 1-12). It should be pointed out that constructing the Anatomy and Physiology buildings and the new Wesley Memorial Hospital on the Emory campus sparked a controversy that smoldered and blazed intermittently for the next thirty years until Eugene Stead spearheaded the development of the 1946 planning report (see pages 90–93). The controversy continued until 1956 (see Chapter 4). Stated simply, the controversy centered on the question whether Emory

University would allocate its resources to develop its medical school in the Grady Memorial Hospital area or would it develop its school on the Emory campus.

A 1922 photograph of the new Wesley Memorial Hospital on the Emory campus is shown in Figure 1-12. Initially, the hospital was used very little by the School of Medicine, and later it almost closed for lack of patients (see pages 14–15).

The photograph shown in Figure 5-84 was made in 1975. Over the years a large number of architectural changes have been made within the hospital, and several wings have been added. It is not possible to photograph the hospital showing all of these additions. Accordingly, separate photographs are shown to illustrate some of the additions.

In the early forties, Mrs. Lettie Pate Whitehead Evans provided the funds to expand the size of the hospital. Mrs. Evans was the widow of Joseph Brown Whitehead Sr., the original bottler of Coca-Cola. The Whitehead Surgical Pavilion was added to Emory University Hospital in 1946.

The A wing "radiology addition"

This addition was completed in 1966.

The G Wing

By the early seventies it was apparent that there was an inadequate number of hospital beds to meet the needs of the enlarging number of faculty members who had joined the Emory University Clinic. Accordingly, plans were made for the addition of an entirely new, seven-story wing to the hospital. The new wing, completed in 1972, was called the G wing.

Plans for the New G Wing of Emory Hospital

I was asked to determine the needs, and to design rough plans, for the floors assigned to medicine within the G wing of Emory University Hospital. I made the following suggestions, all of which were implemented.

Prior to the new development, the house-staff quarters were located in an area of the hospital that was some distance from the patient located on the medical floor. I believed that the house officers assigned to the medical floors should be quartered near the medical patients. Accordingly, special rooms were designed for them.

I suggested that the nursing station, maintenance areas, administrative offices for nurses, monitoring equipment for patients on the floor, and cubicles for house staff and attending physicians be located between the two rows of patients rooms. There were twenty-four rooms and twenty-eight beds to the area. This plan was duplicated on six floors of the hospital.

I was asked to design a plan for the coronary care units and intensive care units to be located in the new G wing. Accordingly, I developed the plan shown in Figure 5-85. The plan was published in the third edition of *The Heart*. The idea was to design a unit that permitted the family members of sick patients to visit their relatives without entering the inside of the unit. This was accomplished by creating a hall that "wrapped around" the unit. A family member could enter the patient's room from the "wrap-around" hallway, and the nurses and physicians could enter the patient's room from inside the unit. A small family waiting area was designed as part of the entrance from the hallway. Two large waiting areas were to be located at the end of the entire floor on each corner of the "wrap-around" hallway. The nurse's station and monitoring equipment were located in the center of the seven-bed unit. This design was costly but was accepted. It then became apparent that, from an architectural point of view, the same plan would have to be followed on three additional floors of the new G wing.

The physicians at Emory University were beginning to see a number of patients who, for various reasons, needed special arrangements. Some of the reasons such a facility was needed are discussed at the end of this section. I was asked to help design a special suite on the seventh floor of the new G wing. I was familiar with the President's Suite at the U.S. Naval Hospital in Bethesda, Maryland. When Lyndon Johnson was admitted to the Naval Hospital in 1955 with his first myocardial infarction, there was no special suite available. He simply used the entire sixteenth floor of the hospital tower. President Roosevelt, who had had the hospital built, wanted only a few rooms on each floor of the tower. As time passed, a new presidential suite was built. I attended President Johnson in the new suite when he was hospitalized there. The plan I proposed for Emory University Hospital, to a large degree, was similar in concept to the presidential suite in the Bethesda Naval Hospital. The suite in Emory Hospital contained a large bedroom with a hospital bed and adjacent bathroom, a dining room, a sitting room, a kitchen, and several additional bedrooms. The facility was to have adequate windows to view the Atlanta skyline.

The house staff at that time criticized the development of such a suite as pampering prominent and well-known people. They reasoned that the money spent there could be used to help less fortunate people. Whereas such an argument can be made, it does not take into account that government officials and business leaders who are not too ill need to continue some of their important work while in the hospital. Prominent officials from this country and from abroad often have "secret service" men assigned to them. These official agents need a place to stay that is near the person they are protecting. A prominent business person needs a place where his or her staff can continue to work under his or her supervision. A prominent actor needs protection from the public at large. It is amazing how everyone in the hospital, including visitors, finds a need to enter a prominent person's room. In other words, certain people need a protected environment if they are to receive the same private treatment other patients receive. Finally, such a facility is not the place where severely ill patients should be treated; such patients need a specialized intensive-care unit with highly specialized nurses.

The Connector (The F Wing)

Prior to 1972, the Department of Medicine had no administrative offices or research space within Emory University Hospital. As chairman of the department, I had a small office in the original Emory University Clinic building, across Clifton Road from the hospital. This office was used exclusively for consultation with private patients.

Because of the obvious need for space within the hospital, I made repeated pleas that the seven-story connector, to be built between the old part of the hospital and the new seven-story G wing, should be designed for medical school use. There was a great need for administrative offices, including an office for the chairman of the Department of Medicine, an office for the chief resident in medicine, offices and research space for certain faculty members, a large conference room, and space for secretaries. The idea was accepted by Dean Richardson and Mr. Woodruff, who was to finance the entire development. The Department of Medicine was allocated two and one-half floors of the new "connector." The second floor was allocated to the nurses, and the remaining two and one-half floors were allocated to the Department of Surgery. I was asked to draw the initial crude plans for the Department of Medicine. In addition to the administrative offices and teaching facilities described above, I asked Spencer King to design four cardiac catheterization laboratories in the space freed by the addition. I also asked the members of the Pulmonary Division to develop plans for a new pulmonary laboratory. The facility was completed in 1972, and I, as chairman, began to spend half my time there. It rapidly became an active facility, and by the late seventies, I was spending three quarters of my time there.

If Stead's 1946 planning report (see page 90) *can be viewed as the "defining moment" for the medical school, the development of space for the administration offices and teaching facilities within Emory University Hospital was the "defining moment" for the Department of Medicine.*

The A wing "southeast quadrant"

The original emergency clinic was redesigned in 1987. Initially called an *emergency clinic*, it was later called a *treatment room*, and major emergencies went to emergency rooms at other hospitals. In the summer of 1996, the facility was redesigned and operated as a fully developed and open *emergency department*. The business offices of the hospital were then located on the second floor of the A wing just above the emergency clinic.

The bridge

The bridge across Clifton Road connecting Emory University Hospital to the Emory Clinic was constructed in 1987. It provided another safe way, in addition to the tunnel, to walk from the hospital to the clinic.

Plans for the new tower (E wing)

The need for more beds at Emory University Hospital continued. Discussions were underway in 1986 for the addition of an eleven-story tower that would be designated the E wing. The magnificent structure was completed in 1988 (see Figure 5-86). It replaced the portion of the hospital originally called the Lucy Elizabeth Pavilion.

The H wing

The new H wing of Emory University Hospital was completed in 1993 (see Figure 5-86). The office suite of the chairman of the Department of Medicine, a classroom, offices for administrative personnel, the hospital medical library, the General Clinical Research Center, facilities for physical therapy, and the hospital cafeteria were moved into this new space. This permitted the reassignment of the space allocated to the Department of Medicine on the fourth floor of the connector (the F wing). A large new cardiac electrophysiology laboratory was built in the space once allocated to the administrative offices of the Department of Medicine. A large cardiology teaching conference room was also designed for the area. The teaching equipment for the room was given by my generous patients, friends, and colleagues. I am honored that the room is known as the Hurst Conference Room. A larger portion of an adjacent wing of the fourth floor was redesigned as a large echocardiographic laboratory.

Other additions

There were other additions to Emory University Hospital, designed to provide excellent space for the support systems of the hospital.

By the early nineties, the Woodruff suite on the seventh floor of the G wing could not meet the needs of the increasing number of patients who needed such a facility. John W. Rollins Sr. pledged his financial support to the renovation of a floor (6A) in Emory University Hospital. The medical and surgical John W. Rollins Pavilion was badly needed for the hospital to offer businessmen and women, government officials, and others from around the world a facility that permits them, when they were medically able, to carry on their work while being treated for their illnesses. The renovation of 6A was completed in 1995. This unique, six-suite facility provides patients with equipment such as a computer, fax machine, and copier, as well as a chef who can prepare special food for international guests.

Saving auditoriums

Plans were not made initially for an auditorium to be located in the original Emory University Clinic building. I urged such a facility, and the Robert Brown Auditorium was finally included.

When the new G wing was added to Emory University Hospital, the auditorium was eliminated. I studied the plans and pointed out repeatedly that we must have an auditorium. I was then asked to design the auditorium in space not originally allocated for such a purpose. I did so.

Although I was no longer chairman of the Department of Medicine, I had become the "auditorium watcher." So, I again pointed out that the plans for the new tower (E wing) revealed that the auditorium had been eliminated. I was asked again to design an auditorium in space not originally allocated for such a purpose.

Number of beds

As this book is written, Emory University Hospital is licensed for 600 beds, of which 200 are assigned to internal medicine and its subspecialists. Specialized units for renal medicine, digestive diseases, cardiology, pulmonary medicine, etc., are located in the hospital. The hospital is able to handle all types of medical problems.

The Uppergate development (as a "part" of Emory University Hospital)

By 1980 we needed more patient rooms at Emory University Hospital. Robert Brown, director of the Emory Clinic, asked me to serve on a committee that redesigned the building known as Uppergate, located across Clifton Road from the hospital. It was to be operated under the rules governing Emory University Hospital. We redesigned a student dormitory across Clifton Road for ambulatory patients who needed special educational instructions. For example, patients with brittle diabetes could be admitted, treated, and taught about their disease. The dining room of the facility could be converted into a classroom. An adequate employees clinic and the student health facility were also included in the renovated space.

This facility worked well until there was a greater need for other types of patients. Accordingly, the original purpose was gradually discarded. Finally, the psychiatric service of Emory University Hospital moved into the facility.

Faculty at Emory University Hospital and Clinic

The faculty in the Department of Medicine who earned their income by attending private patients had offices in the Emory University Clinic across the street from Emory University Hospital and in the hospital itself. Bruce Logue was chief of medicine at Emory University Hospital and head of the Medical Section in the Emory Clinic from the early fifties until 1980.

When Logue retired, I became chief of medicine at Emory University Hospital and head of the Medical Section in the Emory University Clinic from 1980 to 1986. Spalding Schroder was deputy chief of the Medical Section in the Emory University Clinic from 1980 to 1986.

Ernest W. Woodruff Memorial Research Building

The original Ernest W. Woodruff Memorial Research Building was completed in 1954. There have been three subsequent additions to the building, the last of which was completed in 1995. The original building is shown in Figure 5-87A, and the last addition is shown in Figure 5-87B. The construction of the Robert W. Woodruff Health Sciences Center Administration Building (see Figure 5-90) and the O. Wayne Rollins Research Center (see Figure 5-96), plus the renovation of the old Dental School Building, created space for several basic science departments, the dean's administrative offices, and the medical library to move from the Ernest W. Woodruff Memorial Research Building to the new facilities. These moves, plus the enlargement of the Woodruff Memorial Research Building, provided a large amount of research space for the Department of Medicine within the Woodruff Memorial Research Building.

The research building is connected to Emory University Hospital, making it convenient for faculty members who engage in both patient care and research.

Scarborough Memorial Building (Emory Clinic Building A)

A photograph of the building is shown in Figure 5-99. The original Emory Clinic building is shown in Figure 4-10A. There have been several additions to this building, the last of which was completed in 1987. The last addition was a major redesign, in that the entrance to the clinic was changed from facing Clifton Road to the southern side of the original building (see Figure 5-88). Several new parking decks were built over the years, and valet parking became available.

The Anatomy and Physiology Buildings

The John P. Scott Anatomy Building and the T. T. Fishburne Physiology Building were completed in 1917 (see Figures 5-89A and B). They were the first medical school buildings to be built on the Emory campus. At that time, the medical school shared the chemistry building with the university Chemistry Department.

The Williams Building, which connects the Anatomy and Physiology buildings, was constructed in 1970 (see Figure 5-89C). The connector housed several new classrooms and other facilities.

The Robert W. Woodruff Health Sciences Administration Building

The Robert W. Woodruff Health Sciences Center Administration Building was completed in 1978 (see Figure 5-90). In 1997, this facility, one of the largest of its type in the nation, houses the offices of Dr. Michael M. E. Johns, who is executive vice president for health affairs and director of the Robert W. Woodruff Health Sciences Center, as well as the offices of Dr. Thomas J. Lawley, dean of the School of Medicine; Dr. Claudia Adkison, executive associate dean of the School of Medicine; Dr. John H. Stone, associate dean and director of admissions for the School of Medicine; Dr. Jonas A. Shulman, executive associate dean and director of medical education and student affairs; the medical illustrations part of the Department of Biomedical Media; the Health Sciences News and Information Office; the development office of the medical school; the administrative offices for graduate medical education; a large auditorium; several classrooms; and other facilities.

The plaza level of the building is used for large social gatherings related to affairs of the medical center. A number of beautiful statues of historical figures were provided by Dr. John E. Skandalakis, the Chris Carlos Distinguished Professor and director of the Centers for Surgical Anatomy and Technique of Emory University. One three-story wall of the plaza is adorned with large mosaics by Sirio Tonelli, the famous Italian artist. These mosaics, worth millions of dollars, were provided by the patients of Dr. Skandalakis.

Egleston Children's Hospital Before and After 1959

One might ask why there is a discussion of a children's hospital in this book, which deals with the history of the Department of Medicine. Please see the explanation on page 290. Here it is sufficient to state that there were four areas in which the members of the Department of Medicine were initially asked to contribute their talent and resources to the Department of Pediatrics (see pages 291): cardiology, endocrinology, nephrology, and hematology-oncology. Later, as the Department of Pediatrics "came of age," it developed its own Division of Cardiology, Endocrinology, Nephrology, and Hematology-Oncology.

Henrietta Egleston Hospital was named for Thomas Egleston's mother. Mr. Egleston left a bequest at the time of his death that enabled the trustees, whom he had named, to create a children's hospital. The original hospital, built in 1929, was located on Forrest Avenue. The new hospital, supported by the Woodruff Foundation, was built in 1959 on Clifton Road slightly north of, and across the street from, Emory University Hospital. Although Egleston Hospital is governed by a separate board of trustees, there is a contractual relationship between it and Emory University School of Medicine. The hospital grew in size and now has 235 beds (see Figure 5-91). Dr. Richard Blumberg, chairman of the Department of Pediatrics, and Dr. Joe Patterson, chief of pediatrics at Egleston, offered excellent leadership and created a world-class facility.

The Emory Center for Rehabilitation Medicine

The Emory Center for Rehabilitation Medicine was built in 1976 on Clifton Road, across the street from the Robert W. Woodruff Health Sciences Center Administration Building (see Figure 5-92).

This important facility is discussed here for four reasons. It enabled Emory University to further develop its Department of Rehabilitation. It also served as a source of referrals for members of the Department of Medicine and, equally important, provided a place where patients seen on the medical service at Emory University Hospital could be referred for rehabilitative care. Importantly, the Department of Medicine provided the person who became chairman of the Department of Rehabilitation.

In addition, for quite some time, the Department of Medicine supplied house-staff coverage for emergency events that occurred at the Rehabilitation Hospital.

Dr. Gerald F. Fletcher was made professor and chairman of the Department of Rehabilitation Medicine (see Figure 5-93). He served in that position from February 1986 to February 1995. Dr. Fletcher graduated from Emory University School of Medicine in 1961, then served on the medical house staff at Grady, where he became chief resident in medicine in 1967. He served two years as a cardiac fellow at Emory before entering the United States Navy. He was on the faculty as an assistant professor of medicine at the University of California in San Diego before returning to Atlanta in 1969. By then, I had developed a relationship with Georgia Baptist Medical Center similar to the positions created at Piedmont Hospital and Northside Hospital (see page 294). Fletcher accepted the position at Georgia Baptist, where he served as director of internal medicine from 1969 to 1982 and coordinator of cardiovascular services from 1962 to 1986.

Fletcher was appointed a clinical assistant professor of medicine (cardiology) in 1969, promoted to associate professor of medicine (cardiology) in 1972, and professor of medicine (cardiology) in 1975. He and Dr. John Cantwell developed an excellent cardiac rehabilitation program at Georgia Baptist Medical Center. During his active work at that facility, we rotated thirty cardiology fellows through his program.

Fletcher moved to the Emory campus in 1983 as medical director of the Emory Health Enhancement Program, which he supervised in the new George W. Woodruff Physical Education Center.

Fletcher served as acting chairman of the Department of Rehabilitation from February 1985 to February 1986, at which time he became professor and chairman of the Department of Rehabilitation Medicine and Chief of Service at the Emory Center for Rehabilitation Medicine. He joined the staff of the Mayo Clinic in Jacksonville, Florida, in February, 1995.

During Fletcher's career at Emory, he received many research grants and many awards. He edited ten books, wrote ninety-seven scientific articles, and nineteen book chapters. He was a leader in the national and local Heart Association.

The Robert W. Woodruff Health Sciences Center Library

The Calhoun medical library was originally located in the Physiology Building, then later housed in several different places in Emory University Hospital. The library was moved to the Ernest W. Woodruff Memorial Research Building when the latter was completed in 1954. After the dental school closed in 1988, the Dental School Building was renovated, and the medical library was moved there and renamed the Woodruff Health Sciences Center Library (see Figure 5-94).

The library uses two floors of the old Dental School Building. The pink marble, excellent reading rooms, cubicles, and computers literally compel the students and faculty to spend some time in this excellent facility. A memorial room is dedicated to Dr. Abner Wellborn Calhoun.

The other floors of this five-story building house the Center for Ethics in Public Policy and the Professions, the Department of Genetics, psychologists, the central offices for the Physician Assistant Program, offices for radiation control officials, the Centers for Surgical Anatomy and Technique, offices for Continuing Medical Education, offices of former President James Laney, and my own office suite.

The creation of the Robert W. Woodruff Health Sciences Center Library not only provided space for an excellent library but also made room for additional research space in the Woodruff Memorial Research Building. Accordingly, the Department of Medicine gained more space for research.

The O. Wayne Rollins Research Center and the Rollins School of Public Health

The family members of the late O. Wayne Rollins have vision and care about the community in which they live (see Figure 5-95). Although they shun publicity about their benefactions, this book would be incomplete without recognizing their contribution to Emory University.

O. Wayne Rollins was born in Tunnel Hill, Georgia. He attended a one-room schoolhouse and graduated first in his class from Ringgold High School in 1930. His first job was in the winding room of a Chattanooga cotton mill, where he made fifteen cents an hour.

He married Grace Crum of Ooltewah, Tennessee, when he was eighteen years of age (see Figure 5-95). They had two sons, Randall and Gary, who were destined to work in the Rollins companies.

Having begun his career in Delaware, Rollins moved to Atlanta in 1965. He was a brilliant businessman, whose businesses included a radio station, an extermination company (the Orkin Exterminating Company), television stations, oil and gas services, and security systems. He also invested in real estate in Florida and Georgia.

Rollins split his original company into three parts in 1984. Son Gary became president of Rollins, Inc. Son Randall became chairman and CEO of RPC Energy Services. Since Wayne Rollins's death, Randall has also served as chairman and CEO of Rollins, Inc. John Rollins, Wayne's brother, lives in Delaware, where he is CEO of Rollins Truck Leasing, Inc., Rollins Environmental Services, Inc., and Matlack Systems, Inc.

Wayne Rollins was a trustee and, later, trustee emeritus of Emory University until he died on October 11, 1991, at the age of seventy-nine.

Wayne Rollins saw the need for additional research space for the faculty members of Emory University School of Medicine. He and his family provided the financial resources to build the *O. Wayne Rollins Research Center* (see Figure 5-96). Completed in 1990, the building houses the Departments of Pharmacology, Microbiology, and Biochemistry. It also houses the biology and physics departments of the university. President James T. Laney and Dean Richard Krause determined that it would be useful if some of the science departments of the university and some of the basic science departments of the medical school were housed in the same facility. The space to accomplish this was provided in this new building. The photograph shown in Figure 5-95 was made in April 1990 at the dedication of the building.

This excellent facility not only created the badly needed space for the departments mentioned above but also permitted the designated departments to move out of the Woodruff Memorial Research Building, creating additional research space for the Department of Medicine.

After Mr. Rollins died, Mrs. Rollins and their sons created the O. Wayne Rollins Foundation. Mrs. Rollins and her two sons supported the construction of the eleven-story building to house Emory's new Rollins School of Public Health (see Figure 5-97). The building is named the Grace Crum Rollins Building.

The leadership of the Department of Preventive Medicine, chaired by Dr. Thomas Sellers, the nearness of the Centers for Disease Control and Prevention (CDC), and the administrative skill of Dr. Charles Hatcher were combined to spearhead the creation of the Emory School of Public Health. The Rollins family enthusiastically financed the building now named for Grace Crum Rollins and completed in 1994.

The roots for creation of the School of Public Health go back to 1959, when Sellers joined the Department of Medicine. His father was head of the Georgia State Health Department. Sellers became the Director of the Division of Infectious Diseases in the Department of Medicine when Charles LeMaistre moved from that position to become Emory's first chairman of the new Department of Preventive Medicine and Community Health. Sellers later followed LeMaistre as chairman of that department. His relationship to the CDC and his vision undoubtedly planted the seeds from which grew the Rollins School of Public Health. Sellers recalls that Dean Richardson talked to him at the time he became professor and chairman of the Department of Preventive Medicine and Community Health in 1960 about his dreams for a future that would include a School of Public Health in which there was a growing relationship with the Communicable Disease Center.

It should also be noted that the Rollins family's philanthropy includes John W. Rollins's support of the development of the John W. Rollins

Pavilion in Emory University Hospital. See page 336 for a discussion of this unique facility.

The Division of Infectious Diseases of the Department of Medicine, headed by Dr. David Stephens, has developed a close working relationship with the new school. The faculty members of the Rollins School of Public Health serve as a great resource for the members of the Division of Infectious Diseases as well as other divisions. In addition, several members of the Department of Medicine hold joint appointments in the Rollins School of Public Health.

Yerkes Regional Primate Center

Dr. Robert W. Yerkes, a professor of psychobiology at Yale University, created a primate center at Yale in 1930. The laboratory was developed with the financial support of the Rockefeller and Carnegie Foundations and Yale University. Yerkes was convinced that the study of primates would enhance our knowledge of human behavior. When he retired at Yale in 1941, Yale honored him by naming the center the Yerkes Laboratory of Primate Biology. Much of the work was done in laboratories in Orange Park, Florida, where most of the primates were housed.

When Yerkes died in 1956, Yale decided that the distance between the university, in Connecticut, and Orange Park, Florida, was so great that it interfered with the development of an excellent research program. So in 1956, Emory University assumed the administrative responsibility and full ownership of the Orange Park, Florida, facilities. In 1960, the National Institutes of Health developed the Regional Primate Research Centers Program. This program eventually provided funds to move the Orange Park laboratories to Emory University in 1965.

This unique, highly respected facility is an enormous asset to Emory University School of Medicine and its Department of Medicine (see Figures 5-98A and B). Research in endocrine problems, atherosclerosis, AIDS, Parkinson Disease, and other unsolved problems is carried out in this facility.

Future Site for a Building Devoted to Primary Care

By the late eighties it was clear that the Emory Clinic needed to emphasize primary care more than it had previously. The clinic leaders determined that patients could be seen in the Emory Clinic without referrals from other physicians. This decision was influenced by changes occurring in the practice of medicine throughout the nation. In addition, the leaders in the medical school recognized that the house officer programs should encourage medical school graduates to enter the profession of primary care.

As time passed, the Emory Clinic developed satellite clinics in which to deliver primary care. By the early nineties, it seemed wise to develop a facility on the Emory campus that would be filled with clinicians devoted to providing primary and preventive medical care. As this book is written in 1997, the new building is nearing completion (see Figure 5-99).

The new building will house the primary care physicians of the Emory Clinic who are on the Emory campus, additional space for the Rollins School of Public Health, a new auditorium, a demonstration kitchen for nutrition education, a faculty fitness center, and a cardiac rehabilitation center. The facility should become a superb training center for primary care physicians who deliver outpatient care.

Houston Mill House

This historic house was purchased by Emory University in 1959 (see Figure 5-100). The Emory Women's Club restored the house in 1970. The house and grounds are used as a gathering place for Emory faculty, Emory staff, and the Atlanta community. During lunch, which is superb, one may see the president of the University, the vice president for Health Affairs, the dean, or the spouses of colleagues.

This facility was commonly used by the Department of Medicine for "first of the year parties," Christmas parties, special lectures, and occasional weddings.

The house was named for Major Washington Jackson Houston who owned the land in 1860. He built a gristmill on the property but later converted it into a hydroelectric plant. The land was purchased by Harry J. Carr in 1920. Mr. Carr built the beautiful stone house and restored the old mill.

Houston Mill House has, over the years, produced much "togetherness."

The American Cancer Society Home Office

The American Cancer Society moved its national headquarters to a new building on Clifton Road, on land provided by the Woodruff Foundation, in 1989 (see Figure 5-101). Charles Hatcher, who was then vice president of health affairs, deserves much credit for spearheading this development. Although the facility is not officially affiliated with Emory University, the nearness of the facility makes easy access to information regarding cancer that would not otherwise be readily available.

The facility is of considerable help to members of the Division of Hematology and Oncology within the Department of Medicine.

The Centers for Disease Control and Prevention (CDC)

The initials, CDC, originally meant *Communicable Disease Center*. Later, the letters were used to designate the *Centers for Disease Control*. Still later the words—*and Prevention*—were added. A photograph of the building is shown in Figures 5-102A and 5-102B.

The story begins in the thirties, when Robert W. Woodruff was trying to rid Baker County of malaria. He pulled together experts from Emory, the Georgia state government, and the federal government to create the Malaria Field Station in Baker County. Woodruff undoubtedly financed a great deal of the effort. The strategy was successful. It may be assumed that Dr. Glenville Giddings did much of the legwork required to create the Malaria Field Station since he was the liaison between Woodruff and the medical school in other matters, including the testing of the safety of Coca-Cola.

In 1946, the Public Health Service announced that it intended to build a research facility for the study of communicable diseases. Woodruff discussed the matter with Georgia's U.S. senators, Walter George and Richard Russell. Later, Woodruff, who was a Democrat, became friends with President Eisenhower. Eisenhower visited Woodruff at Ichauway, and Woodruff visited Eisenhower at the White House. So, in due time, Woodruff discussed the creation of the CDC with Eisenhower, and in 1960 the federal government announced it would build the facility in Atlanta. Woodruff had given a plot of land on Clifton Road to Emory University for a development that did not take place. This land was then offered to the federal government as the site for the CDC. Boisfeuillet Jones, then working in the Kennedy Administration, was a major mover in bringing the CDC to Clifton Road. The building was completed in 1960, and Lady Bird Johnson dedicated it. She also gave a talk in the Glenn Memorial Church.

The original building did not offer sufficient space for the growing needs of the CDC. The most recent addition to the building was completed in 1996 (see Figure 5-102B). The CDC is the largest federal health facility outside the Washington, D.C., area.

Many of the very competent people who worked at the CDC over the years were given volunteer faculty appointments in the Department of Medicine. They contributed their talent to the educational program at Grady Memorial Hospital and served as a great resource to the members of the Division of Infectious Diseases. Many of them later joined the Department of Medicine in the Division of Infectious Diseases. As an historical matter, we should not forget that in 1957 a branch of the CDC was actually located on the Grady campus, in the former Grady Clay Eye Clinic building. Dr. Jerry Cooper was the leader of the group of workers located there, and Dr. John Galambos was also assigned to that facility. Later, Dr. Sumner Thompson of the CDC, was assigned to work at Grady Hospital in the Division of Infectious Diseases (see page 276). He was a very effective and respected member of the Department of Medicine. Regrettably, he died of a brain tumor in 1995.

The National Audiovisual Center was originally located at the CDC. Dr. James Leiberman was a major mover in assisting the Departments of Medicine and Radiology develop the closed-circuit television system that transmitted medical programs from the Grady auditorium to hospitals within a twenty-five mile radius. This development was the first of its kind. People came from distant places to observe the technology.

The proximity of the CDC to Emory, plus the vision of Thomas Sellers and the leadership of Charles Hatcher, undoubtedly encouraged the discussions that led to the creation of the very successful Rollins School of Public Health.

The New Emory Conference Center and Hotel

The need for an Emory hotel and conference center was recognized in the seventies. By then, the growth of Emory's Postgraduate Educational Programs, plus the needs of the numerous visitors who came to the Centers for Disease Control and Prevention, greatly increased the need for a first-class hotel and conference center. This need was gradually appreciated by officials of the the university. Land was available, and plans were drawn in the late eighties. Because the initial plans were unacceptable to the community (the building's height would spoil the view of the beautiful woods), new plans were drawn and the building was completed in 1994 (see Figure 5-103).

There are 198 hotel rooms in the facility and 20,000 square feet of meeting rooms. The teaching aids in the facility are classified as the most modern, and many postgraduate teaching programs are presented there.

Wesley Woods Geriatric Center and Research Hospital

Wesley Woods, a beautiful geriatric center, became closely affiliated with Emory University in 1985 (see Figures 5-104A). Robert Woodruff supported the development of the facility. Dr. Hugh Wood, former dean of the School of Medicine, was the medical director from 1966 to 1980 and was followed by Dr. Robert Brown (1980 to 1983), Dr. Herbert Karp (1983 to 1991), Dr. Donald E. Manning (1991 to February 1996), and Dr. Larry Tune (March 1996).

Wesley Woods, along with the new geriatric facility at the Veterans Administration Hospital, provided an ideal environment for the development of the Division of Geriatrics in the Department of Medicine (see page 269). In 1983, Dr. Karp became the first director of the Division of Geriatrics in the Department of Medicine. The first medical house officers rotated through these facilities in 1986. The number of medical house officers who rotated through the facilities increased under Karp's direction and the Division of Geriatrics became more formalized. Later, in 1990, Dr. Mario DiGirolamo became the director of the division.

The hundred-bed Geriatric Research Hospital at Wesley Woods was constructed in 1986 (see Figure 5-104B). This enlarged the service and educational opportunities for the development of geriatrics.

The George W. Woodruff Physical Education Center

George W. Woodruff (see Figure 1-22) supplied the funds to create the new Physical Education Center, which replaced the old Emory "field house" in 1983 (see Figure 5-105). The new facility was also designed to house a Health Enhancement Program and Cardiac Rehabilitation Program.

Dr. Gerald F. Fletcher, a member of the Department of Medicine and director of internal medicine at the Georgia Baptist Medical Center, moved to the Emory campus to direct the programs.

Barbara Fletcher, who graduated from the University of South Carolina School of Nursing in 1967 and obtained a master's degree in teaching from the Nell Hodgson Woodruff School of Nursing at Emory in 1972, played a major role in the development of the Health Enhancement Program and Cardiac Rehabilitation Program at the George W. Woodruff Physical Education Center. She was nationally known through her work with the American Heart Association and was another example of the splendid cooperation that existed between Emory nurses and the Department of Medicine. She wrote many scientific articles and patient-directed pamphlets; some of them were written with Julia Purcell and Suzanne Cambre. Their pamphlet on the education of patients following myocardial infarction, *Heart Attack, What Now*, was published by the Georgia chapter of the American Heart Association and has sold over a hundred thousand copies a year in English and Spanish editions, earning large royalties for the Heart Association.

The Nell Hodgson Woodruff School of Nursing

The building for the Nell Hodgson Woodruff School of Nursing was dedicated in 1968 (see Figure 5-106). As I've already stated, no department of medicine can be successful without the help of numerous capable nurses. Accordingly, although indirectly, the Nell Hodgson Woodruff School of Nursing plays an important role in the development and function of the Department of Medicine.

Nell Hodgson Woodruff, the wife of Robert Woodruff, devoted her life to helping others. Doris Lockerman Kennedy wrote of her:

> From this silken cocoon of comfort, she deliberately reached into life-and-death crises in the lives of others, where neither wealth nor rank could match her practical gift for gentle and skillful nurturing. Her compassion was never general; it was always focused and personal.[15]

Robert Woodruff considered "Miss Nellie" a partner. When she died of a cerebral hemorrhage on January 22, 1968, his "partner" was gone, and he never recovered from the loss.

The School of Nursing offers the Bachelor of Science in Nursing degree and the Master of Science degree in the following categories: adult health, advanced nursing practice, community-based nurse practitioners, nurse midwifery, pediatric advanced nursing practice, perinatal-neonatal advanced nursing practice, and patient services administration. The superb faculty has earned an excellent national reputation, and the school is a vital part of the Robert W. Woodruff Health Sciences Center.

The Renovation and Expansion of Grady Hospital

In 1982, William Pinkston, Superintendent of Grady Hospital, began to develop plans for the renovation and expansion of Grady Hospital. Dr. Asa Yancey, who was medical director of Grady Memorial Hospital and associate dean of Emory University School of Medicine, ably represented the medical staff in the planning. Although the hospital was only twenty-five years old, certain parts of the facility were very much out-of-date.

The renovation and expansion of the hospital was expected to cost $69 million. The plans were approved by the Fulton-DeKalb Hospital Authority in 1988, and construction nearing completion in 1995 had reached $336 million (see Figure 5-107).

As of 1997, Emory owns the Henry Woodruff Research Extension Building (the old Gray building) on the Grady campus, as well as the land at the corner of Butler and Armstrong streets where the entire

---

[15] D. L. Kennedy, *Devotedly Miss Nellie* (Atlanta: Emory University, 1982), viii.

Emory School of Medicine was located in 1915. Emory has the use of the Glenn Building and leases the Steiner Building for the use of certain faculty members and for an extra auditorium. Emory also leases space in the United Way Building and is allowed to use space in Feebeck Hall.

In 1997, Emory has a contractual relationship with Grady Memorial Hospital to continue the supervision of certain aspects of patient care. In turn, Grady Memorial Hospital is used as a teaching hospital where certain parts of the educational programs for Emory University medical students, house officers, and fellows are implemented. Unlike in the forties, Emory University Hospital and the Emory Clinic, the Veterans Administration Hospital, and Crawford Long Hospital are used extensively by Emory for the implementation of the educational programs in internal medicine and its subspecialties.

The members of the Department of Medicine located at Grady Memorial Hospital are listed in the discussion that deals with the evolution of the divisions (see pages 240–89). It should be emphasized, however, that faculty members from Emory Hospital and the Emory Clinic, the Atlanta Veterans Administration Hospital, and Crawford Long Hospital are also assigned teaching duties at Grady Memorial Hospital.

Grady Memorial Hospital has been a great asset to Emory University School of Medicine for more than eighty years. Now with its satellite clinics, it continues to be a sorely needed facility for patients who cannot afford private medical care. Great skill will be needed to assure the continued status of the hospital, currently considered to be one of the best of its kind in the nation.

Crawford Long Hospital Before and After 1965

Crawford Long Hospital (see Figure 5-108) was originally named the Davis-Fischer Sanitorium because, in 1908, Drs. E. Campbell Davis and Luther C. Fischer built it for their own patients (Figures 5-109A and B). The hospital was built on Crew Street but moved to 35 Linden Avenue in 1911. An architectural design was used that would allow the hospital to be converted into apartments, because many people believed that a hospital built in the suburbs would fail. A second building, called the B Building, was constructed in 1919, and the Woodruff Building was added in 1945. In 1959, all three structures were brought together by a building that contained the kitchen, dining room, radiology department, and clinical laboratories. The Peachtree Building was added in 1971.

Mrs. Cora Williams, who had served as president of the Georgia, Florida, and Alabama Railroad, established the Jesse Parker Williams Hospital in memory of her husband. Under the terms of her will, the hospital was to provide care for children under the age of twelve and women when their private funds were exhausted. Although she died in 1924, the estate was not settled until 1940. The hospital was built adjacent to Crawford Long Hospital, and arrangements were made for Crawford Long Hospital to provide all support services (nursing, dietary, operating rooms, laundry, laboratory, etc.). When the new Peachtree Building was constructed at Crawford Long Hospital in 1971, the old Jesse Parker Williams Hospital was absorbed into Crawford Long Hospital and became the Jesse Parker Williams Pavilion, providing equal patient capacity as the former hospital.

Dr. E. C. Davis taught at the medical schools that preceded Emory University School of Medicine. Dr. Fischer's great desire was to help patients who were less fortunate than others. I had the following personal experience.

My wife's sister was admitted to Crawford W. Long Hospital in 1947. She had severe brain damage incurred in an automobile wreck. Several weeks passed. I literally lived in her room and nursed her along with private duty nurses. Dr. Fischer called me and her husband to his office and, though we had not asked for it, indicated that he planned to discount her hospital bill. He was a compassionate man. He also revealed that he brought fresh vegetables from his farm to the hospital kitchen so the patients could have excellent food.

Why the Name of the Hospital Was Changed

The name of the hospital was changed to the Crawford W. Long Memorial Hospital in 1932. A prominent surgeon, Dr. Frank K. Boland, documented the evidence that Dr. Crawford W. Long, of Jefferson, Georgia, was the first to use ether as an anesthetic agent. This led to the creation of the statue of Long in the Hall of Fame in Washington, D.C. Dr. Boland spearheaded the movement to change the name of the hospital to honor Crawford W. Long. The Crawford W. Long Museum is located in the hospital.

Dr. Fischer gave the hospital and land to Emory University in 1939. The plan was for the hospital to be governed by a board, which was headed by Dr. Fischer until he died. He stipulated that the hospital should be a teaching hospital for patients of modest financial status.

When Dr. Fischer died in 1953, the governance of the hospital became the responsibility of Emory University. Dr. Wadley Glenn, who had been associate director of the hospital and a member of the Emory Board of Trustees, became the medical director of the hospital (see Figure 5-110). Emory medical students were not assigned there, and there was a separate house-staff program.

During recent years the hospital has been referred to as Crawford Long Hospital of Emory University; the "W." has been eliminated!

Emory Given a Leadership Role at Crawford Long Hospital in 1963
     In 1963, Dean Richardson informed the department chairmen at Emory that the board of trustees had requested that the medical school take over the leadership role in the development of Crawford Long Hospital. I promptly recruited Dr. Harold Ramos to be chief of medicine and director of medical education (see Figure 5-111). He performed well, and in time replaced Dr. Glenn as medical director of the hospital. In 1965, as Emory began to assume a greater leadership role at the hospital, some of the community physicians who used the hospital became concerned that Emory would close the staff to them as Emory had done more than a decade earlier at Emory University Hospital. I met with the medical staff and assured them that as long as I was chairman of the Department of Medicine, excellent, qualified, community physicians would be welcome at Crawford Long Hospital. Emory Clinic physicians would work there, too, but the majority of physicians on the staff would be community physicians. I pointed out that, together, we could create a facility like Barnes Hospital in St. Louis. Community physicians would continue to teach, and their patients would have access to a constantly improving hospital. Dr. Linton Bishop, an Emory medical school graduate and former house officer and cardiac fellow, was enormously helpful in the development (see Figure 5-112). He was a highly respected member of the hospital staff, and when he assured the community physicians that they would not be crowded out of the hospital, their apprehension subsided. As chairman, I had a rule: I did not appoint anyone to the full-time Emory medical staff at Crawford Long Hospital unless Linton Bishop indicated such an individual was needed. Bishop was later appointed to the Emory University Board of Trustees.
     A few members of the Emory faculty were apprehensive about the development, because they thought that Crawford Long Hospital activities would dilute efforts at Emory University Hospital. As time passed, their fear subsided, and those who were initially concerned became vigorous supporters of the development.

Unifying the House-staff Program
     In 1973, the separate house-staff program in medicine at Crawford Long Hospital was discontinued, and the house staff became part of the Emory University Affiliated Hospitals Program in Medicine, which had been created in 1972. As time passed, Crawford Long Hospital gained prominence as an excellent teaching hospital. During the formative years

of the development I had one teaching session each week at Crawford Long Hospital. Now in 1997, I have a teaching session every other week at Crawford Long Hospital.

The development of Crawford Long Hospital gave the Department of Medicine a sense of security, because if anything should happen to the governance of Grady Memorial Hospital or the Veterans Administration Hospital, we now owned and operated two excellent private hospitals—Crawford Long Hospital, licensed for 590 beds (of which about 200 beds were allocated to the medical service), and Emory University Hospital, licensed for 600 beds (of which 200 were allocated to the medical service). If need be, they could serve our needs for students and house staff.

The Creation of the Carlyle Fraser Heart Center

Linton Bishop became the physician and friend of Mr. and Mrs. Carlyle Fraser (see Figures 5-113A and B). Isabel Fraser was a native of Canada, and Carlyle was from upper New York state. They became outstanding citizens of Atlanta. Carlyle Fraser founded the Genuine Parts Company and, by his leadership and business acumen, brought it through the Great Depression to become the largest auto replacement parts company in America. He later served as Fulton County Commissioner and supported Grady Memorial Hospital. He stood strong for progressive, honest government. Isabel Fraser, a nurse, was especially sensitive to medical needs and advocated modern, effective, compassionate health care. Carlyle Fraser died of a myocardial infarction in 1961. In 1973, Isabel Fraser, with advice from her attorney and friend Alex Gaines, and with the support of her children, Nancy Fraser Parker and Richard Fraser, made a substantial gift to establish the Carlyle Fraser Heart Center.

As the Heart Center continued to develop, it attracted generous support from employees of Genuine Parts Company and the Frasers' friends and associates. Outstanding among them were Mrs. Lyman Mauldin, Mrs. Jack Echlin, and Wilton Looney, chairman emeritus of the Genuine Parts Company.

In order to plan the Heart Center, Dr. Wadley Glenn asked for guidance from Drs. Arthur Richardson, Robert Schlant, Dean Warren, Charles Hatcher, Harold Ramos, Linton Bishop, Mr. Dan Barker, and me. We met at breakfast on several occasions and developed a plan that entailed the addition of cardiac catheterization laboratories, cardiac surgical intensive care units, office space, and research laboratories. Cardiology, pulmonary medicine, and cardiac surgery were to be involved. The Carlyle Fraser Heart Center became a reality in 1976, and

Wadley Glenn was named the center's first medical director (see Figure 5-110). I appointed Dr. Arthur Merrill Jr. to direct the cardiac catheterization laboratory, and Drs. Joseph Miller and Joe Craver were recruited by Dr. Charles Hatcher to perform the cardiac surgery. Dr. Doug Morris and Dr. John Hurst Jr. joined the cardiology faculty at Crawford Long Hospital in 1977.

Dr. Byron Williams joined the cardiology staff in nuclear cardiology in 1977. As a cardiac fellow at Emory, he was allowed to study with Barry Zaret at Yale for six months in order to receive additional training in nuclear medicine. Dr. Williams entered the practice of cardiology at St. Joseph's Hospital in 1984 but was asked to rejoin the Emory faculty in 1994. Drs. Henry Liberman and Louis Battey were added to the staff in cardiology. Dr. Randolph Patterson, an Emory graduate who had done outstanding research at the National Heart, Lung and Blood Institute, was also added to the staff. He has become one of the nation's experts in nuclear cardiology.

In keeping with the high standards of the Fraser family, the Heart Center, under the supervision of its own board of directors and the Cardiology Division of Emory University School of Medicine, has attained a strong national reputation and has maintained an excellence that enabled it to attract and support the best clinicians and researchers in both medicine and surgery.

Arthur Merrill Jr. decided to enter practice at Piedmont Hospital in 1978, as did John Hurst. I appointed Dr. Douglas Morris to assume the responsibility of directing the cardiac catheterization laboratory in 1978. He had trained with us, and I recognized his talent. I wanted to keep him on the faculty. His performance as director of the cardiac catheterization laboratory was outstanding.

When Bruce Logue retired from his duties on the Emory campus in 1980, he became director of the Carlyle Fraser Heart Center. His skill and wisdom added significantly to the further development of the Heart Center.

Robert Guyton joined the cardiac surgical staff in 1980. He later became director of the Division of Cardiac Surgery at Emory University but retained his patient care and research base at Crawford Long Hospital. John Gott joined him at Crawford Long Hospital in 1992.

The Carlyle Fraser Heart Center continued to thrive under Logue's direction. When he retired in 1990, Douglas Morris was appointed to the position as the director of the center. Once again, Morris performed extremely well.

Drs. Andrew Taussig and Hall Whitworth joined the faculty and contributed significantly for a few years but eventually entered practice in

Orlando, Florida. Dr. André Churchwell joined the faculty and was a great asset but decided to return to his hometown of Nashville, Tennessee.

Douglas Morris became director of the new Emory Heart Center in 1994, while continuing as director of the Carlyle Fraser Heart Center (see Figure 5-114). My prediction, made in 1978, was realized; Morris was destined to be a leader. Dr. Byron Williams, who missed his contact with house staff and fellows, was asked to rejoin the faculty in 1994 and was named chief of cardiology at Crawford Long Hospital.

Before Isabel Fraser's death, she made another substantial gift to Crawford Long, instructing Linton Bishop to decide how it would be used. He decided to establish and endow the Martha West Looney Chair in Medicine at Crawford Long Hospital honoring the wife of Wilton Looney. Dr. Roland Ingram is the first Martha West Looney Professor of Medicine. The Isabel Fraser Outpatient Center at Crawford Long was named in recognition of Mrs. Fraser's generosity to the hospital.

Other Developments at Crawford Long Hospital

Drs. Gilbert Grossman and Gerald Staton were appointed to develop pulmonary medicine at Crawford Long Hospital, and Dr. Tuncer Someren was appointed to develop renal medicine and renal dialysis.

When Dr. Ramos replaced Dr. Glenn as director of the hospital in 1985, I was asked to appoint a new chief of medicine. The appointment went to Jonas (Jack) Shulman, an infectious disease expert who gave up his position as director of the Division of Infectious Diseases in the Department of Medicine. He was widely acclaimed as a very talented and personable chief. He contributed significantly to an environment of excellence. Later, Drs. James Steinberg and Phyllis Kozarsky joined him.

Dr. R. Carter Davis Jr., a member of the clinical volunteer faculty, developed an excellent gastrointestinal service.

The Emory Departments of Surgery and Obstetrics also developed at Crawford Long Hospital.

A New Office Building at Crawford Long Hospital

A new eight-story office building was added at 25 Prescott Street in 1971. It housed radiation therapy, the library, a 200-seat auditorium, an Emory Clinic business office, and five stories of office space. It is appropriately named the Agnes Raoul Glenn Building in honor of the mother of Dr. Wadley and Mr. Wilbur Glenn, whose generous gift made the building possible.

Excellent Administrative Leadership

Crawford Long Hospital has been blessed with excellent hospital administrators. Dan Barker was one of them (see Figure 5-112). In 1984, he became the overall director of Emory University Hospital and Crawford Long Hospital. Paul Hoffmann was the administrator at Emory University Hospital, and John Henry became the hospital administrator of Crawford Long Hospital. John Henry was outstanding and was destined to follow Dan Barker as the overall administrator for Emory University Hospital and Crawford Long Hospital (see Figure 5-115). Barker and Henry deserve considerable credit for the smooth development of Crawford Long Hospital.

We Are Grateful To –

Wadley Glenn died April 2, 1985. He was a quiet, effective, benevolent member of the Emory Board of Trustees, who gave his money and himself to Crawford Long Hospital. The Woodruff Foundation supported many aspects of the development, and the Carlyle Fraser family contributed mightily to making the hospital an outstanding Emory-owned facility. Wilton Looney was always by the Frasers' side. He, too, with his wife, deserves much credit for the financial support of Crawford Long Hospital.

The Atlanta Veterans Affairs Medical Center

The need for the nation to provide medical care for veterans was recognized in 1811, when the Naval Home was established in Philadelphia. The Soldiers Home was established in 1853 and St. Elizabeth's Hospital in 1855, both in Washington, D.C.

In 1865, President Abraham Lincoln asked Congress "to care for him who shall have borne battle and for his widow, and his orphan." This led to the development of individual homes for sick, disabled, and poor veterans. In 1920 the medical care delivered to veterans was accredited. The Veterans Administration itself was created by President Herbert Hoover in 1930.

The veterans facilities gradually evolved into a national network of hospitals. At the end of World War II, Major General Paul Lawley urged that veterans hospitals should align themselves with medical schools whenever it was possible to do so. This gave birth to dean's committees that became the liaison between the veterans hospitals and the associated medical schools.

The early days of the Veterans Administration Hospital and its relationship to Emory University School of Medicine are discussed in Chapter 4 of this book. In 1960, the plan for a new hospital was approved in Washington. It was mutually advantageous to Emory University and the Atlanta Veterans Hospital for the new hospital to be built near Emory University School of Medicine and Emory University Hospital. I lost two battles in this development. I urged that the new hospital be built as near the Emory University Hospital as possible, in order to interrelate the house-staff coverage and teaching conferences. Instead, the hospital was built two miles away from Emory University Hospital on land bought from Emory University. I was asked, along with the chairman of surgery, to help plan the hospital. I recommended an adequate number of conference rooms, offices for physicians, and adequate research space, all of which were inadequate in the new Grady Hospital. But, my suggestions were not heeded, so when the hospital was built, it was necessary to use a few of the patients' rooms for physicians' offices.

The new hospital, completed in June 1966, was a magnificent twelve-story structure with 550 beds (see Figure 5-116A). Two hundred and thirty beds were allocated to the medical service.

Dr. James Crutcher was chief of the medical service from 1957 until 1974. He was an excellent chief and was highly respected by the medical house staff. He then became associate chief of staff for education. He held that post until 1978, when he was appointed chief medical director of the Veterans Administration in Washington (see Figure 5-116B).

I selected Dr. Joseph Hardison as the new chief of Medicine (see Figure 5-28). Joe graduated from Emory University School of Medicine and had his house-staff training in the Emory-Veterans Administration Hospital program. He is a superb clinician and bedside teacher. He enjoyed working with students and house staff, and they enjoyed working with him. He never tired of his work with students, and in 1996 the students gave him a "teaching award." His thoughtful essays appeared regularly in the *Journal of the American Medical Association*. As chief, he ran an excellent medical service at the Veterans Hospital.

Dr. John Preedy gave up the directorship of the Division of Endocrinology and became the director of research at the Veterans Administration Hospital. In 1982, a badly needed geriatric facility was added to the Veterans Hospital complex. Dr. Hardison was chosen to be Director of this facility. By 1986, when I left the chairmanship, plans were underway for a new research and patient care building. The new building was completed in 1994 (see Figure 5-117).

The Emory Hospital-Veterans Hospital house-staff program was in effect until 1972, when the single, unified Emory University Affiliated Hospitals Program was instituted.

As chairman, I presented a weekly conference at the Veterans Hospital for many years. In 1997, I present one conference there each month.

The members of the Department of Medicine located at the Atlanta Veterans Affairs Hospital in 1986 are listed in the discussion that deals with the Evolution of the Divisions (see pages 240–89).

Over the years, the Atlanta Veterans Administration Hospital has been an enormous asset to the Department of Medicine.

Notes from the Annual Reports
Including a Discussion of the Evolution
of the House-Staff and Fellowship Programs

The president of the University requires that the dean of the School of Medicine submit an annual report that summarizes the activity of the medical school. In order to accomplish this, the dean requests that each department chairman submit to him an annual report that summarizes the activity of the department he or she chairs. I reviewed the annual reports that I prepared. Five reports are missing from the archives, and Dean Richardson did not request a report in 1962–63. My annual reports were 20 to 200 pages long. Accordingly, they cannot be reproduced in their entirety here. In each report, I discussed how we were improving the teaching programs, the research being done, the dire need for more research space, and the appointments and resignations of faculty members. The names of the full-time faculty members, volunteer faculty members, and fellows were listed in the bulletins of the Emory University School of Medicine. The portions of the annual bulletins that are related to the subject are reproduced in Appendixes 8 through 53.

The following paragraphs from three of the annual reports are reproduced because the comments are germane to the description of the department in 1957–58 and to the plans I made prior to relinquishing the chairmanship of the Department of Medicine in 1986.

June 1, 1957–May 31, 1958

The table of organization for the Department of Medicine has been completed. The Department is divided into eight sections and each section has one or more senior members participating in research, teaching and patient care. Fellowship programs are developing in each of these sections. This approach to organization has been very satisfactory. The Department of Medicine is composed of a group of men who stimulate each other and stimulate medical students.

As of September 1, 1958, there were twenty-two (22) full-time members of the Department of Medicine,[16] four (4) part-time members and one hundred

---

[16] Actually, there were only fourteen *active* full-time faculty members.

seventy-four (174) volunteer members, making a total of two hundred (200) members.

June 1, 1984–May 31, 1985

I notified Dean Krause that I will relinquish the Chairmanship of Medicine in August 1986. I will remain Candler Professor of Medicine until 1991. I will continue to render cardiac consultations, teach, and write *The Heart, Medicine for the Practicing Physician,* and begin the *Emory University Journal of Medicine.* By August 1986 I will have been chairman almost 30 years. It has been rewarding and satisfying to be a part of Emory during this period. The school and department are widely acclaimed for the excellence it stands for. I look forward to the years ahead with excitement and will assist the new Chairman in any way he or she wishes. I will turn over to him or her a faculty of 140+, a program of excellent teaching and patient care and the increasing effort in research. Noteworthy is that, through my efforts and those of certain members in the department, I will turn over to the new chairman five unfilled endowed chairs, two endowed by one-half and three additional ones that are highly likely. My dream has been to secure at least one endowed chair for each division. The dream is still the same and I will continue my efforts to accomplish this.

June 1, 1985—May 31, 1986

This is the last Annual Report I will submit. I have been chairman of the Department of Medicine since February 1957. In 1957 there were only about a dozen faculty members at Grady Hospital, Emory Hospital, and the Veterans Administration Hospital. Today there are 147 full-time faculty members. During my tenure as chairman, we moved into the new Grady Hospital and the new Veterans Administration Hospital, began to officially organize Crawford W. Long Hospital, and developed the Emory University Clinic. The house staff program was unified. At an earlier time there were two separate programs— the Emory-VA Program and the Grady Program. Today there is only one house staff program utilizing all four of our facilities with an organized relationship to Piedmont Hospital.

Our patient care program and teaching programs are very strong. In fact, they have gained national recognition. The weakness is inadequate funding for the department as a whole. Too many faculty members earn their salary by patient care services. This limits the amount of time for scholarly work and research. I have always wanted a research-oriented department, and I am proud of the research that has been done. More could have been done if we had adequate research space and financial support for the faculty.

I am extremely pleased that Dr. Juha Kokko has accepted the chairmanship of the department beginning in September, 1986. I knew him as a student and have followed his career with interest. In our numerous talks I am convinced that he will move the department forward as I would like to see it move. He will be given additional funds and space and will develop a more intense research program. I will continue my activities within the Cardiology Division of the

Department of Medicine. Dr. Kokko has requested that I remain as Chief of Cardiology at Emory Hospital and Emory Clinic. I will teach more, see more patients, and write more, including developing the *Emory University Journal of Medicine.*

It is appropriate, I feel, for me to thank all of the faculty and staff for their support throughout my tenure as chairman. I believe, with Dr. Kokko's appointment, the future of the department and school will be in secure and capable hands.

The annual reports highlighted the development of the postgraduate courses. Attendance at the courses reached the level of 500 or more in some courses, and 20 to 70 visiting experts participated in the courses each year.

Grant money for research increased over the years and reached an annual amount of $8-10 million.

Profiles of the interns were prepared for the years 1982–83, 1983–84, and 1984–85. The sheets were detached from the annual reports but were found among them. I suspect the request for the profiles came from Dean Krause, and that they were prepared in 1984 or 1985:

The profiles of interns accepted into the medical house staff for the 1982–1983 period revealed the following. Of 59 interns 17 graduated from Emory and the remainder graduated from a large number of American schools, including Duke, Harvard, Georgetown, University of Pennsylvania, Florida, etc. There were 13 women and 7 minority trainees. Four were in the top 10 percent of the class and 11 were members of Alpha Omega Alpha. Fourteen had received honors in medicine. Twenty-one had done research in medical school and 14 had published the results of their research.

The profile for the interns accepted into the internship program during 1983–1984 revealed the following. Of 59 interns 17 graduated from Emory. The remainder graduated from numerous top American medical schools. There was one excellent foreign graduate from the University of Lebanon. There were 10 women and 9 minority trainees in the group. Three had been in the top 10 percent of their class, nine were members of Alpha Omega Alpha, and 14 had received honors in medicine. Twelve had done research and published.

The profile for the interns accepted into the internship program during 1984–1985 revealed the following. Of 59 interns 23 graduated from Emory. The remaining interns graduated from a large number of American medical schools. There were 18 women and two minority trainees in the group. Four were in the top 10 percent of their graduating class and nine were members of Alpha Omega Alpha honor society.

Eighteen had received honors in medicine. Twenty nine had performed research and 17 had published their work.

The profiles document that interns were selected from an excellent pool of applicants, and that an effort was made to choose the best applicants from numerous excellent medical schools. For nearly thirty years, half of the Emory graduating class applied for an internship in medicine. We received about twenty-five applicants from Emory and accepted about seventeen to twenty of them in our program. This percentage of applicants from Emory continued during the eighties, when other schools were having increasing difficulty recruiting interns in medicine. The residents were chosen from the intern group, and almost all of them remained at Emory. Most fellows were chosen from the Emory house staff, and many faculty members evolved from the house-staff and fellow programs. The house officers knew that if they performed well there would be a place for them. They knew, too, that applicants from other schools and programs were waiting in the wings, should they falter.

Remember, in the early forties, Grady Memorial Hospital, Emory University Hospital, the Veterans Administration Hospital, and Crawford Long Hospital had separate house officer programs. The major program was at Grady Memorial Hospital, and the chairman of the Department of Medicine of Emory had no relationship with Crawford Long Hospital and did not, as far as can be determined, appoint the trainees at Emory University Hospital. Stead, and later Beeson, selected the full-time faculty at the Veterans Administration Hospital. Accordingly, Jack Myers and later Max Michael selected the house officers who worked there. In 1946, Stead appointed Bruce Logue to work at Emory University Hospital and asked him to do two things: to begin a practice of cardiology and to improve the house-staff training. In the early fifties, Max Michael, then chief of medicine at the Veterans Administration Hospital, started the Emory-Veterans Administration house-staff program. This was a step forward, because it improved the experience of the house officers.

In 1957, I recognized that house officers at Grady Hospital were happy and content with their program at Grady Hospital. I believed, however, that they needed experience with private patients. In the beginning, a Grady house officer was permitted to rotate through Emory University Hospital on an elective basis. In 1972, I combined the Grady house-staff and fellows training program with the Emory-Veterans Administration Hospital program to form the Emory University Affiliated Hospitals Program in Internal Medicine. A short time later, when Emory-owned Crawford Long Hospital came under the direct control of Emory, the Crawford Long training program was incorporated in the Emory University Affiliated Hospitals Program in Internal Medicine. This action placed the responsibility of recruitment and appointment of house staff and fellows on the department chairman and his designated associates.

The development of the Emory University Affiliated Hospitals Program in Internal Medicine and its subspecialties had many educational advantages. First of all, this plan offered the trainees experience with a wide variety of patient problems. It also allowed the trainees to be exposed to larger groups of faculty members than was possible in the old system. Each of the four hospitals was different, and this alone broadened the trainees' experience. The new system permitted the chairman and his designated associates to develop a house-staff and fellowship curriculum that fit the desires and needs of the trainees. Secondly, the new program highlighted the fact that Emory University, an educational institution, was responsible for the educational program of the trainees rather than the hospitals.

Early on, each hospital performed the administrative work related to each appointment and paid the salary of the trainee. Early in the program's development, Grady Hospital continued to be the central facility. The other hospitals paid Grady, and Grady paid the house officer. Grady personnel performed the administrative duties associated with the training programs. The final change took place on July 1, 1984, when Emory University School of Medicine assumed the responsibility of performing the administrative duties and paying the trainees. The hospitals, in turn, paid Emory University School of Medicine.

Throughout my chairmanship, I emphasized to Emory officials that the members of the large house-staff and fellowship programs should, when they finished the program, be recognized as Emory University alumni. Each year this dream came closer to being a reality. The 1984 date just mentioned represents the fulfillment of the plan.

The creation of a large and excellent house-staff and fellowship program may be the department's greatest achievement. The trainees taught, did research, and delivered excellent patient care. They contributed mightily to the idea that a teaching hospital is a place where everyone teaches.

Name Changes

Over the years, the names of some of the institutions and buildings that are mentioned in this book have changed. This is one of the reasons the names that are used in one part of the book differ from those used in other parts of the book. Another reason for the difference is that I often used the names that were used in the conversations of the day. For example we commonly say Emory Hospital, although the name is actually

Emory University Hospital. There have been, however, some actual changes in the names of some of the institutions and buildings. They are listed below.

- The name of the Gray Building on the Grady campus was changed to the Woodruff Memorial-Henry Woodruff Extension.
- The name of the Davis-Fischer Sanatorium was changed to Crawford W. Long Hospital. Later the name was changed to Crawford Long Hospital of Emory University.
- The name of the Physiology Building was changed to Physiology and Cell Biology.
- The name of Wesley Memorial Hospital was changed to Emory University Hospital.
- The name of Atlanta Medical College building was changed to Emory University School of Medicine, and later to the Emory Division of Grady Memorial Hospital.
- The Emory University Clinic name was changed to The Emory Clinic.
- The name of the Medical Center was changed to the Woodruff Medical Center and later to the Robert W. Woodruff Health Sciences Center.
- The name of the Communicable Disease Center was changed to Centers for Disease Control, and later to Centers for Disease Control and Prevention.
- The name of the Emory University Dental School Building is currently referred to as "The Old Dental School Building." Rumor has it that a new name is being considered.
- The name of Lawson General Hospital was changed to Lawson Veterans Hospital and then to the Atlanta Veterans Hospital. Later, the name was changed to the Department of Veterans Affairs Medical Center.
- The name of Hughes Spalding Hospital was changed to the Hughes Spalding Children's Hospital.

Benefactors of the Department of Medicine

Many people—students, house officers, fellows, patients, and friends—contributed financial support to the Department of Medicine from 1957 through 1986. Some gifts were small and some large. I thank each contributor with all the emotion I possess. I especially thank Harold Brockey, Asa and Howard Candler, Dr. Tommy Dickinson, Howard and Josephine Dobbs, Florence and Joseph Eichberg, Carlyle and Isabel Fraser, J. B. and Dorothy Fuqua, Martin Guyer, D.D.S., Reunette W. Harris and family, A. Jalil, Dr. Mason Lowance, Bernard Marcus, Louis

Netherland, Carroll and Nancy O'Connor, William and Jean Reid, Julio Mario and Beatrice Santo Domingo, Beverly and Ralph Shere, Rankin Smith, Robert and George Woodruff, and Mack and Grace Worden. These people provided considerable funds for equipment, badly needed space, and endowed chairs within the Department of Medicine.

Silence Please — For Those Who Have Passed

The following full-time faculty members have died: Drs. Charles Brake, James Bradford, George Callaway, Walter Cargill, Bayard Catherwood, James Coberly, Edward R. Dorney, Eugene Ferris, William Friedewald, Benjamin Gendel, Leon Goldberg, Robert Grant, Andreas Gruentzig, Bernard Hallman, E. Garland Herndon Jr., Arthur Merrill Sr., Max Michael, William J. Rawls, J. Spalding Schroder, Sumner Thompson III, James V. Warren, Lamar Waters, Colon H. Wilson, and Hugh Wood.

The following former house officers and fellows have died: Drs. Clark Adair, Pete Brittian, Manley Lanier (Sonny) Carter, Seth Dartley, Alexis Davison, Lloyd Hyde, Iverson Joines, McClaren Johnson Jr., Ray Lanier, Ernest Proctor, Pete Proctor, Jones Skinner, Paul Smith, Theofilos Tsagaris, Malcolm Traxler, William Walter, Stacey White, and Roy Wiggins.

The following members of the administrative staff of the Department of Medicine have died: David Bissett, Alex Nelson, Ruth Strange, and Anne Webb.

Several members of the active volunteer faculty of the Department of Medicine died during my thirty years of chairmanship. Their contribution was deeply appreciated.

The Approaching Storm: Emory is Ready

By 1980, there was abundant evidence that we were entering a new era. Many aspects of our lives were changing. Within that general context, health care was beginning to be viewed as a right by the majority of people in the nation. The delivery of medical service was becoming more complex and more difficult. At the same time the cost of medical care was escalating at an unbelievably high rate. This, for the most part, was the result of medical progress and the cost of high technology. In addition, new methods of financing the cost of being sick were being explored. Simultaneously, there was increasing rebellion against increasing the tax the citizens paid to support medical education, health care, and medical research. Worst of all, and for multiple reasons, patients said they "disliked the medical profession but liked their own doctor."

Relationship to Grady Hospital

For almost three decades, the relationship of Emory University to Grady Memorial Hospital was excellent because of the effective leadership of Dean Richardson of Emory, William Pinkston, who was Superintendent of Grady Hospital, and the Fulton-DeKalb Hospital Authority composed of some of the leading citizens of the two counties. Despite the excellent relationship between Emory and Grady, Dean Richardson always expected the department chairmen to be able to implement their teaching programs elsewhere in our system, if for some reason the clinical departments could not function at Grady. Such a move, however, was never seriously considered during his deanship. By 1986, Dean Krause was having more difficulty with certain aspects of the Emory-Grady relationship. He asked the clinical chairmen to consider how we would function in the future with or without Grady. I believed the Department of Medicine could function effectively by using Emory University Hospital and the Emory Clinic, Crawford Long Hospital, and the Atlanta Veterans Hospital if, for some reason, we were no longer associated with Grady Memorial Hospital. The chairmen of the Departments of Obstetrics and Surgery concluded it would be more difficult for them.

There were new problems at Grady Memorial Hospital. The cost of excellent modern medical care was not being met by the tax paid by the citizens of the two counties, Medicare, Medicaid, and private health insurance. Despite the inadequate budget, many influential citizens of the two counties wanted to decrease the tax paid to operate Grady. In addition, Morehouse School of Medicine wanted an increasing presence and usage of Grady Hospital. Most disturbing of all were the discussion and rumors about the "politicization" of Grady Hospital; the county commissioners were becoming more "interested" in whom they appointed to the Hospital Authority and to the hospital administration. The influence of Emory on the developments at Grady was clearly diminishing. None of these problems existed from 1957 to about 1980. Accordingly, it was possible to carry out the responsibility of running the medical service, teaching, and research without great difficulty. The esprit de corps was superb. Grady was an exciting place. By the eighties, the clouds of change were becoming darker. Obviously, future deans and department chairmen would have to deal with these problems.

Although the Medical Fund helped support the Emory faculty assigned to Grady, the financial and nonfinancial problems at Grady were becoming increasingly serious. Emory, with its plethora of facilities, could, if it became necessary, handle the problems associated with a diminishing presence at Grady Hospital.

The Atlanta Veterans Affairs Hospital

This excellent new facility had been an enormous asset for Emory. The dean's committee functioned well. Accordingly, the relationship between Emory and the Veterans Hospital had always been excellent. By 1986, the plans for a new addition to the hospital were underway. The new addition was needed to increase the space for research and for patient care.

The problem looming at the Veterans Hospital was that the number of veterans who needed hospital and outpatient care was decreasing. There was serious talk of abandoning the veterans health care system and replacing it with a system that permitted veterans to go to private hospitals. There was even talk of closing some of the veterans hospitals. In 1986 these potential problems were recognized. The dean and department chairmen would undoubtedly face this problem in the future. Emory, with two private hospitals under its umbrella, could easily handle any change that might occur at the Veterans Hospital.

Emory University Hospital and Clinic

Emory University Hospital was the "jewel" in Asa Candler's plan for health education, and the Emory Clinic was the "jewel" in Robert W. Woodruff's. These facilities had grown beyond belief, as had the number of buildings used for research and medical school administration. The problems looming in the operation of Emory University Hospital and the Clinic were related to the national change in the delivery of health care and its impact on medical education.

By 1986, most hospitals were becoming massive "intensive care units." Even so, patients were being discharged as quickly as possible, and more and more patients were being treated as outpatients. These actions profoundly influenced educational activities. Patients were commonly admitted to the hospital for a high-tech procedure. This taught the trainees to do procedures but did not teach them the importance of the initial examination of the patient. These problems can be solved by creating an excellent outpatient educational program for students, house staff, and fellows. Emory can be the leader in the nation, because very few excellent outpatient teaching services are currently available elsewhere.

Academic medical centers will survive if they have a large private facility such as the Emory Clinic. This implies that such facilities will be filled with excellent clinicians of every variety who possess the talent to solve any and all medical problems. This being true, it will be the responsibility of the department chairmen of Emory University School of Medicine to recruit clinicians who wish to *teach* and *write*. Even so, the act of appointment will not guarantee that the appointees will be able to find the time to teach and write. As outside forces determine the financial aspects of medical care, a faculty member who wishes to teach and write, may be forced to abandon such a desire because there may be no time available to do so. This problem will be even more difficult to solve as the Emory Clinic develops a large number of satellite clinics. The clinicians who work in the satellite clinics of the future must carry the Emory banner of excellence. They, too, should be encouraged to teach and write. Short of that, they should attend Emory teaching sessions in order to know what Emory does. Whereas such faculty members are needed to keep the academic center financially solvent, they must, even when time to do so is limited, be intimately associated with the academic department of which they are a part.

Crawford Long Hospital

The development of Emory-owned Crawford Long Hospital as an academic facility has been relatively smooth due to the excellent administrative ability of Dan Barker and John Henry and the sage advice of Dr. Linton Bishop. Barker, and later Henry, became the overall superintendent for both Emory University Hospital and Crawford Long Hospital.

There are many members of the Emory Clinic assigned to Crawford W. Long Hospital. The hospital is unique in the Emory system in that community physicians and Emory faculty work in the same facility.

In 1986 there were few problems associated with the metamorphosis of Crawford Long Hospital into an academic institution. In my opinion, the leaders of the future should continue the hospital as an open hospital where Emory faculty and community physicians commingle to create an environment that is different from that of Emory University Hospital, Grady Memorial Hospital, and the Veterans Administration Hospital.

Research

By 1986 the research space had increased considerably at Grady (Henry Woodruff Research Building), on the Emory campus (Ernest Woodruff Memorial Research Building), at the Veterans Hospital, and at Crawford Long Hospital. More research space was planned to be included in the new wing of the Ernest Woodruff Memorial Research Building, and a great deal of research space was planned to be included in the new addition to the Veterans Administration Hospital. More research was being performed at Emory University Hospital in the clinical research facility and in the cardiac catheterization laboratories, and in the Crawford Long research laboratories.

The downside of developments in the research area was the increasing evidence that research funding from the National Institutes of Health was threatened because the citizens at large, and influential political leaders in particular, were demanding tax cuts that would, with the passage of time, impact research funding in a negative way. Should that happen private sources for research could be sought. Philanthropy for research purposes is more difficult to obtain than philanthropy for buildings. One of the problems facing the leaders that follow will be to find the money for research. Whereas money may be found for the support of excellent projects the real need will be to create a system where excellent investigators can be guaranteed a secure long-term future.

Morehouse School of Medicine

Emory's contribution to the development of the Morehouse School of Medicine is discussed on page 297. Emory University and Morehouse will both use Grady Memorial Hospital as a clinical teaching facility. The Deans of the two schools and the Grady administration must work together to create a smooth operation in which patient care and teaching are excellent.

Other Problems

I detected a change in the Department of Medicine as we grew from a small group of 14 faculty members to 147 faculty members. Communication became more difficult. We did not learn as much from each other when we were large as we did when we were small. Units of faculty members tended to become isolated. As years pass more faculty will be added and communication will become even more difficult.

Close to my heart is the changing view some members of the public have about the medical profession. Some say the profession of medicine is a business and should be treated as such. Some demean physicians by calling them "health care providers." Worse than that, some doctors are referred to as "gate keepers." Some patients sue doctors for unjustified reasons. Patients complain that doctors do not treat them with respect and that they do not see them promptly. Emergency rooms are crowded beyond belief, and physicians who work there may not have adequate training in all areas of emergency medicine. The cost of medical care is increasing each year. High technology that has, on the one hand, been responsible for the improvement of medical care, has, on the other hand, increased the cost of medical care. Medical care for the elderly is becoming a major problem, and the medical problems associated with being born and dying are increasing.

The central point of this discussion is that the attitudes and actions of physicians and patients are changing and the cost of medical care continues to rise. The leaders of academic centers of the next decade will be forced to spend a major portion of their time dealing with these problems. It will be difficult for them to teach, deliver personal care to patients, write, perform personal research, and administer a huge department.

Emory's Response to Problems

The problems listed above, as well as others, are faced by all academic centers. Emory, more than any other academic institution, is in an excellent position to manage the problems just mentioned as well as others that are sure to come. Emory is ready.

The Bridge

An effective leader serves as a bridge between one period in time and another period in time. He or she must build a solid platform on which the next leader can implement his or her dreams.

I am comfortable with the idea that the Department of Medicine was better off in 1986 than it was in 1957. Perhaps that is because it was practically nonexistent in 1957 and because *hundreds of devoted people contributed to its development over thirty years.* We all loved Emory. This, more than anything else, contributed to the success that came our way.

The platform on which the new chairman could build included the following:

• The Grady Memorial Hospital training program in medicine for house staff and fellows joined the Emory Hospital-Veterans Hospital program to form the Emory University Affiliated Hospital Programs in Internal Medicine in 1972. The program at Crawford Long Hospital, which had been a separate program, then joined the Emory University Affiliated Hospitals Program in 1973. The consolidation of the former separate programs not only improved efficiency but enabled the chairman to offer every house officer the best of four hospitals. It also offered a secure future should we ever lose the use of any of our facilities.

• The house-staff and fellow teaching program had been ranked among the best in the nation (see profiles of new interns on page 359).

• From 1957 to 1986 about 40 to 50 percent of the members of the senior class at Emory University School of Medicine selected internal medicine, or one of its subspecialties, as their career. Of these, about half of them applied to our program. Even when excellent programs elsewhere were having difficulty recruiting house staff, we had no problem.

• Patients came from all over the nation, and from abroad, for medical care at Emory University Hospital, the Emory Clinic, and Crawford Long Hospital. Patient care was also perceived as being excellent at Grady Hospital and the Atlanta Veterans Hospital.

• The faculty in the Department of Medicine produced many medical textbooks and wrote scientific articles for many journals.

• An increasing amount of research was performed each year in the Department of Medicine. There was perhaps fifty times as much research space available to the Department of Medicine in 1986 as there was in 1957. An enormous amount of new research space was soon to become available for the Department of Medicine. This would be possible because the new Rollins Research building would permit the Departments of Pharmacology, Microbiology, and Biochemistry to move out of the Ernest W. Woodruff Memorial Research Building, leaving space for the Department of Medicine. In addition, a new wing to the Ernest W. Woodruff Memorial Research Building was planned. A large new research facility was also planned at the Veterans Hospital.

• The Emory Clinic was a great success. The ruckus of 1956–57 was almost forgotten in 1986.

• There were fourteen full-time faculty members in the Department of Medicine in 1957. There were 147 full-time faculty members in 1986.

• One hundred and seventy medical house officers and subspecialty fellows were appointed in February 1986 so the new chairman could begin his work in the fall of 1986 with a full house staff.

• The Residency Review Committee reviewed the medical house-staff training program, as well as the programs for all of the medical subspecialists, in early 1986. The programs were all accredited for three additional years. The new chairman would be free of that concern during his early years as chairman.

• Adequate space for the administrative offices of the chairman of the Department of Medicine became available on the fourth floor of Emory University Hospital in 1972. Prior to that, the chairman's major office was in the Glenn Building in the Grady area.

• The following endowed professorships were passed on to the new Chairman:

The Asa Griggs Candler Professor of Medicine. Dr. Juha Kokko, the new chairman of the Department of Medicine, was appointed in 1986.

The R. Bruce Logue Professor of Medicine in Cardiology. Dr. Kokko appointed Dr. R. Wayne Alexander to this professorship.

The J. Willis Hurst Professor of Medicine in Cardiology. Dr. Kokko appointed Dr. Douglas C. Morris to this professorship.

The Mason Lowance Professor of Medicine in Allergy-Immunology. Dr. Kokko will appoint someone to this position in the future.

The Martha West Looney Professor of Medicine in Pulmonary Medicine and Critical Care. Dr. Kokko appointed Dr. Roland H. Ingram to this professorship.

The Frances Kelly Blomeyer Professor of Medicine in Oncology. Dr. Kokko appointed Dr. Lawrence A. Harker to this professorship.

The Carter Smith Sr. Professor of Medicine. This professorship was supported by W. Clair and Reunette W. Harris. Dr. Kokko appointed Dr. William Branch to this professorship.

Dr. Steven W. Schwarzmann Professor of Medicine in Infectious Diseases was financed by George W. Woodruff. Dr. Juha Kokko will make the appointment in the future.

The bridge to the future was made by the "blood, sweat, and tears" of hundreds of people who loved the institution. In 1957 there was little money and very few facilities. By 1996 Emory University ranked sixth among higher education institutions in the nation in the value of its endowment.

Acknowledgments

General References

The sources of the information used to write Chapter 5 of this book were from my own files, the Bulletins of Emory University School of Medicine from 1915 to 1987, my Annual Reports to the Dean from 1956 through 1986 (located in Special Collections of the Woodruff Memorial Library), the Archives of the Woodruff Memorial Health Sciences Center Library, and interviews and letters from others.

The Help of Others

I thank the following individuals for reviewing Chapter 5 of this book: Dr. Paul B. Beeson, Dr. Joseph E. Hardison, Dr. Charles R. Hatcher Jr., Dr. Gary S. Hauk, Dr. William Hollingsworth, Dr. R. Bruce Logue, Mr. J. W. Pinkston Jr., Dr. Thomas F. Sellers Jr., Dr. Mark E. Silverman, Dr. Eugene A. Stead Jr., and Dr. Judson C. Ward Jr.

I thank the following individuals, who either reviewed and corrected certain parts of Chapter 5 or provided information that was necessary for its completion: Mr. Dan Barker, Dr. Linton Bishop, Dr. Edmund Bourke,

Dr. Charles Corley, Dr. Sylvia Crawley, Dr. Mario DiGirolamo, Dr. Michael Duffell, Dr. John Galambos, Dr. Gilbert Grossman, Dr. Dallas Hall, Dr. Lee Hand, Mr. John Henry, Dr. Charles Huguley, Dr. Roland Ingram, Dr. Herbert Karp, Dr. Thomas Lawley, Mr. Larry Minnix, Dr. Stephen Miller, Dr. Neil Moran, Dr. Harold Ramos, Dr. Robert Schlant, Dr. Jonas Shulman, Dr. Corey Slovis, Dr. David Stephens, Dr. John Stone, Dr. Hiram Sturm, Dr. Nanette Wenger, and Dr. Asa Yancey.

Figure 5-1
Dr. J. Willis Hurst was a cardiac fellow with Dr. Paul Dudley White at the Massachusetts General Hospital in 1948 and 1949. Dr. Hurst is seated to the right of Dr. White. Dr. Addison Messer is standing behind Dr. Hurst. The two of them were the last of Dr. White's cardiac fellows. The machine was one of the first instruments used to transmit heart sounds from a patient to an audience.

Figure 5-2
Dr. J. Willis Hurst in 1956, when he was selected to be professor and chairman of the Department of Medicine. His work as chairman began in February 1957 and ended in November 1986. In 1997 he continues to teach and write.

Figure 5-3
 In 1957, Dr. R. Bruce Logue, a cardiologist, was chief of medicine at Emory University Hospital and head of the Medical Section of the Emory University Clinic.

Figure 5-4
 Dr. Charles M. Huguley Jr. In 1957 Dr. Huguley was the hematologist at Emory University Hospital and Clinic.

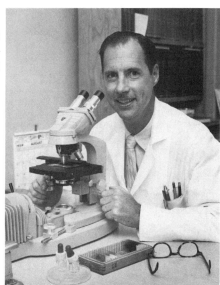

Figure 5-5
 Dr. J. Spalding Schroder. In 1957 Dr. Schroder was the gastroenterologist at Emory University Hospital and Clinic.

Figure 5-6
	Dr. Edward R. Dorney. In 1957 Dr. Dorney, a cardiologist, joined the Department of Medicine of Emory University School of Medicine. He was assigned to Emory University Hospital and Clinic.

Figure 5-7
	Dr. Bernard L. Hallman. In 1957 Dr. Hallman was an endocrinologist at Emory University Hospital and Clinic. He became assistant dean and later associate dean for professional services at Grady Memorial Hospital.

Figure 5-8
	Dr. Benjamin R. Gendel. In 1957 Dr. Gendel, a hematologist, joined the Department of Medicine of Emory University School of Medicine. He was chief of medicine at the Veterans Administration Hospital. He moved to the Glenn Building on the Grady campus and assumed his role as the organizer of the junior and senior medical student program in medicine.

Figure 5-9
Dr. Julius Wenger. In 1957 Dr. Wenger, a gastroenterologist, was located at the Veterans Administration Hospital.

Figure 5-10
Mrs. Ruth Strange. In 1957 Mrs. Strange was the senior secretary, administrative assistant, and business manager of the Department of Medicine. Her office was located in the Glenn Building on the Grady campus.

Figure 5-11
Mrs. Anne S. Webb. In 1958 Mrs. Webb joined the secretarial staff of the Department of Medicine. Her office was located in the Glenn Building on the Grady campus.

Figure 5-12
    Dr. Elbert P. Tuttle Jr. In 1957
Dr. Tuttle, a nephrologist, joined
the Department of Medicine of
Emory University School of Medi-
cine. His office was located in
Grady Memorial Hospital.

Figure 5-13
    Dr. Ross L. McLean. In 1957 Dr. McLean, a
pulmonologist, joined the Department of Medicine of Emory University School of Medicine.
His office was located on the Grady campus.

Figure 5-14
    Dr. Robert H. Franch. In 1957 Dr. Franch,
a cardiologist, joined the Department of Medicine. He developed the cardiac catheterization laboratory in the Woodruff Memorial
Research Building on the Emory campus.
This was the first such laboratory associated
with a private hospital in the city of Atlanta.

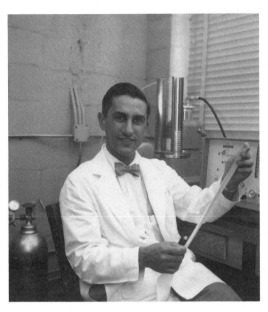

Figure 5-15
Dr. John T. Galambos. In 1957 Dr. Galambos, a gastroenterologist, was appointed to the Department of Medicine of Emory University School of Medicine. His office was located on the Grady campus.

Figure 5-16
Dr. Charles C. Corley Jr. In 1957 Dr. Corley, a hematologist, joined the Department of Medicine of Emory University School of Medicine. His office was located in the Emory University Clinic on the Emory campus.

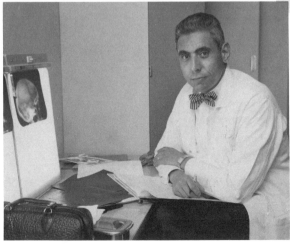

Figure 5-17
Dr. Herbert R. Karp. In 1958 Dr. Karp, a neurologist, joined the Department of Medicine of Emory University School of Medicine. His office was located in Grady Memorial Hospital on the Grady campus.

The Quest for Excellence

Figure 5-18
  Dr. John R. K. Preedy. In 1958 Dr. Preedy, an endocrinologist, joined the Department of Medicine of Emory University School of Medicine. His office was located in the Glenn Building on the Grady campus.

Figure 5-19
  Dr. Robert C. Schlant. In 1958 Dr. Schlant, a cardiologist, joined the Department of Medicine of Emory University School of Medicine. His office was located in Grady Memorial Hospital on the Grady campus.

Figure 5-20
. Dr. Thomas F. Sellers Jr. In 1958 Dr. Sellers, an expert in infectious diseases, joined the Department of Medicine of Emory University School of Medicine. His office was located on the Grady campus.

Figure 5-21
Dr. B. Woodfin Cobbs Jr. In 1958 Dr. Cobbs, a cardiologist, joined the Department of Medicine of Emory University School of Medicine. He was assigned to Emory University Hospital and Clinic.

Figure 5-22A
Postgraduate course entitled "Three Days of Electrolytes," 1957. L–R:
Dr. Milton Krainin, Dr. Charles Whisnant, Dr. George L. Mitchell, Dr. Arnold
Relman, Dr. Ted Danowski, Dr. Elbert Tuttle, Dr. Joe Wilson, Dr. Richard
Johnson. Dr. Arthur Merrill Sr. is behind the microphone.

Figure 5-22B
Postgraduate course entitled "Three Days of Hematology," May 15-16,
1957. L–R: Dr. Charles Huguley, Dr. Benjamin Gendel, Dr. Claude-Staff
Wright, Dr. Spencer Brewer, Dr. Milton Freedman, Dr. Wallace Frommeyer.

Figure 5-22C
Postgraduate course entitled "Cardiac Arrhythmias," October 19–20, 1957. L–R: Dr. Herman Hellerstein, Dr. Calhoun Witham, Dr. Proctor Harvey, Dr. Robert Grant, Dr. Willis Hurst.

Figure 5-22D
Postgraduate course entitled "Liver Disease," December 14–15, 1957. L–R: Dr. David Hein, Dr. Joe Hilsman, Dr. Abner Golden, Dr. Jack D. Myers, Dr. Franz J. Ingelfinger, Dr. David James.

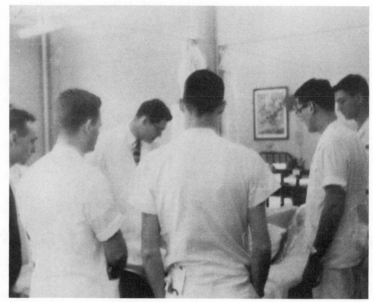

Figure 5-23
    Last ward rounds in old Grady Memorial Hospital, January 27, 1958. L–R: Drs. Ammons, Christy, Hurst, H. C. Ball, Scoggins, and Combs.

Figure 5-24
    The new Grady Memorial Hospital was occupied by patients on January 27, 1958. The hospital cost $22,000,000.

Figure 5-25

Dr. H. Kenneth Walker. Dr. Walker assisted in the day-to-day running of the medical service at Grady Memorial Hospital. His office was located in the Glenn Building on the Grady campus.

Figure 5-26

L–R: Dr. J. Willis Hurst, Dr. W. Dallas Hall, Dr. H. Kenneth Walker, and Mr. J. William Pinkston Jr. The book held by Mr. Pinkston, who was chief executive director of Grady Memorial Hospital, was entitled Clinical Methods. It was edited by Drs. Walker, Hall, and Hurst in 1976. The book was dedicated to Mr. Pinkston as a token of appreciation for his help with the medical service at Grady Memorial Hospital.

Figure 5-27

Dr. David Waters (left) and Dr. Grant Liddle (right), professor and chairman of the Department of Medicine at Vanderbilt University School of Medicine in Nashville, Tennessee. Dr. Liddle was a visiting professor at Emory and presided over the medical house staff research day. Dr. Waters, a cardiology fellow, is receiving the annual medical house staff research award at a banquet which culminated a day when the fellows and house staff presented the results of their research. Dr. Waters eventually became the Director of the Division of Cardiology at the University of Connecticut.

Figure 5-28

Dr. E. Garland Herndon Jr. (shown on the far left) was the first director of the clinical research facility located in Emory University Hospital. Next to him is Dr. James T. Laney (president of Emory University). Dr. R. Bruce Logue is in the white coat, and Dr. Joseph Hardison is shown to the far right.

Figure 5-29

A gathering of four chief residents in medicine at Grady Memorial Hospital. L–R: Dr. Gordon Crowell, Dr. Pete Proctor, Dr. J. Willis Hurst, Dr. Huddie Cheney, and Dr. Marvin M. McCall. Dr. Cheney was the first chief resident in medicine I appointed at Grady Memorial Hospital in 1957. Dr. McCall was chief resident in medicine at Grady Memorial Hospital in 1962, at which time he presented me with a coffee table he had made from the timbers of the old medical school building (see Figure 5-30B).

Figure 5-30A

All that remains of the old Atlanta Medical College, which became the original Emory University School of Medicine. This remnant of a building is located on the corner of Butler and Armstrong Streets.

Figure 5-30B

This coffee table was made by Dr. Marvin McCall during his chief residency at Grady Memorial Hospital in 1962. The table was made from the discarded timbers of the old building that housed the entire Emory University School of Medicine building in 1915.

Figure 5-31

The faculty who participated in the first American Heart Association postgraduate course on March 27–29, 1963. This began a series of national postgraduate courses entitled "Three Days of Cardiology." Back Row: Dr. Charles Butterworth, Dr. Howard Sprague, Dr. Lewis E. January, Dr. J. Willis Hurst, Dr. Frederick J. Levy, Dr. Richard Hurley. Front Row L–R: Dr. Ray W. Gifford Jr., Dr. W. Proctor Harvey, Dr. R. Bruce Logue, Dr. Robert C. Schlant, and Dr. Robert H. Franch.

Figure 5-32

Postgraduate course in coronary angioplasty held September 16–20, 1984. This course was presented by Dr. Andreas Gruentzig, who is shown in the center of the front row, between Dr. Spencer King and Dr. John Douglas.

Figure 5-33
    Dr. Lawrence L. Weed. The originator of the problem-oriented record visited the Department of Medicine on several occasions.

Figure 5-34
    Dr. R. Bruce Logue originated the cardiology fellowship program at Emory University Hospital and Grady Memorial Hospital. He was a major mover in the development of the Emory University Clinic.

Figure 5-35
    Dr. Nanette Kass Wenger. Dr. Wenger joined the Department of Medicine of Emory University School of Medicine in 1959. She became director of the cardiac clinics at Grady Memorial Hospital in 1960.

Figure 5-36
   Dr. Andreas Gruentzig. In 1980 Dr. Gruentzig joined the Department of Medicine of Emory University School of Medicine. He continued the development of coronary angioplasty at Emory University Hospital. He and his wife, Margaret Ann, died in a plane crash in 1985.

Figure 5-37
   Dr. Charles R. Hatcher Jr. was director of the Division of Cardiothoracic Surgery from 1971 to 1990. He was director of Emory University Clinic from 1976 to 1984, then vice president for health affairs and director of the Robert W. Woodruff Health Sciences Center from 1984 to 1996.

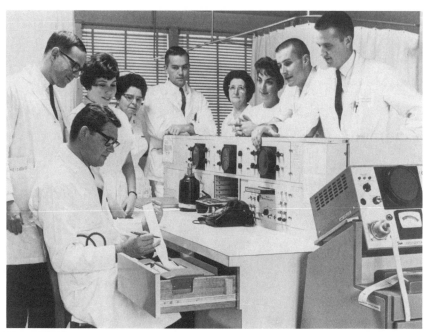

Figure 5-38
Dr. Mark E. Silverman. Dr. Silverman joined the Department of Medicine of Emory University School of Medicine in 1968. He is shown to the far left here when he was a cardiology fellow in 1966. We are shown in the process of checking out the new equipment in the coronary care unit at Grady Memorial Hospital. Dr. Silverman was appointed as an Emory professor at Piedmont Hospital in 1970.

Figure 5-39
Miss Mary Woody. Miss Woody became director of the nursing service and assistant hospital administrator at Grady Memorial Hospital in 1979. In 1984 Miss Woody became director of the nursing service at Emory University Hospital.

Figure 5-40

Grady Memorial Hospital, Department of Medicine, 1957–1958.

Row 1:   Cheney, Maclachlan, Roughton, Foster, Burton, Saffan, Crowell, Graham, Okel, Ammons, Floyd, Rosenberg

Row 2:   Rape, Jones, Everitt, Logue, Preedy, Hurst, Papageorge, Wood, Gendel, Bridges, Taylor, Poole

Row 3:   Tuttle, Robertson, Barbin, Carter, Weeks, Seyffert, Holmes, Howard, Norton, N. Wenger, Lester, Crevasse

Row 4:   Dorney, Hubbard, Trusler, O'Dell, Mason, Strange, Crutcher, J. Wenger, Goza, H. Palmer, LeMaistre

Row 5:   J. Wilson, Bowles, Cary, F. Palmer, Galambos, Robertson, Hallman, Coberly

Row 6:   Schroder, Karp, McLean, Churchwell, Woody, Richardson, W. Brown, Burns, Epes, Milledge

Figure 5-41

Grady Memorial Hospital, Department of Medicine, 1958–1959.

Row 1: Bridges, Okel, Smith, Foster, Williams, Turner, Robertson, Tsagaris, Madden

Row 2: Saffan, Tuttle, Franch, Karp, Hurst, Gendel, Preedy, Churchwell

Row 3: Shinaberger, Lunsford, Guillebeau, L. Jones, Anderson, Callahan, Ammons, Schlant, Pearson, S. Jones, Everitt

Row 4: Mostellar, Scoggins, Christy, Waters, Rogers, D. Johnson, Strozier

Row 5: O'Connell, Rape, Leondardy, Walklett, Perkins, Andrews, Schwartz

Row 6: M. Johnson, Reese, Bowles, Biggers, Craven, MacDonald, Lindsay, Cabaniss

Figure 5-42

Grady Memorial Hospital, Department of Medicine, 1959–1960.

Row 1: Hallman, Cobbs, Dorney, Preedy, Herndon, Crutcher, Hurst, Gendel, Tuttle, J. Wenger, N. Wenger, Galambos, Clinkscales

Row 2: Brown, Scoggins, Churchwell, Jones, Okel, Coberly, Mostellar, Burns, Saffan, Robertson

Row 3: Guillebeau, Haynes, Nahmias, Callaway, Madden, Tope, Christy, McCall, Wiggins, Shell, Waters, Holmes, Rawls, Lindsay, Laughlin, Turner, Leondary

Row 5: Etzenhouser, Jones, Hawkins, Griffin, Block, Parks, Neill, Rhodes

Row 6: Tillman, Lovell, Walker, Trusler, Reese, Shanks

Row 7: Cabaniss, Shinaberger, Belcher, Bridges, Smith, Karp Sellers, Gaston

Figure 5-43
Grady Memorial Hospital, Department of Medicine, 1960–1961.
Row 1: Madden, Wilkinson, Molkner, Heywood, Argy, Free, Block, Bleich, White, J. Steinberg, Crowell
Row 2: Tuttle, J. Wenger, N. Wenger, Galambos, Olansky, Hur, Preedy, McLean, Schlant
Row 3: Farrar, Dillard, Christy, Mostellar, McCall, Neill, Steinberg, Brown, Dorney
Row 4: Abernathy, Tillman, Hargrove, Maner, Rawls, Gaston, Winter, Van Buren, Saffan, Achord
Row 5: Cabaniss, Dunworth, Rhodes, Sadler, Dippy, Walker, Heath, Mendelson, Asada
Row 6: Avret, Proctor, Lee, Afield, Crosswell

Figure 5-44

Grady Memorial Hospital, Department of Medicine, 1961–1962.

Row 1: Tuttle, Gaine, Logue, Karp, White, Crowell, McCall, Hurst, Gendel, Preedy, Schlant, Galambos, N. Wenger, J. Wenger, Goldberg

Row 2: Hall, Ryan, Brylski, McCord, M. Steinberg, Stumb, Paulk, Shuford, Cotts, Mostellar, Tutunji, Greiner

Row 3: Veazey, Avery, Turner, Marine, Smith T, Logan, Glover, Waters, Rhodes, McDonald, Asada

Row 4: Brewer, Reeder, Shanks, Proctor, J. Steinberg, Sbar, Fletcher, Burns

Row 5: Cabaniss, Huff, Foster, Sadler, Hutson

Figure 5-45

Grady Memorial Hospital, Department of Medicine, 1962–1963.

Row 1: Galambos, Goldberg, Bouhuys, Crowell, Hurst, Gendel, Preedy, Wenger, Schlant, Tuttle

Row 2: Rawls, M. Steinberg, Smith T, Flint, Eren, Davis, Kibler, Goldman, Zimmerman, Karp

Row 3: Callaway, Paulk, T. Someren, A. Someren, Dodd, Wight, Graham, Reed, Olansky, Camp

Row 4: Meyer, Vander Els, Sadler, Rhodes, Achord, Huff, Acker, Bryant, Barton, Tartaglia, Long, Jones, Gonzalez

Row 5: Purks, Sellers, J. Steinberg, Lund, Johnson, Hand, Turner, Robinson, Proctor, Fletcher, Dillard

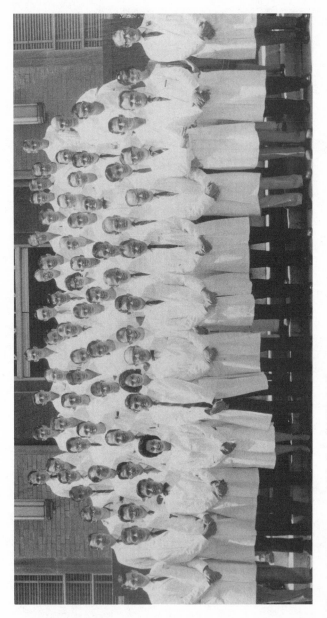

Figure 5-46

Grady Memorial Hospital, Department of Medicine, 1963–1964.

Row 1: Marine, Ramos, Galambos, Wenger, Goldberg, McLean, Hurst, Gendel, Preedy, Bonhuys, Herndon, Schlant

Row 2: Vogler, Hirooka, Huguley, Gaine, Perling, Paulk, Proctor, Brake, Arnold, M. Steinberg

Row 3: Johnson, Turner, Holland, Davis, Oppenheimer, Graham Madden, Dicus, J. Steinberg, Acker, McCullagh

Row 4: Lowrey, Skinner, McNay, Sellers, Hyman, Williams, Laurijssens, Borgman, Silverman, Callaway, Jones, Hall, Camp, Crosthwaite, Block, Van Buren

Row 5: Thompson, Lazarus, Lund, Brawner, Iida, Hand, Kamper J. Turner

Row 6: Ward, Mayer, Sbar, Glancy, Cowan, Davison, Crank, Ballantyne, Lindsay, C. Johnson

Figure 5-47

Grady Memorial Hospital, Department of Medicine, 1964–1965.

Row 1: Wenger, Goldberg, Galambos, Sellers, Hurst, Karp, Gendel, Schlant, Tuttle, Rawls

Row 2: Marine, Ramos, M. Steinberg, J. Steinberg, Glancy, Paulk, McLean, Preedy, Cowan, Kibler

Row 3: Crosthwaite, Ramseur, Bedell, Naiman, Blumenthal, Thomason, Bailey, McCullagh, Hirooka

Row 4: C. Williams, Casey, Vogel, Holland, Gillett, DeSando, Mason, Ammons, MacDonald

Row 5: West, Hyman, Jacobs, Hand, Lathan, Jones, Camp, Van Buren

Row 6: Shepherd, Brylski, Mayer, Callaway, Shuford, C. Johnson, J. Williams

Row 7: Hamilton, Schulze, L. Hyde, Lindsay, Wilson, Sbar, S. Hyde, Crank, Block, M. Johnson, Coulter, Davison, Dorfan, Berger, Douglass, Veazey, Coleman, Dixon, Raymond

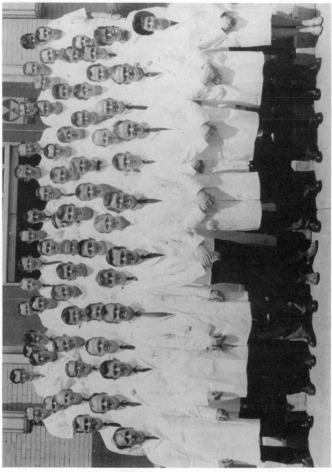

Figure 5-48
Grady Memorial Hospital, Department of
Medicine, 1965–1966.

Row 1: Kibler, Marine, Sellers, Hand, Hurst, Gendel, Schlant, Wenger
Row 2: Beasley, MacDonald, Goldberg, Paulk, Farrar, Steinberg, McPhedran
Row 3: Lindsay, Shuford, Daly, Fletcher, Wells, Eidex
Row 4: F. Jones, Crosthwaite, McCullagh, Lathan, Bussey, Watson, Nutter, Vogel, Galphin
Row 5: Walker, D. Hall, Bobes, Pathak, Madden, Paty, Ramseur, Daniel, Culpepper, Bailey
Row 6: Repass, Bivins, West, Jacobs, Raymond, Romain, R. Jones, Magruder, Lischner, Hamilton
Row 7: MacCannell, McNay, Sonneville, Coulter, Meyer, Veazey, Zimmerman, Azar, J. Hall, Crank, Baskin, Gable, Finley

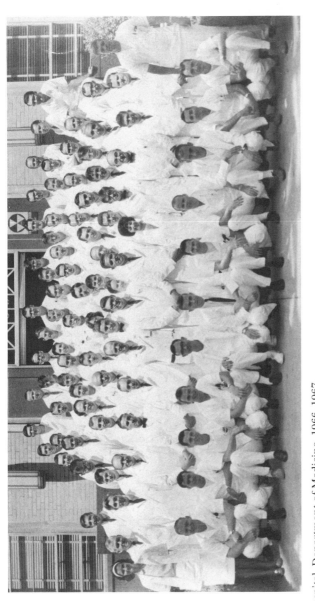

Figure 5-49

Grady Memorial Hospital, Department of Medicine, 1966–1967.

Row 1: G. Jones, Hamilton, Watts, Paty, Forsyth, D. Hall, Bailey, Wells, J. Hall, Gonzalez, Meyer

Row 2: Smith T, C. Wilson, Cobbs, Preedy, Galambos, Ammons, Dorney, Hurst, Crutcher, Wenger, McPhedran, McLean, Farrar, Christy, Lathan

Row 3: Halkos, Alexander, Lindsay, Steinberg, Jacobs, Freeman, Lindsey, Brown, Boring, Karp, Stuart

Row 4: Shepherd, Ward, Hardison, Olansky, Franco, J. Wilson, Kennemer, Macon

Row 5: Rauch, Myerburg, Purvis, Zimmerman, McCoy, Stone, Price, Sullivan, Shinaberger, Sadler

Row 6: Daniel, Lowance, Shulman, Owens, Del Bene, Whaley, R. Jones, Berry, Lischner, Lee, Baskin, Cox, Williams

Row 7: McNabb, Fletcher, Ré, Silverman, Reid, Dimond, Jarrard, Finlay, Sharpe, Frank, Robbins, Munro, Bunn

Figure 5-50

Grady Memorial Hospital, Department of Medicine, 1967–1968.

Row 1: Lindsay, Rahn, C. Wilson, Galambos, Crutcher, Hurst, J. Wenger; Tuttle, Schlant, McPhedran, Ingram

Row 2: J. Wilson, Kelloff, Yeh, Johnson, Munro, Hardison, Jacobs, N. Wenger, Hoagland, Karp, Christy

Row 3: Lee, J. Hall, Crosthwaite, Harris, Williams, Earnest, Sullivan, Goldberg, Olansky, Bergeron

Row 4: Madry, Cherry, Kiley, Schwartz, Wickliffe, Fellner, Holland, Rauch, P. Walter, Stone, Baldwin, Ramos

Row 5: O'Donnell, Whipple, Simanis, Clements, Maniscalco, Purvis, Blumenthal, Lindsey, Paty, Robinson, Fletcher

Row 6: Watts, Bailey, Reid, A. Hall, Krick, Litman, Alexander, Bonanno, Myerburg, Ré, Franco, Hoffman

Row 7: Burns, Daniel, Forsyth, Bryant, Wight, Lowance, Sherr, Flanagan, Silverman, Pike

Row 8: Lischner, Schwarzmann, W. Walter, Baskin, Sadler, Rich, Shulman, Swope, A. Johnson, Hill, Moody, McCullagh, Allee, Lake

Figure 5-51

Grady Memorial Hospital, Department of Medicine, 1968–1969.

Row 1: Davidson, Stone, Skinner, Hurst, Crutcher, Sadler, J. Wenger, Goldberg, Gilbert

Row 2: Huguley, McNay, Schlant, Karp, Galambos, Sullivan, Hardison, N. Wenger, Farrar, J. Shulman, Gendel, Paulk, Barney, P. Walter, Callaway

Row 3: McLean, Clark, Simanis, Fiedelholtz, Wight, Downie, Jacobs, Lindsay, DuBois, Nutter, Buckalew, DiGirolamo

Row 4: Singleton, Whitsett, Spoto, Butcher, Forsyth, Fellner, Ward, Macon, Boring, Marine, Someren, Sellers, Litman, DeSando

Row 5: Unger, C. Johnson, Clements, Pike, West, Miller, M. Shulman, Marcus

Row 6: Burns, Pickett, Cherry, Zendel, Abernathy, Halkos, Yow, Blumenthal, Silverstein, Tierney, Chinoy, Krick

Row 7: Lake, Whipple, Williamson, Reid, Duttera, Graham, Baldwin, Reisman

Row 8: Allee, Hanley, W. Walter, A. Johnson, Collins, Balikian, Sherr, Watts

Figure 5-52
Grady Memorial Hospital, Department of Medicine, 1969–1970.
Row 1:   Davidson, Gilbert, Stone, Paulk, Hall, Clements, Hurst, Wenger, Wilson, Preedy, Schlant, McPhedran, Karp, DiGirolamo
Row 2:   Robertson, Reifler, Cormier, Kravitz, Intravartolo, Kaufman, Kimber, Meyer, Butcher, Siegel, Harper, Franco, Tuttle
Row 3:   Levy, Clark, Dobes, Toole, Cooper, Kassanoff, Rich, Bardack, Goodman, Spoto, Tierney
Row 4:   Manchester, Halkos, Randall, Reiman, Joines, Sachs, Silverstein, Duttera, Hanley, Bloom, Luckey, Gorenberg
Row 5:   Fellner, Petursson, Burns, Singleton, Williamson, Walter, Fiedelholtz, Taranto, Balikian, Miller, Hyde, Simmons

Figure 5-53

Grady Memorial Hospital, Department of Medicine, 1970–1971.

Row 1: Finlay, Walker, Nutter, Preedy, Gendel, Wilson, Hurst, Schlant, Paulk, Gilbert, Wells, Tuttle, Tutunji

Row 2: Weed, McCraw, Lokey

Row 3: Harnisch, Goodman, A. Hall, Nielson, Whaley, Jacobs, Slade, Berberich, Goldman, Baratta, Farrar, N. Kelley, Rice

Row 4: D. Hall, Luckey, Bass, Randall, Harris, Hearne, Kimber, J. Blalock, Zager, Davids, Simmons

Row 5: Waites, A. Kelly, Reifler, Clark, Brereton, Del Bene, Robertson, Meyer, Kirkland, Halushka, Boring, Collins

Row 6: Singleton, Clements, Oak, Longo, Jarrard, T. Blalock, Smallridge, Fellner

Row 7: Geer, Warren, Cernuda, Ratts, Hyde, Dimond, Kiley, Smiley, Wellman, MacNabb, Loucks, Belenkie, Norman

Figure 5-54
Grady Memorial Hospital, Department of Medicine, 1971–1972.
Row 1: Davidson, Silverman, Paulk, Ammons, Hurst, Schlant, Christy, McPhedran, Stone
Row 2: Silvester, Lesser, Randall, J. Wenger, N. Wenger, Goldberg, Walker, Lourie, Longo
Row 3: Luckey, Carliner, Tjandramaga, D. Hall, Rabkin, Kiley, Simanis, Sellers, Del Mazo, Lokey, Lowe, Joines, Fisher
Row 4: Coleman, McCabe, Morse, Ouzts, Abitbol, MacLeod, Lobley, Golden, Hobgood
Row 5: McLean, Weed, Halushka, Levine, Douglas, MacNabb, Fradkin, Hart, Wilber, Simmons, Allee
Row 6: J. Francis, B. Francis, Sawaya, McKenzie, McCraw, Moody, Cantwell, Fletcher, Shulman, Aby
Row 7: MacDonell, Steinberg, Felner, Berberich, Frazier, Carr, Collins, Kelley, Costrini, Wellman

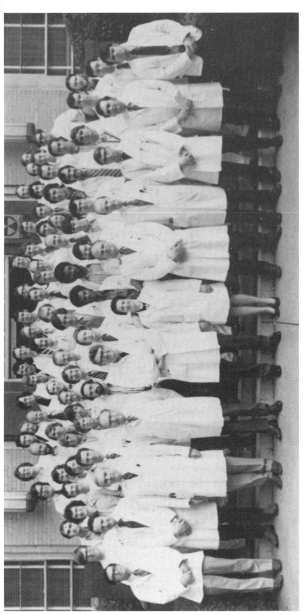

Figure 5-55

Emory University Affiliated Hospitals Program in Internal Medicine and its Subspecialties, Department of Medicine, Emory University School of Medicine, 1972–1973.*

Row 1: Carr, K. Walker, Wilson, Preedy, Hurst, Wenger, Schlant, Dorney, Nutter, Stone, Kiley

Row 2: Nelson, Callaway, Felner, Chambers, Kassan, Maulitz, Eneas, Myron, Miller, Haak, Wilks, Aby, L. Walker

Row 3: Francis, Goldstein, Lutz, Krause, Arnold, Wellman, Wickliffe, McLarin, Tedrick, Costrini

Row 4: Lokey, O'Brien, Honig, Caplan, Burnett, B. Walker, Whitaker, Jarrell, Crickard, Rees, Homey

Row 5: Dimond, Butcher, Morse, O'Connell, Nathan, Kuhn, Lesser, DuBois, Bentch, Davids, Kaliser, Blake, McMillan, Allee

Row 6: Storey, Schuelke, Cantey, Pratt, Moody, Smallridge, Ferguson, Cowan, Cameron, Summers, DuBose, Lancaster, Ouzts, Zamore

*Note the change in title of the picture. The new title signifies the unification of the house-staff program.

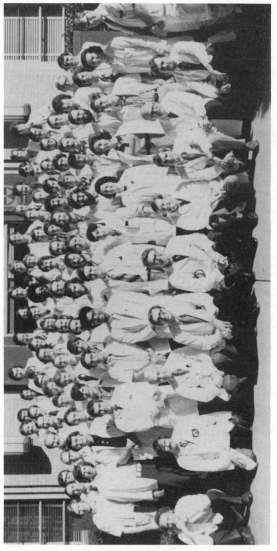

Figure 5-56

Emory University Affiliated Hospitals Program in Internal Medicine and its Subspecialties, Department of Medicine, Emory University School of Medicine, 1973–1974.

Row 1: Walker, Vogel, Wilson, Allee, Hurst, Hardison, DuBose, Schlant, Stone

Row 2: Davids, Abdenour, Favors, Markey, Saiontz, Wenger, Felner, T. Meyer, Greene, Nielson

Row 3: Zamore, Arnold, Ferguson, Tedrick, Mier, Shronts, Carter, Lubin, Morris, Garmany, Hymon

Row 4: Lesser, Cowan, Cox, Strittmitter, Kassan, Cross

Row 5: Pennington, Johnson, Kapernick, Schreeder, Thompson, Drummond, Storey, Chambers, Bentch, Chapman, Minna, McIntyre, Nicholson

Row 6: Aby, S. Sherman, Denniston, Ahrendt, McLarin, Shultz, Brown, Winston, Epstein, Honig, N. Meyer, McCraw

Row 7: Medd, Ritter, Garrett, Barnhart, Miller, Tolin, Whitmire, Wakefield, Freschi, Woodward, Stoller, M. Johnson

Row 8: Whipple, Maniscalco, Bardack, Goldings, Murphree, Lowe, H. Sherman, Yeoman, Chalmers, Pollard, Nathan, Poehlman, Lutz

Figure 5-57
Emory University Affiliated Hospitals Program in Internal Medicine and its Subspecialties, Department of Medicine, Emory University School of Medicine, 1974–1975.

Row 1: DiGirolamo, Goldman, Schlant, Felner, Preedy, Davidson, Hurst, K. Walker, Wilson, Ward, Jacobs, McGowan
Row 2: Balch, Murphree, Whitaker, Denniston, Dewees, Bowman, Favors, Davids, Nutter, Stone, Tuttle, Drake, Greene, Clements
Row 3: Loucks, Wakefield, Shronts, Ferguson, McKeen, King, Knapp, Taub, Coralli, Osburn, Minna, Grass, Mars
Row 4: Johnson, Kelly, Hymon, J. Walker, Meyer, Hobgood, Webb, J. G. Harris, Morris, Lopez, Pickens, McLarin
Row 5: B. Walker, Arnold, Miller, Silvers, Lawson, Perrett, Honig, Schreeder, Siegel, Bussey
Row 6: Miklozek, S. Sherman, Childress, Sidler, C. Epstein, Lewis, Pirkle, Thaler
Row 7: Scott, Darsee, Tolin, Rimland, Drummond, Dennis, Kovaz, Krisle, Kumpuris
Row 8: Sanders, Veluri, Schnell, Lubin, Woodward, Davidson, Bentch, Cleveland, Goldings, Rossner
Row 9: Poehlman, Blackwell, H. Sherman, Thompson, Lutz, Storey, Cameron, Bethel, Arensberg, Mier, Cohen

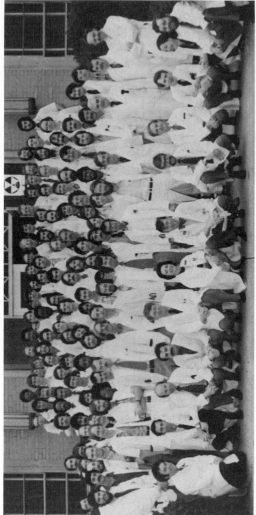

Figure 5-58

Emory University Affiliated Hospitals Program in Internal Medicine and its Subspecialties, Department of Medicine, Emory University School of Medicine, 1975–1976.

Row 1: Goldman, Clements, Wells, Someren, Hurst, Wenger, Hardison, Nutter, Gilbert, Walters, Fellner, Stone
Row 2: Siegel, Grass, Rossing, Stensby, B. Walker, Slovis, Hirsch, Arnold, Mars, Weeks, Ditty, Wilson, Whipple, K. Walker
Row 3: McGowan, Epstein, Lewis, Black, Corry, Miller, Kottle, Bortolozzo, Rose, Mier, Payne, Silvers, Poehlman, Cross, Lutz
Row 4: Fisher, Drake, Lipman, Allen, Richter, Karp, Miklozek, Nelson
Row 5: Kumpuris, Perrone, Veluri, Darsee, Rosman, Webb
Row 6: Francis, Pearlman, Plyasena, Grivas, Eisenband, Perret, Schreeder, Ross, Taub, Drummond, Boehm
Row 7: Walker, Hoopes, Pirkle, Rossner, Blackwell, Hartman, Ramsay, Costrini
Row 8: Holm, Zapf, Schnapper, Lawson, Loucks, Marks, Bethel, Thompson
Row 9: Klingenberg, West Panico, Graham, Smith, H. Osburn, Lubin
Row 10: Howell, Hassinger, Favors, Richardson, Schnell, Dewees, Jacobs, Hollman, Pickens, Markey, Shronts
Row 11: Cleveland, Stein, Rawson, Perrone, DiFulco, Johnson, Thaler, M. Johnson, Blackwell, Remington

Figure 5-59

Emory University Affiliated Hospitals Program in Internal Medicine and its Subspecialties, Department of Medicine, Emory University School of Medicine, 1976–1977.

Row 1: Haynes, Klicpera, J. Felner, Peters, S. Fellner, Nutter, Hand, Hardison, Webb, Dewees, Wilson, Schlant, K. Walker, Faruqui

Row 2: Lutz, Ward, Cooke, Clemmons, Moak, Miklozek, Coryell, Douglass, del Mazo, Wells, D. Davis, Francis, Silvers, Nelsen, Lubin

Row 3: Francis, Nankin, W. Anderson, Ferguson, Anton, Rimland, Blackwell, Anthony, Stensby, Watters, Beard, Maffett

Row 4: Parsons, Clements, Zapf, Darsee, Ware, R. Johnson, Story, Drummond, Gersh, Klingenberg, Kanter, Silverfield, Hoffman

Row 5: Kumpuris, Bromer, Hoyt, Woodward, Black, Rossing, Alimurung, Ouzts, Lipman, Nelson

Row 6: Burnett, Holm, Hotchkiss, Schnapper, Lewis, Dennis, Schnell, Bailey, Role

Row 7: West, DiFulco, Howell, Perrett, Eisenband, Jacobs, Mars, Jones, Hirsh

Row 8: Hethumuni, Payne, Thaler, Coffey, Lipsitt, Bortolazzo, Holmblad, Schmertzler

Row 9: Maurer, Wrenn, Powers, Kovacich, Remington, Dedonis, Graham, Sarma, Cleveland

Row 10: Stackhouse, McGowan, Budell, Hassinger, Slovis, Whatley, Macurak, Smith, Hollman, Hoopes, Flowers, Epstein, Koransky, King, Scheinberg

Hurst is missing from this photograph because of illness.

Figure 5-60

Emory University Affiliated Hospitals Program in Internal Medicine and its Subspecialties, Department of Medicine, Emory University School of Medicine, 1977–1978.

Row 1: McGowan, Rogers, Harris, Hand, Parsons, Tuttle, Francis, Stone, Galambos, Hurst, Drummond, Kovaz, Wenger, Schlant, Davidson, Gilbert, Delcher

Row 2: Lubin, Stensby, Nelson, Kanter, Milstein, Nankin, Ferguson, Scheinberg, Cook, Powers, Wilson, Rossing, Teutsch, DiGirolamo, Nutter

Row 3: Johnson, Fleming, Hall, Rauscher, Lesser, Leavell, Lipman, Wood, Epstein, Nelson, Coffey, Davis, Walker, Jones

Row 4: Ware, Gardner, Corn, Levin, Peltier, Petrini, Prokesch, Klingenberg, Anthony, Perrone, Abela

Row 5: Bell, Corwin, DiFulco, Nolte, Hotz, Bria, Lipsitt, Holm, Hardison, Harvey

Row 6: Feagin, Capogrossi, Maurer, Richter, Floyd, Douglass, West, Jurado, Story, Payne, Ouzts, Liss, Rosman

Row 7: Silverfield, Hotchkiss, del Mazo, Slovis, Woodward, Wrenn, Holmblad, Whatley, Freedman

Row 8: Clemmons, Bradley, Bullock, Lynch, Rawson, Kovacich, Macurak, Cross, Shulman, Black

Row 9: Peters, Odom, Braude, Smith, Stein, Ferguson, Miklozek, Karandanis, Martin, Thompson, Paustian, Stackhouse

Figure 5-61

Emory University Affiliated Hospitals Program in Internal Medicine and its Subspecialties, Department of Medicine, Emory University School of Medicine, 1978–1979.

Row 1: Mars, Goldman, Shulman, Walker, Kann, Jacobs, Hand, Hurst, Hardison, Stone, Wilson, Galambos, Schlant
Row 2: Francis, Hedaya, Paustian, Stensby, Anton, Griffin, Moore, Erb, Stein, McGowan
Row 3: Wiles, Fincher, Peltier, Liss, Abela, Hotchkiss, McMenamin, Darsee, Lipskis, Smith, Johnson, Waites, Lubin
Row 4: Fincher, Wood, Milstein, Colgan, Norton, Shafiq, Vassall, Harrington, Diamond, Taussig, Cowdery, Holm
Row 5: Jacobson, Helken, Schatten, Whitworth, Cohen, Von Berg, Scheinberg, Allyn, Baker, Hall, Clemmons, Cook, Coffey
Row 6: Parson, Steinberg, Herndon, Rossi, Gower, Harris, Harvey, Armstrong, Leavell, Regan, Role
Row 7: Williams, Fein, Smith, Cantrell, Rausher, Drummond
Row 8: Unterman, Bria, Flowers, Lawrence, Silverfield, Holmblad, Fleming, Valadez, Friedman
Row 9: Fowler, Tiliakos, Williams, Odom, Tinsley, Jurado, Rimland, Dedonis, Petrini, O'Neal, G. Austin, C. Austin, Stackhouse
Row 10: Santora, Stark, Taber, Peters, Henderson, Richter, Bradley, Baker, Rossing, Bulloch, Mertesdorf, Grossman, Lynch, St. Amant, Martin, Hoffman, Sendak, Powers, Eckman, Miklozek, Kovalch, Karandanis, White, Cooney

Figure 5-62

Emory University Affiliated Hospitals Program in Internal Medicine and its Subspecialties, Department of Medicine, Emory University School of Medicine, 1979–1980.

Row 1: N. Shulman, Ward, Wenger, B. Francis, K. Walker, Erb, Harvey, Hardison, Mickel, Hotchkiss, Anderson, Wells, Hurst, Lubin, Tuttle, Petrini, J. Shulman, Hand, Schlant, Grossman, Ramos, Goldman, Mars

Row 2: Shafiq, White, Fleming, Mermin, Rossi, O'Neal, Anderson, Capogrossi, Hammond, P. B. Francis, Rogers, Brown, Bonhomme, Jurado

Row 3: Cloninger, Cassell, Alexander, Harris, Moore, Walker, Baker, Herndon, Whitworth, Lipskis, Rimland, Rose, Jenkins, Brown, Greenberg, Wilson, Norton

Row 4: Elsey, Forsthoefel, Peters, Dannehl, Ross, Goldfarb, Hall, Jackson, Tinsley, Stein, Kaplan, McMenamin, Sendak, Ballard, Austin, Taussig, Prokesch, Gower, Holm, McGowan

Row 5: Olmsted, Williams, Glazer, Pilcher, Baker, Polack, Nwasokwa, Steinberg, Wilson, Garner, Wood, Ruderman, Cheney, Lipsitt, Cantrell

Row 6: Henderson, Herd, Vassell, Wolfe, Clark, Davis, Rossi, Champion, Smith, Rauscher, Wagner, Hassett, Martin, Gryza

Figure 5-63
Emory University Affiliated Hospitals Program in Internal Medicine and its Subspecialties, Department of Medicine, Emory University School of Medicine, 1980–1981.

Row 1: Slovis, McCormick, Garner, West, Fisher, Cooke, Musey, Goldman, Hand, Hurst, Hardison, Walker, Herndon, Shulman, Reed, Rosman, Wollam, Wenger, Cobb, Schlant, Ramos, McGowan

Row 2: Martin, Weinberg, Thomas, Herd, Forsthoefel, Rogers, Wagner, Silverman, Rossi, Erb, Allyn, Fein, Hall, Harrison, Smith, Goldberg, Regan, Glaser, Maloney, Rausher, Golden, Lubin

Row 3: Wilson, Elsey, Cloninger, Baker, Olmsted, Simon, Rudert, Gunby, Johnson, Siegel, Durham, Rybolt, Lasker, Burke, Langburg, Karandanis, McGehee, Prokesch, Gower, Lipsitt

Row 4: Anderson, Brown, Certain, Niederman, Franco, Roper, Steinberg, Savage, Cassell, Klingenberg, Jenkins, Hendley, Jackson, Elliott, Szczukowski, Baker, Newman, Sendak, Diamond, Pitts, Wolfe, Gallen, Holm

Row 5: Williams, Brown, Steinberg, Randolph, Lawrence, White, Brown, Whitworth, Belden, Bulloch, Taussig, Parrish, Morris, Conway, Affarah, Battey

Row 6: Ballard, Clemmons, Yanish, Wisebram, Hartmann, Bulger, Bailin, Farley, Pollak, DuVall, Pirkle, Jackson, Fortson

Row 7: Williams, Bronikowski, Nwasokwa, Honig, Mertesdorf, Churchwell, Ferrante, Greenberg, Jurado, Cava, Systrom, Rosing, Rausch, Dannahl, Hoff, Trammell, Milton, Waterman, Moore, Hood, Goldfarb, Tuttle, Prince

Figure 5-64

Emory University Affiliated Hospitals Program in Internal Medicine and its Subspecialties, Department of Medicine, Emory University School of Medicine, 1981–1982.

Row 1: Jaeger, Thomas, Reed, Ramos, Rauscher, Siddiq, Rogers, Hardison, Walker, Hurst, Hand, Aitcheson, Mars, Riddick, Mettler, Hendley, Denson, Hoff

Row 2: Slovis, Tuttle, Shulman, Someren DiGirolamo, Ward, Jacobs, Rimland, Cobb, Ravishankara, Lubin, Systrom, Martin, Hill, Koch

Row 3: Bizzell, Klingenberg, Durham, Andrews, Jackson, Whitworth, Niederman, Sarma, Snead, Hall, Pecora, Szczukowski, Rudert, Schiff, Ballard, Katz, Jacobs, Ramage, Barager

Row 4: Leroy, Bailin, Silverman, Forsthoefel, Rausch, Anderson, Roper, Raizes, Pitts, Hagler, Phelps, Lasker, Murray, Newman

Row 5: Smith, Mixon, Morris, T. Steinberg, Jackson, Boerner, J. Steinberg, Roubey, Hellreich, Brown, Katona, Pollak, Williams, Dannehl, Welch, Neckman

Row 6: Nwasokwa, Harris, Gibson, Pinner, Davis, Jurado, Holland, Eaton, Langburd, Franco, Glazer, Goldfarb, Taussig

Row 7: Milton, Jones-Taylor, Evans, Churchwell, Collins, Brown, O'Donaghue, Burns, Yanish, Bode, Richardson

Row 8: Jones, Cave, Taylor, Haygood, Farley, Burke, Hogan, Maloney, Parrish

Row 9: Gordon, Prince, Anderson, Martinez, King, Harrison, Certain, Casolaro, Davis, Hood, Campbell

Row 10: Routman, Jolly, Rose, Wallace, Gilman, Honig, Hirschbaum, McGhee

Row 11: McGowan, Eckman, Staton, Stein, Weinberg, Sheares, Blincoe, Griffith

Figure 5-65
Emory University Affiliated Hospitals Program in Internal Medicine and Its Subspecialties, Department of Medicine, Emory University School of Medicine, 1982–1983. The increase in size of the program required that we seek a new venue for the annual photograph. The new location, inside Grady Hospital, proved unsatisfactory.

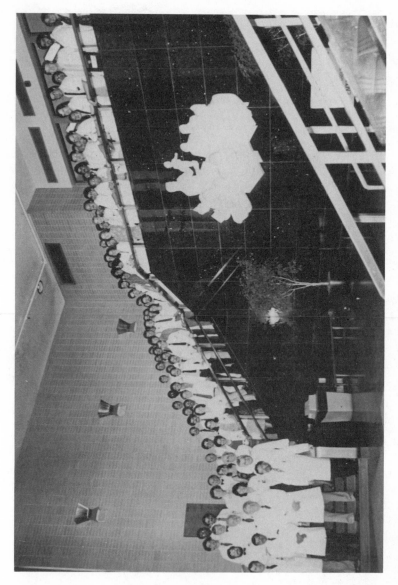

Figure 5-66
Emory University Affiliated Hospitals Program in Internal Medicine and Its Subspecialties, Department of Medicine, Emory University School of Medicine, 1983–1984.

Figure 5-67
Emory University Affiliated Hospitals Program in Internal Medicine and Its Subspecialties, Department of Medicine, Emory University School of Medicine, 1984–1985.

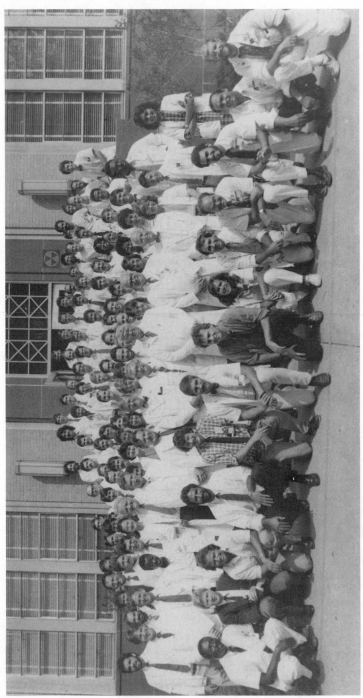

Figure 5-68

Emory University Affiliated Hospitals Program in Internal Medicine and Its Subspecialties, Department of Medicine, Emory University School of Medicine, 1985–1986. Having failed to find a better venue for the annual photograph, as returned to 69 Butler Street, in front of the Glenn Building.

Figure 5-69

Emory University Affiliated Hospitals Program in Internal Medicine and Its Subspecialties, Department of Medicine, Emory University School of Medicine, 1986–1987. Hurst is standing in the center of the first row. Logue is to his right and Kokko to his left. Walker is standing to Kokko's left. This photograph shows the last house staff appointed by Hurst; Dr. Kokko is the new chairman.

The Quest for Excellence

Figure 5-70A
House staff and faculty, Emory-VA Program, 1965–66. Photograph made in front of Emory University Hospital.

Figure 5-70B
This photograph, taken just a few minutes prior to the one shown in Figure 5–70A, and shows that "we were a happy bunch."

424   *The Quest for Excellence*

Figure 5-71
This photograph was shown on the screen when Eugene Stead, former chairman of the Department of Medicine, visited Emory. Its intent was to indicate that Stead's shoes were too big for me (Hurst) to fill. (The photograph is actually John W. Hurst Jr. standing in his father's army boots during a snow storm in Denver, Colorado).

Figure 5-72
Drs. Eugene Stead and Paul Beeson visited Emory at the same time in 1965. L–R: Dr. Robert Schlant, Dr. Maurice Tager, Dr. Eugene Stead, Mrs. Nelie Hurst, Mrs. Eugene Stead, Mrs. Barbara Beeson, Dr. Willis Hurst, and Dr. Paul Beeson.

Figure 5-73
The last time Dr. Eugene Stead visited the Department of Medicine of Emory University School of Medicine was in 1982. The photograph here was made following his discussion at medical grand rounds. On that visit, he gave advice regarding the development of the Division of Geriatrics in the Department of Medicine.

Figure 5-74
Dr. and Mrs. Eugene Stead and Dr. J. Willis Hurst, October 5, 1996, at the Steads' North Carolina home on the shore of Lake Ker.

Figure 5-75
    Mr. Alex N. Nelson. Mr. Nelson, a retired army colonel, became the business manager in the Department of Medicine in 1971. Mr. Nelson was a very capable and likable administrator. He died in 1992.

Figure 5-76
    Mr. Ivan Hawkins. Mr. Hawkins joined the administrative staff of the Department of Medicine in 1980. He managed many of the administrative aspects of the students and house staff. Mr. Hawkins continued in this position following the appointment of Dr. Juha Kokko as chairman of the department. He retired in 1997.

Figure 5-77
    Ms. Carol Miller. Carol joined the secretarial staff of the Department of Medicine in 1964. She was responsible for typing many of the manuscripts and books produced by the Department of Medicine. She continues to work with Dr. J. Willis Hurst and assisted in the preparation of this book.

Figure 5-78
  Mrs. Paula Noriega. Mrs. Noriega joined the secretarial staff of the Department of Medicine in 1974. She remained on the staff for nine years.

Figure 5-79
  Mr. David A. Bissett. Mr. Bissett, a retired army colonel, replaced Mr. Nelson as business manager in the Department of Medicine in 1978. The chief resident in medicine at each of the four hospitals was given an Emory chair each year. Bissett is shown here bringing in an Emory chair to present to one of the chief residents at the annual house-staff breakfast held on the top floor of Grady Memorial Hospital. Mr. Bissett, a superb administrator, died in 1987.

Figure 5-80
   Mrs. Joyce Mundy. Mrs. Mundy joined the secretarial staff in the Department of Medicine in 1981 at Emory University Hospital. She remained in that position until 1986.

Figure 5-81
   Mrs. Billie Hackemeyer. Mrs. Hackemeyer joined the secretarial staff in the Department of Medicine at Grady Memorial Hospital in 1983. She later moved to Emory Hospital, where she became Dr. Juha Kokko's administrative assistant when he became chairman of the department in 1986.

Figure 5-82A
   Mrs. Barbara Brown. Mrs. Brown served admirably as secretary to Dr. J. Willis Hurst in the Emory Clinic.

Figure 5-82B
    Mrs. Joyce White. Mrs. White served admirably as secretary for Dr. J. Willis Hurst in the Emory Clinic.

Figure 5-83
    Emory Clinic Building B was built in 1985. It houses the Emory Eye Center, the Winship Clinic, Outpatient Surgery, and Psychiatry.

Figure 5-84

Emory University Hospital. This aerial photograph of the hospital was made in 1975. Many additions were made to the hospital after 1922, when it was built and named the Wesley Memorial Hospital. These additions are discussed in the text on page 331.

This photograph shows the G wing of the hospital (upper part of photograph) and the connector (F wing). These important additions were made in 1972. Two and one-half floors of the connector were allocated to the Department of Medicine. This was a defining moment for the Department of Medicine, because prior to 1972 there was no space available for the Department within Emory University Hospital.

Later, in 1988, an 11-story tower (E wing) was added to the hospital (see Figure 5-86). The H wing was added in 1993 (see Figure 5-86).

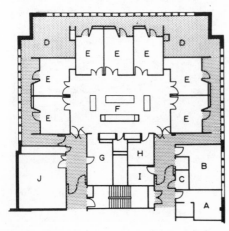

Figure 5-85

The architectural design of the Coronary Care Unit that was built in 1972. This photograph is reproduced with permission from *The Heart: Arteries and Veins*, ed. by J. W. Hurst and R. B. Logue (2d ed., New York: McGraw-Hill 1970), 231.

Figure 5-86
The 11-story patient care tower (E wing) was added to Emory Hospital in 1988. It is shown in the left background. The H wing of Emory Hospital was completed in 1993. It houses the office suite for the chairman of the Department of Medicine, a classroom, offices for administrative personnel, the hospital library, the general clinical research center, facilities for physical therapy, and the hospital cafeteria.

Figure 5-87A
The original Woodruff Memorial Research Building, which is connected to Emory Hospital.

Figure 5-87B
This newest addition to the Woodruff Memorial Research Building was completed in 1995. The E wing to Emory Hospital is to the right.

Figure 5-88
Last addition to Emory Clinic Building A, completed in 1987. The entrance to the building was changed from facing Clifton Road to the southern side of the original building.

Figure 5-89A
The John P. Scott Anatomy Building, completed in 1917.

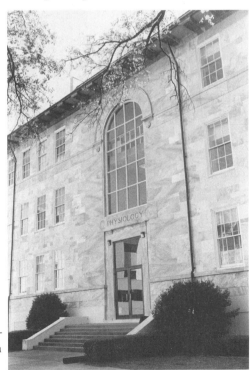

Figure 5-89B
The T. T. Fishburne Physiology Building, completed in 1917.

Figure 5-89C
The connector between the Anatomy and Physiology Buildings was constructed in 1970 and is named in honor of Dr. Harry Williams, a popular
professor of pharmacology.

Figure 5-90
The Robert W. Woodruff Health Sciences Center Administration Building, completed in 1978, is one of the largest medical administration buildings in the nation.

Figure 5-91
  Egleston Children's Hospital as it appeared in 1996.

Figure 5-92
  The Emory Center for Rehabilitation Medicine, completed in 1976.

Figure 5-93
Dr. Gerald F. Fletcher, originally a member of the Department of Medicine, served as chairman of the Department of Rehabilitation Medicine from 1986 to 1995.

Figure 5-94
The Robert W. Woodruff Health Sciences Medical Library is located in the renovated dental school building. This library houses the Abner Wellborn Calhoun Memorial Room.

Figure 5-95
Mr. and Mrs. O. Wayne Rollins. This photograph was taken at the dedication of the O. Wayne Rollins Research Building in 1990.

Figure 5-96
The O. Wayne Rollins Research Center Building was completed in 1990. It houses the Departments of Pharmacology, Microbiology, and Biochemistry. By providing space for these three departments, this important building permitted the development of additional research space for the Department of Medicine within the Woodruff Memorial Research Building.

Figure 5-97
The Grace Crum Rollins School of Public Health. The building was completed in 1994.

Figure 5-98A
Yerkes Regional Primate Research Center (main building).

Figure 5-98B
Yerkes Regional Primate Research Center (field station).

Figure 5-99
When completed, this building will be used for the primary care physicians of the Emory Clinic. The building will be completed in August 1997.

Figure 5-100

Houston Mill House. This historic house has been owned by Emory University since 1959. The house was restored by the Emory Women's Club and is the site of many social events.

Figure 5-101

The American Cancer Society national headquarters building was completed in 1989.

Figure 5-102A
   The original Centers for Disease Control and Prevention, completed in 1959 on land contributed by Mr. Robert W. Woodruff.

Figure 5-102B
   This addition to the Centers for Disease Control and Prevention was completed in 1996.

Figure 5-103
The Emory Conference Center Hotel, completed in 1994.

Figure 104A
Wesley Woods Geriatric Center became closely affiliated with Emory
University in 1985. It is utilized in the training program of the Geriatrics
Division of the Department of Medicine.

Figure 5-104B
The 100-bed Wesley Woods Geriatric and Research Hospital was constructed in 1986.

Figure 5-105
The George W. Woodruff Physical Education Center was completed in 1983. The Health Enhancement and Rehabilitation Program was housed in this facility. The facility is virtually underground and is shown to the left in the upper portion of the photograph.

Figure 5-106
   The Nell Hodgson School of Nursing building, dedicated in 1968.

Figure 5-107
   The newly renovated Grady Memorial Hospital. The plans for the renovation were approved by the Fulton-DeKalb Hospital Authority in 1988.
The construction, which required several years and cost more than $336
million, was completed in 1995. The new outpatient department building
is shown on the right.

Figure 5-108
Crawford W. Long Hospital. The original Crawford W. Long Hospital is on the right, and the Peachtree Building is on the left. Construction of the Peachtree Building was completed in 1971.

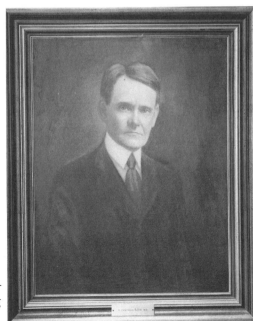

Figure 5-109A
Dr. E. Campbell Davis, co-founder of Crawford Long Hospital.

Figure 5-109B
Dr. Luther C. Fischer, co-founder of Crawford Long Hospital. The original Crawford Long Hospital was named the Davis-Fischer Sanatorium. It was built by Drs. Davis and Fischer. The name was later changed to Crawford W. Long Hospital in honor of the Georgian who was the first to utilize ether anesthesia.

Figure 5-110
This photograph shows Dr. Wadley Glenn, who was the medical director of Crawford W. Long Hospital and a member of the Emory board of trustees. Mrs. Glenn is on the left, and Mrs. Isabel Fraser is on the right.

Figure 5-111
   Dr. Harold S. Ramos became chief of
medicine and director of medical education at Crawford Long Hospital in 1963.

Figure 5-112
   Inspecting the construction of the
Carlyle Fraser Heart Center at Crawford
Long Hospital. Mr. Dan Barker, superin-
tendent of the hospital, is shown in the
center of the photograph. Dr. Wadley Glenn, medical director of Crawford
Long Hospital, is shown on the left. Dr. Linton Bishop, who was a major
mover in the development, is on the right.

The Quest for Excellence

Figure 5-113A
Mr. Carlyle Fraser. The Carlyle Fraser Heart Center is named in honor of him.

Figure 5-113B
Mrs. Isabel Fraser, who helped establish the Carlyle Fraser Heart Center at Crawford Long Hospital.

Figure 5-114
Dr. Douglas C. Morris became director of the Carlyle Fraser Heart Center at Crawford Long Hospital in 1990. In 1994, he moved on to direct the new Emory Heart Center as well. He was appointed the J. Willis Hurst Professor of Medicine in 1996.

Figure 5-115
Mr. John Henry became the administrator for both Emory University Hospital and Crawford Long Hospital in 1995.

Figure 5-116A
The Atlanta Veterans Affairs Hospital, completed in 1966.

Figure 5-116B
Dr. James C. Crutcher was chief of the medical service at the Atlanta Veterans Affairs Medical Center from 1957 to 1974. In 1978 he was appointed chief medical director of the Veterans Administration in Washington, D.C.

Figure 5-117
This addition to the Atlanta Veterans Affairs Medical Center was completed in 1994.

Figure 5-118A
This photograph shows the former Chairman of the Department of Medicine, Dr. J. Willis Hurst, passing the baton to Dr. Juha Kokko, the new chairman of the Department of Medicine. This act actually took place at a dinner at the Cherokee Club in September 1986. The photograph shown above was made in 1995 as a reenactment of the 1986 action.

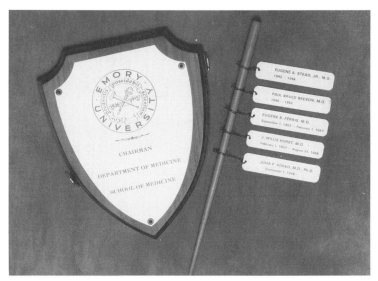

Figure 5-118B
A close-up view of the tags attached to the baton showing the names and dates of those who served as professor and chairman of the Department of Medicine.

EPILOGUE

... It is the personality of the artist or scientist that determines the ultimate character of his work. Therefore, for a historian, the personality of the artist or scientist must be an essential element of study. The historian can do this by recording the impact of a person on his time and future and by tracing his fleeting shadow during his lifetime. Without the human element, history becomes a colorless recitation of facts. This is even more true when dealing with medical science, which has as its final goal the application of science to human beings. The goals of the physician are primarily humanistic.[1]

Richard J. Bing, M.D.

This book chronicles the genesis, evolution, metamorphosis, and growth of Emory University, Emory University School of Medicine, and the Department of Medicine. To quote President Johnson, as he opened the LBJ Library, the tale is told—"with the bark off."

I agree with the epigraph above; "*without the human element, history becomes a colorless recitation of facts.*" Accordingly, when it was possible to do so, I have linked the actions of 1942–1986 to the people who were involved. I have also displayed, as boldly as I can, how progress can be made when an increasing number of devoted people rally around a noble cause. The noble cause was clearly in focus; it was to develop the best Department of Medicine that could be created. *We did not forget that it was the quest for excellence that was important and not the declaration that excellence had been achieved. The quest for excellence in medical matters should never end, and our dissatisfaction with mediocrity should never cease.*

Now, as chairman of the Department of Medicine for the thirty years beginning in 1957 and ending in 1986, I will end this book by repeating some of the remarks I made at the farewell dinner at the Ritz-Carlton Hotel in Buckhead on August 22, 1986. I thanked many people for their help over the years and then addressed my remarks to Juha Kokko:

> Dr. Kokko, my successor, and his wife, Nancy, are here tonight. I have been unable to decide if my feelings are those of a minister who is about to marry an eager couple or the father of the future bride. So I will play both roles. Dr. Kokko—will you take this Department to love and develop, to push forward

---

[1] R. J.Bing, *Cardiology: The Evolution of the Science and the Art* (Switzerland: Harwood Academic Publishers, 1992), xvii. Reproduced with the permission of the publisher and author.

through times of joy and sadness, and be concerned for the Department twenty-four hours a day? The school and Dr. Kokko have already said yes.

It is now time for me to step aside just as the father of the bride steps aside. The father of the bride continues to love the daughter he has given up and will, when called upon, help the marriage in every possible way.

I wish to express my great pleasure that Dr. Kokko will be my successor. He was a student here at Emory, and we have all followed his very successful career. He will, without a doubt, steer the Department into beautiful and exciting waters. Juha, I want you and Nancy to know how happy we are that you will be the next chairman of the Department of Medicine of Emory University.[2]

The photographs shown in Figures 5-118A and 5-118B were made in 1995 (see p. 451). They reproduce an act that took place in the fall of 1986. The members of the Department of Medicine welcomed Dr. and Mrs. Kokko to Emory at a reception at the Cherokee Club. The baton was passed to the new chairman. The little tags on the baton are embossed with the names of the former departmental chairmen and the years they served.

Post-Epilogue (A Personal Note)

I continued my role as Candler Professor of Medicine (Cardiology) and chief of cardiology at Emory University Hospital and the Emory Clinic until 1988. I continued to see patients in consultation until 1991, when Dr. Kokko and Dr. Wayne Alexander, director of the Division of Cardiology, appointed me as consultant to the Division of Cardiology. As such, I teach six to nine sessions each week and write one half of each day. My office suite is on the third floor of the Robert W. Woodruff Health Sciences Center Library (the old dental school building), which is ideal for my efforts.

The Future Is Bright

The benefactors of Emory University have continued to support the dreams of the members of the board of trustees, the president, and the leaders of the various divisions of the university, including the leaders of the Robert W. Woodruff Health Sciences Center. These civic-minded benefactors deserve the gratitude of the community at large. Here are some samples of the developments they have made possible for Emory University and the Robert W. Woodruff Health Science Center.

By the mid-nineties there were fifteen applicants for each of the 114 freshman year positions at Emory University School of Medicine.

---

[2] J. W. Hurst, "The Bridge," in *Notes from a Chairman* (Chicago: Year Book Medical Publishers, 1987), 312–14.

In 1993–94 Emory University School of Medicine ranked twentieth in the nation in federal research funding. This was owing largely to the efforts of Dr. Kokko.

The following information appeared in the January 26, 1996, issue of the *Emory Report.*

> Emory University's endowment of $2.23 billion ranked sixth in the nation. Only Harvard, the Texas system, Yale, Princeton, and Stanford ranked above Emory. Emory had the highest growth rate on invested funds among all universities in the nation. The 32 percent increase in market value was because 1.5 billion dollars were invested in Coca-Cola stock.

The September 3, 1996, issue of the *Emory Report* contained the following announcement.

> The Robert W. Woodruff Foundation, Inc., the Joseph B. Whitehead Foundation, and the Letlee Pate Evans Foundation, long-term friends of Emory, have established the Robert W. Woodruff Health Sciences Fund, Inc., which will provide $3 million each to the Woodruff Health Sciences Center. Half of the annual income will support programs of the Winship Cancer Center.
>
> The foundations jointly designated a portion of their Coca-Cola stock to be set aside in order to establish the new corporation.

The September 10, 1996, issue of the *Atlanta Constitution* carried a story entitled: "Emory Clinic to Build Satellite Facility in North Fulton." The article pointed out that most of the seventeen Emory Clinic satellites were staffed by primary-care physicians. The new facility would be the largest and would provide services in cardiology, neurology, orthopedics, dermatology, and urology, as well as primary care.

The August 25, 1997 issue of *The Emory Report* included the following news:

> Emory tied with five schools for a ninth-place ranking in the national university category of this year's *U.S. News & World Report* annual college quality rankings and had the highest "value-added" factor among the top 25 universities.

The medical school was not mentioned specifically, nor were the departments in the medical school. But as a long-time observer of the Emory scene, I have confidence that the medical school and its Department of Medicine played a considerable role in achieving this ranking.

My View of the Chairmanship

I wish I could do it all again—but the clock is ticking louder now.

Appendixes

A Note of Explanation

• Appendixes 1 through 3 were reproduced from the annual Bulletins of Emory University School of Medicine. The reproductions represent only a fragment of the contents of each of the Bulletins. They were selected for the following reasons.

The Bulletin published in 1915 shows that the school still recognized the Atlanta Medical College. The discussion of Atlanta, the medical school buildings, and the tuition for medical school are interesting.

Emory was still recognizing the Atlanta Medical College in 1917. The discussion about Atlanta, the medical school buildings, and tuition for medical school again make fascinating reading.

The Bulletin published in 1942 can serve as a marker that identifies the period when full-time faculty members were added to the Department of Medicine. Note that the classes were limited to sixty *men.*

• The names of the individuals in leadership positions at Emory University and the Robert W. Woodruff Health Sciences Center and its affiliates from 1915 to 1996 are listed in Appendix 4.

• Parts of the annual Bulletin of Emory University School of Medicine are reproduced in Appendixes 9 through 53. These pages of the Bulletins are reproduced in order to display the names of the department chairmen, the full-time faculty members, the volunteer clinical faculty, and the fellows.

• The photographs appearing in Appendixes 5 through 7 show the deans and department chairmen during the sixties, seventies, and eighties.

• The photograph in Appendix 8 is of a cartoon created by medical student Carl Askren. It shows the department chairman, division directors, and chiefs of the medical services at Emory University Hospital, Grady Memorial Hospital, Crawford Long Hospital, and the Atlanta Veterans Affairs Hospital.

Appendix 1: The following document is copied from a portion of the 1915 Bulletin of Emory University School of Medicine (Appendix 1). Please note that Atlanta Medical College was still mentioned on the face of the Bulletin.

I–4   JULY, 1915   No. 2

BULLETIN
OF
EMORY UNIVERSITY

SCHOOL OF MEDICINE

ATLANTA MEDICAL COLLEGE
ATLANTA, GA.

PUBLISHED QUARTERLY BY EMORY UNIVERSITY
ENTERED AS SECOND-CLASS MATTER JUNE 5, 1915, AT THE POST OFFICE AT
ATLANTA, GA., UNDER ACT OF CONGRESS AUGUST 24, 1912

EMORY UNIVERSITY
THE A. W. CALHOUN MEDICAL LIBRARY

HISTORICAL STATEMENT

Atlanta Medical College. This college was founded in 1854 under the energetic leadership of Doctor J. G. Westmoreland. The first course of lectures was given in the courthouse. In the same year Doctor Westmoreland was elected to the legislature of Georgia, and from that body secured an appropriation of $15,000 with which to aid in erecting the college buildings. The land, corner Butler and Armstrong streets, upon which the present group of college buildings stand, was secured and a substantial building erected. Scarcely was this building completed and equipped, when the Civil

War began. During the war the college buildings were used as a hospital and the surrounding hills were covered with hospital tents, where the blue and gray were cared for side by side. War depleted the professional ranks of the South; physicians were needed in every section and needed quickly. There were students, but no money. The faculty met this emergency in 1865 by re-organizing and reopening the school, and giving two sessions, a winter and summer, a year, allowing the student to graduate after attending two sessions. The expenses of the college were borne by the faculty, who accepted the students' notes for tuition. Few of those notes were ever paid. As the stress of circumstances was relieved, college conditions improved, and yearly sessions were resumed.

The Southern Medical College was organized and chartered in 1878, and continued in successful operation for twenty years.

ATLANTA COLLEGE OF PHYSICIANS AND SURGEONS

In 1898 the faculties of the two schools recognizing the immensely greater value and efficiency of one Medical College in Atlanta, consolidated the two schools as the "Atlanta College of Physicians and Surgeons." This coalition enhanced the prestige of this new school, and stimulated an active interest in the betterment of medical teaching. New buildings were erected and extensive improvements in facilities for teaching and broadening the curriculum were planned and carried out. The college was materially aided by contributions from citizens of Atlanta and from the faculty. Mr. Andrew Carnegie gave $25,000 to establish the "Carnegie Pathological Institute." Doctor A. W. Calhoun contributed $10,000, and the dean, Doctor W. S. Elkin, equipped the Histological Laboratory at an expense of $5,000.

With the establishment of the new laboratories began the employment of salaried "full time" professors.

The Atlanta School of Medicine was established in 1905, and was successful from the start. But the faculties of the two institutions soon recognized the necessity of merging the two schools and forming a strong Medical College with increased resources, teaching ability and clinical facilities. This merger was completed in June, 1913, under the old historic name, "Atlanta Medical College," and occupies the property on Butler street, which was the original site, and has been continuously used for medical teaching since 1854.

MEDICAL DEPARTMENT OF EMORY UNIVERSITY.

The faculty of this institution soon realized that the object of this merger, to organize an institution of dignity and permanent value, whose graduates would receive recognition throughout the United States—an institution so constituted, as to make it a real public asset, and so conducted as to deserve the highest professional and popular commendation, could only be accomplished by securing an endowment, a university connection and greater hospital facilities.

This was accomplished when on June 1, 1915, the Atlanta Medical College was legally made the Medical Department of Emory University, the University taking it over and endowing it with $250,000, in addition to $20,000 previously secured.

By this merger the desires of the Atlanta Medical College have been accomplished, and a great School of Medicine in the Central South has been assured.

It starts anew with an endowment of $270,000. As the Medical Department of a University bearing the name of one of the oldest and best known institutions in the South and which has a large and growing endowment, it enters upon an era of enlarged usefulness.

It has the "Wesley Memorial Hospital," which will at an early day build a two hundred thousand dollar hospital, to be used by the "Atlanta Medical College" as a teaching hospital.

The College now has the privilege of using all the material at Grady Hospital for teaching its classes, about two hundred and fifty beds and an enormous dispensary clinic.

There will be salaried "full time" professors and assistants in the Departments of Anatomy, Physiology, Chemistry, Pathology, Materia Medica and Pharmacology.

This school is now a Class "A" College.

ATLANTA AS A LOCATION

Atlanta is the largest city in Georgia and the surrounding States; it has a population of 200,000, and is a city of diversified interests and industries. The climate of Atlanta is pleasant, lacking both the enervating heat of the lower South and the bitter cold of the North. The Federal Government maintains a military post near Atlanta. The city is the Capital of the State; the railroad center of the South; and one of the most modern and progressive of American cities. The influences in Atlanta are the best. There are many churches which offer special attractions to the medical students. Concerts and lectures add to the interest of student life. The Carnegie Library of Atlanta contains many volumes and is open every day. Living expenses in Atlanta are as reasonable as in most American cities.

The city of Atlanta maintains the Grady Hospital, which takes care of the poor and needy, suffering with diseases common to the central South. In addition, the city maintains a hospital for tuberculous patients, and one for contagious and infectious diseases. In and around the city are nearly 20 other hospitals either under denominational or private control. The Georgia State Board of Health is located in the State Capitol.

The Atlanta Medical College is pre-eminent in this section of the South for its history, its consistent progress, its equipment, and the courses it offers. The College is situated conveniently to the central business section, across the street from the Grady Hospital. It is in reach of the poorer classes needing medical attention. For over sixty years it has maintained a dispensary, which supplies ample material for clinical instruction. The College treats 25,000 to 30,000 patients annually, the patients coming from the State at large as well as from the city.

COLLEGE BUILDINGS

The group of College buildings is situated on a plat of ground about two and a half acres in area at the corner of Butler and Armstrong Streets. This ground has been continually occupied for medical purposes since 1854. It is four blocks from the center of the city, one block from the Auditorium, accessible to street car lines. The buildings, five in number, are arranged on the modern university plan, and are known respectively as the Main Building, situated on the corner, Practical Anatomy

Building, Pathological Institute, and the Microscopic Anatomy Building. In addition, an excellent Animal House is located in the rear of the Pathological Institute. The estimated value of the grounds, buildings and equipment is over a quarter of a million dollars. The buildings are modern and equipped with the latest facilities for teaching medicine in its various branches. They are lighted by gas and electricity, steam heated throughout, and abundantly supplied with hot and cold water. There is an ample supply of individual lockers for the use of students. The College also maintains a Book Store for the convenience of the students where books and materials are sold at regular list prices.

The **Main Building**, erected in 1906, with frontage on Butler Street, has a floor space of approximately 43,000 square feet. The architect of this building, with a member of the Faculty, visited the medical centers of the North and East and examined various college buildings before beginning this one in order that they might secure the most modern ideas of construction and utility. This building is from a composite plan of the best they observed, and is designed for a variety of purposes. On the first floor is the Clinical Dispensary, which consists of two clinic amphitheatres, eight examination rooms and a Pharmacy. Here also are a small clinical laboratory, and a dark room for developing negatives. On the second floor are the Administration Offices, Book Store, Library, Laboratory of Pharmacology, Lecture rooms of Surgery, Medicine and Pharmacology. On the third floor are the laboratories and lecture room of Physiology. Here also is the Surgical Amphitheatre, in connection with which are several examination, sterilization, anaesthetic, recovery and storage rooms and an X-Ray room. The fourth floor, exclusive of the space occupied by the elevation of the Amphitheatre, is taken up by the Laboratories, Lecture room and store rooms of the Chemistry Department.

The **Practical Anatomy Building** is a two-story brick and granite structure, forty by seventy feet, fronting on Butler Street. The basement is devoted to the injection and preservation of cadavers. The floor above is the Dissecting room.

The **Microscopic Anatomy Building** is a two-story brick and granite structure forty by sixty feet, fronting on Armstrong Street. The first floor contains a large lecture room, office of the Professor of Anatomy and a chart room. The second floor contains a large Microscopic Laboratory, Technique Room, Microscope Room and Museum.

The **Pathological Institute** is a three-story brick and granite building, seventy-five feet square, fronting on Butler Street, opposite the Grady Hospital. On the first floor are the offices, Private Laboratories, Museum and Amphitheatre of the Pathological Department. On the second floor is the Pathological Laboratory. On the third floor is the Bacteriological Laboratory.

The **Animal House** is a small brick and concrete building in the rear of the Carnegie Pathological Institute. Its four compartments are adjuncts to Surgery, Pathology, Physiology and Pharmacology. Two concrete frog and turtle ponds furnish materials for work in Physiology and Pharmacology.

FEES AND EXPENSES

Tuition.—The tuition fee for each class is $150.00 per year, entitling the student to all didactic lectures, recitations, quizzes, required laboratory courses and clinics of his class. It is payable in two installments—one-half at the opening of the session, the other half in January before the mid-term examinations.

Dissecting Fee.—The Freshman and Sophomore students are required to pay a dissecting fee of $12.00 per student when they begin dissecting, about November 1st. No one will be allowed to dissect until he has secured his dissecting ticket from the Registrar.

Diploma or Graduation Fee.—Students who apply for the degree of Doctor of Medicine are charged a diploma fee of $25.00, which must be paid to the Registrar on or before April 1st. This fee will not be returned in case an applicant fails to graduate.

Post-Graduate Fee.—Physicians admitted to the general lectures and clinics of this College must pay a fee of $25.00 for attendance throughout all or any portion of the session.

Tuition Fees are not Returnable nor Transferable.—Students withdrawing or receiving their dismissal from the College will not be entitled to any return of fees. Under no circumstances are promissory notes accepted as payment; and no ticket is issued until full payment for the same has been made. Students are advised to pay fees by cash, Postal or Express money orders, or in Atlanta or New York exchange for the exact amount. The College will not endorse nor cash checks for private expenses.

Breakage Deposit.—A deposit of $10.00 is required of all Freshmen and Sophomore students, and $5.00 of all Junior and Senior students at the opening of each session to insure the College against loss of, or damage to, furniture, apparatus, etc. This deposit will be returned at the end of the year after deductions for such damage have been made.

Laboratory work and clinical instruction are especially featured in this institution—and while the laboratories are large, comfortable, superbly equipped and situated in special buildings, there are not extra charges for either laboratory work or other clinical facilities, though this character of work constitutes the most expensive feature of modern medical teaching. Nor are pay quizzes of any kind allowed. This work is directly under the supervision of the Professor of each department.

A student's total outlay of money is represented by the fees as stated, plus his books and necessary living expenses.

BOARD AND LODGING

Good board with lodging will cost from $18.00 to $25.00 per month. Comfortable rooms without board may be had from $5.00 to $10.00 per month. A list of boarding houses, carefully selected, is published just prior to each college session, a copy of which may be had by applying to the Registrar. The students select their choice in regard to location, distance and price.

Students may have their mail directed in care of the "Atlanta Medical College," where it will be delivered to them daily except Sundays and holidays. They should have their addresses changed to their boarding houses as soon as they are permanently located.

Appendix 2: The following document is copied from a portion of the 1917 Bulletin of Emory University School of Medicine (Appendix 2). Please note that Atlanta Medical College was still mentioned on the face of the Bulletin.

Vol. III   JUNE, 1917   No. VI

BULLETIN

OF

EMORY UNIVERSITY

SCHOOL OF MEDICINE

ATLANTA MEDICAL COLLEGE
ATLANTA, GA.

PUBLISHED MONTHLY BY EMORY UNIVERSITY
ENTERED AS SECOND-CLASS MATTER JUNE 5, 1915, AT THE POST OFFICE AT
ATLANTA, GA., UNDER ACT OF CONGRESS OF AUGUST 24, 1912.

HISTORICAL STATEMENT

Atlanta Medical College. This college was founded in 1854 under the leadership of Doctor J. G. Westmoreland. The first course of lectures was given in the courthouse. In the same year Doctor Westmoreland was elected to the legislature of Georgia, and from that body secured an appropriation of $15,000 with which to aid in erecting the college buildings. The land, corner Butler and Armstrong streets, upon which the present group of college buildings stand, was secured and a substantial building erected. Scarcely was this building completed and equipped, when the Civil

War began. During the war the college buildings were used as a hospital and the surrounding hills were covered with hospital tents, where the blue and gray were cared for side by side. War depleted the professional ranks of the South; physicians were needed in every section and needed quickly. There were students, but no money. The faculty met this emergency in 1865 by re-organizing and reopening the school, and giving two sessions, a winter and a summer, a year, allowing the student to graduate after attending two sessions. The expenses of the college were borne by the faculty, who accepted the students' notes for tuition. Few of those notes were ever paid. As the stress of circumstances was relieved, college conditions improved, and yearly sessions were resumed.

The Southern Medical College was organized and chartered in 1878, and continued in successful operation for twenty years.

Atlanta College of Physicians and Surgeons. In 1898 the faculties of the two schools recognizing the immensely greater value and efficiency of one Medical College in Atlanta, consolidated the two schools as the "Atlanta College of Physicians and Surgeons." This coalition enhanced the prestige of the new school, and stimulated an active interest in the betterment of medical teaching. New buildings were erected and extensive improvements in facilities for teaching and broadening the curriculum were planned and carried out. The college was materially aided by contributions from citizens of Atlanta and from the faculty. Mr. Andrew Carnegie gave $25,000 to establish the "Carnegie Pathological Institute." Doctor A. W. Calhoun contributed $10,000, and the dean, Doctor W. S. Elkin, equipped the Histological Laboratory at an expense of $5,000.

With the establishment of the new laboratories began the employment of salaried "full time" professors.

The Atlanta School of Medicine was established in 1905 and was successful from the start. But the faculties of the two institutions soon recognized the necessity of merging the two schools and forming a strong Medical College with increased resources, teaching ability and clinical facilities. This merger was completed in June, 1913, under the old historic name, "Atlanta Medical College," and occupies the property on Butler street, which was the original site, and has been continuously used for medical teaching since 1854.

School of Medicine of Emory University. The faculty of this institution soon realized that the object of this merger, to organize an institution of dignity and permanent value, whose graduates would receive recognition throughout the United States—an institution so constituted, as to make it a real public asset, and so conducted as to deserve the highest professional and popular commendation, could only be accomplished by securing an endowment, a university connection, and greater hospital facilities.

This was accomplished when on June 1, 1915, the Atlanta Medical College was legally made the School of Medicine of Emory University, the University taking it over and endowing it with $250,000, in addition to $20,000 previously secured.

By this merger the desires of the Atlanta Medical College have been accomplished, and a great School of Medicine in the Central South has been assured.

It starts anew with an endowment of $270,000. As the Medical College of a University bearing the name of one of the oldest and best known institutions in the

South, which has a large and growing endowment, it has entered upon an era of enlarged usefulness.

The College utilizes the present Wesley Memorial Hospital, but at an early date there will be erected a new hospital at a cost of two hundred thousand dollars. This new hospital, bearing the old name, and the out-patient building just erected on the grounds of the college, will make in all a commodious group of buildings for clinical instruction.

The College has the privilege of using all the material at Grady Hospital for teaching its classes, about two hundred and fifty beds and an enormous dispensary clinic.

There are salaried "full time" professors, assistants and technicians in the Departments of Anatomy, Physiology, Chemistry, Pathology, and Pharmacology.

This School is a member of the Association of American Medical Colleges and is rated class A by the Council on Education of the American Medical Association.

ATLANTA AS A LOCATION

Atlanta is the largest city in Georgia and the surrounding States; it has a population of 200,000, and is a city of diversified interests and industries. The climate of Atlanta is pleasant, lacking both the enervating heat of the lower South and the bitter cold of the North. The Federal Government maintains a military post near Atlanta. The city is the Capital of the State; the railroad center of the South; and one of the most modern and progressive of American cities. The influences in Atlanta are the best. There are many churches which offer special attractions to the medical students. Concerts and lectures add to the interest of student life. The Carnegie Library of Atlanta contains many volumes and is open every day. Living expenses in Atlanta are as reasonable as in most American cities.

The city of Atlanta maintains the Grady Hospital, which takes care of the poor and needy, suffering with diseases common to the central South. In addition, the city maintains a hospital for tuberculous patients, and one for contagious and infectious diseases. In and around the city are nearly 20 other hospitals either under denominational or private control. The Georgia State Board of Health is located in the State Capitol.

The Atlanta Medical College is pre-eminent in this section of the South for its history, its consistent progress, its equipment and the courses it offers. The College is situated conveniently to the central business section, across the street from the Grady Hospital. It is in reach of the poorer classes needing medical attention. For over sixty years it has maintained a dispensary, which supplies ample material for clinical instruction. The College treats 25,000 to 30,000 patients annually, the patients coming from the State at large as well as from the city.

COLLEGE BUILDINGS

The group of College buildings is situated on a plat of ground over two and a half acres in area at the corner of Butler and Armstrong streets. This ground has been continually occupied for medical purposes since 1854. It is five blocks from the center of the city, one block from the Auditorium, accessible to street car lines. The buildings, four in number, are arranged on the modern university plan, and are known respectively as the Main Building, situated on the corner, Practical Anatomy Building, Pathological Institute, and the new Out-Patient Building. In addition, an excellent Animal House is located in the rear of the Pathological Institute. The estimated value of the grounds, buildings and equipment is over a quarter of a million dollars. The buildings are modern and are equipped with the latest facilities for teaching medicine in its various branches. They are lighted by gas and electricity, steam heated throughout, and are abundantly supplied with hot and cold water. There is an ample supply of individual lockers for the use of students. The College also maintains a Book Store for the convenience of the students where books and materials are sold at regular list prices.

The Main Building, erected in 1906, with frontage on Butler Street, has a floor space of approximately 43,000 square feet. The architect of this building, with a member of the Faculty, visited the medical centers of the North and East and examined various college buildings before beginning this one in order that they might secure the most modern ideas of construction and utility. This building is from a composite plan of the best they observed, and is designed for a variety of purposes. On the second floor are the Administration Offices, Book Store, Library and Lecture rooms of Surgery and Medicine. On the third floor is the Surgical Amphitheatre, in connection with which are several examination, sterilization, anaesthetic, recovery and storage rooms.

The New Medical Buildings. Three of the buildings of this School are located on the Main Campus of the University and are for the instruction of first and second year students. They are similar in architecture and uniform in construction, being built of reinforced concrete with marble veneering. They are listed below:

The Anatomy Building is 140 feet long and 40 feet wide, consisting of three stories and a basement. It also provides for instruction in Bacteriology.

The Chemistry Building is 44 by 159 feet. It is designed eventually to accommodate the academic as well as the medical branches of Chemistry.

The Physiology Building accommodates the departments of Physiology and Pharmacology. Physiology occupies the second and third floors and Pharmacology, the basement and first floor.

The J. J. Gray Clinic Building. This building, which was completed in May, 1917, is a four-story brick and stone structure. It is primarily the out-patient clinic building, though it contains also the dormitory quarters for the hospital internes, and the experimental animal surgery department. The basement is used for the X-Ray Department, the storage room for the Pharmacy, the Dispensary record room, the Pediatric Clinic, the Orthopedic Clinic, and Gymnasium.

On the first floor are the administration office, the pharmacy and the medical and surgical clinics, with the main waiting room.

On the second floor are held the clinics for the various specialties—Neurology, Oto-Rhinolaryngology, Opthalmology, Gynecology and Obstetrics, Genito-Urinary Diseases, and Dermatology.

The third floor consists of twelve dormitory rooms, shower baths, and a club room for the internes.

On the fourth floor, the roof floor, are the paddock for the animals, the sterilizing and operating rooms for experimental surgery.

The elevator shaft runs from the basement to the roof. The building is modern, of reinforced concrete, fire-proof, well ventilated and lighted.

The present dispensary attendance is about 30,000 a year, and it is believed that the new building will enable the staff to handle 50,000 without difficulty.

HOSPITALS

The Grady Hospital was established in 1892 and is under municipal control. It occupies a square on Butler Street across the street from and facing the property of the Atlanta Medical College.

It is constructed on the pavilion plan and has a capacity of two hundred and thirty-five beds. The central administration building has three floors and contains the executive offices and accommodations for the resident medical staff and nurses. Connected with the hospital is a large amphitheatre for medical and surgical clinical instruction and a smaller operating room, and additional rooms for instruments, sterilization of dressings, and giving of anaesthesia, and the preparation of patients for operations. Since its establishment there have been added additional pavilions known as the obstetrical ward, the children's ward and a ward for infectious diseases. In addition a new and magnificent hospital building was completed in 1912, at a cost of over $100,000, and is now in operation. It contains five wards, a number of private rooms, two operating rooms and an open-air ward on the roof. This building is complete in every detail and is furnished throughout with the best and latest hospital equipment. There were treated in this institution last year nearly 7,500 patients. Being directly across the street from the College, it is very convenient to the students of this institution who receive both medical and surgical, clinical and ward instruction at the hospital. There is a training school for nurses connected with the hospital. It also has ample ambulance service.

The Municipal Hospital for Contagious Diseases is under the charge of Dr. J. P. Kennedy, City Health Officer, and through the courtesy of Dr. Kennedy advanced students will be allowed to study contagious diseases at this institution.

St. Joseph's Infirmary is situated on Courtland, corner of Baker Street, and was established in 1880. It is a perfectly equipped and modern institution, accommodating one hundred patients. Three times already has this Infirmary been enlarged, and now an additional building has been erected which has increased the capacity to one hundred. The amount of surgical work performed there is very large. This institution was a large training school for nurses.

Wesley Memorial Hospital is situated on Courtland Street, corner of Auburn avenue, three blocks from the College building. Since its organization in 1905 this hospital has made extensive improvements, putting in a new operating room and has about doubled its capacity, which is fifty beds. This hospital has a training school for nurses. The Trustees will begin the erection of the new Wesley Memorial Hospital at an early date, on or near the site of the medical college. This will be used by the college as a teaching hospital and will afford additional bedside instruction to our students besides that already being done at the Grady Hospital.

The Georgia Baptist Hospital is situated at 69 Luckie Street and has 65 rooms and three large wards with a capacity of ten patients each. The buildings have all the modern equipment necessary for hospital purposes. It also has a training school for nurses.

The Battle Hill Sanitarium for patients suffering with tuberculosis has from 250 to 300 patients, and is at the disposal of the Faculty of this institution for teaching purposes. The Senior class will be taken there by a professor twice a week, the class being divided into small sections for this purpose. Patients in all stages of this disease are cared for at Battle Hill.

The Hospital at the Federal Prison is perfectly equipped and has a capacity of forty beds. In connection with this institution is a modern outdoor tuberculosis camp, with sun parlor, giving an excellent opportunity to observe this plan of treatment.

MacVicar Hospital, situated at 1 Ella Street, was established in 1901 and has a capacity of thirty beds.

With the exception of the last three, these hospitals are centrally located and their phenomenal growth is the best indication of the rapidly increasing clinical facilities of this city.

Use of Hospitals. While the major portion of the hospital instruction is carried on at the Grady Hospital the other hospitals mentioned are utilized to a great extent by the members of our Faculty who are on the Staffs of those hospitals, the Senior Class being taken to them in smell sections.

Anti-Tuberculosis Dispensary. The Clinical material of the anti-tuberculosis dispensary is now at the disposal of the Faculty for teaching purposes.

College Dispensary. The new dispensary building is the first building of the new Wesley Memorial Hospital group. It will serve as a place for diagnosis and treatment of ambulatory cases and as a filter for clinical material for the charity wards of the hospital. It will be officered by the Chief of Clinics, two record clerks, two nurses and a pharmacist and will have a staff of sixty-five attending physicians. There are ten departments:—Medicine, surgery, gynecology and obstetrics, neurology, pediatrics, genito-urinary diseases, dermatology orthopedics, opthalmology and oto-rhino-laryngology. The number of clinics in each department varies from two to five weekly.

Appendix 3: The following document is copied from a portion of the 1942 Bulletin of Emory University School of Medicine (Appendix 3). This document shows the state of the Department of Medicine in 1942 when Dr. Eugene Stead became the first full-time Chairman of the Department.

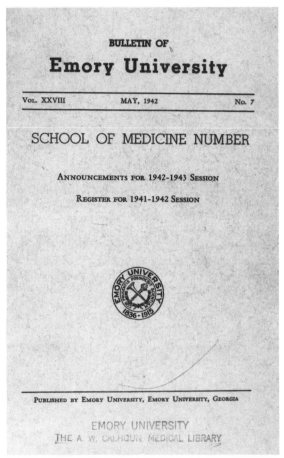

BULLETIN OF
Emory University

VOL. XXVIII   MAY, 1942   No. 7

SCHOOL OF MEDICINE NUMBER

ANNOUNCEMENTS FOR 1942-1943 SESSION

REGISTER FOR 1941-1942 SESSION

PUBLISHED BY EMORY UNIVERSITY, EMORY UNIVERSITY, GEORGIA

EMORY UNIVERSITY
THE A. W. CALHOUN MEDICAL LIBRARY

GENERAL INFORMATION

The School of Medicine of Emory University resulted from the final consolidation of several institutions for medical education which have existed in Atlanta. The history of these developments is outlined below.

The Atlanta Medical College was founded in 1854 under the leadership of Dr. J. G. Westmoreland. The first course of lectures was given in the courthouse. In the same year Dr. Westmoreland was elected to the legislature of Georgia, and from that body secured an appropriation of $15,000 with which to aid in erecting the college buildings. The land at the corner of Butler and Armstrong streets upon which the present group of college buildings stand, was secured and a substantial building erected. Scarcely was this building completed and equipped, when the war between the states began. During the war the college buildings were used as a hospital and the surrounding hills were covered with hospital tents, where the blue and the gray were cared for side by side.

The Southern Medical College was organized and chartered in 1878, and continued in successful operation for twenty years.

In 1898, the faculties of the Atlanta Medical College and of the Southern Medical College consolidated the two schools as the Atlanta College of Physicians and Surgeons. This coalition enhanced the prestige of the new school, and stimulated an active interest in the betterment of medical training. New buildings were erected and extensive improvements in facilities for teaching and broadening the curriculum were planned and carried out. The College was materially aided by contributions from citizens of Atlanta and from the faculty. With the establishment of the new laboratories began the employment of salaried full-time professors.

The Atlanta School of Medicine was established in 1905, and was successful from the start. But its faculty and the faculty of the College of Physicians and Surgeons soon recognized the necessity of merging the two schools and forming a strong medical college with increased resources and facilities. This merger was completed in 1913, under the old historic name, "Atlanta Medical College." The college occupied the property on Butler street, which was the original site, and has been continuously used for medical teaching since 1854.

THE SCHOOL OF MEDICINE OF EMORY UNIVERSITY.—The faculty of the newly organized Atlanta Medical College soon realized that the aims of the merger could be accomplished only by securing an endowment, a university connection, and hospital facilities adapted to teaching purposes. Its ambition was to establish an institution of dignity and permanent value whose graduates would receive recognition throughout the United States—an institution so constituted as to make it a public asset, and so conducted as to deserve the highest professional and public commendation.

Success crowned this ambition when the Atlanta Medical College was legally made the School of Medicine of Emory University in 1915. Becoming thus a part of one of the oldest and best known educational institutions in the South, the medical school entered upon an era of increased usefulness.

The instruction in the first two years, in the elementary branches, was immediately transferred to the University campus in Druid Hills, where the Anatomy, Physiology, and Chemistry buildings had been erected. Upon the completion of the J. J. Gray Clinic building, on Armstrong street, in 1917, most of the third-year work was transferred to these quarters. The work of the fourth year was done in the Grady Hospital and in the main building of the old college at the corner of Butler and Armstrong streets.

Beginning with the session of 1921–1922, the groups of buildings in this locality formerly used for medical teaching only were turned over to the city of Atlanta as the Out-Patient Department, the Entrance Pavilion, and the Colored Section of the Grady Hospital. The care of the patients in these departments is under the exclusive supervision of the faculty of the medical school, offering excellent opportunities for clinical instructions. Space is reserved in the buildings for two lecture rooms, a clinical laboratory, the Dean's office, and the library.

Subsequently, the wards of the white unit of Grady Hospital were reopened to the school for use in clinical instruction. Instruction in this division has increased from year to year until now all services in the white unit as well as the entire colored unit are utilized for teaching purposes. Most of the staff of the white hospital are now members of the Faculty of the School of Medicine.

In its more than eighty years of existence the institution has graduated over 3,200 doctors of medicine. The success of the school during this time is best shown by the records of these men. They fill the cities and country districts of the Southeast and of other sections as practitioners and specialists of the highest type. Many have become leading medical directors, and the alumni of no institution have made better records in the army and navy. Recent graduates secure excellent hospital appointments throughout the country in competitive examinations. The school is a member of the Association of American Medical Colleges, and is fully approved by the Council on Education of the American Medical Association.

At a meeting of the alumni of Emory University in 1914 all alumni of any school which played a part in the formation of the present institution, whether the Atlanta Medical College, the Southern Medical College, the Atlanta College of Physicians and Surgeons, or the Atlanta School of Medicine, were instructed thereafter to sign themselves as graduates of Emory University School of Medicine.

THE EMORY BASE HOSPITAL (EMORY UNIT), known in the U. S. Army as Base Hospital No. 43, was organized in June, 1917, consisting of 36 Medical officers, 100 Red Cross Nurses, 200 Enlisted Men, and 6 Civilians. This was one of the few Base Hospitals from Southern medical colleges sent by the United States Government to France.

In 1922 the Surgeon General authorized the reorganization of the Emory Unit under the name of General Hospital No. 43. Colonel F. K. Boland, Medical Officers Reserve Corps, was made commander of this reserve unit. The War Department subsequently discontinued all reserve hospital units. With the development of world unrest, General Hospital No. 43 was reestablished at Emory in June, 1940, the officers being selected from members of the medical school faculty. In August, 1941, Dr. Ira A. Ferguson succeeded Dr. Daniel C. Elkin as lieutenant colonel, chief of the surgical staff, and director of the unit.

Location

Emory University is situated just outside the city limits of Atlanta, the campus entrance being at 1920 North Decatur Road. At the University is a railroad station, *Emory, Georgia,* on the Seaboard Air Line railroad east of Atlanta; baggage and express should be sent to this station. The post office of the University is *Emory University, Georgia.* Telegraph and telephone communication is available through Atlanta.

The work of the first two years in the School of Medicine is done on the main campus; the work of the third and fourth years is done chiefly at the downtown medical center.

The office of the Dean of the School of Medicine is located at 50 Armstrong Street, S. E., Atlanta.

Grounds and Buildings

The Emory University campus includes acreage in Druid Hills and a city area at the corner of Butler and Armstrong streets, on which is located part of the School of Medicine.

The medical buildings on the campus are:

The John P. Scott Anatomy Building, a four-story building, containing lecture rooms and laboratories for the Departments of Anatomy, Pathology and Bacteriology.

The T. T. Fishburne Physiology Building, a four-story building, occupied by the Departments of Physiology and Pharmacology.

The Chemistry Building, five stories, occupied by the Departments of Chemistry of both the School of Medicine and the College of Arts and Sciences.

The University maintains dormitories and a cafeteria for student use.

EMORY UNIVERSITY HOSPITAL.—In 1922 four units of this splendid plant were completed, and the hospital was opened for patients. Connected with the new hospital is the Lucy Elizabeth Memorial, which is the maternity pavilion, erected by the children of the late Mrs. Asa G. Candler Sr., in memory of their mother.

ATHLETIC FIELD.—A large tract of ground on the campus has been set aside for an athletic field. This field contains a cinder track, space for mass and field sports, basketball, football, and baseball. Excellent tennis courts afford provision for students who desire to participate in this form of athletics. An indoor court has been provided for basketball. An enclosed swimming pool is available throughout the year.

BUILDINGS IN ATLANTA.—In the city are several buildings occupied up to 1921 by the School of Medicine, all of which have been leased to the municipality for the nominal sum of one dollar a year to be used for hospital purposes. They house the negro ward, the negro out-patient department, and the negro school of nursing. These buildings, therefore, form the negro unit of Grady Memorial Hospital, which is the municipal hospital of the City of Atlanta.

Laboratories for Preclinical Sciences

Two modern buildings especially designed for the instruction of medical students in the preclinical branches are located on the campus of the University. These are the John P. Scott Anatomy Building, containing the laboratories of anatomy and pathology, and the T. T. Fishburne Physiology Building, containing the laboratories of physiology and pharmacology. The Department of Bio-Chemistry is housed in the general chemistry building.

Hospitals

The principal teaching units of the school are the Emory University Hospital, which is located on the campus of the University, and Grady Memorial Hospital in the center of Atlanta. The clinical instruction in the first two years is given in the Emory University Hospital, using patients there. Instruction in the third and fourth year is given at Grady Hospital, which is the municipal hospital of the City of Atlanta and includes a hospital for contagious diseases. Its wards and clinics offer a wide variety and abundance of clinical material, both colored and white. In the wards of its combined units approximately 20,000 patients are cared for each year, and its out-patient departments total about 175,000 visits. Instruction is also given at the Henrietta Egleston Memorial Hospital for Children.

Libraries

THE ABNER WELLBORN CALHOUN MEDICAL LIBRARY.—In memory of Dr. A. W. Calhoun, who for thirty-eight years was Professor of Ophthalmology and Oto-Laryngology in the Atlanta Medical College and for many years president of the faculty, this library was re-organized and endowed in 1923 by members of his family. It is located in the Emory University Hospital, convenient to the undergraduate medical students and faculty. It is always open to the medical profession, and the alumni of Emory University especially are invited to visit and use it.

Medical students also have access to the general library of the University, which is housed on the campus.

The medical library contains more than 18,000 volumes and subscribes to 359 current periodicals. The titles include practically all the outstanding journals in every branch of medicine. Complete files of the majority of the important American and English publications have been acquired and foreign files are being purchased as rapidly as possible.

In connection with the Library a medical historical museum has been established and an interesting and valuable collection of old surgical instruments, pictures, manuscripts, etc., has been assembled. The library is anxious to develop this feature, and will welcome contributions of books by local authors, old medical journals, and other materials illustrative of the history and growth of medicine in the South.

The Library of Grady Hospital is maintained jointly by Grady Hospital and the School of Medicine. In addition to the material supplied by the hospital administration it contains literature loaned by the A. W. Calhoun Medical Library. Its reading room is conveniently located for the use of students doing clinical work in the hospital.

Shelves for special reference reading are maintained to supply student needs in the several departments of the school. Provision is also made to transfer, on request, books and journals from the main library for special purposes. This library is in charge of an assistant librarian under the direction of the librarian of the A. W. Calhoun Medical Library.

Endowments

The cost of maintaining a medical school is far in excess of the money paid in the form of tuition by its students. It is therefore necessary to secure additional funds each year to provide an adequate budget. A committee of the medical faculty in co-operation with the administration of the University and an endowment fund committee of interested Atlanta citizens have been working to secure gifts and endowments. Their objective is the development in Atlanta of a medical center as a part of a general university center to serve the Southeast. Many anonymous gifts have been received.

THE JOSEPH BROWN WHITEHEAD PROFESSORSHIP OF SURGERY.—In November, 1939, the Joseph B. Whitehead Foundation, established through the will of the late Joseph B. Whitehead, gave $250,000 as an endowment, the income to be used to support the teaching work and research activities of the "Joseph B. Whitehead Professor of

Surgery." This gift in reality continues the interest which Mr. Whitehead had manifested in surgery. His earlier contributions were given to establish the Joseph B. Whitehead laboratory of surgical research.

During 1940 the Foundation increased the endowment by a gift of an additional $100,000, and also gave $16,500 for expenditure by the department in the current year.

Expenses

University bills for tuition, fees, and dormitory accommodations are payable by the quarter in advance in accordance with the Academic Calendar of the University. If for any reason one is not prepared to pay all charges in advance, arrangements for monthly or other form of partial payment should be made with the Treasurer before the bill becomes due. It is possible to arrange for deferred payments, but there will of necessity be an extra charge.

Matriculation Fee.—A fee of $5.00 is charged for matriculation. It is payable only once.

Tuition and Fees.—The charge for tuition and fees is $112.50 a quarter.

Student Activities Fee.—A fee of $4.50 is collected quarterly for the use of the various student activities.

Hospitalization Fee.—A fee of $2.00 is collected quarterly to cover expenses of hospitalization in case of serious illness.

Damage Deposit.—Every student of the University is required to keep on deposit with the Treasurer the sum of $5.00 as a guarantee against doss or damage of University property entrusted to him. The fee is refundable.

Microscopes.—Each student will be required to provide himself with an acceptable microscope.

Rooms and Board

Dobbs Hall is set aside for the use of graduate and professional students. It contains double and single rooms.

All dormitory rooms are equipped with the necessary furniture, but students supply their own pillows, bed linen, and towels.

Charges for rooms are by the quarter in accordance with the University calendar. Charges in Dobbs Hall for each occupant, based on room selected, are:

     Double room $22.50
     Double corner room 25.50
     Single room 30.00

The dormitories open on the first day of the scholastic year. They are closed during the Christmas holidays and during the summer intermissions in June and September.

Meals may be obtained in a modern cafeteria on the campus at a cost of $17.00 to $25.00 a month.

RESERVATION OF ROOMS.—All requests for reservation of dormitory rooms should be made to *The Registrar, Emory University, Ga.* The fee required for reservation is five dollars; remittance should be made by check or money order payable to Emory University. The reservation fee is credited to the applicant, and will apply on his dormitory account.

Students who prefer will experience no difficulty in getting rooms, or room and board, in the vicinity of the University.

Admission

Correspondence in regard to entrance as well as applications for admission should be addressed to *The Director of Admissions, Emory University, Georgia.*

The first-year class is limited to sixty men. Since many more than this number apply for admission each year, it is necessary to reject many well qualified applicants. It is a general policy to confine acceptances to residents of the Southeast. Satisfactory completion of all pre-medical requirements in a fully accredited institution is an indispensable prerequisite for consideration. Superior ability as shown by grades on college work and by the aptitude test, seriousness of purpose, and personal qualifications that indicate fitness for the profession are determining factors in the selection of matriculants.

The necessary information concerning an applicant's previous education, together with the application form, should be submitted as early as possible and in any case not later than five months before opening of a session. The applicant will be notified as promptly as possible if he is accepted, but frequently several weeks must elapse before final action can be taken.

Only men are admitted.

The details of the entrance requirements are as follows:

1. As evidence of preliminary education, an applicant must present a certificate of at least fifteen units from an accredited high school, and in addition a certificate from an approved literary or scientific college showing that he has been in attendance there at least three years and has credits in physics, inorganic and organic chemistry, biology, and English, with sufficient other work to make a minimum total of ninety semester hours. No entrance conditions whatever can be allowed nor can any substitutions be made for the required subjects.

2. All applicants are required to take the Medical Aptitude Test formulated by the Association of American Medical Colleges. This should be taken in the school where the applicant completes his premedical training.

3. Personal interviews are required of all applicants. These are arranged by the Dean with members of the faculty or representatives of the school.

4. The laws of the State of Georgia require that every application for admission be examined and approved by the State Entrance Examiner. A fee of $2.00 is required for this examination. Applicants are to forward two copies of their entrance credentials direct to the Director of Admissions. If the applicant is accepted he will then be requested to send a check (or money order payable at Athens, Ga.) to cover the inspection fee. The proper documents will then be forwarded to the State Examiner.

Appendix 4: Governance

EMORY UNIVERSITY

CHAIRMEN, BOARD OF TRUSTEES, EMORY UNIVERSITY

Asa Griggs Candler	1915–1929
Charles Howard Candler	1929–1957
Henry L. Bowden	1957–1980
Robert Strickland	1980–1995
Bradley Currey Jr.	1995–present

PRESIDENTS OF EMORY UNIVERSITY

Harvey W. Cox	1942–1943
Goodrich C. White	1944–1957
S. Walter Martin	1958–1963
Sanford S. Atwood	1964–1976
James T. Laney	1977–1993
William M. Chace	1994–present

VICE PRESIDENT FOR HEALTH AFFAIRS*

Boisfeuillet Jones	1955–1961
Orie E. Myers Jr.	1961–1973
E. Garland Herndon Jr.	1973–1983
Charles R. Hatcher Jr.	1984–1996
Michael M. E. Johns	1996–present

CHAIRMEN, WOODRUFF HEALTH SCIENCES CENTER BOARD

James D. Robinson Jr.	1965–1967
William R. Bowdoin	1968–1983
James B. Williams	1984–present

EMORY UNIVERSITY SCHOOL OF MEDICINE

DEANS

W. Simpson Elkin	1915–1925
Russell H. Oppenheimer	1925–1945
Eugene A. Stead Jr.	1945–1946
R. Hugh Wood	1946–1955
Arthur P. Richardson	1956–1979
James F. Glenn	1980–1983
George W. Brumley	4/4/83 (Acting)

---

* Various titles have been used to designate the position Vice President for Health Affairs. As the medical center evolved the title also evolved, so that in 1997 it is designated as "Executive Vice President for Health Affairs and Director of the Robert W. Woodruff Health Sciences Center."

Richard M. Krause   1983–1989
Jeffrey L. Houpt   1989–1996
Thomas J. Lawley   1996–present

EMORY UNIVERSITY HOSPITAL

ADMINISTRATORS

Walker White   1922–1925
Russell H. Oppenheimer   1925–1937
Robert S. Hudgins   1937–1942
Robert F. Whitaker   1942–1952
Burwell W. Humphrey   1953–1976
W. Daniel Barker   1977–1978
Paul B. Hoffmann   1978–1988
W. Daniel Barker   1988–1989
Donald E. Wells   1989–1994
John D. Henry   1995–present

MEDICAL DIRECTORS

Russell H. Oppenheimer   1937–1945
J. Elliott Scarborough   1945–1966
E. Garland Herndon Jr.   1966–1983
Garland D. Perdue   1983–1993
John L. Waller   1993–1995
Robert B. Smith III   1995–present

CRAWFORD W. LONG HOSPITAL

ADMINISTRATORS

Luther C. Fischer   1908–1953
Wadley R. Glenn   1953–1972
W. Daniel Barker   1972–1984
John D. Henry   1984–present

MEDICAL DIRECTORS

Edward C. Davis   1908–1931
Lutcher C. Fischer   1931–1946
Wadley R. Glenn   1946–1985
Harold S. Ramos   1985–present

DIRECTORS OF HOSPITALS

Mr. Dan Barker was the overall Director of Emory and Crawford Long Hospitals from May 1984 to March 1991. Following this Mr. Don Wells at Emory and Mr. John Henry at Crawford Long reported to Dr. Charles Hatcher. John Henry became the Chief Executive Officer for both hospitals in 1995.

EMORY CLINIC

DIRECTORS

R. Hugh Wood	1953–1957
J. Elliott Scarborough	1957–1966
Robert L. Brown	1966–1976
Charles R. Hatcher Jr.	1976–1984
Garland D. Perdue	1984–1993
Rein Saral	1993–present

GRADY MEMORIAL HOSPITAL

CHAIRMEN, THE FULTON-DEKALB HOSPITAL AUTHORITY

Thomas K. Glenn	1941–1946
Hughes Spalding	1947–1958
Fred J. Turner	1959–1961
W. O. Duvall	1962–1964
Edgar J. Forio	1965–1968
Robert S. Regenstein	1969–1983
Edward C. Loughlin Jr.	1983–1991
Robert L. Brown Jr.	1992–present

MEDICAL DIRECTORS

Joseph Hines, M.D.	1932–37
Julian Jarman, M.D.	1962–65
Douglas B. Kendrick	1967–72
Asa G. Yancey Sr.	1972–1/1/1989
Hamilton E. Holmes	1/2/1989–1995
Gail V. Anderson	Acting 1995
(Title changed to Chief of Staff)	1996–present

SUPERINTENDENTS/EXECUTIVE DIRECTORS/PRESIDENTS

Albert Frensch	6/2/1892–10/31/1892
Thomlinson Fort Brewster	11/1/1892–1906
W. B. Summerall	Dates unknown
R. A. Bartholomew	1919
Steve Johnston	1920–1931
John B. Franklin	1931–1938
Joseph Hines	1938–1939
J. Moss Bealor	1939–1943
Frank Wilson Sr.	1943–1964
J. W. Pinkston Jr.	1964–1989
Robert B. Johnson	1989–1993
Donald F. Snell (Acting)	1993–1994
Edward J. Renford	April 1994–present

DEPARTMENT OF VETERANS AFFAIRS

DIRECTORS

Horace B. Cupp	1946–1951
John G. Hood	1952–1957
W. H. Thiele	1957–1959
Hardy A. Kemp	1959–1962
John G. Hood	1963–1974
Julian A. Jarman	1975–1976
P. K. Whiteside	1976–1979
James S. Dooley	1979–1980
Glenn Alred Jr.	1980–1992
Larry R. Deal	1992–1995
Robert A. Perreault	1996–present

CHIEFS OF STAFF*

Julian A. Jarman	1963–1975
Lewis Jones	1975–1979
A. Wendell Musser	1980–1993
P. Bailey Francis	1993–present

---

* Prior to 1963 the Chief of Staff position was rotated through the clinical services.

Appendix 5:

Department chairmen of Emory University School of Medicine in the early sixties.

Back row left-to-right: Dr. John E. Steinhaus, Chairman of the Department of Anesthesiology; Dr. Richard W. Blumberg, Chairman of the Department of Pediatrics; Dr. F. Phinizy Calhoun Jr., Chairman of the Department of Ophthalmology; Dr. James A. Bain, Director of Basic Health Sciences; Dr. Geoffrey Bourne, Chairman of the Department of Anatomy; Dr. John D. Martin Jr., Chairman of the Department of Surgery; Dr. S. Heinz Weens, Chairman of the Department of Radiology; Dr. Neil C. Moran, Chairman of the Department of Pharmacology; Dr. J. Willis Hurst, Chairman of the Department of Medicine; Dr. Thomas F. Sellers Jr., Chairman of the Department of Preventive Medicine and Community Health; Dr. John T. Ellis, Chairman of the Department of Pathology; Dr. Alfred E. Wilhelmi, Chairman of the Department of Biochemistry; Dr. J. Dan Thompson, Chairman of the Department of Gynecology and Obstetrics.

Front row left-to-right: Dr. J. Elliott Scarborough, Director of the Emory University Clinic; Mr. Henry L. Bowden, Chairman of the Board of Trustees of Emory University; Dr. Bernard L. Hallman, Associate Dean, School of Medicine, Mrs. Marian Richardson; Dr. Arthur P. Richardson, Dean of Emory University School of Medicine; Dr. Evangeline T. Papageorge, Associate Dean, Emory University School of Medicine; Mr. Orie E. Myers Jr., Vice-President for Health Affairs; Ms. Mildred Jordan, Head Librarian, Emory University School of Medicine.

Missing from the photograph are: Dr. Morris Tager, Chairman of the Department of Microbiology; Dr. Gerhard Brecher, Chairman of the Department of Physiology; Dr. Bernard C. Holland, Chairman of the Department of Psychiatry; Dr. Mieczyslaw Peszczynski, Department of Physical Medicine.

Appendix 6:

Department chairmen of Emory University School of Medicine in the early seventies. Back row left-to-right: Dr. J. Dan Thompson, Chairman of the Department of Gynecology and Obstetrics; Dr. Bernard C. Holland, Chairman of the Department of Psychiatry; Dr. John E. Steinhaus, Chairman of the Department of Anesthesiology; Dr. Michael B. Gravanis, Chairman of the Department of Pathology; Dr. H. Earl Jones, Chairman of the Department of Dermatology; Dr. J. Willis Hurst, Chairman of the Department of Medicine; Dr. Thomas F. Sellers, Chairman of the Department of Preventive Medicine and Community Health; Dr. Herbert R. Karp, Chairman of the Department of Neurology; Dr. Dwight Cavanaugh, Chairman of the Department of Ophthalmology; Dr. W. Dean Warren, Chairman of the Department of Surgery; Dr. J. Robin DeAndrade, Chairman of the Department of Orthopedics; Dr. James A. Bain, Director of Basic Health Sciences; Dr. Neil C. Moran, Chairman of the Department of Pharmacology.

Front row left-to-right: Dr. Morris Tager, Chairman of the Department of Microbiology; Dr. Heinz S. Weens, Chairman of the Department of Radiology; Dr. Jack Kostyo, Chairman of the Department of Physiology; Dr. Arthur P. Richardson, Dean, School of Medicine; Dr. Richard W. Blumberg, Chairman of the Department of Pediatrics; Dr. Jerome Sutin, Chairman of the Department of Anatomy; Dr. Elmer C. Hall, Chairman of the Department of Biometry. The portrait of Mr. Robert W. Woodruff is seen in the background.

Missing from this photograph are: Dr. Alfred E. Wilhelmi, Chairman of the Department of Biochemistry, and Dr. Mieczyslaw Peszczynski, Chairman of the Department of Physical Medicine.

Appendix 7

Department chairmen of Emory University School of Medicine, May 2, 1983.

Back row left-to-right: Dr. Richard S. Riggins, Chairman of the Department of Orthopedics; Dr. Earl Jones, Chairman of the Department of Dermatology; Dr. Donald O. Nutter, Senior Associate Dean for Research Programs and Faculty Affairs; Dr. William J. Casarella, Chairman of the Department of Radiology; Dr. George W. Brumley, Chairman of the Department of Pediatrics.

Middle row left-to-right: Dr. Michael B. Gravanis, Chairman of the Department of Pathology; Dr. John E. Steinhaus, Chairman of the Department of Anesthesiology; Dr. Thomas F. Sellers Jr., Chairman of the Department of Preventive Medicine and Community Health; Dr. Donald B. McCormick, Chairman of the Department of Biochemistry; Dr. John K. Spitznagel, Chairman of the Department of Microbiology; Dr. J. Willis Hurst, Chairman of the Department of Medicine.

Front row left-to-right: Dr. Jerome Sutin, Chairman of the Department of Anatomy; Dr. J. Dan Thompson, Chairman of the Department of Gynecology and Obstetrics; Dr. W. Dean Warren, Chairman of the Department of Surgery; Dr. James F. Glenn, Dean, Emory University School of Medicine; Dr. Robert B. Gunn, Chairman of the Department of Physiology; Dr. Neil C. Moran, Chairman of the Department of Pharmacology.

Missing from this photograph are: Dr. Elmer C. Hall, Chairman of the Department of Biometry, Dr. Herbert R. Karp, Chairman of the Department of Neurology, Dr. H. Dwight Cavanagh, Chairman of the Department of Ophthalmology, Dr. Bernard C. Holland, Chairman of the Department of Psychiatry, and Dr. J. Robin deAndrade, Chairman of the Department of Rehabilitation Medicine.

Appendix 8:

The above cartoons of the department chairman, division directors within the Department of Medicine, and chiefs of medicine were drawn by senior medical student Carl Askrens in 1984.

Top row left-to-right: Dr. J. Willis Hurst, Chairman of the Department of Medicine; Dr. Edmund Bourke, Director of the Division of Nephrology; Dr. G. Michael Duffell, Director of the Division of Pulmonary Diseases; Dr. John T. Galambos, Director of the Division of Digestive Diseases; Dr. W. Dallas Hall Jr., Director of the Division of General Medicine and Director of the Division of Hypertension; Dr. W. Lee Hand, Director of Infectious Diseases; Dr. Charles M. Huguley Jr., Director of the Division of Hematology and Oncology; Dr. Herbert R. Karp, Director of the Division of Genetics; Dr. Lawrence S. Phillips, Director of the Division of Endocrinology and Metabolism; Dr. Robert C. Schlant, Director of the Division of Cardiology; Dr. Colon H. Wilson, Director of the Division of Rheumatology and Immunology; Dr. Joseph E. Hardison, Chief of Medicine at the Veterans Administration Medical Center; Dr. Harold S. Ramos, Chief of Medicine at Crawford Long Hospital; and Dr. Jonas A. Shulman. Dr. Shulman was destined to follow Dr. Harold S. Ramos as chief of medicine at Crawford Long Hospital; Dr. H. Kenneth Walker, Assistant to the Chairman and Assistant Chief of Medicine, Grady Memorial Hospital.

Appendix 9: Bulletin of Emory University School of Medicine, which lists the full-time and clinical volunteer faculty members of the Department of Medicine in 1942.

MEDICINE
INTERNAL MEDICINE

Eugene A. Stead Jr., B.S., M.D., *Professor of Medicine; Chairman of the Department*
Russell H. Oppenheimer, A.B., M.D., *Professor of Medicine*
Cyrus W. Strickler, M.D., *Professor of Clinical Medicine*
James E. Paullin, A.B., M.D., LL.D., *Professor of Clinical Medicine*
Avary M. Dimmock, M.D., *Associate Professor of Clinical Medicine*
Glenville Giddings, M.D., *Associate Professor of Clinical Medicine*
Carl C. Aven, M.D., *Associate Professor of Clinical Medicine*
Justin Andrews, Ph.B., ScD., *Associate Professor of Public Health*
Charles H. Paine, M.D., *Assistant Professor of Clinical Medicine*
John B. Fitts, A.B., M.D., *Assistant Professor of Clinical Medicine*
Henry C. Sauls, M.D., *Assistant Professor of Clinical Medicine*
Edgar D. Shanks, M.D., Assistant *Professor of Clinical Medicine*
*Harold M. Bowcock, M.S., M.D., *Assistant Professor of Clinical Medicine*

Associates in Medicine

L. M. Blackford, B.S., M.D., M.Sc.Med.	R. S. Leadingham, M.D.
Allen H. Bunch, A.B., M.D.	J. M. Monfort, A.B., M.D.
Hal M. Davison A.B., M.D.	R. Hugh Wood, M.D.

Instructors in Medicine

F. M. Atkins, A.B., M.D.	J. C. Masser, B.S., M.D.
T. L. Byrd, M.D.	W. R. Minnich, B.S., M.D.
T. S. Claiborne, A.B., M.D.	V. E. Powell, B.S., M.D.
M. S. Dougherty, B.S., M.D.	J. L. Richardson, B.S., M.D.
C. H. Holmes, B.S., M.D.	Carter Smith, B.S., M.D.
G. F. Klugh Jr., B.S., M.D.	C. W. Strickler Jr., M.D.
	E. Van Buren, B.S., M.D.

Assistants in Medicine

E. B. Agnor, B.Ph., M.D.	† A. Park McGinty, B.S., M.D.
Z. A. Allen, M.D.	A. J. Merrill, B.S., M.D.
John W. Allgood, B.S., M.D.	† Gene Nardin, A.B., M D.
E. A. Bancker, B.S., M.D.	Harry Parks, B.S., M.D.
C. F. Barnett, B.S., M.D.	Claud T. Prevost, M.D.
Martin S. Belle, A.B., M.D.	Laurence B. Reppert, M.D.
† W. R. Crowe, M.D.	Maurice Rich, B.S. M.D.
J. K. Fancher, A.B., M.D.	Charles F. Stone Jr., M.D.
† A. W. Hobby, M.D.	W. H. Trimble, B.S., M.D.
C. L. Laws, M.D.	James V. Warren, A.B., M.D.
† R. Bruce Logue, B.S., M.D.	James I. Weinberg, B.S., M.D.
M. I. Lowance, B.S., M.D.	Robert L. Whipple, B.S., M.D.
	B. P. Wolff, B.S., M.D.
	Mrs. Wallace Cooper, *Secretary*

---

* On leave of absence.
† Called to active military duty.

Appendix 10: Bulletin of Emory University School of Medicine, which lists the full-time and clinical volunteer faculty members of the Department of Medicine in 1943.

MEDICINE
INTERNAL MEDICINE

Eugene A. Stead Jr., B.S., M.D., Professor of Medicine; Chairman of the Department
Cyrus W. Strickler, M.D., Professor of Clinical Medicine
James E. Paullin, A.B., M.D., LL.D., Professor of Clinical Medicine
Russell H. Oppenheimer, A.B., M.D., Professor of Clinical Medicine
Glenville Giddings, M.D., Associate Professor of Clinical Medicine
Avary M. Dimmock, M.D., Associate Professor of Clinical Medicine
Carl C. Aven, M.D., Associate Professor of Clinical Medicine
† Justin Andrews, Ph.B., Sc.D., Associate Professor of Public Health
Paul B. Beeson, M.D., C.M., Assistant Professor of Medicine
Charles H. Paine, M.D., Assistant Professor of Clinical Medicine
John B. Fitts, A.B., M.D., Assistant Professor of Clinical Medicine
Henry C. Sauls, M.D., Assistant Professor of Clinical Medicine
Edgar D. Shanks, M.D., Assistant Professor of Clinical Medicine

Associates in Medicine

† L. M. Blackford B.S., M.D., M.Sc.Med.
Allen H. Bunce, A.B, M.D.
Hal M. Davison, A.B., M.D.
R. S. Leadingham, M.D.

Joseph C. Massee, B.S., M.D.
† J. M. Monfort, A.B., M.D.
Carter Smith, B.S., M.D.
Ebert Van Buren, B.S., M.D.
† R. Hugh Wood, M.D.

Instructors in Medicine

F. M. Atkins, A B., M.D.
T. L. Byrd, M.D.
† T. S. Claiborne, A B, M.D.
† M. S. Dougherty, B.S., M.D.
C. H. Holmes, B.S., M.D.
† G. F. Klugh Jr., B.S., M.D.

† Bruce Logue, B.S., M.D.
A. J. Merrill, B.S., M.D.
W. R Minnich, B.S., M.D.
† V. E. Powell, B.S., M.D.
J. L. Richardson, B.S., M.D.
† C. W. Strickler Jr., M.D.
J. V. Warren, A.B., M.D.

Assistants in Medicine

† E. B. Agnor, Ph.B., M.D.
E. A. Allen, M.D.
E. S. Armstrong, M.D.
E. A. Bancker, B.S., M.D.
C. F. Barnett, B.S., M.D.
T. T. Blalock, M.D.
E. S. Brannon, A.M., M.D.
† W. R. Crowe, M.D.
Roy W. Eastwood, A.B., M.D.
J. K. Fancher, A.B., M.D.
Harvey Hamff, A.B., M.D.
Albert Heyman, B.S., M.D.
John B. Hickam, AB, M.D.
† A. W. Hobby, M.D.

C. L. Laws, M.D.
M. L. Lowance, B.S., M.D.
T. E. McGeachy, A.B., M.D.
† A. Park McGinty, B.S., M.D.
W. B. McMath, B.S., M.D.
E. S. Miller, M.D.
† Gene Nardin, A.B., MD.
† Harry Parks, B.S., M.D,
Claud T. Prevost, B.S., M.D.
† C. F. Stone Jr., M.D.
† W. H. Trimble, B.S., M.D.
† James L. Weinberg, B.S., M.D.
R. L. Whipple, B.S., M.D.
† B. P. Wolff, B.S., M.D.

---

† Called to active military duty.

The Quest for Excellence

Appendix 11: Bulletin of Emory University School of Medicine, which lists the full-time and clinical volunteer faculty members of the Department of Medicine in 1944.

MEDICINE
INTERNAL MEDICINE

Eugene A. Stead Jr., B.S., M.D., *Professor of Medicine; Chairman of the Department*
Cyrus W. Strickler, M.D., *Professor of Clinical Medicine*
James E. Paullin, A.B., M.D., LL.D., *Professor of Clinical Medicine*
Russell H. Oppenheimer, A.B., M.D., *Professor of Clinical Medicine*
Glenville Giddings, M.D., *Associate Professor of Clinical Medicine*
Henry C. Sauls, M.D., *Associate Professor of Clinical Medicine*
† Justin Andrews, Ph.B., Sc.D., *Associate Professor of Public Health*
Paul B. Beeson, M.D., C.M., *Assistant Professor of Medicine*
Charles H. Paine, M.D., *Assistant Professor of Clinical Medicine*
John B. Fitts, A.B., M.D., *Assistant Professor of Clinical Medicine*
Joseph C. Massee, B.S., M.D., *Assistant Professor of Clinical Medicine*
Ebert Van Buren, B.S., M.D., *Assistant Professor of Clinical Medicine*

Associates in Medicine

† L. M. Blackford, B.S., M.D., M.Sc.Med.   † J. M. Monfort, A.B., M.D.
Roy S. Leadingham, M.D.   † Carter Smith, B.S., M.D.
Arthur J. Merrill, B.S., M.D.   † R. Hugh Wood, M.D.

Instructors in Medicine

Evert A. Bancker, B.S., M.D.   † Bruce Logue, B.S., M.D.
T. Luther Byrd, M.D.   † W. R. Minnich, B.S., M.D.
† T. S. Claiborne, A.B., M D   † V. E. Powell, B.S., M.D.
† M. S. Dougherty, B.S., M.D.   J. L. Richardson, B.S., M.D.
Harvey Hamff, A.B., M.D.   † C. W. Strickler Jr., M.D.
Albert Heyman, B.S., M.D.   J. V. Warren, A.B., M.D.
                        R. L. Whipple Jr., B.S., M.D.

Assistants in Medicine

† E. B. Agnor, Ph.B., M.D.   M. I. Lowance, B.S., M.D.
H. Homer Allen, M.D.   T. E. McGeachy, A.B., M.D.
E. S. Armstrong, M.D.   † A. Park McGinty, B.S., M.D.
Crawford F. Barnett, B.S., M.D.   C. J. McLoughlin, A.B., M.D.
John E. Beck, B.S., M.D.   E. S. Miller, M.D.
† T. T. Blalock, M.D.   † Gene Nardin, A.B., M.D.
E. S. Brannon, M.A., M.D.   F. L. Neely, A.B., M.D.
† W. R. Crowe, M.D.   Harry Parks, B.S., M.D.
I. M. Gibson, M.A., M.D.   † C. P. Stone Jr., M.D.
J. F. Hackney, M.D.   † W. H. Trimble, B.S., M.D.
† A. W. Hobby, M.D.   † J. I. Weinberg, B.S., M.D.
Eugenia Jones, B.S., M.A., D.SC., M.D.   † B. P. Wolff, B.S., M.D.

---

† Called to active military duty.

Appendix 12: Bulletin of Emory University School of Medicine, which lists the full-time and clinical volunteer faculty members of the Department of Medicine in 1945.

MEDICINE
Departmental Staff

Eugene A. Stead Jr., B.S., M.D., *Professor of Medicine; Chairman of the Department*
Cyrus W. Strickler, M.D., *Professor of Clinical Medicine*
James E. Paullin, A.B., M.D., LL.D., *Professor of Clinical Medicine*
Russell H. Oppenheimer, A.B., M.D., *Professor of Clinical Medicine*
Glenville Giddings, M.D., *Associate Professor of Clinical Medicine*
Henry C. Sauls, M.D., *Associate Professor of Clinical Medicine*
*Justin Andrews, Ph.B., Sc.D., *Associate Professor of Public Health*
Paul B. Beeson, M.D., C.M., *Associate Professor of Medicine*
Charles H. Paine, M.D., *Assistant Professor of Clinical Medicine*
John B. Fitts, A.B., M.D., *Assistant Professor of Clinical Medicine*
Joseph C. Massee, B.S., M.D., *Assistant Professor of Clinical Medicine*
Ebert Van Buren, B.S., M.D., *Assistant Professor of Clinical Medicine*
Arthur J. Merrill, B.S., M.D., *Assistant Professor of Medicine*

Associates

*L. M. Blackford, B.S., M.D, M.Sc.Med.
Roy S. Leadingham, M.D.
*J. M. Monfort, A.B., M.D.
*Carter Smith, B.S., M.D.
*R. Hugh Wood, M.D.

Instructors

Evert A. Bancker, B.S., M.D.
E. S. Brannon, A.M., M.D.
T. Luther Byrd, M.D.
*T. S. Claiborne, A.B., M.D.
*M. S. Dougherty, B.S., M.D.
Harvey Hamff, A.B., M.D.
Albert Heyman, B.S., M.D.
*Bruce Logue, B.S., M.D.
*W. R. Minnich, B.S., M.D.
*V. E. Powell, B.S., M.D.
J. L. Richardson, B.S., M.D.
*C. W. Strickler Jr., M.D.
J. V. Warren, A.B., M.D.
R. L. Whipple Jr., B.S., M.D.

Assistants

*E. B. Agnor, Ph.B., M.D.
Eustace A. Allen, A.B., M.D.
E. S. Armstrong, M.D.
Maxwell R. Berry, Ph.D., M.D.
*T. T. Blalock, M.D.
W. R. Crowe, M.D.
J. F. Hackney, M.D.
J. Frank Harris, M.D.
*A. W. Hobby, M.D.
Eugenia Jones, A.M., D.Sc., M.D.
M. I. Lowance, B.S., M.D.
T. E. McGeachy, A.B., M.D.
*A. Park McGinty, B.S., M.D.
C. J. McLoughlin, A.B., M.D.
*Gene Nardin, A.B, M.D.
F. L. Neely, A.B., M.D.
Harry Parks, B.S., M.D.
*C. F. Stone Jr., M.D.
*W. H. Trimble, B.S., M.D.
*J. I. Weinberg, B.S., M.D.
*B. P. Wolff, B.S., M.D.

* In military service

Appendix 13: Bulletin of Emory University School of Medicine, which lists the full-time and clinical volunteer faculty members of the Department of Medicine in 1946.

MEDICINE
Departmental Staff

Eugene A. Stead Jr., B.S., M.D., *Professor of Medicine; Chairman of the Department*
Paul B. Beeson, M.D., C.M., *Professor of Medicine; Assistant Professor of Bacteriology*
James E. Paullin, A.B., M.D., LL.D., *Professor of Clinical Medicine*
Russell H. Oppenheimer, A.B., M.D., *Professor of Clinical Medicine*
William F. Friedewald, B.S., M.D., *Associate Professor of Medicine; Professor of Bacteriology and Immunology*
R. Hugh Wood, M.D., *Associate Professor of Clinical Medicine*
Glenville Giddings, M.D., *Associate Professor of Clinical Medicine*
Henry C. Sauls, M.D., *Associate Professor of Clinical Medicine*
Justin Andrews, B.Ph., Sc.D., *Associate Professor of Public Health*
Joseph C. Massee, B.S., M.D., *Assistant Professor of Clinical Medicine*
Ebert Van Buren, B.S., M.D., *Assistant Professor of Clinical Medicine*
Charles H. Paine, B.S., M.D., *Assistant Professor of Clinical Medicine*
John B. Fitts, A.B., M.D., *Assistant Professor of Clinical Medicine*
Arthur J. Merrill, B.S., M.D., *Assistant Professor of Clinical Medicine*

Associates

L. M. Blackford, B.S., M.D., M.Sc.Med.   Roy S. Leadingham, M.D.
Frank L. Engel, A.B., M.D.   J. M. Monfort, A.B., M.D.
                     Carter Smith, B.S., M.D.

Instructors

Evert A. Bancker, B.S., M.D.   Bruce Logue, B.S., M.D.
T. S. Claiborne, A.B., M.D.   W. R. Minnich, B.S., M.D.
M. S. Dougherty, B.S., M.D.   V. E. Powell, B.S., M.D.
Harvey Hamff, A.B., M.D.   J. L. Richardson, B.S., M.D.
Albert Heyman, B.S., M.D.   C. W. Strickler Jr., M.D.
Byron J. Hoffman, A.B., M.D.   J. V. Warren, A.B., M.D.
Charles Huguley, A.B., M.D.   R. L. Whipple Jr., B.S., M.D.

Assistants

E. B. Agnor, B.Ph., M.D.   M. I. Lowance, B.S., M.D.
Eustace A. Allen, A.B., M.D.   T. E. McGeachy, A.B., M.D.
E. S. Armstrong, M.D.   A. Park McGinty, B.S., M.D.
John E. Beck, B.S., M.D.   C. J. McLoughlin, A.B., M.D.
Maxwell R. Berry, M.D., Ph.D.   Rudolph J. Marshall, M.D.
T. T. Blalock, M.D.   Max Michael, B.S., M.D.
Max M. Blumberg, B.S., M.D.   Gene Nardin, A.B., M.D.
W. R. Crowe, M.D.   F. L. Neely, A.B., M.D.
J. F. Hackney, M.D.   Harry Parks, B.S., M.D.
J. Frank Harris, A.B., M.D.   James F. Schieve, M.D.
Lamont Henry, B.S., M.D.   C. F. Stone Jr., M.D.
A. W. Hobby, M.D.   W. H. Trimble, B.S., M.D.
Eugenia Jones, B.S., A.M., D.Sc., M.D.   J. I. Weinberg, B.S., M.D.
William R. Kay, B.S., M.D.   B. P. Wolff, B.S., M.D.

Appendix 14: Bulletin of Emory University School of Medicine, which lists the full-time and clinical volunteer faculty members of the Department of Medicine in 1947.

MEDICINE
Departmental Staff

Paul B. Beeson, M.D., C.M., *Professor of Medicine; Chairman of the Department*
James E. Paullin, A.B., M.D., LL.D., *Professor of Clinical Medicine*
Russell H. Oppenheimer, A.B., M.D., *Professor of Clinical Medicine*
R. Hugh Wood, M.D., *Professor of Clinical Medicine*
William H. Friedewald, B.S., M.D., *Associate Professor of Medicine; Professor of Bacteriology and Immunology*
James V. Warren,[1] A.B., M.D., *Associate Professor of Medicine; Professor of Physiology*
Glenville Giddings, M.D., *Associate Professor of Clinical Medicine*
Henry C. Sauls, M.D., *Associate Professor of Clinical Medicine*
William A. Smith, B.S., M.D., *Associate Professor of Clinical Medicine (Neurology)*
Richard B. Wilson, B.S., M.D., *Associate Professor of Clinical Medicine (Neurology)*
Arthur J. Merrill, B.S., M.D., *Assistant Professor of Medicine*
Joseph C. Massee, B.S., M.D., *Assistant Professor of Clinical Medicine*
Ebert Van Buren, B.S., M.D., *Assistant Professor of Clinical Medicine*
Charles H. Paine, B.S., M.D., *Assistant Professor of Clinical Medicine*
John B. Fitts, A.B., M.D., *Assistant Professor of Clinical Medicine*
Herbert S. Alden, B.S., M.D., *Assistant Professor of Clinical Medicine (Dermatology)*

Associates

L. M. Blackford, B.S., M.D., Sc.Med.
William L. Dobes, A.B., M.D.
 (Dermatology)
Hugh E. Hailey, A.B., M.D.
 (Dermatology)
Roy S. Leadingham, M.D.

R. Bruce Logue, B.S., M.D.
Max Michael, B.S., M.D.
J. Merrell Monfort, A.B., M.D.
Philip H. Nippert, B.S., M.D.
 (Dermatology)
Carter Smith, B.S., M.D.

Instructors

Evert A. Bancker, B.S., M.D.
T. Sterling Claiborne, A.B., M.D.
Robert P. Grant,[1] A.B., M.D.
L. Harvey Hamff, A.B., M.D.
Albert Heyman, B.S., M.D.
Byron J. Hoffman, A.B., M.D.
David F. James, B.S., M.D.
Edward S. Miller, M.D.

William R. Minnich, B.S., M.D.
Vernon E. Powell, B.S., M.D.
Joseph L. Rankin, A.B., M.D.
 (Dermatology)
Jeff L. Richardson, B.S., M.D.
Charles F. Stone Jr., M.D.
Cyrus W. Strickler Jr., M.D.
Robert L. Whipple Jr., B.S., M.D.

Assistants

Elbert B. Agnor, Ph.B., M.D.
Eustace A. Allen, A.B., M.D.

Edward S. Armstrong, M.D.
John E. Beck, B.S., M.D.

Maxwell R. Berry, M.D., Ph.D.
Tully T. Blalock, M.D.
Max M. Blumberg, B.S., M.D.
Philip K. Bondy, A.B., M.D.
Sandy B. Carter, B.S., M.D.
William R. Crowe, M.D.
Edgar M. Dunstan, B.S., A.M., M.D.
J. Frank Harris, A.B., M.D.
J. Lamont Henry, B.S., M.D.
A. Worth Hobby, M.D.
William H. Hooten, A.B., M.D.
Eugenia C. Jones, B.S., A.M., D.Sc., M.D.
Mason I. Lowance, B.S., M.D.

T. English McGeachy, A.B., M.D.
A. Park McGinty, B.S., M.D.
Christopher J. McLoughlin, A.B., M.D.
Joseph P. Melvin, M.S., M.D.
F. Levering Neely, A.B., M.D.
Harry Parks, B.S., M.D.
Caroline K. Pratt, A.B., M.D.
Harry J. Price, M.D.
C. Purcell Roberts, A.B., M.D.
J. Spalding Schroder, A.B., M.D.
Hyman Stillerman, M.S., M.D.
William H. Trimble, B.S., M.D.
James I. Weinberg, B.S., M.D.

Bernard P. Wolff, B.S., M.D.

------

[1]Appointment effective July 1, 1947.

Appendix 15: Bulletin of Emory University School of Medicine, which lists the full-time faculty members and resident teaching assistants of the Department of Medicine in 1948.

MEDICINE

Professors: Paul B. Beeson (Chairman), Russell H. Oppenheimer, James E. Paullin, R. Hugh Wood

Associate Professors: William F. Friedewald, Glenville Giddings, Richard B. Wilson (Neurology), James V. Warren

Assistant Professors: Herbert S. Alden (Dermatology), John B. Fitts, Joseph C. Massee, Arthur J. Merrill, Charles H. Paine, Carter Smith, William A. Smith (Neurology), Ebert Van Buren

Associates: L. Minor Blackford, William L. Dobes (Dermatology), Hugh E. Hailey (Dermatology), Albert Heyman, David F. James, Roy S. Leadingham, R. Bruce Logue, Max Michael, J. Merrell Monfort, Philip H. Nippert (Dermatology)

Instructors: Evert A. Bancker, Walter M. Bartlett, Walter L. Bloom, John F. Busey, T. Sterling Claiborne, Hortense E. Garver (Clinical Pathology), Robert P. Grant, L. Harvey Hamff, Lamont Henry, Byron J. Hoffman, Charles M. Huguley, Edward S. Miller, William R. Minnich, John L. Patterson Jr., Vernon E. Powell, Joseph L. Rankin (Dermatology), John C. Ransmeier, Jefferson L. Richardson, Charles F. Stone Jr., Cyrus W. Strickler Jr., Robert L. Whipple Jr.

Assistants: Elbert B. Agnor, Eustace A. Allen, Adward S. Armstrong, John S. Atwater, J. Gordon Barrow, John E. Beck, Maxwell R. Berry Jr., Tully T. Blalock, Max M. Blumberg, C. Daniel Burge, Sandy B. Carter, William R. Crowe, Edgar M. Dunstan, J. Frank Harris, A. Worth Hobby, Eugenia C. Jones, Mason I. Lowance, T. English McGeachy, A. Park McGinty, Christopher J. McLoughlin, Chester W. Morse, F. Levering Neely, Harry Parks, Caroline K. Pratt, Harry J. Price, C. Purcell Roberts, J. Spalding Schroder, Hyman Stillerman, Lloyd F. Timberlake, William H. Trimble, James I. Weinberg, Bernard P. Wolff

Resident Teaching Assistants—
  At *Grady Memorial Hospital:* Philip Bondy, Arthur Codington, Elizabeth Gambrell, Frank M. Geiser, H. H. Turner
  At *Emory University Hospital:* Clyde Tomlin,[1] Hugh P. Smith Jr., John Withington

---

[1] Resigned January 1, 1948.

Appendix 16: Bulletin of Emory University School of Medicine, which lists the full-time and clinical volunteer faculty members, and resident teaching assistants of the Department of Medicine in 1949.

MEDICINE

Paul B. Beeson, M.D., C.M., *Professor of Medicine; Chairman of the Department*
Russell H. Oppenheimer, A.B., M.D., *Professor of Clinical Medicine*
James E. Paullin, A.B., M.D., LL.D., *Professor of Clinical Medicine*
R. Hugh Wood, M.D., *Professor of Clinical Medicine*
William F. Friedewald, B.S., M.D., *Associate Professor of Medicine*
Glenville Giddings, M.D., *Associate Professor of Clinical Medicine*
William A. Smith, B.S., M.D., *Associate Professor of Clinical Medicine (Neurology)*
James V. Warren, A.B., M.D. *Associate Professor of Medicine*
Richard B. Wilson, B.S., M.D. *Associate Professor of Clinical Medicine (Neurology)*
Herbert S. Alden, B.S., M.D., *Assistant Professor of Clinical Medicine (Dermatology)*
John B. Fitts, A.B., M.D., *Assistant Professor of Clinical Medicine*
Joseph C. Massee, B.S., M.D., *Assistant Professor of Clinical Medicine*
Arthur J. Merrill, B.S., M.D., *Assistant Professor of Medicine*
Max Michael, B.S., M.D., *Assistant Professor of Clinical Medicine*
Charles H. Paine, B.S., M.D., *Assistant Professor of Clinical Medicine*
Carter Smith, B.S., M.D., *Assistant Professor of Clinical Medicine*
Ebert Van Buren, B.S., M.D., *Assistant Professor of Clinical Medicine*

Associates

L. Minor Blackford, BS., M.D., M.Sc.Med.
William L. Dobes, A.B., M.D.
  (Dermatology)
Hugh E. Hailey, A.B., M.D.
  (Dermatology)
Albert Heyman, B.S., M.D.

David F. James, B.S., M.D.
Roy S. Leadingham,[1] M.D.
R. Bruce Logue, B.S., M.D.
J. Merrell Monfort, A.B., M.D.
Philip H. Nippert, B.S., M.D.
  (Dermatology)

Instructors

Evert A. Bancker, B.S., M.D.
Walter M. Bartlett, B S., M.D.
Walter L. Bloom, M.D.
John F. Busey, B.S., M.D.
Walter H. Cargill, B.S., M.D.
T. Sterling Claiborne, A.B. M.D.
Martin M. Cummings, B.S. M.D.
Hortense E. Garver, M.S.
  (Clinical Pathology)
Robert P. Grant, A.B., M.D.
L Harvey Hamff, A.B., M.D.
Lamont Henry, B.S., M.D.

Byron J. Hoffman, A.B., M.D.
Charles M. Huguley, A.B., M.D.
Edward S. Miller,[2] M.D.
William R. Minnich B.S., M.D.
John L. Patterson Jr., A.B., M.D.
Vernon E. Powell, B.S., M.D.
Joseph L. Rankin, A.B., M.D.
  (Dermatology)
John C. Ransmeier, A.B., M.D.
Jefferson L. Richardson, B.S., M.D.
Charles F. Stone Jr., M.D.
Cyrus W. Strickler Jr., MD.

Robert L. Whipple Jr., B.S., M.D.

Assistants

Guy H. Adams, A.B., M.D.
Elbert B. Agnor, Ph.B., M.D.
Eustace A. Allen, A.B., M.D.
Edward S. Armstrong,[3] LL.D.
John S. Atwater, A.B., M.D., M.Sc.Med.
J. Gordon Barrow, B.S., M.D.
John E. Beck, B.S. M.D.
Maxwell R. Berry Jr., M.D., Ph.D.
Tully T. Blalock, M.D.
Max M. Blumberg, B.S., M.D.
Charles E. Brown, A.M., M.D.
C. Daniel Burge, B.S., M.D.
John J. Butler, A.B., M.D.
Sandy B. Carter, B.S., M.D.
William R. Crowe, M.D.
Edgar M. Dunstan, A.M., M.D.
Edwin C. Evans, B.S., M.D.
Frank M. Geiser, B.S., M.D.
David R. Ginder,[4] A.B., M.D.
O. Eugene Hanes, A.B., M.D.
J. Frank Harris, A.B., M.D.
A. Worth Hobby, M.D.
Eugenia C. Jones, A.M., D.Sc., M.D.

Harold B. Levin, M.D. *(Dermatology)*
Louis K. Levy, M.D.
Mason I. Lowance, B.S., M.D.
T. English McGeachy, A.B., M.D.
A. Park McGinty, B.S., M.D.
Christopher J. McLoughlin, A.B., M.D.
Clarence W. Mills, B.S., M.D.
Chester W. Morse, A.B., M.D.
F. Levering Neely, A.B., M.D.
Fenwick T. Nichols, B.S., M.D.
Harry Parks, B.S., M.D.
William L. Paullin Jr., M.D.
Caroline K. Pratt, A.B., M.D.
Harry J. Price, M.D.
C. Purcell Roberts, A.B., M.D.
J. Spalding Schroder, A.B., M.D.
Joseph A. Schwartz, B.S., M.D.
John deR. Slade, A.B., M.D.
Hyman Stillerman, M.S., M.D.
Lloyd F. Timberlake, A.B., M.D.
William H. Trimble, B.S., M.D.
James I. Weinberg, B.S., M.D.
Bernard P. Wolff, B.S., M.D.

Resident Teaching Assistants

At Grady Memorial Hospital:

William H. Dean, A.B., M.D.
Donald Faulkner, B.S., M.D.

W. Elizabeth Gambrell, Ph.D., M.D.
H. H. Turner, M.D.

At Emory University Hospital:

William J. Senter, B.S., M.D.

Robbins Research Fellow

Francis Fitzhugh, A.B., M.D.

---

[1] On leave of absence.
[2] Resigned July 1, 1948.
[3] Resigned August 1, 1948.
[4] Appointment effective July 1, 1949.

Appendix 17: Bulletin of Emory University School of Medicine, which lists the full-time and clinical volunteer faculty members, and resident teaching assistants of the Department of Medicine in 1950.

MEDICINE

Paul B. Beeson, M.D., C.M., *Professor of Medicine, Chairman of the Department*
Russell H. Oppenheimer, A.B., M.D., *Professor of Clinical Medicine*
R. Hugh Wood, M.D., *Professor of Clinical Medicine*
F. William Sunderman, *Professor of Clinical Medicine (Clinical Pathology)*
William F. Friedewald, B.S., M.D., *Associate Professor of Medicine*
James V. Warren, A.B., M.D., *Associate Professor of Medicine*
Glenville Giddings, M.D., *Associate Professor of Clinical Medicine*
William A. Smith, B.S., M.D., *Associate Professor of Clinical Medicine (Neurology)*
Richard B. Wilson, B.S., M.D., *Associate Professor of Clinical Medicine (Neurology)*
Arthur J. Merrill, B.S., M.D., *Assistant Professor of Medicine*
Herbert S. Alden, B.S., M.D., *Assistant Professor of Clinical Medicine (Dermatology)*
John B. Fitts, A.B., M.D., *Assistant Professor of Clinical Medicine*
Joseph C. Massee, B.S., M.D., *Assistant Professor of Clinical Medicine*
Max Michael Jr., B.S., M.D., *Assistant Professor of Clinical Medicine*
Charles H. Paine, B.S., M.D., *Assistant Professor of Clinical Medicine*
Carter Smith, B.S., M.D., *Assistant Professor of Clinical Medicine*
Ebert Van Buren, B.S., M.D., *Assistant Professor of Clinical Medicine*

Associates

L. Minor Blackford, B.S., M.D., M.Sc.Med.
Philip K. Bondy, A.B., M.D.
William L. Dobes, A.B., M.D.
  (Dermatology)
Robert P. Grant, A.B., M.D.
Hugh E. Hailey, A.B., M.D. *(Dermatology)*
Albert Heyman, B.S., M.D.

Charles M. Huguley Jr., A.B., M.D.
David F. James, B.S., M.D.
Roy S. Leadingham,[1] MD.
R. Bruce Logue, B.S., MD.
J. Merrell Monfort, A.B., M.D.
Philip H. Nippert, B.S., M.D.
  (Dermatology)

Robert L. Whipple Jr., B.S., M.D.

Instructors

Elbert B. Agnor, Ph.B., M.D.
Evert A. Bancker, B.S., M.D.
J. Gordon Barrow, B.S., M.D.
Walter M. Bartlett, B.S., M.D.
Walter L. Bloom, M.D.
John F. Busey,[2] B.S., M.D.
Walter H. Cargill, B.S., M.D.
T. Sterling Claiborne, A.B., M.D.
Martin M. Cummings, B.S, M.D.
Richard E. Felder,[3] A.B., M.D.
W. Elizabeth Gambrell, Ph.D., M.P.H., M.D.

Hortense E. Garver, M.S. *(Clinical Pathology)*
L. Harvey Hamff, A.B., M.D.
Lamont Henry, B.S., M.D.
Byron J. Hoffman, A.B., M.D.
William R. Minnich, B.S., M.D.
John L. Patterson Jr., A.B., M.D.
Vernon E. Powell B.S., M.D.
Joseph L. Rankin, A.B., M.D.
  (Dermatology)
John C. Ransmeier, A.B., M.D.

Jefferson L. Richardson, B.S., M.D.
J. Spalding Schroder, A.B., M.D.

Charles F. Stone Jr., M.D.
Cyrus W. Strickler Jr., M.D.

Assistants

Guy H. Adams, A.B., M.D.
Eustace A. Allen, A.B., M.D.
John S. Atwater, A.B., M.D., M.Sc.Med.
John E. Beck, B.S., M.D.
Maxwell R. Berry Jr., M.D., Ph.D.
Tully T. Blalock, M.D.
Max M. Blumberg, B.S., M.D.
Charles E. Brown, A.M., M.D.
C. Daniel Burge, B.S., M.D.
John J. Butler,[4] A.B., M.D.
Sandy B. Carter, B.S., M.D.
William R. Crowe, M.D.
David B. Dennison, B.S., M.D.
Edgar M. Dunstan, A.M., M.D.
Edwin C. Evans, B.S., M.D.
Milton H. Freedman, B.S., M.D.
Frank M. Geiser, B.S., M.D.
David R. Ginder, A.B., M.D.
O. Eugene Hanes, A.B., M.D.
J. Frank Harris, A.B., M.D.
Joseph H. Hilsman Jr., B.S., M.D.
A. Worth Hobby, M.D.
David James Hughes, M.D.
J. Willis Hurst, B.S., M.D.
Eugenia C. Jones, A.M., D.Sc., M.D.

Harold B. Levin, M.D. *(Dermatology)*
Louis K. Levy, M.D.
Mason I. Lowance, B.S., M.D.
T. English McGeachy, A.B., M.D.
A. Park McGinty, B.S., M.D.
Christopher J. McLoughlin, A.B., M.D.
Clarence W. Mills, B.S., M.D.
Chester W. Morse, A.B., M.D.
Michael V. Murphy Jr., B.S., M.D.
F. Levering Neely, A.B., M.D.
Fenwick T. Nichols Jr.[5] B.S., M.D.
Harry Parks, B.S., M.D.
William L. Paullin Jr., M.D.
Caroline K. Pratt, A.B., M.D.
Harry J. Price, M.D.
C. Purcell Roberts, A.B., M.D.
Joseph A. Schwartz, B.S., MD.
John deR. Slade, A.B., M.D.
Hyman B. Stillerman, M.S., M.D.
Lloyd F. Timberlake, A.B., M.D.
William H. Trimble, B.S., M.D.
Paul D. Vella, A.B., M.D.
James I. Weinberg, B.S., M.D.
Bernard P. Wolff, B.S., M.D.

Resident Teaching Assistants

At Grady Memorial Hospital:
Richard E. Felder, A.B., M.D.

At Emory University Hospital:
John K. Davidson, B.S., M.D.

At Lawson Veterans Hospital:
William B. Fackler Jr., B.S., M.D.

---

[1] On leave of absence.
[2] Resigned March 1, 1950.
[3] Appointment effective July 1, 1950.
[4] Resigned June 1, 1949.
[5] Resigned July 1, 1949.

Appendix 18: Bulletin of Emory University School of Medicine, which lists the full-time and clinical volunteer faculty members, and resident teaching assistants of the Department of Medicine in 1951.

MEDICINE

Paul B. Beeson, *Professor of Medicine; Chairman of the Department*

Professor: Rolla E. Dyer

Professors (Clinical): Russell H. Oppenheimer, R. Hugh Wood, F. William Sunderman *(Clinical Pathology)*

Associate Professors: William F. Friedewald, James V. Warren

Associate Professors (Clinical): Glenville Giddings, William A. Smith *(Neurology)*, Richard B. Wilson *(Neurology)*

Assistant Professors: Albert Heyman, David F. James, R. Bruce Logue, Arthur J. Merrill

Assistant Professors (Clinical): Herbert S. Alden *(Dermatology)*, W. Roy Mason, Joseph C. Massee, Max Michael, Vernon E. Powell, Carter Smith, Elbert Van Buren

Associates: L. Minor Blackford, Walter L. Bloom, Philip K. Bondy, William L. Dobes *(Dermatology)*, Robert P. Grant,[1] Hugh E. Hailey *(Dermatology)*, Charles M. Huguley Jr., J. Merrell Monfort, Philip H. Nippert *(Dermatology)*, Robert L. Whipple Jr.

Instructors: Elbert B. Agnor, Evert A. Bancker, J. Gordon Barrow, Walter M. Bartlett,[2] Charles E. Brown, C. Daniel Burge, Walter H. Cargill, T. Sterling Claiborne, Martin M. Cummings, Richard E. Felder, W. Elizabeth Gambrell, Hortense E. Garver *(Clinical Pathology)*, David R. Ginder, L. Harvey Hamff, J. Frank Harris, David L. Hearin *(Dermatology)*, Lamont Henry, Joseph H. Hilsman, Byron J. Hoffman, J. Willis Hurst, William R. Minnich, John L. Patterson Jr., Joseph L. Rankin *(Dermatology)*, John C. Ransmeier,[3] Jefferson L. Richardson, J. Spalding Schroder, Charles F. Stone Jr., Cyrus W. Strickler Jr.

Assistants: Guy H. Adams, Eustace A. Allen, John S. Atwater, John E. Beck, Maxwell R. Berry Jr., Tully T. Blalock, William E. Bloomer, Max M. Blumberg, Sandy B. Carter, William R. Crowe, David B. Dennison, Joseph T. Doyle, Edgar M. Dunstan, Edwin C. Evans, Milton H. Freedman, Frank M. Geiser, Franklin H. Goodwin, O. Eugene Hanes, A. Worth Hobby, David James Hughes,[2] Eugenia C. Jones, Alvin D. Josephs, Harold B. Levin *(Dermatology)*, Louis K. Levy, Bernard S. Lipman, Mason I. Lowance, T. English McGeachy, A. Park McGinty, Christopher J. McLoughlin, William B. Martin, Clarence W. Mills, Chester W. Morse, Michael V. Murphy Jr., F. Levering Neely, Harry Parks, William L. Paullin, Caroline K. Pratt, Harry J. Price, C. Purcell Roberts, Joseph A. Schwartz,[4] John deR. Slade, Wyman P. Sloan Jr., Hyman B. Stillerman, Lloyd F. Timberlake, William H. Trimble, Paul D. Vella, James I. Weinberg, J. Grant Wilmer, Bernard P. Wolff

Research Fellows: Clayton R. Sikes, T. Whatley Duke, Francis W. Fitzhugh

Resident Teaching Assistants:

At *Grady Memorial Hospital:* Daniel D. Hankey

At *Emory University Hospital:* Henry S. Jennings Jr., Grattan C. Woodson Jr.

At *Lawson Veterans Hospital:* Charles M. Jennings

---

[1] Resigned July 16, 1960.
[2] In military service.

[3] Resigned February 1, 1951.
[4] Resigned July 15, 1950.

Appendix 19: Bulletin of Emory University School of Medicine which lists the full-time and clinical volunteer faculty members, and Research Fellows of the Department of Medicine in 1952.

MEDICINE

Paul B. Beeson,[1] *Professor of Medicine; Chairman of the Department*
Professors: Rolla E. Dyer, Russell H. Oppenheimer, James V. Warren,[2] R. Hugh Wood
Associate Professors: William F. Friedewsld, R. Bruce Logue, Arthur J. Merrill, Max Michael Jr.
Associate Professors (Clinical): C. Glenville Giddings, William A. Smith *(Neurology)*, Richard B. Wilson *(Neurology)*
Assistant Professors: Walter L. Bloom, Philip K. Bondy,[3] Albert Heyman, David F. James
Assistant Professors (Clinical): Herbert S. Alden *(Dermatology)*, W. Roy Mason Jr., Joseph C. Massee, Vernon E. Powell, Carter Smith, Ebert Van Buren
Associates: J. Gordon Barrow, L. Minor Blackford, Walter H. Cargill, T. Sterling Claiborne, Martin M. Cummings, William L. Dobes *(Dermatology)*, Hugh E. Hailey *(Dermatology)*, L. Harvey Hamff, Charles M. Huguley Jr., J. Merrell Monfort, Philip H. Nippert *(Dermatology)*, J. Spalding Schroder, Charles F. Stone Jr., Robert L. Whipple Jr.
Instructors: Elbert B. Agnor, John S. Atwater, Evert A. Bancker, Tully T. Blalock, Charles E. Brown, C. Daniel Burge, E. Napier Burson Jr., Joseph T. Doyle, Richard E. Felder, W. Elizabeth Gambrell, Hortense E Garver *(Clinical Pathology)*, David R. Ginder, J. Frank Harris, David L. Hearin *(Dermatology)*, Lamont Henry, Joseph H. Hilsman Jr., Byron J. Hoffman, J. Willis Hurst *(Cardiology)*, Henry S. Jennings, William R. Minnich, F. Levering Neely, John L. Patterson Jr., William L. Paullin Jr., Harry J. Price, Joseph L. Rankin *(Dermatology)*, Cyrus W. Strickler Jr.
Assistants: Guy H. Adams, Eustace A. Allen, John E. Beck, Williaza E. Bloomer, Max M. Blumberg, Sandy B. Carter, William R. Crowe, William J. Dean, David B. Dennison, Edgar M. Dunstan, Edwin C. Evans, Milton H. Freedman, Frank M. Geiser, Glenville A. Giddings, Franklin H. Goodwin,[4] O. Eugene Hanes, Haygood N. Hill, Eugenia C. Jones, Alvin D. Josephs, Harold B. Levin *(Dermatology)*, Louis K. Levy, Bernard S. Lipman, Mason I. Lowance, A. Park McGinty, Christopher J. McLoughlin, William B. Martin,[5] Clarence W. Mills, Chester W. Morse, Michael V. Murphy Jr., Harry Parks, Caroline K. Pratt,[6] C. Purcell Roberts, John deR. Slade, Wyman P. Sloan Jr., Hyman B. Stillerman, Lloyd F. Timberlake, Clyde E. Tomlin, William H. Trimble, Paul D. Vella, James I. Weinberg, J. Grant Wilmer, Bernard P. Wolff
Research Fellows: Louis L. Battey, Francis W. Fitzhugh Jr., Bernard L. Hallman, Ralph A. Huie, Charles Lepine, Gratton C. Woodson Jr.[7]

---

[1] Resigned March 31, 1952.
[2] Resigned August 1, 1952.
[3] Resigned July 1, 1952.
[4] Resigned August 1, 1951.

[5] Resigned November 28, 1951.
[6] Died May 22, 1951.
[7] In military service.

Appendix 20: Bulletin of Emory University School of Medicine, which lists the full-time and clinical volunteer faculty members, and research fellows of the Department of Medicine in 1953.

MEDICINE

Eugene B. Ferris Jr., *Professor of Medicine; Chairman of the Department*
Professors: Rolla E. Dyer, Russell H. Oppenheimer, R. Hugh Wood
Associate Professors: William F. Friedewald, R. Bruce Logue, Arthur J. Merrill, Max Michael Jr.
Associate Professors (Clinical): Herbert S. Alden (Dermatology), C. Glenville Giddings, Joseph C. Massee, Carter Smith, William A. Smith (Neurology), Richard B. Wilson (Neurology)
Assistant Professors: Walter L. Bloom, Albert A. Brust, Albert Heyman, Charles M. Huguley Jr., J. Spalding Schroder
Assistant Professors (Clinical): L. Minor Blackford, T. Sterling Claiborne, Martin M. Cummings, William L. Dobes (Dermatology), L. Hanvey Hamff, David F. James, Emanuel E. Mandel, W. Roy Mason Jr., Philip H. Nippert (Dermatology), Vernon E. Powell, Charles F. Stone Jr., Ebert Van Buren, Robert L. Whipple Jr.
Associates: J. Gordon Barrow, Tully T. Blalock, Charles E. Brown, C. Daniel Burge, E. Napier Burson Jr., Walter H. Cargill, Richard E. Felder, W. Elizabeth Gambrell, Hugh E. Hailey (Dermatology), J. Frank Harris, Lamont Henry, Joseph H. Hilsman Jr., Byron J. Hoffman, J. Willis Hurst (Cardiology), J. Merrell Monfort, F. Levering Neely, William L. Paullin Jr., Joseph L. Rankin (Dermatology)
Instructors: Guy H. Adams, Elbert B. Agnor, Eustace A. Allen, John S. Atwater, Evert A. Bancker, John E. Beck, William E. Bloomer, Max M. Blumberg, Sandy B. Carter, Gerald B. Cooper, William R. Crowe, David B. Dennison, Edgar M. Dunstan, Edwin C. Evans, Francis W. Fitzhugh Jr., Milton H. Freedman, Hortense E. Garver (Clinical Pathology), Glenville A. Giddings, David R. Ginder, Bernard L. Hallman, O. Eugene Hanes, David L. Hearin (Dermatology), Haywood N. Hill, Ralph A. Huie, Henry S. Jennings, Eugenia C. Jones, Alvin D. Josephs, James A. Kaufman, Harold B. Levin (Dermatology), Louis K. Levy, Bernard S. Lipman, Mason I. Lowance, A. Park McGinty, Christopher J. McLoughlin, Clarence W. Mills, William R. Minnich, Chester W. Morse, Michael V. Murphy Jr., Gene Nardin, Harry Parks, John L. Patterson Jr., Harry J. Price, Arthur M. Pruce, C. Purcell Roberts, John deR. Slade, Wyman P. Sloan, Hyman B. Stillerman, Cyrus W. Strickler Jr., Lloyd F. Timberlake, William H. Trimble, Margaret J. Wall, James I. Weinberg, Edward McM. West, J. Grant Wilmer, Bernard P. Wolff, Edgar Woody Jr.
Research Fellows: Charles Ballentine, Marguerite L. Candler, Manuel N. Cooper, William J. Dean, Remo J. DiSalvo, Harold T. Dodge, Robert W. Ferguson, Claude H. Fowler Jr., Thomas L. Gorsuch, I. B. Harrison, George L. Mitchell Jr., Warren G. Sarrell

Appendix 21: Bulletin of Emory University School of Medicine, which lists the full-time and clinical volunteer faculty members and fellows of the Department of Medicine in 1954.

MEDICINE

Eugene B. Ferris Jr., *Professor of Medicine; Chairman of the Department*
Professors: Rolla E. Dyer, Russell H. Oppenheimer, R. Hugh Wood
Associate Professors: R. Bruce Logue, Arthur J. Merrill, Max Michael Jr.
Associate Professors (Clinical): Herbert S. Alden (Dermatology), William F. Friedewald, C. Glenville Giddings, Joseph C. Massee, Carter Smith, William A. Smith (Neurology), Richard B. Wilson (Neurology)
Assistant Professors: Walter L. Bloom, Albert A. Brust, Albert Heyman,[1] Charles M. Huguley Jr., J. Spalding Schroder
Assistant Professors (Clinical): L. Minor Blackford, T. Sterling Claiborne, William L. Dobes (Dermatology), L. Harvey Hamff, David F. James, Emanuel E. Mandel, W. Roy Mason Jr., Philip H. Nippert (Dermatology), John H. Peters (Internal), Vernon E. Powell, Charles F. Stone Jr., Ebert Van Buren, Robert L. Whipple Jr.
Associates: J. Gordon Barrow, Tully T. Blalock, Charles E. Brown,[2] C. Daniel Burge, E. Napier Burson Jr., Walter H. Cargill, Richard E. Felder, W. Elizabeth Gambrell, Hugh E. Hailey (Dermatology), J. Frank Harris, Lamont Henry, Joseph H. Hilsman Jr., Byron J. Hoffman, J. Willis Hurst (Cardiology), J. Merrell Monfort, F. Levering Neely, William L. Paullin Jr., Joseph L. Rankin (Dermatology)
Instructors: Guy H. Adams, Elbert B. Agnor, Eustace A. Allen, Thomas J. Anderson Jr., John S. Atwater, Evert A. Bancker, John E. Beck, Linton H. Bishop Jr., William E. Bloomer, Max M. Blumberg, Estelle P. Boynton, H. Eugene Brown, E. Fred Campbell, Marguerite L. Candler, Sandy B. Carter, Gerald R. Cooper, Manuel N. Cooper, William R. Crowe, David B. Dennison, Remo J. DiSalvo, Edgar M. Dunstan, Walter F. Edmundson II, Edwin C. Evans, Francis W. Fitzhugh Jr.,[2] Francis T. Flood,[3] Claude H. Fowler Jr., Milton H. Freedman, Hortense E. Garver (Clinical Pathology), Robert I. Gibbs Jr., Glenville A. Giddings, David R. Ginder, Thomas A. Haedicke, Bernard L. Hallman, O. Eugene Hanes, Daniel D. Hankey, David L. Hearin (Dermatology), David E. Hein, Haywood N. Hill, David J. Hughes, Ralph A. Huie Jr., Henry S. Jennings Jr.,[4] Carl C. Jones Jr., Eugenia C. Jones, Alvin D. Josephs, James A. Kaufman, Harold B. Levin (Dermatology), Louis K. Levy, Bernard S. Lipman, Mason I. Lowance, A. Park McGinty, Christopher J. McLoughlin, Clarence W. Mills, William R. Minnich, George L. Mitchell Jr., Chester W. Morse, Michael V. Murphy Jr.,[2] Gene Nardin, Sidney Olansky, Harry Parks, Arthur M. Pruce, C. Purcell Roberts, Warren G. Sarrell, Legh R. Scott, John deR. Slade, Wyman P. Sloan, Hyman B. Stillerman, Cyrus W. Strickler Jr., Lloyd F. Timberlake, William H. Trimble, Margaret J. Wall, James I. Weinberg, Edward McM. West, J. Grant Wilmer, Joseph S. Wilson, Bernard P. Wolff, Edgar Woody Jr.
Fellows: Freeman H. Cary, Remo J. DiSalvo, James D. Evans, Oscar W. Freeman, Thomas C. Hill Jr., Charles D. Hollis, Thomas D. Johnson, Herbert R. Karp, Milton J. Krainin, Lawrence E. Lamb, Robert F. Leyen, Hugh K. Sealy Jr., Benjamin T. White

---

[1] Resigned January 1, 1954.
[2] On military leave of absence.
[3] Resigned November 25, 1953.
[4] Resigned November 15, 1953.

Appendix 22: Bulletin of Emory University School of Medicine, which lists the full-time and clinical volunteer faculty members and fellows of the Department of Medicine in 1955.

MEDICINE

Eugene B. Ferris Jr., *Professor of Medicine; Chairman of the Department*
Professors: Rolla E. Dyer, Russell H. Oppenheimer,[1] R. Hugh Wood
Professor (Clinical): Benjamin R. Gendel[2]
Associate Professors: R. Bruce Logue, Arthur J. Merrill, Max Michael Jr.[3]
Associate Professors (Clinical): Herbert S. Alden (Dermatology), William F. Friedewald, C. Glenville Giddings, Joseph C. Massee, Carter Smith, William A. Smith (Neurology), Richard B. Wilson (Neurology)
Assistant Professors: Walter L. Bloom, Albert A. Brust, Noble O. Fowler, Charles M. Huguley Jr., Charles A. LeMaistre, J. Spalding Schroder
Assistant Professors (Clinical): Carl C. Aven, L. Minor Blackford, T. Sterling Claiborne, William L. Dobes (Dermatology), L. Harvey Hamff, David F. James, Emanuel E. Mandel,[4] W. Roy Mason Jr., Philip H. Nippert (Dermatology), John H. Peters (Internal), Vernon E. Powell, Charles F. Stone Jr., Ebert Van Buren, Robert L. Whipple Jr.
Associates: J. Gordon Barrow, Tully T. Blalock, Charles E. Brown, C. Daniel Burge, E. Napier Burson Jr., Walter H. Cargill, Richard E. Felder, W. Elizabeth Gambrell, Hugh E. Hailey (Dermatology), J. Frank Harris, Lamont Henry, Joseph H. Hilsman Jr., Byron J. Hoffman, J. Willis Hurst (Cardiology),[5] J. Merrell Monfort, F. Levering Neely, William L. Paullin Jr., Joseph L. Rankin (Dermatology)
Instructors: Guy H. Adams, Elbert B. Agnor, Henry C. Alexander Jr., Eustace A. Allen, Thomas J. Anderson Jr., John S. Atwater, Evert A. Bancker, William H. Baria,[5] John E. Beck, Alfred M. Bennett, Linton H. Bishop Jr., William E. Bloomer, Max M. Blumberg, Estelle P. Boynton, H. Eugene Brown: E. Fred Campbell,[6] Marguerite L. Candler, Sandy B. Carter, Freeman H. Cary,[5] L. Guy Chelton, Noah H. Chiles, Gerald R. Cooper, Manuel N. Cooper, William R. Crowe, James C. Crutcher, David B. Dennison, Remo J. DiSalvo,[7] F. William Dowda, Edgar M. Dunstan, Walter F. Edmundson II,[8] Edwin C. Evans, Harold A. Ferris, Francis W. Fitzhugh Jr., Claude H. Fowler Jr., Milton H. Freedman, Hortense E. Garver (Clinical Pathology), Robert I. Gibbs Jr., Glenville A. Giddings, David R. Ginder, Thomas A. Haedicke, James A. Hagans, Bernard L. Hallman, O. Eugene Hanes, Daniel D. Hankey, David L. Hearin (Dermatology), David E. Hein, Haywood N. Hill, Thomas C. Hill Jr., Edward H. Hook Jr., David J. Hughes, Ralph A. Huie Jr., Carl C. Jones Jr., Eugenia C. Jones, Alvin D. Josephs, James A. Kaufman, Milton J. Krainin, Harold B. Levin (Dermatology), Louis K. Levy, Bernard S. Lipman, Grady E. Longino, Mason I. Lowance, A. Park McGinty, Christopher J. McLoughlin, Clarence W. Mills, William R. Minnich, George L. Mitchell Jr., Chester W. Morse, Michael V. Murphy Jr., Ralph A. Murphy Jr., Gene Nardin, Sidney Olansky, Harry Parks, Arthur M. Pruce, C. Purcell Roberts, Warren G. Sarrell,[9] Legh R. Scott, John deR. Slade, Wyman P. Sloan, Hyman B. Stillerman, Cyrus W. Strickler Jr., Paul Teplis, Lloyd F. Timberlake, Clyde E. Tomlin, William H. Trimble, Margaret J. Wall, James I. Weinberg, John G.

Wells, Edward McM. West, Ben T. White, J. Grant Wilmer, Joseph S. Wilson, Bernard P. Wolff, Grattan C. Woodson, Edgar Woody Jr.

Fellows: Elizabeth Adams, Ernest W. Beasley Jr., Alfred M. Bennett, Med Scott Brown, Peter J. Cline, William S. Dingledine, James A. Hagans, Thomas C. Hill Jr., Milton J. Krainin, Joseph T. Melton, Samuel O. Poole, Ruben E. Smith, Charles L. Whisnant Jr., Joseph A. Wilber, Earl E. Yantis

---

[1] Resigned August 21, 1954.

[2] Appointment effective June 1, 1955.

[3] Resigned June 20, 1954.

[4] Resigned July 1, 1954.

[5] On military leave of absence.

[6] Resigned June 21, 1954.

[7] Resigned June 30, 1954.

[8] Resigned July 23, 1954.

[9] Appointment expired July 1, 1954.

Appendix 23: Bulletin of Emory University School of Medicine, which lists the full-time and clinical volunteer faculty members and fellows of the Department of Medicine in 1956.

MEDICINE

Eugene B. Ferris Jr., *Professor of Medicine; Chairman of the Department*
Professors: Rolla E. Dyer, R. Hugh Wood
Professor (Clinical): Benjamin R. Gendel
Associate Professors: Walter L. Bloom, Albert A. Brust, Charles A. LeMaistre, R. Bruce Logue
Associate Professors (Clinical): Herbert S. Alden (Dermatology), William F. Friedewald, Glenville Giddings, Joseph C. Massee, Arthur J. Merrill, John H. Peters, Carter Smith, William A. Smith (Neurology), Richard B. Wilson (Neurology)
Assistant Professors: Noble O. Powler, Charles M. Huguley Jr., J. Spalding Schroder
Assistant Professors (Clinical): Carl C. Aven, J. Gordon Barrow, L. Minor Blackford, T. Sterling Claiborne, Gerald R. Cooper, William L. Dobes (Dermatology), L. Harvey Hamff, David F. James, W. Roy Mason Jr., Philip H. Nippert (Dermatology), Vernon E. Powell, Charles F. Stone Jr., Ebert Van Buren, Robert L. Whipple Jr.
Associates: Eustace A. Allen, Thomas J. Anderson Jr., Tully T. Blalock, Charles E. Brown, C. Daniel Burge, E. Napier Burson Jr., Walter H. Cargill, James C. Crutcher, Richard E. Felder, W. Elizabeth Gambrell, Hugh E. Hailey (Dermatology), Bernard L. Hallman, J. Frank Harris, Lamont Henry, Joseph H. Hilsman Jr., Byron J. Hoffman, J. Willis Hurst, J. Merrell Monfort, Chester W. Morse, Gene Nardin, F. Levering Neely, Harry Parks, William L. Paullin Jr., Joseph L. Rankin (Dermatology), John deR. Slade, Hyman B. Stillerman, Lloyd F. Timberlake, Edgar Woody Jr.
Instructors: Charles D. Adams, Guy H. Adams, Elbert B. Agnor, Henry C. Alexander Jr.,[1] C. Raymond Arp, John S. Atwater, Evert A. Bancker, William H. Baria,[2] Ernest W. Beasley Jr., John E. Beck, Alfred M. Bennett, Maxwell Berry, Linton H. Bishop Jr., William E. Bloomer, Max M. Blumberg, Estelle P. Boynton, H. Eugene Brown, Marguerite L. Candler, Frank P. Cantrell, Sandy B. Carter, Freeman H. Cary,[2] L. Guy Chelton, Noah H. Chiles, Peter J. Cline, Robert P. Coggins, Manuel N. Cooper, William R. Crowe, Joseph A. Cruise, C. Warren Davidson, David B. Dennison, Edward R. Dorney, F. William Dowda, Walter S. Dunbar, Edgar M. Dunstan, Edwin C. Evans, Harold A. Ferris, Francis W. Fitzhugh Jr., Luther G. Fortson Jr., Claude H. Fowler Jr., Milton H. Freedman, Hortense E. Garver (Clinical Pathology), Robert I. Gibbs Jr., Glenville A. Giddings, David R. Ginder, Thomas A. Haedicke,[3] James A. Hagans,[1] O. Eugene Hanes, Daniel D. Hankey, Byron F. Harper Jr., David L. Hearin (Dermatology), David E. Hein, Haywood N. Hill, Thomas C. Hill Jr.,[1] A. Worth Hobby, Edward W. Hook Jr., David J. Hughes, Ralph A. Huie Jr., Carl C. Jones Jr., Eugenia C. Jones, Alvin D. Josephs, James A. Kaufman, Milton J. Krainin,[3] Harold B. Levin (Dermatology), Louis K. Levy, Bernard S. Lipman, Grady E. Longino,[4] Mason I. Lowance, John M. McCoy, A. Park McGinty, Christopher J. McLoughlin, Clarence W. Mills, William R. Minnich, George L. Mitchell Jr., Michael V. Murphy Jr., Ralph A. Murphy Jr., Sidney Olansky,[5] Lamar B. Peacock, Arthur M. Pruce, Purcell

Roberts, Legh R. Scott Jr., Thomas B. Sharp Jr., Wyman P. Sloan Jr., Cyrus W. Strickler Jr., Paul Teplis, Nathaniel S. Thornton, Clyde E. Tomlin,[6] Margaret J. Wall, James I. Weinberg, John G. Wells, Edward McM. West, Ben T. White II,[5] Joseph A. Wilber, J. Grant Wilmer, Joseph S. Wilson, Bernard P. Wolff, Grattan C. Woodson Jr., John T. Yauger

Fellows: Elizabeth K. Adams,[1] Med Scott Brown,[1] A. Grigg Churchwell, William S. Dingledine, Robert H. Franch, John T. Galambos, William R. Hancock, Edward W. Hook, William B. Hudgins, Richard H. Johnson, James W. Lea Jr., William M. Madison Jr., Joseph T. Melton,[3] B. Waldo Moore Jr., Samuel O. Poole,[3] Shirley L. Rivers, Thomas F. Sellers Jr., Reuben E. Smith,[2] John A. Ward, Donald E. Warren, Charles L. Whisnant Jr.,[3] Earl E. Yantis[3]

---

[1] Appointment expired July 1, 1955.
[2] On military leave of absence.
[3] Resigned September 16, 1955.
[4] Resigned September 20, 1955.
[5] Resigned July 14, 1955.
[6] Appointment expired September 11, 1955.

Appendix 24: Bulletin of Emory University School of Medicine, which lists the full-time and clinical volunteer faculty members and fellows of the Department of Medicine in 1957.

Medicine

J. Willis Hurst, *Professor of Medicine; Chairman of the Department*[1]
Professors: Rolla E. Dyer, R. Hugh Wood
Professor (Clinical): Benjamin R. Gendel
Associate Professors: Walter L. Bloom,[2] Albert A. Brust, Charles A. LeMaistre, R. Bruce Logue (Cardiology), Noble O. Fowler
Associate Professors (Clinical): Herbert S. Alden (Dermatology), William F. Friedewald, Glenville Giddings, Joseph C. Massee, Arthur J. Merrill, John H. Peters,[3] Carter Smith, William A. Smith (Neurology), Richard B. Wilson (Neurology)
Assistant Professors: Charles M. Huguley Jr., J. Spalding Schroder
Assistant Professors (Clinical): Carl C. Aven Jr., J. Gordon Barrow, L. Minor Blackford, T. Sterling Claiborne, Gerald R. Cooper, William L. Dobes (Dermatology), L. Harvey Hamff, David F. James, W. Roy Mason Jr., Philip H. Nippert (Dermatology), Vernon E. Powell, Charles F. Stone Jr., Ebert Van Buren, Julius Wenger, Robert L. Whipple Jr.
Associates: Eustace A. Allen, Thomas J. Anderson Jr., Alfred M. Bennett, Tully T. Blalock, Charles E. Brown, H. Eugene Brown, C. Daniel Burge, E. Napier Burson Jr., Walter H. Cargill, James C. Crutcher, Edward R. Dorney, Richard E. Felder, W. Elizabeth Gambrell, Hugh E. Hailey (Dermatology), Bernard L. Hallman, J. Frank Harris, David E. Hein, Lamont Henry, Joseph H. Hilsman Jr., Byron J. Hoffman, Clarence W. Mills, J. Merrell Monfort, Chester W. Morse, Gene Nardin, F. Levering Neely, Harry Parks, William L. Paullin Jr., Joseph L. Rankin (Dermatology), John deR. Slade, Hyman B. Stillerman, Lloyd F. Timberlake, Joseph S. Wilson, Edgar Woody Jr.
Instructors: Charles D. Adams, Elizabeth K. Adams, Guy H. Adams, Elbert B. Agnor, C. Raymond Arp, John S. Atwater, Evert A. Bancker, William H. Baria,[4] Ernest W. Beasley Jr., John E. Beck, Maxwell Berry, Linton H. Bishop Jr., William E. Bloomer, Max M. Blumberg, Estelle P. Boynton, Spencer S. Brewer Jr., Marguerite L. Candler, Craig G. Cantrell,[5] Frank P. Cantrell,[6] Sandy B. Carter, Freeman H. Cary, H. Guy Chelton, Noah H. Chiles,[7] A. Grigg Churchwell, Maurice L. B. Clarke, Peter J. Cline, James C. Coberly, Robert P. Coggins, Manuel N. Cooper, William R. Crowe, Joseph S. Cruise, C. Warren Davidson, David B. Dennison, F. William Dowda, Walter S. Dunbar, Edgar M. Dunstan, Edwin C. Evans, Harold A. Ferris, Francis W. Fitzhugh Jr., Luther G. Fortson Jr., Claude H. Fowler Jr., Robert H. Franch, Milton H. Freedman, Robert I. Gibbs Jr., Glenville A. Giddings, David R. Ginder, O. Eugene Hanes, Daniel D. Hankey, Byron F. Harper Jr., David L. Hearin (Dermatology), Haywood N. Hill, A. Worth Hobby, Edward W. Hook,[8] David S. Hubbard,[5] William B. Hudgins, Ralph A. Huie Jr., Carl C. Jones, Eugenia C. Jones, Alvin D. Josephs, James A. Kaufman, Milton J. Krainin, Harold B. Levin (Dermatology), Louis K. Levy, Bernard S. Lipman, Mason I. Lowance, John M. McCoy, A. Park McGinty, Christopher J. McLoughlin, William R. Minnich, George

Appendixes 505

L. Mitchell Jr., B. Waldo Moore, Michael V. Murphy Jr., Ralph A. Murphy Jr., Abraham M. Oshlag, Lamar B. Peacock, Arthur M. Pruce, Walton H. Reeves, Shirley L. Rivers, Purcell Roberts, Legh R. Scott Jr., Thomas F. Sellers Jr.,[9] Thomas B. Sharp Jr., Wyman P. Sloan Jr., Cyrus W. Strickler Jr., Paul Teplis, Nathaniel S. Thornton, William R. Vogler Jr., Margaret J. Wall, Bruce S. Webster, James I. Weinberg, John G. Wells, Edward McM. West, Harold W. Whiteman, Joseph A. Wilber,[8] J. Grant Wilmer, Charles L. Whisnant, Bernard P. Wolff, Grattan C. Woodson Jr., John T. Yauger

Fellows: John B. Bewick, Jack H. Burnett Jr., Charles C. Corley, John T. Galambos, F. Dempsey Guillebeau, William R. Hancock,[8] Timothy Harden, Richard H. Johnson,[8] James W. Lea Jr.,[8] William M. Madison Jr.,[8] James M. Majors, James W. Mosley, Paul W. Seavey, Jean S. Staton, Warren D. Stribling, W. Yates Trotter, John A. Ward, Donald E. Warren,[8] Walter Wiegel

---

[1] Eugene B. Ferris Jr., Professor of Medicine and Chairman of the Department, resigned February 1, 1957.
[2] Appointment expired February 2, 1957.
[3] Resigned May 15, 1957.
[4] On military leave of absence.
[5] Appointment expires June 30, 1957.
[6] Resigned August 20, 1956.
[7] Resigned February 1, 1957.
[8] Appointment expired June 30, 1956.
[9] Appointment expires July 1, 1957.

Appendix 25: Bulletin of Emory University School of Medicine, which lists the full-time and clinical volunteer faculty members and fellows of the Department of Medicine in 1958.

MEDICINE

J. Willis Hurst, *Professor of Medicine; Chairman of the Department*
Professors: Benjamin R. Gendel, R. Bruce Logue (Cardiology), R. Hugh Wood
Professor (Clinical): Rolla E. Dyer
Associate Professors: Albert A. Brust,[1] Noble O. Fowler,[2] Charles M. Huguley Jr., Charles A. LeMaistre, Ross L. McLean, J. Spalding Schroder
Associate Professors (Clinical): Herbert S. Alden (Dermatology), J. Gordon Barrow, Gerald R. Cooper, William F. Friedewald, Glenville Giddings, L. Harvey Hamff, Joseph C. Massee, Arthur J. Merrill, Carter Smith, William A. Smith (Neurology), Richard B. Wilson (Neurology)
Assistant Professors: H. Eugene Brown, Bernard L. Hallman, Herbert R. Karp (Neurology), John R. K. Preedy, Elbert P. Tuttle Jr.
Assistant Professors (Clinical): Carl C. Aven, L. Minor Blackford, T. Sterling Claiborne, James C. Crutcher, William L. Dobes (Dermatology), David F. James, W. Roy Mason Jr., Philip H. Nippert (Dermatology), Vernon E. Powell, Charles F. Stone Jr., Ebert Van Buren, Julius Wenger, Robert L. Whipple Jr.
Associates: Eustace A. Allen, Thomas J. Anderson Jr., C. Raymond Arp, John S. Atwater, Ernest W. Beasley Jr., Alfred M. Bennett,[3] Linton H. Bishop Jr., Tully T. Blalock, Spencer S. Brewer Jr., Charles E. Brown, C. Daniel Burge, E. Napier Burson Jr., Marguerite L. Candler, Walter H. Cargill, Freeman H. Cary, James C. Coberly, Manuel N. Cooper, William R. Crowe, Edward R. Dorney, F. William Dowda, Walter S. Dunbar, Edwin C. Evans, Richard E. Felder, Harold A. Ferris, Francis W. Fitzhugh Jr., Milton H. Freedman, John T. Galambos, W. Elizabeth Gambrell, Robert I. Gibbs Jr., Hugh E. Hailey (Dermatology), Daniel D. Hankey, J. Frank Harris, David L. Hearin (Dermatology), David E. Hein, Lamont Henry, Haywood N. Hill, Joseph H. Hilsman Jr., A. Worth Hobby, Byron J. Hoffman, David J. Hughes, Ralph A. Huie Jr., Carl C. Jones Jr., James A. Kaufman, Milton J. Krainin, Harold B. Levin (Dermatology), Louis K. Levy, Bernard S. Lipman, A. Park McGinty, Christopher J. McLoughlin, Clarence W. Mills, George L. Mitchell Jr., J. Merrell Monfort, Chester W. Morse, Michael V. Murphy Jr., Ralph A. Murphy Jr., Gene Nardin, F. Levering Neely, Harry Parks, William L. Paullin Jr., Lamar B. Peacock, Joseph L. Rankin (Dermatology), Shirley L. Rivers, Purcell Roberts, John deR. Slade, Wyman P. Sloan Jr., Hyman B. Stillerman, Paul Teplis, Nathaniel S. Thornton, Lloyd F. Timberlake, Charles L. Whisnant Jr., Joseph S. Wilson, Bernard P. Wolff, Grattan C. Woodson Jr., Edgar Woody Jr., John T. Yauger
Instructors: Charles D. Adams (Dermatology), Elizabeth K. Adams, Guy H. Adams, Elbert B. Agnor, Evert A. Bancker, William H. Baria,[4] John E. Beck, Maxwell Berry, William E. Bloomer, Max M. Blumberg, Estelk P. Boynton,[5] Sandy B. Carter, H. Guy Chelton, Huddie L. Cheney,[6] A. Grigg Churchwell, Maurice L. B. Clarke, Peter J. Cline, Claud P. Cobb Jr., Robert P. Coggins, Charles C. Corley, Joseph S. Cruise, C. Warren Davidson, Nicholas E. Davies, David B. Dennison, Edgar M. Dunstan,

Luther G. Fortson Jr., Claude H. Fowler Jr., Robert H. Franch, Glenville A. Giddings. David R. Ginder,[7] Halcott T. Haden,[7] William R. Hancock. O. Eugene Hanes, Byron F. Harper Jr., William B. Hudgins, Henry S. Jennings Jr., Eugenia C. Jones, Alvin D. Josephs, Houston W. Kitchin, Constantine P. Lampros, Mason I. Lowance, John M. McCoy, George R. Mayfield,[8] William R. Minnich, James B. Minor, B. Waldo Moore Jr., Abraham M. Oshlag, Samuel O. Poole, Arthur M. Pruce, W. Harrison Reeves, Legh R. Scott Jr., Thomas B. Sharp Jr., Jean S. Staton, Warren D. Stribling III, Cyrus W. Strickler Jr., Hiram M. Sturm (Cardiology), William R. Vogler Jr., Margaret J. Wall, John A. Ward, Bruce S. Webster, James I. Weinberg, John G. Wells, Edward McM. West, Harold W. Whiteman Jr., W. Talbert Williams, J. Grant Wilmer

Fellows: Pat S. Barrow,[5] John B. Bewick,[9] Jack H. Burnett Jr.,[9] Lamar E. Crevasse Jr., Louis B. Daniel,[5] George M. Goza Jr., F. Dempsey Guillebeau,[9] Timothy Harden,[9] David Hubbard, Martha J. McAnulty, James M. Major, James W. Mosely, Ernest E. Proctor, Henry Randall, Mason G. Robertson, Paul W. Seavey,[9] W. Yates Trotter Jr., Walter Weigel[9]

---

[1] Resigned July 31, 1957
[2] Resigned September 30, 1957
[3] Resigned May 31, 1957
[4] On military leave of absence.
[5] Resigned August 31, 1957.
[6] Appointment expires June 30, 1958.
[7] Resigned December 31, 1957.
[8] Resigned January 31, 1958.
[9] Appointment expired June 30, 1957.

Appendix 26: Bulletin of Emory University School of Medicine, which lists the full-time and clinical volunteer faculty members and fellows of the Department of Medicine in 1959.

MEDICINE

J. Willis Hurst, *Professor of Medicine; Chairman of the Department*
Professors: Benjamin R. Gendel, R. Bruce Logue (Cardiology), R. Hugh Wood
Professor (Clinical): Rolla E. Dyer
Associate Professors: Charles M. Huguley Jr., Charles A. LeMaistre, Ross L. McLean, John R. K. Preedy, J. Spalding Schroder
Associate Professors (Clinical): Herbert S. Alden (Dermatology), J. Gordon Barrow, Gerald R. Cooper, William F. Friedewald, Glenville Giddings, L. Harvey Hamff, Joseph C. Massee, Arthur J. Merrill, Carter Smith, William A. Smith (Neurology), Richard B. Wilson (Neurology)
Assistant Professors: H. Eugene Brown, A. Grigg Churchwell, Edward R. Dorney, John T. Galambos, Bernard L. Hallman, Herbert R. Karp (Neurology), Robert C. Schlant, Thomas F. Sellers Jr., Elbert P. Tuttle Jr.
Assistant Professors (Clinical): Carl C. Aven, L. Minor Blackford, T. Sterling Claiborne, James C. Crutcher, William L. Dobes (Dermatology), Euclid G. Herndon Jr., David F. James, W. Roy Mason Jr., Philip H. Nippert (Dermatology), Vernon E. Powell, Charles F. Stone Jr., Ebert Van Buren, Julius Wenger, Robert L. Whipple Jr.
Associates: Eustace A. Allen, Thomas J. Anderson Jr., C. Raymond Arp, John S. Atwater, Ernest W. Beasley Jr., Linton H. Bishop Jr., Tully T. Blalock, Spencer S. Brewer Jr., Charles E. Brown, C. Daniel Burge, E. Napier Burson Jr., Marguerite L. Candler, Walter H. Cargill, Freeman H. Cary, James C. Coberly, Manuel N. Cooper, William R. Crowe, F. William Dowda, Walter S. Dunbar, Edwin C. Evans, Richard E. Felder, Harold A. Ferris, Francis W. Fitzhugh Jr., Milton H. Freedman, W. Elizabeth Gambrell, Robert I. Gibbs Jr., Hugh E. Hailey (Dermatology), Daniel D. Hankey, J. Frank Harris, David L. Hearin (Dermatology), David E. Hein, Lamont Henry, Haywood N. Hill, Joseph H. Hilsman Jr., A. Worth Hobby, Byron J. Hoffman, David J. Hughes, Ralph A. Huie Jr., Carl C. Jones Jr., James A. Kaufman, Milton J. Krainin, Harold B. Levin (Dermatology), Louis K. Levy, Bernard S. Lipman, A. Park McGinty, Christopher J. McLoughlin, Clarence W. Mills, George L. Mitchell Jr., J. Merrell Monfort, Chester W. Morse, Michael V. Murphy Jr., Ralph A. Murphy Jr., F. Levering Neely, Harry Parks, William L. Paullin Jr., Lamar B. Peacock, Joseph L. Rankin (Dermatology), Shirley L. Rivers, Purcell Roherts, John deR. Slade, Wyman P. Sloan Jr., Hyman B. Stillerman, Paul Teplis, Nathaniel S. Thornton, Lloyd F. Timberlake, Charles L. Whisnant Jr., Joseph S. Wilson, Bernard P. Wolff, Grattan C. Woodson Jr., Edgar Woody Jr., John T. Yauger
Instructors: Charles D. Adams (Dermatology), Elizabeth K. Adams, Guy H. Adams, Elbert B. Agnor, Evert A. Bancker, John E. Beck, Maxwell Berry, William E. Bloomer, Max M. Blumberg, Sandy B. Carter, L. Guy Chelton, Maurice L. B. Clarke, Peter J. Cline, Claud P. Cobb Jr., B. Woodfin Cobbs Jr. (Cardiology), Robert P. Coggins, Charles C. Corley Jr., Joseph S. Cruise, Robert P. Cunningham, C. Warren Davidson, Nicholas E. Davies, David B. Dennison, Edgar W. Dunstan, Luther G.

Appendixes 509

Fortson Jr., Robert H. Franch, Glenville A. Giddings, George M. Goza Jr., William R. Hancock, O. Eugene Hanes, Byron F. Harper Jr., David S. Hubbard, W. Baird Hudgins, John L. Jacobs, Henry S. Jennings Jr., McClaren Johnson Sr., Richard H. Johnson, Alvin D. Josephs, Houston W. Kitchin, Mason I. Lowance, Martha J. McAnulty, John W. McCoy, Preston R. Miller Jr., William R. Minnich, James B. Minor, B. Waldo Moore Jr., Abraham M. Oshlag, Rosemonde S. Peltz, Samuel O. Poole, Ernest E. Proctor (Cardiology), Arthur M. Pruce, Henry Randall, W. Harrison Reeves, Legh R. Scott Jr., Thomas B. Sharp Jr., Jean S. Staton, Warren D. Stribling III, Cyrus W. Strickler Jr., Hiram M. Sturm (Cardiology), Margaret J. Wall, John A. Ward, Bruce S. Webster, James I. Weinberg, John G. Wells, Edward McM. West, Harold W. Whiteman Jr., Joseph A. Wilber, Edward H. Williams Jr., W. Talbert Williams, J. Grant Wilmer

Fellows: John C. Ammons Jr., Thomas C. Dickinson, Laurie L. Dozier Jr., Freeman Epes, Thomas E. Fulmer, F. Dempsey Guillebeau, R. Lanier Jones Jr., Martha S. G. Lovell, Lewis Lunsford Jr., David O. MacLachlan, Brigette B. Nahmias, Hugh O. Pearson Jr., Carroll B. Quinlan, Benjamin D. Saffan, James H. Shinaberger, Sanford A. Shmerling, Nanette K. Wenger

Appendix 27: Bulletin of Emory University School of Medicine, which lists the full-time and clinical volunteer faculty members and fellows of the Department of Medicine in 1960.

MEDICINE

J. Willis Hurst, *Professor of Medicine; Chairman of the Department*

Professors: Benjamin R. Gendel, R. Bruce Logue (Cardiology), Sidney Olansky (Dermatology), R. Hugh Wood

Professor (Clinical): Rolla E. Dyer

Associate Professors: Charles M. Huguley Jr., Ross L. McLean, John R. K. Preedy, J. Spalding Schroder

Associate Professors (Clinical): Herbert S. Alden (Dermatology), J. Gordon Barrow, Gerald R. Cooper, William F. Friedewald, L. Harvey Hamff, Joseph C. Massee, Arthur J. Merrill, Carter Smith, William A. Smith (Neurology), Richard B. Wilson (Neurology)

Assistant Professors: H. Eugene Brown, A. Grigg Churchwell, James C. Crutcher, Edward R. Dorney, Robert H. Franch, John T. Galambos, Bernard L. Hallman, Euclid G. Herndon Jr., Herbert R. Karp (Neurology), Robert C. Schlant, Thomas F. Sellers Jr., Elbert P. Tuttle Jr.

Assistant Professors (Clinical): Carl C. Aven, T. Sterling Claiborne, William L. Dobes (Dermatology), David F. James, W. Roy Mason Jr., Philip H. Nippert (Dermatology), Vernon E. Powell, Charles F. Stone Jr., Ebert Van Buren, Julius Wenger, Robert L. Whipple Jr.

Associates: Eustace A. Allen, Thomas J. Anderson Jr., C. Raymond Arp, John S. Atwater, Ernest W. Beasley Jr., Linton H. Bishop Jr., Tully T. Blalock, Spencer S. Brewer Jr., Charles E. Brown, C. Daniel Burge, E. Napier Burson Jr., Marguerite L. Candler, Freeman H. Cary, B. Woodfin Cobbs Jr. (Cardiology), James C. Coberly, Manuel N. Cooper, Charles C. Corley Jr., William R. Crowe, F. William Dowda, Walter S. Dunbar, Edwin C. Evans, Richard E. Felder, Harold A. Ferris, Francis W. Fitzhugh Jr., Milton H. Freedman, W. Elizabeth Gambrell, Robert I. Gibbs Jr., Hugh E. Hailey (Dermatology), Daniel D. Hankey, J. Frank Harris, David L. Hearin (Dermatology), David E. Hein, Lamont Henry, Haywood N. Hill, Joseph H. Hilsman Jr., A. Worth Hobby, Byron J. Hoffman, David J. Hughes, Ralph A. Huie Jr., Carl C. Jones Jr., James A. Kaufman, Milton J. Krainin, Harold B. Levin (Dermatology), Louis K. Levy, Bernard S. Lipman, A. Park McGinty, Christopher J. McLoughlin, Clarence W. Mills, George L. Mitchell Jr., J. Merrell Monfort, Chester W. Morse, Michael V. Murphy Jr., Ralph A. Murphy Jr., F. Levering Neely, Harry Parks, William L. Paullin Jr., Lamar B. Peacock, Joseph L. Rankin (Dermatology), Shirley L. Rivers, Purcell Roberts, John deR. Slade, Wyman P. Sloan Jr., Hyman B. Stillerman, Paul Teplis, Nathaniel S. Thornton, Lloyd F. Timberlake, Charles L. Whisnant Jr., Joseph S. Wilson, Bernard P. Wolff, Grattan C. Woodson Jr., Edgar Woody Jr., John T. Yauger

Instructors: Charles D. Adams (Dermatology), Elizabeth K. Adams, Guy H. Adams, Elbert B. Agnor, Evert A. Bancker, John E. Beck, Maxwell Berry, William E. Bloomer, Max M. Blumberg, Sandy B. Carter, L. Guy Chelton, Maurice L. B. Clarke, Peter J. Cline, Claud P. Cobb Jr., Robert P. Coggins, Joseph S. Cruise, Robert P.

Cunningham, C. Warren Davidson, Nicholas E. Davies, David B. Dennison, Edgar M. Dunstan, Luther G. Fortson Jr., Glenville A. Giddings, George M. Goza Jr., Harold A. Gussack, O. Eugene Hanes, John N. Harbour, Timothy Harden Jr., Byron F. Harper Jr., David S. Hubbard, W. Baird Hudgins, John L. Jacobs, Henry S. Jennings Jr., McClaren Johnson Sr., Richard H. Johnson, Samuel H. Jones Jr., Alvin D. Josephs, Houstin W. Kitchin, Mason I. Lowance, Martha J. McAnulty, John M. McCoy, Preston R. Miller Jr., William R. Minnich, James B. Minor, B. Waldo Moore Jr., Abraham M. Oshlag, Rosemonde S. Peltz, Samuel O. Poole, Ernest E. Proctor (Cardiology), Arthur M. Pruce, Henry Randall, W. Harrison Reeves, Gilbert M. Schiff, Legh R. Scott Jr., Sanford A. Shmerling, Jean S. Staton, Warren D. Stribling III, Cyrus W. Strickler Jr., Carlos A. Stuart, Hiram M. Sturm (Dermatology), Suzanne Trusler, Margaret J. Wall, John A. Ward, Bruce S. Webster, James I. Weinberg, John G. Wells, Nanette K. Wenger, Harold W. Whiteman, Joseph A. Wilber, W. Talbert Williams, J. Grant Wilmer

Fellows: Henry A. Bridges, G. Harmon Brown, Donald C. Chait, Grady S. Clinkscales Jr., F. Dempsey Guillebeau, John G. Leonardy, Brigitte B. Nahmias, Benjamin B. Okel, James M. Parks, Robert J. Robertson Jr., Donald G. Rosenberg, Benjamin D. Saffan, Thomas B. Sharp Jr., J. Orson Smith Jr., Calvin L. Thrash Jr., Samuel P. Tillman, Theofilos J. Tsagaris, Daniel R. Turner, Roy A. Wiggins

Appendix 28: Bulletin of Emory University School of Medicine, which lists the full-time and clinical volunteer faculty members and fellows of the Department of Medicine in 1961.

MEDICINE

J. Willis Hurst, *Professor of Medicine; Chairman of the Department*

Professors: Benjamin R. Gendel, R. Bruce Logue (Cardiology), Sidney Olansky (Dermatology), R. Hugh Wood

Professor (Clinical): Rolla E. Dyer

Associate Professors: Charles M. Huguley Jr., Ross L. McLean, John R. K. Preedy, J. Spalding Schroder

Associate Professors (Clinical): Herbert S. Alden (Dermatology), J. Gordon Barrow, Gerald R. Cooper, William F. Friedewald, L. Harvey Hamff, Joseph C. Massee, Arthur J. Merrill, Carter Smith, William A. Smith (Neurology), Richard B. Wilson (Neurology)

Assistant Professors: H. Eugene Brown, A. Grigg Churchwell, James C. Crutcher, Edward R. Dorney, Robert H. Franch, John T. Galambos, Leon I. Goldberg, Bernard L. Hallman, E. Garland Herndon Jr., Herbert R. Karp (Neurology), Robert C. Schlant, Thomas F. Sellers Jr., Elbert P. Tuttle Jr., Julius Wenger

Assistant Professors (Clinical): Carl C. Aven, T. Sterling Claiborne, William L. Dobes (Dermatology), David F. James, W. Roy Mason Jr., Philip H. Nippert (Dermatology), Vernon E. Powell, Charles F. Stone Jr., Ebert Van Buren, Robert L. Whipple Jr.

Associates: Eustace A. Allen, Thomas J. Anderson Jr., C. Raymond Arp, John S. Atwater, Ernest W. Beasley Jr., Linton H. Bishop Jr., Tully T. Blalock, Spencer S. Brewer Jr., Charles E. Brown, C. Daniel Burge, E Napier Burson Jr., Marguerite L. Candler, B. Woodfin Cobbs Jr. (Cardiology), James C. Coberly, Manuel N. Cooper, Charles C. Corley Jr., William R. Crowe, F. William Dowda, Walter S. Dunbar, Edwin C. Evans, Richard E. Felder, Harold A. Ferris, Francis W. Fitzhugh Jr., Milton H. Freedman, W. Elizabeth Gambrell, Robert I. Gibbs Jr., Hugh E. Hailey (Dermatology), Daniel D. Hankey, J. Frank Harris, David L. Hearin (Dermatology), David E. Hein, Lamont Henry, Haywood N. Hill, Joseph H. Hilsman Jr., A. Worth Hobby, Byron J. Hoffman, David J. Hughes, Ralph A. Huie Jr., Carl C. Jones Jr., James A. Kaufman, Milton J. Krainin, Harold B. Levin (Dermatology), Louis K. Levy, Bernard S. Lipman, A. Park McGinty, Christopher J. McLoughlin, Clarence W. Mills, J. Merrell Monfort, Chester W. Morse, Michael V. Murphy Jr., Ralph A. Murphy Jr., F. Levering Neely, Harry Parks, William L. Paullin Jr., Lamar B. Peacock, Joseph L. Rankin (Dermatology), Shirley L. Rivers, Purcell Roberts, John deR. Slade, Wyman P. Sloan Jr., Hyman B. Stillerman, Paul Teplis, Nathaniel S. Thornton, Lloyd F. Timberlake, Charles L. Whisnant Jr., Joseph S. Wilson, Bernard P. Wolff, Grattan C. Woodson Jr., Edgar Woody Jr., John T. Yauger

Instructors: Charles D. Adams (Dermatology), Elizabeth K. Adams, Guy H. Adams, Elbert B. Agnor, Evert A. Bancker, John E. Beck, J. Norman Berry, Maxwell Berry, William E. Bloomer, Max M. Blumberg, Sandy B. Carter, Donald C. Chait, L. Guy Chelton, Maurice L. B. Clarke, Peter J. Cline, Claud P. Cobb Jr., Robert P. Coggins, Joseph S. Cruise, Robert P. Cunningham, C. Warren Davidson, Nicholas E. Davies,

David B. Dennison, Edgar M. Dunstan, Louis H. Felder, Luther G. Fortson Jr., Glenville A. Giddings, Harold A. Gussack, Chenault W. Hailey, O. Eugene Hanes, John H. Harbour, Timothy Harden Jr., Byron F. Harper Jr., Donald C. Hartzog Jr., Joseph A. Hertell, David S. Hubbard, Robert W. Hubbell, W. Baird Hudgins, John L. Jacobs, Henry S. Jennings Jr., McClaren Johnson Sr., Richard H. Johnson, Alvin D. Josephs, Houston W. Kitchin, Mason I. Lowance, Martha J. McAnulty, John M. McCoy, Claude F. McCuiston, Preston R. Miller Jr., William R. Minnich, James B. Minor, B. Waldo Moore Jr., Zebulon V. Morgan Jr., James R. Neill, Leszek Ochota, Abraham M. Oshlag, Rosemonde S. Peltz, Samuel O. Poole, Ernest E. Proctor (Cardiology), Arthur M. Pruce, Henry Randall, W. Harrison Reeves, Gilbert M. Schiff, Legh R. Scott Jr., Sanford A. Shmerling, Jean S. Staton, Warren D. Stribling III, Cyrus W. Strickler Jr., Carlos A. Stuart, Hiram M. Sturm (Dermatology), Suzanne Trusler, Margaret J. Wall, John A. Ward, Bruce S. Webster, James I. Weinberg, John G. Wells, Nanette K. Wenger, Harold W. Whiteman, Roy Wiggins, Joseph A. Wilber, W. Talbert Williams, J. Grant Wilmer

Fellows: Andrew H. Abernathy III, James Achord, Frederico Arthes, Makoto Asada, C. Harmon Brown, E. Eddy Burns, C. Daniel Cabaniss, Walter E. Dippy, J. Harper Gaston, C. Wallace Harper, Frederick D. Maner, Marvous E. Mostellar, Benjamin B. Okel, Owen Reese Jr., Robert J. Robertson Jr., Benjamin D. Saffan, James Z. Shanks, Joel S. Steinberg, Marta C. Steinberg, Charles B. Upshaw Jr., Frances C. Walker, Lamar H. Waters, Thorne S. Winter III, Asbury D. Wright Jr.

Appendix 29: Bulletin of Emory University School of Medicine, which lists the full-time and clinical volunteer faculty members and fellows of the Department of Medicine in 1962.

MEDICINE

J. Willis Hurst, *Professor of Medicine; Chairman of the Department*

Professors: Benjamin R. Gendel, R. Bruce Logue, Sidney Olansky, R. Hugh Wood

Professors (Clinical): Rolla E. Dyer, Arthur J. Merrill

Associate Professors: H. Eugene Brown, James C. Crutcher, Edward R. Dorney, John T. Galambos, Bernard L. Hallman, Charles M. Huguley Jr., Herbert R. Karp, Ross L. McLean, John R. K. Preedy, Robert C. Schlant, J. Spalding Schroder, Elbert P. Tuttle Jr., Julius Wenger

Associate Professors (Clinical): Herbert S. Alden, J. Gordon Barrow, Gerald R. Cooper, William F. Friedewald, L. Harvey Hamff, Joseph C. Massee, Carter Smith, William A. Smith, Richard B. Wilson

Assistant Professors: A. Grigg Churchwell, James C. Coberly, Robert M. Franch, Leon I. Goldberg, E. Garland Herndon Jr., Thomas F. Sellers Jr.

Assistant Professors (Clinical): Carl C. Aven, T. Sterling Claiborne, William L. Dobes, David F. James, W. Roy Mason Jr., Philip H. Nippert, Vernon E. Powell, Charles F. Stone Jr., Ebert Van Buren, Robert L. Whipple Jr.

Associates: Eustace A. Allen, Thomas J. Anderson Jr., John S. Atwater, Ernest W. Beasley Jr., Linton H. Bishop Jr., Tully T. Blalock, Spencer S. Brewer Jr., Charles E. Brown, C. Daniel Burge, E. Napier Burson Jr., Marguerite L. Candler, B. Woodfin Cobbs Jr., Manuel N. Cooper, Charles C. Corley Jr., William R. Crowe, F. William Dowda, Walter S. Dunbar, Edwin C. Evans, Richard E. Felder, Harold A. Ferris, Francis W. Fitzhugh Jr., Milton H. Freedman, W. Elizabeth Gambrell, Robert I. Gibbs Jr., Hugh E. Hailey, Daniel D. Hankey, J. Frank Harris, David L. Hearin, David E. Hein, Lamont Henry, Haywood N. Hill, Joseph H. Hilsman Jr., A. Worth Hobby, Byron J. Hoffman, David J. Hughes, Ralph A. Huie Jr., Carl C. Jones Jr., James A. Kaufman, Milton J. Krainin, Harold B. Levin, Louis K. Levy, Bernard S. Lipman, A. Park McGinty, Christopher J. McLoughlin, Clarence W. Mills, J. Merrell Monfort, Chester W. Morse, Michael V. Murphy Jr., Ralph A. Murphy Jr., F. Levering Neely, Harry Parks, William L. Paullin Jr., Lamar B. Peacock, Joseph L. Rankin, Shirley L. Rivers, Purcell Roberts, John deR. Slade, Wyman P. Sloan Jr., Hyman B. Stillerman, Paul Teplis, Nathaniel A. Thornton, Lloyd F. Timberlake, John A. Ward, Charles L. Whisnant Jr., Joseph S. Wilson, Bernard P. Wolff, Grattan C. Woodson Jr., Edgar Woody Jr., John T. Yauger

Instructors: Charles D. Adams, Elizabeth K. Adams, Guy H. Adams, Elbert B. Agnor, Bernard L. Albert, Evert A. Bancker, Gerhard O. Bern, J. Norman Berry, Maxwell Berry, Max M. Blumberg, Leonard Brown, Sandy B. Carter, Donald C. Chait, L. Guy Chelton, Maurice L. B. Clarke, Peter J. Cline, Claud P. Cobb Jr., Robert P. Coggins, Gordon C. Crowell, Joseph S. Cruise, Robert P. Cunningham, C. Warren Davidson, Nicholas E. Davies, David B. Dennison, Edgar M. Dunstan, Louis H. Felder, Robert M. Fine, Luther G. Fortson Jr., Eli A. Friedman, Glenville A. Giddings, Harold A. Gussack, Chenault W. Hailey, O. Eugene Hanes, John H. Harbour, Timothy Harden

Jr., Byron F. Harper Jr., Joseph A. Hertell, David S. Hubbard, Robert W. Hubbell, W. Baird Hudgins, John L. Jacobs, Henry S. Jennings Jr., McClaren Johnson Sr., Richard H. Johnson, Alvin D. Josephs, Houston W. Kitchin, John G. Leonardy, Mason I. Lowance, Frank S. MacDonell, Marvin M. McCall III, John M. McCoy, Claude F. McCuiston, Preston R. Miller Jr., George T. Mims Jr., William R. Minnich, James B. Minor, B. Waldo Moore Jr., Zebulon V. Morgan Jr., Leszek Ochota, Benjamin B. Okel, Abraham M. Oshlag, Rosemonde S. Peltz, Samuel O. Poole, Ernest E. Proctor, Arthur M. Pruce, Henry Randall, W. Harrison Reeves, Benjamin D. Saffan, Gilbert M. Schiff, Legh R. Scott Jr., Sanford A. Shmerling, Jean S. Staton, Joel S. Steinberg, Warren D. Stribling III, Cyrus W. Strickler Jr., Carlos A. Stuart, Hiram M. Sturm, Suzanne Trusler, Charles B. Upshaw Jr., William Ralph Vogler Jr., Margaret J. Wall, Lamar H. Waters, Bruce S. Webster, James I. Weinberg, John G. Wells, Nanette K. Wenger, Harold W. Whiteman, Roy A. Wiggins, Joseph A. Wilber, W. Talbert Williams, J. Grant Wilmer

Fellows: James L. Achord, Makoto Asada, Edwin T. Avret, Robert S. Bryant Jr., Zeb C. Burton Jr., C. Daniel Cabaniss, James H. Christy, William A. Dickinson Jr., William E. Farrar Jr., Richard S. Foster, Saul J. Grosberg, Glenn E. McCormick Jr., Robert H. McDonald Jr., F. Debele Maner, Marvous E. Mostellar, William C. Rape, William J. Rawls, John H. Sadler, Carlos R. Salgado, James Z. Shanks, Marta Steinberg, Julius W. Welborn Jr.

Appendix 30: Bulletin of Emory University School of Medicine, which lists the full-time and clinical volunteer faculty members and fellows of the Department of Medicine in 1963.

MEDICINE

J. Willis Hurst, *Professor of Medicine; Chairman of the Department*
Professors: Benjamin R. Gendel, Herbert R. Karp, R. Bruce Logue, Sidney Olansky, R. Hugh Wood
Professors (Clinical): Rolla E. Dyer, Arthur J. Merrill
Associate Professors: H. Eugene Brown, James C. Crutcher, Edward R. Dorney, Robert H. Franch, John T. Galambos, Bernard L. Hallman, E. Garland Herndon Jr., Charles M. Huguley Jr., Ross L. McLean, John R. K. Preedy, Robert C. Schlant, J. Spalding Schroder, Elbert P. Tuttle Jr., Julius Wenger
Associate Professors (Clinical): Herbert S. Alden, J. Gordon Barrow, T. Sterling Claiborne, Gerald R. Cooper, William L. Dobes, William F. Friedewald, L. Harvey Hamff, David F. James, Joseph C. Massee, Carter Smith, William A. Smith, Charles F. Stone, Richard B. Wilson
Assistant Professors: Arend Bouhuys, B. Woodfin Cobbs Jr., James C. Coberly, Charles C. Corley, Leon I. Goldberg, Robert F. Kibler, Harold S. Ramos, Thomas F. Sellers Jr.
Assistant Professors (Clinical): Thomas J. Anderson Jr., Carl C. Aven, Linton H. Bishop Jr., Tully T. Blalock, Spencer S. Brewer Jr., Charles E. Brown, C. Daniel Burge, E. Napier Burson Jr., A. Grigg Churchwell, F. William Dowda, Walter S. Dunbar, Edwin C. Evans, Harold A. Ferris, Francis W. Fitzhugh Jr., Milton H. Freedman, Daniel D. Hankey, David E. Hein, Lamont Henry, Haywood N. Hill, David J. Hughes, Carl C. Jones Jr., Louis K. Levy, Bernard S. Lipman, W. Roy Mason Jr., A. Park McGinty, Clarence W. Mills, Michael V. Murphy Jr., F. Levering Neely, Philip H. Nippert, Harry Parks, Lamar B. Peacock, Vernon E. Powell, John deR. Slade, Wyman P. Sloan Jr., Hyman B. Stillerman, Paul Teplis, Lloyd F. Timberlake, Ebert Van Buren, Robert L. Whipple Jr., Charles L. Whisnant Jr., Joseph A. Wilber, Joseph S. Wilson, Gratton C. Woodson Jr., Edgar Woody Jr., John T. Yauger
Associates: Eustace A. Allen, John S. Atwater, Ernest W. Beasley Jr., J. Norman Berry, Marguerite L. Candler, Donald C. Chait, William R. Crowe, Nicholas E. Davies, Louis H. Felder, W. Elizabeth Gambrell, Robert I. Gibbs Jr., Harold A. Gussack, Byron F. Harper Jr., J. Frank Harris, David L. Hearin, Joseph H. Hilsman Jr., A. Worth Hobby, Byron J. Hoffman, David S. Hubbard, Ralph A. Huie Jr., Richard H. Johnson, James A. Kaufman, Milton J. Krainin, Harold B. Levin, John M. McCoy, Preston R. Miller Jr., James B. Minor, J. Merrell Monfort, B. Waldo Moore Jr., Zebulon V. Morgan Jr., Chester W. Morse, Ralph A. Murphy Jr., William L. Paullin Jr., Rosemonde S. Peltz, Joseph L. Rankin, W. Harrison Reeves, Shirley L. Rivers, C. Purcell Roberts, Jean S. Staton, Carlos A. Stuart, Hiram M. Sturm, Nathaniel A. Thornton, John A. Ward, Bruce S. Webster, Nanette K. Wenger, Harold W. Whiteman, Bernard P. Wolff
Instructors: James L. Achord, Charles D. Adams, Elizabeth K. Adams, Guy H. Adams, Elbert B. Agnor, Bernard L. Albert, Mary Lou Applewhite, Evert A. Bancker,

Gerhard O. Bern, Maxwell Berry, Max M. Blumberg, Philip S. Brachman, Leonard Brown, James A. Bryan II, C. Daniel Cabaniss, Sandy B. Carter, L. Guy Chelton, Maurice L. B. Clarke, Peter J. Cline, Claud P. Cobb Jr., Robert P. Coggins, Gordon C. Crowell, Joseph S. Cruise, Robert P. Cunningham, C. Warren Davidson, David B. Dennison, Edgar M. Dunstan, Robert M. Fine, Luther G. Fortson Jr., Eli A. Friedman, Stephen E. Furst, Edwin J. Galler, Glenville A. Giddings, Chenault W. Hailey, O. Eugene Hanes, John H. Harbour, Timothy Harden Jr., Joseph A. Hertell, Robert W. Hubbell, W. Baird Hudgins, John L. Jacobs, Henry S. Jennings Jr., McClaren Johnson Sr., Alvin D. Josephs, Houston W. Kitchin, James W. Lea Jr., John G. Leonardy Jr., Mason I. Lowance, Frank S. MacDonell, Glenn E. McCormick, Claude F. McCuiston, George Mims Jr., William R. Minnich, James W. Mosley, Marvous E. Mostellar, Carl W. Norden, Leszek Ochota, Benjamin B. Okel, Marian F. Olansky, Abraham M. Oshlag, Malcolm I. Page, Samuel O. Poole, Ernest E. Proctor, Arthur M. Pruce, A. Henry Randall Jr., William J. Rawls, Donald H. Rockwell, Benjamin D. Saffan, Gilbert M. Schiff, Legh R. Scott Jr., James Z. Shanks, Sanford A. Shmerling, Carl G. Silverman, Joel S. Steinberg, Warren D. Stribling III, Cyrus W. Strickler Jr., Suzanne Trusler, Charles B. Upshaw Jr., Fred T. Valentine, William R. Vogler, Margaret J. Wall, William C. Waters III, James I. Weinberg, John G. Wells, J. Herbert West, Roy A. Wiggins, W. Talbert Williams, J. Grant Wilmer

Fellows: James J. Acker, Hrair M. Balikian, Dorothg Brinsfield, James R. Brylski, Leonard L. Cotts, Sacit Eren, Richard S. Foster, Wray A. Hammer, Julian Johnson, Hurley D. Jones, Robert H. McDonald (Medicine-Pharmacology), John L. McNay Jr. (Medicine-Pharmacology), William C. Rape, John H. Sadler, Carlos R. Salgado, Ayten Someren, Tuncer Someren, Marta C. Steinberg, Joseph M. Turner, Julius W. Welborn Jr., Alfred M. Zimmerman (Medicine-Pharmacology)

Appendix 31: Bulletin of Emory University School of Medicine, which lists the full-time and clinical volunteer faculty members and fellows of the Department of Medicine in 1964.

MEDICINE

J. Willis Hurst, *Professor of Medicine; Chairman of the Department*

Professors: Benjamin R. Gendel, Herbert R. Karp, R. Bruce Logue, Sidney Olansky, R. Hugh Wood

Professors (Clinical): Rolla E. Dyer, Arthur J. Merrill

Associate Professors: H. Eugene Brown, James C. Crutcher, Edward R. Dorney, Robert H. Franch, John T. Galambos, Bernard L. Hallman, E. Garland Herndon Jr., Charles M. Huguley Jr., Robert F. Kibler, Ross L. McLean, John R. K. Preedy, Robert C. Schlant, J. Spalding Schroder, Elbert P. Tuttle Jr., Julius Wenger

Associate Professors (Clinical): Herbert S. Alden, J. Gordon Barrow, T. Sterling Claiborne, Gerald R. Cooper, William L. Dobes, William F. Friedewald, L. Harvey Hamff, David F. James, Joseph C. Massee, Carter Smith, William A. Smith, Charles F. Stone Jr., Richard B. Wilson

Assistant Professors: Arend Bouhuys, B. Woodfin Cobbs Jr., James C. Coberly, Charles C. Corley Jr., Leon I. Goldberg, Irving Green, Harold S. Ramos, Thomas F. Sellers Jr.

Assistant Professors (Clinical): Thomas J. Anderson Jr., Carl C. Aven, Linton H. Bishop Jr., Tully T. Blalock, Spencer S. Brewer Jr., Charles E. Brown, C. Daniel Burge, E. Napier Burson Jr., A. Grigg Churchwell, F. William Dowda, Walter S. Dunbar, Edwin C. Evans, Harold A. Ferris, Francis W. Fitzhugh Jr., Milton H. Freedman, Daniel D. Hankey, David E. Hein, Lamont Henry, Haywood N. Hill, David J. Hughes, Carl C. Jones Jr., Louis K. Levy, Bernard S. Lipman, W. Roy Mason Jr., A. Park McGinty, Clarence W. Mills, Michael V. Murphy Jr., F. Levering Neely, Philip H. Nippert, Harry Parks, Lamar B. Peacock, Vernon E. Powell, John deR. Slade, Wyman P. Sloan Jr., Hyman B. Stillerman, Paul Teplis, Lloyd F. Timberlake, Ebert Van Buren, Robert L. Whipple Jr., Charles L. Whisnant Jr., Joseph A. Wilber, Joseph S. Wilson, Gratton C. Woodson Jr., Edgar Woody Jr., John T. Yauger

Associates: James L. Achord, Eustace A. Allen, Mary Lou Applewhite, John S. Atwater, Ernest W. Beasley Jr., J. Norman Berry, Marguerite L. Candler, Donald C. Chait, William R. Crowe, Nicholas E. Davies, Louis H. Felder, W. Elizabeth Gambrell, Robert I. Gibbs Jr., Harold A. Gussack, Byron F. Harper Jr., J. Frank Harris, David L. Hearin, Joseph H. Hilsman Jr., A. Worth Hobby, Byron J. Hoffman, David S. Hubbard, Ralph A. Huie Jr., Richard H. Johnson, James A. Kaufman, Milton J. Krainin, James W. Lea Jr., Harold B. Levin, John M. McCoy, Alexander M. McPhedran, Preston R. Miller Jr., James B. Minor, J. Merrell Monfort, B. Waldo Moore Jr., Zebulon V. Morgan Jr., Chester W. Morse, Ralph A. Murphy Jr., William L. Paullin Jr., Rosemonde S. Peltz, Joseph L. Rankin, William J. Rawls, W. Harrison Reeves, Shirley L. Rivers, C. Purcell Roberts, Jean S. Staton, Joel S. Steinberg, Carlos A. Stuart, Hiram M. Sturm, Nathaniel A. Thornton, John A. Ward, William C. Waters III, Bruce S. Webster, Nanette K. Wenger, Harold W. Whiteman, Bernard P. Wolff

Instructors: Charles D. Adams, Elizabeth K. Adams, Guy H. Adams, Elbert B. Agnor, Evert A. Bancker, Gerhard O. Bern, Maxwell Berry, Max M. Blumberg, Philip S. Brachman, Leonard Brown, James A. Bryan II, C. Daniel Cabaniss, Sandy B. Carter, L. Guy Chelton, Maurice L. B. Clarke, Peter J. Cline, Claud P. Cobb Jr., Robert P. Coggins, Harry A. Cooper, Leonard L. Cotts, Joseph S. Cruise, Robert P. Cunningham, C. Warren Davidson, David B. Dennison, John S. Dodd Jr., Edgar M. Dunstan, Marvin F. Engle, Robert M. Fine, Luther G. Fortson Jr., Stephen E. Furst, Edwin J. Galler, Glenville A. Giddings, Chenault W. Hailey, O. Eugene Hanes, John H. Harbour, Timothy Harden Jr., Joseph A. Hertell, Robert W. Hubbell, W. Baird Hudgins, John L. Jacobs, Henry S. Jennings, McClaren Johnson Sr., Alvin D. Josephs, Houston W. Kitchin, John G. Leonardy Jr., Mason I. Lowance, Frank S. MacDonell, Glenn E. McCormick, Claude F. McCuiston, George Mims Jr., William R. Minnich, M. Brittain Moore Jr., James W. Mosley, Marvous E. Mostellar, Carl W. Norden, Benjamin B. Okel, Marian F. Olansky, Abraham M. Oshlag, Bernard H. Palay, Samuel O. Poole, Ernest E. Proctor, Herbert D. Proctor, Arthur M. Pruce, A. Henry Randall Jr., Robert A. Reich, Donald H. Rockwell, Benjamin D. Saffan, C. Vernon Sanders, W. Eugene Sanders, Legh R. Scott Jr., James Z. Shanks, Sanford A. Shmerling, Carl G. Silverman, Warren D. Stribling III, Cyrus W. Strickler Jr., Abraham M. Tornow, Suzanne Trusler, Charles B. Upshaw Jr., Fred T. Valentine, William R. Vogler, Margaret J. Wall, James I. Weinberg, John G. Wells, J. Herbert West, Roy A. Wiggins, W. Talbert Williams, J. Grant Wilmer.

Fellows: James J. Acker, John C. Ammons, Hrair M. Balikian, Charles A. Brake, James N. Brawner III, James R. Brylski, Zeb C. Burton Jr., Charles M. Cowan, Shia H. Elson, Sacit Eren, M. Patricia Gaine, Tsutomu Hirooka, McClaren Johnson Jr., Hurley D. Jones, J. Sherwood Jones Jr., Marc J. Laurijssens, Joseph Lindsay Jr., Michael E. Lowrey, Walter B. Mayer Jr., Melvin B. Meyer, John L. McNay Jr., E. Alan Paulk Jr., Carlos R. Salgado, Victor E. Schulze Jr., Ayten Someren, Tuncer Someren, Marta C. Steinberg, B. Dolores Stough, Malcolm H. Williams, James W. Williamson, A. Marvin Zimmerman

Appendix 32: Bulletin of Emory University School of Medicine, which lists the full-time and clinical volunteer faculty members and fellows of the Department of Medicine in 1965.

MEDICINE

J. Willis Hurst, *Professor of Medicine; Chairman of the Department*
Professors: Benjamin R. Gendel, Herbert R. Karp, R. Bruce Logue, Sidney Olansky, R. Hugh Wood
Professors (Clinical): Rolla E. Dyer, Arthur J. Merrill, William A. Smith
Associate Professors: H. Eugene Brown, James C. Crutcher, Edward R. Dorney, Robert H. Franch, John T. Galambos, Leon I. Coldberg, Bernard L. Hallman, E. Garland Herndon Jr., Charles M. Huguley Jr., Robert F. Kibler, Ross L. McLean, John R. K. Preedy, Robert C. Schlant, J. Spalding Schroder, Elbert P. Tuttle Jr., Julius Wenger
Associate Professors (Clinical): Herbert S. Alden, J. Gordon Barrow, T. Sterling Claiborne, Gerald R. Cooper, William L. Dobes, William F. Friedewald, L. Harvey Hamff, David F. James, Joseph C. Massee, Carter Smith, Charles F. Stone Jr., Richard B. Wilson
Assistant Professors: B. Woodfin Cobbs Jr., James C. Coberly, Charles C. Corley Jr., Harold S. Ramos, Thomas F. Sellers Jr., Nanette K. Wenger, Harry L. Williams
Assistant Professors (Clinical): Thomas J. Anderson Jr., Carl C. Aven, Linton H. Bishop Jr., Tully T. Blalock, Spencer S. Brewer Jr., Charles E. Brown, C. Daniel Burge, E. Napier Burson Jr., A. Grigg Churchwell, F. William Dowda, Walter S. Dunbar, Edwin C. Evans, Harold A. Ferris, Francis W. Fitzhugh Jr., Milton H. Freedman, Daniel D. Hankey, David E. Hein, Lamont Henry, Haywood N. Hill, David J. Hughes, Carl C. Jones Jr., Louis K. Levy, Bernard S. Lipman, W. Roy Mason Jr., A. Park McGinty, Michael V. Murphy Jr., F. Levering Neely, Philip H. Nippert, Harry Parks, Lamar B. Peacock, Vernon E. Powell, John deR. Slade, Wyman P. Sloan Jr., Hyman B. Stillerman, Paul Teplis, Lloyd F. Timberlake, Ebert Van Buren, Robert L. Whipple Jr., Charles L. Whisnant Jr., Joseph A. Wilber, Joseph S. Wilson, Gratton C. Woodson Jr., Edgar Woody Jr., John T. Yauger
Associates: James L. Achord, Eustace A. Allen, Mary Lou Applewhite, John S. Atwater, Ernest W. Beasley Jr., J. Norman Berry, Marguerite L. Candler, Donald C. Chait, William R. Crowe, Nicholas E. Davies, Louis H. Felder, W. Elizabeth Gambrell, Robert I. Gibbs Jr., Harold A. Gussack, Byron F. Harper Jr., J. Frank Harris, David L. Hearin, Joseph H. Hilsman Jr., A. Worth Hobby, Byron J. Hoffman, David S. Hubbard, Ralph A. Huie Jr., Richard H. Johnson, James A. Kaufman, Milton J. Krainin. James W. Lea Jr., Harold B. Levin, John M. McCoy, Alexander M. McPhedran, William M. Marine, Preston R. Miller Jr., James B. Minor, J. Merrell Monfort, B. Waldo Moore Jr., Zebulon V. Morgan Jr., Chester W. Morse, Ralph A. Murphy Jr., William L. Paullin Jr., Rosemonde S. Peltz, Joseph L. Rankin, William J. Rawls, W. Harrison Reeves, Shirley L. Rivers, C. Purcell Roberts, Jean S. Staton, Joel S. Steinberg, Carlos A. Stuart, Hiram M. Sturm, Nathaniel A. Thornton, William R. Vogler, John A. Ward, William C. Waters III, Bruce S. Webster, Harold W. Whiteman, Bernard P. Wolff.

Instructors: Charles D. Adams, Elizabeth K. Adams, Guy H. Adams, Elbert B. Agnor, Harold Asher, Edwin T. Avret, Evert A. Bancker, Gerhard O. Bern, Maxwell Berry, Max M. Blumberg, Philip S. Brachman, Charles A. Brake, C. Daniel Cabaniss, Sandy B. Carter, L. Guy Chelton, James H. Christy, Maurice L. B. Clarke, Peter J. Cline, Claud P. Cobb Jr., Robert P. Coggins, Harry A. Cooper, Leonard L. Cotts, Joseph S. Cruise, Robert P. Cunningham, C. Warren Davidson, David B. Dennison, John S. Dodd Jr., Edgar M. Dunstan, Theodore C. Eickhoff, Marvin F. Engle, Robert M. Fine, Luther G. Fortson Jr., Stephen E. Furst, Edwin J. Galler, Glenville A. Giddings, David L. Glancy. Martin I. Goldstein, Chenault W. Hailey, O. Eugene Hanes, John H. Harhour, Timothy Harden Jr., Joseph A. Hertell, Robert W. Hubbell, W. Baird Hudgins, John L. Jacobs, Henry S. Jennings Jr., McClaren Johnson Sr., Alvin D. Josephs, Houston W. Kitchin, John G. Leonardy Jr., Mason I. Lowance, Frank S. MacDonell. Glenn E. McCormick Jr., Claude F. McCuiston, John L. McNay Jr., George T. Mims Jr., William R. Minnich, James W. Mosley, Marvous E. Mostellar, Carl W. Norden, Benjamin B. Okel, Marian F. Olansky, Abraham M. Oshlag, Bernard H. Palay, Samuel O. Poole, Ernest E. Proctor, Arthur M. Pruce, A. Henry Randall Jr., Robert A. Reich, Stewart R. Roberts Jr., Benjamin D. Saffan, C. Vernon Sanders, Legh R. Scott Jr., James Z. Shanks, Sanford A. Shmerling, Warren D. Stribling III, Cyrus W. Strickler Jr., Abraham M. Tornow, Charles B. Upshaw Jr., Fred T. Valentine, Margaret J. Wall, James I. Weinberg, John G. Wells, J. Herbert West, Roy A. Wiggins, W. Talbert Williams, J. Grant Wilmer, Thorne S. Winter III

Fellows: Andrew H. Abernathy III, John C. Ammons, James D. Armistead, John R. Arnold, Alfred D. Beasley, Rodney A. Block, James N. Brawner III, James R. Brylski, George M. Callaway Jr., Charles M. Cowan, R. Paul Crank Jr., Alexis H. Davison, Valdir deP. Furtado, Phillip E. Gertler, Tsutomu Hirooka, Julian Jacobs, Samuel R. Lathan Jr., Arthur A. Madden, W. Brem Mayer Jr., Melvin B. Meyer, Roy W. Miller, Henry G. Palmer Jr., E. Alan Paulk Jr., G. David Raymond, Paul H. Robinson, Sheldon S. Sbar, Marta C. Steinberg, B. Dolores Stough, James K. VanBuren, Jay D. Williams Jr., James W. Williamson, A. Marvin Zimmerman

Appendix 33: Bulletin of Emory University School of Medicine, which lists the full-time and clinical volunteer faculty members and fellows of the Department of Medicine in 1966.

MEDICINE

J. Willis Hurst, *Professor of Medicine; Chairman of the Department*

Professors: Benjamin R. Gendel, Herbert R. Karp, R. Bruce Logue, Sidney Olansky

Professors (Clinical): J. Gordon Barrow, T. Sterling Claiborne, Rolla E. Dyer, David F. James, Joseph C. Massee, Arthur J. Merrill, Carter Smith, William A. Smith

Associate Professors: H. Eugene Brown, B. Woodfin Cobbs Jr., Charles C. Corley Jr., James C. Crutcher, Edward R. Dorney, Robert H. Franch, John T. Galambos, Leon I. Goldberg, Bernard L. Hallman, E. Garland Herndon Jr., John G. Hood, Charles M. Huguley Jr., Robert F. Kibler, Ross L. McLean, John R. K. Preedy, Thomas F. Sellers Jr., Robert C. Schlant, J. Spalding Schroder, Elbert P. Tuttle Jr., Julius Wenger

Associate Professors (Clinical): Herbert S. Alden, Thomas J. Anderson Jr., Linton H. Bishop Jr., Spencer S. Brewer Jr., C. Daniel Burge, E. Napier Burson Jr., Gerald R. Cooper, William L. Dobes, F. William Dowda, Milton H. Freedman, William F. Friedewald, L. Harvey Hamff, Daniel D. Hankey, David E. Hein, Lamont Henry, Haywood N. Hill, David J. Hughes, Louis K. Levy, Bernard S. Lipman, F. Levering Neely, Harry Parks, W. Harrison Reeves, Wyman P. Sloan Jr., Charles F. Stone Jr., Paul Teplis, Joseph S. Wilson, Richard B. Wilson

Assistant Professors: James L. Achord, James C. Coberly, James W. Lea Jr., Alexander M. McPhedran, Harold S. Ramos, James H. Shinaberger, Joel S. Steinberg, John A. Ward, William C. Waters III, Nanette K. Wenger, Harry L. Williams, Colon H. Wilson Jr.

Assistant Professors (Clinical): Carl C. Aven, J. Norman Berry, Tully T. Blalock:, Charles E. Brown, Donald C. Chait, A. Grigg Churchwell, Nicholas E. Davies, Walter S. Dunbar, Edwin C. Evans, Harold A. Ferris, Robert M. Fine, Francis W. Fitzhugh Jr., Robert I. Gibbs Jr., Byron F. Harper Jr., David S. Hubbard, Carl C. Jones Jr., A. Park McGinty, W. Roy Mason Jr., James B. Minor, James W. Mosley, Michael V. Murphy Jr., Philip H. Nippert, Lamar B. Peacock, Vernon E. Powell, Bryan W. Robinson, John deR. Slade, Jean S. Staton, Hyman B. Stillerman, Hiram M. Sturm, Lloyd F. Timberlake, Ebert Van Buren, Robert L. Whipple Jr., Charles Whisnant Jr., Harold W. Whiteman, Joseph A. Wilber, Gratton C. Woodson Jr., Edgar Woody Jr., John T. Yauger

Visiting Assistant Professor: Bjorn Erik Roos

Associates: John C. Ammons, Charles A. Brake, James H. Christy, W. Edmund Farrar Jr., John L. McNay Jr., Keith L. MacCannell, William M. Marine, Shirley L. Rivers, William R. Vogler

Associates (Clinical): Eustace A. Allen, John S. Atwater, Ernest W. Beasley Jr., Marguerite L. Candler, William R. Crowe, John S. Dodd Jr., Louis H. Felder, Stephen E. Furst, W. Elizabeth Gambrell, Harold A. Gussack, J. Frank Harris, David L. Hearin, Joseph H. Hilsman Jr., A. Worth Hobby, Byron J. Hoffman, Ralph A. Huie Jr., Richard H. Johnson, James A. Kaufman, Milton J. Krainin, John G.

Leonardy, Harold B. Levin, John M. McCoy, Preston R. Miller Jr., J. Merrell Monfort, B. Waldo Moore Jr., Zebulon V. Morgan Jr., Chester W. Morse, Ralph A. Murphy Jr., Benjamin B. Okel, William L. Paullin Jr., Rosemonde S. Peltz, Joseph L. Rankin, Robert A. Reich, C. Purcell Roberts, Stewart R. Roberts Jr., C. Vernon Sanders, Legh R. Scott Jr., Sanford A. Shmerling, Carlos A. Stuart, Nathaniel A. Thornton, Abraham M. Tornow, Charles B. Upshaw Jr., J. Grant Wilmer, Thorne S. Winter III, Bernard P. Wolff

Instructors: Gerhard O. Bern, George M. Callaway Jr., Gilbert D. Grossman, W. Lee Hand, Joseph Lindsay Jr., Alexander S. McKinney, Marian F. Olansky, Marta C. Steinberg

Instructors (Clinical): Charles D. Adams, Elizabeth K. Adams, Elbert B. Agnor, Harold Asher, Edwin T. Avret, Evert A. Bancker, Maxwell Berry, Max M. Blumberg, Philip S. Brachman, C. Daniel Cabaniss, Sandy B. Carter, L. Guy Chelton, Allan L. Cline, Peter J. Cline, Claud P. Cobb Jr., Robert P. Coggins, Harry A. Cooper, Leonard L. Cotts, Joseph S. Cruise, Robert P. Cunningham, C. Warren Davidson, David B. Dennison, Edgar M. Dunstan, Theodore C. Eickoff, Shia H. Elson, Marvin F. Engle, Luther G. Fortson Jr., Edwin J. Galler, Glenville A. Giddings, David L. Glancy, Martin I. Goldstein, Chenault W. Hailey, O. Eugene Hanes, John H. Harbour, Timothy Harden Jr., Clark W. Heath Jr., Joseph A. Hertell, Robert W. Hubbell, W. Baird Hudgins, John L. Jacobs, Henry S. Jennings Jr., McClaren Johnson Sr., Alvin D. Josephs, Houston W. Kitchin, Mason I. Lowance, Frank S. MacDonell, Glenn E. McCormick Jr., Claude F. McCuiston, George T. Mims Jr., William R. Minnich, Marvous E. Mostellar, Abraham M. Oshlag, Bernard H. Palay, Samuel O. Poole, Ernest E. Proctor, Arthur M. Pruce, A. Henry Randall Jr., Benjamin D. Saffan, James Z. Shanks, Warren D. Stribling III, Cyrus W. Strickler Jr., Daniel R. Turner, James K. Van Buren, Margaret J. Wall, James I. Weinberg, John G. Wells, J. Herbert West, Roy A. Wiggins, Malcolm H. Williams, W. Talbert Williams

Fellows: Gordon J. Azar, Alfred D. Beasley, Robert M. Boger, James A. Butts, James L. Crosthwait, Thomas G. Douglass, Maxwell A. Eidex, Ruth G. Freeman, Valdir de Paula Furtado, Robert L. Galphin Jr., Robert C. Grant, Joseph E. Hardison, McClaren Johnson Jr., Frederic G. Jones, Jack W. MacDonald, Arthur A. Madden, W. Brem Mayer Jr., Melvin B. Meyer, S. R. Pathak, G. David Raymond, Victor E. Schulze Jr., Richard L. Shepherd, Fuller A. Shuford, Carter Smith Jr., P. Frank Sonneville, B. Dolores Stough, P. Burt Veazey, Russell W. Wallace Jr., David T. Watson, Charles M. Wender, H. Lake Westfall Jr.

Appendix 34: Bulletin of Emory University School of Medicine, which lists the full-time and clinical volunteer faculty members and fellows of the Department of Medicine in 1967.

MEDICINE

J. Willis Hurst *Professor of Medicine; Chairman of the Department*

Professors: James C. Crutcher (Pulmonary Disease), John T. Galambos (Gastroenterology), Benjamin R. Gendel (Hematology), Leon I. Goldberg (Clinical Pharmacology), E. Garland Herndon Jr. (Renal Disease and Inorganic Metabolism), Charles M. Huguley Jr. (Hematology), Herbert R. Karp (Neurology), R. Bruce Logue (Cardiology), Ross L. McLean (Pulmonary Disease), Sidney Olansky (Dermatology), John R. K. Preedy (Endocrinology), Robert C. Schlant (Cardiology), J. Spalding Schroder (Gastroenterology), Thomas F. Sellers Jr. (Infectious Disease), Elbert P. Tuttle Jr. (Renal Disease and Inorganic Metabolism)

Professor Emeritus: R. Hugh Wood (Active in 1967–68)

Professors (Clinical): J. Gordon Barrow, T. Sterling Claiborne, Rolla E. Dyer, David F. James, Henry J. L. Marriott, Joseph C. Massee, Arthur J. Merrill, Carter Smith, William A. Smith

Associate Professors: H. Eugene Brown, B. Woodfin Cobbs Jr. (Cardiology), Charles C. Corley Jr. (Hematology), Edward R. Dorney (Cardiology), Robert H. Franch (Cardiology), Bernard L. Hallman, John G. Hood, Robert F. Kibler (Neurology), Julius Wenger (Gastroenterology)

Associate Professors (Clinical): Herbert S. Alden, Thomas J. Anderson Jr., Linton H. Bishop Jr., Spencer S. Brewer Jr., C. Daniel Burge, E. Napier Burson Jr., Gerald R. Cooper, William L. Dobes, F. William Dowda, Milton H. Freedman, William F. Friedewald, L. Harvey Hamff, Daniel D. Hankey, David E. Hein, Lamont Henry, Haywood N. Hill, David J. Hughes, Louis K. Levy, Bernard S. Lipman, F. Levering Neely, Harry Parks, W. Harrison Reeves, Wyman P. Sloan Jr., Charles F. Stone Jr., Paul Teplis, Joseph S. Wilson, Richard B. Wilson

Assistant Professors: James L. Achord (Gastroenterology), James C. Coberly, R. Paul Crank (Cardiology), James W. Lea Jr. (Hematology), William M. Marine (Infectious Disease), John L. McNay (Clinical Pharmacology), Alexander H. McPhedran (Neurology), Harold S. Ramos, Bryan W. Robinson (Neurology), James H. Shinaherger (Renal Disease and Inorganic Metabolism), John A. Ward (Endocrinology), William C. Waters III (Renal Disease and Inorganic Metabolism), Nanette K. Wenger (Cardiology), Harry L. Williams (Clinical Pharmacology), Colon H. Wilson Jr. (Rheumatology)

Assistant Professors (Clinical): Carl C. Aven, J. Norman Berry, Tully T. Blalock, Charles E. Brown, Donald C. Chait, A. Grigg Churchwell, Nicholas E. Davies, Walter S. Dunbar, Edwin C. Evans, Harold A. Ferris, Robert M. Fine, Francis W. Fitzhugh Jr., Rohert I. Gibbs Jr., Byron F. Harper Jr., David S. Hubbard, Carl C. Jones Jr., W. Roy Mason Jr., A. Park McGinty, James B. Minor, James W. Mosley, Michael V. Murphy Jr., Philip H. Nippert, Lamar B. Peacock, Vernon E. Powell, John deR. Slade, Jean S. Staton, Hyman B. Stillerman, Hiram M. Sturm, Lloyd F. Timberlake, Ebert Van

Buren, Robert L. Whipple Jr., Charles L. Whisnant Jr., Harold W. Whiteman, Joseph
A. Wilber, Grattan C. Woodson Jr., Edgar Woody Jr., John T. Yauger
Visiting Clinical Assistant Professor: Eigill F. Hvidberg
Associates: John C. Ammons (Neurology), Charles A. Brake, James H. Christy
(Endocrinology), W. Edmund Farrar Jr. (Infectious Disease), Shirley L. Rivers
(Hematology), William R. Vogler (Hematology)
Associates (Clinical): Eustace A. Allen, John S. Atwater, Ernest W. Beasley Jr.,
Marguerite L. Candler, William R. Crowe, John S. Dodd Jr., Louis H. Felder,
Stephen E. Furst, W. Elizabeth Gambrell, Harold A. Gussack, J. Frank Harris, David
L. Hearin, Joseph H. Hilsman Jr., A. Worth Hobby, Byron J. Hoffman, Ralph A.
Huie Jr., Richard H. Johnson, James A. Kaufman, Milton J. Krainin, John C.
Leonardy Jr., Harold B. Levin, John M. McCoy, Preston R. Miller Jr., J. Merrell
Monfort, B. Waldo Moore Jr., Zebulon V. Morgan Jr., Chester W. Morse, Ralph A.
Murphy Jr., Benjamin B. Okel, William L. Paullin Jr., Rosemond S. Peltz, Joseph L.
Rankin, Robert A. Reich, C. Purcell Roberts, Stewart R. Roberts Jr., C. Vernon
Sanders, Legh R. Scott Jr., Sanford A. Shmerling, Carlos A. Stuart, Nathaniel A.
Thornton, Abraham M. Tornow, Charles B. Upshaw Jr., J. Grant Wilmer, Thorne S.
Winter III, Bernard P. Wolff
Instructors: Gerhard O. Bern, George M. Callaway Jr. (Renal Disease and Inorganic
Metabolism), W. Dallas Hall Jr., Joseph E. Hardison, Julian Jacobs (Hematology),
Lewis E. Jones, Joseph Lindsay Jr. (Cardiology), Alexander S. McKinney
(Neurology), Marian F. Olansky (Dermatology), Paul H. Robinson, John H. Sadler
(Renal Disease and Inorganic Metabolism), B. Dolores Stough
Instructors (Clinical): Andrew H. Abernathy, Charles D. Adams, Elizabeth K. Adams,
Elbert B. Agnor, Harold Asher, Edwin T. Avret, Evert A. Bancker, Maxwell Berry,
Max M. Blumberg, Philip S. Brachman, C. Daniel Cabaniss, Sandy B. Carter, L. Guy
Chelton, Peter J. Cline, Claud P. Cobb Jr., Robert P. Coggins, Harry A. Cooper,
Leonard L. Cotts, Joseph S. Cruise, Robert P. Cunningham, C. Warren Davidson,
Brown W. Dennis, David B. Dennison, H. Bruce Dull, Edgar M. Dunstan, Theodore
C. Eickhoff, Shia H. Elson, Marvin F. Engel, Leonard Fishman, Paul E. Fitzpatrick,
Luther G. Fortson Jr., Edwin J. Galler, David L. Glancy, Martin I. Goldstein,
Chenault W. Hailey, O. Eugene Hanes, John H. Harbour, Timothy Harden Jr.,
Charles E. Harrison Jr., Clark W. Heath Jr., Joseph A. Hertell, Robert W. Hubbell,
W. Baird Hudgins, John L. Jacobs, Henry S. Jennings Jr., McClaren Johnson Sr.,
Alvin D. Josephs, Houston W. Kitchin, Mason I. Lowance, Frank S. MacDonell
Glenn E. McCormick Jr., Claude F. McCuiston, George T. Mims Jr., William R.
Minnich, Marvous E. Mostellar, Abraham M. Oshlag, Bernard H. Palay, Samuel O.
Poole, Ernest E. Proctor, Arthur M. Pruce, A. Henry Randall Jr., Benjamin D.
Saffan, James Z. Shanks, Jerome H. Siegel, Warren D. Stribling III, Cyrus W.
Strickler Jr., Daniel R. Turner, James K. Van Buren, Margaret J. Wall, James I.
Weinberg, John G. Wells, J. Herbert West, Roy A. Wiggins, Malcolm H. Williams, W.
Talbert Williams
Fellows: James F. Alexander, Mahlon H. Barlow Jr., Alfred D. Beasley, John D. Boyett,
Neil C. Brown. Locke Y. Carter, I. Sylvia Crawley, James L. Crosthwait, Gerald F.
Fletcher, Ruth G. Freeman, Charles A. Gilbert, Alexander A. Halkes, Alfred H.
Kennemer, I. Lehman Lindsey Jr., W. Brem Mayer Jr., William H. McCullagh,
Howard G. Munro, Robert J. Myerburg, Albert Nantel, John A. Paar, S. R. Pathak,

The Quest for Excellence

Everett C. Price, Robert C. Robbins, Richard L. Shepherd, W. Ferrell Shuford Jr., Mark E. Silverman, John H. Stone III, William H. Stuart, Dean R. Taylor, Russell W. Wallace Jr., Patricia B. Wilber, John L. Wilson

Appendix 35: Bulletin of Emory University School of Medicine, which lists the full-time and clinical volunteer faculty members and fellows of the Department of Medicine in 1968.

MEDICINE

J. Willis Hurst, *Professor of Medicine; Chairman of the Department*
Professors: James C. Crutcher (Pulmonary Disease), Edward R. Dorney (Cardiology), John T. Galambos (Gastroenterology), Benjamin R. Gendel (Hematology), Leon I. Goldberg (Clinical Pharmacology), E. Garland Herndon Jr. (Renal Disease and Inorganic Metabolism), Robert J. Hoagland, Charles M. Huguley Jr. (Hematology), Herbert R. Karp (Neurology), Robert F. Kibler (Neurology), R. Bruce Logue (Cardiology), Ross L. McLean (Pulmonary Disease), Sidney Olansky (Dermatology), John R. K. Preedy (Endocrinology), Robert C. Schlant (Cardiology), J. Spalding Schroder (Gastroenterology), Thomas F. Sellers Jr. (Infectious Disease), Elbert P. Tuttle Jr. (Renal Disease and Inorganic Metabolism)
Professors Emeriti: Rolla E. Dyer, R. Hugh Wood (Active in 1968–69)
Professors (Clinical): J. Gordon Barrow, T. Sterling Claiborne, David F. James, Henry J. L. Marriott, Joseph C. Massee, Arthur J. Merrill, Carter Smith, William A. Smith
Associate Professors: H. Eugene Brown, B. Woodfin Cobbs Jr. (Cardiology), Charles C. Corley Jr. (Hematology), Peter G. Dayton (Clinical Pharmacology), Robert H. Franch (Cardiology), Bernard L. Hallman, John G. Hood, John L. McNay Jr. (Clinical Pharmacology), Harold S. Ramos, Julius Wenger (Gastroenterology)
Visiting Associate Professor: John T. Riggin Jr.
Associate Professors (Clinical): Herbert S. Alden, Thomas J. Anderson Jr., Linton H. Bishop Jr., Spencer S. Brewer Jr., C. Daniel Burge, E. Napier Burson Jr., Gerald R. Cooper, William L. Dobes, F. William Dowda, Milton H. Freedman, William F. Friedewald, L. Harvey Hamff, Daniel D. Hankey, David E. Hein, Lamont Henry, Haywood N. Hill, David J. Hughes, Louis K. Levy, Bernard S. Lipman, F. Levering Neely, Harry Parks, W. Harrison Reeves, Wyman P. Sloan Jr., Charles F. Stone Jr., Paul Teplis, Joseph S. Wilson, Richard B. Wilson
Assistant Professors: James L. Achord (Gastroenterology), John C. Ammons (Neurology), Vardaman M. Buckalew (Renal Disease and Inorganic Metabolism), James H. Christy (Endocrinology), James C. Coberly, W. Edmund Farrar Jr. (Infectious Disease), Charles A. Gilbert (Cardiology), Roland F. Ingram Jr. (Clinical Physiology), Joseph Lindsay Jr. (Cardiology), William M. Marine (Infectious Disease), Alexander M. McPhedran (Neurology), Bryan W. Robinson (Neurology), John H. Sadler (Renal Disease and Inorganic Metabolism), James F. Schwartz (Neurology), William R. Vogler (Hematology), John A. Ward (Endocrinology), William C. Waters III (Renal Disease and Inorganic Metabolism), Nanette K. Wenger (Cardiology), H. Jordan Whyte (Dermatology), Harry L. Williams (Clinical Pharmacology), Colon H. Wilson (Rheumatology)
Assistant Professors (Clinical): Carl C. Aven, J. Norman Berry, Tully T. Blalock, Charles E. Brown, Donald C. Chait, A. Grigg Churchwell, R. Paul Crank, Nicholas E. Davies, Walter S. Dunbar, Edwin C. Evans, Harold A. Ferris, Robert M. Fine, Francis W. Fitzhugh Jr., Robert I. Gibbs Jr., Byron F. Harper Jr., David S. Hubbard, Carl C.

Jones Jr., W. Roy Mason Jr., A. Park McGinty, James B. Minor, James W. Mosley, Michael V. Murphy Jr., Philip H. Nippert, Lamar B. Peacock, Vernon E. Powell, Shirley Rivers, John deR. Slade, Jean S. Staton, Hyman B. Stillerman, Hiram F. Sturm, Lloyd F. Timberlake, Ebert Van Buren, Robert L. Whipple Jr., Charles L. Whisnant Jr., Harold W. Whiteman, Joseph A. Wilber, Grattan C. Woodson Jr., Edgar Woody Jr., John T. Yauger

Associates: John R. Boring III (Infectious Disease), Charles A. Brake, George M. Callaway (Renal Disease and Inorganic Metabolism), June W. Gray, Joseph E. Hardison, Julian Jacobs, Alexander S. McKinney (Neurology), Donald O. Nutter (Cardiology), Paul W. Seavey, Jonas Shulman (Infectious Disease), Tuncer Someren

Associates (Clinical): Eustace A. Allen, John S. Atwater, Ernest W. Beasley Jr., Marguerite L. Candler, William R. Crowe, John S. Dodd Jr., Louis H. Felder, Stephen E. Furst, W. Elizabeth Gambrell, Harold A. Gussack, J. Frank Harris, David L. Hearin, Joseph H. Hilsman Jr., A. Worth Hobby, Byron J. Hoffman, Ralph A. Huie Jr., Richard H. Johnson, James A. Kaufman, Milton J. Krainin, John G. Leonardy Jr., Harold B. Levin, John M. McCoy, Preston R. Miller Jr., J. Merrell Monfort, B. Waldo Moore Jr., Zebulon V. Morgan Jr., Chester W. Morse, Ralph A. Murphy Jr., Benjamin B. Okel, William L. Paullin Jr., Rosemond S. Peltz, Joseph L. Rankin, Robert A. Reich, C. Purcell Roberts, Stewart R. Roberts Jr., C. Vernon Sanders, Legh R. Scott Jr., Sanford A. Shmerling, Carlos A. Stuart, Nathaniel A. Thornton, Abraham M. Tornow, Charles B. Upshaw Jr., J. Grant Wilmer, Thorne S. Winter III, Bernard P. Wolff

Instructors: Hrair M. Balikian (Endocrinology), Gerhard O. Bern, I. Sylvia Crawley (Cardiology), Gerald F. Fletcher, Herbert A. Goodman, Edwin J. Macon (Renal Disease and Inorganic Metabolism), W. Brem Mayer (Neurology), Marian F. Olansky (Dermatology), William L. Pomeroy Jr., Paul H. Robinson (Cardiology)

Instructors (Clinical): Andrew H. Abernathy, Charles D. Adams, Elizabeth K. Adams, Elbert B. Agnor, Harold Asher, Edwin T. Avret, Evert A. Bancker, Maxwell Berry, Allan C. Bleich, Max M. Blumberg, Philip S. Brachman, Louis C. Brown, C. Daniel Cabaniss, Sandy B. Carter, L. Guy Chelton, Peter J. Cline, Claud P. Cobb Jr., Harry A. Cooper, Robert B. Copeland, Leonard L. Cotts, Paul Calvin Cronce, Joseph S. Cruise, Robert P. Cunningham, C. Warren Davidson, Brown W. Dennis, David B. Dennison, H. Bruce Dull, Edgar M. Dunstan, Shia H. Elson, Marvin F. Engel, Leonard Fishman, Paul E. Fitzpatrick, Luther G. Fortson Jr., Edwin J. Galler, Phillip E. Gertler, David L. Glancy, Martin I. Goldstein, Chenault W. Hailey, O. Eugene Hanes, John H. Harbour, Timothy Harden Jr., Charles E. Harrison Jr., Clark W. Heath Jr., Joseph A. Hertell, Robert W. Hubbell, W. Baird Hudgins, John L. Jacobs, Henry S. Jennings Jr., McLaren Johnson Sr., Lewis E. Jones, Alvin D. Josephs, Houston W. Kitchin, Mason I. Lowance, Frank S. MacDonell, Glenn E. McCormick Jr., Claude F. McCuiston, George T. Mims Jr., William R. Minnich, Marvous E. Mostellar, Abraham M. Oshlag, Bernard H. Palay, William M. Pavlovsky, Samuel O. Poole, Ernest E. Proctor, Arthur M. Pruce, A. Henry Randall Jr., Benjamin D. Saffan, James Z. Shanks, Jerome H. Siegel, Warren D. Stribling III, Cyrus W. Strickler Jr., Daniel R. Turner, James K. Van Buren, Margaret J. Wall, James I. Weinberg, John G. Wells. J. Herbert West, Roy A. Wiggins, Malcolm H. Williams, W. Talbert Williams

Fellows: James F. Alexander, Marsha F. Armstrong, M. Thomas Bailey Jr., Brian J. Baldwin, Joseph A. Bonanno, Comer Cherry, Michael Duffell, Susan K. Fellner, John C. Hall, Charles H. Hamilton, Jim A. Harris, Sam E. Hyde III, Allen H. Johnson, George W. Jones Jr., Michael S. Landy, I. Lehman Lindsey Jr., George I. Litman, Robert J. Myerburg, Charles J. Owens, Donald W. Paty, W. Lanier Pearce, Everett C. Price, Karl H. Rahn, Stephen W. Schwarzmann, Michael G. Shulman, Mark E. Silverman, James K. Stokes, John H. Stone III, William H. Stuart, Gerald L. Summer, Robert C. Talley, H. Leonard Turner, Stewart Wald, H. Kenneth Walker, Russell W. Wallace Jr., Paul F. Walter, Garrison G. Watts Jr., Patricia B. Wilber, John L. Wilson, Billy K. Yeh

Electronics Associate: James W. Kinard

Appendix 36: Bulletin of Emory University School of Medicine, which lists the full-time and clinical volunteer faculty members and fellows of the Department of Medicine in 1969.

MEDICINE

J. Willis Hurst, *Professor of Medicine; Chairman of the Department*
Professors: J. C. Crutcher (Pulmonary Disease), E. R. Dorney (Cardiology), J. T. Galambos (Digestive Diseases), B. R. Gendel (Hematology), L. I. Goldberg (Clinical Pharmacology), E. G. Herndon Jr. (Nephrology and Inorganic Metabolism), C. M. Huguley Jr. (Hematology), H. R. Karp (Neurology), R. F. Kibler (Neurology), R. B. Logue (Cardiology), R. L. McLean (Pulmonary Disease), S. Olansky (Dermatology), J. R. K. Preedy (Endocrinology), D. Rudman (Clinical Research Facility), R. C. Schlant (Cardiology), J. S. Schroeder (Digestive Diseases), T. F. Sellers Jr. (Infectious Disease), E. P. Tuttle (Nephrology and Inorganic Metabolism)
Professors Emeriti: R. E. Dyer, R. H. Wood (Active in 69–70)
Professors (Clinical): J. G. Barrow, T. S. Claiborne, D. F. James, H. J. L. Marriott, A. J. Merrill, C. Smith, W. A. Smith
Associate Professors: H. E. Brown, V. M. Buckalew (Nephrology and Inorganic Metabolism), B. W. Cobbs Jr. (Cardiology), C. C. Corley Jr. (Hematology), J. K. Davidson (Endocrinology), P. G. Dayton (Clinical Pharmacology), M. Di Girolamo (Endocrinology), R. H. Franch (Cardiology), B. L. Hallman, J. G. Hood, R. H. Ingram Jr. (Clinical Physiology), J. L. McNay Jr. (Clinical Pharmacology), A. M. McPhedran (Neurology), H. S. Ramos, N. S. Skinner Jr. (Clinical Physiology), W. C. Waters III (Nephrology and Inorganic Metabolism), J. Wenger (Cardiology), N. K. Wenger (Cardiology)
Visiting Associate Professor: J. T. Riggin Jr.
Associate Professors (Clinical): H. S. Alden, T. J. Anderson Jr., L. H. Bishop Jr., S. S. Brewer Jr., C. D. Burge, E. N. Burson Jr., G. R. Cooper, W. L. Dobes, F. W. Dowda, M. H. Freedman, W. F. Friedewald, L. H. Hamff, D. D. Hankey, D. E. Hein, L. Henry, H. N. Hill, D. J. Hughes, L. K. Levy, B. S. Lipman, F. L. Neely, H. Parks, W. H. Reeves, W. P. Sloan Jr., C. F. Stone Jr., P. Teplis, J. S. Wilson, R. B. Wilson
Assistant Professors: J. L. Achord (Digestive Diseases), S. Akgun (Clinical Research Facility), J. C. Ammons (Neurology), J. R. Boring III (Infectious Disease), A. C. Brown (Dermatology), J. H. Christy (Endocrinology), J. C. Coberly, D. C. Collins (Endocrinology), W. E. Farrar Jr. (Infectious Disease), L. A. Garcia (Clinical Research Facility), C. A. Gilbert (Cardiology), J. Lindsay (Cardiology), W. M. Marine (Infectious Disease), D. O. Nutter (Cardiology), E. A. Paulk Jr. (Cardiology), J. H. Sadler (Nephrology and Inorganic Metabolism), J. F. Schwartz (Neurology), J. A. Shulman (Infectious Disease), J. H. Stone III, J. A. Vogler (Hematology), J. A. Ward (Endocrinology), H. L. Williams (Clinical Pharmacology), C. H. Wilson Jr. (Rheumatology)
Assistant Professors (Clinical): C. C. Aven, J. N. Berry, T. T. Blalock, C. E. Brown, D. C. Chait, A. G. Churchwell, R. P. Crank, N. E. Davies, W. S. Dunbar, E. C. Evans, H. A. Ferris, R. M. Fine, F. W. Fitzhugh Jr., R. I. Gibbs Jr., B. F. Harper Jr., J. W. Hirsch, D. S. Hubbard, C. C. Jones Jr., W. R. Mason Jr., A. P. McGinty, J. B. Minor, J. W.

Mosley, M. V. Murphy Jr., P. H. Nippert, L. B. Peacock, V. E. Powell, S. Rivers, J. deR. Slade, J. S. Staton, H. B. Stillerman, H. F. Sturm, L. F. Timberlake, E. Van Buren, R. L. Whipple Jr., C. L. Whisnant Jr., H. W. Whiteman H. J. Whyte, J. A. Wilber, G. C. Goodson Jr., E. Woody Jr., J. T. Yauger

Associates: G. M. Callaway Jr. (Nephrology and Inorganic Metabolism), J. Gray, J. E. Hardison (Hematology), J. Jacobs (Hematology), E. J. Macon (Nephrology and Inorganic Metabolism), A. S. McKinney (Neurology), J. Perel (Clinical Pharmacology), T. Someren (Nephrology and Inorganic Metabolism)

Associates (Clinical): E. A. Allen, J. S. Atwater, E. W. Beasley Jr., M. L. Candler, W. R. Crowe, J. S. Dodd Jr., L. H. Felder, S. E. Furst, W. E. Gambrell, H. A. Gussack, J. F. Harris, D. L. Hearin, J. H. Hilsman Jr., A. W. Hobby, B. J. Hoffman, R. A. Huie Jr., R. H. Johnson, J. A. Kaufman, M. J. Krainin, J. G. Leonardy Jr., H. B. Levin, J. M. McCoy, P. R. Miller Jr., J. M. Monfort, B. W. Moore Jr., Z. V. Morgan Jr., C. W. Morse, R. A. Murphy Jr., B. B. Okel, W. L. Paullin Jr., R. S. Peltz, J. L. Rankin, R. A. Reich, C. P. Roberts, S. R. Roberts Jr., C. V. Sanders, L. R. Scott Jr., S. A. Shmerling, C. A. Stuart, N. A. Thornton, A. M. Tornow, C. B. Upshaw Jr., J. G. Wilmer, T. S. Winter III, B. P. Wolff

Instructors: H. Balikian (Endocrinology), G. O. Bern, M. A. Eidex, E. J. Malveaux Sr., W. B. Mayer (Neurology), M. F. Olansky (Dermatology), P. H. Robinson (Cardiology), R. Wallace Jr. (Neurology)

Instructors (Clinical): A. H. Abernathy, C. D. Adams, E. K. Adams, E. B. Agnor, H. Asher, E. T. Avret, E. A. Bancker, M. Berry, A. C. Bleich, M. M. Blumberg, E. C. Borden, P. S. Brachman, L. C. Brown, J. A. Bryan, C. D. Cabaniss, S. B. Carter, L. G. Chelton, P. J. Cline, C. P. Cobb Jr., H. A. Cooper, R. B. Copeland, L. L. Cotts, P. C. Cronce, J. S. Cruise, R. P. Cunningham, C. W. Davidson, B. W. Dennis, D. B. Dennison, H. B. Dull, E. M. Dunstan, S. Elson, M. F. Engel, B. L. Evatt, L. Fishman, P. E. Fitzpatrick, L. G. Fortson Jr., E. J. Galler, P. E. Gertler, D. L. Glancy, M. I. Goldstein, C. W. Hailey, O. E. Hanes, J. H. Harbour, T. Harden Jr., C. T. Harding, C. E. Harrison Jr., C. J. Hatem, C. W. Heath Jr., J. A. Hertell, V. N. Houck, R. W. Hubbell, W. B. Hudgins, H. I. Hurtig, J. L. Jacobs, H. S. Jennings Jr., M. Johnson Sr., G. W. Jones Jr., L. E. Jones, A. D. Josephs, S. H. King, H. W. Kitchin, M. S. Landy, W. H. Likosky, M. I. Lowance, F. S. MacDonell, G. E. McCormick Jr., C. F. McCuiston, G. T. Mims Jr., W. R. Minnich, T. P. Monath, M. E. Mostellar, A. M. Oshlag, B. H. Palay, W. M. Pavlovsky, S. O. Poole, E. E. Proctor, A. M. Pruce, A. H. Randall Jr., R. H. Rubin, B. D. Saffan, J. Z. Shanks, J. H. Siegel, W. D. Stribling III, C. W. Strickler Jr., D. M. Taylor, D. R. Turner, J. K. Van Buren, M. J. Wall, J. I. Weinberg, J. G. Wells, J. H. West, R. A. Wiggins, M. H. Williams, W. T. Williams

Electronics Associate: J. W. Kinard (Research Specialist)

Fellows: J. L. Barney, B. J. Baldwin, H. J. Baskin, G. D. Bellward, J. B. Blumenthal, D. W. Clark, J. M. D'Angelo, W. L. Deardorff, R. E. Dubois, M. Duffell, M. C. Dunaway, F. Fiedelholtz, D. H. Forsyth, R. D. Franco, B. Gillett, R. R. Goodin, G. R. Grant Jr., J. C. Hall, S. E. Hyde III, T. V. Inglesby, A. H. Johnson, L. D. Johnson, S. B. King III, I. L. Lindsey Jr., G. I. Litman, D. C. Markle, J. F. Meyer, R. J. Noble, D. W. Paty, A. M. Petty III, M. K. Petursson, K. H. Rahn, P. K. Ré, R. G. Sachs, S. W. Schwarzmann, M. G. Shulman, H. R. Silverstein, J. Simanis, W. H. Stuart, G. L. Summer, R. C. Talley, S. Wald, H. K. Walker, P. F. Walter, W. H. Walter III, G. G. Watts, R. A. Weaver, E. B. Weisman, T. P. Wight Jr., P. B. Wilber

Appendix 37: Bulletin of Emory University School of Medicine, which lists the full-time and clinical volunteer faculty members and fellows of the Department of Medicine in 1970.

MEDICINE

J. Willis Hurst, *Professor of Medicine; Chairman of the Department*

Professors: J. C. Crutcher (Pulmonary Disease), E. R. Dorney (Cardiology), R. H. Franch (Cardiology), J. T. Galambos (Digestive Diseases), B. R. Gendel (Hematology), L. I. Goldberg (Clinical Pharmacology), E. G. Herndon (Nephrology and Inorganic Metabolism), C. M. Huguley Jr. (Hematology), H. R. Karp (Neurology), R. F. Kibler (Neurology), R. B. Logue (Cardiology), J. L. McNay Jr. (Clinical Pharmacology), S. Olansky (Dermatology), J. R. K. Preedy (Endocrinology), D. Rudman (Clinical Research Facility), R. C. Schlant (Cardiology), J. S. Schroder (Digestive Diseases), T. F. Sellers Jr. (Infectious Disease), E. P. Tuttle Jr. (Nephrology and Inorganic Metabolism), J. Wenger (Digestive Diseases)

Professors Emeriti: R. E. Dyer, J. G. Hood, R. H. Wood (Active in 1970–71)

Professors (Clinical): J. G. Barrow, T. S. Claiborne, D. F. James, H. J. L. Marriott, A. J. Merrill, C. Smith Sr., W. A. Smith

Associate Professors: J. L. Achord (Digestive Diseases), J. C. Ammons (Neurology), J. R. Boring III (Infectious Disease), H. E. Brown, V. M. Buckalew Jr. (Nephrology and Inorganic Metabolism), B. W. Cobbs Jr. (Cardiology), C. C. Corley Jr. (Hematology), J. K. Davidson (Endocrinology), P. G. Dayton (Clinical Pharmacology), M. Di Girolamo (Endocrinology), W. E. Farrar (Infectious Disease), B. L. Hallman, R. H. Ingram Jr. (Pulmonary), W. M. Marine (Infectious Disease), A. M. McPhedran (Neurology), H. S. Ramos, J. H Sadler (Nephrology and Inorganic Metabolism), J. A. Shulman (Infectious Disease), N. S. Skinner Jr. (Clinical Physiology), J. A. Ward (Endocrinology), W. C Waters III (Nephrology and Inorganic Metabolism), N. K. Wenger (Cardiology), C. H. Wilson Jr. (Rheumatology)

Associate Professors (Clinical): H. S. Alden, T. J. Anderson Jr., L. H. Bishop Jr., S. S. Brewer Jr., C. D. Burge, E. N. Burson Jr., G. R. Cooper, W. L. Dobes, F. W. Dowda, M. H. Freedman, W. F. Friedewald, L. H. Hamff, D. D. Hankey, D. E. Hein, L. Henry, H. N. Hill, D. J. Hughes, L. K. Levy, B. S. Lipman, F. L. Neely, H. Parks, W. H. Roevca, W. P Sloan Jr., C. F. Stone Jr., P. Teplis, J. S. Wilson, R. B. Wilson

Assistant Professors: C. D. Cabaniss (Cardiology), H. M. Balikian (Endocrinology), A. C. Brown (Dermatology), E. A. Bruckner (Hematology), G. M. Callaway (Nephrology and Inorganic Metabolism), J. H. Christy (Endocrinology), J. C. Coberly, D. C. Collins (Endocrinology), I. S. Crawley (Cardiology), S. A. Cucinell (Clinical Pharmacology), G. M. Duffell (Pulmonary), C. A. Gilbert (Cardiology), W. D. Hall (Nephrology and Inorgamc Metabolism), J. E. Hardison (Hematology), J. Jacobs (Hematology), J. Lindsay Jr. (Cardiology), E. J. Macon (Nephrology and Inorganic Metabolism), Y. I. Mapp (Hematology), A. S. McKinney (Neurology), D. O. Nutter (Cardiology), E. A. Paulk Jr. (Cardiology), P. H. Robinson (Cardiology), J. F. Schwanz (Neurology), P. W. Seavey, M. E. Silverman (Cardiology), J. H. Stone (Cardiology), W. R. Vogler (Hematology), H. L. Williams (Clinical Pharmacology)

Assistant Professors (Clinical): C. C. Aven, M. P. Berenson, J. N. Berry, T. T. Blalock, H. H. Brill, C. E. Brown, D. C. Chait, R. R. Copeland, R. P. Crank, N. E. Davies, W. S. Dunbar, E. C. Evans, H. A. Ferris, A. Fiedotin, R. M. Fine, F. W. Fitzhugh Jr., G. F. Fletcher, R. I. Gibbs Jr., B. F. Harper Jr., J. W. Hirsch, D. S. Hubbard, C. C. Jones Jr., W. R. Mason Jr., A. P. McGinty, J. B. Minor, J. W. Mosley, M. V. Murphy Jr., P. H. Nippert, L. B. Peacock, V. E. Powell, S. Rivers, J. deR. Slade, J. S. Staton, H. B. Stillerman, H. F. Sturm, L. F. Timberlake, E. Van Buren, R. L. Whipple Jr., C. L. Whisnant Jr., H. W. Whiteman, H. J. Whyte, J. A. Wilber, G. C. Goodson Jr., E. Woody Jr., J. T. Yauger

Associates: S. W. Ahn, J. W. Gray, W. B. Mayer (Neurology), J. N. Perel (Clinical Pharmacology), T. Someren (Nephrology and Inorganic Metabolism), F. Tutunji (Cardiology)

Associates (Clinical): E. A. Allen, J. S. Atwater, E. W. Beasley Jr., M. L. Candler, W. R. Crowe, J. S. Dodd Jr., L. H. Felder, S. E. Furst, W. E. Gambrell, H. A. Gussack, J. F. Harris, D. L. Hearin, J. H. Hilsman Jr., A. W. Hobby, B. J. Hoffman, R. A. Huie Jr., R. H. Johnson, J. A. Kaufman, M. J. Krainin, J. G. Leonardy Jr., H. B. Levin, J. M McCoy, P. R. Miller Jr., J. M. Monfort, B. W. Moore Jr., Z. V. Morgan Jr., C. W. Morse, R. A. Murphy Jr., B. B. Okel, W. L. Paullin Jr., R. S. Peltz, J. L. Rankin, R. A. Reich, C. P. Roberts, C. V. Sanders, L. R. Scott Jr., S. A. Shmerling, C. A. Stuart, N. A. Thornton, A. M. Tornow, C. B. Upshaw Jr., J. G. Wilmer, T. S. Winter III, B. P. Wolff

Instructors: S. D. Clements, C. F. Demoise, M. A. Eidex, L. A. Gardberg, L. E. Jones, E. J. Malveaux Sr., M. F. Olansky (Dermatology), R. A. Weaver

Instructor Emeritus (Clinical): C. W. Strickler Jr.

Instructors (Clinical): A. H. Abernathy, C. D. Adams, E. K. Adams, E. B. Agnor, H. Asher, D. F. Austin, E. T. Avret, E. A. Bancker, F. Barnett Jr., M. Berry, A. C. Bleich, M. M. Blumberg, E. C. Borden, P. S. Brachman, G. F. Brooks Jr., L. C. Brown, J. A. Bryan, A. L. Brodsky, T. M. Buchanan, C. C. Butler, S. B. Carter, G. Chelton, P. J. Cline, C. P. Cobb Jr., J. D. Coonrod, H. A. Cooper, J. L. Cooper, L. L. Cotts, P. C. Cronce, J. S. Cruise, R. P. Cunningham, C. W. Davidson, B. W. Dennis, D. B. Dennison, J. A. Donadio, R. E. Drusin, H. B. Dull, E. M. Dunstan, S. H. Elson, M. F. Engle, B. L. Evatt, L. Fishman, P. E. Fitzpatrick, L. G. Fortson Jr., D. H. Forsyth, E. J. Galler, R. A. Garibaldi, P. E. Gertler, D. L. Glancy, M. I. Goldstein, D. S. Gordon, C. W. Hailey, J. C. Hall, O. E. Hanes, J. H. Harbour, T. Harden Jr., C. T. Harding, C. E. Harrison Jr., C. J. Hatem, C. W. Heath Jr., J. A. Hertell, A. R. Hinman, V. W. Houck, R. W. Hubbell, W. B. Hudgins, H. I. Hurtig, J. L. Jacobs, H. S. Jennings, McC. Johnson Sr., McC. Johnson Jr., G. W. Jones Jr., L. E. Jones, J. B. Kahn, S. H. King, H. W. Kitchin, T. E. Kohn, M. S. Landy, B. C. Lanier, S. R. Lathan, W. H. Likosky, R. A. Liss, M. I. Lowance, C. T. Lucas, F. S. MacDonell, D. M. Mackey, R. R. Masden, A. Mallory, G. E. McCormick, C. F. McCuiston, J. E. McGowan Jr., G. T. Mims, W. R. Minnich, T. P. Monath, M. E. Mostellar, A. M. Oshlag, R. L. Pace, B. H. Palay, W. M. Pavlovsky, S. O. Poole, E. E. Proctor, A. M. Pruce, A. H. Randall, S. B. Reller, R. H. Rubin, B. D. Saffan, J. D. Schmale, A. L. Schroeter, J. Z. Shanks, J. H. Siegal, B. D. Silverman, A. Sommer, C. Smith Jr., W. D. Stribling III, D. M. Taylor, D. R. Turner, R. H. Turner, T. M. Tuthill, J. K. Van Buren, M. J. Wall, R. B. Wallace, J. I. Weinberg, J. G. Wells, H. J. West, K. A. Western, S. E. Wiegand, R. A. Wiggins, M. H. Williams, W. T. Williams, S. A. Wyll

Electronics Associate: J. W. Kinard (Research Specialist)

Fellows: B. J. Baldwin (Cardiology), J. B. Blumenthal (Cardiology), D. W. Clark (Clinical Pharmacology), P. G. Cohen (Nephrology and Inorganic Metabolism), E. A. Cucinell (Clinical Pharmacology), J. M. D'Angelo (Hematology), R. E. DuBois (Infectious Disease), S. K. Fellner (Nephrology and Inorganic Metabolism), F. Fiedelholtz (Cardiology), D. G. Finlay Jr. (Clinical Pharmacology), R. D. Franco (Neurology), B. M. Gillett (Neurology), R. R. Goodin (Cardiology), A. A. Halkos (Cardiology), H. G. Hanley (Cardiology), H. T. Harper III (Cardiology), C. Hobbs (Digestive Diseases), T. V. Inglesby (Cardiology), W. F. Jacobs (Cardiology), S. B. King III (Cardiology), A. D. Lewis (Dermatology), J. H. Manchester (Cardiology), J. F. Meyer (Cardiology), D. W. Paty (Neurology), O. V. Preli (Cardiology), R. B. Randall (Cardiology), T. E. Ratts (Cardiology), P. K. Re (Neurology), F. D. Rose (Cardiology), R. G. Sachs (Cardiology), W. Siegel (Cardiology), H. R. Silverstein (Cardiology), C. M. Singleton (Rheumatology), G. F. Slade (Neurology), E. Spoto (Cardiology), H. K. Stonecipher (Cardiology), W. M. Turner (Nephrology and Inorganic Metabolism), H. K. Walker (Neurology), W. H. Walter III (Cardiology), E. B. Weisman (Cardiology), J. H. West (Hematology), T. L. Whitsett (Clinical Pharmacology), P. B. Wilber (Cardiology)

Appendix 38: Bulletin of Emory University School of Medicine, which lists the full-time and clinical volunteer faculty members and fellows of the Department of Medicine in 1971.

MEDICINE

J.Willis Hurst, *Professor of Medicine; Chairman of the Department*

Professors: C. C. Corley Jr. (Hematology), J. C. Crutcher (Pulmonary Disease), J. K. Davidson, E. R. Dorney (Cardiology), R. H. Franch (Cardiology), J. T. Galambos (Digestive Diseases), B. R. Gendel (Genetics and Hematology), L. I. Goldberg (Clinical Pharmacology), E. G. Herndon Jr. (Nephrology and Inorganic Metabolism), C. M. Huguley Jr. (Hematology), R. H. Ingram Jr. (Pulmonary Disease), H. R. Karp (Neurology), R. F. Kibler (Neurology), R. B. Logue (Cardiology), J. L. McNay Jr. (Clinical Pharmacology), S. Olansky (Dermatology), J. R. K. Preedy (Endocrinology), D. Rudman (Clinical Research Facility), R. C. Schlant (Cardiology), J. S. Schroder (Digestive Diseases), T. F. Sellers Jr. (Infectious Disease), N. S. Skinner (Clinical Physiology), E. P. Tuttle Jr. (Nephrology and Inorganic Metabolism), J. Wenger (Digestive Diseases)

Professors Emeriti: R. E. Dyer, J. G. Hood, R. H. Wood

Professors (Clinical): 1J. G. Barrow, T. S. Claiborne, D. F. James. H. J. L. Marriott, A. J. Merrill, C. Smith Sr., W. A. Smith

Associate Professors: J. L. Achord (Digestive Diseases), J. C. Ammons (Neurology), J. R. Boring III (Infectious Disease), H. E. Brown, V. M. Buckalew Jr. (Nephrology and Inorganic Metabolism), J. H. Christy (Endocrinology), B. W. Cobbs Jr. (Cardiology), P. G. Dayton (Clinical Pharmacology), M. Di Girolamo (Endocrinology), W. E. Farrar Jr. (Infectious Disease), C. A. Gilbert (Cardiology), B. L. Hallman, W. M. Marine (Infectious Disease), A. M. McPhedran (Neurology), D. O. Nutter (Cardiology), E. A. Paulk Jr. (Cardiology), H. S. Ramos, J. H. Sadler (Nephrology and Inorganic Metabolism), J. A. Shulman (Infectious Disease), W. R. Vogler (Hematology), J. A. Ward (Endocrinology), N. K. Wenger (Cardiology), H. L. Williams (Clinical Pharmacology), C. H. Wilson Jr. (Rheumatology)

Associate Professors (Clinical): H. S. Alden, T. J. Anderson Jr., L. H. Bishop, S. S. Brewer Jr., C. D. Burge, N. Burson Jr., G. R. Cooper, W. L. Dobes, F. W. Dowda, M. H. Freedman, W. F. Friedewald, D. D. Hankey, D. E. Hein, L. Henry, D. J. Hughes, L. K. Levy, B. Lipman, F. L. Neely, H. Parks, W. H. Reeves, W. P. Sloan, C. F. Stone Jr., P. Teplis, W. C. Waters III, J. S. Wilson, R. B. Wilson

Assistant Professors: C. J. Barry (Nephrology and Inorganic Metabolism), A. C. Brown (Dermatology), E. A. Bruckner (Hematology), C. D. Cabaniss (Cardiology), F. M. Callaway Jr. (Nephrology and Inorganic Metabolism), J. C. Coberly, D. C. Collins (Endocrinology), I. S. Crawley (Cardiology), S. A. Cucinell (Clinical Pharmacology), G. M. Duffell (Pulmonary Disease), L. J. Elsas, G. F. Fletcher (Cardiology), M. B. Gravanis, G. D. Grossman (Pulmonary Disease), W. D. Hall Jr. (Nephrology and Inorganic Metabolism), W. L. Hand (Infectious Disease), J. E. Hardison (Hematology), Z. H. Israili (Clinical Pharmacology), J. Jacobs (Hematology), E. J. Macon (Nephrology and Inorganic Metaboliam), A. S. McKinney (Neurology), J. N. Perel (Clinical Pharmacology), P. H. Robinson (Cardiology), J. F. Schwartz

(Neurology), S. W. Schwarzman (Infectious Disease), P. W. Seavey, M. E. Silvermann (Cardiology), T. Someren (Nephrology and Inorganic Metabolism), J. H. Stone (Cardiology), M. V. Teem (Digestive Diseases), P. F. Walter (Cardiology), J. O. Wells (Nephrology and Inorganic Metabolism)

Assistant Professors (Clinical): C. C. Aven, M. P. Berenson, J. N. Berry, T. T. Blalock, H. H. Brill, C. E. Brown, C. C. Butler, D. C. Chait, R. B. Copeland, P. C. Crank, N. E. Davies, W. S. Dunbar, H. A. Ferris Jr., A. Fiedotin, R. Fine, F. W. Fitzhugh Jr., R. I. Gibbs, B. F. Harper Jr., H. N. Hill, J. W. Hirsch, D. S. Hubbard, C. C. Jones Jr., W. R. Mason Jr., W. B. Mayer, J. B. Minor, M. V. Murphy, P. H. Nippert, L. B. Peacock, V. E. Powell, S. L. Rivers, J. deR. Slade, J. S. Staton, H. B. Stillerman, H. M. Sturm, L. F. Timberlake, E. Van Buren, R. L. Whipple Jr., C. L. Whisnant Jr., H. W. Whiteman, H. J. Whyte, J. A. Wilber, G. Woodson Jr., E. Woody, J. T. Yauger

Associates: S. W. Ahn, M. O. Read (Nephrology and Inorganic Metabolism), F. J. Tutunji (Cardiology)

Associates (Clinical): E. A. Allen, J. S. Atwater, E. W. Beasley, M. Candler, W. R. Crow, A. Curley, J. S. Dodd Jr., L. H. Felder, W. E. Gambrell, H. A. Gussack, J. F. Harris, D. L. Hearin, C. W. Heath Jr., J. H. Hilsman, A. W. Hobby, B. J. Hoffman, R. A. Huie Jr., R. H. Johnson, J. A. Kaufman, M. J. Krainin, J. G. Leonardy Jr., H. B. Levin, J. M. McCoy, P. R. Miller Jr., J. M. Monfort, B. W. Moore, Z. V. Morgan, C. W. Morse, R. A. Murphy, B. B. Okel, W. L. Paullin, R. Peltz, J. L. Rankin, R. A. Reich, P. Roberts, C. V. Sanders, L. R. Scott, S. A. Shmerling, C. Stuart, N. A. Thornton, A. M. Tornow, C. B. Upshaw Jr., J. G. Wilmer, T. S. Winter, B. P. Wolff

Instructors: G. O. Bern, S. C. Davis Jr., C. F. Demoise, E. J. Malveaux (Clinical Pharmacology), M. Olansky (Dermatology), W. Siegel (Cardiology), H. K. Walker (Neurology), R. A. Weaver (Pulmonary Disease), L. W. Whatley (Nephrology and Inorganic Metabolism)

Instructor Emeritus (Clinical): C. W. Strickler Jr.

Instructors (Clinical): A. H. Abernathy, C. D. Adams, E. K. Adams, E. B. Agnor, H. Asher, E. A. Bancker, C. F. Barnett Jr., D. Berd, M. Berry, A. C. Bleich, M. M. Blumberg, E. C. Borden, P. S. Brachman, A. L. Brodsky, L. C. Brown, J. A. Bryan, T. M. Buchanan, C. C. Butler, S. B. Carter, G. Chelton, P. J. Cline, C. P. Cobb Jr., P. G. Cohen, B. P. Conway, H. A. Cooper, J. L. Cooper, L. L. Cotts, T. L. Crews, P. C. Cronce, J. S. Cruise, R. P. Cunningham, C. W. Davidson, B. W. Dennis, D. B. Dennison, H. B. Dull, E. M. Dunstan, M. A. Eidex, S. H. Elson, M. F. Engle, J. M. Felner, L. Fishman, P. E. Fitzpatrick, D. H. Forsyth, L. G. Fortson Jr., C. C. Fulkerson, E. J. Galler, R. A. Garibaldi, P. E. Gertler, D. L. Glancy, N. I. Goldman, M. I. Goldstein, D. S. Gordon, M. G. Grand, C. Hailey, L. D. Haley, J. C. Hall, O. E. Hanes, J. H. Harbour, T. Harden, C. T. Harding, C. E. Harrison Jr., C. J. Hatem, C. W. Heath Jr., J. A. Hertell, A. R. Hinman, V. W. Houck, R. W. Hubbell, D. H. Huber, W. B. Hudgins, M. A. Jablow, J. L. Jacobs, H. S. Jennings Jr., McC. Johnson Sr., McC. Johnson Jr., G. W. Jones, L. E. Jones, J. B. Kahn, A. S. Kaiser, S. H. King, H. W. Kitchin, T. E. Kohn, M. S. Landy Jr., B. G. Lanier, S. R. Latham, W. H. Likosky, R. A. Liss, M. I. Lowance, C. T. Lucas, F. S. MacDonell D. M. Mackey, D. G. Maki, G. E. McCormick, C. F. McCuiston, J. E. McGowen, G. D. Miller, G. T. Mims, W. R. Minnich, D. S. Misfeldt, T. P. Monath, M. E. Mostellar, R. G. Offut, A. M. Oshlag, R. L. Pace, B. H. Palay, W. M. Pavlovsky, L. S. Phillips, S. O. Poole, A. M. Pruce, F. S. Rhame, A. H. Randall, R. H. Rubin, A. H. Rudolph, B. D. Saffan, A. L.

Schroeter, S. H. Schwartz, J. Z. Shanks J. H. Siegel, B. D. Silverman, J. W. Singer, C. Smith Jr., R. W. Smith III, A. Sommer, J. W. Spitzberg, W. D. Stribling III, W. H. Stuart, A. T. Taylor, D. M. Taylor, D. R. Turner, T. M. Tuthill, J. K. Van Buren, M. J. Wall, R. B. Wallace, J. I. Weinberg. J. G. Wells. J. H. West, K. A. Western, S. E. Wiegand, R. A. Wiggins, W. S. Wilborn, M. H. Williams, W. T. Williams, S. A. Wyll *Fellows:* P. Ahmann, P. B. Albright, I. Belenkie. S. Berberich, J. C. Buell, D. W. Clark, S. D. Clements, L. E. Cooper, J. S. Cranman, R. F. Croke, W. G. Edwards, S. Fellner, M. L. Fisher, R. D. Franco, L. J. Gardberg, B. M. Gillett, P. J. Goldman, J. H. Hall III, H. C. Hanley, T. V. Inglesby, I. W. Joines, R. Jones, I. Kassanoff, L. R. Kirkland, W. D. Kistler Jr., M. R. Longo Jr., D. B. McCraw, J. F. Meyer, J. B. Oak, O. V. Preli, A. Raizner, R. B. Randall Jr., T. E. Ratts, P. Re, F. D. Rose, J. Schmale, G. Slade, R. B. Smiley Jr., E. Spoto Jr., P. Wilber, J. R. Zager, S. Zimmerman

Appendix 39: Bulletin of Emory University School of Medicine, which lists the full-time and clinical volunteer faculty members and fellows of the Department of Medicine in 1972.

MEDICINE

J. Willis Hurst, *Professor of Medicine; Chairman of the Department*
Professors: Benjamin R. Gendel, Herbert R. Karp, R. Bruce Logue, Sidney Olansky
Professors (Clinical): J. Gordon Barrow, T. Sterling Claiborne, Rolla E. Dyer, David F. James, Joseph C. Massee, Arthur J. Merrill, Carter Smith, William A. Smith
Associate Professors: H. Eugene Brown, B. Woodfin Cobbs Jr., Charles C. Corley Jr., James C. Crutcher, Edward R. Dorney, Robert H. Franch, John T. Galambos, Leon I. Goldberg, Bernard L. Hallman, E. Garland Herndon Jr., John G. Hood, Charles M. Huguley Jr., Robert F. Kibler, Ross L. McLean, John R. K. Preedy, Thomas F. Sellers Jr., Robert C. Schlant, J. Spalding Schroder, Elbert P. Tuttle Jr., Julius Wenger
Associate Professors (Clinical): Herbert S. Alden, Thomas J. Anderson Jr., Linton H. Bishop Jr., Spencer S. Brewer Jr., C. Daniel Burge, E. Napier Burson Jr., Gerald R. Cooper, William L. Dobes, F. William Dowda, Milton H. Freedman, William F. Friedewald, L. Harvey Hamff, Daniel D. Hankey, David E. Hein, Lamont Henry, Haywood N. Hill, David J. Hughes, Louis K. Levy, Bernard S. Lipman, F. Levering Neely, Harry Parks, W. Harrison Reeves, Wyman P. Sloan Jr., Charles F. Stone Jr., Paul Teplis, Joseph S. Wilson, Richard B. Wilson
Assistant Professors: James L. Achord, James C. Coberly, James W. Lea Jr., Alexander M. McPhedran, Harold S. Ramos, James H. Shinaberger, Joel S. Steinberg, John A. Ward, William C. Waters III, Nanette K. Wenger, Harry L. Williams, Colon H. Wilson Jr.
Assistant Professors (Clinical): Carl C. Aven, J. Norman Berry, Tully T. Blalock, Charles E. Brown, Donald C. Chait, A. Grigg Churchwell, Nicholas E. Davies, Walter S. Dunbar, Edwin C. Evans, Harold A. Ferris, Robert M. Fine, Francis W. Fitzhugh Jr., Robert I. Gibbs Jr., Byron F. Harper Jr., David S. Hubbard, Carl C. Jones Jr., A. Park McGinty, W. Roy Mason Jr., James B. Minor, James W. Mosley, Michael V. Murphy Jr., Philip H. Nippert, Lamar B. Peacock, Vernon E. Powell, Bryan W. Robinson, John deR. Slade, Jean S. Staton, Hyman B. Stillerman, Hiram M. Sturm, Lloyd F. Timberlake, Ebert Van Buren, Robert L. Whipple Jr., Charles Whisnant Jr., Harold W. Whiteman, Joseph A. Wilber, Gratton C. Woodson Jr., Edgar Woody Jr., John T. Yauger
Visiting Assistant Professor: Bjorn Erik Roos
Associates: John C. Ammons, Charles A. Brake, James H. Christy, W. Edmund Farrar Jr., John L. McNay Jr., Keith L. MacCannell, William M. Marine, Shirley L. Rivers, William R. Vogler
Associates (Clinical): Eustace A. Allen, John S. Atwater, Ernest W. Beasley Jr., Marguerite L. Candler, William R. Crowe, John S. Dodd Jr., Louis H. Felder, Stephen E. Furst, W. Elizabeth Gambrell, Harold A. Gussack, J. Frank Harris, David L. Hearin, Joseph H. Hilsman Jr., A. Worth Hobby, Byron J. Hoffman, Ralph A. Huie Jr., Richard H. Johnson, James A. Kaufman, Milton J. Krainin, John G.

Leonardy, Harold B. Levin, John M. McCoy, Preston R. Miller Jr., J. Merrell Monfort, B. Waldo Moore Jr., Zebulon V. Morgan Jr., Chester W. Morse, Ralph A. Murphy Jr., Benjamin B. Okel, William L. Paullin Jr., Rosemonde S. Peltz, Joseph L. Rankin, Robert A. Reich, C. Purcell Roberts, Stewart R. Roberts Jr., C. Vernon Sanders, Legh R. Scott Jr., Sanford A. Shmerling, Carlos A. Stuart, Nathaniel A. Thornton, Abraham M. Tornow, Charles B. Upshaw Jr., J. Grant Wilmer, Thorne S. Winter III, Bernard P. Wolff

Instructors: Gerhard O. Bern, George M. Callaway Jr., Gilbert D. Grossman, W. Lee Hand, Joseph Lindsay Jr., Alexander S. McKinney, Marian F. Olansky, Marta C. Steinberg

Instructors (Clinical): Charles D. Adams, Elizabeth K. Adams, Elbert B. Agnor, Harold Asher, Edwin T. Avret, Evert A. Bancker, Maxwell Berry, Max M. Blumberg, Philip S. Brachman, C. Daniel Cabaniss, Sandy B. Carter, L. Guy Chelton, Allan L. Cline, Peter J. Cline, Claud P. Cobb Jr., Robert P. Coggins, Harry A. Cooper, Leonard L. Cotts, Joseph S. Cruise, Robert P. Cunningham, C. Warren Davidson, David B. Dennison, Edgar M. Dunstan, Theodore C. Eickoff, Shia H. Elson, Marvin F. Engle, Luther G. Fortson Jr., Edwin J. Galler, Glenville A. Giddings, David L. Glancy, Martin I. Goldstein, Chenault W. Hailey, O. Eugene Hanes, John H. Harbour, Timothy Harden Jr., Clark W. Heath Jr., Joseph A. Hertell, Robert W. Hubbell, W. Baird Hudgins, John L. Jacobs, Henry S. Jennings Jr., McClaren Johnson Sr., Alvin D. Josephs, Houston W. Kitchin, Mason I. Lowance, Frank S. MacDonell, Glenn E. McCormick Jr., Claude F. McCuiston, George T. Mims Jr., William P. Minnich, Marvous E. Mostellar, Abraham M. Oshlag, Bernard H. Palay, Samuel O. Poole, Ernest E. Proctor, Arthur M. Pruce, A. Henry Randall Jr., Benjamin D. Saffan, James Z. Shanks, Warren D. Stribling III, Cyrus W. Strickler Jr., Daniel R. Turner, James K. Van Buren, Margaret J. Wall, James I. Weinberg, John G. Wells, J. Herbert West, Roy A. Wiggins, Malcolm H. Williams, W. Talbert Williams

Fellows: Gordon J. Azar, Alfred D. Beasley, Robert M. Boger, James A. Butts, James L. Crosthwait, Thomas G. Douglass, Maxwell A. Eidex, Ruth G. Freeman, Valdir de Paula Furtado, Robert L. Galphin Jr., Robert C. Grant, Joseph E. Hardison, McClaren Johnson Jr., Frederic G. Jones, Jack W. MacDonald, Arthur A. Madden, W. Brem Mayer Jr., Melvin B. Meyer, S. R. Pathak, G. David Raymond, Victor E. Schulze Jr., Richard L. Shepherd, Fuller A. Shuford, Carter Smith Jr., P. Frank Sonneville, B. Dolores Stough, P. Burt Veazey, Russell W. Wallace Jr., David T. Watson, Charles M. Wender, H. Lake Westfall Jr.

Appendix 40: Bulletin of Emory University School of Medicine, which lists the full-time and clinical volunteer faculty members and fellows of the Department of Medicine in 1973.

MEDICINE

J. W. Hurst, *Professor of Medicine; Chairman of the Department*

Professors: V. M. Buckalew Jr. (Nephrology and Inorganic Metabolism), B. W. Cobbs (Cardiology), C. C. Corley Jr. (Hematology), J. C. Crutcher (Pulmonary), J. K. Davidson (Endocrinology), P. G. Dayton (Clinical Pharmacology), E. R. Dorney (Cardiology), R. H. Franch (Cardiology), J. T. Galambos (Digestive Disease), L. I. Goldberg (Clinical Pharmacology), B. L. Hallman, E. G. Herndon Jr. (Nephrology and Inorganic Metabolism), C. M. Huguley Jr. (Hematology), R. H. Ingram Jr. (Pulmonary), H. R. Karp (Neurology), R. F. Kibler (Neurology), R. B. Logue (Cardiology), J. L. McNay Jr. (Clinical Pharmacology), S. Olansky (Dermatology), J. R. K. Preedy (Endocrinology), D. Rudman (Clinical Research Facility), R. C. Schlant (Cardiology), J. S. Schroder (Digestive Disease), T. F. Sellers Jr. (Infectious Disease), N. S. Skinner (Clinical Physiology), E. P. Tuttle Jr. (Nephrology and Inorganic Metabolism), J. Wenger (Digestive Disease), N. K. Wenger (Cardiology)

Professors Emeriti: J. G. Hood, R. H. Wood (Active in 1971–72)

Professors (Clinical): H. S. Alden, J. G. Barrow, T. S. Claiborne, W. L. Dobes, L. H. Hamff, H. N. Hill, H. J. L. Marriott, A. J. Merrill, C. Smith Sr., W. A. Smith

Associate Professors: J. C. Ammons (Neurology), J. R. Boring III (Infectious Disease), A. C. Brown (Dermatology), H. E. Brown, J. H. Christy (Endocrinology), D. C. Collins (Endocrinology), M. Di Girolamo (Endocrinology), G. F. Fletcher (Cardiology), C. A. Gilbert (Cardiology), J. E. Hardison (Hematology), J. Jacobs (Hematology), D. E. McFarlin (Neurology), A. M. McPhedran (Neurology), D. O. Nutter (Cardiology), E. A. Paulk, H. S. Ramos, J. A. Shulman (Infectious Disease), W. R. Vogler (Hematology), J. A. Ward (Endocrinology), H. L. Williams (Clinical Pharmacology), C. H. Wilson Jr. (Rneumatology)

Associate Professors (Clinical): T. J. Anderson Jr., L. H. Bishop, S. S. Brewer Jr., C. E. Brown, C. D. Burge, E. N. Burson Jr., G. R. Cooper, F. W. Dowda, E. C. Evans, M. H. Freedman, W. F. Friedewald, D. D. Hankey, D. E. Hein, L. Henry, D. J. Hughes, L. K. Levy, B. S. Lipman, A. P. McGinty, F. L. Neely, H. Parks, W. H. Reeves, S. L. Rivers, W. P. Sloan, C. F. Stone Jr., H. M. Sturm, P. Teplis, W. C. Waters III, J. A. Wilber, J. S. Wilson, R. B. Wilson, G. C. Woodson Jr.

Assistant Professors: E. A. Bruckner (Hematology), C. D. Cabaniss (Cardiology), G. M. Callaway Jr. (Nephrology and Inorganic Metabolism), J. C. Coberly, I. S. Crawley (Cardiology), G. M. Duffell (Pulmonary), L. J. Elsas II, S. K. Fellner (Nephrology and Inorganic Metabolism), G. D. Grossman (Pulmonary), W. D. Hall Jr. (Nephrology and Inorganic Metabolism), W. L. Hand (Infectious Disease), Z. H. Israili (Clinical Pharmacology), J. W. Keller (Hematology), S. B. King (Cardiology), E. J. Macon (Nephrology and Inorganic Metabolism), A. S. McKinney (Neurology), J. M. Perel (Clinical Pharmacology), A. L. Plummer (Pulmonary), P. H. Robinson (Cardiology), J. F. Schwartz (Neurology), S. W. Schwarzmann (Infectious Disease), P. W. Seavey, M. E. Silverman (Cardiology), T. Someren (Nephrology and Inorganic

Metabolism), J. H. Stone (Cardiology), M. V. Teem (Digestive Disease), H. K. Walker (Neurology), P. F. Walter (Cardiology), J. O. Wells (Nephrology and Inorganic Metabolism)

Assistant Professors (Clinical): C. C. Aven, M. P. Berenson, J. N. Berry, T. T. Blalock, H. H. Brill, C. C. Butler, D. C. Chait, R. B. Copeland, R. P. Crank, P. C. Cronce, N. E. Davies, W. S. Dunbar, H. A. Ferris, A. Fiedotin, R. M. Fine, L. Fishman, F. W. Fitzhugh Jr., R. I. Gibbs, H. A. Gussack, B. F. Harper Jr., C. W. Heath Jr., J. W. Hirsch, D. S. Hubbard, C. C. Jones Jr., J. G. Leonardy Jr., W. R. Mason Jr., W. B. Mayer, J. B. Minor, Z. V. Morgan Jr., M. V. Murphy, P. H. Nippert, L. B. Peacock, R. S. Peltz, B. D. Saffan, M. G. Schultz, L. R. Scott Jr., S. A. Shmerling, J. deR. Slade, J. S. Staton, H. B. Stillerman, L. F. Timberlake, G. B. Upshaw Jr., E. Van Buren, R. L. Whipple Jr., C. L. Whisnant Jr., H. W. Whiteman, H. J. Whyte, J. G. Wilmer, E. Woody, J. T. Yauger

Associate: S. W. Ahn

Associates (Clinical): E. A. Allen, J. S. Atwater, E. W. Beasley, M. L. Candler, W. R. Crowe, A. H. Davison, J. S. Dodd Jr., L. H. Felder, W. E. Gambrell, J. C. Hall, J. F. Harris, D. L. Hearin, J. H. Hilsman, A. W. Hobby, B. J. Hoffman, R. A. Huie Jr., R. H. Johnson, J. A. Kaufman, M. J. Krainin, S. R. Lathan, H. B. Levin, J. M. McCoy, P. R. Miller Jr., J. M. Monfort, B. W. Moore Jr., C. W. Morse, R. A. Murphy, B. B. Okel, W. L. Paulin Jr., J. L. Rankin, R. A. Reich, C. P. Roberts, C. V. Sanders, C. A. Stuart, W. H. Stuart, D. M. Taylor, N. A. Thornton, A. M. Tornow, J. K. Van Buren, T. S. Winters, B. P. Wolff

Instructors: G. O. Bern, S. C. Davis Jr., J. D. Cooper, E. D. Hobgood (Endocrinology), L. E. Jones, R. C. MacDonell, E. J. Malveaux (Clinical Pharmacology), W. McDonald, M. Olansky, R. B. Randall Jr., W. H. Spruell (Rheumatology), T. B. Tjandramaga (Clinical Pharmacology), R. A. Weaver

Instructors (Clinical): A. H. Abernathy, C. D. Adams, E. K. Adams, E. B. Agnor, H. Asher, E. T. Avret, M. T. Bailey, E. A. Bancker, C. F. Barnett Jr., D. Berd, M. Berry, A. C. Bleich, M. M. Blumberg, J. B. Blumenthal, E. C. Borden, P. S. Brachman, J. N. Brawner III, L. C. Brown, J. A. Broyles III, J. A. Bryan, S. B Carter, G. Chelton, P. J. Cline, C. P. Cobb Jr., P. G. Cohen, B. F. Conway, H. A. Cooper, J. L. Cooper, L. L. Cotts, T. L. Crews, J. S. Cruise, R. P. Cunningham, C. W. Davidson, W. W. Davis, B. W. Dennis, D. B. Dennison, H. B. Dull, E. M. Dunstan, M. A. Eidex, S. H. Elson, M. F. Engle, P. E. Fitzpatrick, D. H. Forsyth, L. G. Fortson Jr., R. D. Franco, M. Frank III, C. C. Fulkerson, E. J. Galler, P. E. Gertler, B. M. Gillett, D. L. Glancy, R. H. Glew, N. I. Goldman, D. S. Gordon, M. G. Grand, C. W. Hailey, L. D. Haley, O. E. Hanes, J. H. Harbour, T. Harden, C. T. Harding, C. E. Harrison Jr., C. J. Hatem, J. A. Hertell, W. A. Howard, R. W. Hubbel, W. B. Hudgins, M. A. Jablow, J. L. Jacobs, H. S. Jennings Jr., McC. Johnson Sr., McC. Johnson Jr., R. E. Johnson, G. W. Jones, S. H. King, M. S. Landy Jr., B. G. Lanier, M. I. Lowance, F. S. MacDonell, D. M. Mackey, G. E. McCormick, C. F. McCuiston, G. D. Miller, W. R. Minnich, T. P. Monath, M. E. Mostellar, A. M. Oshlag R. L. Pace, B. H. Palay, W. M. Pavlovsky, S. O. Poole, A. M. Pruce, A. H. Randall, F. S. Rhame, P. A. Rice, R. H. Rubin, A. H. Rudolph, R. M. Schmidt, A. L. Schroeter, S. H. Schwartz, J. Z. Shanks, J. H. Siegel, J. W. Singer, R. B. Smiley, C. Smith Jr., R. W. Smith III, J. W. Spitzberg, W. D. Stribling III, A. T. Taylor, D. R. Turner, T. M. Tuthill, G. E. Vanderpool, J. H.

Walker, M. J. Wall, R. W. Wallace, J. I. Weinberg, J. G. Wells, J. H. West, R. A. Wiggins, W. S. Wilborn, M. H. Williams, W. T. Williams

Fellows: P. Ahmann, T. Akiyama, J. G. Allee, A. T. Allen III, I. Belenkie, S. N. Berberich, P. E. Berry, A. B. Brady Jr., A. G. Brandau, S. C. Campbell, J. D. Cantwell, N. H. Carliner, J. T. Carpenter Jr., M. L. Carr, C. E. Cernuda, D. W. Clark, E. H. Coleman, L. E. Cooper, R. P. Croke, J. del Mazo, K. A. Dimond, G. D. Finlay Jr., M. L. Fisher, V. L. Flatt, J. E. Frazier II, W. W. Fridy Jr., R. B. Geer, T. D. Golden, N. Gupta, J. H. Hall III, N. J. Hart, J. A. Hoole, G. T. Jarrard Jr., I. W. Joines II, W. D. Kistler, J. M. Lesser, M. R. Longo Jr., D. B. McCraw, D. E. McMartin, J. N. Mahmoud, R. R. Masden, J. Mu, W. C. Pierson, M. L. Purvis, S. W. Rabkin, A. Raizner, T. L. Ratts, H. C. Robertson III, J. I. Sawaya, M. Shoji, D. L. Steinberg, R. L. Warren, W. H. Whaley, C. N. Williamson, J. Zager

Appendix 41: Bulletin of Emory University School of Medicine, which lists the full-time and clinical volunteer faculty members and fellows of the Department of Medicine in 1974.

MEDICINE

J. W. Hurst, *Professor of Medicine; Chairman of the Department*
Professors: V. M. Buckalew Jr. (Nephrology and Inorganic Metabolism), B. W. Cobbs (Cardiology), C. C. Corley Jr. (Hematology), J. C. Crutcher (Pulmonary), J. K. Davidson (Endocrinology), P. G. Dayton (Clinical Pharmacology), E. R. Dorney (Cardiology), R. H. Franch (Cardiology), J. T. Galambos (Digestive Disease), L. I. Goldberg (Clinical Pharmacology), B. L. Hallman, E. G. Herndon Jr. (Nephrology and Inorganic Metabolism), C. M. Huguley Jr. (Hematology), R. H. Ingram Jr. (Pulmonary), H. R. Carp (Neurology), R. F. Kibler (Neurology), R. B. Logue (Cardiology), J. L. McNay Jr. (Clinical Pharmacology), S. Olansky (Dermatology), J. R. K. Preedy (Endocrinology), D. Rudman (Clinical Research Facility), R. C. Schlant (Cardiology), J. S. Schroder (Digestive Disease), T. F. Sellers Jr. (Infectious Disease), E. P. Tuttle Jr. (Nephrology and Inorganic Metabolism), J. Wenger (Digestive Disease), N. K. Wenger (Cardiology)
Probssors Emeriti: J. G. Hood, R. H. Wood (Active in 1972–73)
Professors (Clinical): H. S. Alden, J. G. Barrow, T. S. Claiborne, W. L. Dobes, L. H. Hamff, H. N. Hill, H. J. L. Marriott, C. Smith Sr., W. A. Smith
Professor Emeritus (Clinical): A. J. Merrill
Associate Professors: J. C. Ammons (Neurology), J. R. Boring III (Infectious Disease), A. C. Brown (Dermatology), H. E. Brown, G. M. Callaway (Nephrology and Inorganic Metabolism), J. H. Christy (Endocrinology), D. C. Collins (Endocrinology), M. DiGirolamo (Endocrinology), G. F. Fletcher (Cardiology), C. A. Gilbert (Cardiology), W. D. Hall (Nephrology and Inorganic Metabolism), J. E. Hardison (Hematology), J. Jacobs (Hematology), E. J. Macon (Nephrology and Inorganic Metabolism), W. M. Marine (Infectious Disease), D. E. McFarlin (Neurology), A. S. McKinney (Neurology), A. M. McPhedran (Neurology), D. A. Nutter (Cardiology), E. A. Paulk Jr. (Cardiology), H. S. Ramos (Cardiology), J. F. Schwartz (Neurology), P. W. Seavey, J. A. Shulman (Infectious Disease), J. H. Stone III (Cardiology), C. L. Vogel (Hematology and Oncology), R. Vogler (Hematology), J. A. Ward (Endocrinology), C. H. Wilson (Rheumatology)
Associate Professors (Clinical): T. J. Anderson Jr., L. H. Bishop, S. S. Brewer Jr., C. E. Brown, C. D. Burge, E. N. Burson Jr., G. R. Cooper, R. B. Copeland, F. W. Dowda, E. C. Evans, R. M. Fine, M. H. Freedman, W. F. Friedewald, D. D. Hankey, D. E. Hein, D. J. Hughes, L. K. Levy, B. S. Lipman, A. P. McGinty, F. L. Neely, H. Parks, W. H. Reeves, S. L. Rivers, W. P. Sloan, C. F. Stone Jr., H. M. Sturm, P. Teplis, W. C. Waters III, J. A. Wilber, J. S. Wilson, R. B. Wilson, G. C. Woodson Jr.
Assistant Professors: E. A. Bruckner (Hematology), C. D. Cabaniss (Cardiology), D. W. Clark (Cardiology), S. D. Clements (Cardiology), J. C. Coberly, I. S. Crawley (Cardiology), G. M. Duffell (Pulmonary Disease), A. O. Feingold (Ambulatory Care), S. K. Fellner (Nephrology and Inorganic Metabolism), J. A. Goldman (Rheumatology), M. B. Gravanis, B. H. Green-Plauth (Internal Medicine), G. D.

Grossman (Pulmonary Diseases), W. L. Hand (Infectious Disease), Z. H. Israili (Clinical Pharmacology), J. W. Keller (Hematology), S. B. King (Cardiology), J. B. McGowan (Infectious Disease), A. J. Merrill Jr., J. M. Perel (Clinical Pharmacology), A. L. Plummer (Pulmonary Diseases), P. H. Robinson (Cardiology), B. J. Rosenbaum, S. W. Schwarzmann (Infectious Disease), B. D. Silverman (Cardiology), M. E. Silverman (Cardiology), T. Someren (Nephrology and Inorganic Metabolism), F. G. Strauss (Nephrology and Inorganic Metabolism), H. K. Walker (Neurology), P. F. Walter (Cardiology), J. O. Wells (Nephrology and Inorganic Metabolism)

Assistant Professors (Clinical): C. C. Aven, M. P. Berenson, J. N. Berry, T. T. Blalock, H. H. Brill, C. C. Butler, D. C. Chait, R. P. Crank, P. C. Cronce, N. E. Davies, W. S. Dunbar, H. A. Ferris, A. Fiedotin, R. M. Fine, L. Fishman, F. W. Fitzhugh Jr., R. I. Gibbs, H. A. Gussack, B. F. Harper Jr., C. W. Heath Jr., J. W. Hirsch, D. S. Hubbard, C. C. Jones Jr., J. E. Lee, J. G. Leonardy Jr., W. R. Mason Jr., W. B. Mayer, J. B. Minor, Z. V. Morgan Jr., M. V. Murphy, B. B. Nahmias, P. H. Nippert, L. B. Peacock, R. S. Peltz, R. B. Randall, B. D. Saffan, M. G. Schultz, L. R. Scott Jr., S. A. Shmerling, J. deR. Slade, J. S. Staton, H. B. Stillerman, H. W. Swann, L. F. Timberlake, G. B. Upshaw Jr., E. Van Buren, R. L. Whipple Jr., C. L. Whisnant Jr., H. W. Whiteman, H. J. Whyte, J. G. Wilmer, E. Woody, J. T. Yauger

Associates: S. W. Ahn, R. B. Chawla, S. C. Davis Jr.

Associates (Clinical): E. A. Allen, Harold Asher, J. S. Atwater, E. W. Beasley, M. L. Candler, W. R. Crowe, A. H. Davison, J. S. Dodd Jr., L. H. Felder, W. E. Gambrell, J. C. Hall, J. F. Harris, D. L. Hearin, J. H. Hilsman, A. W. Hobby, B. J. Hoffman, R. A. Huie Jr., R. H. Johnson, J. A. Kaufman, M. J. Krainin, S. R. Lathan, H. B. Levin, J. M. McCoy, P. R. Miller Jr., J. M. Monfort, B. W. Moore Jr., C. W. Morse, R. A. Murphy, B. B. Okel, W. L. Paulin Jr., J. L. Rankin, R. A. Reich, C. P. Roberts, C. V. Sanders, C. A. Stuart, W. H. Stuart, D. M. Taylor, N. A. Thornton, A. M. Tornow, J. K. Van Buren, T. S. Winters, B. P. Wolff

Instructors: G. O. Bern, M. L. Carr, E. Hobgood, L. E. Jones, J. D. Kiley, E. Malveaux Sr., T. B. Tjandramaga, R. A. Weaver, L. W. Whatley

Instructors (Clinical): A. H. Abernathy, C. D. Adams, E. K. Adams, E. B. Agnor, P. D. Anderson, J. H. Armstrong, E. T. Avret, M. T. Bailey, E. A. Bancker, C. F. Barnett Jr., D. Berd, M. Berry, J. H. Blalock, A. C. Bleich, M. M. Blumberg, J. B. Blumenthal, E. C. Borden, P. S. Brachman, J. N. Brawner III, L. C. Brown, T. M. Brown Jr., J. A. Broyles III, J. A. Bryan, J. D. Cantwell, S. B. Carter, L. G. Chelton, P. J. Cline, C. P. Cobb Jr., P. G. Cohen, R. A. Cohen, B. F. Conway, H. A. Cooper, J. L. Cooper, L. E. Cooper, W. S. Corrie, L. L. Cotts, T. L. Crews, J. S. Cruise, R. P. Cunningham, C. W. Davidson, W. W. Davis, B. W. Dennis, D. B. Dennison, H. B. Dull, E. M. Dunstan, J. D. Eckstein, M. A. Eidex, S. H. Elson, M. F. Engle, L. E. Falls, E. Fitzpatrick, D. H. Forsyth, L. G. Fortson Jr., R. D. Franco, M. Frank III, C. C. Fulkerson, E. J. Galler, R. J. Gerdes, P. E. Gertler, B. M. Gillett, D. L. Glancy, R. H. Glew, G. C. Goldman, N. I. Goldman, M. I. Goldstein, D. S. Gordon, M. G. Grand, R. L. Green, C. W. Hailey, L. D. Haley, O. E. Hanes, J. H. Harbour, T. Harden Jr., C. T. Harding, C. E. Harrison Jr., C. J. Hatem, D. M. Henshaw, J. A. Hertell, V. N. Houck, W. A. Howard, R. W. Hubbell, W. B. Hudgins, M. A. Jablow, J. L. Jacobs, H. S. Jennings Jr., McC. Johnson Sr., McC. Johnson Jr., R. E. Johnson, I. W. Joines, G. W. Jones, H. S. Kahn, S. H. King, H. W. Kitchin, S. J. Kraus, M. S. Landy Jr., B. G. Lanier, M. I. Lowance, F. S. MacDonell, L. A. Mack, D. M. Mackey, P. MacWilliams, G. E. McCormick, C. F.

McCuiston, G. D. Miller, G. T. Mims Jr., W. R. Minnich, T. P. Monath, M. E. Mostellar, A. M. Oshlag, R. L. Pace, B. H. Palay, D. J. Pirozzi, S. O. Poole, A. M. Pruce, A. H. Randall, F. S. Rhame, P. A. Rice, R. H. Rubin, A. H. Rudolph, R. A. Schmidt A. L. Schroeter, S. H. Schwartz, J. Z. Shanks, J. H. Siegel, J. W. Singer, G. J. Smallberg, R. B. Smiley, C. Smith Jr., R. W. Smith III, W. D. Stribling, A. T. Taylor, J. D. Todino, S. J. Toporoff, D. R. Turner, T. M. Tuthill, G. E. Vanderpool, J. M. Walker, M. J. Wall, R. W. Wallace, J. B. Walter, J. I. Weinberg, E. B. Weisman, J. G. Wells, J. H. West, W. H. Whaley, C. L. Whisnant, R. A. Wiggins, W. S. Wilborn, M. H. Williams, W. T. Williams

Fellows: P. Ahman, J. G. Allee, E. U. Blalock, A. S. Blaustein, A. B. Brady Jr., A. G. Brandau, W. S. Brooks Jr., N. H. Caplan, N. H. Carliner, J. T. Carpenter, G. N. Chant, M. A. Chorches, J. A. Corso, K. A. Dimond, J. S. Douglas, C. T. Durham, J. M. Epstein, J. Felner, M. Fisher, J. E. Francis, J. E. Frazier II, W. Fridy Jr., R. L. Garber, T. Golden, J. H. Hall III, B. D. Harnsberger, N. J. Hart, L. C. Hopkins, J. P. Jones, G. J. Kaplan, D. Karandanis, S. H. Kaufman, C. N. Kelley, M. W. Kilgore, G. Kozma, A. E. Kravitz, J. M. Lesser, C. R. Lobley, E. K. Lominack, D. S. MacLeod, J. N. Mahmoud, D. E. McMartin, C. Moody, J-y Mu, C. A. Perlino, W. C. Pierson, N. A. Price, M. L. Purvis, S. D. Rauch Jr., N. W. Robie, J. Sawaya, M. Shoji, J. Simanis, W. H. Smiley, D. L. Steinberg, R. S. Summers, M. J. Sylvester, S. N. Tewari, M. L. Throne, J. C. Toole, H. W. Wallach, C. N. Williamson, E. F. Winton, S. P. Zimmerman

546   *The Quest for Excellence*

Appendix 42: Bulletin of Emory University School of Medicine, which lists the full-time and clinical volunteer faculty members and fellows of the Department of Medicine in 1975.

MEDICINE

J. W. Hurst, *Professor of Medicine; Chairman of the Department*
Professors: B. W. Cobbs Jr. (Cardiology), C. C. Corley Jr. (Hematology and Oncology), J. C. Crutcher (Pulmonary Disense), J. K. Davidson (Endocrinology), P. G. Dayton (Clinical Pharmacology), E. R. Dorney (Cardiology), R. H. Franch (Cardiology), J. T. Galambos (Digestive Diseases), L. I. Goldberg (Clinical Pharmacology), B. L. Hallman, E. G. Herndon Jr. (Nephrology and Inorganic Metabolism), C. M. Huguley Jr. (Hematology and Oncology), H. R. Karp (Neurology), R. F. Kibler (Neurology), R. B. Logue (Cardiology), J. L. McNay Jr. (Clinical Pharmacology), S. Olansky (Dermatology), J. R. K. Preedy (Endocrinology), D. Rudman (Clinical Research Facility), R. C. Schlant (Cardiology), J. S. Schroder (Digestive Diseases), T. F. Sellers Jr. (Infectious Disense), E. P. Tuttle Jr. (Nephrology and Inorganic Metabolism), J. Wenger (Digestive Diseases), N. K. Wenger (Cardiology)
Professors Emeriti: J. G. Hood, R. H. Wood (Active in 1973–74)
Professors (Clinical): H. S. Alden, J. G. Barrow, T. S. Claiborne, W. L. Dobes, L. H. Hamff, H. J. L. Marriott, C. Smith Sr., W. A. Smith
Professor Emeritus (Clinical): A. J. Merrill
Associate Professors: J. C. Ammons (Neurology), J. R. Boring (Infectious Disease), A. C. Brown (Dermatology), C. D. Cabaniss (Cardiology), G. M. Callaway Jr. (Nephrology and Inorganic Metabolism), J. H. Christy (Endocrinology), D. C. Collins (Endocrinology), M. DiGirolamo (Endocrinology), G. M. Duffell (Pulmonary Disease), G. F. Fletcher (Cardiology), C. A. Gilbert (Cardiology), G. D. Grossman (Pulmonary Disease), W. D. Hall Jr. (Nephrology and Inorganic Metabolism), J. E. Hardison (Hematology and Oncology), T. Hersh (Digestive Disenses), J. Jacobs (Hematology and Oncology), E. J. Macon (Nephrology and Inorganic Metabolism), W. M. Marine (Infectious Disease), D. E. McFarlin (Neurology), A. S. McKinney (Neurology), D. O. Nutter (Cardiology), H. S. Ramos (Cardiology), P. H. Robinson (Cardiology), P. W. Seavey (Ambulatory Medicine), J. F. Schwartz (Neurology), J. A. Shulman (Infectious Disease), M. E. Silverman (Cardiology), J. H. Stone (Ambulatory Medicine), C. L. Vogel (Hematology and Oncology), W. R. Vogler (Hematology and Oncology), J. A. Ward (Endocrinology), C. H. Wilson Jr. (Rheumatology), R. E. Yodaiken (Endocrinology)
Associate Professors (Clinical): T. J. Anderson Jr., L. H. Bishop, S. S. Brewer Jr., C. E. Brown, C. D. Burge, E. N. Burson Jr., G. R. Cooper, R. B. Copeland, F. W. Dowda, E. C. Evans, R. M. Fine, M. H. Freedman, W. F. Friedewald, D. D. Hankey, D. E. Hein, D. J. Hughes, L. K. Levy, B. S. Lipman, A. P. McGinty, F. L. Neely, H. Parks, E. A. Paulk, W. H. Reeves, S. L. Rivers, W. P. Sloan, C. F. Stone Jr., H. M. Sturm, P. Teplis, W. C. Waters III, J. A. Wilber, J. S. Wilson, R. B. Wilson, G. C. Woodson Jr.
Assistant Professors: W. S. Brooks (Digestive Diseases), E. A. Bruckner (Hematology and Oncology), D. L. Camenga (Neurology), N. H. Carliner, D. W. Clark, S. D. Clements (Cardiology), J. C. Coberly (General Medicine), I. S. Crawley (Cardiology), R. S.

Douthard (Ambulatory Medicine), L. J. Elsas (Hematology and Oncology), A. O. Feingold (Ambulatory Medicine), S. K. Fellner (Nephrology and Inorganic Metabolism), J. M. Felner (Cardiology), J. Goldman (Rheumatology), B. H. Greene-Plauth (Ambulatory Medicine), W. L. Hand (Infectious Disease), Z. H. Israili (Clinical Pharmacology), J. W. Keller (Hematology and Oncology), S. B. King (Cardiology), L. R. Kirkland (Ambulatory Medicine), R. C. MacDonell Jr. (Nephrology and Inorganic Metabolism), D. B. McCraw (Cardiology), J. B. McGowan (Infectious Disease), A. J. Merrill Jr. (Cardiology), C. A. Perlino (Infectious Disease), A. L. Plummer (Pulmonary Disease), S. R. Roberts (Pulmonary Disease), B. J. Rosenbaum (Nephrology and Inorganic Metabolism), S. W. Schwarzmann (Infectious Disease), D. C. Silcox (Rheumatology), B. D. Silverman (Cardiology), J. Smith T (Ambulatory Medicine), T. Someren (Nephrology and Inorganic Metabolism), F. G. Strauss (Nephrology and Inorganic Metabolism), H. K. Walker (Neurology), P. F. Walter (Cardiology), R. A. Weaver (Infectious Disease), J. O. Welis (Nephrology and Inorganic Metabolism), L. W. Whatley (Nephrology and Inorganic Metabolism), I. Willis (Dermatology)

Assistant Professors (Clinical): C. C. Aven, M. P. Berenson, J. N. Berry, T. T. Blalock, A. G. Brandau, H. H. Brill, C. C. Butler, D. C. Chait, R. P. Crank, P. C. Cronce, N. E. Davies, W. S. Dunbar, H. A. Ferris, A. Fiedotin, L. Fishman, F. W. Fitzhugh Jr., R. I. Gibbs, D. S. Gordon, H. A. Gussack, B. F. Harper Jr., C. W. Heath Jr., J. W. Hirsch, D. S. Hubbard, C. C. Jones Jr., M. Kozower, J. E. Lee, J. G. Leonardy Jr., W. R. Mason Jr., W. B. Mayer, J. B. Minor, Z. V. Morgan Jr., M. V. Murphy, B. B. Nahmias, P. H. Nippert, L. C. Norins, E. Oran, L. B. Peacock, R. S. Peltz, J. M. Perel, R. B. Randall, B. D. Saffan, M. G. Schultz, L. R. Scott Jr., S. A. Shmerling, J. deR. Slade, J. S. Staton, M. B. Stillerman, J. W. Swann, L. F. Timberlake, C. B. Upshaw Jr., E. Van Buren, R. L. Whipple Jr., C. L. Whisnant Jr., H. W. Whiteman, H. J. Whyte, J. G. Wilmer, E. Woody, J. T. Yauger

Associates: R. K. Chawla, F. C. H. Chou (Neurology), S. C. Davis Jr., N. B. Shulman

Associates (Clinical): E. A. Allen, Harold Asher, J. S. Atwater, E. W. Beasley, M. L. Candler, W. R. Crowe, A. H. Davison, J. S. Dodd Jr., L. H. Felder, W. E. Gambrell, J. C. Hall, J. F. Harris, D. L. Hearin, J. H. Hilsman, A. W. Hobby, B. J. Hoffman, R. A. Huie Jr., R. H. Johnson, J. A. Kaufman, M. J. Krainin, S. R. Lathan, H. B. Levin, J. M. McCoy, P. R. Miller Jr., J. M. Monfort, B. W. Moore Jr., C. W. Morse, R. A. Murphy, B. B. Okel, W. L. Paulin Jr., J. L. Rankin, R. A. Reich, C. P. Roberts, C. V. Sanders, C. A. Stuart, W. H. Stuart, D. M. Taylor, N. A. Thornton, A. M. Tornow, J. K. Van Buren T. S. Winters, B. P. Wolff

Instructors: J. G. Allee, J. A. Broyles III, R. F. Cunningham, J. B. DuBose, S. B. Heymsfield, L. E. Jones, J. N. Mahmoud, E. J. Malveaux Sr., C. M. Rogers, M. Shoji, S. A. Wohlgemuth

Instructors (Clinical): A. H. Abernathy, C. D. Adams, E. K. Adams, E. B. Agnor, P. D. Anderson, J. H. Armstrong, E. T. Avret, M. T. Bailey, E. A. Bancker, C. F. Barnett Jr., G. O. Bern, M. Berry, J. H. Blalock, A. C. Bleich, M. M. Blumberg, J. B. Blumenthal, E. C. Borden, P. S. Brachman, J. N. Brawner III, T. M. Brown Jr., J. A. Bryan, J. D. Cantwell, S. B. Carter, L. C. Chelton, P. J. Cline, C. P. Cobb Jr., P. G. Cohen, R. A. Cohen, B. F. Conway, D. L. Cooper, H. A. Cooper, J. L. Cooper, L. E. Cooper, W. S. Corrie, L. L. Cotts, T. L. Crews, J. S. Cruise, R. P. Cunningham, C. W. Davidson, W. W. Davis, B. W. Dennis, D. B. Dennison, W. L. Dobes Jr., H. B. Dull, E. M.

Dunstan, J. D. Eckstein, M. A. Eidex, S. H. Elson, M. F. Engle, L. E. Falls, L. K. Feinerman, D. J. Filip, E. Fitzpatrick, D. H. Forsyth, L. G. Fortson Jr., R. D. Franco, M. Frank III, C. C. Fulkerson, E. J. Galler, R. J. Gerdes, P. E. Gertler, B. M. Gillett, D. L. Glancy, R. H. Glew, G. C. Goldman, N. I. Goldman, M. I. Goldstein, M. G. Grand, R. L. Green, C. W. Hailey, L. D. Haley, O. E. Hanes, J. H. Harbour, T. Harden Jr., C. T. Harding, C. E. Harrison Jr., C. J. Hatem, D. M. Henshaw, J. A. Hertell, V. N. Houck, W. A. Howard, R. W. Hubbell, W. B. Hudgins, M. A. Jablow, J. L. Jacobs, N. F. Jacobs, H. S. Jennings Jr., McC. Johnson Sr., R. E. Johnson, I. W. Joines, G. W. Iones, H. S. Kahn, R. E. Kaufman, E. C. Kelly III, S. H. King, H. W. Kitchin, R. H. Koenig, T. E. Kohn, A. E. Kravitz, G. D. Kumin, M. S. Landy Jr., B. G. Lanier, D. C. Lowance, M. I. Lowance, F. S. MacDonell, P. MacWilliams, G. E. McCormick, C. F. McCuiston, F. M. Melewicz, G. D. Miller, G. T. Mims Jr., W. R. Minnich, T. P. Monath, M. E. Mostellar, A. M. Oshlag, R. L. Pace, B. H. Palay, S. O. Poole, A. M. Pruce, F. C. Rabb, A. H. Randali, R. K. Re, F. S. Rhame, N. W. Robie, R. H. Rubin, A. H. Rudolph, R. A. Schmidt, J. Z. Shanks, A. H. Shaw, J. H. Siegel, R. B. Smiley, C. Smith Jr., R. W. Smith III, D. R. Stickney, W. D. Stribling, M. L. Throne, J. D. Todino, S. J. Toporoff, D. R. Turner, T. M. Tuthill, G. E. Vanderpool, J. M. Walker, M. J. Wall, R. W. Wallace, J. B. Walter, J. I. Weinberg, E. B. Weisman, J. G. Wells, J. H. West, W. H. Whaley, C. L. Whisnant, R. A. Wiggins, W. S. Wilborn, M. H. Williams, W. T. Williams

Fellows: G. T. Abernathy, C. W. Anderson, W. R. Back, E. U. Blalock, T. T. Blalock Jr., R. M. Boozer, W. S. Brooks, D. R. Butcher, R. A. Calloway, M. L. Carr, N. G. Chant, M. A. Chorches, E. H. Coe, J. Correa, J. A. Corso, J. Z. Davids, D. W. DeBra Jr., J. S. Douglas, D. P. DuBois, C. T. Durham, K. Ehanispoor, J. Epstein, J. S. Fantz, R. P. Foa, J. E. Francis, E. D. Harnsberger, J. G. Harris, S. P. Harwood, R. L. Haynes, L. T. Hefner, N. Holtz, L. C. Hopkins, J. P. Jones, L. J. Kanter, G. J. Kaplan, D. Karandanis, M. W. Kilgore, G. Kozma, L. M. Lesser, J. L. Lokey, D. S. MacLeod, K. M. Michaelides, H. G. Mond, C. L. Moody, D. C. Morris, J. B. Oak, R. D. Oakley, H. W. Overbeck, J. A. Payne, J. R. Pine, S. D. Rauch, G. M. Rich, D. Schlossberg, D. A. Siddiqui, W. H. Smiley, M. R. Sorrell, R. S. Summers, M. J. Sylvester A. I. Taranto, S. E. Thompson III, S. C. Tindall, J. C. Toole. F. G. Vincenti, A. Vissy, D. D. Waters, C. W. Wickliffe, E. F. Winton, R. L. Wolfson, S. A. Zendel, S. R. Zimmerman

Appendix 43: Bulletin of Emory University School of Medicine, which lists the full-time and clinical volunteer faculty members and fellows of the Department of Medicine in 1976.

MEDICINE

J. W. Hurst, *Professor of Medicine; Chairman of the Department*

Professors: B. W. Cobbs Jr. (Cardiology), C. C. Corley Jr. (Hematology and Oncology), J. C. Crutcher (Pulmonary Disease), J. K. Davidson (Endocrinology), P. G. Dayton (Clinical Pharmacology), E. R. Dorney (Cardiology), R. H. Franch (Cardiology), J. T. Galambos (Digestive Diseases), C. A. Gilbert (Cardiology), B. L. Hallman, E. G. Herndon Jr., (Nephrology and Inorganic Metabolism), Theodore Hersh (Digestive Diseases), C. M. Huguley Jr. (Hematology and Oncology), H. R. Karp (Neurology), R. F. Kibler (Neurology), R. B. Logue (Cardiology), D. O. Nutter (Cardiology), S. Olansky (Dermatology), J. R. K. Preedy (Endocrinology), D. Rudman (Clinical Research Facility), R. C. Schlant (Cardiology), J. S. Schroder (Digestive Diseases), T. F. Sellers Jr. (Infectious Disease), J. A. Shulman (Infectious Disease), E. P. Tuttle Jr. (Nephrology and Inorganic Metabolism), J. Wenger (Digestive Diseases), N. K. Wenger (Cardiology), C. H. Wilson (Rheumatology)

Professors Emeriti: J. G. Hood, R. H. Wood (Active in 1974–75)

Professors (Clinical): H. S. Alden, J. C. Barrow, T. S. Claiborne, W. L. Dobes, L. H. Hamff, H. J. L. Marriott, C. Smith Sr., W. A. Smith

Professor Emeritus (Clinical): A. J. Merrill

Associate Professors: J. C. Ammons (Neurology), J. R. Boring (Infectious Disease), C. D. Cabaniss (Cardiology), G. M. Callaway Jr. (Nephrology and Inorganic Metabolism), J. H. Christy (Endocrinology), D. C. Collins (Endocrinology), I. S. Crawley (Cardiology), M. DiGirolamo (Endocrinology), G. M. Duffell (Pulmonary Disease), G. F. Fletcher (Cardiology), G. D. Grossman (Pulmonary Disease), W. D. Halt Jr. (Nephrology and Inorganic Metabolism), W. L. Hand (Infectious Disease), J. E. Hardison (Hematology and Oncology), Z. H. Israili (Clinical Pharmacology), J. Jacobs (Hematology and Oncology), H. R. Kann (Hematology), E. J. Macon (Nephrology and Inorganic Metabolism), W. M. Marine (Infectious Disease), A. S. McKinney (Neurology), M. R. Moore (Hematology), H. S. Ramos (Cardiology), P. H. Robinson (Cardiology), P. W. Seavey (Ambulatory Medicine), J. F. Schwartz (Neurology), N. B. Shulman (Nephrology and Inorganic Metabolism), M. E. Silverman (Cardiology), J. H. Stone (Ambulatory Medicine), C. L. Vogel (Hematology and Oncology), W. R. Vogler (Hematology and Oncology), H. K. Walker (Neurology), P. F. Walter (Cardiology), J. A. Ward (Endocrinology), R. G. Yodaiken

Associate Professors (Clinical): T. J. Anderson Jr., L. H. Bishop, S. S. Brewer Jr., C. E. Brown, C. D. Burge, E. N. Burson Jr., G. R. Cooper, R. B. Copeland, F. W. Dowda, E. C. Evans, R. M. Fine, M. H. Freedman, W. F. Friedewald, D. D. Hankey, D. E. Hein, A. L. Hitzelberger, D. J. Hughes, L. K. Levy, B. S. Lipman, A. P. McGinty, F. L. Neely, H. Parks, E. A. Paulk, W. H. Reeves, S. L. Rivers, W. P. Sloan, C. F. Stone Jr., H. M. Sturm, P. Teplis, W. C. Waters III, J. A. Wilber, J. S. Wilson, R. B. Wilson, G. C. Woodson Jr.

Assistant Professors: W. S. Brooks (Digestive Diseases), J. A. Broyles (Dermatology), D. L. Camenga (Neurology), R. K. Chawla (Clinical Research Facility), S. D. Clements (Cardiology), J. C. Coberly (General Medicine), J. S. Douglas (Cardiology), R. S. Douthard (Ambulatory Medicine), J. B. DuBose III (General Medicine), L. J. Elsas (Hematology and Oncology), A. O. Feingold (Ambulatory Medicine), P. B. Francis, S. K. Fellner (Nephrology and Inorganic Metabolism), J. M. Felner (Cardiology), M. F. Gentry (General Medicine), J. A. Goldman (Rheumatology), B. H. Greene-Plauth (Ambulatory Medicine), L. T. Heffner (Hematolgy), L. C. Hopkins (Neurology), J. W. Keller (Hematology and Oncology), C. M. Kim (Ambulatory Medicine), S. B. King (Cardiology), L. R. Kirkland (Ambulatory Medicine), R. C. MacDonell Jr. (Nephrology and Inorganic Metabolism), D. B. McCraw (Cardiology), J. R. McGowan (Infectious Disease), W. R. Mason (General Medicine), A. J. Merrill Jr. (Cardiology), D. C. Morris (Cardiology), P. I. Musey (Endocrinology), C. W. Oettinger III (Infectious Disease), K. O'Malley (Clinical Pharmacology), A. L. Plummer (Pulmonary Disease), S. R. Roberts (Pulmonary Disease), B. J. Rosenbaum (Nephrology and Inorganic Metabolism), S. W. Schwarzmann (Infectious Disease), M. Shoji (Clinical Research Facility), B. D. Silverman (Cardiology), J. Smith T (Ambulatory Medicine), T. Someren (Nephrology and Inorganic Metabolism), R. A. Weaver (Infectious Disease), J. O. Wells (Nephrology and Inorganic Metabolism), L. W. Whatley (Nephrology and Inorganic Metabolism), C. W. Wickliffe (Cardiology), P. J. Wiesner, W. S. Wilborn, I. Willis (Dermatology), E. F. Winton (Hematology and Oncology)

Assistant Professors (Clinical): C. C. Aven, M. P. Berenson, J. N. Berry, T. T. Blalock, J. M. Bradford (Biomedical Engineering), A. G. Brandau, H. H. Brill, C. C. Butler, M. D. Byrd, N. H. Carliner, D. C. Chait, R. P. Crank, P. C. Cronce, N. E. Davies, W. S. Dunbar, H. A. Ferris, A. Fiedotin, L. Fishman, F. W. Fitzhugh Jr., R. I. Gibbs Jr., D. S. Gordon, H. A. Gussack, L. D. Haley, R. F. Hansen, B. F. Harper Jr., C. W. Heath Jr., J. W. Hirsch, K. A. Hoose, D. S. Hubbard, C. C. Jones Jr., J. R. Karansky, M. Kozower, J. E. Lee, J. G. Leonardy Jr., W. C. Maloy, W. B. Mayer, J. B. Minor, Z. V. Morgan Jr., M. V. Murphy, B. B. Nahmias, P. H. Nippert, L. C. Norins, E. Oran, L. B. Peacock, R. S. Peltz, J. M. Perel, R. B. Randall, M. J. Ravry, B. D. Saffan, M. G. Schultz, L. R. Scott Jr., P. K. Shaw, S. A. Shmerling, J. deR. Slade, J. S. Staton, M. B. Stillerman, J. W. Swann, L. F. Timberlake, C. B. Upshaw Jr., E. Van Buren, R. L. Whipple Jr., C. L. Whisnant Jr., H. W. Whiteman, H. J. Whyte, J. G. Wilmer, E. Woody, J. T. Yauger

Associates: C. S. Chou (Neurology), F. C. H. Chou (Neurology), S. C. Davis Jr., S. B. Heymsfield

Associates (Clinical): E. A. Allen, Harold Asher, J. S. Atwater, E. W. Beasley, M. L. Candler, W. R. Crowe, A. H. Davison, J. S. Dodd Jr., L. H. Felder, W. E. Gambrell, J. C. Hall, J. F. Harris, D. L. Hearin J. H. Hilsman, A. W. Hobby, B. J. Hoffman, R. A. Huie Jr., R. H. Johnson, J. A. Kaufman, M. J. Krainin, S. R. Lathan, H. B. Levin, J. M. McCoy, P. R. Miller Jr., J. M. Monfort, B. W. Moore Jr., C. W. Morse, R. A. Murphy, B. B. Okel, W. L. Paullin Jr., J. L. Rankin, R. A. Reich, C. P. Roberts, C. V. Sanders, C. A. Stuart, W. H. Stuart, D. M. Taylor, N. A. Thornton, A. M. Tornow, J. K. Van Buren, T. S. Winter, B. P. Wolff

Instructors: R. Atluri, R. F. Cunningham, J. Z. Davids, L. E. Falls, V. R. Harrell, E. P. Hobgood, L. E. Jones, H. S. Kahn, E. J. Malveaux, J. W. Mier, D. H. Murphree, M. F. Olansky, C. M. Rogers, W. W. Walker, R. L. Whipple III, J. A. Whitaker III, A. A. Zaki
Instructors (Clinical): A. H. Abernathy, C. D. Adams, E. K. Adams, E. B. Agnor, P. D. Anderson, J. H. Armstrong, E. T. Avret, M. T. Bailey, C. F. Barnett Jr., G. O. Bern, M. Berry, J. H. Blalock, A. C. Bleich, M. M. Blumberg, J. B. Blumenthal, E. C. Borden, P. S. Brachman, J. N. Brawner III, J. A. Bryan, D. M. Burns, J. D. Cantwell, S. B. Carter, L. C. Chelton, P. J. Cline, J. O. Clune, C. P. Cobb Jr., P. G. Cohen, R. A. Cohen, D. L. Cooper, H. A. Cooper, J. L. Cooper, L. E. Cooper, L. L. Cotts, T. L. Crews, J. S. Cruise, R. P. Cunningham, C. W. Davidson, W. W. Davis, D. W. DeBra, B. W. Dennis, D. B. Dennison, W. L. Dobes Jr., H. B. Dull, E. M. Dunstan J. D. Eckstein, M. A. Eidex, S. H. Elson, M. F. Engle, L. K. Feinerman, D. J. Filip, E. Fitzpatrick, D. H. Forsyth, L. G. Fortson Jr., R. D. Franco, M. Frank III, E. J. Galler, R. J. Gerdes, P. E. Gertler, B. M. Gillett, D. E. Girard, D. L. Glancy, R. H. Glew, T. D. Golden, G. C. Goldman, N. I. Goldman, M. I. Goldstein, R. L. Green, C. W. Hailey, O. E. Hanes, J. H. Harbour, T. Harden Jr., C. T. Harding, C. E. Harrison Jr., C. J. Hatem, D. M. Henshaw, J. A. Hertell, V. N. Houck, R. W. Hubbell, W. B. Hudgins, M. A. Jablow, J. L. Jacobs, N. F. Jacobs, H. S. Jennings Jr., McC. Johnson Sr., R. E. Johnson, I. W. Joines, G. W. Jones, R. E. Kaufman, E. C. Kelly III, H. W. Kitchin, R. H. Koenig, A. E. Kravits, G. D. Kumin, M. S. Landy Jr., B. G. Lanier, D. C. Lowance, M. I. Lowance, F. S. MacDonell, P. MacWilliams, G. E. McCormick, C. F. McCuiston, F. M. Melewicz, G. D. Miller, G. T. Mims Jr., W. R. Minnich, T. P. Monath, M. E. Mostellar, A. M. Oshlag, R. L. Pace, B. H. Palay, S. O. Poole, A. M. Pruce, F. C. Rabb, A. H. Randall Jr., R. K. Re, F. S. Rhame, R. H. Rubin, A. H. Rudolph, R. M. Schmidt, J. Z. Shanks, A. H. Shaw, J. H. Siegel, R. B. Smiley Jr., C. Smith Jr., R. W. Smith III, D. R. Stickney, W. D. Stribling, M. L. Throne, S. C. Tindall, J. D. Todino, S. J. Toporoff, D. R. Turner, T. M. Tuthill. G. E. Vanderpool, J. M. Walker, M. J. Wall, R. W. Wallace, J. B. Walter. J. I. Weinberg, J. G. Wells, J. H. West, W. H. Whaley, R. A. Wiggins, M. H. Williams, W. T. Williams
Fellows: G. T. Abernathy, S. J. Alexander, C. W. Anderson, R. A. Bardack, P. J. Barry, B. N. Basuray, W. N. Bloch Jr., R. J. Brooker, T. M. Brown Jr., D. R. Butcher, J. A. Chiapella, S. P. Childress, R. D. Cohen, C. A. Droulias, D. P. DuBois, A. M. A. Faruqui, G. P. Fisher, R. P. Foa, J. E. Freschi, J. H. Gilliam III, R. W. Goldstein, L. S. Goodman, S. S. Hartman, S. P. Harwood, L. A. J. Higginson, N. Holtz, J. T. Horney, J. W. Hurst Jr., G. J. Kaplan, G. L. Karcioglu, W. R. Kenney, S. P. Kottle, G. Kozma, L. M. Lesser, A. M. Levine, H. H. Lopez, D. A. Lowe, J. L. McCans, C. A. McConnell, B. Maniscalco, O. P. Matthews Jr., K. M. Michaelides, D. C. Morris, R. S. Morse, W. J. Nicholson, M. A. Norman, J. B. Oak, W. A. Olson, C. A. Osmon, J. R. Pine, K. H. K. Piyasena, K. O. Rees, G. M. Rich, D. Schlossberg, J. L. Segal, J. A. Settle Jr., C. Sillipat, M. Sorrell, M. J. Sylvester, A. I. Taranto, P. N. Temsey-Armos, S. E. Thompson III, N. Vicuna-Fernandez, F. G. Vincente, S. Wallace, D. D. Waters, F. J. Wierichs Jr., S. A. Zendel

Appendix 44: Bulletin of Emory University School of Medicine, which lists the full-time and clinical volunteer faculty members and fellows of the Department of Medicine in 1977.

MEDICINE

J. W. Hurst, *Professor of Medicine; Chairman of the Department*

Professors: J. H. Christy (Endocrinology), B. W. Cobbs Jr. (Cardiology), C. C. Corley Jr. (Hematology and Oncology), J. C. Crutcher (Pulmonary Diseases), J. K. Davidson (Endocrinology), P. G. Dayton (Clinical Pharmacology), M. DiGirolamo (Endocrinology), E. R. Dorney (Cardiology), G. F. Fletcher (Cardiology), R. H. Franch (Cardiology), J. T. Galambos (Digestive Diseases), C. A. Gilbert (Cardiology), B. L. Hallman (General Medicine), E. G. Herndon Jr. (Nephrology and Inorganic Metabolism), T. Hersh (Digestive Diseases), C. M. Huguley Jr. (Hematology and Oncology), R. B. Logue (Cardiology), D. O. Nutter (Cardiology), S. Olansky (Dermatology), J. R. K. Preedy (Endocrinology), H. S. Ramos (Cardiology), D. Rudman (Clinical Research Facility/Nutrition), R. C. Schlant (Cardiology), J. S. Schroder (Digestive Diseases), T. F. Sellers Jr. (Infectious Diseases), J. A. Shulman (Infectious Diseases), E. P. Tuttle Jr. (Nephrology and Inorganic Metabolism), John A. Ward (Endocrinology), J. Wenger (Digestive Diseases), N. K. Wenger (Cardiology), C. H. Wilson Jr. (Rheumatology)

Professors Emeriti: J. G. Hood, R. H. Wood (Active in 1976–77)

Professors (Clinical): H. S. Alden, J. G. Barrow, L. H. Bishop Jr., L. H. Hamff, H. J. L. Marriott, H. Parks, C. Smith Sr., L. W. Sullivan, J. W. Sweeney

Professors Emeriti (Clinical): T. S. Claiborne, J. C. Massee, A. J. Merrill Sr.

Associate Professors: J. R. Boring (Infectious Diseases), G. M. Callaway Jr. (Nephrology and Inorganic Metabolism), D. C. Collins (Endocrinology), I. S. Crawley (Cardiology), G. M. Duffell (Pulmonary Diseases), S. K. Fellner (Nephrology and Inorganic Metabolism), G. D. Grossman (Pulmonary Diseases), W. D. Hall Jr. (Nephrology and Inorganic Metabolism), W. L. Hand (Infectious Diseases), J. E. Hardison (Hematology and Oncology), Z. H. Israili (Clinical Pharmacology), J. Jacobs (Hematology and Oncology), H. E. Kann Jr. (Hematology and Oncology), S. B. King III (Cardiology), E. J. Macon (Nephrology and Inorganic Metabolism), A. L. Plummer (Pulmonary Diseases), P. H. Robinson (Cardiology), P. W. Seavey, M. E. Silverman (Cardiology), J. H. Stone III, W. R. Vogler (Hematology and Oncology), H. K. Walker (Neurology), P. F. Walter (Cardiology), J. O. Wells (Nephrology and Inorganic Metabolism), I. Willis (Dermatology)

Associate Professors (Clinical): T. J. Anderson Jr., J. N. Berry, S. S. Brewer Jr., C. E. Brown, C. D. Burge, E. N. Burson Jr., C. D. Cabaniss, G. R. Cooper, R. B. Copeland, N. E. Davies, F. W. Dowda, E. C. Evans, A. Fiedotin, R. M. Fine, M. H. Freedman, W. F. Friedewald, D. D. Hankey, B. F. Harper Jr., D. E. Hein, A. L. Hitzelberger, D. J. Hughes, B. S. Lipman, A. P. McGinty, F. L. Neely, E. A. Paulk, W. H. Reeves, S. L. Rivers, W. P. Sloan, J. S. Staton, C. F. Stone Jr., H. M. Sturm, P. Teplis, C. Upshaw Jr., W. C. Waters III, J. A. Wilber, J. S. Wilson, G. C. Woodson Jr.

Associate Professor Emeritus (Clinical): L. K. Levy

Assistant Professors: B. A. Blumenstein, J. M. Bradford (Pulmonary Diseases), W. S. Brooks Jr. (Digestive Diseases), S. Chang (Cardiology), R. K. Chawla (Clinical Research Facility/Nutrition), S. D. Clements Jr. (Cardiology), J. del Mazo (Digestive Diseases), J. S. Douglas Jr. (Cardiology), R. S. Douthard, A. G. Dunston, L. J. Elsas II (Medical Genetics), A. O. Feingold, J. M. Felner (Cardiology), P. B. Francis (Pulmonary Diseases), M. F. Gentry, J. A. Goldman (Rheumatology), M. B. Gravanis, B. H. Greene-Plauth, L. T. Heffner Jr. (Hematology and Oncology), S. B. Heymsfield (Clinical Research Facility/Nutrition), E. L. Hochgelerent (Nephrology and Inorganic Metabolism), H. Jinich (Digestive Diseases), L. E. Jones, D. Karandanis, J. W. Keller (Hematology and Oncology), C. M. Kim, L. R. Kirkland, R. C. MacDonell Jr. (Nephrology and Inorganic Metabolism), W. R. Mason, J. E. McGowan Jr. (Infectious Diseases), A. J. Merrill Jr. (Cardiology), M. R. Moore (Hematology and Oncology), D. C. Morris (Cardiology), P. I. Musey (Endocrinology), D. W. Nixon (Hematology and Oncology), C. W. Oettinger II (Nephrology and Inorganic Metabolism), C. A. Perlino (Infectious Diseases), D. J. Pirozzi (Dermatology), C. M. Rogers, B. J. Rosenbaum (Nephrology and Inorganic Metabolism), S. W. Schwarzmann (Infectious Diseases), N. B. Shulman (Nephrology and Inorganic Metabolism), B. D. Silverman (Cardiology), T. Someren (Nephrology and Inorganic Metabolism), S. F. Stein (Hematology and Oncology), R. A. Weaver (Infectious Diseases), L. W. Whatley (Nephrology and Inorganic Metabolism), W. S. Wilborn, E. F. Winton (Hematology and Oncology)

Assistant Professors (Clinical): J. T. Apgar, H. Asher, C. C. Aven, R. A. Bardack, M. P. Berenson, J. G. Black, T. T. Blalock, J. B. Blumenthal, A. G. Brandau, H. H. Brill, J. A. Broyles III, C. C. Butler, M. D. Byrd, S. B. Carter Jr., H. L. Casey, D. C. Chait, R. P. Crank, T. L. Crews, P. C. Cronce, R. C. Davis Jr., W. S. Dunbar, M. J. Duttera Jr., P. D. Espy, L. S. Feinsmith, L. Fishman, F. W. Fitzhugh Jr., D. H. Forsyth, M. Frank III, R. I. Gibbs Jr., G. J. Giesler Jr., D. S. Gordon, H. A. Gussack, L. D. Haley, J. C. Hall, R. F. Hansen, C. W. Heath Jr., J. W. Hirsch, K. E. Holtzapple, K. A. Hoose, D. S. Hubbard, C. C. Jones Jr., R. H. Kelleher, J. R. Koransky, M. Kozower, J. G. Leonardy Jr., W. C. Maloy, G. C. Miller, J. B. Minor, Z. V. Morgan Jr., M. V. Murphy Jr., B. B. Nahmias, P. H. Nippert, L. C. Norins, R. J. O'Brien, E. Oran, L. B. Peacock, R. S. Peltz, V. T. Peng, J. M. Perel, B. F. Pike, R. B. Randall, M. J. R. Ravry, P. J. Rodzewicz, C. M. Rogers, W. E. Rogers, T. J. Romano, R. W. Ryder, B. D. Saffan, C. V. Sanders, M. G. Schultz, N. H. Schwartz, L. R. Scott Jr., P. K. Shaw, S. A. Shmerling, D. C. Silcox, G. B. Skipworth, J. DeR. Slade, R. C. Slaton, C. Smith Jr., J. Smith T, D. L. Steinberg, J. R. Stone, J. W. Swann, S. L. Swartz, D. M. Taylor, M. V. Teem, S. E. Thompson III, L. F. Timberlake, E. B. Weisman, C. L. Whisnant Jr., H. J. Whyte, C. W. Wickliffe, P. J. Wiesner, E. Woody Jr., J. T. Yauger

Assistant Professor Emeritus (Clinical): E. M. Dunstan

Associates: S. C. Davis Jr., A. A. Zaki

Associates (Clinical): E. A. Allen, J. S. Atwater, E. W. Beasley Jr., M. L. Candler, W. R. Crowe, A. H. Davison, J. S. Dodd Jr., L. H. Felder, W. E. Gambrell, J. F. Harris, D. L. Hearin, J. H. Hilsman Jr., A. W. Hobby, B. J. Hoffman, R. A. Huie Jr., R. H. Johnson, J. A. Kaufman, M. J. Krainin, S. R. Lathan, H. B. Levin, J. M. McCoy, P. R. Miller Jr., J. M. Monfort, B. W. Moore Jr., C. W. Morse, R. A. Murphy Jr., B. B. Okel, W. L. Paullin Jr., J. L. Rankin, R. A. Reich, E. J. Reiner, C. P. Roberts, C. A. Stuart, N. A. Thornton, A. M. Tornow, E. Van Buren, J. K. Van Buren, T. S. Winter III, B. P. Wolff

554 *The Quest for Excellence*

Instructors: R. F. Cunningham (Clinical Pharmacology), A. G. Dunston, L. E. Falls (Rheumatology), S. S. Hethumuni, E. Hobgood (Endocrinology), E. J. Malveaux (Clinical Pharmacology), R. L. Mars, K. M. Michaelides (Digestive Diseases), J. W. Mier, C. L. Miklozek, D. H. Murphree, M. F. Olansky, F. Rodriguez, W. W. Walker, D. M. Webb, R. L. Whipple III

Instructors (Clinical): A. H. Abernathy III, C. D. Adams, E. K. Adams, E. B. Agnor, P. D. Anderson, S. Arnon, E. T. Avret, M. T. Bailey, C. F. Barnett Jr., H. J. Baskin, G. O. Bern, M. Berry, J. H. Blalock, A. C. Bleich, L. Blonde, M. M. Blumberg, E. C. Borden, P. S. Brachman, J. N. Brawner III, J. A. Bryan, P. Bunvasaranand, D. M. Burns, A. E. Buxton, J. D. Cantwell, S. B. Carter Sr., L. G. Chelton, M. A. Chorches, P. J. Cline, J. O. Clune, C. P. Cobb Jr., P. G. Cohen, R. A. Cohen, D. L. Cooper, H. A. Cooper, J. L. Cooper, L. E. Cooper, L. L. Cotts, J. S. Cruise, R. P. Cunningham, C. W. Davidson, W. W. Davis, D. W. DeBra, B. W. Dennis, D. B. Dennison, W. L. Dobes Jr., H. B. Dull, E. M. Dunstan, M. A. Eidex, S. H. Elson, M. F. Engel, L. K. Feinerman, P. E. Fitzpatrick, L. G. Fortson Jr., E. J. Galler, R. J. Gerdes, P. E. Gertler, D. E. Girard, D. L. Glancy, R. H. Glew, T. D. Golden, G. C. Goldman, N. I. Goldman, M. I. Goldstein, R. L. Green, B. Hafkin, C. W. Hailey, R. W. Haley, O. E. Hanes, J. H. Harbour, T. Harden Jr., C. E. Harrison Jr., C. J. Hatem, M. A. W. Hattwick, D. M. Henshaw, J. A. Hertell, C. H. Hoke, V. N. Houck, R. W. Hubbell, W. B. Hudgins, M. A. Jablow, J. L. Jacobs, N. F. Jacobs Jr., H. S. Jennings Jr., M. Johnson Sr., R. E. Johnson, I. W. Joines II, G. W. Jones Jr., R. E. Kaufman. E. C. Kelly III, K. R. Kennedy, H. W. Kitchin, G. S. Kleris, G. D. Kumin, M. S. Landy Jr., B. G. Lanier, D. C. Lowance, M. I. Lowance, F. S. MacDonell, P. MacWilliams, G. E. McCormick Jr., C. F. McCuiston, F. M. Melewicz, G. D. Miller, G. T. Mims Jr., M. E. Mostellar, A. M. Oshlag, R. L. Pace, L. G. Pack, B. H. Palay, S. O. Poole, A. M. Pruce, F. C. Rabb, A. H. Randall Jr., V. L. Randolph, F. S. Rhame, R. H. Rubin, A. H. Rudolph, M. J. Safra, R. M. Schmidt, J. Z. Shanks, A. H. Shaw, J. H. Siegel, R. B. Smiley Jr., R. W. Smith III, D. R. Stickney, W. D. Stribling III, D. W. Thompson, M. L. Throne, J. D. Todino, S. J. Toporoff, D. R. Turner, T. M. Tuthill, G. E. Vanderpool, M. J. Wall, J. B. Walter, J. I. Weinberg, J. G. Wells, J. H. West, W. H. Whaley, R. A. Wiggins, M. H. Williams, W. T. Williams

Instructor Emeritus (Clinical): C. W. Strickler Jr.

Research Associates: P. R. Garrett, G. L. Karcioglu, C. A. Osmon

Fellows: D. M. Ackerman, F. M. Alimurung, D. Arensberg, R. S. Arnold, F. J. Barry, M. R. Beard, W. N. Bloch Jr., J. J. Boylan, D. S. Brandenburg, J. A. Bretza, H. J. Brody, R. J. Brooker, T. M. Brown Jr., B. A. Cassidy, J. F. Cotant Jr., J. A. Drummond, A. M. Faruqui, R. W. Goldstein, L. S. Goodman, H. Hayashi, G. D. Hethumuni, L. A. Higginson, E. C. Honig, J. T. Horney, J. W. Hurst Jr., K. K. Joshi, W. B. Kelley, W. R. Kenny, G. M. Krisle III, D. J. Little, H. H. Lopez, D. A. Lowe, J. F. Lutz, D. H. Magill III, O. P. Matthews Jr., G. A. Micheletti Jr., J. S. Miller, V. C. Musey, M F. Nathan, W. J. Nicholson, D. E. Noble, W. A. Olson, D. B. Pakkala, G. B. Pelletier, J. R. Pine, K. H. Piyasena, J. H. Poehlman, K. O. Rees, D. Rimland, W. G. Rogers, J. A. Settle Jr., W. P. Stallings, F. D. Stegall, D. L. Tedrick, L. C. Teixeira, P. N. Temsey-Armos, R. C. Terrill, J. A. Walker, S. W. Wallace, M. L. Westphal, J. A. Whitaker III, J. O. White, R. C. Woodward, C. L. Yarbrough

Appendix 45: Bulletin of Emory University School of Medicine, which lists the full-time and clinical volunteer faculty members and fellows of the Department of Medicine in 1978.

MEDICINE

J. W. Hurst, *Professor of Medicine; Chairman of the Department*

Professors: J. H. Christy (Endocrinology), D. C. Collins* (Endocrinology), B. W. Cobbs Jr. (Cardiology), C. C. Corley Jr. (Hematology and Oncology), J. C. Crutcher* (Pulmonary Diseases), J. K. Davidson (Endocrinology), P. G. Dayton (Clinical Pharmacology), M. DiGirolamo (Endocrinology), E. R. Dorney (Cardiology), G. F. Fletcher (Cardiology), R. H. Franch* (Cardiology), J. T. Galambos (Digestive Diseases), C. A. Gilbert (Cardiology), W. D. Hall (Hypertension), B. L. Hallman* (General Medicine), E. G. Herndon Jr.* (Nephrology and Inorganic Metabolism), T. Hersh (Digestive Diseases), C. M. Huguley Jr. (Hematology and Oncology), R. B. Logue (Cardiology), D. O. Nutter* (Cardiology), S. Olansky (Dermatology), J. R. K. Preedy* (Endocrinology), H. S. Ramos* (Cardiology), D. Rudman* (Clinical Research Facility/Nutrition), R. C. Schlant (Cardiology), J. S. Schroder (Digestive Diseases), T. F. Sellers Jr.* (Infectious Diseases), J. A. Shulman* (Infectious Diseases), J. H. Stone III* (General Medicine), E. P. Tuttle Jr. (Nephrology and Inorganic Metabolism), J. A. Ward (Endocrinology), J. Wenger (Digestive Diseases), N. K. Wenger (Cardiology), C. H. Wilson Jr.* (Rheumatology)

Professors Emeriti: J. G. Hood, R. H. Wood*

Professors (Clinical): H. S. Alden, J. G. Barrow, L. H. Bishop Jr., L. H. Hamff, B. S. Lipman, H. J. L. Marriott, H. Parks, C. Smith Sr., L. W. Sullivan, J. W. Sweeney

Professors Emeriti (Clinical): T. S. Claiborne, J. C. Massee, A. J. Merrill Sr.

Associate Professors: J. R. Boring III* (Infectious Diseases), G. M. Callaway Jr. (Nephrology and Inorganic Metabolism), S. D. Clements Jr. (Cardiology), I. S. Crawley (Cardiology), G. M. Duffell (Pulmonary Diseases), S. K. Fellner (Nephrology and Inorganic Metabolism), J. A. Goldman (Rheumatology), G. D. Grossman (Pulmonary Diseases), W. L. Hand* (Infectious Diseases). J. E. Hardison (Hematology and Oncology), Z. H. Israili* (Clinical Pharmacology), J. Jacobs (Hematology and Oncology), H. Jinich (Digestive Diseases), H. E. Jones (Dermatology), H. E. Kann Jr. (Hematology and Oncology), J. W. Keller (Hematology and Oncology), S. B. King III* (Cardiology), E. J, Macon (Nephrology and Inorganic Metabolism), J. E. McGowan Jr.* (Infectious Diseases), A. J. Merrill Jr. (Cardiology), A. L. Plummer (Pulmonary Diseases), P. H. Robinson (Cardiology), S. W. Schwarzmann* (Infectious Diseases), P. W. Seavey (General Medicine), M. E. Silverman (Cardiology), W. R. Vogler (Hematology and Oncology), H. K. Walker (Neurology), P. F. Walter (Cardiology), J. O. Wells (Nephrology and Inorganic Metabolism), I. Willis (Dermatology)

Associate Professors (Clinical): T. J. Anderson Jr., J. N. Berry, S. S. Brewer Jr., C. E. Brown, C. D. Burge, E. N. Burson Jr., C. D. Cabaniss, G. R. Cooper, R. B. Copeland, N. E. Davies, F. W. Dowda, E. C. Evans, A. Fiedotin, R. M. Fine, M. H. Freedman, W. F. Friedewald, D. D. Hankey, B. F. Harper Jr., D. E. Hein, A. L. Hitzelberger, D. J. Hughes, A. P. McGinty, F. L. Neely, E. A. Paulk, W. H. Reeves, S. L. Rivers, W. P.

556   *The Quest for Excellence*

Sloan, J. S. Staton, C. F. Stone Jr., H. M. Sturm, P. Teplis, C. Upshaw Jr., W. C. Waters III, J. A. Wilber, J. S. Wilson, G. C. Woodson Jr.

Associate Professor Emeritus (Clinical): L. K. Levy

Assistant Professors: W. A. Artis (Dermatology), B. A. Blumenstein* (Nephrology and Inorganic Metabolism), J. M. Bradford (Pulmonary Diseases), W. S. Brooks Jr. (Digestive Diseases), W. J. Budell (General Medicine), R. K. Chawla (Clinical Research Facility/Nutrition), J. C. Coberly,* H. K. Delcher (Endocrinology), J. delMazo (Digestive Diseases), J. S. Douglas Jr.* (Cardiology), R. S. Douthard, L. J. Elsas II* (Medical Genetics), A. M. A. Faruqui (Cardiology), J. M. Felner (Cardiology), P. B. Francis (Pulmonary Diseases), M. F. Gentry* (General Medicine), M. B. Gravanis,* B. H. Greene-Plauth (General Medicine), R. L. Haynes (Pulmonary Diseases), L. T. Heffner Jr. (Hematology and Oncology), S. B. Heymsfield (Clinical Research Facility/Nutrition), E. L. Hochgelerent (Nephrology and Inorganic Metabolism), L. E. Jones* (General Medicine), D. Karandanis (General Medicine), C. M. Kim, L. R. Kirkland (General Medicine), R. C. Long (Hematology and Oncology), M. F. Lubin (General Medicine), R. C. MacDonell Jr.* (Nephrology and Inorganic Metabolism), M. J. Markey (General Medicine), W. R. Mason (General Medicine), M. R. Moore (Hematology and Oncology), D. C. Morris (Cardiology), P. I. Musey (Endocrinology), S. M. Nasrallah (Digestive Diseases), D. W. Nixon (Hematology and Oncology), C. W. Oettinger II (Nephrology and Inorganic Metabolism), C. A. Perlino (Infectious Diseases), J. R. Pine (Pulmonary Diseases), D. J. Pirozzi (Dermatology), S. R. Roberts Jr.* (Pulmonary Diseases), C. M. Rogers (General Medicine), J. I. Sawaya (Cardiology), M. Shoji* (Hematology), N. B. Shulman (Nephrology and Inorganic Metabolism), B. D. Silverman (Cardiology), T. Someren (Nephrology and Inorganic Metabolism), S. F. Stein (Hematology and Oncology), L. W. Whatley* (Nephrology and Inorganic Metabolism), W. `S. Wilborn, E. F. Winton (Hematology and Oncology), R. C. Woodward (General Medicine), S. G. Yeoman (General Medicine), R. M. York (Hematology and Oncology)

Assistant Professors (Clinical): J. T. Apgar, K. F. W. Armbruster, H. Asher, R. A. Bardack, M. P. Berenson, J. G. Black, T. T. Blalock, J. B. Blumenthal, A. G. Brandau, H. H. Brill, J. A. Broyles III, C. C. Butler, M. D. Byrd, J. D. Cantwell, J. B. Carr, S. B. Carter Jr., H. L. Casey, D. C. Chait, T. S. Claiborne Jr., D. S. Clark, R. P. Crank, T. L. Crews, P. C. Cronce, R. C. Davis Jr., R. E. Dixon, W. L. Dobes, W. S. Dunbar, M. J. Duttera Jr., E. Dyckman, P. D. Espy, A. O. Feingold, L. S. Feinsmith, L. Fishman, F. W. Fitzhugh Jr., D. H. Forsyth, M. Frank III, W. K. Galen, R. I. Gibbs Jr., G. J. Giesler Jr., R. W. Goldstein, D. S. Gordon, H. A. Gussack, L. D. Haley, J. C. Hall, R. F. Hansen, C. W. Heath Jr., J. W. Hirsch, K. E. Holtzapple, K. A. Hoose, C. C. Jones Jr., R. M. Kelleher, W. R. Kenny, J. D. Kiley, F. LaCamera Jr., J. G. Leonardy Jr., J. L. Lokey, W. C. Maloy, J. S. McDougal, G. C. Miller, J. B. Minor, Z. V. Morgan Jr., M. V. Murphy Jr., B. B. Nahmias, P. H. Nippert, L. C. Norins, R. G. Oatfield, R. J. O'Brien, E. Oran, L. B. Peacock, R. S. Peltz, V. T. Peng, J. M. Parel, B. F. Pike, R. B. Randall, M. J. R. Ravry, P. J. Rodzewicz, T. J. Romano, S. J. Rosenbloom, R. W. Ryder, B. D. Saffan, C. V. Sanders, D. R. Schaberg, R. M. Schmidt, M. G. Schultz, N. H. Schwartz, L. R. Scott Jr., P. K. Shaw, S. A. Shmerling G. B. Skipworth, J. deR. Slade, R. C. Slaton, C. Smith Jr., J. Smith T, T. J. Spira, C. T. Stafford, D. L. Steinberg, J. R. Stone, J. W. Swann, S. L. Swartz, D. M. Taylor, M. V. Teem Jr., M. F. Tenholder, S. E.

Thompson III, L. F. Timberlake, E. Van Buren, J. B. Walter, R. A. Weaver, E. B. Weisman, J. J. Wellman, R. L. Whipple III, C. L. Whisnant Jr., H. J. Whyte, C. W. Wickliffe, P. J. Wiesner, E. Woody Jr., J. T. Yauger
Assistant Professor Emeritus (Clinical): E. M. Dunstan
Associates: R. A. Bethel, S. C. Davis Jr. (General Medicine), A. A. Zaki (General Medicine)
Associates (Clinical): E. A. Allen, J. S. Atwater, E. W. Beasley Jr., M. L. Candler, W. R. Crowe, A. H. Davison, J. S. Dodd Jr., L. H. Felder, W. E. Gambrell, J. F. Harris, J. H. Hilsman Jr., B. J. Hoffman, R. A. Huie Jr., R. H. Johnson, J. A. Kaufman, M. J. Krainin, S. R. Lathan, H. B. Levin, J. M. McCoy, P. R. Miller Jr., J. M. Monfort, B. W. Moore Jr., C. W. Morse, R. A. Murphy Jr., B. B. Okel, W. L. Paullin Jr., J. L. Rankin, R. A. Reich, E. J. Reiner, C. P. Roberts, T. K. Ruebush II, M. S. Shaw, C. A. Stuart, N. A. Thornton, A. M. Tornow, J. K. Van Buren, T. S. Winter III, B. P. Wolff
Instructors: R. F. Cunningham (Clinical Pharmacology), S. P. Dewees (General Medicine), L. E. Falls (Rheumatology), A. Grushka (Digestive Diseases), E. Hobgood (Endocrinology), S. S. Lee (General Medicine), J. F. Lutz (General Medicine), C. L. Miklozek (General Medicine), M. F. Olansky,* F. Rodriguez, D. M. Webb (General Medicine)
Instructors (Clinical): A. H. Abernathy III, C. D. Adams, E. K. Adams, E. B. Agnor, P. D. Anderson, S. Arnon, E. T. Avret, M. T. Bailey, C. F. Barnett Jr., H. J. Baskin, G. O. Bern, M. Berry, J. H. Blalock, A. C. Bleich, M. M. Blumberg, E. C. Borden, P. S. Brachman, J. N. Brawner III, J. A. Bryan, P. Bunyasaranand, D. M. Burns, A. E. Buxton, S. B. Carter Sr., L. G. Chelton, M. A. Chorches, P. J. Cline, C. P. Cobb Jr., P. G. Cohen, R. A. Cohen, D. L. Cooper, H. A. Cooper, J. L. Cooper, L. E. Cooper, L. L. Cotts, J. S. Cruise, C. W. Davidson, W. W. Davis, D. W. DeBra, B. W. Dennis, D. B. Dennison, H. B. Dull, M. A. Eidex, S. H. Elson, L. K. Feinerman, P. E. Fitzpatrick, L. G. Fortson Jr., E. J. Galler, R. J. Gerdes, P. E. Gertler, D. L. Glancy, R. H. Glew, T. D. Golden, G. C. Goldman. N. I. Goldman, M. I. Goldstein, B. Hafkin, C. W. Hailey, R. W. Haley, O. E. Hanes, J. H. Harbour, T. Harden Jr., C. E. Harrison Jr., M. A. W. Hattwick, D. M. Henshaw, J. A. Hertell, T. G. Hill, C. H. Hoke, V. N. Houck, R. W. Hubbell, W. B. Hudgins, M. A. Jablow, J. L. Jacobs, H. S. Jennings Jr., M. Johnson Sr., I. W. Joines II, G. W. Jones Jr., E. C. Kelly III, H. W. Kitchin, G. S. Kleris, G. D. Kumin, M. S. Landy Jr., B. G. Lanier, H. H. Lopez, D. C. Lowance, M. I. Lowance, F. S. MacDonell, P. MacWilliams, G. E. McCormick Jr., C. F. McCuiston, F. M. Melewicz, G. D. Miller, G. T. Mims Jr., C. B. Mosher, M. E. Mostellar, A. M. Oshlag, R. L. Pace, B. H. Palay, S. O. Poole, N. A. Price, A. M. Pruce, F. C. Rabb, A. H. Randall Jr., V. L. Randolph, F. S. Rhame, R. H. Rubin, M. J. Safra, S. H. Schwartz, J. Z. Shanks, J. H. Siegel, M. S. Siegel, R. B. Smiley Jr., R. W. Smith III, D. R. Stickney, W. D. Stribling III, D. W. Thompson, M. L. Throne, J. D. Todino, S. J. Toporoff, D. R. Turner, T. M. Tuthill, G. E. Vanderpool, M. J. Wall, J. G. Wells, J. H. West, W. H. Whaley, R. A. Wiggins, M. H. Williams, W. T. Williams, J. M. Wolff
Instructors Emeriti (Clinical): E. A. Bancker, C. W. Strickler Jr.
Fellows: D. M. Ackerman, B. N. Alimurung, F. M. Alimurung, D. Arensberg, R. S. Arnold, D. A. Atefi, S. M. Barolsky, W. J. Bennett, W. N. Bloch Jr., D. S. Brandenburg, H. J. Brody, M. Capogrossi-Colognesi, W. R. Carlisle, B. A. Cassidy, S. P. Childress, J. T. Cook, R. W. Corwin, J. F. Cotant Jr., P. A. DuBose, A. B. Filstein,

D. G. Fisher, J. B. Francis, P. R. Garrett Jr., J. H. Gilliam III, S. S. Hartman, G. D. Hethumuni, N. F. Jacobs, M. J. Johnson, K. K. Joshi, J. Juarez-Uribe, W. B. Kelley, F. Khorfan, G. B. Knowlton, J. R. Koransky, S. P. Kottle, G. M. Krisle III, C. A. Latting, H. A. Liberman, M. T. Logsdon, D. H. Magill III, R. L. Mars, H. H. McIlwain, J. O. McLean, T. P. Meyer, G. A. Micheletti, J. S. Miller, V. C. Musey, M. F. Nathan, C. M. Nielson, M. A. Norman, W. A. Olson, H. G. Ouzts, G. B. Pelletier, M. S. Perkel, F. M. Pickens, J. H. Poehlman, C. M. Reimer, D. Rimland, W. G. Rogers, H. N. Sacks, P. R. Sarma, P. J. Scheinberg, H. I. Sherman, S. W. Sherman, V. G. Soules, W. P. Stallings, F. D. Stegall, D. L. Tedrick, L. C. Teixeira, J. G. Thompson Jr., J. L. Turner, M. L. Westphal, J. A. Whitaker III

---

*Joint appointment.

Appendix 46: Bulletin of Emory University School of Medicine, which lists the full-time and clinical volunteer faculty members and fellows of the Department of Medicine in 1979.

Medicine

J. W. Hurst, *Professor of Medicine; Chairman of the Department*

Professors: J. H. Christy (Endocrinology), D. C. Collins* (Endocrinology), B. W. Cobbs Jr. (Cardiology), C. C. Corley Jr. (Hematology and Oncology), J. C. Crutcher* (Pulmonary Diseases), J. K. Davidson (Endocrinology), P. G. Dayton* (Clinical Pharmacology), M. DiGirolamo* (Endocrinology), E. R. Dorney (Cardiology), G. F. Fletcher (Cardiology), R. H. Franch* (Cardiology), J. T. Galambos (Digestive Diseases), C. A. Gilbert (Cardiology), W. D. Hall (Hypertension), B. L. Hallman* (General Medicine), J. E. Hardison (Hematology and Oncology), E. G. Herndon Jr.* (Nephrology and Inorganic Metabolism), T. Hersh (Digestive Diseases), C. M. Huguley Jr. (Hematology and Oncology), J. Jacobs (Hematology and Oncology), R. B. Logue (Cardiology), D. O. Nutter* (Cardiology), J. R. K. Preedy* (Endocrinology), H. S. Ramos* (Cardiology), D. Rudman* (Clinical Research Facility/Nutrition), R. C. Schlant (Cardiology), J. S. Schroder (Digestive Diseases), T. F. Sellers Jr.* (Infectious Diseases), J. A. Shulman* (Infectious Diseases), M. E. Silverman (Cardiology), J. H. Stone III* (General Medicine), E. P. Tuttle Jr. (Nephrology and Inorganic Metabolism), W. R. Vogler (Hematology and Oncology), J. A. Ward (Endocrinology), J. Wenger (Digestive Diseases), N. K. Wenger (Cardiology), C. H. Wilson Jr.* (Rheumatology)

Professors Emeriti: J. G. Hood, R. H. Wood*

Professors (Clinical): J. G. Barrow, L. H. Bishop Jr., L. H. Hamff, B. S. Lipman, H. J. L. Marriott, H. Parks, C. Smith Sr., L. W. Sullivan

Professors Emeriti (Clinical): T. S. Claiborne, J. C. Massee, A. J. Merrill Sr.

Associate Professors: J. R. Boring III* (Infectious Diseases), G. M. Callaway Jr. (Nephrology and Inorganic Metabolism), S. D. Clements Jr. (Cardiology), I. S. Crawley (Cardiology), G. M. Duffell (Pulmonary Diseases), S. K. Fellner (Nephrology and Inorganic Metabolism), J. M. Felner (Cardiology), J. A. Goldman (Rheumatology), G. D. Grossman (Pulmonary Diseases), W. L. Hand* (Infectious Diseases), Z. H. Israili* (Clinical Pharmacology), H. Jinich (Digestive Diseases), H. E. Kann Jr. (Hematology and Oncology), J. W. Keller (Hematology and Oncology), S. B. King III* (Cardiology), E. J. Macon (Nephrology and Inorganic Metabolism), J. E. McGowan Jr.* (Infectious Diseases), A. J. Merrill Jr. (Cardiology), M. R. Moore (Hematology and Oncology), D. W. Nixon (Hematology and Oncology), A. L. Plummer (Pulmonary Diseases), P. H. Robinson (Cardiology), S. W. Schwarzmann* (Infectious Diseases), P. W. Seavey (General Medicine), H. K. Walker (Neurology), P. F. Walter (Cardiology), J. O. Wells (Nephrology and Inorganic Metabolism)

Associate Professors (Clinical): T. J. Anderson Jr., J. N. Berry, S. S. Brewer Jr., C. E. Brown, S. J. Brunjes, C. D. Burge, E. N. Burson Jr., C. D. Cabaniss, G. R. Cooper, R. B. Copeland, N. E. Davies, F. W. Dowda, E. C. Evans, A. Fiedotin, M. H. Freedman, W. F. Friedewald, D. S. Gordon, D. D. Hankey, B. F. Harper Jr., D. E. Hein, A. L. Hitzelberger, D. J. Hughes, A. P. McGinty, F. L. Neely, E. A. Paulk, W. H.

Reeves, W. P. Sloan, J. S. Staton, C. F. Stone Jr., P. Teplis, C. Upshaw Jr., W. C. Waters III, J. A. Wilber, J. S. Wilson, G. C. Woodson Jr.

Associate Professor Emeritus (Clinical): L. K. Levy

Assistant Professors: D. Arensberg (Cardiology), J. Bergman (General Medicine), B. A. Blumenstein* (Hypertension), J. M. Bradford (Pulmonary Diseases), W. S. Brooks Jr. (Digestive Diseases), W. J. Budell (General Medicine), R. K. Chawla (Clinical Research Facility/Nutrition), J. C. Coberly*, J. D. Cooper (Nephrology and Inorganic Metabolism), R. S. Cross (General Medicine), H. K. Delcher (Endocrinology), J. delMazo (Digestive Diseases), S. P. Dewees (General Medicine), J. S. Douglas Jr.* (Cardiology), R. S. Douthard, L. J. Elsas II* (Medical Genetics), P. B. Francis (Pulmonary Diseases), M. F. Gentry* (General Medicine), M. B. Gravanis,* B. H. Greene-Plauth (General Medicine), L. T. Heffner Jr. (Hematology and Oncology), S. B. Heymsfield (Clinical Research Facility/Nutrition), E. L. Hochgelerent (Nephrology and Inorganic Metabolism), L. E. Jones* (General Medicine), D. Karandanis (General Medicine), L. R. Kirkland (General Medicine), R. C. Long (Hematology and Oncology), M. F. Lubin (General Medicine), R. C. MacDonell Jr.* (Nephrology and Inorganic Metabolism), W. R. Mason (General Medicine), S. B. Miller (Rheumatology), D. C. Morris (Cardiology), P. I. Musey (Endocrinology), S. M. Nasrallah (Digestive Diseases), C. W. Oettinger II (Nephrology and Inorganic Metabolism), C. A. Perlino (Infectious Diseases), J. R. Pine (Pulmonary Diseases), D. Rimland (Infectious Diseases), S. R. Roberts Jr.* (Pulmonary Diseases), F. Rodriguez, C. M. Rogers (General Medicine), M. Shoji* (Hematology), N. B. Shulman (Hypertension), B. D. Silverman (Cardiology), T. Someren (Nephrology and Inorganic Metabolism), S. F. Stein (Hematology and Oncology), P. L. Werner (Endocrinology), L. W. Whatley* (Nephrology and Inorganic Metabolism), C. Whitsett* (Hematology and Oncology), W. S. Wilborn, E. F. Winton (Hematology and Oncology), E. L. Wollam (Hypertension), R. M. York (Hematology and Oncology)

Assistant Professors (Clinical): M. D. Alexander Jr., L. J. Anderson, D. J. Appelrouth, K. F. W. Armbruster, H. Asher, R. A. Bardack, M. P. Berenson, R. A. Bethel, J. G. Black, T. T. Blalock, J. B. Blumenthal, R. M. Boger, A. G. Brandau, D. S. Brandenburg, H. H. Brill, C. Broome, C. F. Burnett III, W. B. Burns Jr., C. C. Butler, M. D. Byrd, J. D. Cantwell, J. B. Carr, S. B. Carter Jr., H. L. Casey, D. C. Chait, R. W. Chapman, T. S. Claiborne Jr., M. L. Cohen, R. P. Crank, T. L. Crews, B. G. Cucher, L. J. D'Angelo, R. C. Davis Jr., D. E. DiSantis, R. E. Dixon, W. S. Dunbar, M. J. Duttera Jr., E. Dyckman, W. A. Eyzaguirre, A. O. Feingold, L. S. Feinsmith, F. W. Fitzhugh Jr., D. H. Forsyth, M. Frank III, W. K. Galen, R. I. Gibbs Jr., G. J. Giesler Jr., S. A. Goings, R. W. Goldstein, H. A. Gussack, J. C. Hall, R. F. Hansen, R. L. Haynes, C. W. Heath Jr., J. W. Hirsch, K. A. Hoose, N. F. Jacobs Jr., M. J. Jolivette Jr., C. C. Jones Jr., W. E. Jones, R. A. Kaslow, S. S. Katz, W. R. Kenny, J. D. Kiley, M. J. Krainin, F. LaCamera Jr., J. G. Leonardy Jr., J. L. Lokey, W. C. Maloy, M. J. Markey, W. J. Martone, W. M. McClellan, J. S. McDougal, K. M. Michaelides, G. C. Miller, J. B. Minor, Z. V. Morgan Jr., M. V. Murphy Jr., B. B. Nahmias, P. H. Nippert, L. C. Norins, R. G. Oatfield, E. Oran, L. B. Peacock, A. S. Peiken, R. S. Peltz, J. M. Perel, B. F. Pike, R. B. Randall, M. J. R. Ravry, H. F. Retailliau, P. J. Rodzewicz, T. J. Romano, B. J. Rosenbaum, S. J. Rosenbloom, R. W. Ryder, B. D. Saffan, C. V. Sanders, D. R. Schaberg, R. M. Schmidt, M. G. Schultz, N. H. Schwartz, L. R. Scott

Jr., J. E. Seals, P. K. Shaw, S. A. Shmerling, J. deR. Slade, C. Smith Jr., J. Smith T,
T. J. Spira, C. T. Stafford, D. L. Steinberg, J. R. Stone, D. M. Taylor, M. V. Teem Jr.,
S. E. Thompson III, L. F. Timberlake, E. Van Buren, J. B. Walter, R. A. Weaver, E. B.
Weisman, J. J. Wellman, R. L. Whipple III, C. L. Whisnant Jr., C. W. Wickliffe, P. J.
Wiesner, E. Woody Jr., J. T. Yauger
Assistant Professor Emeritus (Clinical): E. M. Dunstan
Associates: R. W. Altemose (Hematology and Oncology), W. H. Cleveland
(Nephrology), S. C. Davis Jr. (General Medicine), A. A. Francendese, C. S.
Goldsand (Nephrology), E. D. Himot (Nephrology), C. R. Hines (Hematology and
Oncology), D. H. Lawson (Hematology and Oncology), H. A. Liberman
(Cardiology), R. L. Mars (Nephrology), H. H. McIlwain (Rheumatology and
Immunology), V. C. Musey (Endocrinology), R. J. O'Brien (Pulmonary Diseases), G.
Panahi (Rheumatology and Immunology), M. S. Perkel (Digestive Diseases), J. F.
Plowden (Hematology and Oncology), F. J. Rogers (Cardiology), M. E. Rose
(Hematology and Oncology), F. J. Schreiber (Hematology and Oncology), M. C.
Schwarz (Hematology and Oncology), S. M. Shlaer, J. A. Stone (Hematology and
Oncology)
Associates (Clinical): J. S. Atwater, E. W. Beasley Jr., M. L. Candler, W. R. Crowe, A. H.
Davison, J. S. Dodd Jr., L. H. Felder, W. E. Gambrell, J. F. Harris, J. H. Hilsman Jr.,
B. J. Hoffman, R. A. Huie Jr., R. H. Johnson, J. A. Kaufman, S. R. Lathan, J. M.
McCoy, P. R. Miller Jr., J. M. Monfort, B. W. Moore Jr., C. W. Morse, R. A. Murphy
Jr., B. B. Okel, W. L. Paullin Jr., R. A. Reich, E. J. Reiner, C. P. Roberts, T. K.
Ruebush II, M. S. Shaw, C. A. Stuart, N. A. Thornton, A. M. Tornow, J. K. Van
Buren, T. S. Winter III B. P. Wolff
Instructors: R. F. Cunningham (Clinical Pharmacology), J. A. Drummond (General
Medicine), E. Hobgood (Endocrinology), E. C. Honig, J. D. Johnson,* H. S. Kahn,*
J. M. Kovaz (General Medicine), S. K. Lee (General Medicine), M. F. Olansky,*
H. G. Ouzts (General Medicine), P. J. Scheinberg (General Medicine)
Instructors (Clinical): A. H. Abernathy III, C. D. Adams, E. K. Adams, E. B. Agnor, P. D.
Anderson, S. Arnon, E. T. Avret, M. T. Bailey, C. F. Barnett Jr., G. O. Bern, M. Berry,
J. H. Blalock, A. C. Bleich, M. M. Blumberg E. C. Borden, P. S. Brachman, J. N.
Brawner III, J. A. Bryan, D. M. Burns, S. B. Carter Sr., L. G. Chelton, M. A.
Chorches, P. J. Cline, C. P. Cobb Jr., P. G. Cohen, R. A. Cohen, H. A. Cooper, L. E.
Cooper, L. L. Cotts, J. S. Cruise, C. W. Davidson, W. W. Davis, D. W. DeBra, B. W.
Dennis, D. B. Dennison, H. B. Dull, M. A. Eidex, S. H. Elson, P. E. Fitzpatrick, L. G.
Fortson Jr., E. J. Galler, R. J. Gerdes, P. E. Gertler, D. L. Glancy, R. H. Glew, T. D.
Golden, G. C. Goldman, N. I. Goldman, A. S. Grivas Jr., B. Hafkin, C. W. Hailey,
O. E. Hanes, J. H. Harbour, T. Harden Jr., C. E. Harrison Jr., M. A. W. Hattwick,
D. M. Henshaw, J. A. Hertell, T. G. Hill, C. H. Hoke, V. N. Houck, R. W. Hubbeil,
W. B. Hudgins, M. A. Jablow, J. L. Jacobs, H. S. Jennings Jr., M. Johnson Sr., I. W.
Joines II, G. W. Jones Jr., G. S. Kahn, E. C. Kelly III, A. M. Kimball, H. W. Kitchin,
G. D. Kumin, M. S. Landy Jr., B. G. Lanier, H. H. Lopez, D. C. Lowance, M. I.
Lowance, F. S. MacDonell, P. MacWilliams, G. E. McCormick Jr., C. F. McCuision,
F. M. Melewicz, G. D. Miller, G. T. Mims Jr., M. E. Mostellar, A. M. Oshlag, R. L.
Pace, B. H. Palay, Q. R. Pirkle Jr., S. O. Poole, N. A. Price, A. M. Pruce, F. C. Rabb,
A. H. Randall Jr., F. S. Rhame, R. H. Rubin, M. J. Safra, S. H. Schwartz, J. Z. Shanks,
J. H. Siegel, M. S. Siegel, R. B. Smiley Jr., R. W. Smith III, D. R. Stickney, W. D.

Stribling III, M. L. Throne, J. D. Todino, S. J. Toporoff, D. R. Turner, T. M. Tuthill, G. E. Vanderpool, M. J. Wall, J. G. Wells, J. H. West, W. H. Whaley, R. A. Wiggins, M. H. Williams, W. T. Williams, J. M. Wolff

Instructors Emeriti (Clinical): E. A. Bancker, C. W. Strickler Jr.

Fellows: B. N. Alimurung, J. S. Alizadeh, S. M. Barolsky, W. J. Bennett, M. C. Capogrossi, R. W. Carlisle, J. A. Chiapella, W. R. Corwin, J. R. Darsee, J. S. Dennis, R. Dronavailli, P. A. DuBose, R. M. Eisenband, R. C. Ferguson, J. B. Francis, R. J. Friedman, J. H. Gilliam III, B. G. Hymon, M. J. Johnson, J. Juarez-Uribe, J. Kirby, W. S. Knapp, G. B. Knowlton, J. R. Koransky, C. A. Latting, C. W. McLarin, J. O. McLean, R. L. Mars, T. P. Meyer, C. L. Mikolich, N. B. Nicoloff, W. A. Olson, G. B. Pelletier, P. S. Perret, F. M. Pickens, B. D. Remington, J. W. Ross, S. D. Rossner, H. N. Sacks, M. H. Sanders, H. I. Sherman, S. W. Sherman, Y. K. Siddiq, G. L. Simone, O. Sofer, C. B. Teutsch, J. L. Turner, D. M. Webb, J. W. Whitaker, B. R. Williams Jr., E. H. Willard III

---

*Joint appointment.

Appendix 47: Bulletin of Emory University School of Medicine, which lists the full-time and clinical volunteer faculty members and fellows of the Department of Medicine in 1980.

MEDICINE

J. W. Hurst, *Professor of Medicine; Chairman of the Department*

Professors: J. H. Christy (Endocrinology), D. C. Collins* (Endocrinology), B. W. Cobbs Jr. (Cardiology), C. C. Corley Jr. (Hematology and Oncology), J. C. Crutcher* (Pulmonary Diseases), J. K. Davidson (Endocrinology), M. DiGirolamo* (Endocrinology), E. R. Dorney (Cardiology), G. F. Fletcher (Cardiology), R. H. Franch* (Cardiology), J. T. Galambos (Digestive Diseases), W. D. Hall Jr. (Hypertension), B. L. Hallman* (General Medicine), J. E. Hardison (Hematology and Oncology), E. G. Herndon Jr.* (Nephrology and Inorganic Metabolism), T. Hersh (Digestive Diseases), C. M. Huguley Jr. (Hematology and Oncology), J. Jacobs (Hematology and Oncology), R. B. Logue (Cardiology), D. O. Nutter* (Cardiology), J. R. K. Preedy* (Endocrinology), H. S. Ramos* (Cardiology), D. Rudman* (Clinical Research Facility/Nutrition), R. C. Schlant (Cardiology), J. S. Schroder (Digestive Diseases), T. F. Sellers Jr.* (Infectious Diseases), J. A. Shulman* (Infectious Diseases), M. E. Silverman (Cardiology), J. H. Stone III* (General Medicine), E. P. Tuttle Jr. (Nephrology and Inorganic Metabolism), W. R. Vogler (Hematology and Oncology), J. A. Ward (Endocrinology), J. Wenger (Digestive Diseases), N. K. Wenger (Cardiology), C. H. Wilson Jr.* (Rheumatology)

Professors Emeriti: J. G. Hood, R. H. Wood*

Professors (Clinical): J. G. Barrow, L. H. Bishop Jr., C. A. Gilbert, L. H. Hamff, B. S. Lipman, H. J. L. Marriott, H. Parks, C. Smith Sr., L. W. Sullivan

Professors Emeriti (Clinical): T. S. Claiborne, J. C. Massee, A. J. Merrill Sr.

Associate Professors: J. R. Boring III* (Infectious Diseases), G. M. Callaway Jr. (Nephrology and Inorganic Metabolism), R. K. Chawla (Clinical Research Facility/Nutrition), S. D. Clements Jr. (Cardiology), I. S. Crawley (Cardiology), P. C. Davidson, G. M. Duffell (Pulmonary Diseases), S. K. Fellner (Nephrology and Inorganic Metabolism), J. M. Felner (Cardiology), P. B. Francis (Pulmonary Diseases), J. A. Goldman (Rheumatology), G. D. Grossman (Pulmonary Diseases), W. L. Hand (Infectious Diseases), S. B. Heymsfield (Clinical Reaearch Facility/Nutrition), Z. H. Israili* (Clinical Pharmacology), H. E. Kann Jr. (Hematology and Oncology), J. W. Keller (Hematology and Oncology), S. B. King III* (Cardiology), E. J. Macon (Nephrology and Inorganic Metabolism), J. E. McGowan Jr.* (Infectious Diseases), M. R. Moore (Hematology and Oncology), D. W. Nixon (Hematology and Oncology), A. L. Plummer (Pulmonary Diseases), P. H. Robinson (Cardiology), S. W. Schwarzmann* (Infectious Diseases), P. W. Seavey (General Medicine), H. K. Walker (Neurology), P. F. Walter (Cardiology), J. O. Wells (Nephrology and Inorganic Metabolism), E. F. Winton (Hematology and Oncology)

Associate Professors (Clinical): T. J. Anderson Jr., J. N. Berry, S. S. Brewer Jr., C. E. Brown, C. D. Burge, E. N. Burson Jr., C. D. Cabaniss, G. R. Cooper, R. B. Copeland, N. E. Davies, F. W. Dowda, E. C. Evans, A. Fiedotin, M. H. Freedman, W. F.

564   *The Quest for Excellence*

Friedewald, D. S. Gordon, D. D. Hankey, B. F. Harper Jr., D. E. Hein, A. L. Hitzelberger, A. P. McGinty, A. J. Merrill Jr., F. L. Neely, E. A. Paulk, W. H. Reeves, W. P. Sloan, J. S. Staton, C. F. Stone Jr., P. Teplis, C. Upshaw Jr., W. C. Waters III, J. A. Wilber, J. S. Wilson, G. C. Woodson Jr.

Associate Professor Emeritus (Clinical): L. K. Levy

Assistant Professors: D. Arensberg (Cardiology), J. Bergman (General Medicine), B. A. Blumenstein* (Hypertension), J. M. Bradford Jr. (Pulmonary Diseases), W. S. Brooks Jr. (Digestive Diseases), J. W. Budell (General Medicine), C. F. Burnett III (General Medicine), J. D. Cooper (Nephrology and Inorganic Metabolism), R. S. Cross (General Medicine), H. K. Delcher (Endocrinology), J. delMazo (Digestive Diseases), S. P. DeWees (General Medicine), J. S. Douglas Jr.* (Cardiology), R. S. Douthard (General Medicine), J. R. Eckman (Hematology), L. J. Elsas II* (Medical Genetics), C. B. Evans (General Medicine), M. F. Gentry* (General Medicine), M. B. Gravanis,* G. H. Greene-Plauth (General Medicine), L. T. Heffner Jr. (Hematology and Oncology), E. L Hochgelerent (Nephrology and Inorganic Metabolism), R. P. Holm (General Medicine), J. W. Hurst Jr. (Cardiology), L. E. Jones (General Medicine), D. Karandanis (General Medicine), L. R. Kirkland (General Medicine), C. A. Klingenberg (General Medicine), W. M. Lieppe (Cardiology), R. C. Long (Hematology and Oncology), M. F. Lubin (General Medicine), R. L. Mars (Nephrology and Inorganic Metabolism), W. R. Mason (General Medicine), S. B. Miller (Rheumatology), D. C. Morris (Cardiology), P. I. Musey (Endocrinology), V. C. Musey (Endocrinology), S. M. Nasrallah (Digestive Diseases), C. W. Oettinger II (Nephrology and Inorganic Metabolism), J. H. Oh (Nephrology), M. S. Perkel (Digestive Diseases), C. A. Perlino (Infectious Diseases), J. R. Pine (Pulmonary Diseases), J. J. Regan (General Medicine), S. P. Riepe, D. Rimland (Infectious Diseases), S. R. Roberts Jr.* (Pulmonary Diseases), C. M. Rogers (General Medicine), M. B. Sabom (Cardiology), P. R. Sarma (Hematology and Oncology), M. Shoji* (Hematology and Oncology), N. B. Shulman (Hypertension), T. Someren (Nephrology and Inorganic Metabolism), S. F. Stein (Hematology and Oncology), L. W. Whatley* (Nephrology and Inorganic Metabolism), C. Whitsett* (Hematology and Oncology), E. L. Wollam (Hypertension), R. M. York (Hematology and Oncology)

Assistant Professors (Clinical): L. J. Anderson, D. J. Appelrouth, K. F. W. Armbruster, H. Asher, R. A. Bardack, M. P. Berenson, R. A. Bethel, J. G. Black, T. T. Blalock, J. B. Blumenthal, R. M. Boger, N. J. Bozzini, A. G. Brandau, D. S. Brandenburg, H. H. Brill, C. Broome, W. B. Burns Jr., C. C. Butler, M. D. Byrd, J. D. Cantwell, J. B. Carr, S. B. Carter Jr., H. L. Casey, D. C. Chait, R. W. Chapman, T. S. Claiborne Jr., J. I. Clark, M. L. Cohen, J. A. Corso, R. P. Crank, T. L. Crews, B. G. Cucher, L. J. D'Angelo, R. C. Davis Jr., J. E. Dawson Jr., D. E. DiSantis, R. E. Dixon, W. S. Dunbar, M. J. Duttera Jr., E. Dyckman, W. A. Eyzaguirre, A. O. Feingold, L. S. Feinsmith, F. W. Fitzhugh Jr., D. H. Forsyth, M. Frank III, W. K. Galen, R. I. Gibbs Jr., G. J. Geisler Jr., S. A. Goings, R. W. Goldstein, H. A. Gussack, J. C. Hall, R. F. Hansen, W. K. Harper, S. S. Hartman, R. L. Haynes, C. W. Heath Jr., C. A. Henderson, J. W. Hirsch, K. A. Hoose, N. F. Jacobs Jr., M. J. Jolivette Jr., C. C. Jones Jr., W. E. Jones, R. A. Kaslow, S. S. Katz, W. R. Kenny, J. D. Kiley, J. R. Koransky, M. J. Krainin, F. LaCamera Jr., J. G. Leonardy Jr., M. R. Levine, J. L. Lokey, C. E. Lopez, D. H. Magill III, W. C. Maloy, G. L. Mandell, S. Margolis, M. J. Markey, W. J. Martone,

W. M. McClellan, D. B. McCraw, J. S. McDougal, K. M. Michaelides, G. C. Miller, J. S. Miller, J. B. Minor, Z. V. Morgan Jr., M. V. Murphy Jr., B. B. Nahmias, P. H. Nippert, L. C. Norins, E. Oran, H. G. Ouzts, L. B. Peacock, A. S. Peiken, R. S. Peltz, J. M. Perel, B. F. Pike, R. B. Randall, M. J. R. Ravry, H. F. Retailliau, F. Rodriguez, P. J. Rodzewicz, T. J. Romano, B. J. Rosenbaum, S. J. Rosenbloom, R. H. Roswell, R. W. Ryder, H. N. Sacks, B. D. Saffan, C. V. Sanders, D. R. Schaberg, R. M. Schmidt, M. G. Shultz, N. H. Schwartz, L. R. Scott Jr., J. E. Seals, P. K. Shaw, S. W. Sherman, S. A. Shmerling, M. G. Shulman, B. D. Silverman, J. deR. Slade, C. Smith Jr., J. Smith T, W. B. Spearman, T. J. Spira, C. T. Stafford, D. L. Steinberg, J. R. Stone, D. M. Taylor, M. V. Teem Jr., S. E. Thompson III, L. F. Timberlake, E. Van Buren, J. B. Walter, D. T. Watson, R. A. Weaver, E. B. Weisman, J. J. Wellman, R. L. Whipple III, C. L. Whisnant Jr., C. W. Wickliffe, P. J. Wiesner, E. Woody Jr., J. T. Yauger

Assistant Professor Emeritus (Clinical): E. M. Dunstan

Associates: R. W. Altemose (Hematology and Oncology), M. L. Black, R. M. Boozer, W. H. Cleveland (Nephrology), S. C. Davis Jr. (General Medicine), R. V. Dronavalli (Rheumatology), A. A. Francendese (Endocrinology), R. H. Gersh (Hematology), C. S. Goldsand (Nephrology), M. A. Goldsmith (Clinical Research Facility), E. D. Himot (Nephrology), D. H. Lawson (Hematology and Oncology), G. Panahi (Rheumatology and Immunology), K. Ramacharyulu (Nephrology), M. E. Rose (Hematology and Oncology), E J. Schreiber (Hematology and Oncology), J. A. Stone (Hematology and Oncology)

Associates (Clinical): J. S. Atwater, E. W. Beasley Jr., M. L. Candler, W. R. Crowe, A. H. Davison, J. S. Dodd Jr., L H. Felder, W. E. Gambrell, J. F. Harris, J. H. Hilsman Jr., B. J. Hoffman, R. A. Huie Jr., R. H. Johnson, J. A. Kaufman, S. R. Lathan, J. M. McCoy, P. R. Miller Jr., J. M. Monfort, B. W. Moore Jr., C. W. Morse, R. A. Murphy Jr., B. B. Okel, W. L. Paulin Jr., R. A. Reich, E. J. Reiner, C. P. Roberts, T K. Ruebush II, M. S. Shaw, C. A. Stuart, N. A. Thornton, A. M. Tornow, J. K. Van Buren, T. S. Winter III, B. P. Wolff,

Instructors: R. F. Cunningham (Clinical Pharmacology), J. R. Darsee, E. Hobgood (Endocrinology), E. C. Honig, J. D. Johnson,* H. S. Kahn,* S. K. Lee (General Medicine), M. F. Olansky,* G. C. Richter, Y. K. Siddiq (Endocrinology), J. G. Stensby, T. F. Waites

Instructors (Clinical): A. H. Abernathy III, C. D. Adams, E. K Adams, E. B. Agnor, P. D. Anderson, S. Arnon, E. T. Avret, M. T. Bailey, C. F. Barnett Jr., G. O. Bern, M. Berry, J. H. Blalock, A. C. Bleich, M. M. Blumberg, E. C. Borden, P. S. Brachman, J. N. Brawner III, J. A. Bryan, D. M. Burns, H. N. Camp, S. B. Carter Sr., L. G. Chelton, M. A. Chorches, P. J. Cline, C. P. Cobb Jr., P. G. Cohen, R. A. Cohen, H. A. Cooper, L. E. Cooper. L. L. Cotts, J. S. Cruise, C. W. Davidson, W. W. Davis, D. W. DeBra, B. W. Dennis, D. B. Dennison, H. B. Dull, M. A. Eidex, S. H. Elson, P. E. Fitzpatrick, L. G. Fortson Jr., E. J. Galler, R. J. Gerdes, P. E. Gertler, D. L. Glancy, R. H. Glew, T. D. Golden, G. C. Goldman, N. I. Goldman, A. S. Grivas Jr., B. Hafkin, C. W. Hailey, O. E. Hanes, J. H. Harbour, T. Harden Jr., C. E. Harrison Jr., M. A. W. Hattwick, D. M. Henshaw, J. A. Hertell, T. G. Hill, C. H. Hoke, V. N. Houck, R. W. Hubbell, W. B. Hudgins, M. A. Jablow, J. L. Jacobs, H. S. Jennings Jr., M. Johnson Sr., I. W. Joines II, G. W. Jones Jr., G. S. Kahn, E. C. Kelly III, A. M. Kimball, H. W. Kitchin, G. D. Kumin, M. S. Landy Jr., B. G. Lanier, H. H. Lopez, D. C. Lowance, M. I. Lowance, F. S. MacDonell, P. MacWilliams, G. E. McCormick Jr., C. F.

McCuiston, F. M. Melewicz, G. D. Miller, G. T. Mims Jr., M. E. Mostellar, A. M. Oshlag, R. L. Pace, B. H. Palay, Q. R. Pirkle Jr., S. O. Poole, N. A. Price, A. M. Pruce, F. C. Rabb, A. H. Randall Jr., F. S. Rhame, R. H. Rubin, M. J. Safra, S. H. Schwartz, J. Z. Shanks, J. H. Siegel, M. S. Siegel, R. B. Smiley Jr., R. W. Smith III, D. R. Stickney, W. D. Stribling III, M. L. Throne, J. D. Todino, S. J. Toporoff, D. R. Turner, T. M. Tuthill, G. E. Vanderpool, J. G. Wells, J. H. West, W. H. Whaley, R. A. Wiggins, M. H. Williams, W. T. Williams, J. M. Wolff

Instructors Emeriti (Clinical): E. A. Bancker, C. W. Strickler Jr.

Fellows: B. N. Alimurung, S. P. Allen, W. S. Arnold, R. X. Atluri, N. S. Bass, R. L. Brown S. J. Bryda, A. V. Burnstein, J. E. Carruth, J. R. Darsee, J. S. Dennis, J. A. Drummond, R. M Eisenband, R. D. Ferguson, S. C. Ferguson, R. J. Friedman, J. Graham, D. A. Goldenberg, E. H. Hirsh, J. L. Hollman, J. R. Hutcheson, B. G. Hymon, R. E. Johnson, J. Juarez-Uribe, W. S. Knapp, M. L. Knudtson, M. A. Kukuka, H. A. Liberman, R. C. Lipman, H. J. Marchand, I. E. Mayer, C. W. McLarin, J. O. McLean, J. R. Mikolich, C. L. Miklozek, N. B. Nicoloff, R. G. Nankin, S. K. Naidu, P. S. Pérrett, D. Y. Rawson, G. W. Reader, B. D. Remington, J. W. Ross, S. D. Rossner, Y. Saad-Dine, P. J. Scheinberg, E. J. Schelbar, G. L. Simone, O. Soffer, T. F. Waites, J. D. Ware, D. M. Webb, S. E. Webster, J. W. Whitaker, E. H. Willard III, B. R. Williams Jr.

---

*Joint appointment.

Appendix 48: Bulletin of Emory University School of Medicine, which lists the full-time and clinical volunteer faculty members and fellows of the Department of Medicine in 1981.

MEDICINE

J. W. Hurst, *Professor of Medicine; Chairman of the Department*
Professors: J. H. Christy (Endocrinology), D. C. Collins* (Endocrinology), B. W. Cobbs Jr. (Cardiology), C. C. Corley Jr. (Hematology and Oncology), J. C. Crutcher* (Pulmonary Diseases), J. K. Davidson (Endocrinology), M. DiGirolamo* (Endocrinology), E. R. Dorney (Cardiology), G. F. Fletcher (Cardiology), R. H. Franch* (Cardiology), J. T. Galambos (Digestive Diseases), W. D. Hall Jr., (Hypertension), B. L Hallman* (General Medicine), W. L. Hand* (Infectious Diseases), J. E. Hardison (Hematology and Oncology), E. G. Herndon Jr.* (Nephrology and Inorganic Metabolism), T. Hersh (Digestive Diseases), C. M. Huguley Jr. (Hematology and Oncology), J. Jacobs (Hematology and Oncology), R. B. Logue (Cardiology), D. O. Nutter* (Cardiology), J. R. K. Preedy* (Endocrinology), H. S. Ramos (Cardiology), D. Rudman* (Clinical Research Facility/Nutrition), R. C. Schlant (Cardiology), J. S. Schroder (Digestive Diseases), T. F. Sellers Jr.* (Infectious Diseases), J. A. Shulman* (Infectious Diseases), M. E. Silverman (Cardiology), J. H. Stone III (General Medicine), E. P. Tuttle Jr. (Nephrology and Inorganic Metabolism), W. R. Vogler (Hematology and Oncology), H. K. Walker (Neurology), J. A. Ward (Endocrinology), J. Wenger (Digestive Diseases), N. K. Wenger (Cardiology), C. H. Wilson Jr.* (Rheumatology)
Professors Emeriti: J. G. Hood, R. H. Wood
Professors (Clinical): J. G. Barrow, L. H. Bishop Jr., C. A. Gilbert, L. H. Hamff, B. S. Lipman, H. J. L. Marriott, F. C. McDuffie, H. Parks, V. Slamecka, C. Smith Sr., L. W. Sullivan
Professors Emeriti (Clinical): T. S. Claiborne, J. C. Massee, A. J. Merrill Sr.
Associate Professors: J. R. Boring III* (Infectious Diseases), G. M. Callaway Jr. (Nephrology and Inorganic Metabolism), R. K. Chawla* (Clinical Research Facility/Nutrition), S. D. Clements Jr. (Cardiology), I. S. Crawley (Cardiology), P. C. Davidson, G. M. Duffell (Pulmonary Diseases), S. K. Fellner (Nephrology and Inorganic Metabolism), J. M. Felner (Cardiology), P. B. Francis (Pulmonary Diseases), J. A. Goldman (Rheumatology), G. D. Grossman* (Pulmonary Diseases), S. B. Heymsfield (Clinical Research Facility/Nutrition), Z. H. Israili* (Clinical Pharmacology), J. W. Keller (Hematology and Oncology), S. B. King III* (Cardiology), E. J. Macon (Nephrology and Inorganic Metabolism), J. E. McGowan Jr.* (Infectious Diseases), M. R. Moore (Hematology and Oncology), S. M. Nasrallah (Digestive Diseases), D. W. Nixon (Hematology and Oncology), A. L. Plummer (Pulmonary Diseases), E. H. Robinson (Cardiology), S. W. Schwarzmann* (Infectious Diseases), P. W. Seavey (General Medicine), S. F. Stein (Hematology and Oncology), P. F. Walter (Cardiology), J. O. Wells (Nephrology and Inorganic Metabolism), E. F. Winton (Hematology and Oncology)
Associate Professors (Clinical): T. J. Anderson Jr., J. N. Berry, S. S. Brewer Jr., C. E. Brown, C. D. Burge, E. N. Burson Jr., C. D. Cabaniss, G. R. Cooper, R. B. Copeland,

N. E. Davies, J. del Mazo, F. W. Dowda, E. C. Evans, A. Fiedotin, M. H. Freedman, W. F. Friedewald, D. S. Gordon, D. D. Hankey, B. F. Harper Jr., D. E. Hein, H. E. Kann Jr., A. P. McGinty, A. J. Merrill Jr., F. L. Neely, E. A. Paulk, W. H. Reeves, W. P. Sloan, J. S. Staton, C. F. Stone Jr., P. Teplis, C. Upshaw Jr., W. C. Waters III, J. A. Wilber, J. S. Wilson, G. C. Woodson Jr.

Associate Professor Emeritus (Clinical): L. K. Levy

Assistant Professors: D. Arensberg (Cardiology), R. Atluri (General Medicine), J. Bergman (General Medicine), B. A. Blumenstein* (Hypertension), R. M. Boozer, J. M. Bradford Jr. (Pulmonary Diseases), W. S. Brooks Jr. (Digestive Diseases), J. W. Budell (General Medicine), C. F. Burnett III (General Medicine), J. D. Cooper (Nephrology and Inorganic Metabolism), R. W. Corwin (Pulmonary Diseases), D. C. Davis (General Medicine), S. C. Davis Jr. (General Medicine), H. K. Delcher (Endocrinology), J. S. Douglas Jr.* (Cardiology), R. S. Douthard (General Medicine), J. R. Eckman (Hematology), L. J. Elsas II* (Medical Genetics), A. A. Francendese, M. F. Gentry* (General Medicine), M. B. Gravanis*, G. H. Greene-Plauth (General Medicine), L. T. Heffner Jr. (Hematology and Oncology), E. Hobgood (Endocrinology), E. L. Hochgelerent (Nephrology and Inorganic Metabolism), R. P. Holm (General Medicine), E. G. Honig, E. M. Hoyt Jr., D. Karandanis (General Medicine), L. R. Kirkland (General Medicine), C. A. Klingenberg (General Medicine), H. A. Liberman (Cardiology), R. C. Long (Hematology and Oncology), M. F. Lubin (General Medicine), J. F. Lutz (Cardiology), R. L. Mars (Nephrology and Inorganic Metabolism), W. R. Mason (General Medicine), S. B. Miller (Rheumatology), D. C. Morris (Cardiology), P. I. Musey (Endocrinology), C. Musey (Endocrinology), C. W. Oettinger II (Nephrology and Inorganic Metabolism), J. H. Oh (Nephrology), M. S. Perkel (Digestive Diseases), C. A. Perlino (Infectious Diseases), J. R. Pine* (Pulmonary Diseases), D. A. Rajapakse (Rheumatology), S. P. Riepe, D. Rimland (Infectious Diseases), S. R. Roberts Jr.* (Pulmonary Diseases), C. M. Rogers* (General Medicine), M. B. Sabom (Cardiology), P. R. Sarma (Hematology and Oncology), M. Shoji* (Hematology and Oncology), N. B. Shulman (Hypertension), Y. K. Siddiq (Endocrinology), D. B. Simon (General Medicine), C. M. Slovis (General Medicine), O. Soffer (Nephrology and Inorganic Metabolism), T. Someren (Nephrology and Inorganic Metabolism), S. E. Thompson III (Infectious Diseases), L. W. Whatley (Nephrology and Inorganic Metabolism), C. Whitsett* (Hematology and Oncology), B. R. Williams Jr. (Cardiology), E. L. Wollam (Hypertension), R. M. York (Hematology and Oncology)

Assistant Professors (Clinical): L. J. Anderson, D. J. Appelrouth, K. F. W. Armbruster, H. Asher, G. L. August, R. A. Bardack, M. P. Berenson, J. G. Black, T. T. Blalock, J. B. Blumenthal, R. M. Boger, N. J. Bozzini, A. G. Brandau, D. S. Brandenburg, H. H. Brill, C. Broome, E. C. Burdette II, W. B. Burns Jr., C. C. Butler, M. D. Byrd, J. D. Cantwell, J. B. Carr, S. B. Carter Jr., H. L. Casey, D. C. Chait, R. W. Chapman, T. S. Claiborn Jr., J. I. Clark, W. H. Cleveland, M. L. Cohen, J. A. Corso, R. P. Crank, T. L. Crews, B. G. Cucher, R. C. Davis Jr., J. E. Dawson Jr., T. J. DiFulco, D. E. DiSantis, R. E. Dixon, W. S. Dunbar, M. J. Duttera Jr., E. Dyckman, C. B. Evans, W. A. Eyzaguirre, A. O. Feingold, L. S. Feinsmith, F. W. Fitzhugh Jr., D. H. Forsyth, M. Frank III, R. I. Gibbs Jr., G. J. Geisler Jr., S. A. Goings, R. W. Goldstein, H. A. Gussack, J. C. Hall, R. F. Hansen, W. K. Harper, S. S. Hartman, R. L. Haynes, C. W.

Heath Jr., C. A. Henderson, J. W. Hirsch, K. A. Hoose, J. W. Hurst Jr., N. F. Jacobs
Jr., M. J. Jolivett Jr., C. C. Jones Jr., W. E. Jones, R. A. Kaslow, S. S. Katz, W. R.
Kenny, J. D. Kiley, J. R. Koransky, M. J. Krainin, F. LaCamera Jr., W. M. Lieppe, J. G.
Leonardy Jr., M. R. Levine, J. L. Lokey, C. E. Lopez, D. H. Magill III, W. C. Maloy,
G. L. Mandell, S. Margolis, M. J. Markey, W. J. Martone, W. M. McClatchey, W. M.
McClellan, D. B. McCraw, J. S. McDougal, K. M. Michaelides, G. C. Miller, J. S.
Miller, J. B. Minor, Z. V. Morgan Jr., M. V. Murphy Jr., B. B. Nahmias, L. C. Norins,
R. J. O'Brien, E. Oran, H. G. Ouzts, L. B. Peacock, A. S. Pelken, R. S. Peltz, B. F.
Pike, R. B. Randall, M. J. R. Ravry, H. F. Retailliau, F. Rodriguez, P. J. Rodzewicz,
T. J. Romano, B. J. Rosenbaum, S. J. Rosenbloom, R. H. Roswell, R. W. Ryder, H. N.
Sacks, B. D. Saffan, G V. Sanders, D. R. Schaberg, R. M. Schmidt, M. G. Shultz, N. H.
Schwartz, L. R. Scott Jr., J. E. Seals, P. K. Shaw, S. W. Sherman, S. A. Shmerling,
M. G. Shulman, B. D. Silverman, J. deR. Slade, C. Smith Jr., J. Smith T, W. B.
Spearman, T. J. Spira, D. L. Steinberg, D. M. Taylor, M. V. Teem Jr., L. F.
Timberlake, E. Van Buren, J. P. Vansant, J. B. Walter, D. T. Watson, R. A. Weaver,
E. B. Weisman, J. J. Wellman, R. L. Whipple III, C. L. Whisnant Jr., C. W. Wickliffe,
P. J. Wiesner, R. M. Winslow, E. Woody Jr., J. T. Yauger
Assistant Professor Emeritus (Clinical): E. M. Dunstan
Senior Associate: V. R. Gramling
Associates (Clinical): J. S. Atwater, E. W. Beaaley Jr., M. L. Candler-Ballard, W. R. Crowe,
A. H. Davison, J. S. Dodd Jr., L. H. Felder, W. E. Gambrell, J. F. Harris, J. H. Hilsman
Jr., B. J. Hoffman, R. A. Huie Jr., R. H. Johnson, J. A. Kaufmann, S. R. Lathan, J. M.
McCoy, P. R. Miller Jr., J. M. Monfort, B. W. Moore Jr., C. W. Morse, R. A. Murphy
Jr., B. B. Okel, W. L Paulin Jr., R. A. Reich, E J. Reiner, C. P. Roberts, T. K. Ruebush
II, M. S. Shaw, C. A. Stuart, N. A. Thornton, A. M. Tornow, J. K. Van Buren, T. S.
Winter III, B. P. Wolff
Instructors: T. K. Colgan (General Medicine), R. F. Cunningham (Clinical
Pharmacology), J. B. Francis, R. S. Hotchkiss (General Medicine), J. D. Johnson*,
H. S. Kahn*, D. H. Lawson (Hematology and Oncology), S. K. Lee (General
Medicine), M. F. Olansky*, W. A. Peters, J. A. Richmond, H. E Sours
(Endocrinology), K. Wright (Endocrinology)
Instructors (Clinical): A. H. Abernathy III, E. K. Adams, E. B. Agnor, P. D. Anderson, S.
Arnon, E. T. Avret, M. T. Bailey, C. F. Barnett Jr., W. B. Bassett Jr., G. O. Bern, M.
Berry, J. H. Blalock, A. C. Bleich, M. M. Blumberg, P. S. Brachman, J. N. Brawner
III, J. A. Bryan, D. M. Burns, H. N. Camp, S. B. Carter Sr., L. G. Chelton, M. A.
Chorches, P. J. Cline, C. P. Cobb Jr., P. G. Cohen, R. A. Cohen, H. A. Cooper, L. E
Cooper, J. S. Cruise, C. W. Davidson, W. W. Davis, D. W. DeBra. B. W. Dennia, D. B.
Dennison, M. A. Eidex, S. H. Elson, P. E. Fitzpatrick, L. G. Fortson Jr., E. J. Galler,
R. J. Gerdes, P. E. Gertler, T. D. Golden, N. I. Goldman, A. S. Grivas Jr., B. Hafkin,
R. W. Haley, O. E. Hanes, J. H. Harbour, T. Harden Jr., C. E. Harrison Jr., J. A.
Hertell, C. H. Hoke, V. N. Houk, R. W. Hubbell, W. B. Hudgins, J. L. Jacobs, H. S.
Jennings Jr., M. Johnson Sr., I. W. Joines II, G. W. Jones Jr., A. M. Kimball, H. W.
Kitchin, G. D. Kumin, M. S. Landy Jr., B. G. Lanier, H. H. Lopez, D. C. Lowance,
M. I. Lowance, C. F. McCuiston, F. M. Melewicz, G. D. Miller, G. T. Mims Jr., M. E.
Mostellar, A. M. Oshlag, R. L. Pace, B. H. Palay, Q. R. Pirkle Jr., S. O. Poole, N. A.
Price, A. M. Pruce, A. H. Randall Jr., R. H. Rubin, M. J. Safra, S. H. Schwartz, J. Z.
Shanks, M. S. Siegel, R. B. Smiley Jr., R. W. Smith III, D. R. Stickney, W. D. Stribling

III, M. L. Throne, J. D. Todino, S. J. Toporoff, D. R. Turner, G. E. Vanderpool, J. G. Wells, J. H. West, W. H. Whaley, R. A. Wiggins, W. T. Williams, J. M. Wolff
Instructors Emeriti (Clinical): E. A. Bancker, C. W. Strickler Jr.
Fellows: H. B. Affarah (Nephrology), B. N. Alimurung (Cardiology), S. P. Allen (Cardiology), H. Alpert (Pulmonary Diseases), W. S. Arnold (Cardiology), P. S. Balasubramaniam (Hematology/Oncology), N. S. Bass (Rheumatology), E. N. Bassey (Nephrology), M. L. Black (Hematology/Oncology), J. H. Brewer (Infectious Diseases), R. L. Brown (Rheumatology), B. Bruot (Endocrinology), D. Bryansmith (Hematology/Oncology), S. Bryda (Endocrinology), A. V. Burnstein (Digestive Diseases), J. E. Carruth (Cardiology), T. Cartwright (Hematology/Oncology), P. M. Caruso (Cardiology), K. R. Chary (Nephrology), J. B. Clemons (Digestive Diseases), T. K. Colgan (Cardiology), J. L. Dedonis (Cardiology), J. S. Dennis (Cardiology), P. L. Douglass (Cardiology), S. C. Ferguson (Digestive Diseases), R. Ferguson (Cardiology), C. Flowers (Cardiology), R. H. Gersh (Hematology/Oncology), D. A. Goldenberg (Digestive Diseases), M. Gur-Lavi (Rheumatology), J. Hollman (Cardiology), E. H. Hirsh (Digestive Diseases), J. R. Hoopes (Cardiology), R. E. Johnson (Cardiology), R. Jurado (Infectious Diseases), H. R. Khalil (Hematology), W. S. Knapp (Cardiology), M. L. Knudtson (Cardiology), G. G. Krishna (Nephrology), M. A. Kutcher (Cardiology), M. A. Libow (Cardiology), R. C. Lipman (Cardiology), C. W. McLarin (Cardiology), J. R. Mikolich (Cardiology), I. E. Mayer (Digestive Diseases), A. R. Morales (Rheumatology), P. L. Murphy (Cardiology), R. G. Nankin (Cardiology), N. B. Nicoloff (Cardiology), R. C. Prokesch (Infectious Diseases), C. F. Quinn (Cardiology), C. W. Reader (Cardiology), H. W. Rosman (Cardiology), J. Regjn (Hematology/Oncology), S. D. Rossner (Cardiology), Y. Saad-Dine (Endocrinology), J. Schelbar (Pulmonary Diseases), P. W. Siegel (Digestive Diseases), G. L. Simone (Cardiology), W. E. Story (Cardiology), N. A. Tiliakos (Rheumatology), T. F. Waltes (Cardiology), S. E. Webster (Infectious Diseases)

---

*Joint appointment.

Appendix 49: Bulletin of Emory University School of Medicine, which lists the full-time and clinical volunteer faculty members and fellows of the Department of Medicine in 1982.

MEDICINE

J. W. Hurst, *Charles Howard Candler Professor of Medicine; Chairman of the Department*
Professors: J. H. Christy (Endocrinology), D. C. Collins* (Endocrinology), B. W. Cobbs Jr. (Cardiology), C. C. Corley Jr. (Hematology/Oncology), J. K. Davidson (Endocrinology), M. DiGirolamo* (Endocrinology), E. R. Dorney (Cardiology), G. F. Fletcher (Cardiology), R. H. Franch* (Cardiology), J. T. Galambos (Digestive Diseases), A. R. Gruentzig* (Cardiology), W. D. Hall Jr. (Hypertension), B. L. Hallman* (General Medicine), W. L. Hand* (Infectious Diseases), J. E. Hardison* (Hematology/Oncology), E. G. Herndon Jr.* (Nephrology and Inorganic Metabolism), T. Hersh (Digestive Diseases), C. M. Huguley Jr. (Hematology/Oncology), J. Jacobs (Hematology/Oncology), S. B. King III* (Cardiology), D. O. Nutter* (Cardiology), J. R. K. Preedy (Endocrinology), H S. Ramos* (Cardiology), D. Rudman* (Clinical Research Facility/Nutrition), R. C. Schlant (Cardiology), J. S. Schroder (Digestive Diseases), T. F. Sellers Jr.* (Infectious Diseases), J. A. Shulman* (Infectious Diseases), M. E. Silverman (Cardiology), J. H. Stone III* (General Medicine), E. P. Tuttle Jr. (Nephrology and Inorganic Metabolism), W. R. Vogler (Hematology/Oncology), H. K. Walker (Neurology), P. F. Walter (Cardiology), J. A. Ward (Endocrinology), J. Wenger (Digestive Diseases), N. K. Wenger (Cardiology), C. H. Wilson Jr.* (Rheumatology)
Professors Emeriti: J. G. Hood, R. B. Logue, R. H. Wood
Professors (Clinical): J. G. Barrow, L. H. Bishop Jr., R. B. Copeland, J. C. Crutcher, C. A. Gilbert, L. H. Hamff, B. S. Lipman, F. C. McDuffie, H. J. L. Marriott, H. Parks, V. Slamecka, C. Smith Sr., L. W. Sullivan
Professors Emeriti (Clinical): T. S. Claiborne, J. C. Massee, A. J. Merrill Sr.
Associate Professors: B. A. Blumenstein* (Hypertension), J. R. Boring III* (Infectious Diseases), W. S. Brooks Jr. (Infectious Diseases), G. M. Callaway Jr. (Nephrology and Inorganic Metabolism), R. K. Chawla* (Clinical Research Facility/Nutrition), S. D. Clements Jr. (Cardiology), I. S. Crawley (Cardiology), P. C. Davidson, J. S. Douglas Jr.,* G. M. Duffell (Pulmonary Diseases), J. R. Eckman (Hematology), S. K. Fellner (Nephrology and Inorganic Metabolism), J. M. Felner (Cardiology), P. B. Francis (Pulmonary Diseases), J. A. Goldman (Rheumatology), G. D. Grossman* (Pulmonary Diseases), S. B. Heymsfield (Clinical Research Facility/Nutrition), Z. H. Israili* (Clinical Pharmacology), D. Karandanis (General Medicine), J. W. Keller (Hematology/Oncology), E. J. Macon (Nephrology and Inorganic Metabolism), J. E. McGowan Jr.* (Infectious Diseases), M. R. Moore (Hematology/Oncology), D. C. Morris (Cardiology), S. M. Nasrallah (Digestive Diseases), D. W. Nixon (Hematology/Oncology), C. A. Perlino (Infectious Disease), A. L. Plummer (Pulmonary Diseases), P. H. Robinson (Cardiology), C. M. Rogers* (General Medicine), S. W. Schwarzmann* (Infectious Diseases), P. W. Seavey (General Medicine), M. Shoji* (Hematology/Oncology), S. F. Stein (Hematology/On-

572 The Quest for Excellence

cology), J. O. Wells (Nephrology and Inorganic Metabolism), E. F. Winton (Hematology/Oncology)

Associate Professors (Clinical): T. J. Anderson Jr., J. N. Berry, S. S. Brewer Jr., C. E. Brown, C. D. Burge, E. N. Burson Jr., C. D. Cabaniss, G. R. Cooper, N. E. Davies, J. del Mazo, F. W. Dowda, E. C. Evans, B. L. Evatt, A. Fiedotin, M. H. Freedman, W. F. Friedewald, D. S. Gordon, D. D. Hankey, B. F. Harper Jr., D. E. Hein, H. E. Kann Jr., A. P. McGinty, A. J. Merrill Jr., F. L. Neely, E. A. Paulk, W. H. Reeves, W. P. Sloan, J. S. Staton, C. F. Stone Jr., P. Teplis, C. Upshaw Jr., W. C. Waters III, J. A. Wilber, J. S. Wilson, G. C. Woodson Jr.

Associate Professor Emeritus (Clinical): L. K. Levy

Assistant Professors: D. Arensberg (Cardiology), R. Atluri (General Medicine); J. Bergman (General Medicine), R. M. Boozer, J. M. Bradford Jr. (Pulmonary Diseases), J. W. Budell (General Medicine), C. F. Burnett III (General Medicine), J. D. Cooper (Nephrology and Inorganic Metabolism), D. C. Davis (General Medicine), S. C. Davis Jr. (General Medicine), H. K. Delcher (Endocrinology), R. S. Douthard (General Medicine), L. J. Elsas II* (Medical Genetics), A. A. Francendese, M. F. Gentry* (General Medicine), M. J. Gilman, M. B. Gravanis*, B. H. Greene-Plauth (General Medicine), L. T. Heffner Jr. (Hematology/Oncology), E. Hobgood (Endocrinology), E. L. Hochgelerent (Nephrology and Inorganic Metabolism), R. P. Holm (General Medicine), E. G. Honig, L. R. Kirkland (General Medicine), C. A. Klingenberg (General Medicine), H. A. Liberman (Cardiology), R. C. Long (Hematology/Oncology), M. F. Lubin (General Medicine), J. F. Lutz (Cardiology), R. L. Mars (Nephrology and Inorganic Metabolism), W. R. Mason (General Medicine), S. B. Miller (Rheumatology), P. I. Musey (Endocrinology), V. C. Musey (Endocrinology), C. W. Oettinger II (Nephrology and Inorganic Metabolism), J. H. Oh (Nephrology), J. B. Orlin*, M. S. Perkel (Digestive Diseases), J. R. Pine* (Pulmonary Diseases), D. A. Rajapakse (Rheumatology), S. P. Riepe, D. Rimland (Infectious Diseases), S. R. Roberts Jr.* (Pulmonary Diseases), M. B. Sabom (Cardiology), P. R. Sarma (Hematology/Oncology), N. B. Shulman (Hypertension), Y. K. Siddiq (Endocrinology), D. B. Simon (General Medicine), C. M. Slovis (General Medicine), O. Soffer (Nephrology and Inorganic Metabolism), T. Someren (Nephrology and Inorganic Metabolism), S. E. Thompson III (Infectious Diseases), L. W. Whatley* (Nephrology and Inorganic Metabolism), C. Whitsett* (Hematology/Oncology), B. R. Williams Jr. (Cardiology), S. M. Wodicka (General Medicine), E. L. Wollam (Hypertension), K. Wright (Endocrinology), R. M. York (Hematology/Oncology)

Assistant Professors (Clinical): L. J. Anderson, D. J. Appelrouth, K. F. W. Armbruster, H. Asher, G. L. August, R. A. Bardack, M. P. Berenson, J. G. Black, T. T. Blalock, J. B. Blumenthal, R. M. Boger, N. J. Bozzini, A. G. Brandau, D. S. Brandenburg, H. H. Brill, C. Broome, E. C. Burdette II, W. B. Burns Jr., C. C. Butler, M. D. Byrd, J. D. Cantwell, J. B. Carr, S. B. Carter Jr., D. C. Chait, R. W. Chapman, T. S. Claiborne Jr., J. I. Clark, W. H. Cleveland, M. L. Cohen, J. A. Corso, R. P. Crank Jr., T. L. Crews, B. G. Cucher, R. C. Davis Jr., J. E. Dawson Jr., T. J. DiFulco, D. E. DiSantis, W. S. Dunbar, M. J. Duttera Jr., E. Dyckman, C. B. Evans, W. A. Eyzaguirre, A. O. Feingold, L. S. Feinsmith, F. W. Fitzhugh Jr., D. H. Forsyth, M. Frank III, R. I. Gibbs Jr., G. J. Geisler Jr., S. A. Goings, R. W. Goldstein, H. A. Gussack, J. C. Hall, R. F. Hansen, S. S. Hartman, R. L. Haynes, C. W. Heath Jr., C. A. Henderson, J. W.

Hirsch, K. A. Hoose, J. W. Hurst Jr., N. F. Jacobs Jr., M. J. Jolivette Jr., C. C. Jones Jr., W. E. Jones, R. A. Kaslow, S. S. Katz, W. R. Kenny, J. D. Kiley, J. R. Koransky, M. J. Krainin, W. M. Lieppe, J. G. Leonardy Jr., M. R. Levine, J. L. Lokey, C. E. Lopez, D. C. Lowance, D. H. Magill III, W. C. Maloy, G. L. Mandell, S. Margolis, M. J. Markey, W. J. Martone, W. M. McClatchey, W. M. McClellan, D. B. McCraw, J. S. McDougal, K. M. Michaelides, G. C. Miller, J. S. Miller, J. B. Minor, F. A. Moorhead, Z. V. Morgan Jr., M. V. Murphy Jr., B. B. Nahmias, M. C. Newton Jr., L. C. Norins, R. J. O Brien, E. Oran, H. G. Ouzts, L. B. Peacock, A. S. Peiken, R. S. Peltz, B. F. Pike, R. B. Randall Jr., M. J. R. Ravry, H. F. Retailliau, F. Rodriguez, P. J. Rodzewicz, T. J. Romano, B. J. Rosenbaum, S. J. Rosenbloom, R. W. Ryder, H. N. Sacks, B. D. Saffan, C. V. Sanders, D. R. Schaberg, M. G. Shultz, N. H. Schwartz, L. R. Scott Jr., J. E. Seals, P. K. Shaw, S. W. Sherman, S. A. Shmerling, M. G. Shulman, B. D. Silverman, J. deR. Slade, C. Smith Jr., J. Smith T, W. B. Spearman, T. J. Spira, D. L. Steinberg, D. M. Taylor, M. V. Teem Jr., L. F. Timberlake, E. Van Buren, J. P. Vansant, J. B. Walter, D. T. Watson, R. A. Weaver, E. B. Weisman, J. J. Weilman, W. H. Whaley, R. L. Whipple III, C. L. Whisnant Jr., C. W. Wickliffe, P. J. Wiesner, R. M. Winslow, E. Woody Jr., J T. Yauger

Assistant Professor Emeritus (Clinical): E. M. Dunstan

Senior Associates: V. R. Gramling, J. R. Morgan

Associates (Clinical): J. S. Atwater, E. W. Beasley Jr., M. L. Candler-Ballard, W. R. Crowe, A. H. Davison, J. S. Dodd Jr., L. H. Felder, W. E. Gambrell, J. F. Harris, J. H. Hilsman Jr., B. J. Hoffman, R. A. Huie Jr., R. H. Johnson, J. A. Kaufmann, S. R. Lathan, J. M. McCoy, P. R. Miller Jr., J. M. Monfort, B. W. Moore Jr., C. W. Morse, R. A. Murphy Jr., B. B. Okel, W. L. Paulin Jr., R. A. Reich, E. J. Reiner, C. P. Roberts, T. K. Ruebush II, M. S. Shaw, C. A. Stuart, A. M. Tornow, J. K. Van Buren, T. S. Winter III, B. P. Wolff

Instructors: N. S. Bass, A. V. Burnstein, D. B. Cooke, T. K. Garner, P. A. Herndon, H. S. Kahn,* D. H. Lawson (Hematology/Oncology), S. K. Lee (General Medicine), M. F. Olansky,* J. A. Richmond, H. S. Rosman (Endocrinology)

Instructors (Clinical): A. H. Abernathy III, E. K. Adams, E. B. Agnor, R. G. Albright Jr., P. D. Anderson, S. Arnon, W. S. Arnold, J. E. Averett Jr., E. T. Avret, M. T. Bailey Jr., C. F. Barnett Jr., W. B. Bassett Jr., G. O. Bern, M. Berry, J. H. Blalock, A. C. Bleich, M. M. Blumberg, P. S. Brachman, J. N. Brawner III, J. A. Bryan, D. M. Burns, H. N. Camp, S. B. Carter Sr., L. G. Chelton, M. A. Chorches, P. J. Cline, C. P. Cobb Jr., P. G. Cohen, R. A. Cohen, H. A. Cooper, L. E. Cooper, J. S. Cruise, C. W. Davidson, W. W. Davis, D. W. DeBra Jr., B. W. Dennis, D. B. Dennison, M. A. Eidex, S. H. Elson, P. E. Fitzpatrick, L. G. Fortson Jr., E. J. Galler, R. J. Gerdes, P. E. Gertler, T. D. Golden N. I. Goldman, A. S. Grivas Jr., B. Hafkin, R. W. Haley, O. E. Hanes, J. H. Harbour, T. Harden Jr., C. E. Harrison Jr., J. H. Harvey, J. A. Hertell, C. H. Hoke, V. N. Houk, R. W. Hubbell, W. B. Hudgins, J. L. Jacobs, H. S. Jennings Jr., M. Johnson Sr. G. W. Jones Jr., A. M. Kimball, H. W. Kitchin, W. S. Knapp, G. D. Kumin, M. S. Landy, B. G. Lanier, H. H. Lopez, M. I. Lowance, J. L. Luetkemeyer, C. F. McCuiston, F. M. Melewicz, G. D. Miller, G. T. Mims Jr., M. E. Mostellar, C. M. Nielson, A. M. Oshlag, R. L. Pace, B. H. Palay, D. S. Perling, Q. R. Pirkle Jr., S. O. Poole, N. A. Price, A. M. Pruce, A. H. Randall Jr., R. S. Robbins, S. D. Rossner, R. H. Rubin, W. B. Ruderman, M. J. Safra, S. H. Schwartz, J. Z. Shanks, M. S. Siegel, G. L. Simone, R. B. Smiley Jr., R. W. Smith III, D. E. Snyder Jr., D. R. Stickney, W. D.

Stribling III, M. L. Throne, S. J. Toporoff, D. R. Turner, G. E. Vanderpool, J. G. Wells, J. H. West, R. A. Wiggins, W. T. Williams, J. M. Wolff

Instructors Emeriti (Clinical): E. A. Bancker, C. W. Strickler Jr.

Fellows: H. B. Affarah (Nephrology), D. Allegra (Infectious Diseases), H. Alpert (Pulmonary Diseases), C. Austin (Hematology/Oncology), J. Axelson (Endocrinology), D. Bartley (Infectious Diseases), E. Bassey (Nephrology), B. Bruot (Endocrinology), D. Bryansmith (Hematology/Oncology), G. Bulloch (Cardiology), T. Cartwright (Hematology), P. Caruso (Cardiology), R. Chernecky (Digestive Diseases), J. B. Clemmons (Digestive Diseases), T. Colgan (Cardiology), A. Cook (Cardiology), D. Crandall (Endocrinology), J. Dedonis (Cardiology), P. Douglass (Cardiology), C. Flowers (Cardiology), F. Font (Rheumatology/Immunology), A. Freedman (Hematology/Oncology), S. Fried (Endocrinology), E. Gardner (Digestive Diseases), M. Gur-Lavi (Rheumatology/Immunology), D. Hall (Cardiology), S. Harrington (Digestive Diseases), M. Harris (Cardiology), J. Hollman (Cardiology), J. Hoopes (Cardiology), R. Johnson (Cardiology), R. Jurado (Infectious Diseases), M. Knudtson (Cardiology), M. Kutcher (Cardiology), A. Landis (Hematology), R. Laurens (Pulmonary), M. Libow (Cardiology), M. Lipsitt (Cardiology), D. Lipskis (Cardiology), D. Lynch (Hematology), E. Manolas (Cardiology), D. Martin (Digestive Diseases), J. McClelland (Cardiology), B. Meier (Cardiology), F. Miller (Clinical Research), J. Montagnino (Cardiology), J. Moore (Digestive Diseases), R. Morales (Rheumatology/Immunology), P. Murphy (Cardiology), G. Myerson (Rheumatology/Immunology), R. Paustian (Cardiology), G. Pilcher (Cardiology), R. Prokesch (Infectious Diseases), C. Quinn (Cardiology), D. Rausher (Digestive Diseases), W. Reader (Cardiology), J. Regan (Hematology), R. Rose (Infectious Diseases), P. Siegel (Digestive Diseases), W. Story (Cardiology), A. Thomley (Cardiology), N. Tiliakos (Rheumatology), N. Trask (Cardiology), M. Wilson (Endocrinology), R. Wrenn (Endocrinology)

---

*Joint appointment.

Appendix 50: Bulletin of Emory University School of Medicine, which lists the full-time and clinical volunteer faculty members and fellows of the Department of Medicine in 1983.

MEDICINE

J. W. Hurst, *Charles Howard Candler Professor of Medicine; Chairman of the Department*
Professors: J. H. Christy (Endocrinology), D. C. Collins* (Endocrinology), B. W. Cobbs Jr. (Cardiology), C. C. Corley Jr. (Hematology and Oncology), J. K. Davidson (Endocrinology), M. DiGirolamo* (Endocrinology), E. R. Dorney (Cardiology), J. M. Felner (Cardiology), G. F. Fletcher (Cardiology), R. H. Franch* (Cardiology), J. T. Galambos (Digestive Diseases), D. S. Gordon*, A. R. Gruentzig* (Cardiology), R. B. Gunn*, W. D. Hall Jr. (Hypertension), B. L. Hallman* (General Medicine), W. L. Hand (Infectious Diseases), J. E. Hardison* (General Medicine), E. G. Herndon Jr.* (Nephrology and Inorganic Metabolism), T. Hersh (Digestive Diseases), C. M. Huguley Jr. (Hematology and Oncology), J. Jacobs (Hematology and Oncology), S. B. King III* (Cardiology), J. E. McGowan Jr.* (Infectious Diseases), D. O. Nutter* (Cardiology), J. R. K. Preedy* (Endocrinology), H. S. Ramos* (Cardiology), D. Rudman (Clinical Research Facility/Nutrition), R. C. Schlant (Cardiology), J. S. Schroder (Digestive Diseases), T. F. Sellers Jr.* (Infectious Diseases), J. A. Shulman* (Infectious Diseases), M. E. Silverman (Cardiology), J. H. Stone III* (General Medicine), E. P. Tuttle Jr. (Nephrology and Inorganic Metabolism), W. R. Vogler (Hematology and Oncology), H. K. Walker (Neurology), P. F. Walter (Cardiology), J. A. Ward (Endocrinology), J. Wenger (Digestive Diseases), N. K. Wenger (Cardiology), C. H. Wilson Jr.* (Rheumatology)
Professors Emeriti: E. A. Bancker, T. S. Claiborne, E. M. Dunstan, W. E. Gambrell, J. G. Hood, R. B. Logue, W. R. Mason, J. C. Massee, A. J. Merrill Sr., C. W. Strickler Jr., R. H. Wood
Professors (Clinical): L. H. Bishop Jr., R. B. Copeland, J. C. Crutcher, C. A. Gilbert, L. H. Hamff, B. S. Lipman, F. C. McDuffie, H. J. L. Marriott, H. Parks, V. Slamecka, C. Smith Sr., L. W. Sullivan
Clinical Professors Emeriti: J. G. Barrow, D. D. Hankey, L. K. Levy, A. P. McGinty, F. L. Neely
Associate Professors: D. Arensberg (Cardiology), B. A. Blumenstein* (Hypertension), J. R. Boring III* (Infectious Diseases), W. S. Brooks Jr. (Infectious Diseases), G. M. Callaway Jr. (Nephrology and Inorganic Metabolism), R. K. Chawla* (Clinical Research Facility/Nutrition), S. D. Clements Jr. (Cardiology), I. S. Crawley (Cardiology), P. C. Davidson, J. S. Douglas Jr.*, G. M. Duffell (Pulmonary Diseases), J. R. Eckman (Hematology), S. K. Fellner (Nephrology and Inorganic Metabolism), P. B. Francis (Pulmonary Diseases), M. F. Gentry* (General Medicine), J. A. Goldman (Rheumatology), B. H. Greene-Plauth (General Medicine), G. D. Grossman* (Pulmonary Diseases), L. T. Heffner Jr., (Hematology and Oncology), S. B. Heymsfield (Clinical Research Facility/Nutrition), Z. H. Israili* (Clinical Pharmacology), D. Karandanis (General Medicine), J. W. Keller (Hematology and Oncology), E. J. Macon (Nephrology and Inorganic Metabolism), M. R. Moore (Hematology and Oncology), D. C. Morris (Cardiology), D. W. Nixon (Hematology

and Oncology), J. H. Oh* (Nephrology), C. A. Perlino (Infectious Diseases), A. L. Plummer (Pulmonary Diseases), P. H. Robinson (Cardiology), C. M. Rogers* (General Medicine), S. W. Schwarzmann* (Infectious Diseases), P. W. Seavey (General Medicine), M. Shoji* (Hematology and Oncology), N. B. Shulman, S. F. Stein (Hematology and Oncology), S. E. Thompson III (Infectious Diseases), J. O. Wells (Nephrology and Inorganic Metabolism), E. F. Winton (Hematology and Oncology), R. M. York (Hematology and Oncology)

Associate Professors (Clinical): T. J. Anderson Jr., J. N. Berry, S. S. Brewer Jr., C. E. Brown, C. D. Burge, E. N. Burson Jr., C. D. Cabaniss, G. R. Cooper, N. E. Davies, J. del Mazo, F. W. Dowda, E. C. Evans, B. L. Evatt, A. Fiedotin, M. H. Freedman, B. F. Harper Jr., D. E. Hein, H. E. Kann Jr., A. J. Merrill Jr., E. A. Paulk, W. H. Reeves, J. S. Staton, C. F. Stone Jr., P. Teplis, C. Upshaw Jr., W. C. Waters III, J. A. Wilber, J. S. Wilson, G. C. Woodson Jr.

Assistant Professors: R. Atluri (General Medicine), R. P. Bain*, G. R. Banks, R. M. Boozer, J. W. Budell (General Medicine), C. F. Burnett III (General Medicine), A. V. Burnstein, D. C. Davis (General Medicine), S. C. Davis Jr. (General Medicine), H. K. Delcher (Endocrinology), R. S. Douthard (General Medicine), L. J. Elsas II* (Medical Genetics), M. J. Gilman, M. B. Gravanis*, E. Hobgood (Endocrinology), E. G. Honig, L. R. Kirkland (General Medicine), C. A. Klingenberg (General Medicine), D. H. Lawson (Hematology and Oncology), H. A. Liberman (Cardiology), R. C. Long (Hematology and Oncology), M. F. Lubin (General Medicine), J. F. Lutz (Cardiology), R. L. Mars (Nephrology and Inorganic Metabolism), S. B. Miller (Rheumatology), V. C. Musey (Endocrinology), C. W. Oettinger II (Nephrology and Inorganic Metabolism), J. B. Orlin*, M. S. Perkel (Digestive Diseases), J. R. Pine* (Pulmonary Diseases), D. A. Rajapakse (Rheumatology), J. A. Richmond, S. P. Riepe, D. Rimland (Infectious Diseases), S. R. Roberts Jr.* (Pulmonary Diseases), M. B. Sabom (Cardiology), P. R. Sarma (Hematology and Oncology), Y. K. Siddiq (Endocrinology), D. B. Simon (General Medicine), C. M. Slovis (General Medicine), O. Soffer (Nephrology and Inorganic Metabolism), T. Someren (Nephrology and Inorganic Metabolism), L. W. Whatley* (Nephrology and Inorganic Metabolism), C. Whitsett* (Hematology and Oncology), B. R. Williams Jr. (Cardiology), S. M. Wodicka (General Medicine), E. L. Wollam (Hypertension), K. Wright (Endocrinology)

Assistant Professors (Clinical): L. J. Anderson, D. J. Appelrouth, H. Asher, G. L. August, R. A. Bardack, M. P. Berenson, J. Birge, J. G. Black, T. T. Blalock, J. B. Blumenthal, R. M. Boger, N. J. Bozzini, A. G. Brandau, D. S. Brandenburg, H. H. Brill, C. Broome, E. C. Burdette II, W. B. Burns Jr., C. C. Butler, M. L. Butler, M. D. Byrd, J. D. Cantwell, J. B. Carr, S. B. Carter Jr., D. C. Chait, R. W. Chapman, T. S. Claiborne Jr., J. I. Clark, W. H. Cleveland, J. D. Cooper, J. A. Corso, R. P. Crank Jr., T. L. Crews, B. G. Cucher, R. C. Davis Jr., J. E. Dawson Jr., T. J. DiFulco, D. E. DiSantis, W. S. Dunbar, M. J. Duttera Jr., E. Dyckman, C. B. Evans, W. A. Eyzaguirre, A. O. Feingold, L. S. Feinsmith, F. W. Fitzhugh Jr., D. H. Forsyth, M. Frank III, R. I. Gibbs Jr., G. J. Geisler Jr., S. A. Goings, R. W. Goldstein, H. A. Gussack, R. F. Hansen, S. S. Hartman, R. L. Haynes, C. A. Henderson, J. W. Hirsch, K. A. Hoose, J. M. Hughes, J. W. Hurst Jr., N. F. Jacobs Jr., C. C. Jones Jr., S. S. Katz, W. R. Kenny, J. D. Kiley, J. R. Koransky, M. J. Krainin, W. M. Lieppe, J. G. Leonardy Jr., M. R. Levine, J. L. Lokey, C. E. Lopez, D. C. Lowance, D. H. Magill III, W. C. Maloy,

S. Margolis, M. J. Markey, W. J. Martone, W. M. McClatchey, W. M. McClellan, D. B. McCraw, J. S. McDougal, K. M. Michaelides, G. C. Miller, J. S. Miller, F. A. Moorhead, Z. V. Morgan Jr., M. V. Murphy Jr., B. B. Nahmias, M. C. Newton Jr., L. C. Norins, R. J. O'Brien, E. Oran, H. G. Ouzts, L. B. Peacock, A. S. Peiken, B. F. Pike, R. B. Randall Jr., M. J. R. Ravry, W. J. Rawls, H. F. Retailliau, F. Rodriguez, P. J. Rodzewicz, B. J. Rosenbaum, S. J. Rosenbloom, H. N. Sacks, B. D. Saffan, C. V. Sanders, M. G. Shultz, N. H. Schwartz, L. R. Scott Jr., P. K. Shaw, S. W. Sherman, S. A. Shmerling, M. G. Shulman, B. D. Silverman, J. deR. Slade, C. Smith Jr., J. Smith T, W. B. Spearman, T. J. Spira, D. L. Steinberg, D. M. Taylor, M. V. Teem Jr., L. F. Timberlake, E. Van Buren, J. P. Vansant, J. B. Walter, D. T. Watson, E. B. Weisman, J. J. Wellman, W. H. Whaley, R. L. Whipple III, C. L. Whisnant Jr., C. W. Wickliffe, P. J. Wiesner, R. M. Winslow, R. C. Woodward, E. Woody Jr., J. T. Yauger

Senior Associates: J. M. Bradford Jr. (Pulmonary Diseases), V. R. Gramling, J. F. Morgan, P. I. Musey*

Associates: D. B. Bryansmith, D. P. Hall, H. W. Smith III, A. S. Taussig, D. S. Thomas

Associates (Clinical): J. S. Atwater, E. W. Beasley Jr., M. L. Candler-Ballard, W. R. Crowe, A. H. Davison, J. S. Dodd Jr., L. H. Felder, J. F. Harris, B. J. Hoffman, R. A. Huie Jr., R. H. Johnson, J. A. Kaufmann, S. R. Lathan, J. M. McCoy, P. R. Miller Jr., J. M. Monfort, B. W. Moore Jr., R. A. Murphy Jr., B. B. Okel, W. L. Paulin Jr., R. A. Reich, E. J. Reiner, C. A. Stuart, J. K. Van Buren, T. S. Winter III

Instructors: P. H. D'Amato (Cardiology), H. S. Kahn*, S. K. Lee (General Medicine), P. H. Meadors (General Medicine), M. F. Olansky*, G. W. Staton, N. A. Tiliakos

Instructors (Clinical): A. H. Abernathy III, E. K. Adams, E. B. Agnor, R. G. Albright Jr., D. Aldarondo, S. Arnon, W. S. Arnold, J. E. Averett Jr., E. T. Avret, M. T. Bailey Jr., C. F. Barnett Jr., W. B. Bassett Jr., G. O. Bern, J. H. Blalock, A. C. Bleich, M. M. Blumberg, P. S. Brachman, J. N. Brawner III, J. A. Bryan, D. M. Burns, H. N. Camp, S. B. Carter Sr., L. G. Chelton, M. A. Chorches, T. E. Clark, P. J. Cline, C. P. Cobb Jr., P. G. Cohen, R. A. Cohen, L. E. Cooper, J. S. Cruise, C. W. Davidson, W. W. Davis, D. W. DeBra Jr., B. W. Dennis, M. A. Eidex, S. H. Elson, P. E. Fitzpatrick, L. G. Fortson Jr., E. J. Galler, P. E. Gertler, T. D. Golden, N. I. Goldman, A. S. Grivas Jr., B. Hafkin, R. W. Haley, J. H. Harbour, T. Harden Jr., C. E. Harrison Jr., J. H. Harvey, J. A. Hertell, C. H. Hoke, V. N. Houk, R. W. Hubbell, W. B. Hudgins, G. W. Jones Jr., H. W. Kitchin, W. S. Knapp, K. K. Kroenke, G. D. Kumin, M. S. Landy, B. G. Lanier, H. H. Lopez, M. I. Lowance, C. F. McCuiston, C. W. McLarin, G. T. Mims Jr., C. M. Nielson, A. M. Oshlag, R. L. Pace, B. H. Palay, K. A. Peroutka, Q. R. Pirkle Jr., S. O. Poole, N. A. Price, R. C. Prokesch, A. M. Pruce, A. H. Randall Jr., R. S. Robbins, S. D. Rossner, R. H. Rubin, W. B. Ruderman, M. J. Safra, S. H. Schwartz, J. Z. Shanks, G. L. Simone, R. B. Smiley Jr., C. N. Smith, G. A. Smith, R. W. Smith III, D. E. Snider Jr., W. H. Spruell, D. R. Stickney, W. D. Stribling III, M. L. Throne, S. J. Toporoff, D. R. Turner, G. E. Vanderpool, J. G. Wells, J. H. West, S. White, R. A. Wiggins, W. T. Williams, J. M. Wolff

Fellows: H. B. Affarah (Nephrology), C. Austin (Hematology and Oncology), J. Axelson (Endocrinology), D. Bartley (Infectious Diseases), L. Battey Jr. (Cardiology), C. Bredlau (Cardiology), B. Bruot (Endocrinology), G. Bulloch (Cardiology), J. Campbell (Cardiology), R. Chernecky (Digestive Diseases), J. Cherner (Digestive Diseases), A. Chiaramida (Cardiology), D. Cohen (Nephrology), T. Colgan (Cardiology), D. Collins (Hematology), A. Cook (Cardiology), D. Cooke

(Cardiology), R. Coralli (Cardiology), P. Douglas (Cardiology), R. Dretler (Infectious Diseases), F. Eickman (Cardiology), B. Erb (Cardiology), B. Fisher (Cardiology), F. Font (Rheumatology), A. Freedman (Hematology and Oncology), S. Fried (Endocrinology), E. Gardner (Digestive Diseases), S. Harrington (Digestive Diseases), M. Harris (Cardiology), D. Helfman (Endocrinology), J. Hill (Endocrinology), J. Hollman (Cardiology), J. Hoopes (Cardiology), T. Ischinger (Cardiology), W. Jacobs (Cardiology), P. Jolly (Hematology and Oncology), L. Kaplan (Pulmonary Diseases), A. Landis (Hematology and Oncology), R. Laurens (Pulmonary Diseases), T. Lawrence (Rheumatology), M. Lemay (Cardiology), M. Libow (Cardiology), M. Lipsitt (Cardiology), D. Lipskis (Cardiology), D. Martin (Digestive Diseases), J. McClelland (Cardiology), B. Meier (Cardiology), J. Moore (Digestive Diseases), C. Mullen (Pulmonary Diseases), P. Murphy (Cardiology), G. Myerson (Rheumatology), R. Paustian (Cardiology), S. Pember (Endocrinology), E. Phillips (Cardiology), C. Quinn (Cardiology), J. Rainer (Cardiology), D. Rausher (Digestive Diseases), R. Rose (Infectious Diseases), R. Savage (Cardiology), F. Schnell (Hematology), T. Steinberg (Infectious Diseases), W. Story (Cardiology), A. Thomley (Cardiology), R. Toro (Rheumatology), N. Trask (Cardiology), S. White (Rheumatology), H. Whitworth (Cardiology), M. Wood (Nephrology)

---

*Joint appointment.

Appendix 51: Bulletin of Emory University School of Medicine, which lists the full-time and clinical volunteer faculty members and fellows of the Department of Medicine in 1984.

MEDICINE

J. W. Hurst, *Charles Howard Candler Professor of Medicine; Chairman of the Department*
Professors: J. H. Christy (Endocrinology), S. D. Clements Jr. (Cardiology), D. C. Collins* (Endocrinology), B. W. Cobbs Jr. (Cardiology), C. C. Corley Jr. (Hematology and Oncology), I. S. Crawley (Cardiology), J. K. Davidson (Endocrinology), M. DiGirolamo* (Endocrinology), E. R. Dorney (Cardiology), J. M. Felner (Cardiology), G. F. Fletcher (Cardiology), R. H. Franch* (Cardiology), J. T. Galambos (Digestive Diseases), D. S. Gordon*, A. R. Gruentzig* (Cardiology), R. B. Gunn*, W. D. Hall Jr. (Hypertension), W. L. Hand (Infectious Diseases), J. E. Hardison* (General Medicine), E. G. Herndon Jr.* (Nephrology and Inorganic Metabolism), T. Hersh (Digestive Diseases), C. M. Huguley Jr. (Hematology and Oncology), J. Jacobs (Hematology and Oncology), S. B. King III* (Cardiology), J. E. McGowan* (Infectious Diseases), D. W. Nixon (Hematology and Oncology), D. O. Nutter* (Cardiology), J. R. K. Preedy (Endocrinology), H. S. Ramos* (Cardiology), D. Rudman (Clinical Research Facility/Nutrition), R. C. Schlant (Cardiology), J. S. Schroder (Digestive Diseases), P. W. Seavey (General Medicine), T. F. Sellers Jr.* (Infectious Diseases), J. A. Shulman* (Infectious Diseases), M. E. Silverman (Cardiology), J. H. Stone III* (General Medicine), E. P. Tuttle Jr. (Nephrology and Inorganic Metabolism), W. R. Vogler (Hematology and Oncology), H. K. Walker (Neurology), P. F. Walter (Cardiology), J. A. Ward (Endocrinology), J. Wenger (Digestive Diseases), N. K. Wenger (Cardiology), C. H. Wilson Jr.* (Rheumatology)
Professors Emeriti: E. A. Bancker, T. S. Claiborne, E. M. Dunstan, W. E. Gambrell, J. G. Hood, R. B. Logue, W. R. Mason, J. C. Massee, A. J. Merrill Sr., C. W. Strickler Jr., R. H. Wood
Professors (Clinical): L. H. Bishop Jr., R. B. Copeland, J. C. Crutcher, C. A. Gilbert, L. H. Hamff, F. C. McDuffie, H. J. L. Marriott, H. Parks, V. Slamecka, C. Smith Sr., L. W. Sullivan
Professors Emeriti (Clinical): J. G. Barrow, D. D. Hankey, L. K. Levy, B. S. Lipman, A. P. McGinty, F. L. Neely
Associate Professors: D. Arensberg (Cardiology), B. A. Blumenstein* (Hypertension), J. R. Boring III* (Infectious Diseases), W. S. Brooks Jr. (Infectious Diseases), G. M. Callaway Jr. (Nephrology and Inorganic Metabolism), R. K. Chawla*, (Clinical Research Facility/Nutrition), P. C. Davidson, H. K. Delcher (Endocrinology), J. S. Douglas Jr.*, G. M. Duffell (Pulmonary Diseases), J. R. Eckman (Hematology), S. K. Fellner (Nephrology and Inorganic Metabolism), P. B. Francis (Pulmonary Diseases), M. F. Gentry* (General Medicine), B. H. Greene-Plauth (General Medicine), G. D. Grossman* (Pulmonary Diseases), L. T. Heffner Jr., (Hematology and Oncology), S. B. Heymsfield (Clinical Research Facility/Nutrition), Z. H. Israili* (Clinical Pharmacology), D. Karandanis (General Medicine), J. W. Keller (Hematology and Oncology), M. F. Lubin (General Medicine), E. J. Macon (Nephrology and Inorganic Metabolism), M. R. Moore (Hematology and

Oncology), D. C. Morris (Cardiology), J. H. Oh* (Nephrology), C. A. Perlino (Infectious Diseases), J. R. Pine (Pulmonary Diseases), A. L. Plummer (Pulmonary Diseases), D. Rimland (Infectious Diseases), P. H. Robinson (Cardiology), C. M. Rogers* (General Medicine), S. W. Schwarzmann* (Infectious Diseases), M. Shoji* (Hematology and Oncology), N. B. Shulman, S. F. Stein (Hematology and Oncology), S. E. Thompson III (Infectious Diseases), J. O. Wells (Nephrology and Inorganic Metabolism), E. F. Winton (Hematology and Oncology), R. M. York (Hematology and Oncology)

Associate Professsors (Clinical): T. J. Anderson Jr., J. N. Berry, S. S. Brewer Jr., C. E. Brown, C. D. Burge, E. N. Burson Jr., N. E. Davies, J. del Mazo, F. W. Dowda, E. C. Evans, B. L. Evatt, A. Fiedotin, M. H. Freedman, B. F. Harper Jr., D. E. Hein, H. E. Kann Jr., A. J. Merrill Jr., W. H. Reeves, J. S. Staton, C. F. Stone Jr., P. Teplis, C. Upshaw Jr., W. C. Waters III, J. A. Wilber, J. S. Wilson, G. C. Woodson Jr.

Assistant Professors: C. T. Aitcheson, R. P. Bain*, R. M. Boozer, D. C. Davis (General Medicine), S. C. Davis Jr. (General Medicine), R. S. Douthard (General Medicine), L. J. Elsas II* (Medical Genetics), M. J. Gilman, M. B. Gravanis*, E. Hobgood (Endocrinology), E. G. Honig, L. R. Kirkland (General Medicine), C. A. Klingenberg (General Medicine), D. H. Lawson (Hematology and Oncology), H. A. Liberman (Cardiology), J. F. Lutz (Cardiology), R. L. Mars (Nephrology and Inorganic Metabolism), P. H. Meadors (General Medicine), S. B. Miller (Rheumatology), V. C. Musey (Endocrinology), B. B. Nahmias*, C. W. Oettinger II (Nephrology and Inorganic Metabolism), M. S. Perkel (Digestive Diseases), D. A. Rajapakse (Rheumatology), J. A. Richmond*, S. P. Riepe, S. R. Roberts Jr.* (Pulmonary Diseases), M. B. Sabom (Cardiology), P. R. Sarma (Hematology and Oncology), Y. K. Siddiq (Endocrinology), D. B. Simon (General Medicine), C. M. Slovis* (General Medicine), O. Soffer (Nephrology and Inorganic Metabolism), T. Someren (Nephrology and Inorganic Metabolism), G. W. Staton, D. S. Stephens, N. A. Tiliakos, L. W. Whatley (Nephrology and Inorganic Metabolism), C. Whitsett* (Hematology and Oncology), B. R. Williams Jr. (Cardiology), S. M. Wodicka (General Medicine), E. L. Wollam (Hypertension), K. Wright (Endocrinology)

Assistant Professors (Clinical): L. J. Anderson, D. J. Appelrouth, H. Asher, G. L. August, R. A. Bardack, M. P. Berenson, J. G. Black, J. B. Blumenthal, R. M. Boger, G. R. Botstein, N. J. Bozzini, A. G. Brandau, D. S. Brandenburg, H. H. Brill, C. Broome, E. C. Burdette II, W. B. Burns Jr., C. C. Butler, M. L. Butler, M. D. Byrd, J. D. Cantwell, S. B. Carter Jr., D. C. Chait, R. W. Chapman, T. S. Claiborne Jr., J. I. Clark, W. H. Cleveland, J. D. Cooper, J A. Corso, R. P. Crank Jr., T. L. Crews, B. G. Cucher, R. C. Davis Jr., J. E. Dawson Jr., T. J. DiFulco, D. E. DiSantis, W. S. Dunbar, M. J. Duttera Jr., C. B. Evans, W. A. Eyzaguirre, A. O. Feingold, L. S. Feinsmith, F. W. Fitzhugh Jr., M. Frank III, G. J. Giesler Jr., S. A. Goings, R. W. Goldstein, H. A. Gussack, R. F. Hansen, S. S. Hartman, R. L. Haynes, C. A. Henderson, J. W. Hirsch, K. A. Hoose, J. M. Hughes, J. W. Hurst Jr., N. F. Jacobs Jr., C. C. Jones Jr., S. S. Katz, W. R. Kenny, J. D. Kiley, J. R. Koransky, M. J. Krainin, W. M. Lieppe, J. G. Leonardy Jr., L. M. Lesser, M. R. Levine, J. L. Lokey, C. E. Lopez, D. C. Lowance, D. H. Magill III, W. C. Maloy, S. Margolis, M. J. Markey, W. J. Martone, W. M. McClatchey, W. M. McClellan, D. B. McCraw, J. S. McDougal, K. M. Michaelides, G. C. Miller, J. S. Miller, F. A. Moorhead, Z. V. Morgan Jr., M. C. Newton Jr., L. C. Norins, R. J. O'Brien, E. Oran, H. G. Ouzts, L. B. Peacock, A. S. Peiken, B. F. Pike, R. B. Randall

Jr., M. J. R. Ravry, W. J. Rawls, H. F. Retailliau, F. Rodriguez, P. J. Rodzewicz, B. J. Rosenbaum, S. J. Rosenbloom, H. N. Sacks, B. D. Saffan, C. V. Sanders, M. G. Shultz, N. H. Schwartz, S. W. Sherman, S. A. Shmerling, M. G. Shulman, B. D. Silverman, J. deR. Slade, C. Smith Jr., W. B. Spearman, T. J. Spira, D. L. Steinberg, D. M. Taylor, M. V. Teem Jr., L. F. Timberlake, E. Van Buren, J. P. Vansant, J. B. Walter, D. T. Watson, E. B. Weisman, J. J. Wellman, W. H. Whaley, R. L. Whipple III, C. W. Wickliffe, P. J. Wiesner, R. M. Winslow, R. C. Woodward, E. Woody Jr., J. T. Yauger

Senior Associates: W. A. Alexander Jr., S. C. Brown-Johnson J. M. Bradford Jr., (Pulmonary Diseases), J. W. Budell (General Medicine), V. R. Gramling, J. F. Morgan, P. I. Musey*

Associates: M. W. Forsthoefel, J. O. Hill, R. L. Jurado, M. T. Riddick, S. M. Schwartz, J. P. Steinberg, H. B. Whitworth Jr., M. E. Wilson*

Associates (Clinical): J. S. Atwater, E. W. Beasley Jr., M. L. Candler-Ballard, W. R. Crowe, A. H. Davison, J. S. Dodd Jr., L. H. Felder, R. A. Huie Jr., R. H. Johnson, J. A. Kaufmann, S. R. Lathan, J. M. McCoy, P. R. Miller Jr., B. W. Moore Jr., R. A. Murphy Jr., B. B. Okel, W. L. Paulin Jr., R. A. Reich, E. J. Reiner, C. A. Stuart, J. K. Van Buren, T. S. Winter III

Instructors: P. H. D'Amato (Cardiology), H. S. Kahn*, S. K. Lee (General Medicine), M. F. Olansky*

Instructors (Clinical): A. H. Abernathy III, R. G. Albright Jr., W. S. Arnold, J. E. Averett Jr., E. T. Avret, M. T. Bailey Jr., C. F. Barnett Jr., W. B. Bassett Jr., G. O. Bern, J. H. Blalock, A. C. Bleich, P. S. Brachman, J. N. Brawner III, M. E. Brown, H. N. Camp, M. A. Chorches, T. E. Clark, P. J. Cline, C. P. Cobb Jr., P. G. Cohen, R. A. Cohen, L. E. Cooper, J. S. Cruise, C. W. Davidson, W. W. Davis, D. W. DeBra Jr., S. H. Elson, A. B. Fishmen, P. E. Fitzpatrick, L. G. Fortson Jr., E. J. Galler, T. K. Garner, P. E. Gertler, T. D. Golden, N. I. Goldman, A. S. Grivas Jr., B. Hafkin, R. W. Haley, J. H. Harbour, T. Harden Jr., C. E. Harrison Jr., J. A. Hertell, V. N. Houk, R. W. Hubbell, W. B. Hudgins, G. W. Jones Jr., W. S. Knapp, K. K. Kroenke, G. D. Kumin, M. S. Landy, B. G. Lanier, M. A. Lipsitt, H. H. Lopez, M. I. Lowance, C. F. McCuiston, C. W. McLarin, G. T. Mims Jr., B. H. Palay, K. A. Peroutka, Q. R. Pirkle Jr., S. O. Poole, N. A. Price, R. C. Prokesch, A. M. Pruce, C. F. Quinn, A. H. Randall Jr., D. B. Rausher, R. S. Robbins, S. D. Rossner, R. H. Rubin, W. B. Ruderman, S. H. Schwartz, J. Z. Shanks, G. L. Simone, R. B. Smiley Jr., C. N. Smith, R. W. Smith III, D. E. Snider Jr., W. H. Spruell, W. D. Stribling III, M. L. Throne, S. J. Toporoff, D. R. Turner, G. E. Vanderpool, J. G. Wells, J. H. West, S. White, R. A. Wiggins, W. T. Williams, J. M. Wolff

Fellows: H. B. Affarah (Nephrology), E. Baetti (Rheumatology), L. Battey Jr. (Cardiology), W. Blincoe (Cardiology), C. Bredlau (Cardiology), G. Bulloch (Cardiology), J. Campbell (Cardiology), R. Cassell (Hematology and Oncology), J. Cherner (Digestive Diseases), A. Chiaramida (Cardiology), A. Churchwell (Cardiology), K. Cloninger (Cardiology), D. Cohen (Nephrology), D. Collins (Hematology), A. Cook (Cardiology), D. Cooke (Cardiology), R. Coralli (Cardiology), R. Dretler (Infectious Diseases), F. Eickman (Cardiology), B. Erb (Cardiology), B. Fisher (Cardiology), A. Grothe (Endocrinology), W. Guest (Pulmonary Diseases), D. Hall (Cardiology), D. Hartle (Endocrinology), D. Helfman (Endocrinology), R. Hermann (Hematology and Oncology), J. Hill

(Endocrinology), W. Hollinger (Pulmonary Diseases), T. Ischinger (Cardiology), W. Jacobs (Cardiology), A. Johnson (Digestive Diseases), P. Jolly (Hematology and Oncology), L. Kaplan (Pulmonary Diseases), P. Katona (Infectious Diseases), E. Katz (Digestive Diseases), P. Kirschbaum (Cardiology), W. Knopf (Cardiology), P. Kozarsky (Infectious Diseases), C. Lawrence (Rheumatology), T. Lawrence (Rheumatology), M. Lemay (Cardiology), D. Lipskis (Cardiology), A. Lopez-Enriquez (Hematology), G. Mason (Pulmonary Diseases), D. Martin (Digestive Diseases), K. McClelland (Cardiology), B. Meier (Cardiology), D. Miller (Cardiology), C. Mullen (Pulmonary Diseases), P. Nwasokwa (Cardiology), R. Paustian (Cardiology), S. Pember (Endocrinology), D. Peteet (Hematology and Oncology), E. Phillips (Cardiology), G. Pilcher (Cardiology), S. Powelson (Cardiology), J. Rainer (Cardiology), C. Rudert (Digestive Diseases), R. Savage (Cardiology), F. Schnell (Hematology), S. Schwartz (Endocrinology), B. Simmons (Infectious Diseases), M. Sineway (Pulmonary Diseases), H. Smith III (Cardiology), T. Steinberg (Infectious Diseases), A. Taussig (Cardiology), A. Thomley (Cardiology), R. Toro (Rheumatology), S. Tripodis (Digestive Diseases), S. White (Rheumatology), H. Whitworth (Cardiology), D. Wisebram (Digestive Diseases), M. Wood (Nephrology)

---

*Joint appointment.

Appendix 52: Bulletin of Emory University School of Medicine, which lists the full-time and clinical volunteer faculty members and fellows of the Department of Medicine in 1985.

MEDICINE

J. W. Hurst, *Charles Howard Candler Professor of Medicine; Chairman of the Department*
Professors: J. E. Bourke (Nephrology & Inorganic Metabolism), J. H. Christy (Endocrinology), S. D. Clements Jr. (Cardiology), D. C. Collins* (Endocrinology), B. W. Cobbs Jr. (Cardiology), C. C. Corley Jr. (Hematology and Oncology), I. S. Crawley (Cardiology), J. K. Davidson (Endocrinology), M. DiGirolamo* (Endocrinology), E. R. Dorney (Cardiology), J. M. Felner (Cardiology), G. F. Fletcher (Cardiology), R. H. Franch* (Cardiology), J. T. Galambos (Digestive Diseases), D. S. Gordon* (Hematology), A. R. Gruentzig* (Cardiology), R. B. Gunn*, W. D. Hall Jr. (Hypertension), W. L. Hand (Infectious Diseases), J. E. Hardison* (General Medicine), E. G. Herndon Jr.* (Nephrology and Inorganic Metabolism), T. Hersh (Digestive Diseases), C. M. Huguley Jr. (Hematology and Oncology), J. Jacobs (Hematology and Oncology), H. R. Karp* (Gerontology), S. B. King III* (Cardiology), R. M. Krause (Infectious Diseases), J. E. McGowan* (Infectious Diseases), D. W. Nixon (Hematology and Oncology), D. O. Nutter* (Cardiology), L. S. Phillips* (Endocrinology), J. R. K. Preedy (Endocrinology), H. S. Ramos* (Cardiology), R. C. Schlant (Cardiology), J. S. Schroder (Digestive Diseases), P. W. Seavey (General Medicine), T. F. Sellers Jr.* (Infectious Diseases), J. A. Shulman* (Infectious Diseases), M. E. Silverman (Cardiology), J. H. Stone III* (General Medicine), E. P. Tuttle Jr. (Nephrology and Inorganic Metabolism), W. R. Vogler (Hematology and Oncology), H. K. Walker* (Neurology), P. F. Walter (Cardiology), J. A. Ward (Endocrinology), J. Wenger (Digestive Diseases), N. K. Wenger (Cardiology), C. H. Wilson Jr.* (Rheumatology)
Professors Emeriti: E. A. Bancker, T. S. Claiborne, E. M. Dunstan, W. E. Gambrell, B. L. Hallman, R. B. Logue, W. R. Mason, J. C. Massee, A. J. Merrill Sr., C. W. Strickler Jr., R. H. Wood
Professors (Clinical): L. H. Bishop Jr., R. B. Copeland, J. C. Crutcher, C. A. Gilbert, L. H. Hamff, F. C. McDuffie, H. J. L. Marriott, H. Parks, V. Slamecka, C. Smith Sr., L. W. Sullivan
Professors Emeriti (Clinical): J. G. Barrow, C. E. Brown, D. D. Hankey, L. K. Levy, B. S. Lipman, A. P. McGinty, F. L. Neely
Associate Professors: D. Arensberg (Cardiology), J. R. Boring III* (Infectious Diseases), W. S. Brooks Jr. (Infectious Diseases), G. M. Callaway Jr. (Nephrology and Inorganic Metabolism), R. K. Chawla*, (Clinical Research Facility/Nutrition), P. C. Davidson, H. K. Delcher (Endocrinology), J. S. Douglas Jr.*, G. M. Duffell (Pulmonary Diseases), J. R. Eckman (Hematology), P. B. Francis (Pulmonary Diseases), M. F. Gentry* (General Medicine), B. H. Greene-Plauth (General Medicine), G. D. Grossman* (Pulmonary Diseases), L. T. Heffner Jr., (Hematology and Oncology), S. B. Heymsfield (Clinical Research Facility/Nutrition), Z. H. Israili* (Clinical Pharmacology), D. Karandanis (General Medicine), J. W. Keller (Hematology and Oncology), M. F. Lubin (General Medicine), J. F. Lutz (Cardiology), E. J. Macon

(Nephrology and Inorganic Metabolism), S. B. Miller (Rheumatology), M. R. Moore (Hematology and Oncology), D. C. Morris (Cardiology), J. H. Oh* (Nephrology), C. A. Perlino (Infectious Diseases), J. R. Pine (Pulmonary Diseases), A. L. Plummer (Pulmonary Diseases), S. P. Riepe (Digestive Diseases), D. Rimland (Infectious Diseases), P. H. Robinson (Cardiology), C. M. Rogers* (General Medicine), S. W. Schwarzmann* (Infectious Diseases), M. Shoji* (Hematology and Oncology), N. B. Shulman, S. F. Stein (Hematology and Oncology), S. E. Thompson III (Infectious Diseases), J. O. Wells (Nephrology and Inorganic Metabolism), E. F. Winton (Hematology and Oncology), E. L. Wollam (Hypertension), R. M. York (Hematology and Oncology)

Associate Professsors (Clinical): T. J. Anderson Jr., J. N. Berry, S. S. Brewer Jr., C. D. Burge, E. N. Burson Jr., N. E. Davies, J. del Mazo, F. W. Dowda, E. C. Evans, B. L. Evatt, A. Fiedotin, M. H. Freedman, B. F. Harper Jr., D. E. Hein, H. E. Kann Jr., A. J. Merrill Jr., W. H. Reeves, J. S. Staton, C. F. Stone Jr., P. Teplis, C. Upshaw Jr., W. C. Waters III, J. A. Wilber, J. S. Wilson, G. C. Woodson Jr.

Assistant Professors: R. P. Bain*, R. M. Boozer, V. D. Bourke (Nephrology and Inorganic Metabolism), R. V. Clark (Endocrinology), P. H. D'Amato (Cardiology), D. C. Davis (General Medicine), S. C. Davis Jr. (General Medicine), R. S. Douthard (General Medicine), L. J. Elsas II* (Medical Genetics), M. J. Gilman, M. B. Gravanis*, E. Hobgood (Endocrinology), E. G. Honig, L. R. Kirkland (General Medicine), C. A. Klingenberg (General Medicine), D. H. Lawson (Hematology and Oncology), H. A. Liberman (Cardiology), R. L. Mars (Nephrology and Inorganic Metabolism), D. M. Martin (Digestive Diseases), P. H. Meadors (General Medicine), V. C. Musey (Endocrinology), B. B. Nahmias, C. W. Oettinger II (Nephrology and Inorganic Metabolism), D. A. Rajapakse (Rheumatology), J. A. Richmond*, S. R. Roberts Jr.* (Pulmonary Diseases), P. R. Sarma (Hematology and Oncology), Y. K. Siddiq (Endocrinology), D. G. Simon (General Medicine), C. M. Slovis* (General Medicine), O. Soffer (Nephrology and Inorganic Metabolism), T. Someren (Nephrology and Inorganic Metabolism), G. W. Staton, D. S. Stephens, N. A. Tiliakos, L. W. Whatley (Nephrology and Inorganic Metabolism), C. Whitsett* (Hematology and Oncology), S. M. Wodicka (General Medicine), K. Wright (Endocrinology)

Assistant Professors (Clinical): L. J. Anderson, D. J. Appelrouth, H. Asher, G. L. August, R. A. Bardack, A. V. Baute, M. P. Berenson, J. G. Black, J. B. Blumenthal, R. M. Boger, G. R. Botstein, A. G. Brandau, D. S. Brandenburg, H. H. Brill, C. Broome, E. C. Burdette II*, W. B. Burns Jr., C. C. Butler, M. L. Butler, M. D. Byrd, J. D. Cantwell, S. B. Carter Jr., D. C. Chait, R. W. Chapman, T. S. Claiborne Jr., J. I. Clark, W. H. Cleveland, J. D. Cooper, J. A. Corso, T. L. Crews, B. G. Cucher, R. C. Davis Jr., J. E. Dawson Jr., T. J. DiFulco, D. E. DiSantis, W. S. Dunbar, M. J. Duttera Jr., C. B. Evans, W. A. Eyzaguirre, A. O. Feingold, L. S. Feinsmith, F. W. Fitzhugh Jr., M. Frank III, G. J. Giesler Jr., S. A. Goings, R. W. Goldstein, H. A Gussack, R. F. Hansen, S. S. Hartman, R. L. Haynes, C. A. Henderson, E. H. Hirsh, J. W. Hirsch, K. A. Hoose, J. M. Hughes, J. W. Hurst Jr., N. F. Jacobs Jr., C. C. Jones Jr., S. S. Katz, W. R. Kenny, J. D. Kiley, J. R. Koransky, S. P. Kottle, M. J. Krainin, W. M. Lieppe, J. G. Leonardy Jr., L. M. Lesser, M. R. Levine, J. L. Lokey, C. E. Lopez, D. C. Lowance, D. H. Magill III, W. C. Maloy, S. Margolis, M. J. Markey, W. J. Martone, W. M. McClatchey, W. M. McClellan, D. B. McCraw, J. S. McDougal, K. M. Michaelides, G. C. Miller, J. S.

Miller, Z. V. Morgan Jr., M. C. Newton Jr., L. C. Norins, R. J. O'Brien, E. Oran, H. G. Ouzts, L. B. Peacock, A. S. Peiken, B. F. Pike, R. B. Randall Jr., M. J. R. Ravry, W. J. Rawls, H. F. Retailliau, F. Rodriguez, P. J. Rodzewicz, B. J. Rosenbaum, S. J. Rosenbloom, M. B. Sabom, H. N. Sacks, B. D. Saffan, C. V. Sanders, M. G. Shultz, N. H. Schwartz, S. W. Sherman, S. A. Shmerling, M. G. Shulman, B. D. Silverman, J. deR. Slade, C. Smith Jr., W. B. Spearman, T. J. Spira, D. L. Steinberg, D. M. Taylor, M. V. Teem Jr., L. F. Timberlake, E. Van Buren, J. P. Vansant, J. B. Walter, D. T. Watson, E. B. Weisman, J. J. Wellman, W. H. Whaley, R. L. Whipple III, C. W. Wickliffe, P. J. Wiesner, R. M. Winslow, R. C. Woodward, E. Woody Jr., J. T. Yauger

Senior Associates: W. A. Alexander Jr., S. C. Brown-Johnson, J. M. Bradford Jr., (Pulmonary Diseases), J. W. Budell (General Medicine), C. F. Burnett III, S. D. Eilen (Cardiology), S. Goldstein, V. R. Gramling (Oncology), J. F. Morgan, P. I. Musey*, N. B. Watts (Endocrinology), G. G. Woodson III (General Medicine)

Associates: H. B. Affarah, L. L. Battey Jr., B. C. Donohue, T. L. Eglin, C. M. Franco, M. S. Goldfarb, J. O. Hill, R. L. Jurado, J. D. Lowdon, G. K. Morris, M. T. Riddick, R. L. Schleicher, S. M. Schwartz, C. L. Weston, M. E. Wilson*, M. J. Yanish

Associates (Clinical): E. W. Beasley Jr., M. L. Candler-Ballard, W. R. Crowe, A. H. Davison, J. S. Dodd Jr., L. H. Felder, R. A. Huie Jr., R. H. Johnson, J. A. Kaufmann, S. R. Lathan, J. M. McCoy, P. R. Miller Jr., B. W. Moore Jr., R. A. Murphy Jr., B. B. Okel, W. L. Paulin Jr., R. A. Reich, E. J. Reiner, C. A. Stuart, J. K. Van Buren, T. S. Winter III

Instructors: R. A. Cohen (Digestive Diseases), H. S. Kahn*, S. K. Lee (General Medicine), M. F. Olansky*

Instructors (Clinical): A. H. Abernathy III, R. G. Albright Jr., W. S. Arnold, J. E. Averett Jr., E. T. Avret, M. T. Bailey Jr., C. F. Barnett Jr., W. B. Bassett Jr., J. H. Blalock, A. C. Bleich, P. S. Brachman, J. N. Brawner III, M. E. Brown, H. N. Camp, M. A. Chorches, T. E. Clark, P. J. Cline, C. P. Cobb Jr., H. J. Cohen, P. G. Cohen, A. J. Cook Jr., L. E. Cooper, J. S. Cruise, C. W. Davidson, W. W. Davis, D. W. DeBra Jr., R. H. Dretler, R. M. Eisenband, S. H. Elson, A. B. Fishmen, P. E. Fitzpatrick, L. G. Fortson Jr., A. Freedman, E. J. Galler, T. K. Garner, P. E. Gertler, T. D. Golden, N. I. Goldman, A. S. Grivas Jr., B. Hafkin, R. W. Haley, J. H. Harbour, T. Harden Jr., C. E. Harrison Jr., J. A. Hertell, V. N. Houk, R. W. Hubbell, W. B. Hudgins, G. W. Jones Jr., W. S. Knapp, G. D. Kumin, A. M. Landis, M. S. Landy, B. G. Lanier, T. M. Lee, M. A. Lipsitt, H. H. Lopez, M. I. Lowance, C. F. McCuiston, C. W. McLarin, G. T. Mims Jr., B. H. Palay, K. A. Peroutka, Q. R. Pirkle Jr., S. O. Poole, N. A. Price, R. C. Prokesch, A. M. Pruce, C. F. Quinn, A. H. Randall Jr., D. B. Rausher, R. S. Robbins, S. D. Rossner, R. H. Rubin, S. H. Schwartz, J. Z. Shanks, M. S. Shaw, G. L. Simone, R. B. Smiley Jr., C. N. Smith, R. W. Smith III, D. E. Snider Jr., W. H. Spruell, W. D. Stribling III, M. L. Throne, S. J. Toporoff, D. R. Turner, M. I. Unterman, G. E. Vanderpool, J. G. Wells, J. H. West, S. White, R. A. Wiggins, W. T. Williams, J. M. Wolff

Fellows: R. S. Allen (Hematology), H. V. Anderson, S. W. Anderson (Cardiology), J. Audeh (Hematology), E. Baetti (Rheumatology), L. Battey Jr. (Cardiology), B. Berkowitz (Pulmonary Diseases), W. Blincoe (Cardiology), C. Bredlau (Cardiology), E. D. Butler (Rheumatology), J. Campbell (Cardiology), R. Cassell (Hematology and Oncology), A. Churchwell (Cardiology), K. Cloninger (Cardiology), J. B. Cohn (Hematology and Oncology), R. Coralli (Cardiology), J. C. Durham (Infectious

Diseases), F. Eickman (Cardiology), B. Erb (Cardiology), M. Erbland (Pulmonary Diseases), M. M. Farley (Infectious Diseases), B. Fisher (Cardiology), A. M. Fixelle (Digestive Diseases), W. T. Fowler (Endocrinology), P. R. Girard (Endocrinology), M. Glazer (Cardiology), W. Guest (Pulmonary Diseases), D. Hall (Cardiology), D. Hartle (Endocrinology), R. Hermann (Hematology and Oncology), R. D. Hill (Cardiology), J. Hill (Endocrinology), R. D. Hoff (Cardiology), G. Hoffmeister (Cardiology), W. Hollinger (Pulmonary Diseases), R. R. Hood (Cardiology), W. Jacobs (Cardiology), A. Johnson (Digestive Diseases), P. Jolly (Hematology and Oncology), P. Katona (Infectious Diseases), E. Katz (Digestive Disases), E. M. Kennedy (Infectious Diseases), P. Kirschbaum (Cardiology), W. Knopf (Cardiology), P. Kozarsky (Infectious Diseases), C. Lawrence (Rheumatology), P. P. Leimgruber, M. Lemay (Cardiology), M. A. Libow, A. Lopez-Enriquez (Hematology), W. P. Maier (Rheumatology), G. Mason (Pulmonary Diseases), P. J. Micale (Cardiology), C. R. Miles (Hematology), D. D. Miller (Cardiology), A. L. Niederman (Cardiology), P. Nwasokwa (Cardiology), W. L. Olmsted (Cardiology), S. Pember (Endocrinology), D. Peteet (Hematology and Oncology), P. G. Phelps (General Medicine), E. Phillips (Cardiology), G. Pilcher (Cardiology), S. Powelson (Cardiology), Y. Pertuz (Nephrology), J. Rainer (Cardiology), J. H. Reed (Endocrinology), C. Rudert (Digestive Diseases), S. Schwartz (Endocrinology), B. Simmons (Infectious Diseases), M. Sineway (Pulmonary Diseases), H. Smith III (Cardiology), R. E. Stein (Digestive Diseases), T. Steinberg (Infectious Diseases), C. M. Talano, S. V. Thacker (Endocrinology), S. Tripodis (Digestive Diseases), J. L. Vivas (Rheumatology), S. White (Rheumatology), D. Wisebram (Digestive Diseases), H. B. Whitworth Jr. (Cardiology), M. Yanish (Hematology)

---

*Joint appointment.

Appendix 53: Bulletin of Emory University School of Medicine, which lists the full-time and clinical volunteer faculty members and fellows of the Department of Medicine in 1986.

MEDICINE

J. W. Hurst, Charles Howard Candler Professor of Medicine; Chairman of the Department
Professors: J. E. Bourke (Nephrology & Inorganic Metabolism), J. H. Christy (Endocrinology), S. D. Clements Jr. (Cardiology), D. C. Collins* (Endocrinology), B. W. Cobbs Jr. (Cardiology), C. C. Corley Jr. (Hematology and Oncology), I. S. Crawley (Cardiology), J. K. Davidson (Endocrinology), M. DiGirolamo* (Endocrinology), E. R. Dorney (Cardiology), J. M. Felner (Cardiology), G. F. Fletcher (Cardiology), R. H. Franch* (Cardiology), J. T. Galambos (Digestive Diseases), D. S. Gordon* (Hematology), A. R. Gruentzig* (Cardiology), R. B. Gunn*, W. D. Hall Jr. (Hypertension), W. L. Hand (Infectious Diseases), J. E. Hardison* (General Medicine), T. Hersh (Digestive Diseases), C. M. Huguley Jr. (Hematology and Oncology), J. Jacobs (Hematology and Oncology), H. R. Karp* (Gerontology), S. B. King III* (Cardiology), J. E. McGowan* (Infectious Diseases), D. W. Nixon (Hematology and Oncology), L. S. Phillips* (Endocrinology), J. R. K. Preedy (Endocrinology), H. S. Ramos* (Cardiology), R. C. Schlant (Cardiology), J. S. Schroder (Digestive Diseases), P. W. Seavey (General Medicine), T. F. Sellers Jr.* (Infectious Diseases), J. A. Shulman* (Infectious Diseases), M. E. Silverman (Cardiology), J. H. Stone III* (General Medicine), E. P. Tuttle Jr. (Nephrology and Inorganic Metabolism), W. R. Vogler (Hematology and Oncology), H. K. Walker* (Neurology), P. F. Walter (Cardiology), J. A. Ward (Endocrinology), J. Wenger (Digestive Diseases), N. K. Wenger (Cardiology)
Professors Emeriti: E. A. Bancker, T. S. Claiborne, E. M. Dunstan, W. E. Gambrell, B. L. Hallman, R. B. Logue, W. R. Mason, J. C. Massee, A. J. Merrill Sr., C. W. Stricker Jr.
Professors (Clinical): J. N. Berry, L. H. Bishop Jr., R.B. Copeland, J. C. Crutcher, N. E. Davies, C. A. Gilbert, L. H. Hamff, B. F. Harper Jr., F. C. McDuffie, H. J. L. Marriott, H. Parks, V. Slamecka, J. S. Staton, L. W. Sullivan, P. Teplis, C. H. Wilson Jr.
Professors Emeriti (Clinical): J. G. Barrow, C. E. Brown, D. D. Hankey, L. K. Levy, B. S. Lipman, A. P. McGinty, F. L. Neely, C. Smith Sr.
Associate Professors: D. Arensberg (Cardiology), H. J. Berger*, J. R. Boring III* (Infectious Diseases), W. S. Brooks Jr. (Infectious Diseases), G. M. Callaway Jr. (Nephrology and Inorganic Metabolism), R. K. Chawla (Endocrinology), J. S. Douglas Jr.*, G. M. Duffell (Pulmonary Diseases), J. R. Eckman* (Hematology), P. B. Francis (Pulmonary Diseases), M. F. Gentry* (General Medicine), B. H. Greene-Plauth (General Medicine), G. D. Grossman* (Pulmonary Diseases), L. T. Heffner Jr., (Hematology and Oncology), S. B. Heymsfield (Endocrinology), H. Israili, D. Karandanis (General Medicine), J. W. Keller (Hematology and Oncology), M. F. Lubin (General Medicine), J. F. Lutz (Cardiology), E. J. Macon (Nephrology and Inorganic Metabolism), R. L. Mars (Nephrology and Inorganic Metabolism), S. B. Miller (Rheumatology), M. R. Moore (Hematology and Oncology), D. C. Morris (Cardiology), S. R. Newcom, J. H. Oh* (Nephrology), R. E. Patterson* (Cardiology), C. A. Perlino (Infectious Diseases), J. R. Pine (Pulmonary Diseases),

A. L. Plummer (Pulmonary Diseases), S. P. Riepe (Digestive Diseases), D. Rimland (Infectious Diseases), P. H. Robinson (Cardiology), C. M. Rogers* (General Medicine), S. W. Schwarzmann* (Infectious Diseases), M. Shoji* (Hematology and Oncology), N. B. Shulman, C. M. Slovis* (General Medicine), S. F. Stein (Hematology and Oncology), S. E. Thompson III (Infectious Diseases), J. O. Wells (Nephrology and Inorganic Metabolism), E. F. Winton* (Hematology and Oncology), E. L. Wollam (Hypertension), R. M. York (Hematology and Oncology) *Associate Professsors (Clinical):* T. J. Anderson Jr., S. S. Brewer Jr., C. D. Burge, E. N. Burson Jr., P. C. Davidson, H. K. Delcher, J. del Mazo, F. W. Dowda, E. C. Evans, B. L. Evatt, A. Fiedotin, M. H. Freedman, D. E. Hein, H. E. Kann Jr., A. J. Merrill Jr., W. H. Reeves, C. F. Stone Jr., C. Upshaw Jr., W. C. Waters III, J. A. Wilber, J. S. Wilson, G. C. Woodson Jr.

Assistant Professors: R. P. Bain*, V. D. Bourke (Nephrology & Inorganic Metabolism), R. V. Clark (Endocrinology), P. H. D'Amato (Cardiology), P. D. Dass (Nephrology), D. C. Davis (General Medicine), S. C. Davis Jr. (General Medicine), B. C. Donohue (Cardiology), R. S. Douthard (General Medicine), L. J. Elsas II* (Medical Genetics), R. J. Gebhart, S. P. Gebhart, M. J. Gilman, M. B. Gravanis*, E. Hobgood (Endocrinology), E. G. Honig, L. R. Kirkland (General Medicine), D. H. Lawson (Hematology and Oncology), H. A. Liberman (Cardiology), P. H. Meadors (General Medicine), V. C. Musey (Endocrinology), B. B. Nahmias, C. W. Oettinger II (Nephrology and Inorganic Metabolism), D. A. Rajapakse (Rheumatology), J. A. Richmond*, S. R. Roberts Jr.* (Pulmonary Diseases), P. R. Sarma (Hematology and Oncology), Y. K. Siddiq (Endocrinology), D. G. Simon (General Medicine), O. Soffer (Nephrology and Inorganic Metabolism), T. Someren (Nephrology and Inorganic Metabolism), R. G. Spanheimer, G. W. Staton, D. S. Stephens, N. A. Tiliakos, N. B. Watts (Endocrinology), L. W. Whatley (Nephrology and Inorganic Metabolism), C. Whitsett* (Hematology and Oncology), S. M. Wodicka (General Medicine), K. Wright (Endocrinology)

Assistant Professors (Clinical): A. H. Abernathy III, C. T. Aitcheson, J. F. Alderete, L. J. Anderson, D. J. Appelrouth, H. Asher, G. L. August, R. A. Bardack, A. V. Baute, M. P. Berenson, J. G. Black, J. B. Blumenthal, R. M. Boger, G. R. Botstein, A. G. Brandau, D. S. Brandenburg, J. N. Brawner III, H. H. Brill, C. Broome, E. C. Burdette II*, W. B. Burns Jr., C. C. Butler, M. D. Byrd, J. D. Cantwell, S. B. Carter Jr., D. C. Chait, R. W. Chapman, T. S. Claiborne Jr., J. I. Clark, W. H. Cleveland, J. D. Cooper, J. A. Corso, T. L. Crews, B. G. Cucher, R. C. Davis Jr., J. E. Dawson Jr., T. J. DiFulco, D. E. DiSantis, W. S. Dunbar, M. J. Duttera Jr., S. H. Elson, C. B. Evans, W. A. Eyzaguirre, A. O. Feingold, L.-S. Feinsmith, F. W. Fitzhugh Jr., M. Frank III, G. J. Giesler Jr., S. A. Goings, R. W. Goldstein, H. A. Gussack, R. F. Hansen, S. S. Hartman, R. L. Haynes, C. A. Henderson, E. H. Hirsh, J. W. Hirsch, K. A. Hoose, J. M. Hughes, J. W. Hurst Jr., N. F. Jacobs Jr., C. C. Jones Jr., G. W. Jones Jr., S. S. Katz, W. R. Kenny, J. D. Kiley, C. A. Klingenberg, W. S. Knapp, J. R. Koransky, S. P. Kottle, M. J. Krainin, J. G. Leonardy Jr., L. M. Lesser, M. R. Levine, J. L. Lokey, C. E. Lopez, D. C. Lowance, D. H. Magill III, W. C. Maloy, S. Margolis, M. J. Markey, D. M. Martin, W. J. Martone, W. M. McClatchey, W. M. McClellan, D. B. McCraw, J. S. McDougal, C. W. McLarin, K. M. Michaelides, G. C. Miller, J. S. Miller, Z. V. Morgan Jr., M. C. Newton Jr., L. C. Norins, R. J. O'Brien, E. Oran, H. G. Ouzts, L. B. Peacock, A. S. Peiken, B. F. Pike, R. B. Randall Jr., D. B. Rausher, M. J. R. Ravry,

W. J. Rawls, H. F. Retailliau, F. Rodriguez, P. J. Rodzewicz, B. J. Rosenbaum, S. J. Rosenbloom, S. D. Rossner, M. B. Sabom, H. N. Sacks, B. D. Saffan, C. V. Sanders, M. G. Shultz, N. H. Schwartz, S. W. Sherman, S. A. Shmerling, M. G. Shulman, B. D. Silverman, G. L. Simone, J. deR. Slade, C. Smith Jr., W. B. Spearman, T. J. Spira, D. L. Steinberg, D. M. Taylor, M. V. Teem Jr., L. F. Timberlake, E. Van Buren, J. P. Vansant, J. B. Walter*, D. T. Watson, E. B. Weisman, J. J. Wellman, W. H. Whaley, R. L. Whipple III, C. W. Wickliffe, P. J. Wiesner, R. M. Winslow, R. C. Woodward, E. Woody Jr., J. T. Yauger

Senior Associates: L. L. Battey Jr., S. L. Brody, S. C. Brown-Johnson, J. M. Bradford Jr., (Pulmonary Diseases), J. W. Budell (General Medicine), R. J. Coralli, S. D. Eilen (Cardiology), S. Goldstein, V. R. Gramling (Oncology), R. D. Hansen, J. O. Hill, N. W. Holland Jr., P. E. Kozarsky, W. P. Maier, C. S. Rudert (Digestive Diseases), S. A. West (General Medicine), D. C. Wolf, G. B. Woodson III (General Medicine)

Associates: E. A. Baetti, A. S. Burris, S. C. M. DiRusso, M. E. Eaton, T. L. Eglin, M. D. Glazer, M. D. Hunter, R. L. Jurado, P. P. Leimgruber, J. D. Lowdon, S. O'Donoghue, M. A. Parker, R. L. Schleicher, N. S. Welch Jr., C. L. Weston, M. E. Wilson*

Associates (Clinical): E. W. Beasley Jr., M. L. Candler-Ballard, W. R. Crowe, A. H. Davison, J. S. Dodd Jr., L. H. Felder, R. A. Huie Jr., R. H. Johnson, J. A. Kaufmann, S. R. Lathan, J. M. McCoy, P. R. Miller Jr., B. W. Moore Jr., R. A. Murphy Jr., B. B. Okel, W. L. Paulin Jr., R. A. Reich, E. J. Reiner, C. A. Stuart, J. K. Van Buren, T. S. Winter III

Instructors: H. S. Kahn*, S. K. Lee (General Medicine), M. F. Olansky*, T. F. Smith

Instructors (Clinical): R. G. Albright Jr., W. S. Arnold, J. E. Averett Jr., E. T. Avret, M. T. Bailey Jr., D. A. Baldrich, C. F. Barnett Jr., W. B. Bassett Jr., D. E. Bild, J. H. Blalock, A. C. Bleich, P. S. Brachman, M. E. Brown, H. N. Camp, M. A. Chorches, T. E. Clark, P. J. Cline, C. P. Cobb Jr., H. J. Cohen, P. G. Cohen, R. A. Cohen, A. J. Cook Jr., L. E. Cooper, C. W. Davidson, W. W. Davis, D. W. DeBra Jr., B. R. Dix, P. L. Douglass, R. H. Dretler, R. M. Eisenband, B. J. Erb, A. B. Fishmen, P. E. Fitzpatrick, C. Flowers, L. G. Fortson Jr., A. Freedman, M. Friedman, R. N. Fullerton Jr., E. J. Galler, T. K. Garner, P. E. Gertler, T. D. Golden, N. I. Goldman, A. S. Grivas Jr., B. Hafkin, J. H. Harbour, T. Harden Jr., M. D. Harris, C. E. Harrison Jr., J. A. Hertell, V. N. Houk, R. W. Hubbell, W. B. Hudgins, W. M. Hudson Jr., A. E. Karpas, E. Katz III, G. D. Kumin, A. M. Landis, M. S. Landy, B. G. Lanier, T. M. Lee, M. A. Lipsitt, H. H. Lopez, M. I. Lowance, C. F. McCuiston, G. T. Mims Jr., B. H. Palay, Q. R. Pirkle Jr., S. O. Poole, N. A. Price, R. C. Prokesch, A. M. Pruce, C. F. Quinn, A. H. Randall Jr., R. S. Robbins, R. H. Rubin, S. H. Schwartz, J. Z. Shanks, F. E. Shaw Jr., M. S. Shaw, V. E. Silverman, R. B. Smiley Jr., C. N. Smith, R. W. Smith III, D. E. Snider Jr., W. H. Spruell, W. D. Stribling III, R. A. Strikas, M. L. Throne, S. J. Toporoff, D. R. Tumer, M. I. Unterman, G. E. Vanderpool, J. G. Wells, J. H. West, S. White, R. A. Wiggins, W. T. Williams, D. L. Wisebram, J. M. Wolff,

Fellows: P. Abi-Mansur (Cardiology), W. A. Alexander Jr. (Infectious Diseases), R. S. Allen (Hematology/Oncology), H. V. Anderson (Cardiology), S. W. Anderson (Cardiology), J. Audeh (Hematology/Oncology), E. Beasley (Endocrinology), B. Berkowitz (Pulmonary Diseases), W. Blincoe (Cardiology), W. R. Bray (Pulmonary Diseases), C. Bredlau (Cardiology), A. S. Burris, E. D. Butler (Rheumatology), J. F. Campbell (Infectious Diseases), G. Cash (Cardiology), M. Certain (Cardiology), A.

Churchwell (Cardiology), K. Cloninger (Cardiology), J. B. Cohn (Hematology/ Oncology), J. C. Durham (Infectious Diseases), M. Erbland (Pulmonary Diseases), M. M. Farley (Infectious Diseases), A. M. Fixelle (Digestive Diseases), C. Franco (Hematology/Oncology), M. Garcia-Caro (Rheumatology), J. H. Garten (Digestive Diseases), E. W. Glaser (Endocrinology), M. Glazer (Cardiology), M. Goldfarb (Cardiology), M. I. Golding (Digestive Diseases), B. J. Gottschalk (Hematology/ Oncology), K. E. Griffith (Digestive Diseases), B. J. Grossman (Hematology/ Oncology), R. D. Hill (Cardiology), R. D. Hoff (Cardiology), J. Hoffmeister (Cardiology), W. N. Holland (Geriatrics), J. W. Hollman (Infectious Diseases), R. Hood (Cardiology), G. E. Katz (Cardiology), E. Kennedy (Infectious Diseases), P. J. Kertes (Cardiology), P. Kirschbaum (Cardiology), W. Knopf (Cardiology), P. P. Leimgruber (Cardiology), E. Lominack (Cardiology), W. Maier (Rheumatology), P. J. Micale (Cardiology), C. R. Miles (Hematology), D. D. Miller (Cardiology), L. H. Mufson (Cardiology), T. G. Murray (Pulmonary Diseases), A. Mustaq (Endocrinology), C. Neckman (Cardiology), A. L. Niederman (Cardiology), O. Nwasokwa (Cardiology), W. L. Olmsted (Cardiology), M. Parker (Endocrinology), M. Pecora (Cardiology), R. L. Perez (Rheumatology), Y. Pertuz (Nephrology), G. F. Pilcher (Cardiology), S. J. Pollak (Cardiology), J. H. Reed (Endocrinology), J. F. Reinus (Digestive Diseases), M. T. Riddick (Digestive Diseases), G. Roubin (Cardiology), R. Schleicher (Endocrinology), S. Schwartz (Endocrinology), D. Shonkoff (Cardiology), H. W. B. Smith III (Cardiology), D. B. Southern (Cardiology), H. Spilker (Cardiology), R. E. Stein (Digestive Diseases), J. D. Talley III (Cardiology), S. V. Thacker (Endocrinology), J. Vigoreaux (Cardiology), J. L. Vivas (Rheumatology), D. J. Vrooman (Pulmonary Diseases), H. T. Walpole Jr. (Cardiology), J. P. Waring (Digestive Diseases), N. S. Welch Jr., H. Whitworth (Cardiology), C. I. Wilmer (Cardiology), M. Wilson (Endocrinology)

---

*Joint appointment.

Index of Names

The following index references all parts of the main text (pp. vii–455) except the annual group photographs, plus the administrators listed in Appendix 4 "Governance" (pp. 476–479).

Blincoe, Homer P. "Butch," 15, 87
Bloom, Walter, 124, 125, 149, 150, 161, 170, 204
Blumberg, Richard W., 50, 204, 210, 339
Bogle, Charles W., III, 236
Boland, Frank K., 350
Bondy, Philip, 78, 96, 124, 127, 129, 264
Bone, David, 258, 290
Bonkovsky, Herbert, 223, 228, 264
Boring, John, 274, 317
Bouhuys, Arend, 283
Bourke, Edmund, 280, 317, 370
Bowden, Henry L., 476
Bowdoin, William R., 476
Brake, Charles, 267, 363
Branch, William 268, 370
Brandeau, Gordon, 248
Brannon, E. S., 75, 79, 242, 292
Braunwald, Eugene, 283
Brecher, Gerhart, 288
Brelsford, Ted, xiii
Brewer, Spencer, 380fig
Brewster, Thomlinson Fort, 478
Brinsfield, Dorothy, 275, 290
Brittian, Pete, 363
Brockey, Harold, 259, 362
Brody, Steve, 268
Brooks, Scott, 263
Brown, A. C., 261
Brown, Barbara, 326, 428fig
Brown, Eugene, 97, 267
Brown, Robert L., 87, 160, 269, 346, 478
Brown, Robert L., Jr., 478
Broyles, John, 261
Bruckner, E. V., 271
Brumley, George W., 476
Brust, Al, 149, 150, 204
Bryan, Patsy, 236
Buckalew, Vardaman, 278, 318
Budell, William, 268
Burchell, Howard, 197, 202
Burns, Carol, xi
Butterworth, Charles, 387fig

—C—

Cabaniss, Dan, 318
Calhoun, Abner Wellborn, 341

Calhoun, Phinizy, 82, 90, 93
Calkins, Evan, 284
Callaway, George, 279, 363
Cambre, Suzanne, 347
Candler, Asa Griggs, 4, 5, 15–26, 44, 48, 58fig, 59fig, 327, 362, 476
Candler, Charles Howard, 16, 23–25, 42, 50, 362, 476
Candler, Lucy Elizabeth, 16, 18, 59fig
Candler, Martha Beall, 17
Candler, Mrs. Charles Howard, 152
Candler, Samuel Charles, 16, 17
Candler, Warren Akin, 4, 5, 22, 24, 58fig
Candler Family, v
Cantey, Robert, 318
Cantrell, Craig, 208
Cantwell, John, 294, 340
Cargill, Walter, 97, 129, 150, 205, 363
Carlyle, Thomas, v
Carr, Harry J., 344
Carr, Virginia, xi
Carrel, Alexis, 288
Carter, Jimmy, 321
Carter, Manley Lanier (Sonny), 363
Cary, Freeman, 129, 246
Casarella, William, 292
Catherwood, Bayard, 266, 363
Caton, William, 150, 161, 170
Chace, William M., xiii, 476
Chang, Sonia, 249
Chawla, R. K., 266
Cheney, Huddie, 208, 227, 385fig
Chisholm, Barney, 174
Christian, Henry, 70, 71
Christy, James, 265, 291, 382fig
Churchill, Winston, 10, 102
Churchwell, André, 256, 354
Churchwell, Grigg, 151, 209, 282
Clark, Dwight W., 247
Clark, Richard, 266
Clements, Stephen D., Jr., 237, 249
Cobb, Ty, 41
Cobbs, B. Woodfin, Jr., 210, 248, 379fig
Coberly, James, 129, 363
Cohen, Mandel, 195
Collins, Delwood, 265
Combs, Dr., 382fig

Staton, Gerald, 284, 354
Stead, Emily, 69
Stead, Eugene Auson, 69
Stead, Eugene A., Jr., xi, xii, xiii, 1, 13,
    33, 34, 46, 49, 51, 62fig, 69–72, 75, 77,
    79, 81, 82, 84, 86–90, 93–96, 98, 108,
    109fig, 116, 125, 139, 178, 197, 198,
    203, 231, 242, 243, 269, 293, 322, 324,
    331, 370, 424fig, 425fig, 476
Stead, Evelyn, 94, 324, 424fig
Stead, William, 97
Stein, Sidney, 271
Steinberg, James, 354
Steinhaus, John, 292
Stephens, David S., 277, 319, 343, 371
Stephenson, Lois, 158
Süllerman, Hyman, 274
Stone, Charles, 293
Stone, John H., 240, 249, 267, 319, 321,
    338, 371
Strange, Ruth, 207, 325, 326, 363, 375fig
Strickland, Robert, 476
Strickler, Cyrus W., Jr., 31, 51
Strickler, Cyrus W., Sr., 8, 14, 30, 32, 47,
    49, 60fig, 61fig
Strickler, Mary, 30
Sturm, Hiram, 260, 371
Summerall, W. B., 478
Sydenstricker, V. P., 194
Symbas, Peter, 258, 290

—T—

Tager, Maurice, 424fig
Talley, J. David, 227, 319
Talley, Robert C., 287, 318, 319
Taussig, Andrew, 256, 353
Teem, Martin, 263
Thiele, W. H., 479
Thomas, Lewis, 224
Thompson, J. Dan, 210, 292
Thompson, Sumner E., III, 276, 346, 363
Thoreau, Henry, 324
Thorn, George, 77
Thredgill, Rader, 306
Thurman, Anna, 30
Tierney, Larry, 321
Tiliakos, Nicholas, 285

Tindall, George, 291
Titus, Louisa, 266
Titus, Rosemary, 266
Todd, Dorothy, 326
Tomlin, Clyde, 245
Tonelli, Sirio, 338
Townsend, Roy, 174
Traxler, Malcolm, 363
Tsagaris, Theofilos, 363
Tune, Larry, 347
Turner, Fred J., 478
Turner, "Uncle Allen," 2, 4, 16, 47
Tuttle, Elbert, 214
Tuttle, Elbert, Jr., 151, 209, 278, 279, 287,
    291, 319, 376fig, 380fig

—V—

Vanderbilt, Cornelius, 4
Venable, Willis E., 19, 20
Vogler, Ralph, 271
Volpitto, Perry, 194, 292

—W—

Walker, H. Kenneth, 217–19, 237, 239,
    305, 306, 312, 321, 325, 383fig, 383fig
Walker, Thomas, 232
Walker, Woolfolk, 20
Waller, John L., 477
Walter, Paul F., 248
Walter, William, 363
Ward, John, 265
Ward, Judson C., Jr., xiii, 51, 108, 139,
    178, 370
Warren, Dean, 229, 264, 352
Warren, Donald, 281
Warren, Gloria, 94
Warren, James V., 74–77, 79, 80, 96, 108,
    124, 130, 159, 242, 292, 363
Warren, Roy, 220
Waters, David, 319, 384fig
Waters, Lamar, 363
Waters, William C., III, 279, 321
Watts, Nelson, 266
Webb, Anne S., 207, 325, 375fig
Weed, Lawrence L., 237, 389fig
Weens, Heinz S., 75, 79, 80, 159, 235,
    242, 292